For Complete Mastery Over **Written & Spoken** English

Phrasal Verbs *in* Daily Use

JK Arora
(MA, BEd)

Arihant Publications (I) Pvt Ltd, Meerut

Delhi Office: 4577/15, Ramchhaya, Agarwal Road, Darya Ganj, New Delhi - 2
Phone : 011-23280316, 47630600 ; Fax : 011-43540876

Head Office : Kalindi, TP Nagar, Meerut, Phone : 0121-2401479, 2512970, 2402029 ;
Fax : 0121-2401648, Email : info@arihantbooks.com

卐 **Zonal & Regional Offices :**

North Zone **Agra**: 8/195, New Engineers' Colony, Kaushalpur, Agra, Ph. 0562 – 6451531, Email: arihant_agra02@yahoo.co.in; **Delhi–1 (for Delhi & NCR) :** 4577/15, Ramchhaya, Agarwal Road, Darya Ganj, New Delhi – 110002, Ph. 011 – 23280316, Fax. 011 – 43540876, Email: arihant_delhi07@yahoo.co.in; **Delhi–2 (for Haryana, Himachal, J&K & Punjab) :** 4577/15, Ramchhaya, Agarwal Road, Darya Ganj, New Delhi – 110002, Ph. 011 – 23280316, Fax. 011 – 43540876, Email: arihant_delhi07@yahoo.co.in **Jaipur**: C–8, Link Road, Jalupura MD Road, Near Hotel Apoorva, Jaipur – 302 001 (Raj), Ph. 0141 – 4033077, Email : deepmahur85@gmail.com; **Kota**: 5-J-18, Talwardi, Behind T.T. Hospital, Kota–324009 (Rajasthan.), 0744–2406760, Email : arihant_kota@yahoo.co.in; **Lucknow**: C – 22,Vijay Laxmi Transport Building, Transport Nagar, Kanpur Road, Lucknow – 226 012 (UP), Ph. 0522 – 6459009, Fax : 0522-4028575, Email : arihant_lko@yahoo.com; **Haldwani**: Raja Enterprises, Varun Complex, Rampur Road, Haldwani (Uttrakhand), Ph. 05946 – 235456 ; Email : arihant_kashipur@yahoo.co.in; **Meerut**: Kalindi, TP Nagar, Meerut, Ph: 0121-6534323, Email: arihant_meerutbranch@yahoo.co.in.

East Zone **Bhubaneshwar**: 14, Shahid Nagar, Bhubaneshwar – 751007 (Orissa), Ph. 064 – 2503050, 09938211103, Email : bhubaneshwar@arihantbooks.com; **Kolkata**: 4, Tottee Lane, Kolkata – 700016 (WB), Ph. 033 – 22526713, Fax. 033 – 22523564, Email: arihant_kol@yahoo.co.in; **Guwahati**: Aastha Towers, Ist Floor, Module No. XIII, CK Road, Pan Bazar, Guwahati – 781 001, (Asom) Ph. 0361 – 2731599, E-mail : arihant_guwahati@yahoo.co.in; **Patna**: Gangotri Complex, U/465, Lohia Nagar, Kankarbagh, Patna – 20 (Bihar), Ph. 0612 – 2360623, Email: cafpatna@rediffmail.com.

Central Zone **Nagpur**: 27, Nathuji Pise Complex, Opp. Mokshadham, New Gate, Beside Hanuman Mandir, Great Nag Road, Nagpur – 14, (Maharashtra), Ph. 0712 – 2748211 ; Email : arihant_nagpur1@yahoo.co.in.

South Zone **Hyderabad**: Plot No.–115, SBI Colony, Kavadiguda, Near Sri Satya Sai Temple, Hyderabad–500020, Ph. 040 – 65347774, 66107772, Email: hyd.arihant@gmail.com; **Bengaluru**: 362, 10th Main, 2nd Cross, Ist Block, Basaveshwara Nagar, Bengaluru-560079, Mob : +919242693192

卐 **Price** : Rs 150.00

卐 **Laser Typesetting** : Arihant DTP Unit, Meerut

PO No. : TXT-59-T057823-3-24

For further information on
Arihant Group, visit log in : www.arihantbooks.com

Preface

Have you ever found it difficult to understand English in magazines, newspapers, books, on TV or on the radio? Then you probably need to improve your knowledge of phrasal verbs. Most qualified and experienced English language teachers will tell you that any successful English course should include phrasal verbs from elementary level and beyond. They are also an important part of all major English language tests, be it competitive for recruitments or entrances for higher studies.

This book, the 'Dictionary of Phrasal Verb' is ideal for any English language student, from high school level and beyond. The text has been presented alphabetically so that it becomes easy to use and adapt. It is also suitable for use by teachers in the classroom for students of all ages & groups. The book is even ideal for use along with other texts as part of a course of study.

Sincere efforts have been taken in coinage of the content, but always there is a scope for improvement. We invite and welcome any feedback & suggestions for the improvement of this book in subsequent editions.

JK Arora

Content

Phrasal verbs beginning with

1 Words Beginning With–A

Abide by : adhere to; accept. ***Ex 1.*** I shall certainly *abide by* my promise.

Ex 2. We shall ***abide*** by the referee's decision.

Account for : (a) explain. ***Ex.*** Her illness *accounts for* her absence.

(b) give a satisfactory record of. ***Ex.*** The cashier could not *account for* the deficit in our bank balance.

(c) destroy something or kill somebody. ***Ex 1.*** Two masked intruders were *accounted for* by our security guards. ***Ex 2.*** Our anti-aircraft guns *accounted for* five enemy bombers.

Account to : give explanation. ***Ex.*** you will have to *account to* me if anything happens to this child while he is in your care.

Act as : perform the role or functions of somebody/something. ***Ex.*** I don't understand their language; you will have to *act as* interpreter.

Act for : represent somebody; perform somebody's duties, etc. on his behalf. ***Ex.*** During his illness, his solicitor has been *acting for* him in his business affairs.

Act on : (a) take action in accordance with or as a result of something.

Ex 1. *Acting on information* received, the police raided the club.

Ex 2. She always acts on my advice.

(b) have an effect on. ***Ex.*** It amply deserves to be borne in mind that alcohol acts on the brain.

Act out : act a part in a real-life situation and for some purpose; do or present something in a theatrical way. ***Ex 1.*** She *acted out* all that had happened to her. ***Ex 2.*** He *acted out* his injured innocence.

Act up : (a) respond aptly. ***Ex.*** When the children tease him, he does not know how to *act up*.

(b) behave in an annoying way. ***Ex.*** If you scold your child, he will only start *acting up*.

(c) perform erratically. ***Ex.*** As my car has started *acting up*, it badly needs servicing.

Adapt for : (a) modify. ***Ex.*** My novel has been *adapted for* television.

(b) make suitable for a new situation. ***Ex.*** This machine has been *adapted for* use underwater.

Adapt to : make fit. ***Ex.*** *Adapt* this building to the needs of the old people who will live in it.

Adapt from : translate. ***Ex.*** This play has been skilfully *adapted from* the original.

Adapt oneself to : adjust. ***Ex.*** He *adapted himself* quickly to the new climate.

Add in : include something. ***Ex.*** Please *add in* these items in order to complete the list.

Add to : increase. ***Ex 1.*** The bad weather only *added* to our difficulties. ***Ex 2.*** The recent excavations have *added* greatly to our knowledge of life in ancient India.

Add up : (a) make sense. ***Ex.*** His story just does not *add up*-he must be lying.

(b) assess. ***Ex.*** *Add up* all the advantages and disadvantages, and try to come to a conclusion.

Add up to : indicate something. ***Ex 1.*** These clues do not really add up to very much. ***Ex 2.*** The evidence wholly *adds* up to a case of murder.

Address oneself to : tackle something. ***Ex 1.*** When will you *address yourself* to the main item on the agenda? ***Ex 2.*** There are two questions to which I shall *address myself* in this lecture.

Admit of : leave room for. ***Ex.*** Action on this matter *admits* of no delay.

Agree with : (a) suit somebody's health or digestion. ***Ex.*** The humid climate did not *agree with* him.

(b) match; be consistent with. ***Ex.*** His account of the affair does not *agree with* mine.

(c) coincide with. ***Ex.*** His explanation *agrees with* the facts of the case.

(d) approve of. ***Ex 1.*** I don't *agree with* people smoking all day long.

(e) correspond in number, person, etc. ***Ex.*** The verb *agrees with* its subject in number and person.

Aim at : direct at somebody. ***Ex.*** My remarks were not *aimed at* you.

Allow for : take into account. ***Ex 1.*** It will take you half an hour to get to the airport, *allowing for* traffic delays. ***Ex 2.*** When making up this kind of material, you should *allow for* shrinkage in the wash.

Allow of : permit. ***Ex 1.*** The facts *allow* of only one explanation. ***Ex 2.*** His responsible position *allowed of* no unseemly behaviour in public. ***Ex 3.*** Her income *allows of* no extravagance in her way of living.

Amount to : (a) be equal to. ***Ex 1.*** His total worldly possessions *amounted to* little more than the clothes he stood up in. ***Ex 2.*** What you say *amounts to* a direct accusation.

(b) total; add up to. ***Ex.*** Our information does not *amount to* much.

(c) become successful. ***Ex.*** He will never do anything, and he will never *amount to* anything.

Answer back : (a) defend oneself. ***Ex.*** It is unfair to attack a person in the newspaper when he cannot *answer back*.

(b) speak rudely when being scolded or criticised. ***Ex.*** When your wife scolds you, you should not *answer back*.

Answer for : (a) be responsible for. ***Ex.*** Don't forget that one day you will have to *answer for* your foolish behaviour.

(b) speak in support of somebody/something. ***Ex.*** As I have known her for many years, I can certainly *answer for* her honesty.

Answer to : (a) obey. ***Ex.*** Whom do you *answer to* in your new job?

(b) try to explain. ***Ex.*** One day you will have to *answer to* a higher authority for your sins of ommission and commission.

(c) correspond to. ***Ex.*** A man *answering to* the police description was arrested in Patna last night.

Ante up : (a) make initial stake. ***Ex.*** They *anted up* and started to play.

(b) contribute a sum of money. ***Ex.*** The government *anted up* to the tune of ten million rupees.

(c) stake in order to start a game. ***Ex.*** They each *anted up* twenty rupees.

(d) pay. ***Ex.*** They finally *anted up* fifty thousand rupees for the use of the premises.

Apply to : (a) concerns; be relevant to. ***Ex.*** These rules do not *apply to* this case.

(b) concentrate thought and energy on. ***Ex.*** We must *apply* our minds *to* finding a solution to the problem.

(e) make particular use of. ***Ex.*** The results of this research can be *applied to* new developments in technology.

(d) put on, spread on. ***Ex.*** The lotion should be *applied* sparingly to the skin.

Approve of : (a) like, admire. ***Ex 1.*** His mother-in-law does not exactly approve of him. ***Ex 2.*** I *approve of* your trying to earn some money; but please don't neglect your studies.

(b) confirm; accept. ***Ex 1.*** The minutes of the last meeting were *approved of* by the board of directors. ***Ex 2.*** Don't expect him to *approve of* your design straight away.

Ask after : request information about somebody's health. ***Ex 1.*** He always *asks after* you in his letters. ***Ex 2.*** I *asked after* his children.

Ask in : invite. ***Ex 1.*** We *asked her* in for coffee. ***Ex 2.*** *Ask* your friend *in*; I would like to meet him.

Ask of : request somebody to behave; expect of. ***Ex 1.*** May I *ask* a favour *of* you? ***Ex 2.*** Are not you *asking* rather a lot *of* your son-expecting him to be top of his class in every subject?

Ask out : invite to go out. ***Ex 1.*** I have been *asked out* for the evening by the boy next door. ***Ex 2.*** When she discovered that her husband had *asked* his charming lady secretary *out* to dinner, she was furious.

Attach oneself to : join as a companion or member, in an unwelcome manner. ***Ex.*** A young man *attached himself* to me at the party and I could not get rid of him.

Attach to : (a) consider as having. ***Ex.*** too much importance should not be *attached to* the reports of impending revolution in that country.

(b) consider as being attributable or applicable. ***Ex.*** No suspicion can be *attached to* the accountant.

(c) be applicable or attributable to. ***Ex.*** The main credit for the party's electoral success *attaches to* the coolness and confidence of its leader.

Attend on/upon : (a) tend; look after. ***Ex.*** Two nurses *attended* night and day *on* the dying statesman.

(b) accompany. ***Ex.*** Many difficulties and dangers *attended upon* his singlehanded voyage round the world.

Attend to : (a) pay attention to. ***Ex.*** If you don't *attend to* your teacher, you will never learn anything.

(b) look after; take care of. ***Ex 1.*** If you go out, who will attend to the baby? ***Ex 2.*** An experienced assistant *attended to* the important customers.

Awake to : become aware of; realise. ***Ex.*** He *awoke to* the possible dangers.

Awaken somebody to : cause somebody to become aware of something. ***Ex 1.*** We should *awaken* the society *to* the dangers of drugs. ***Ex 2.*** I have *awaken* him *to* the fact that there is no easy way to success.

---

2 Words Beginning With–B

Back away : move backwards in fear or dislike. ***Ex.*** The frightened child *backed away* from the horse.

Back down : give up a claim to something; yield. ***Ex 1.*** I proved that I was right and my critics had to *back down*. ***Ex 2.*** The trade union expects the management to *back down*. ***Ex 3.*** He is too proud to *back down* and admit mistakes.

Back out : withdraw from. ***Ex 1.*** He has decided to *back out* of the project. ***Ex 2.*** It is too late to *back out* of the deal now.

Back up : support or encourage somebody/something. ***Ex 1.*** I always *back up* my friends. ***Ex 2.*** I shall *back* your story *up*, if they ask me about it.

Bail out : help in an emergency. ***Ex.*** I shall surely *bail* you *out* of the problem.

Bale out : leave by parachute. ***Ex.*** The crew *baled out* of the blazing plane.

Ball up : spoil; ruin. ***Ex.*** He *balled up* the whole thing, and the scheme failed.

Bamboozle into : trick somebody into doing something. ***Ex.*** She *bamboozled* me *into* believing that she had lost all her money.

Bandy about : pass on a rumour, etc. in a thoughtless way. ***Ex 1.*** The stories being *bandied about* are completely false. ***Ex 2.*** Your name is being *bandied about* as the next Chairman of the Company.

Bang about/around : move about noisily. ***Ex.*** The children *banged about* upstairs.

Bang away : shoot continuously. ***Ex.*** The soldiers were *banging away* at the target.

Bang into : meet by chance. ***Ex.*** I *banged into* him after many a year.

Bang out : produce. ***Ex.*** He *banged out* an article on the typewriter.

Bank on : base hopes on. ***Ex 1.*** I am *banking on* your assistance. ***Ex 2.*** He is *banking on* you to help him. ***Ex 3.*** He was *banking on* the train being on time.

Bank up : (a) form into a heap or ridge. ***Ex.*** Seaweed *banks up* along the water's edge.

(b) heap with fuel to ensure that a fire burns slowly for a long time. ***Ex.*** Don forget to *bank up* the fire before you go to bed.

Bargain away : give away. ***Ex.*** The leaders *bargained away* the freedom of their people.

Bargain for : expect. ***Ex.*** The examination was more difficult than I had *bargained for*.

Bargain on : be prepared for; expect. ***Ex.*** He did not *bargain on* his father returning so soon.

Barge about : move heavily and clumsily. ***Ex.*** The boys *barged about*, making a lot of noise.

Barge in/into : enter or interrupt something rudely or clumsily. ***Ex 1.*** I tried to stop him coming through the door but he just *barged in*. ***Ex 2.*** Don't *barge into* our conversation.

Bark out : say something in a sharp harsh voice. ***Ex.*** The captain *barked out* an order.

Barricade in : keep somebody in by making a barricade. ***Ex.*** They *barricaded themselves in* their rooms.

Barricade off : block with a barricade. ***Ex.*** The police *barricated off* the entrance to the park.

Bash in/down : case something to collapse by striking it violently. ***Ex 1.*** He *bashed in* the lid of the box. ***Ex 2.*** They *bashed* the door down.

Bash up : treat somebody violently. ***Ex.*** He was *bashed up* in the playground by some older boys.

Batten on : thrive or live well at the expense of somebody/something. ***Ex.*** She avoided having to work by *battening on* her boy-friends.

Batter down : flatten something by hitting it repeatedly. ***Ex.*** Let us *batter* the door *down*.

Batter to : cause something to become a specified shape by hitting it hard. ***Ex.*** The victim's face was *battered to* a pulp. ***Ex.*** The huge waves *battered* the wrecked ship *to* pieces.

Bawl out : scold somebody severely. ***Ex.*** He was *bawled out* for inefficiency.

Bear away/off : seize and carry away. ***Ex 1.*** They *bore off* several captives. ***Ex 2.*** She *bore away* the first prize.

Bear down : defeat or overcome somebody. ***Ex.*** I am sure he will *bear down* the enemy.

Bear down on : move quickly and threatening towards somebody/something. ***Ex.*** The angry farmer was *bearing down* on us.

Bear on : relate to something; affect something. ***Ex.*** These matters *bear on* the welfare of the community.

Bear out : support somebody; confirm something. ***Ex.*** The other witnesses will *bear out* what I say.

Bear up : be strong enough not to despair; cope; manage. ***Ex.*** He is *bearing up* well against all his misfortunes.

Bear with : tolerate somebody/something patiently. ***Ex.*** I must *bear with* her during this difficult period.

Beat down : (a) force an entry by hitting repeatiedly. ***Ex.*** The thieves had *beaten* the door *down*.

(b) flatten something. ***Ex.*** The wheat had been *beaten down* by the rain.

Beat into/to : bring somebody to a specified state by hitting repeatedly. ***Ex 1.*** The dog was *beaten to* death. ***Ex 2.*** The children were *beaten into* submission.

Beat off : drive somebody/something away by fighting. ***Ex.*** The attacker was *beaten off*.

Beat out : (a) produce (a rhythm) by drumming. ***Ex.*** He *beat out* a tune on a tin can.

(b) extinguish (a fire) by beating. ***Ex.*** They *beat* the flames *out*.

(c) removes something by striking with a hammer, etc. ***Ex.*** The mechanic *beat out* the dent in the car's wing.

Beat to : arrive at a place before somebody. ***Ex.*** I shall *beat* you *to* the top of the hill.

Beat up : hit, kick or thrash somebody severely. ***Ex.*** He was badly *beaten up* by a gang of thugs.

Beaver away : work hard. ***Ex.*** He has been *beavering away* at this job for hours.

Bed down : settle for the night. ***Ex.*** The soldiers *bedded down* in a barn.

Beef up : add force or weight to something. ***Ex.*** The new evidence *beefed up* our case.

Begg off : ask to be excused from doing something. ***Ex.*** He promised to attend the meeting but then *begged off*.

Believe in : (a) feel sure of existence of. ***Ex.*** I *believe in* God, the Greatest. ***Ex.*** Do you *believe in* ghosts ?

(b) trust somebody/something; feel sure of worth or truth of. ***Ex.*** I *believe in* her good character. ***Ex.*** He *believes in* getting plenty of exercise.

Believe of : accept that somebody is capable of a particular action, etc. ***Ex.*** If I had not seen him doing it, Iwould never have *believed* it *of* him.

Belly out : swell out. ***Ex 1.*** The sails *bellied out*. ***Ex 2.*** The wind *bellied out* the sails.

Bend to : (a) submit to something. ***Ex.*** He *bent to* my will.

(b) force somebody to submit to one's will. ***Ex.*** I *bent* him *to* my will.

Be bent on : be determined on. ***Ex.*** He is *bent on* winning at all costs.

Bind over : warn somebody that he will appear in court again if he breaks the law. ***Ex.*** The magistrate *bound* him *over* to keep the peace for a year.

Bite off : cut something off by biting. ***Ex.*** He *bit off* a large chunk of an apple.

Blast away/down : break something by blasting. ***Ex.*** The explosion *blasted* the door *down*.

Blast off : be launched by the firing of rockets. ***Ex.*** The rocket *blasted off* at noon.

Blaze away : fire continuously with guns. ***Ex.*** Our gunners kept *blazing away* at the enemy.

Blaze up : (a) burst into flames. ***Ex.*** The fire *blazed up* when he added paraffin.

(b) suddenly become angry. ***Ex.*** He *blazed up* without warning.

Blend in : (a) mix harmoniously. ***Ex.*** The new office block does not *blend in* with its surroundings.

(b) add another ingredient to something and mix the two. ***Ex.*** Melt the butter and then *blend in* the flour.

Blink away/back : try to control or hide by blinking. ***Ex.*** Although in pain, she bravely *blinked back* her tears.

Block off : separate using a solid barrier. ***Ex.*** Police *blocked off* the street after the explosion.

Bloom with : be in a healthy or flourishing condition. ***Ex.*** They were *blooming with* health and happiness.

Blot out : (a) cover or hide with a blot. ***Ex.*** Several words in the letter had been *blotted out*.

(b) hide something completely. ***Ex.*** Thick cloud *blotted out* the view.

Blow down/off : move or be moved by the force of mind, etc. ***Ex 1.*** His hat *blew off*. ***Ex 2.*** Many chimneys *blew down* during the strom. ***Ex 3.*** He *blew* the dust *off* the book.

Blow in/into : arrive or enter suddenly. ***Ex.*** Let me know who has just *blown in*.

Blow out : be extiguished by the wind, etc. ***Ex.*** He opened the door and the candle *blew out*.

Blow over : pass away without having a serious effect. ***Ex 1.*** The storm *blew over* in the night. ***Ex 2.*** The scandal will soon *blow over*.

Blow up : (a) explode; be destroyed by an explosion. ***Ex 1.*** The bomb *blew up*. ***Ex 2.*** A policeman was killed when his body-trapped car *blew up*.

(b) start suddenly with force. ***Ex.*** A storm is *blowing up*.

(c) lose one's temper. ***Ex.*** I am sorry I *blew up* at you.

(d) reprimand somebody severely. ***Ex.*** She got *blown up* by her boss for being late.

(e) destroy something by an explosion. ***Ex.*** The police station was *blown up* by terrorists. .

(f) exaggerate or inflate something. ***Ex 1.*** Her abilities as an actress have been greatly *blown up* by the popular press. ***Ex 2.*** The whole affair was *blown up* out of all proportion.

Bluff into : make somebody believe or do something by deceiving him. ***Ex.*** They were *bluffed into* believing that we were not ready for the attack.

Blurt out : say something suddenly and tactlessly. ***Ex.*** He *blurted out* the bad news before I could stop him.

Bluster one's way out of something : try to escape from something by talking aggressively, boastfully, etc. ***Ex.*** He always tries to *bluster his way out of* difficult situations.

Bob up : come to the surface quickly. ***Ex.*** She dived below the surface, then *bobbed up* like a cork again a few seconds later.

Boil away : boil until nothing remains; evaporate. ***Ex.*** The water in the kettle had all *boiled away*.

Boil down : summarise something; condence something. ***Ex.*** Please *boil* that article *down* to 400 words.

Boil down to : be summarised as something. ***Ex.*** The issue really *boils down to* a clash between left and right.

Boil over : (a) boil and flow over the side of a pan, etc. ***Ex.*** The milk is *boiling over*.

(b) explode; reach a point of crisis. ***Ex.*** The crisis is in danger of *boiling over* into civil war.

Boo off : force somebody to leave by booing. ***Ex.*** The actors were *booed off* the stage.

Book in : (a) register at a hotel, an airport, etc. ***Ex.*** He *booked in* at the Ashoka Hotel.

(b) make a reservation for somebody at a hotel, etc. ***Ex.*** We have *booked* you *in* at the Hotel Inn for four nights.

Boot out of : (a) throw somebody out by force. ***Ex.*** His father *booted* him *out of* the house.

(b) dismiss somebody from a job. ***Ex.*** He has been *booted out of* his job.

Bottle up : restrain or suppress feelings. ***Ex.*** Instead of discussing their problems, they *bottle up* all their anger and resentment.

Bounce along/down/into : move with up and down motion. ***Ex 1.*** He came *bouncing into* the room. ***Ex 2.*** The car *bounced along* the bumpy mountain road.

Bounce back : recover well after a setback. ***Ex 1.*** Share prices *bounced back* this morning. ***Ex 2.*** She has had many misfortunes in her life but she always *bounces back*.

Bow out : (a) withdraw from something. ***Ex.*** I am *bowing out* of this project-I don't approve of it.

(b) retire from an important position. ***Ex.*** After thirty years in politics, he is finally *bowing out*.

Bow to : submit to something; accept something. ***Ex 1.*** You have to *bow to* his greater experience. ***Ex 2.*** We must *bow to* the inevitable. ***Ex 3.*** We are tired of having to *bow to* authority.

Bowl along/down : move fast and smoothly. ***Ex.*** We are *bowling along* the motorway at fifty kilometres per hour.

Bowl over : astound somebody; surprise somebody greatly. ***Ex.*** W were *bowled over* by the news of her marriage.

Box in/up : shut somebody/something in a small space. ***Ex 1.*** He feels *boxed in*, living in that tiny flat. ***Ex 2.*** She hates being *boxed up* in an office all day.

Break away : (a) escape suddenly. ***Ex.*** The prisoner *broke away* from his guards.

(b) leave a political party. ***Ex.*** Several Janata Dal MPs *broke away* to join the Samajvadi Party.

(c) leave a state to form a new one. ***Ex.*** A province has *broken away* to form a new state.

Break down : (a) cease to function. ***Ex 1.*** The telephone system has *broken down*. ***Ex 2.*** Our car *broke down* on the motorway.

(b) fail; collapse. **Ex 1.** Negotiations between the two sides have *broken down*. ***Ex 2.*** If law and order break down, anarchy will result.

(c) become very bad. ***Ex.*** Her health condition *broke down* under the pressure of work.

(d) lose control of one's feelings. ***Ex.*** He *broke down* and wept when he heard the bad news.

(e) make something collapse by striking it hard. ***Ex.*** Firemen had to *break* the door *down* to reach the people trapped inside.

(f) overcome; cause something to collapse; conquer or destroy something. ***Ex 1.*** We *broke down* their resistance. ***Ex 2.*** She *broke down* her shyness. ***Ex 3.*** Let us *break down* the barriers of fear and hostility which divide the two communities.

Break in : (a) enter a building by force. ***Ex.*** Burglars had *broken in* while we were out of station. .

(b) interrupt or disturb something ***Ex.*** Please don't *break in* on our conversation.

Break into : (a) enter something by force. ***Ex.*** His house was *broken into* by burglars last night.

(b) suddenly begin. ***Ex.*** As the Prime Minister's car arrived, the crowd *broke into* loud applause.

(c) suddenly change (from a slower to faster pace). ***Ex.*** The man *broke into* a run when he saw the police.

Break off : (a) stop speaking. ***Ex.*** He *broke off* in the middle of a sentence.

(b) become separated. ***Ex.*** The door handle has *broken off*.

(c) end something suddenly; discontinue something. ***Ex 1.*** We have *broken off* diplomatic relations with that country. ***Ex 2.*** They have *broken off* their engagement.

Break out : (a) start suddenly. ***Ex 1.*** Fire *broke out* during the night. ***Ex 2.*** Rioting *broke out* between rival groups of fans. ***Ex 3.*** When did the war *break out*?

(b) escape from a place by using force. ***Ex.*** Many a prisoner *broke out* of the jail.

Break out in : (a) suddenly became covered in something. ***Ex.*** His face *broke out in* a rash.

(b) suddenly begin to show strong feelings. ***Ex.*** She *broke out in* a rage.

Break through : (a) make new and important discoveries. ***Ex.*** Scientists are beginning to *break through* in the fight against cancer.

(b) make a way through something using force. ***Ex.*** Demonstrators *broke through* the police cordon.

(c) appear rom behind (clouds). ***Ex.*** The sun *broke through* at last in the afternoon.

Break up : (a) disperse; go away in different directions. ***Ex.*** The meeting *broke up* at 11 o'clock.

(b) begin holidays when school closes at the end of term. ***Ex.*** When do you *break up* for Diwali?

(c) become very weak; collapse. ***Ex.*** He was *breaking up* under the strain.

(d) (of a period of fine weather) : end. ***Ex.*** The weather shows signs of *breaking up*.

(e) come to an end. ***Ex.*** Their marriage is *breaking up*.

(f) cause something to come to an end. ***Ex.*** They decided to *break up* the partnership.

(g) disperse or scatter something by using force. ***Ex.*** Police were called in to *break up* the meeting.

(h) divide something by means of analysis, an administrative decision, etc.

Ex 1. Sentences can be *broken up* into clauses. ***Ex 2.*** The government has *broken up* the large private estates.

(i) end a relationship with sb. ***Ex.*** She has just *broken up* with her boyfriend.

Break with : (a) end a relationship with sb. ***Ex.*** He has just *broken with* his girlfriend.

(b) give up something; abandon something. ***Ex 1.*** Don't *break with* old traditions. ***Ex 2.*** It is very difficult to *break with* old habits.

Breathe into : fill with. ***Ex.*** The new managing director has *breathed* fresh life *into* the company.

Breeze along/in/through: move in a cheerful carefree way. ***Ex 1.*** Look who has just *breezed in*. ***Ex 2.*** She *breezes through* life, never worrying about anything.

Brew up : prepare a drink of tea. ***Ex.*** The campers were *brewing up* outside their tents.

Bridle at : show anger, resentment, etc. ***Ex.*** She *bridled at* your offensive remarks.

Bring about : (a) cause to happen. ***Ex 1.*** The accident was *brought about* by his recklessness. ***Ex 2.*** The government will *bring about* changes in the electoral system.

(b) change direction of movement. ***Ex 1.*** The helmsman *brought* us *about* and we went scudding off in a new direction. ***Ex 2.*** He *brought* the boat *about* and headed for safety.

Bring along on : (a) help, encourage, to develop. ***Ex.*** They are trying to *bring along* two promising young swimmers.

(b) help to grow more quickly. ***Ex.*** The fine weather will *bring* the crops *along* very nicely.

Bring along : conduct from one place to another. ***Ex 1.*** You can *bring* your wife *along* to the party if you like. ***Ex 2.*** I want to *bring* him *along* to see you.

Bring around/round : (a) conduct or lead sb. to a place. ***Ex 1.*** Do *bring* your mother *around* one evening. We are longing to meet her. ***Ex 2.*** You are welcome to *bring* your guests *around* to our place.

(b) convert sb. to one's own point of view. ***Ex 1.*** Father was not keen on the project, but we managed to *bring* him *around*. ***Ex 2.*** I easily *brought* her *around* to our way to thinking.,

Bring away : return home having formed a particular impression, etc. ***Ex.*** We *brought away* rather mixed impressions of our holiday in Kashmir.

Bring back : (a) restore borrowed property. ***Ex.*** Please *bring back* the book tomorrow.

(b) cause to return. ***Ex.*** He has gone away from home and nothing will *bring* him *back* again.

(c) reintroduce something. ***Ex 1.*** I am very much in favour of *bringing back* the death penalty. ***Ex 2.*** They voted against *bringing back* the capital punishment.

(d) recall to mind. ***Ex.*** The old photograph *brought back* many happy memories of my childhood.

Bring before : present for discussion, decision or judgement. ***Ex 1.*** We should have a word together now; the matter is being *brought before* the committee tomorrow forenoon. ***Ex 2.*** He was *brought before* the court and found guilty.

Bring down : (a) cause to fall from the sky by destroying, killing or wounding. ***Ex.*** Several enemy aircrafts were intercepted and *brought down*.

(b) land. ***Ex.*** The pilot *brought* his crippled plane *down* in a field.

(c) cause to fall over and stop. ***Ex.*** We managed to *bring down* two of the deer, even though they were running fast.

(d) cause the defeat or fall of sb; overthrow sb. ***Ex 1.*** People say that the scandal may *bring down* the government. ***Ex 2.*** The defection of a large number of back-benchers *brought down* the last government.

(e) reduce; lower. ***Ex 1.*** Grocers have agreed to *bring down* the cost of several basic commodities. ***Ex 2.*** Demand has been *brought down* by increases in imports. ***Ex 3.*** Suitable steps should be taken as early as possible to *bring down* the cost of living.

Bring forth : produce something. ***Ex 1.*** Trees *bring forth* fruit. ***Ex 2.*** Can you *bring forth* any sparkling new suggestions for improving our product? ***Ex 3.*** He *brought forth* a new plan, just as unworkable as the old one.

Bring forward : (a) raise, propose or present for discussion. ***Ex 1.*** At our next social welfare meeting, he is proposing to *bring forward* the question of developing the women welfare centre. ***Ex 2.*** She *brought forward* a new proposal.

(b) transfer to an earlier date; advance something. ***Ex 1.*** Clocks and watches should be *bright forward* one hour from midnight today. ***Ex 2.*** Because of the possibility of a clash with another event, we have decided to *bring* the dinner party *forward* from the 9th to the 2nd April. ***Ex 3.*** The meeting has been *brought forward* from the 12th August to the 6th August.

(c) carry or transfer a total from the foot of one page (in a ledger) to the top of the next; or from the account for one period to the account for another. ***Ex.*** A credit balance of two thousand rupees was *brought forward* from his May account.

(d) record that correspondence, etc. is to be produced for sb's attention at a future date. ***Ex 1.*** Please *bring* this letter *forward* on the 5th of the next month. ***Ex 2.*** I *brought* this *forward* yesterday, and she has done nothing about it.

Bring in : (a) gather; harvest. ***Ex.*** Weather forecast assure us of a few more days of fine weather in which to *bring in* the harvest.

(b) earn; produce; yield. ***Ex 1.*** My freelance work *brings* me *in* ten thousand rupees a month. ***Ex 2.*** She does odd jobs that *bring* her *in* about two thousand rupees a month.

(c) give sb a part to play in some scheme; give sb a position of advantage; introduce sb as an adviser, etc. ***Ex 1.*** They have *brought in* a public relations man to advise on press coverage. ***Ex 2.*** Experts should be *brought in* to advise the government on matters relating to kidnapping for ransom.

(d) arrest; bring to a police station for questioning. ***Ex 1.*** If you see anyone loitering near the bank, *bring* him *in*. ***Ex 2.*** Two suspicious characters were *brought in* yesterday.

(e) (legislation) introduce. ***Ex 1.*** The government *brought in* a bill to improve road safety. ***Ex 2.*** Legislation is being *brought in* to revise the Homicide Act.

(f) pronounce a verdict on an accused person. ***Ex 1.*** The judge *brought in* a verdict that he was guilty of murder. ***Ex 2.*** The magistrate *brought in* a verdict that she had died from falling off the roof of her house.

Bring in on : let sb participate in something; inform sb of something. ***Ex 1.*** People, who are most likely to be affected, must be *brought in on* our proposals from the beginning. ***Ex 2.*** Local residents were angry at not being *brought in on* the new housing scheme.

Bring off : (a) rescue from a ship; carry to safety. ***Ex 1.*** The passengers and crew were *brought off* by the Yarmouth lifeboat. ***Ex 2.*** The coastguards have *brought* all the crew *off*, and the ship is sinking by the bows.

(b) succeed in something. ***Ex 1.*** She *brought* the deal *off* in a spectacular way. ***Ex 2.*** Don't trust him to *bring* it *off*. ***Ex 3.*** It was indubitably a difficult task, but I *brought* it *off*.

Bring on : (a) lead to, result in or cause something. ***Ex 1.*** This kind of weather often *brings on* hay fever. ***Ex 2.*** He was out in the rain all day, and this *brought on* a bad cold. ***Ex 3.*** She suffered from nervous tension *brought on* by overwork.

(b) help to develop or improve. ***Ex.*** The coach *brought on* a few promising young persons in the reserve team.

(c) cause to grow rapidly. ***Ex.*** The hot weather is *bringing* the wheat *on* nicely.

(d) cause something to happen to oneself or sb else. ***Ex.*** You have *brought* shame and disgrace on yourself and your family.

(e) introduce. ***Ex.*** He *brought on* the guest speaker, amid tremendous applause.

Bring out : (a) cause to strike; to withdraw labour. ***Ex 1.*** He has *brought* the clerical staff *out* on strike. ***Ex 2.*** It started as a strike in the foundry; then that *brought out* most of the assembly workers as well.

(b) help to lose shyness or reserve. ***Ex 1.*** She is a retiring sort of girl, but I am doing my best to *bring* her *out*. ***Ex 2.*** Sushila is very shy. Try to *bring* her *out*.

(c) introduce to society as a debutante. ***Ex.*** She is *bringing out* her eldest daughter next season.

(d) cause something to open, appear or flower. ***Ex 1.*** The hot weather has *brought out* all the blossom on the fruit trees. ***Ex 2.*** Will the sunshine *bring out* the rose?

(e) publish something. ***Ex.*** Ramesh Publishing House has *brought out* an immensely valuable and useful book titled 'Word Power'.

(f) produce something. ***Ex 1.*** our company is *bringing out* a new Sports car next month. ***Ex 2.*** New personal computers are *brought out* almost daily.

(g) show something clearly; reveal something. ***Ex.*** The enlargement has *brought out* the details in the photograph.

(h) speak, utter. ***Ex.*** He did not finish the sentence because if he had *brought out* the word, it would probably have made him cry.

(i) reveal; make clear or explicit. ***Ex.*** The meaning of the poem was admirably *brought out* by Mridula Devi who is indisputably an erudite scholar.

(j) elicit something; cause a quality to be seen in sb; call forth. ***Ex 1.*** Bear in mind that a crisis brings out the best. ***Ex 2.*** Disaster *bring out* all that was best in the family.

Bring out in : cause sb to be partially covered with. ***Ex 1.*** Don't allow her to get excited : it *brings* her *out in* a nervous rash. ***Ex 2.*** The scorching heat *brought* him *out in* a rash.

Bring out/out of : cause to leave; carry from. ***Ex 1.*** They gathered up the few-belongings that they had managed to *bring out of* the burning house. ***Ex 2.*** She rummaged about in the attic and *brought out* a pile of old documents.

Bring over : (a) cause sb to come from overseas; accompany sb travelling or settling overseas. ***Ex.*** He has been teaching in India for over a couple of years. Next summer he hopes to *bring* his family *over* from France.

(b) make sb change his way of thinking, loyalties, etc. ***Ex 1.*** Try to *bring* him *over* to our cause. ***Ex 2.*** The rebel leader abruptly changed sides, *bringing* most of his fellow dissidents *over* with him. ***Ex 3.*** I don't think that many of the people in the centre can be *brought over* the government side.

Bring round : cause sb to regain consciousness after fainting. ***Ex.*** Six young, well-dressed women fainted in the blistering heat but were quickly *brought round* by the doctor.

Bring round to : direct a conversation to a particular subject. ***Ex 1.*** He keeps trying to *bring* the conversation *round to* politics. ***Ex 2.*** I *brought* the discussion *round to* co-education.

Bring through : save sb; help sb to recover; be responsible for sb's recovery or survival. ***Ex 1.*** It is needless to say that only cool heads will *brings* us *through* this crisis. ***Ex 2.*** She was very badly injured, but the doctors *brought* her *through.*

Bring together : reconcile two parties who are in conflict; end a quarrel. ***Ex 1.*** I shall do my best to *bring* the two parties *together.* ***Ex 2.*** He is trying to *bring* the two sides to the dispute *together* to discuss a new formula.

Bring under : (a) subdue sb; bring sb under control. ***Ex 1.*** Please let me know how the rebels were quickly *brought under.* ***Ex 2.*** The police handled the situation tactfully. The rioters were *brought under* completely.

(b) include something within a category. ***Ex.*** The points to be discussed at the meeting can be *brought under* four main headings.

Bring up : (a) raise, rear or educate sb. ***Ex 1.*** The rich, pious widow adopted two little girls and *brought* them *up.* ***Ex 2.*** The fact of being *brought up* in a shabby and dirty town was another thing that helped us to be competitive. ***Ex 3.*** How many children have you *brought up*? ***Ex 4.*** His parents died when he was a child and he was *brought up* by his paternal uncle.

(b) teach or persuade sb in the course of his upbringing to something. ***Ex 1.*** He had been *brought up* to think that his parents always knew best. ***Ex 2.*** You should *bring up* your sons to stand on their own feet. ***Ex 3.*** He was *brought up* to respect authority.

(c) raise, or call attention to something. ***Ex 1.*** I *bring* this story up now only to compare my experience with that of some uphappy fellow on the Staff Selection Commission. ***Ex 2.*** These are matters that you can *bring up* at the next meeting stated for Friday, the 9th instant. ***Ex 3.*** I think we are agreed on the main points. Does anyone want to *bring up* anything further?

(d) cause to appear for trial. ***Ex 1.*** They were *brought up* for causing a disturbance and obstructing the police. ***Ex 2.*** She was *brought up* on a charge of drunken driving.

(e) vomit something. ***Ex 1.*** He *brought up* his food. ***Ex 2.*** She keeps *bringing up* everything they give her.

(f) make remarks or movement stop suddenly. ***Ex 1.*** We were *brought up* short; by a sudden bellow from our friend. ***Ex 2.*** His remark *brought* me *up* with a jerk. ***Ex 3.*** What *brought* me *up* short and made my irritation evaporate was the sight of two bulging sacks lying at his feet.

(g) move or call (soldiers, guns, etc.) to the front line. ***Ex.*** We need to *bring up* more tanks.

Bring up against: make sb face or confront sh/sth. ***Ex 1.*** He was *brought up against* his wife's fear and mistrust of strange people. ***Ex 2.*** Working in a multiracial community had *brought* him *up against* the realities of intolerance. ***Ex 3.*** Working in the slums *brought* me *up against* the realities of poverty.

Bring up to : bring to an acceptable level or standard. ***Ex.*** His work in Hindi needs to be *brought up to* the standard of the others.

Bristle with: (a) display a frightening or impressive array of; be fraught with; have a large number of something. ***Ex 1.*** None can deny the fact that the problem *bristles with* difficulties. ***Ex 2.*** The trenches were *bristling with* machine-guns. ***Ex 3.*** The first chapter, which *bristles with* names, is essentially a regimented history of the purely scientific side of the missile project.

(b) show or display in an extreme form. ***Ex 1.*** Just mention her name to him and he positively *bristles with* anger. ***Ex 2.*** She *bristled with* Indignation when I told her not to make friends with that rich, handsome young man.

Brood on/over: .think about something for a long time in a troubled or resented way. ***Ex 1.*** It does not help to *brood on* your mistakes. ***Ex 2.*** Don't *brood over* the past. **Ex 3.** I don't know what she is *brooding on.*

Brown off : bore; annoy; dishearten; frustrate. ***Ex 1.*** You look *browned off*, miss Sweety. Can I help? ***Ex 2.*** This kind of job really *browns* me *off*. ***Ex 3.*** He is *browned off* with working so hard for so little money.

Brush aside : (a) push to one side as being lighter or weaker than oneself. ***Ex.*** The enemy column *brushed aside* our defence and advanced east.

(b) disregard; treat as of little or no importance; pay little or no attention to. ***Ex 1.*** She *brushed aside* most of my objections to her plan. ***Ex 2.*** You should *brush aside* your own interest for the good of the nation as a whole.

Brush down : (a) clean by thorough brushing. ***Ex.*** Your coat needs *brushing down* : it is covered with fluff.

(b) scold. Ex. The games instructor *brushed* him *down* for not turning out for training.

Brush off : (a) remove something from something. ***Ex 1.*** He *brushed* mud *off* his trousers. ***Ex 2.*** She *brushed* the fly *off* her face.

(b) ignore sb; refuse to listen to sb; jilt, reject; avoid meeting or forming a relationship with sb. ***Ex 1.*** His girlfriend has just *brushed* him *off*. ***Ex 2.*** I am very keen on her but she is always *brushing* me *off*.

Brush past : touch sb/sth lightly while moving close to him/it. ***Ex 1.*** She *brush past* him without saying a word. ***Ex 2.*** A cat *brushed past* her leg in the darkness.

Brush up : study, practise or revise a skill in order to the proficient in it once again. ***Ex 1.*** His spoken Arabic was hurriedly *brushed up* before he took off on a sales tour of the Middle East. ***Ex 2.*** You must *brush up* your French before you go to Paris.

Bubble over : reach a climax; rise to a peak. ***Ex.*** Boundless excitement seemed to *bubble over* inside that bubbly young woman.

Bubble over with : display a great deal of. ***Ex.*** He is *bubbling over with* enthusiasm for the proposed trip to Tokyo.

Bubble up : rise to the surface in bubbles and/or with the sound of bursting bubbles. *Ex.* The warm gases *bubbled up* through the water.

Buck up : (a) make or become more lively or cheerful. ***Ex 1.*** The news that she is calling at our place this afternoon, has *bucked* us all *up*. ***Ex 2.*** It was absolutely clear that his visit had *bucked* her *up* to a very great extent. ***Ex 3.*** *Buck up*! Things are not as bad as you think.

(b) make haste: hurry up. ***Ex 1.*** *Buck up*! We are going to be late ***Ex 2.*** You will have to *buck up* if you want to catch that train.

Buckle down to : start something in a determined way. ***Ex 1.*** He is not like to *buckle down to* the job. ***Ex 2.*** She is really *buckling down to* her new job. ***Ex 3.*** You cannot play around with this assignment : it is something that needs to be *buckled down* to seriously.

Buckle to : (a) make a special effort in the face of difficulties. ***Ex.*** The childern had to *buckle to* while their mother was in hospital.

(b) get busy. ***Ex.*** They *buckled to* and finished the work assigned to them.

Bugger about/around : (a) behave in a foolish or irresponsible way. ***Ex 1.*** Now stop *buggering about*, Nithish. I have got work to do. ***Ex 2.*** If you carry on *buggering around* with those matches, you are likely to set the house on fire.

(b) treat sb in a foolish or casual way; behave as though one had a poor estimate of sb's worth, etc. ***Ex 1.*** She is sick of being *buggered about* by the company. ***Ex 2.*** I bluntly told my employer not to *bugger* me *about* even in the least. ***Ex 3.*** Don't try to be clever with him. If he thinks you are *buggering* him *around*, he will clobber you.

Bugger off : go away; leave; clear off. ***Ex 1.*** *Bugger off* and leave me alone. ***Ex 2.*** He had *buggered off* before I had a chance to get a word in. ***Ex 3.*** I was only four minutes late but they had all *buggered off*.

Bugger up : spoil; ruin; make a mess of. ***Ex 1.*** Don't go fiddling around with that spanner - you will *bugger* the whole works *up*. ***Ex 2.*** Things can easily be *buggered up* by twits like you.

Build in/into : make a firm and necessary part of something. ***Ex.*** The landlord insisted on *building into* our agreement a clause for bidding us to sublet.

Build on : (a) use something as a foundation for further progress. ***Ex.*** In their latest design, the company is clearly *building on* the tremendous success of previous years.

(b) base something on something. ***Ex 1.*** My argument is *built on* sound logic. ***Ex 2.*** Don't *build* your hopes *on* the economic strength of the country.

Build up : (a) accumulate, so as to form a block; become greater or more numerous. ***Ex 1.*** Traffic is *building up* on roads into the city.***Ex 2.*** On the 15 August, traffic *built up* along the roads to the Red Fort. ***Ex 3.*** Tension is *building up* in the heart of the town.

(b) become more intense. ***Ex.*** Tension *built up* as the crisis approached.

(c) make healthier. ***Ex.*** As per medical advice, you need more protein to *build* you *up*.

(d) speak in glowing terms of sb/sth; speak with great praise about sh/sth, ***Ex 1.*** Don't *build* me *up* too much : I am really not that talented. ***Ex 2.*** He was not half the performer he was *build up* to be. ***Ex 3.*** The fihn was *build up* to be a masterpiece, but I found it very disappointing.

(e) become concentrated. ***Ex 1.*** Enemy forces are *building up* in the hills. ***Ex 2.*** Clouds are *building up* over the sea.

(f) develop. ***Ex.*** He has *built up* a remarkable physique by following these exercises.

(g) amass. ***Ex.*** They have *built up* quite a fortune in that business.

(h) acquire. ***Ex.*** She hopes to *build up* a reputation for honesty, integrity and intellectual ability.

Build up into : come or put together to form a whole. ***Ex.*** Eventually, these books will *build up into* a fine library.

Bulk out : make something bigger or thicker. ***Ex.*** You should add extra pages to *bulk* the book *out*.

Bulldoze into : (a) force sb to do something, by frightening him. ***Ex.*** They *bulldozed* me *into* signing the agreement.

(b) put something with force in the specified direction. ***Ex.*** She *bulldozed* her way *into* the meeting hall.

Bully into : force sb to do something, by frightening him. ***Ex.*** The general manager tried to *bully* his men *into* working harder by threatening them with dismissal.

Bum around : wander or hang about idly; travel around or spend time doing nothing in particular. ***Ex 1.*** He *bummed around* in Europe for six months. ***Ex 2.*** He just *bums around*, living from day to day.

Bumble about/along : act or move in a clumsy disorganised manner. ***Ex 1.*** The professor *bumbled* absent-mindedly *along* the road to the airport. ***Ex 2.*** She *bumbles about*, doing everything wrong.

Bump along/down: move with a jolting action. ***Ex.*** The old bus *bumped along* the mountain road.

Bump into: meet sb. by chance. ***Ex.*** Can you guess whom I *bumped into* this forenoon?

Bump off : kill or murder sb. ***Ex.*** Why did you *bump* him *off*?

Bump up : increase or raise something. ***Ex 1.*** They have *bumped up* prices of several household commodities. ***Ex 2.*** Do you want to *bump up* your income?

Buoy up : (a) keep cheerful or content. ***Ex.*** He was *buoyed up* by thinking that he might manage to get married himself.

(b) encourage sb; raise the hopes or spirits of sb. ***Ex.*** We felt *buoyed up* by the good news.

Burn out: (a) ruin one's health through overwork, etc. ***Ex 1.*** The last time I saw him, he looked completely *burned out*. ***Ex 2.*** If you don't give up this evening work, you will *burn* yourself *out*.

(b) die, burn to an end. ***Ex 1.*** His anger seems to have *burned out*. ***Ex 2.*** Her enthusiasm has *burned out*.

Burn with : be filled with, or consumed by. ***Ex.*** She *burned with* longing for her absent lover.

Burst in : enter suddenly. ***Ex.*** The police *burst in* through the door and arrested the gang.

Burst in on : interrupt .sb/sth by arriving suddenly. ***Ex 1.*** Why did you *burst in on* the meeting? ***Ex 2.*** You should not have *burst in on* us without knocking.

Burst into : (a) begin, suddenly and/or violently, to cry, laugh, sing, etc. ***Ex 1.*** Anandi, who has been nervous and jumpy lately, suddenly *burst into* tears. ***Ex 2.*** Why did you *burst into* a guffaw?

(b) begin, suddenly and violently, to burn. ***Ex.*** The aircraft crashed and *burst into* flames.

(c) begin suddenly to flower. ***Ex.*** The orchards seemed to have *burst into* blossom overnight.

Burst out : exclaim; declare suddenly and with feeling. ***Ex 1.*** She *burst out* crying. ***Ex 2.*** He angrily *burst out*, why don't you stop pretending that you know all the answers?

Burst out/out of: leave abruptly and/or violently. ***Ex.*** The gate suddenly gave way and an angry crowd *burst out of* the yard.

Burst out of : grow too big or fat for. ***Ex.*** All the children were *bursting out of* their school uniforms.

Burst through : make an opening and come through it with sudden violence. ***Ex.*** Desperate efforts were made to seal off the gap *through* which the enemy troops had *burst*.

Burst upon: occur suddenly to; draw on/upon sb. ***Ex 1.*** The truth of what his wife had been saying suddenly *burst upon* him. ***Ex 2.*** When did the varacity of the case *burst upon* you?

Burst with: show an abundance of. ***Ex.*** It is said that both of you are *bursting with* health and good looks.

Bury (oneself) in : (a) go to a place where one will meet few people. ***Ex 1.*** He *buried himself in* the village to pen a book. ***Ex 2.*** What made her go and *bury herself in* the country ?

(b) become deeply involved in something; concentrate deeply on something. ***Ex 1.*** In the evenings, he *buries himself* in his books. ***Ex 2.*** Right after dinner, he would go into the study and *bury himself* in his paper-work. ***Ex 3.*** Don't disturb me : I am *buried* in the crossword.

Bust up: cause something to end; disrupt something; break up. ***Ex 1.*** Why did they *bust up* the meeting? ***Ex 2.*** It was his drinking that *busted up* their marriage. ***Ex 3.*** Everything was fine between those two friends until that stunningly beautiful woman stepped in an *busted* them *up*.

Note : The word bust-up is a noun. It means *violent quarrel*. ***Ex 1.*** Therewas a *bust-up* between those two young men over a property dispute. ***Ex 2.*** We heard a tremendous *bust-up* going on in the next room.

Butt in : (a) interrupt a conversation. ***Ex 1.*** I wish you would not keep *butting in* when we are in the middle of a conversation. ***Ex 2.*** He always *butts in* when we are talking. ***Ex 3.*** May I *butt in* on your conversation? ***Ex 4.*** Don't *butt in* like that when I am speaking. **(b)** meddle, intervene, interfere. ***Ex 1.*** It is better that his affairs should be handled by one man. It makes confusion if someone else *butts in*. ***Ex 2.*** Of course, I don't want to *butt in* on the technical side.

Butter up : flatter sb with a view to obtaining favours, etc. ***Ex 1.*** Don't *butter* me *up*. I hate hypocrisy. ***Ex 2.*** Look at him *buttering up* the general manager. ***Ex 3.*** I have seen her *buttering up* the boss.

Butter up to : try to get close to sb by flattering him insincerely. ***Ex.*** Don't bother *buttering up to* me. I am too old a hand to be won over by flattery.

Button up : complete something successfully; conclude or finalise something. ***Ex 1.*** Prompt and proper steps should be taken to *button up* the deal with three days. ***Ex 2.*** When was the matter *buttoned up*?

Buy in : buy a stock of something (as a precaution in the event of a shortage). ***Ex 1.*** People *bought in* stocks of tinned goods in anticipation of food rationing. ***Ex 2.*** Let us *buy in* coal for the ensuing winter.

Buy off : persuade sb, by paying hiin money, not to act against one's interest. ***Ex 1.*** Don't ignore her threats to lodge a report against you : she will have to be *bought off*. ***Ex 2.*** If you are trying to *buy* me *off*, I am afraid you have; to the wrong person. ***Ex 3.*** Unless he drops the charge, we shall have to *buy* him *off*.

Buy out : pay sb to give up a post, or a share in a business; obtain control by buying all shares. ***Ex 1.*** New members can join by *buying out* an existing member at the current price of units. ***Ex 2.*** Having *bought out* all his partners, he now owns the whole company. ***Ex 3.*** The bigger company has *bought out* all the shareholders of the smaller one.

Buy up : buy all or as much as possible of something; obtain complete financial control over something. ***Ex 1.*** A Calcutta businessman has *bought up* the entire company. ***Ex 2.*** All the land for miles around has been *bought up* by one of my fast friends. ***Ex 3.*** Let us *buy up* all available land around New Delhi. ***Ex 4.*** Speculators are trying to *buy up* supplies of raw materials.

Buzz about/around: move quickly and busily. ***Ex.*** Madhu Malti *buzzed around* the kitchen making proper preparations for the dinner parry

Buzz off : go away; leave. ***Ex 1.*** *Buzz off* and leave me alone. ***Ex 2.*** He just *buzzed off* and left his wife to cope with the house and children.

---

3 *Words Beginning With–C*

Cage in : make somebody feel that he is in a cage. ***Ex.*** In that office, I felt terribly *caged in.*

Cake in/with: cover something thickly with something that becomes hard when dry. ***Ex 1.*** His shoes were *caked with* mud. ***Ex 2.*** When he arrived home from the match, he was *caked in* mud from head to foot.

Calculate on : depend or rely on. ***Ex.*** We cannot *calculate on* having good weather for the party.

Call about : visit somebody to discuss something. ***Ex.*** I have been asked by our general manager to *call about* your outstanding debt on the cooker.

Call at : visit a place. ***Ex.*** I shall *call at* your house tomorrow at 4.30 p.m.

Call away : summon by calling. ***Ex 1.*** He was *called away* by his friends. ***Ex 2.*** The doctor was *called away* a few minutes ago.

Call by : visit a place or a person briefly when passing by a house, etc. ***Ex 1.*** I shall *call by* on my way home. ***Ex 2.*** Please remain at home at four o'clock this evening. I shall *call by* and pick up my books and clothes.

Call down : (a) reprimand or scold somebody severely. ***Ex.*** They really *called* me *down* for doing that.

(b) summon, invoke: ***Ex.*** The old man *called down* curses on his enemies.

Call for : (a) require, demand or need something. ***Ex 1.*** This job *calls for* a man of considerable initiative, tact and resourcefulness. ***Ex 2.*** The work *calls for* endurance and patience. ***Ex 3.*** The situation *calls for* prompt action. ***Ex 4.*** You have got the job; this *calls for* a celebration. ***Ex 5.*** That rude remark was not *called for.*

(b) go to somebody's house to take him somewhere; go to a house, shop, etc. to collect something. ***Ex 1.*** What time shall I *call for* you tomorrow? ***Ex 2.*** The goods will be *called for* by our servant. ***Ex 3.*** She *called for* the books she had lent me.

Call forth : (a) demand, bring into play; cause to appear; elicit. ***Ex 1.*** His speech *called forth* an angry response from the audience. ***Ex 2.*** The dark days of 1942 *called forth* the best in the character of the Indian people. ***Ex 3.*** The emergency *called forth* reserves of energy which he did not know he possessed. ***Ex 4.*** His behaviour *called forth* numerous protests.

(b) produce and use. ***Ex.*** You will have to *call forth* all your energy.

Call in : (a) request, order, the return of something. ***Ex 1.*** The army *called in* all the unwanted ammunition. ***Ex 2.*** The library *called in* all overdue books. .

(b) stop at one place on the way to another. ***Ex.*** *call in* this evening, if you can; I have something important to discuss.

Call off : (a) stop or give the order to stop. ***Ex.*** As we were getting too far from our factory premises, I decided to *call* my workers *off*.

(b) order somebody to stop attacking, worrying or searching somebody. ***Ex.*** Please *call* your dog *off*–it is frightening the children.

(c) cancel, abandon or drop something. ***Ex 1.*** They should *call off* this competition for her love. ***Ex 2.*** I don't see any point in going on with our idea of a picnic, therefore *called off* the programme. ***Ex 3.*** Let us call it off. ***Ex 4.*** The workers have decided to *call off* their strike. ***Ex 5.*** The match was *called off* because of bad weather.

Call on : visit a person. ***Ex.*** She *called on* me yesterday for about an hour.

Call out : (a) give a greeting, make a request, etc. in a loud voice. ***Ex 1.*** Good morning, he *called out* to me. ***Ex 2.*** If you want anything from the shop, just *call out* and I shall bring it.

(b) state, declare, in a loud voice. ***Ex.*** Please keep quiet while I *call out* the names of the successful candidates.

(c) order or advise to go on strike. ***Ex 1.*** The trade union leaders *called* the workers *out* on strike. ***Ex 2.*** Bus-drivers may be *called out* on strike in support of their recent wage-claim.

(d) summon from a place. ***Ex 1.*** Doctors are often *called out* in the middle of the night. ***Ex 2.*** A practical joker picked up the telephone and *called out* the fire-brigade. ***Ex 3.*** The government will *call out* the army, as and when necessary.

(e) shout, try to attract attention; cry out. ***Ex.*** The starving peasants *called out* for food and clothes.

Call over : (a) visit casually. ***Ex.*** He *called over* to see us yesterday.

(b) call in sequence. ***Ex.*** He *called over* all the names on the list.

Call round : pay a visit to. ***Ex 1.*** Do *call round* when you have the time. We are at home most evenings. ***Ex 2.*** I shall *call round* at my brother's house this afternoon to pick up the dictionary.

Call up : (a) reach, communicate with, by telephone. ***Ex 1.*** I shall *call* you *up* if I need your help. ***Ex 2.*** I tried to *call* you *up* last night, but no one answered the phone.

(b) summon for military or national service. ***Ex 1.*** The general *called up* reinforcements. ***Ex 2.*** He was *called up* right at the beginning of the war. ***Ex 3.*** The army is *calling up* reservists in case of emergency.

(c) recall to memory. ***Ex.*** The sound of happy laughter *called up* memories of his childhood.

Call upon : (a) invoke. ***Ex.*** The government hopes that it will not be necessary to *call upon* emergency powers.

(b) invite, request. ***Ex 1.*** I now *call upon* the Chairman to address the meeting. ***Ex 2.*** I shall now *call upon* Mr. Himdri Datta to propose a vote of thanks to the committee.

(c) urge or appeal to somebody. ***Ex 1.***We shall have to *call upon* our friends to help us. ***Ex 2.*** The deputation *called upon* the mayor to invite his co-operation in their work. **Ex 3.** I feel *called upon* to warn you that you will be punished if you don't attend office both regularly and punctually.

Camp up : overact to an absurd degree, and in such a way as to please an unsophisticated audience. ***Ex.*** If the play is intrinsically bad, you will never turn it into a success by *camping* it *up* like that.

Cancel out : be equal to something in force and effect; counterbalance something. ***Ex 1.*** Her kindness and generosity *cancel out* her occasional flashes of temper. ***Ex 2.*** Your arguments *cancel* each other *out*. ***Ex 3.*** Your present behaviour *cancels out* any past help you gave us.

Cannon against : collide heavily with somebody/something. ***Ex 1.*** Don't do anything to *cannon against* national unity and integrity. ***Ex 2.*** The interests of two countries *cannon against* each other.

Care for : (a) like or love. ***Ex.*** He *cares for* her very deeply.

(b) look after: take *care* of; be responsible *for*. ***Ex.*** who will *care for*, him if his wife dies?

Carp at/about : complain continually about unimportant matters. ***Ex 1.*** She is always *carping at* her husband. ***Ex 2.*** Don't waste time *carping about* his laziness.

Carry along: help to continue or complete a task etc; give encouragement or support to. ***Ex 1.*** The amateur footballtearn was *carried along* by the enthusiasm of its supporters and finally defeated the more highly-rated professional club. ***Ex 2.*** His firm belief that he was on the threshold of a great discovery *carried* him *along*.

Carry away : move or fill somebody with emotion, so that he no longer has full control over his thoughts etc. ***Ex 1.*** When she starts to sing, she just *carries* you *away*. ***Ex 2.*** He tends to get *carried away* when watching wrestling on T.Y.***Ex 3.*** Don't get *carried away* with childish enthusiasm.

Carry back : take somebody back in memory; cause to remember. ***Ex 1.*** The sound of seagulls *carried* me *back* to my childhood holidays by the sea. ***Ex 2.*** The sight of the place *carried* him *back* to his childhood.

Carry forward : transfer the total of figures in a column or on a page to a new column or page. ***Ex 1.*** The money was *carried forward* to the next month. ***Ex 2.*** It is no use *carrying* this debt *folward*; we might as well write it off. ***Ex 3.*** He was *carried forward* on a wave of popular feeling.

Carry off : (a) win. ***Ex.*** She *carried off* most of the prizes for swimming.

(b) handle a situation successfully. ***Ex.*** He *carried* the speech *off* well despite feeling very nervous.

Carry on : (a) continue doing something. ***Ex.*** Please *carry* on working as usual while I am away.

(b) fuss, quarrel, argue, behave noisily. ***Ex 1.*** The children have been *canying on* a bit. ***Ex 2.*** He was *carrying on* about his pen.

(c) maintain. ***Ex.*** Life on earth is not going to be impossible, but it will have to be *carried on* in far less favourable circumstances.

(d) conduct, hold. ***Ex.*** You should not *carry on* long conversation with your friends when someone else is waiting to use the telephone.

(e) transact. ***Ex 1.*** We *carried on* our business in an honest manner. ***Ex 2.*** A great many shady businesses are *carried on* through the advertisement columns of respectable newspapers.

(f) have an irregular affair with. ***Ex 1.*** People say that she is *carrying on* with her boss. ***Ex 2.*** It is really shocking that your husband is *carrying on* with the lovely woman next door. ***Ex 3.*** They have been *carrying on* for years.

Carry out : (a) fulfil something; do something as required. ***Ex 1.*** He did not carry out my instructions. ***Ex 2.*** I *carried out* the project without difficulty. ***Ex 3.*** You should *carry out* your promises.

(b) perform or conduct. ***Ex 1.*** The police *carried out* an extensive search for the murderer. ***Ex 2.*** Extensive tests have been *carried out* on the patient.

Carry over : (a) retain as an item to be dealt with at a later date. ***Ex.*** I propose that some minor matters on the agenda should be *carried over* for consideration at the next meeting of the committee.

(b) continue. ***Ex.*** Would you please *carry* the report *over* on to the next page.

(c) forward to the next balance sheet. ***Ex.*** He *carried* the money *over* to the next month.

Carry through : (a) sustain; help to survive difficult period. ***Ex.*** Her dogged determination *carried* her *through* the ordeal.

(b) complete something successfully. ***Ex 1.*** These aims will be *carried through* to the end. ***Ex 2.*** They *carried* the plan *through* to the last letter. ***Ex 3.*** I began the scheme but my wife *carried* it *through*. ***Ex 4.*** It is a difficult job but he is the person to *carry* it *through*.

Carry with : (a) obtain or keep the support of; persuade somebody to follow, agree with one. ***Ex.*** The Prime Minister appears to be *carrying* the whole youth of the country *with* him.

(b) be always aware or reminded of; retain. ***Ex.*** I shall always *carry with* me the memory of the sufferings he had to face in his childhood.

Carve out : make, build, a career as a result or great effort. ***Ex 1.*** He *carved out* a name for himself as ajournalist. ***Ex 2.*** He *carved out* a career for himself as an actor, though at first he hardly earned enough to keep body and soul together.

Carve-up : dismember; divide something into parts or slices. ***Ex 1.*** The territory was *carved up* by the occupying powers. ***Ex 2.*** The companies *carved up* the market to suit themselves. ***Ex 3.*** The victors mercilessly *carved up* the defeated country, each taking an equal share.

Cast in : get the benefit of; exploit for profit; take advantages of. ***Ex 1.*** The shopkeepers are *cashing in* on temporary shortages by raising prices. ***Ex 2.*** You should not try to *cash in* on the fact that she likes you.

Cash about/around for : try to find or think of something hurriedly or in an emergency. ***Ex 1.*** He *cast about* in his mind for some plausible excuse for not turning up at the meeting. ***Ex 2.*** He *cast about* desperately *for* something to say. ***Ex 3.*** The suspect *cast about for* some way of escaping from the police-car.

Cast aside : discard; remove; throw off; abandon. ***Ex 1.*** She has *cast* her old friends *aside*. ***Ex 2.*** He *cast aside* all his inhibitions. ***Ex 3.*** As soon as he inherited his father's fortune, he *cast* his old friends *aside*.

Cast away : leave somebody somewhere as a result of a shipwreck. ***Ex.*** Many people were *cast away* on a desert island.

Cast back : (a) look back. ***Ex.*** He *cast back* in his mind to the last war,trying to remember exact dates.

(b) direct to the past. ***Ex 1.*** He *cast back* his mind to earlier days. ***Ex 2.*** She *cast* her thoughts *back* to happier times.

Cast down : (a) lower. ***Ex.*** She *cast* her eyes *down* shyly.

(b) be depressed or unhappy; demoralise or discourage. ***Ex 1.*** He feels rather *cast down* at the moment. ***Ex 2.*** I am not easily *cast down*. ***Ex 3.*** He was not easily *cast down*, but circumstances combined to depress him.

Cast off : (a) release the ropes or cables used to hold a boat or ship in position alongside a quay etc. ***Ex 1.*** The order was given to *cast off* and soon the ship was moving away from the quay. ***Ex 2.*** The men *cast off* and began rowing out to sea.

(b) abandon or reject somebody/something. ***Ex 1.*** People say that she has *cast off* four boy-friends in a month. ***Ex 2.*** When he grows tired of a woman, he just *casts* her *off* like an old coat.

(c) remove temporarily or permanently; take off and throw aside carelessly. ***Ex 1.*** He *cast off* his clothes and dived into the cool water of the lake. ***Ex 2.*** Some people *cast off* clothing long before it is worn out.

Cast out : expel; drive away. ***Ex 1.*** As the members of the association did not like his behaviour, they *cast* him *out*. ***Ex 2.*** The old animals were *cast out* from the herd. ***Ex 3.*** He was said to be able to *cast out* demons.

Cast round for : try to find or seek hurriedly or in an emergency; cast I about for.***Ex.*** I *cast round for* a reasonable excuse to leave my guests. In the end, I simply walked out.

Cast up : (a) direct upwards. ***Ex.*** He *cast* his eyes *up* to heaven and asked for patience.

(b) calculate. ***Ex.*** He tried to *cast up* the whole complicated thing.

(c) refer to constantly, in reproach. ***Ex 1.*** She goes on *casting up* his old infidelities. ***Ex 2.*** He always *casts up* at her the fact that she crashed the car. ***Ex 3.*** Don't *cast* that *up* at me the whole time.

(d) throw, deposit upon ***Ex.*** The shipwrecked sailors were *cast up* on the shore of a desert island.

Catch at : try to seize something. ***Ex.*** He *caught at* the branch but could not reach it.

Catch on : (a) understand something. ***Ex 1.*** Are you very quick to *catch on*? ***Ex 2.*** He is not doltish (foolish) : he will *catch on* what you are doing. ***Ex 3.*** He followed the conversation rather blankly for a while, then his expression changed. He was *catching on.*

(b) become popular or fashionable. ***Ex 1.*** It is said that mini-skirts first *caught on* in the 1960's. ***Ex 2.*** We thought of opening a restaurant downstairs, but the suggestion never *caught on* with the older committee members. ***Ex 3.*** The fashion of wearing loose clothes is *catching on.*

Catch out : (a) show that somebody is ignorant or doing something wrong. ***Ex 1.*** Ask me anything you like-you won't *catch* me *out*. ***Ex 2.*** He tried to *catch* me *out* with his smart questions.

(b) discover, trap. ***Ex 1.*** Be careful, or they will *catch* you *out* telling lies. ***Ex 2.*** She was *caught out* cheating in the examination.

(c) dismiss a batsman by catching the ball after he has touched it with his bat and before it touches the ground. ***Ex.*** Three of the batsmen were *caught out* by the wicket-keeper.

Catch-up : (a) seize, gather to oneself, hastily. ***Ex 1.*** The woman caught up her basket and ran out of the shop before anyone could stop her. ***Ex 2.*** He *caught* the child *up* in his arms.

(b) raise and fasten something hanging free or loose. ***Ex 1.*** Her hair was *caught up* with a long pin. ***Ex 2.*** She *caught up* her hair into a bun.

(c) trap. ***Ex 1.*** He had *caught* his coat *up* in the chain of his bicycle, and this caused the accident. ***Ex 2.*** She disentangled the sleeve of her jumper, which has got *caught up* in a rose bush.

(d) make special efforts to do something which has been left undone, or neglected. ***Ex 1.*** My secretary had to work in the lunch hour to *catch up* on his neglected filing. ***Ex 2.*** I have got a lot of work to *catch up* on.

(e) reach and sometimes overtake somebody who is ahead; reach the same stage as somebody. ***Ex 1.*** Go on in front. I shall soon *catch* you *up*. ***Ex 2.*** After missing a term through illness, he had to work hard in order to *catch up* with the others. ***Ex 3.*** I expect he will *catch up* on lost time by working harder. ***Ex 4.*** He says he just cannot *catch up* with his work.

Catch up on : (a) overtake; defeat; change a person's outlook or way of life. ***Ex 1.*** It appears that marriage has *caught up* on him. ***Ex 2.*** I think her past is beginning to *catch up* on her.

(b) acquire information about something belatedly. ***Ex.*** Come over for a chat, so that we can *catch up* on each other's news.

Cater for : expect. ***Ex 1.*** He did not *cater for* all these problems when he bought this shop. ***Ex 2.*** She said she had not *catered for* the interference of colleagues when she took the job.

Cater to : try to satisfy a particular need or demand. ***Ex.*** Some of the newspapers are always *catering to* people's love of scandal.

Cave in : (a) collapse; fall inwards. ***Ex.*** The roof of the tunnel *caved in* on the workmen.

(b) yield; collapse morally under some kind of pressure. ***Ex 1.*** Under close questioning, the suspect *caved in* and confessed all his misdemeanours. ***Ex 2.*** He *caved in* under the weight of her complaints. ***Ex 3.*** Don't expect the government to *cave in* on this issue. ***Ex 4.*** Enemy resistance soon *caved in*.

Centre in/on/upon : have somebody/something as its centre or main concern or theme; be concentrated or concentrate on somebody/something. ***Ex 1.*** My research-was *centered on* the social effects of unemployment. ***Ex 2.*** Public interest *centres upon* the outcome of next week's by-election. ***Ex 3.*** All his interests have *centred in* the people's methods of agriculture.

Centre on/round : have, fix, as its centre; revolve about/around; cause to revolve about/around. ***Ex 1.*** The social life of the village *centres round* the local sports club. ***Ex 2.*** He became involved in the whirlpool of activity which *centred round* Mahatma Gandhi. ***Ex 3.*** To give access to markets, the newtndustries had been *centred on* a motorway junction.

Chain down : hold or keep down with chains. ***Ex.*** They decided to *chain* the prisoners *down*.

Chain up : restrain movement by means of a chain, or chains. ***Ex.*** That dog ought to be *chained up*; it is dangerous.

Chalk out : draw the outline of something with chalk. ***Ex 1.*** Goalposts were roughly *chalked out* on the playground wall. ***Ex 2.*** To explain his design to the visitors, the architect *chalked out* a simple plan on the blackboard.

Chalk up : (a) mark up with chalk. ***Ex.*** He *chalked up* their names on a blackboard.

(b) mark a score. ***Ex.*** The numbers were *chalked up* as the results came in.

(c) achieve or register a success. ***Ex 1.*** Our team has *chalked up* its fifth win in a row. ***Ex 2.*** Their team *chalked up* another victory last week.

(d) give credit to somebody or somebody's account for something. ***Ex.*** They willingly *chalked up* ₹ 500 worth of sales to me.

Chance on : happen to meet or find; meet by accident. ***Ex.*** I *chanced on* her last week for the first time in about five years.

Change back/into : (a) return to one's former shape, character, etc. ***Ex.*** Cats can never *change back into* kittens.

(b) take off one's clothes and put on others that one was wearing earlier. ***Ex.*** Can I *change back into* my jeans now?

Change down : engage a lower gear when driving a car, etc. ***Ex 1.*** The driver *changed down* from third to second gear. ***Ex 2.*** He did not *change down* quickly.

Change into : (a) alter; transform. ***Ex 1.*** As the magician waved his wand, the four mice *changed into* splendid white horses. ***Ex 2.*** His sickness *changed* him *into* a miserable, demanding old man. ***Ex 3.*** He suddenly *changed* from a well-behaved child *into* a loutish adolescent.

(b) break a large unit of money into smaller ones; give for the currency of one country the equivalent currency of another. ***Ex 1.*** You can *change* your money *into* the local currency at the airport. ***Ex 2.*** Could you *change* this five-hundred rupee note *into* ten-rupee notes for me, please?

(c) put on a garment, or garments having removed another, or others. ***Ex 1.*** Just a minute, I shall *change into* something smarter. ***Ex 2.*** Just let me *change into* something less formal. ***Ex 3.*** You must *change into* a clean dress beiore we go out.

Change out of : remove a garment, or garments in order to put on another, or others. ***Ex.*** Let us go for a walk. All right; I shall just *change out of* these old things.

Change over to : adopt something new or different; change one's activity or profession. ***Ex 1.*** I used to take tea at breakfast, but I have *changed over to* coffee. ***Ex 2.*** We have just *changed over* from gas *to* electricity. ***Ex 3.*** That country has *changed over* from military *to* democratic rule.

Change over/round : (a) exchange places, positions or roles; change places with. ***Ex 1.*** I would like to drive the car into Shimla, so if you will stop at the next parking-place, we shall *change over*. ***Ex 2.*** You and Ramesh should *change round*, you need more experience of office routine.

(b) change positions, change ends. ***Ex.*** After a certain number of points, the players *changed round*, so that neither could benefit unduly from the wind or the position of the sun.

Change up : move to a higher gear. ***Ex.*** The driver *changed up* from second to third gear.

Channel off : divert. ***Ex.*** They tried to *channel off* some of the revenue earmarked for ornaments and use it to alleviate poverty.

Charge up : record something as a debt to be paid by somebody. ***Ex 1.*** Please *charge* these goods *up* to my account. ***Ex 2.*** Tell him to *charge* the meal *up* to the company.

Charge with : (a) accuse of. ***Ex 1.*** The policeman *charged* him *with* driving a car while under the influence of alcohol. ***Ex 2.*** The offence *with* which he is *charged* carries a heavy penalty.

(b) fill; make heavy. ***Ex 1.*** His entry on stage had once again *charged* the scene *with* dramatic tension. ***Ex 2.*** The atmosphere was tense and *charged with* fear.

(c) allot a duty or responsibility to somebody. ***Ex 1.*** Rajni was *charged with* a very important mission. ***Ex 2.*** The young officer was *charged with* the task of taking 100 prisoners to the rear.

Charm from/out of : get something from somebody/something by using charm. ***Ex 1.*** He could *charm* the birds *out of* the trees. ***Ex 2.*** She managed to *charm* the little girl down *from* the top of the ladder.

Chase about/around : rush or hurry. ***Ex.*** He has been *chasing about* town all morning looking for an exquisite present for her.

Chase around after : occupy one's time and energy with or in pursuit of. ***Ex.*** If he did not spend so much of his time *chasing around* after girls, he might have some chance of getting through his B.A. examination.

Chase away/out : force somebody/something to run away; drive somebody/something away. ***Ex 1.*** He *chased* the cat *out* into the garden. ***Ex 2.*** The little boy *chased* the cat *out* of the kitchen.

Chase up : (a) contact somebody and try to obtain money, information, etc. ***Ex.*** *chase up* the clients with outstanding debts.

(b) try to investigate something or make something happen more quickly. ***Ex.*** Who will *chase up* the delayed order?

Chat up : chat to somebody in a friendly or flirtatious manner in order to gain his or her confidence. ***Ex 1.*** I saw him *chatting up* with a charming girl last evening. ***Ex 2.*** She was being *chatted up* by a bearded youth when I arrived on the scene.

Cheat at : play unfairly. ***Ex.*** He was asked to resign from the club when he was discovered *cheating at* cards.

Cheat of : prevent from. ***Ex 1.*** The cat was *cheated* of its prey by the warning cries of the parent birds. ***Ex 2.*** It was the lack of a proper education, *of* which he had been *cheated* by his parents' penury (extreme poverty).

Cheat out of : prevent somebody from having something, in an unfair or a dishonest way. ***Ex 1.*** She was *cheated out of* her rightful inheritance. ***Ex 2.*** Don't *cheat* him *out of* his honest earnings.

Check in at : (a) register as a guest at a hotel or as a passenger at an airport. ***Ex 1.*** He *checked in at* the hotel on Monday, the 12th April, 1992, at 6 p.m. ***Ex 2.*** They had an accident on the road and did not *check in at* their hotel until after midnight.

(b) arrange a place for. ***Ex.*** I shall *check* you *in at* one of the best hotels.

Check in : leave or accept something for safe keeping in a cloak room or left luggage office. ***Ex.*** Is there a place we can *check in* our coats?

Check off : (a) mark items on a list as correct or as having been dealt with ***Ex 1.*** Please *check off* these parcels before they are despatched. ***Ex 2.*** He *checked* their names *off* as they went aboard the plane.

(b) go off duty. ***Ex.*** He *checked off* at eight o'clock.

Check on : verify ***Ex.*** He wanted to find out whether the children had their coats or not; he looked in the cloakroom to *check on* that.

Check out : (a) make a systematic inspection of a number of listed things. ***Ex 1.*** When all the instruments had been *checked out* according to the established routine, the pilot signalled that he was ready for take-off. ***Ex 2.*** We should *check* the whole place *out,* in case it has been bugged.

(b) leave a hotel, etc. ***Ex.*** He *checked out* last night, and left no forwarding address.

(c) assist departure of. ***Ex 1.*** We *checked* them *out* this morning. ***Ex 2.*** The airline has *checked* their luggage *out.*

(d) confirm by carefully checking. ***Ex 1.*** Would you *check out* these names and numbers, please? ***Ex 2.*** Ask him to *check* the information *out* for us.

Check over : examine something to find out if it is correct. ***Ex 1.*** The secretary always *checked over* the letters before putting them on the director's desk. ***Ex 2.*** *Check* the manuscript *over* carefully before passing it to the typist. ***Ex 3.*** I would like you to *check over* the proofs of this book. ***Ex 4.*** He *checked over* the names on the list to ensure that everything was correct.

Check up : examine; make a check. ***Ex 1.*** I shall just *check up* and find out if he is still here. ***Ex 2.*** The doctor will *check up* on how things are going with you. ***Ex 3.*** The company will *check up* on the estimates for the next year.

Check up on : investigate; test. ***Ex 1.*** The police are *checking up on* him. ***Ex 2.*** You should *check up on* this story before you print it.

Cheer on : encourage somebody to make greater efforts by cheering. ***Ex.*** The crowd *cheered* the runners *on* as they started on the last lap of the race.

Cheer up : become happier or more cheerful. ***Ex 1.*** Try and *cheer up* a bit; life is not that bad. ***Ex 2.*** You look as though you need to be *cheered up*. ***Ex 3.*** I sent her a Get Well card to *cheer* her *up*. ***Ex 4.*** I expect he will *cheer up* when he sees the new car. ***Ex 5.*** She tried to *cheer* them *up* with funny stories.

Cheese off : make somebody bored, frustrated or annoyed. ***Ex 1.*** He is cheesed off with his job. ***Ex 2.*** What finally *cheesed* me *off* was being passed over when the director's job fell vacant. ***Ex 3.*** Tell me how she *cheesed* you *off*.

Chew over : consider slowly and carefully. ***Ex 1.*** I shall give you till tomorrow to *chew* the matter *over*.

Chew up : (a) spoil. ***Ex.*** The machine *chewed up* the paper.

(b) reprimand. ***Ex.*** The general manager really *chewed* us *up* yesterday because of what we did.

Chicken out : decide not to do something because one is afraid; lose courage; dodge or escape like a frightened chicken. ***Ex 1.*** He had an appointment to see the dentist but he *chickened out* at the last moment. ***Ex 2.*** He is a coward, and he will *chicken out* if he can. ***Ex 3.*** They feared that their allies would *chicken out* at the last moment.

Chime in : interrupt a conversation. ***Ex 1.*** He kept *chiming in* with his own opinions. ***Ex 2.*** She *chimed in* with some ideas of her own. ***Ex 3.*** Can you think of some ready way of stopping him from *chiming in*?

Chime in with : fit or suit something. ***Ex 1.*** It is good that your plans *chime in with* ours. ***Ex 2.*** What he had said *chimed in* perfectly *with* her own immediate reaction.

Chip away at : continuously break off small pieces from something. ***Ex 1.*** The sculptor *chipped away* steadily *at* the stone. ***Ex 2.*** He was *chipping away at* a block of marble with a chisel.

Chip in : join in or interrupt a conversation. ***Ex 1.*** He *chipped in* with several complaints of his own. ***Ex 2.*** She *chipped in* with some interesting remarks. ***Ex 3.*** Who asked you to *chip in* with your opinion?

Chip in with : contribute money. ***Ex.*** I *chipped in with* hundred rupees towards his retirement present. ***Ex 2.*** If everyone *chips in with* a tenner, we will be able to buy her an exquisite present on the happy occasion of her seventeenth birthday.

Chisel out of : cheat or swindle somebody; obtain by a trick, or deceit. ***Ex 1.*** Watch that fellow. He will *chisel* you *out of* every paisa you have got, if you are not careful. ***Ex 2.*** A swindler *chiselled* him *out of* ten thousand rupees.

Chivvy along : continuously urge somebody to do something, often in an annoying way. ***Ex 1.*** His father kept on *chivvying* him *along* to get his hair cut. ***Ex 2.*** He *chivvied* the children *along* as fast as he could, ***Ex 3.*** The workers were getting tired of being *chivvied along* by their contractor.

Choke back : restrain or suppress something. ***Ex 1.*** When he saw the pitiful condition of the children in the orphanage, he could not *choke back* her tears. ***Ex 2.*** Please try to *choke back* your anger.

Choke down : (a) swallow something with difficulty. ***Ex.*** He did not like the food but he managed to *choke* it *down*.

(b) accept, with humiliation. ***Ex.*** He *choked down* the insult at the meeting of the board of directors last evening.

Choke off : (a) interrupt somewhat rudelyor abruptly. ***Ex 1.*** He *choked off* when I was penning a letter to a fast friend of mine. ***Ex 2.*** Don't *choke off* when he is busy.

(b) reprimand somebody severely for doing something. ***Ex 1.*** He choked off his son for disobedience. ***Ex 2.*** I was *choked off* by father for borrowing the car without permission.

(e) cut off or sever something by some violent action. ***Ex.*** Our army has *choked off* the enemy's supplies.

Chop about : keep changing from one thing to another, from one direction to another. ***Ex.*** First you say you want to be a doctor; then you are going to be a teacher; then you think you will join the Army; I wish you would not *chop about* so much.

Chop at : aim blows at something with an axe, a knife, etc. ***Ex.*** He was *chopping at* the tree with an axe.

Chop back : economise. ***Ex.*** We shall have to *chop back* on expenditure this month.

Chop down : cause something to fall down by cutting it at the base. ***Ex 1.*** I am going to *chop down* some of the old apple trees; they have almost stopped producing fruit.

Chop off : remove something from something by cutting with an axe, etc. ***Ex 1.*** These branches are overhanging the road; *chop* them *off*. ***Ex 2.*** The executioner *chopped* his head *off*.

Chop up : (a) divide. ***Ex.*** They have apparently decided to *chop up* the company into smaller units.

(b) cut into small pieces with a heave knife, or axe. ***Ex.*** As the furniture is old and useless, you should *chop* it *up* for firewood.

Chuck away : (a) fail to take advantage of. ***Ex.*** He *chucked away* his opportunity of making a career for himself in the Civil Sece.

(b) not use properly; throwaway. ***Ex.*** There were plenty of people ready to *chuck* his money *away*, but few to stand by him when he ended up bankrupt.

Chuck away on : marry, keep company with, squander one's time, energy or money on, somebody who is unworthy of one in the opinion of others. ***Ex.*** He was a nincompoop (fool) to *chuck* himself *away on* such a frivolous woman.

Chuck out : remove forcibly; expel; force to go. ***Ex 1.*** They *chucked* her *out* of the college for being a bad influence. ***Ex 2.*** He did not leave of his own free will; he was *chucked out*. ***Ex 3.*** They were *chucked out* of the club for being too rowdy. ***Ex 4.*** He failed in his examinations, and was *chucked out* of university.

Chuck up : abandon, leave; resign from. ***Ex 1.*** He *chucked up* the work and went to another town. ***Ex 2.*** He just *chucked up* his job at the factory and said he intended never to work again.

Chug along : move along slowly accompanied by the short dull repeated noise of the engine. ***Ex 1.*** The old ship *chugged along* the river. ***Ex 2.*** As we neared the harbour, a large boat came *chugging along*.

Chum up : become very friendly with; get on friendly terms with. ***Ex 1.*** Those two boys seem to leave *chummed up* pretty quickly. ***Ex 2.*** She *chummed up* with another new girl. ***Ex 3.*** Do you want to *chum up* with that charming young woman ?

Churn out : produce regularly and in large quantities, usually of bad quality. ***Ex 1.*** I dislike to *churn out* romantic novels. ***Ex 2.*** They wen *churning out* consumer goods faster than the market could absorl them. ***Ex 3.*** That author has *churned out* a lot of rubbish in his time

Claim back : ask for something to be returned. ***Ex.*** You can *claim* your money *back* if the goods are damaged.

Clam up : become totally uncommunicative, through fear; suspicion distrust, etc. ***Ex 1.*** They say that he always *clammed up* when the asked him about his wife. ***Ex 2.*** Don't *clam up* just when the story is getting interesting.

Clamp down on : become stricter about something; use one's authority against somebody or to prevent or suppress something. ***Ex 1.*** The government should *clamp down on* the corrupt officers and officials ***Ex 2.*** The authorities concerned should *clamp down on* violence in television programmes.

Clap in/into : put swiftly in/into jail, etc, often without trial. ***Ex.*** The suspects were *clapped in* prison and kept there for months without trial.

Clap on : (a) put on hastily. ***Ex.*** He *clapped* his hat *on* and strode angril from the room.

(b) add something to the price of something, in an unwelcome way. ***Ex.*** The government has *clapped on* an extra two rupees on a kilogra of sugar.

Clap out : feel completely worn out or exhausted. ***Ex.*** I feel really *clappe out* today.

Clash with : (a) join in rigorous argument with; disagree seriously abou something. ***Ex.*** The Prime Minister *clashed with* the leader of the Opposition on the question of unemployment.

(b) happen inconveniently at the same time as something else. ***Ex 1.*** It is a pity that the two concerts *clash with* each other; I wanted to go to both of them. ***Ex 2.*** Your dinner party *clashes with* a wedding I am going to.

(c) not match or harmonise. ***Ex 1.*** The colour of the wallpaper *clashes with* the carpet. ***Ex 2.*** The red of her scarf *clashes with* the purple of her hat.

Clatter across : move across making a clatter. ***Ex.*** The children *clattered across* the street.

Clean down : clean thoroughly, from top to bottom. ***Ex 1.*** He *cleaned* the car *down* last night. ***Ex 2.*** My mother always insists on *cleaning* the whole house *down* at least once a month.

Clean from : remove something from something by wiping, brushing or scraping. ***Ex.*** She *cleaned* the dirt *from* her finger-nails.

Clean out : clean the inside of something thoroughly. ***Ex.*** When were the stables last *cleaned out*?

Clean out/out of : take all a person's money or stock. ***Ex 1.*** I have not a rupee left; buying all those books has completely *cleaned* me *out*. ***Ex 2.*** The burglars *cleaned* her *out* of all her jewellery and money. ***Ex 3.*** The tobacconist was *cleaned out* of cigarettes by people who expected the price to go up.

Clean up : (a) make a place clean by removing dirt, etc; remove dirt, rubbish, etc. from a place to clean it. ***Ex 1.*** Now that the party is over, shall we *clean up*? ***Ex 2.*** She *cleaned* the place *up* after the children's party.

(b) get rid of something; make a place free of something; remove criminals, harmful influences, etc. from something. ***Ex 1.*** The Chief Minister of Delhi is determined to *clean up* the city. ***Ex 2.*** The police should take stern steps to *clean up* the town.

(c) suppress an enemy, usually small groups still resisting after a major advance; mop up. ***Ex.*** Our army *cleaned up* the remnants of the enemy trapped in certain areas in the western sector after the war between the two countries was over.

(d) make or win a lot of money. ***Ex.*** The fact that you have *cleaned up* an enormous fortune, has gladdened me beyond expression in language.

(e) get washed. ***Ex 1.*** I am just going home to *clean up*. ***Ex 2.*** Just give me five minutes to *clean* myself *up*; I am covered in mud. ***Ex 3.*** How long will you take to *clean* yourself *up*?

Clear away : remove objects in order to leave a clear space. ***Ex.*** The maid will *clear* these dishes *away*; then we will be able to work at the table.

Clear of : declare to be free from. ***Ex 1.*** The signalman was *cleared of* all responsibility for the railway accident. ***Ex 2.*** The accusations you are making relate to charges *of* which my client has been *cleared*.

Clear off : (a) run away; go away. You have no right to be here. Clear off. ***Ex 1.*** He *cleared off* as soon as he saw the policeman coming. ***Ex 2.*** When the man saw the policeman, he *cleared off* as fast as his legs could carry him.

(b) complete the payment of something. ***Ex 1.*** He has at last *cleared off* all his debts. ***Ex 2.*** When will you *clear off* all your hire purchase payments?

Clear out : (a) make something empty or tidy by removing what is inside it; clean by clearing thoroughly. ***Ex 1.*** The maid *cleared out* the cup-boards. ***Ex 2.*** Who will *clear out* the attic?

(b) remove; evict. ***Ex 1.*** He *cleared* the people *out of* the room. ***Ex 2.*** They have *cleared* all the tenants *out* of those houses.

(c) leave a place. ***Ex.*** I am fed up with being told what I can do and what I cannot do; I am *clearing out*.

Clear out/out of : leave quickly. ***Ex 1.*** If you have any sense, you will *clear out* before my father comes home from work. ***Ex 2.*** Tell him to *clear out* of this place before he causes any more trouble.

Clear up : (a) improve; become fine or bright. ***Ex 1.*** The weather was bad early this morning but it *cleared up* before ten o'clock. ***Ex 2.*** I think the weather will soon *clear up*.

(b) disappear as good health returns. ***Ex.*** Has your rash *cleared up* yet?

(c) make things tidy or orderly; remove rubbish, etc. ***Ex 1.*** We cannot go until all the bitter has been *cleared up*. ***Ex 2.*** Don't expect us to *clear up* that mess you are making. ***Ex 3.*** Please *clear up* before you leave this place.

(d) remove doubt about something; solve something. ***Ex 1.*** The police hope to *clear* the matter *up* within a couple of days. ***Ex 2.*** It is a mystery that has never been *cleared up*. ***Ex 3.*** Can you *clear up* this misunderstanding? ***Ex 4.*** I decided to go and see her, and get the point *cleared up* quickly; before trouble arose.

Clear with : have somebody/something inspected or approved by somebody in authority. ***Ex 1.*** You will have to *clear* it *with* the general manager. ***Ex 2.*** Have these cameras been *cleared with* the Custom Department? ***Ex 3.*** Get the visitors *cleared with* the security officer before you take them to the Minister's Office.

Climb down : admit a mistake; retract; withdraw from a position in an argument, etc. ***Ex 1.*** As new facts became known, the government was forced to *climb down* over its handling of the spy scandal. ***Ex 2.*** When he was proved wrong by the new evidence, he was forced to *climb down* and accept that he was mistaken.

Clip out of : remove something from something else with scissors, etc. ***Ex.*** I told him to *clip* the article on interview techniques *out of* today's Amrit Bazar Patrika.

Clock in/on : record the time of one's arrival at work by putting a card in a machine with a clock. ***Ex.*** Workers are expected to *clock in* at 8.30 a.m. every working day.

Clock out/off : record the time of one's departure from work by putting a card in a machine which stamps the time on the card. ***Ex 1.*** Workers usually *clock out* at 5.30 p.m. ***Ex 2.*** They *clocked* the men *out* at 6 p.m.

Close around/over : surround and enclose or grip. ***Ex 1.*** His hand *closed over* the money. ***Ex 2.*** She felt my arms *close around* her.

Close down : (a) stop broadcasting. ***Ex 1.*** Television *closed down* for the night just after 12.30 a.m. ***Ex 2.*** It is midnight and we are now *closing down*.

(b) stop functioning or operating; shut down. ***Ex 1.*** The factory had to *close down* through lack of orders. ***Ex 2.*** Many businesses have *closed down* because of the recession. ***Ex 3.*** He has *closed down* his business in Patna. ***Ex 4.*** We have decided to *close* that branch *down*.

Close in : (a) draw nearer to, or around somebody so as to attack or seize him. ***Ex.*** The enemy is *closing in*.

(b) surround or envelop somebody/something; approach. ***Ex 1.*** Darkness was gradually closing in. ***Ex 2.*** The night *closed in* again as the little oasis of light receded. ***Ex 3.*** The evening is *closing in*. ***Ex 4.*** When winter *closed in*, with constant rain, I sent for a waterproof suit.

(c) (of days) : get shorter. ***Ex.*** The days are *closing in* now that winter is nearly here.

Close in on/upon: encircle; tighten the circle round. ***Ex.*** Our army is now *closing in upon* the militants.

Close up : (a) heal. ***Ex 1.*** The wound took a long time to *close up*. ***Ex 2.*** The cut in his arm has begun to *close up*.

(b) come, or bring something closer together. ***Ex 1.*** The officer ordered the soldiers to *close up*. ***Ex 2.*** The marching men had to *close up* to let the oncoming convoy go past.'

(c) shut something temporarily. ***Ex 1.*** Sorry; madam, we are *closing up* for lunch. ***Ex 2.*** He *closes* the shop *up* at 8.30 p.m. ***Ex 3.*** These flowers *close up* at night.

(d) shut up for an indefinite period. ***Ex 1.*** The manager *closes up*; he is always the last to leave. ***Ex 2.*** She *closes* the office *up* at 6.30 p.m.

Close with : (a) grapple with. ***Ex.*** The wrestler *closed with* his opponent.

(b) start fighting. ***Ex.*** After a long period of shelling, our infantry surged forward and *closed with* the enemy in hand-to-hand fighting.

(c) agree on a price; strike a bargain with. ***Ex.*** After a good deal of discussion over the value of the car, I finally *closed with* him at a reasonable figure.

Cloud over : become cloudy. ***Ex.*** The sky has *clouded over*.

Clown about/around : act in a foolish way. ***Ex 1.*** Stop *clowning about*. ***Ex 2.*** Make it a point never to *clown around* in the presence of ugly girls or old women.

Club together: make contributions of money, so that the total sum can be used for a specific purpose. ***Ex 1.*** The employees of the company *clubbed together* to buy the managing director an exquisite present. ***Ex 2.*** We have *clubbed together* to help her with her debts. ***Ex 3.*** Let us *club together* to present a diamond necklace to her on the happy occasion of her nineteenth birthday to be celebrated on Tuesday; the 12th instant, with great gay, gaiety and gusto.

Clue in : provide with necessary information. ***Ex.*** Please *clue* me *in* on what you are doing, so that I can help you.

Clue up : provide with necessary information for professional purposes; make somebody well-informed. ***Ex 1.*** She is really *clued up* on politics. ***Ex 2.*** Are you very much *clued up* on electronics?

Cluster around/round : gather round in clusters or small groups; surround closely. ***Ex 1.*** Mohini highly admired the roses *clustering round* the door of our cottage. ***Ex 2.*** We *clustered around* to listen to him. ***Ex 3.*** Reporters *clustered around* the distinguished visitor from France. ***Ex 4.*** The village *clusters round* the Hanuman Temple.

Clutter up : (a) occupy space, giving a room, house, etc. an untidy appearance. ***Ex 1.*** Objects of every kind *cluttered up* the entrance to the house, so that it was almost impossible to get in. ***Ex 2.*** The passage was *cluttered up* with stacks of old books and pictures. ***Ex 3.*** Don't *clutter up* my desk; I have just tidied it.

(b) (of knowledge, information, etc.) : exist copiously but in a muddled way in somebody's mind. ***Ex 1.*** His head is *cluttered up* with all manner of useless information. ***Ex 2.*** Is your head *cluttered up* with useless facts ? ***Ex 3.*** Her writing style is *cluttered up* with fancy expressions.

Coast along : ride or drive without much effort or, in the case of a car, without using the engine. ***Ex 1.*** We *coasted along* on our bicycles with the wind behind us. ***Ex 2.*** As the fuel-gauge pointed to empty, I switched off the engine whenever I could and just *coasted along.*

Coax out of/from : obtain something from somebody by gentle persuasion. ***Ex 1.*** I *coaxed* a smile *from* her. ***Ex 2.*** I had to *coax* the information *out of* Chameli Devi.

Cock up : (a) raise. ***Ex.*** The horse *cocked up* its ears when it heard the loud noise.

(b) bungle; mess up; spoil or ruin. ***Ex.*** The travel agent completely *cocked up* the arrangements for our excursion.

Colour in : fill a particular area, shape, etc. with colour. ***Ex.*** The child *coloured in* all the shapes on the page with a crayon.

Colour up : (a) blush; go red in the face as a result of shyness, feelings of guilt or embarrassment. ***Ex 1.*** Why did she *colour up* at the mention of your name? ***Ex 2.*** She *coloured up* at his unseemly remarks.

(b) exaggerate; distort. ***Ex.*** There is no gainsaying the fact that some journalists like to *colour* their stories up with lurid details of people's private lives.

Comb through : search thoroughly. ***Ex.*** She *combed through* the files searching for evidence of fraud against you.

Come about: (a) happen. ***Ex 1.*** Can you tell me how the accident *came about*? ***Ex 2.*** I know nothing about how the accident *came about.* ***Ex 3.*** How did it *come about* that he knew where we were?

(b) change direction of movement. ***Ex 1.*** We *came about* and went off on a new track. ***Ex 2.*** The ship *came about* and headed back for safety.

Come across : (a) be understood or communicated. ***Ex.*** The preacher spoke for a long time but his meaning did not really *come across.*

(b) make an impression; be received. ***Ex 1.*** She *came across* as a sympathetic person. ***Ex 2.*** Your speech on India's Foreign Policy *came across* well. ***Ex 3.*** He *comes across* badly in interviews.

(c) meet or find by chance. ***Ex 1.*** I *came across* an old college friend in university Street this morning. ***Ex 2.*** I *came across* some old photographs in a drawer of his desk.

Come across with : give or hand over. ***Ex 1.*** She owes me ten thousand rupees but I doubt if she will ever *come across* with it. ***Ex 2.*** He *came across* with the names of his accomplices in the bank robbery.

Come after : (a) chase or pursue. ***Ex.*** As soon as we started across the field, the farmer *came after* us waving a big stick.

(b) follow in sequence. ***Ex.*** The foreign tourist says that the cheese *comes after* pudding in his country.

Come along : (a) arrive; appear. ***Ex.*** She is not married yet. She is waiting for the right person to *come along*.

(b) hurry up; be quick; try harder. ***Ex 1.*** *Come along*, boys. ***Ex 2.*** *Come along*, Maya; we cannot wait all day.

(c) attend. ***Ex 1.*** May my brother *come along* to the meeting as well? ***Ex 2.*** We are having a few persons in for tea tomorrow. Do *come along* if you are free.

(d) accompany. ***Ex.*** Would you *come along* with me, please?

(e) make progress. ***Ex 1.*** His broken arm is *coming along* quite well. ***Ex 2.*** His work is *coming along* well. ***Ex 3.*** He has begun to *come along* very well in English since the new tutor was appointed.

(f) grow; develop. ***Ex 1.*** Our roses are *coming along* well nicely. ***Ex 2.*** Those seedlings are *coming along* well in the greenhouse.

Come along with : move somewhere quickly. ***Ex.*** I asked him to *come along with* me to the restaurant to have a cup of tea. Coine apart: break or fall into pieces; disintegrate. ***Ex 1.*** The machine *came apart* when he started it up. ***Ex 2.*** I did not drop the plate: it just *came apart* in my hands.

Come at : (a) attack. ***Ex.*** She *came at* me with a big strick.

(b) discover; ascertain. ***Ex 1.*** The purpose of the official inquiry is to *come at* the true facts of the case. ***Ex 2.*** It is a universally accepted veracity that the truth is often difficult to *come at*. ***Ex 3.*** It is difficult to *come at* the exact facts.

(c) find; get hold of. ***Ex.*** He looked for that article, but could not *come at* it anywhere.

Come away : (a) become detached. ***Ex 1.*** The plaster had started to *come away* from the wall. ***Ex 2.*** I pulled the rotten wood and it *came away* without difficulty. ***Ex 3.*** His heel has come away from the rest of the shoe.

(b) leave. ***Ex.*** He had to *come away* before the end of the play.

Come away with : leave a place with. ***Ex.*** I *came away* with the distinct impression that all was not well with their marriage.

Come back : (a) return. ***Ex 1.*** I *came back* very late last night. ***Ex 2.*** Please *come back* to what you were saying a moment ago.

(b) become popular, successful or fashionable. ***Ex 1.*** Baggy trousers are starting to *come back*. ***Ex 2.*** Long skirts have been out of fashion for a long time, but they are *coming back*.

(c) be restored or reintroduced. ***Ex.*** There are many people in the country who would be glad to see the death penalty *come back* of certain offences.

(d) return to memory. ***Ex 1.*** Her face is *coming back* to me no ***Ex 2.*** The language I used to speak at my primary school *came back* me. ***Ex 3.*** At first I could not remember why everything seemeds familiar, then it all *came back.*

Come back at : reply to somebody forcefully or angrily. ***Ex 1.*** He *came back* at the speaker with some sharp questions. ***Ex 2.*** When charged with the crime, he *came back* at us furiously.

Come back to : reply somebody about something after a period of time ***Ex.*** Can I *come back to* you on that subject later?

Come before : (a) be presented to somebody/something for discussion decision or judgement. ***Ex.*** The case *comes before* the court next week.

(b) have greater importance than somebody/something els ***Ex 1.*** Fighting poverty and unemployment should *come before* all other political considerations. ***Ex 2.*** The building or homes, hospital and schools should *come before* the building of new office blocks.

Come between : interfere in the affairs of; cause the separation or estrangement of two persons. ***Ex 1.*** The lovers swore to let nothing and nobody *come between* them. ***Ex 2.*** It is often dangerous, and never wise to *come between* a man and his wife. ***Ex 3.*** I vehemently hate, anything to *come between* us.

Come between somebody and something : prevent somebody from doing or having something. ***Ex 1.*** I am not going to let a small matte like that *come between me and my sleep.* ***Ex 2.*** I don't let anything *come between me and my daily walk.*

Come by : (a) obtain. ***Ex 1.*** How did you *come by* this excellent painting. ***Ex 2.*** Jobs are very hard to *come by* these days. ***Ex 3.*** He says honestly came by that money.

(b) receive something by chance. ***Ex.*** How did she *come by* that scratch on her cheek?

Come down : (a) drop or fall. ***Ex 1.*** The snow *came down* thick and fast. ***Ex 2.*** The rain *came down* in torrents.

(b) collapse. ***Ex.*** The ceiling of their house *came down* last night.

(c) become lower; fall. ***Ex 1.*** Her temperature *came down* in the morning. ***Ex 2.*** His weight is slowly *coming down.* ***Ex 3.*** The price of petrol is *coming down.* ***Ex 4.*** Petrol is *coming down* in price.

(d) land or fall from the sky. ***Ex 1.*** We were forced to *come down* in a field. ***Ex 2.*** Four of our fighters *came down* inside enemy lines.

(e) make a present of money, give money to somebody. ***Ex.*** Just when I was at my wits' end wondering how to pay my bills, my old aunt *came down* handsomely; she sent me a cheque for ten thousand rupees.

(f) reach a .decision: decide to exert one's influece. ***Ex.*** The Chief Minister *came down* heavily on my side, and the Chief Secretary was routed.

Come down from : come from one place to another. ***Ex.*** When did you *come down from* Calcutta?

Come down on : (a) rebuke somebody; criticise severely for some fault. ***Ex.*** Don't *come down* too hard *on* her.

(b) punish somebody. ***Ex.*** The courts are *coming down* heavily *on* young offenders.

(c) demand money or payment from. ***Ex 1.*** His creditors *came down on* him for prompt payment of his bills, when they heard of his financial difficulties. ***Ex 2.*** He *came down on* the driver of the car for heavy damages.

Come down to : (a) be passed from one generation to another. ***Ex.*** These are the stories that *came down to* us from our forefathers.

(b) boil down to; be able to be summarised as something; be a question of something. ***Ex 1.*** It *comes down to* two choices : You can either stay here and obey me, or leave and never return. ***Ex 2.*** The whole dispute *comes down to* a power struggle between management and trade unions.

(c) be forced by poverty, etc. to do something that one would never do normally; be reduced to. ***Ex 1.*** He has *come down to* begging. ***Ex 2.*** I never thought that she would *come down to* asking my advice about her affairs.

(d) reach as far down as. ***Ex.*** Her hair *comes down to* her waist.

Come down with : (a) become ill with. ***Ex 1.*** He *came down with* flu, and was unable to go to work. ***Ex 2.*** As I *came down with* a severe attack of malarial fever, I could not, as originally planned, go on a tour of the various places of historical importance in the country.

(b) payout. ***Ex.*** She *came down with* six thousand rupees at last.

Come forth : emerge. ***Ex.*** I had very great hopes of his speech last night, but nothing new *came forth*.

Come forward : (a) present oneself; move to the fore; make oneself known. ***Ex 1.*** He has *come forward* with an offer of help. ***Ex 2.*** Will you *come forward* as a candidate in the local elections? ***Ex 3.*** The police have asked witnesses of the accident to *come forward* and help them with their inquiries.

(b) be raised for discussion. ***Ex.*** The matter was deferred at last evening's meeting, but will *come forward* at our next session on Monday; the 14th instant, at 4.30 p.m.

Come from : (a) have as one's birthplace or place of residence. ***Ex 1.*** He *comes from* Turkey. ***Ex 2.*** Where do you *come from*?

(b) be a product of. ***Ex 1.*** Milk *comes from* cows and buffaloes. ***Ex 2.*** Most of the dates eaten in India *come from* Iraq. ***Ex 3.*** These toys *come from* Japan.

Come from/of : (a) be descended from. ***Ex 1.*** She *comes from* a long line *of* actresses. ***Ex 2.*** He *comes of* an aristocratic family.

(b) be the result of *Ex 1.* I wonder if anything will *come of* our teaparty. *Ex 2.* Carry on with your present research. Nothing but good can *come of* it.

Come in : (a) become fashionable. *Ex 1.* Do you know exactly when wigs first *came in*, in this country? *Ex 2.* I expect long skirts will *come in* again soon.

(b) become seasonable or available. *Ex 1.* Apples do not *come in* before October. *Ex 2.* We have not any cotton curtains in stockjust at present; but they should *come in* any moment now.

(c) gain power. *Ex 1.* When the present government *came in*, the country was in a very difficult financial situation. *Ex 2.* The Communists *came in* at the last election.

(d) finish a race. *Ex 1.* Please tell me which horse *came in* first. *Ex 2.* Where did he *come in* second or third? *Ex 3.* He led most of the way but suddenly lost his strength and *came in* last.

(e) be received as income. *Ex.* He has five thousand rupees a month *coming in* from his investments.

(f) get some advantage from; have a part to play in. *Ex.* I understand the scheme perfectly, but I cannot see where I *come in*.

(g) move towards the land. *Ex 1.* Don't stay on the rocks too long, the tide is *coming in* fast, and you might get cut off. *Ex 2.* The tide is out now, but it starts to *come in* at about six o'clock.

(h) be received; reach the office, editor's desk, etc. *Ex.* News is *coming in* of a serious train crash in Muradnagar.

(i) continue with, or contribute to, a commentary, discussion, etc. *Ex 1.* Would you like to *come in* at this point, Mr. Himadri Datta? *Ex 2.* I should like to *come in* here, as I happen to know a good deal about how people live in these high-rise flats.

Come in for : be the object of something; attract something; receive something. *Ex 1.* She *came in* for a lot of criticism. *Ex 2.* The young artist's pictures *came in* for a great attention. *Ex 3.* The government's foreign policy has *come in for* a storm .of criticism from the newspapers.

Come in on : have a part or share in something; join something. *Ex.* If you want to *come in on* the venture, you must decide now.

Come in with: join somebody in a venture, scheme, etc. *Ex.* You can *come in with* us if you can contibute sixty thousand rupees.

Come into : inherit something. *Ex 1.* He *came into* a fortune when his uncle died. *Ex 2.* He has *come into* a lot of money from his old aunt's estate. *Ex 3.* I don't *come into* my share of the legacy until I am twenty-one.

Come of : (a) be the result of. *Ex 1.* No harm can *come of* tryping. *Ex 2.* This is what *comes of* being over-confident. *Ex 3.* He promised to help, but I don't think anything will *come of* it.

(b) be descended from. ***Ex.*** He comes of a noble family.

Come off : (a) fall from. ***Ex 1.*** He *came off* his horse when it refused to jump over a fence. ***Ex 2.*** He *came off* his bicycle on his way to school.

(b) become detached or separated from something. ***Ex 1.*** When I tried to lift the jug, the handle *came off*. ***Ex 2.*** Abutton has *come off* her coat.

(c) be removable. ***Ex 1.*** These knobs do not *come off*, they are fixed on permanently. ***Ex 2.*** The lid of this tin won't *come off* for me; can you move it?

(d) take place; happen. ***Ex 1.*** When is your wedding coming off ? ***Ex 2.*** Did your proposed trip to Ankara ever *come off*? ***Ex 3.*** His marriage did not *come off*; his fiancee broke off the engagement at the last minute.

(e) be successful; have the intended effect or result. ***Ex 1.*** Her attempt to break the world record nearly *came off*. ***Ex 2.*** The film does quite *come off*. ***Ex 3.*** His plans did not *come off*. **Ex 4.** Their attempt to rob him did not *come off*.

(f) fare; get on. ***Ex 1.*** He *came off* well by comparison with the others. ***Ex 2.*** He always *comes off* badly in fights. ***Ex 3.*** Let me know who *came off* best in the debate. ***Ex 4.*** How did you *come off* in the affair?

(g) have finished doing something. ***Ex.*** He had just *come off* an assignment which had taken him half way round the world.

(h) be removed from a price. ***Ex 1.*** I am waiting until Budget Day to see if something will *come off* the price of cars. ***Ex 2.*** I have heard that two rupes a gallon is *coming off* the price of petrol. ***Ex 3.*** Under the new rules, the import tariff *comes off* certain kinds of goods.

(i) disappear. ***Ex 1.*** These stains will not *come off*. ***Ex 2.*** The marks *came off* after some rubbing.

Come on : (a) leave a place in order to arrive at a destination later than somebody else. ***Ex.*** You had better go to the station now; I shall *come on* later.

(b) be cheerful or strong. ***Ex.*** *Come on*, try it again.

(c) start. ***Ex 1.*** It *come on* to rain. ***Ex 2.*** He feels a cold *coming on*. ***Ex 3.*** My throat is dry,and a bit sore; perhaps I have got a cold *coming on*.

(d) begin to arrive. ***Ex 1.*** The travellers wanted to reach the hotel before night *came on*. ***Ex 2.*** Winter is coming on : you can feel it in the air. ***Ex 3.*** Night is *coming on*.

(e) begin. ***Ex.*** Just as we were beginning to enjoy ourselves, the rain *came on* and spoilt everything.

(f) begin to bowl. ***Ex 1.*** Their best man *came on* to bowl. ***Ex 2.*** He *came on* to bowl after the tea interval.

(g) appear on (the stage in a play, concert, opera etc.). ***Ex.*** When Dilip Kumar *came on* for the first time, the audience lustily appluaded.

(i) be shown or performed. ***Ex 1.*** The film does not *come on* until nine o'clock, so there is plenty of time for us to get to the cinema. ***Ex 2.*** There is a very good play *coming on* at the Odeon next week.

(j) be considered (by a court). ***Ex 1.*** His case *comes on* this afternoon.***Ex 2.*** They have been waiting for a long time for their case to *come on.*

(k) continue to advance. ***Ex.*** The soldiers *came on* in the face of heavy fire.

(l) progress, develop. ***Ex 1.*** How are your potatoes *coming on*? ***Ex 2.*** Are your plans *coming on* all right?

Come on/upon: (a) encounter; find or meet by chance. ***Ex 1.*** As we turned the corner, we *came on* a group of men who were waiting for the restaurant to open. ***Ex 2.*** I *came upon* several children playing in the street. ***Ex 3.*** I *came on* this old edition of Rabindra Nath Tagore's works while I was going through some trunks in the attic of my aunt's house.

(b) affect; strike. ***Ex.*** Many misfortunes *came upon* the poor during that harsh winter.

Come out : (a) strike; stop work. ***Ex 1.*** The workers of our factory have *come out* to a man. ***Ex 2.*** The dockers have *come out* on strike.

(b) leave, be released from prision. ***Ex.*** He got a four-year imprisonment, but he may *come out* early for good conduct.

(c) be formally introduced to high society. ***Ex 1.*** Sundari Devi *came out* last season. ***Ex 2.***When will your eldest daughter *come out*?

(d) flower; appear; begin to grow; blossom. ***Ex 1.*** The roses have *come out* early this year. ***Ex 2.*** The crocuces *came out* late this year because of the cold weather.

(e) become visible; appear. ***Ex 1.*** The rain stopped and the sun *came out.* ***Ex 2.*** The stars *come out* at night. ***Ex 3.*** During the morning the sky was overcast, but in the afternoon the sun *came out.* ***Ex 4.*** My youngest grandson loved to watch the stars *come out* at night.

(f) be produced or published; appear in the shops. ***Ex 1.*** She wants to know when my book on 'Interview Techniques' is *coming out.* ***Ex 2.*** That magazine *comes out* once a week. ***Ex 3*** .. Our News Panorama, a magazine of current affairs, both national and international, *comes out* once a month.

(g) be told; be disclosed, revealed; become known. ***Ex 1.*** It *came out* that she had been telling a pack of lies. ***Ex 2.*** The full story relating to the murder of an industrial tycoon *cames out* at the trial. ***Ex 3.*** The news has just *come out* that our P.M.is visiting America next week.

(h) be revealed or shown up clearly. ***Ex 1.*** Everyone *come out* well in the wedding photograph except the bride. ***Ex 2.*** His arrogance *comes out* in every speech he makes. ***Ex 3.*** Her best qualities *come out* in a crisis. ***Ex 4.*** The meaning of the poem does not really *come out* in your interpretation.

(i) be spoken. ***Ex 1.*** His statement did not *come out* quite as he had intended. ***Ex 2.*** No sooner had the words *come out* than I regretted my indiscretion in speaking them. ***Ex 3.*** The things he had prepared to say fled from him, and instead words *came out* which had no origin in his conscious mind.

(j) become clear or explicit. ***Ex.*** I think the inner meaning of the composition *comes out* very clearly in your interpretation.

(k) emerge. ***Ex 1.*** At such testing times, only the good in him *came out*, and none of the bad. ***Ex 2.*** Did you see the low cunning *coming out* in him as he sang the praises of the clapped-out car he was trying to sell ?

(l) produce a satisfactory answer; be solved. ***Ex 1.*** I can not make this equation *come out*. ***Ex 2.*** Can you help me with this sum, please? It won't *come out*. (rn) be announced or declared. ***Ex.*** When do the psychology results *come out*? (n) have a specified position in a test, examination, etc. ***Ex 1.*** My grandson *came out* first in the examination. ***Ex 2.*** They were very disappointed when their lovely eldest daughter *came out* bottom in the examination.

Come out against : say publicly that one is opposed to something. ***Ex.*** In his speech to the Lok Sabha, the Law Minister *came out* clearly *against* any change to the existing law.

Come out at : amount to a particular cost or sum; work out at; be calculated at. ***Ex 1.*** What is the cost of putting your car back on the road going to *come out at*? ***Ex 2.*** The total cost *comes out at* sixty thousand rupees.

Come out for : leave home for an excursion, etc. ***Ex.*** Would you like to *come out for* a drive in the country?

Come out in : become partially covered in (spot, pimples, etc.) ***Ex 1.*** He *came out in* a rash last night. ***Ex 2.*** Hot weather makes her *come out in* a rash. ***Ex 3.*** Shortly after I had eaten the lobster, I came out in pimples. ***Ex 4.*** He has begun to *come out in* spots.

Come out/out of : (a) leave, emerge, from. ***Ex 1.*** He has *come out of* the ordeal well. ***Ex 2.*** We were caught up in a rush of people *coming out of* the football ground. ***Ex 3.*** Police went into the house to try to persuade the man to *come out*.

(b) leave the place where it has been fixed. ***Ex 1.*** The little girl's front tooth *came out* when she bit the apple. ***Ex 2.*** As the screw was rusty, it did not *come out of* the wall.

(c) disappear with cleaning. ***Ex 1.*** Do you think these ink-marks wi *come out of* my dress if I boil it? ***Ex 2.*** The colours in these material are guaranteed not to *come out.*

Come out with : say something; utter something. ***Ex 1.*** He *came out with* stream of abuse. ***Ex 2.*** Mridula Devi sometimes *comes out with* the most extraordinary remarks. ***Ex 3.*** He *came out with* a string of four-letter words that brought blushes to many of the elderly ladies present. ***Ex 4.*** He *came out with* some funny ideas. ***Ex 5.*** You never know what that child will *come out with* next.

Come over : (a) try to impress, persuade, etc. by assuming a false manner or behaving in an insincere way. ***Ex 1.*** It gives me a pain in the neck watching that dolt *coming* it *over* people who are ten times better at the job than he is. ***Ex 2.*** She tries to win sympathy by *coming* the manager *over* everybody. ***Ex 3.*** Just let him try *coming* the boss *over* me.

(b) visit somebody. ***Ex 1.*** If you can get leave, please *come over* this weekend. ***Ex 2.*** My French pen-friend is *coming over* for a holiday this summer.

(c) overtake, seize, affect. ***Ex 1.*** A fit of dizziness *came over* him. ***Ex 2.*** A fit of stubbornness *came over* him and he refused to have anything further to do with the project. ***Ex 3.*** I have never seen her looking so cheerful. What has *come over* her?

(d) feel or become. ***Ex.*** I thought of this, and thought of that, and altogether I *came over* quite absent-minded.

Come over to : change from one side, opinion, etc. to another. ***Ex 1.*** He will never *come over to* our side. ***Ex 2.*** At a curcial point in the war, one of the enemy's most powerful allies *came over to* our side. ***Ex 3.*** How would you like to *come over to* company? You could double your salary within a year.

Come round : (a) recure; arrive. ***Ex 1.*** The Commonwealth Prime Minister's Conference *comes round* next month. ***Ex 2.*** Diwali seems to *come round* quicker every year.

(b) regain consciousness. ***Ex.*** Pour some water on his face-he will soon *come round.*

(c) visit somebody or a place within the same town or city. ***Ex. 1.*** She will *come round* to our house this evening. ***Ex 2.*** Do *come round* and see us sometime.

(d) recover one's good humour; become happy again after being in a bad mood. ***Ex 1.*** He is sulking because his parents would not let him go to the pictures; he will soon *come round.* ***Ex 2.*** Don't scold the boy; he will *come round* in time.

(e) be converted to somebody else's opinion or views; change attitude. ***Ex 1.*** I shall never *come round* to your way of thinking.

Come round to : (a) reach the point of doing something after procrastination or unavoidable delay; do something after a long time. ***Ex 1.*** It was several weeks before I eventually *came round to* answering his letter. ***Ex 2.*** When he finally *came round to* writing the letter, he found his feelings were easier to express than he had expected.

(b) be converted to somebody else's opinion or views; change attitude; begin to accept or appreciate; agree after disagreeing. ***Ex 1.***I shall never *come round to* your way of thinking. ***Ex 2.*** She is slowly *coming round to* my point of view.

Come through : (a) survive; recover from serious illness-mental or physical; avoid serious injury. ***Ex 1.*** He is very ill but doctors expect him to *come through*. ***Ex 2.*** With such a weak heart, he was lucky to *come through* the operation. ***Ex 3.*** I have *come through* two world wars. ***Ex 4.*** She was involved in an accident, but she *came through* without even a scratch.

(b) arrive by telephone, radio, etc. or through official channels. ***Ex 1.*** A message is just *coming through*. ***Ex 2.*** Your posting has just *come through*; you are going to Chennai.

Come to : (a) recover consciousness. ***Ex.*** When he *came to*, he could not, for a moment, recognise his surroundings.

(b) (of boat, ship) stop. ***Ex.*** A police patrol boat hailed to us to *come to*.

(c) be equal to; amount to. ***Ex 1.*** The bill *came to* four thousand rupees. ***Ex 2.*** I never expected those few items to *come to* so much.

(d) occur to somebody. ***Ex.*** The idea *came to* me two hours ago. It suddenly *came to* him that he had been wrong all along.

(e) reach a particular situation or state of affairs. ***Ex 1.*** The doctors will operate if it proves necessary-but it may not *come to* that. ***Ex 2.*** Things have *come to* such a state in the company that he is thinking of resigning.

(f) be given or left to somebody as an inheritance. ***Ex 1.*** The farm *came to* him on his father's death. ***Ex 2.*** He has a lot of money *coming to* him when his uncle dies.

Come to with : approach, tackle with. ***Ex 1.*** The young scientist *came to* the subject *with* a fresh, lively mind. ***Ex 2.*** The attitude *with* which you *come to* your new job is all-important.

Come together : be reconciled; settle differences. ***Ex I*** doubt if the divorced couple will *come together* again, even for the sake of the children.

Come under : (a) be included within a certain category. ***Ex 1.*** What heading does this *came under*? ***Ex 2.*** Articles on farming *come under* agriculture.

(b) be the target of. ***Ex.*** We *came under* heavy enemy fire.

Come up : (a) come upstairs. ***Ex.*** Please don't wait down there; *come* straight *up*.

(b) appear above the soil; begin to grow. ***Ex.*** I sowed some radish seeds two weeks ago, but they have not *come up* yet.

(c) (of the sun); rise. *Ex.* We watched the sun *come up*.

(d) be mentioned or discussed; arise. ***Ex 1.*** The question of drug taking is bound to *come up* at the next conference. ***Ex 2.*** That subject *came up* in conversation.

(e) ***Ex.*** His name *came up* whenever the matter ofIndian missiles was discussed.

(f) come to be considered by a court; appear in court. ***Ex.*** Her divorce case *comes up* next week.

(g) move; be transported. ***Ex 1.*** All our supplies have to *come up* by this single railway. ***Ex 2.*** Roads and bridges were destroyed to prevent the enemy's reserves from *coming up*.

(h) rise through water to or above the surface. *Ex.* He breathed like a diver *coming up* for air.

(i) occur; arise. ***Ex 1.*** I shall let you know as soon as a vacancy *comes up*. ***Ex 2.*** Something urgent has *come up*; I shall not be able to see you tonight.

(j) win (in a lottery) : appear (by chance). ***Ex 1.*** My number *came up* and I won fifty lakh rupees. ***Ex 2.*** One of his bonds *came up* in the last draw; he won a ten-thousand-rupee prize. ***Ex 3.*** He is very lucky; he is always *coming up* on the football pools.

Come up against : be faced with or opposed by. ***Ex 1.*** We expect to *come up against* a lot of opposition to the scheme. ***Ex 2.*** Your carefree nature often *comes up against* the problem of money.

Come up for : be considered as an applicant or a candidate. ***Ex 1.*** He *comes up for* re-election next year. ***Ex 2.*** Members of the faculty *come up for* election to the Board of Studies every two years.

Come up to : (a) approach; move towards. ***Ex.*** The beggar *come up to* me with outstretched hand.

(b) reach up as far as. ***Ex.*** The water *came up to* my neck.

(c) reach an acceptable level or standard. ***Ex 1.*** Her performance did not really *come up to* her usual high standard. ***Ex 2.*** For one reason or another, their holiday in Kashmir did not *come up to* expectations.

Come up with : produce or find. ***Ex 1.*** He *came up with* a new idea for boosting sales. ***Ex 2.*** Some people apparently have an almost uncanny ability to *come up with* the right answer. ***Ex 3.*** Scientists will have to *come up with* new methods of increasing the world's food supply.

Come within : come near enough. ***Ex 1.*** No aircraft *came within* range. ***Ex 2.*** A naval patrol *came within* view of our observation post.

Complain of : mention some pain, discomfort, etc. ***Ex.*** The patient is *complaining of* acute stomach pain.

Cone off : mark or separate something with cones. ***Ex 1.*** They *coned off* a section of motorway during repairs. ***Ex 2.*** They should *cone off* parking spaces that must not be used.

Confide in : trust somebody enough to tell a secret to him. ***Ex.*** There is no one here I can *confide in*.

Conjure up : make something appear as a picture in the mind; evoke, suggest, a mental picture. ***Ex 1.*** This is a tune which *conjures up* pleasant memories. ***Ex 2.*** The speaker's words *conjured up* a vision of perfect world, where every man loved his neighbour.

Conk out : (a) (of machine); stop functioning. ***Ex.*** My car *conked out* at the crossroads.

(b) (of people) : become exhausted; fall asleep; faint or die. ***Ex 1.*** Grandfather usually *conks out* (*i.e.* sleeps) for a couple of hours or so after lunch. ***Ex 2.*** ft is hard for him to get to work and he nearly *conked out* a few weeks ago with a severe attack of influenza.

Contract out/out of : withdraw from an agreement which applies to a large group. ***Ex 1.*** You can *contract out of* the pension scheme if you wish. ***Ex 2.*** I had several tenants *contracting out of* their obligations.

Cook up : concoct; invent, something in order to deceive. ***Ex 1.*** In order to avoid going to the meeting, he *cooked up* an excuse about being ill. ***Ex 2.*** I don't like *cooking up* stories just to help you out of a difficult situation ***Ex 3.*** If she meets a man who suits her, she will soon *cook up* a resemblance to her ideal mate.

Cool down/off : make or become calm, less excited or less enthusiastic. ***Ex 1.*** She has *cooled off* a lot towards me. ***Ex 2.*** She is very angry; don't speak to her until she has *cooled down* a bit. ***Ex 3.*** People say that ten days injail *cooled* him *off* to a very great extent. ***Ex 4.*** Put them in a cell for an hour or two ... that will *cool* them *down*. ***Ex 5.*** Keep these two persons apart until they have *cooled down* a bit.

Coop up : confine; restrict the freedom of somebody/something by keeping him/it inside. ***Ex 1.*** I have been *cooped up* all day. ***Ex 2.*** He has been *cooped up* in his room for days. ***Ex 3.*** I sometimes feel really *cooped up* in this tiny house.

Cop out of : (a) fail to do what one ought to do, through fear. ***Ex.*** He was boasting about how brave he was at the start, but *copped out of* it at the finish.

(b) withdraw. ***Ex.*** He *copped out of* his responsibilities.

Cork up : suppress, feelings, etc. ***Ex 1.*** Don't *cork* it all *up* : if you feel angry; show it. ***Ex 2.*** She has *corked up* her feelings for years. ***Ex 3.*** It is very bad for you to *cork* your emotions *up*.

Cotton on : become fully aware of; come to understand or realize something. ***Ex 1.*** At last, she was *cottoned on* to what they mean. ***Ex 2.*** He seems to be very slow in *cottoning on* to the significance of the new tax laws. ***Ex 3.*** He did not *cotton on* what she was trying to do to him.

Cotton to : take a linking to somebody; like somebody/something. ***Ex.*** don't *cotton to* your scheme.

Cough up : say or produce something reluctantly. ***Ex 1.*** He had to *cough up* a sum of five lakh rupees as ransom for the release of his son who was kidnapped by dacoits a fortnight ago. ***Ex 2.*** He owes me money, but he won't cough up. ***Ex 3.*** Come on, *cough up* : who broke the cup ***Ex 4.*** She asked a sum of money which was nearly the maximum that would *cough up*.

Count against : be considered, consider, as a factor against somebody ***Ex 1.*** His inability to arrive at work on time *counted against* him whe he asked for promotion. ***Ex 2.*** Your criminal record will *count against* you in finding a job. ***Ex 3.*** She is young and inexperienced, but please do not *count* that *against* her.

Count among : be regarded/regard somebody/something as one of the stated group. ***Ex 1.*** I no longer *count* you *among* my friends. ***Ex 2.*** He *counts among* the most gifted to the current generation of writers ***Ex 3.*** There was a time when I was proud to *count* him *among* ill staunch supporters.

Count for : be of importance. ***Ex 1.*** He seems to *count for* quite a lot in his company. ***Ex 2.*** When it came to money, all his friendly promise *counted for* little. ***Ex 3.*** That does not *count for* much in India. ***Ex 4.*** She says that all your hard work *count for* nothing.

Count in : include somebody/something. ***Ex 1.*** See how many plates we have, but don't *count in* the cracked ones. ***Ex 2.*** If you are all going to, the party, you can *count* me *in*. ***Ex 3.*** I want you to *count* me *in* on this project.

Count on : rely on somebody/something confidence. ***Ex 1.*** You can *count on* my full co-operation in this regard. ***Ex 2.*** As he is unreliable, don't *count on* his help. ***Ex 3.*** Don't *count on* a salary increase this year. ***Ex 4.*** You can always *count on* me for financial assistance when you are in difficulties.

Count out : (a) count things one by one, slowly. ***Ex.*** The old lad laboriously *counted out* forty rupees and gave this amount to her grandson.

(b) count up to ten over a boxer who has been knocked down, signifying his defeat. ***Ex.*** The referee *counted* him *out* in the first round.

(c) not include somebody/something. ***Ex 1.*** You can *count* me *out* of this little plan of yours. ***Ex 2.*** If it is going to be a rowdy party, you can *count* me *out*.

Count towards : be included as. ***Ex.*** These payments will *count towards* your pension.

Count upto : add upto : ***Ex.*** These small contributions soon *count upto* a sizeable amount.

Cover for : do somebody's work, duties, etc. during his absence. ***Ex 1.*** I shall *cover for* Maya Devi while she is out of station on tour.

Cover against : insure against loss, etc. ***Ex.*** They are fully *covered against* fire and theft.

Cover in : put a protective cover over: ***Ex 1.*** We decided to *cover in* the passage between the main building an the annexe. ***Ex 2.*** They are having the terrace *covered in*. ***Ex 3.*** They have *covered in* the whole market.

Cover in/with : protect with, coat with; make dirt, etc. fly and fall on. ***Ex 1.*** The walls had been *covered with* a green paint. ***Ex 2.*** A passing lorry ran through a puddle and *covered* us *in* mud from head to foot.

Cover over/up : hide from view; protect with clothing, etc. ***Ex 1.*** I am glad to see that the police have *covered* the blood-stains *over*. ***Ex 2.*** *Cover* the baby's feet *up*; he will catch cold. ***Ex 3.*** It is cold and you should *cover up* warmly. ***Ex 4.*** He *covered* the child *up* with a blanket.

Cover up : hide the true state of affairs on one's own or somebody else's behalf; conceal a mistake, something illegal, etc. ***Ex 1.*** The inefficient who successfully *cover up* are those who know how to put on a big display of efficiency when it will be noticed, and let the rest go hang. ***Ex 2.*** If I am late tomorrow, please *cover up* for me. ***Ex 3.*** There are too many people in this office trying to *cover up* the mistakes of the past few years.

Note : The word *cover up* is a noun used in the sense of act of concealing a mistake, something illegal, and so on. ***Ex.*** She said nothing was stolen, but that is just a *cover up*.

Cow into : intimidate somebody; make somebody do as one wants by frightening him. They were *cowed into* total submission.

Ex 2. He is not the kind of man who is likely to be *cowed into* submission. ***Ex 3.*** She was wholly *cowed into* by the dacoits, threats of dire consequences.

Crab about : grumble; criticise; complain. ***Ex.*** The boss is always *crabbing about* my work.

Crack down : impose more severe treatment or restriction on someb? dy/something. Police are *cracking down* on drug dealers. ***Ex 2.*** The income tax commissioner *cracked down* on the tax evaders.

Note: The word *crack down* is a noun. It denotes severe measures to restrict or discourage undesirable or criminal people or action. ***Ex.*** The income tax department should carry out frequent *crack downs* on tax evasion.

Crack up : (a) lose one's health or mental stability; break down. ***Ex 1.*** You will *crack up* if you go on working so hard. ***Ex 2.*** I must be *cracking up*, because I am beginning to forget everything I should be doing. ***Ex 3.*** If she goes on working and worrying as she has been doing, she is bound to *crack up* sooner or later. ***Ex 4.*** What has come over you? This is not the time to *crack up*.

(b) break up; disintegrate; shatter; Suddenly, without warning, the plane seemed to *crack up* as it was about to take off.

(c) praise highly. Swimming is not all it is *cracked up* to be, in m opinion. I do not know why young Champa is cracked up as paragon of beauty and virtues.

Note : *Crack up*, as a noun means *loss of physical or mental health*. ***Ex 1.*** He suffers from a *crack up* owing to overwork. ***Ex 2.*** What is the cause of his *crack up*?

Cram for : learn a lot of facts in a short time for an examination. ***Ex.*** He is *cramming for* a chemistry test.

Cram with : put or concentrate a great deal or too much of something. The book titled 'Improve Your Vocabulary' is *crammed with* valuabl information about innumerable, highly useful topics relating to verious competitive examinations conducted by U.P.S.C., S.S.C., and many other recruitment agencies for different services.

Crash about : move about in a clumsy, noisy manner, knocking things over and so on. Why do you *crash about* I've that as soon as you ge home from school?

Crash out : sleep in an improvised bed, when very tired. ***Ex.*** May I *crash out* on your floor tonight?

Crawl to : act in a humble, submissive manner towards somebody to obtain favours, ***Ex 1.*** The general manager lost the respect of his staff when they saw him crawling to the Chairman. ***Ex 2.*** She is always *crawling to* the boss. ***Ex 3.*** If there is anyting he despises, it is being *crawled to* by people wishing to curry favour.

Credit with : believe somebody to possess or be capable of. ***Ex 1.*** I don't *credit* him *with* being able to jump onto a moving bus at this age. ***Ex 2.*** What on earth did you put your finger in the boiling water for? I *credited* you *with* more common sense than that.

Creep in/into : (a) enter very quietly. ***Ex 1.*** The erring husband, returning home at one a.m. removed his shoes and *crept in* as silently as he could. ***Ex 2.*** She *crept into* the room and kissed the sleeping child.

(b) enter imperceptibly. ***Ex 1.*** You should awlays try to argue calmly and not allow any unpleasantness or bitterness to *creep in*. ***Ex 2.*** Once complications are allowed to *creep in*, the outcome is in danger. ***Ex 3.*** A distinct note of acrimony had *crept into* their conversation.

Creep over : affect gradually. ***Ex.*** They *crept over* him, vaguely at first and then more strongly, the suspicion that he was being deliberately poisoned.

Creep up : approach silently or unobserved. ***Ex 1.*** We *crept up* and, peering through the brambles, saw they were having a picnic. ***Ex 2.*** I dislike the feeling of being *creep up* on. Why don't you walk in boldly, and say what you have to say?

Creep up on : approach imperceptibly. ***Ex.*** The years went by and all the time the day for him to retire from the army inexorably *crept up on* him.

Cringe before/to : behave in a timid, cowardly or ingratiating way. ***Ex 1.*** He is always cringing to the managing director. ***Ex 2.*** I don't *cringe before* anybody.

Crock up : become or make weak or useless. ***Ex 1.*** A lot of people *crock up* suddenly these days-it is the effect of modern living, sedentary work and an over-rich diet. ***Ex 2.*** The news of his son's sad and sudden demise finally *crocked* him *up*.

Crop up : appear or happen unexpectedly. ***Ex 1.*** Something has *cropped up* and I shall not be able to see you tonight. ***Ex 2.*** The same problems keep *cropping up*, off and on. ***Ex 3.*** Some difficult questions *crop up* at this point. ***Ex 4.*** All sorts of difficulties *cropped up*. ***Ex 5.*** That subject *cropped up* as we walked. ***Ex 6.*** Wherever I went in America, the names of Mahatma Gandhi and Netaji Subhash Bose kept *cropping up*. ***Ex 7.*** The pills must be good because the name was always *cropping up* in the newspapers. ***Ex 8.*** Please stay at home tomorrow. I shall call you if anything *crops up* in the office.

Cross in : oppose, thwart; obstruct. ***Ex 1.*** People say that she has been *crossed in* love. ***Ex 2.*** He *crosses* me *in* everything. ***Ex 3.*** He is a friendly enough person, so long as you don't *cross* him *in* business plans.

Cross off : remove something from a list, etc. by putting a line through it. ***Ex 1.*** You can *cross* him name *off* the list, as he is not coming. ***Ex 2.*** I found that my name had been *crossed off* the list of players, and somebody else's substituted.

Cross out : delete. ***Ex 1.*** Ten words have been *crossed out*. ***Ex 2.*** The teacher had *crossed out* much of what the boy had written. ***Ex 3.***

The envelope arrived with the old address *crossed out*, and the new one written alongside it.

Crow over : boast about a victory; taunt an enemy, rival or opponent with his defeat; express gleeful triumph about one's success, etc. ***Ex 1.*** He won the competition and kept *crowing over* his rivals. ***Ex 2.*** It is unwise to *crow* too noisily *over* a defeated enemy. ***Ex 3.*** Don't *crow over* her disappointment.

Crowd in on : come into the mind in large numbers. ***Ex 1.***Happy memories of his boyhood *crowded in on* him. ***Ex 2.*** Scenes of his past life came *crowding in on* the drowning man. ***Ex 3.*** His sins of omission and commission *crowded in on* the condemned man when he was being taken to the gallows to be hanged.

Crowd in/into : (a) move in large numbers into a relatively small space. ***Ex 1.*** We had all *crowded into* her small drawing-room. ***Ex 2.*** Hundreds of people *crowded into* the village hall to hear the local M.P.

(b) put many people or things into a small space or period of time; cram somebody/something into something. ***Ex 1.*** They *crowd* people *into* the buses. ***Ex 2.*** Guests were *crowded into* the few remaining rooms. ***Ex 3.*** He *crowds* too much detail *into* his paintings. ***Ex 4.*** Can you manage to *crowd* a few persons more *in.*

Crowd out/out of : (a) be the cause of keeping people out of a place; keep somebody/something out of a space by filling it oneself. ***Ex 1.*** The restaurant's regular customers are being *crowded out* by tourist. ***Ex 2.*** Pressure on study-space has *crowded out* new students from many university libraries.

(b) prevent somebody/something from operating successfully. ***Ex.*** Small shops are being *crowded out* by the big supermarkets.

(c) push aside. ***Ex 1.*** My article on India's Foreign Policy was *crowded out of* yesterday's edition. ***Ex 2.*** It is my firm belief that we have been deliberately *crowded out of* the project.

Crowd round : form a large group round. ***Ex 1.***Why do people *crowd round*, staring stupidly, whenever there is an accident? ***Ex 2.*** Passersby *crowded round* the policeman as he made his arrest.

Crown with : (a) form or cover the top of something. ***Ex 1.*** The hill is *crowned with* a wood. ***Ex 2.*** Her head is *crowned with* beautiful fair hair.

(b) complete or conclude something in a worthy or perfect way. My efforts were finally *crowned with* success.

Crumple up : collapse; come suddenly to an end. ***Ex 1.*** His resistance to our proposal has *crumpled up*. ***Ex 2.*** He just *crumpled up* when the bullet hit him.

Crush in/into : enter; or cause to, too small a space. ***Ex 1.*** As soon as the train stopped, about five hundred people tried to *crush in*. ***Ex 2.*** More than thirty head of cattle had been *crushed into* a lorry that was only big enough to take twenty. ***Ex 3.*** You cannot *crush* forty people *into* such a tiny room.

Crush out/out of : remove something by pressing or squeezing. ***Ex 1*** . He *crushed* the juice *out of* oranges. ***Ex 2.*** When I last saw him, he looked like a man who had got the spirit *crushed out of* him.

Cry down : belittle; give little importance to; say that something is not very good, important, etc.; decry; criticise, ***Ex 1.*** Don't *cry down* his real achievements. ***Ex 2.*** Nobody should *cry down* the efforts of the government to improve the lot of working people. ***Ex 3.*** He is in the habit of *crying* everyone *down*.

Cry off : (a) withdraw one's support. ***Ex.*** He promised to support me, but he *cried off* at the last moment.

(b) withdraw from something one has promised to do. ***Ex.*** I said I would go, but had to *cry off* at the last moment.

(c) withdraw from. ***Ex.*** He *cried off* the project and left his friends in great difficulty.

Cry out for : demand something; require something. ***Ex 1.*** People are *crying out for* free and fair elections. ***Ex 2.*** The present system is *crying out for* early reform. ***Ex 3.*** The business is just *crying out for* some capital.

Cry up : consider; praise. ***Ex.*** He is not all he is *cried up* to be

Crystallize into : become clear and definite. ***Ex.*** His vague ideas *crystallized into* a definite plan.

Cuddle up : nestle; lie close and comfortably; draw closer to another person for warmth or comfort. ***Ex 1.*** The child *cuddled up* to her mother. ***Ex 2.*** Most mothers enjoy being *cuddled up* to. ***Ex 3***. They *cuddled up* under the blanket.

Cull from : select or obtain something from various different sources. ***Ex.*** This information has been *culled from* various reference books.

Curl up : (a) lie or sit with curved back and one's legs drawn up close to the body. ***Ex 1.*** The child *curled up* in bed. ***Ex 2.*** The cat had *curled up* in front of the fire. ***Ex 3.*** His little son *curled up* with a book. ***Ex 4.*** She *curled* herself *up* in the big armchair.

(b) rise or ascend in curling movements. ***Ex.*** The smoke *curled up* from the chimney.

(c) bend at the waist. ***Ex.*** A blow to the stomach made him *curl up*.

(d) make or feel very embarrased. ***Ex.*** Your bad jokes always makes me *curl up*.

(e) laugh or cause somebody to laugh heartily. ***Ex.*** I just *curled up* when I saw her dressed as a clown.

Cursed with : be unfortunate in having; be afflicted with. ***Ex1.*** He is *cursed with* bad health. ***Ex 2.*** Are you *cursed with* a violent temper? ***Ex 3.*** Mohini seems to be *cursed with* the ability to see the other fellow's point of view, with the result that she has no firm opinions on anything.

Curtain off : separate or divide something with a curtain, or curtains. ***Ex.*** A corner of the room had been *curtained off* as kind of improvised wardrobe.

Cut across : (a) not correspond to; act in a manner contrary to. ***Ex.*** Opinion on this issue *cuts across* traditional political boundaries.

(b) take a short route across. ***Ex.*** He usually *cuts across* the park on his way home.

(e) Interrupt. ***Ex 1.*** His decision will *cut across* our basic plan. ***Ex 2.*** The wall *cuts across* our line of vision.

Cut along : go quickly. ***Ex*** *Cut along* and ask her if she needs my help.

Cut at : attempt to sever, open or wound somebody/something with a knife, etc. ***Ex 1.*** His attacker *cut at* him with a big knife. ***Ex 2.*** He *cut* desperately *at* the rope in an attempt to free his foot. ***Ex 3.*** One of the men *cut at* her with a razor; the blade nicked the skin.

Cut away : remove something by cutting. ***Ex 1.*** A few villagers *cut away* all the dead branches from the tree. ***Ex 2.*** The surgeon *cut away* the tumour with expert skill.

Cut back : (a) prune something; shorten by cutting off shoots and branches close to the stem. ***Ex 1.*** The gardener *cut back* our rose bush. ***Ex 2.*** He decided to *cut* the plants *back* in order to improve their growth later in the season.

(b) lower the rate of; reduce something considerably. ***Ex 1.*** Owing to the unfavourable economic climate, the motor-car industry has *cut back* production by twenty per cent. ***Ex 2.*** If you don't sell more goods, you will have to *cut back* production.

(c) return quickly. ***Ex.*** He *cut back* through the woods to where he had been standing before.

Note : The word *cut back* is used as a noun to mean reduction. ***Ex.*** The government will have to resort to *cut back* in public spending.

Cut down : (a) fell; cause something to fall down by cutting it at the base. ***Ex 1.*** He *cut down* many a tree yesterday. ***Ex 2.*** I was distressed to find that all the mango trees had been *cut down.*

(b) kill somebody. ***Ex 1.*** He was *cut down* by cancer at an early age. ***Ex 2.*** His son was *cut down* in the war in the full vigour of his manhood.

(c) consume, use or buy less; reduce the amount or quantity of. ***Ex 1.*** We must *cut* our expenses *down* somehow. ***Ex 2.*** The doctor told me to *cut down* my consumption of fat. ***Ex 3.*** He has decided to *cut down* his expenses. ***Ex 4.*** She is finding out ways and means to *cut down* her abnormal weight.

(d) reduce the length of; shorten something. ***Ex 1.*** If you can *cut* your article *down* to about one thousand words, we shall publish it in our next issue. ***Ex 2.*** The tailor *cut* the dress *down*. ***Ex 3.*** We ought to *cut down* the volume of work.

(e) persuade somebody to reduce a price. ***Ex 1.*** He was asking two lakh rupees for the car, but I succeeded in *cutting* him *down* by twenty thousand rupees. ***Ex 2.*** The tourist *cut* the hawker *down* to six hundred rupees for the vase.

Cut from : remove somebody/something from a larger object by cutting. ***Ex 1.*** He *cut* a branch *from* that tree. ***Ex 2.*** The injured driver was *cut from* the wreckage of his car.

Cut in : (a) interrupt another person or a conversation between two other persons. ***Ex 1.*** She always *cuts in* when other people are talking. ***Ex. 2*** Don't *cut in* our conversation.

(b) overtake a vehicle and turn dangerously into its path. ***Ex 1.*** Impatient drivers who habitually *cut in* are bound to cause an accident sooner or later. ***Ex 2.*** The lorry overlook me and then *cut in*.

(c) include somebody as a member of a group engaged in some profit making activity, and in return for an initial contribution of money; advice or service. ***Ex 1.*** Next time you form a syndicate, don't forget to *cut* me *in*. ***Ex 2.*** I would like to be *cut in* on this project. ***Ex.3*** As he is dishonest, we must not *cut* him *in* on our scheme.

(d) intervene. ***Ex.*** I think I ought to *cut in* what they are doing.

(e) move to intercept. ***Ex.*** The police car *cut in* ahead of the escaping robbers.

Cut in/into : divide by cutting. ***Ex 1.*** The warship hit the submarine amid ships and *cut* it *in* two. ***Ex 2.*** *Cut* the paper *into* two-centimetre strips, and then I shall explain how the game is played.

Cut into : (a) make an incision in; start to divide up, carve or slice. ***Ex 1.*** As the young girl *cut into* her birthday-cake, everyone cheered and clapped their hands. ***Ex 2.*** The knife easily *cut into* the butter.

(b) interrupt. ***Ex 1.*** His unwelcome voice *cut* gratingly *into* their quiet discussion. ***Ex 2.*** He *cut into* our conversation many a time.

Cut off : (a) remove something. by cutting. ***Ex 1.*** Let him *cut* the top *off*. ***Ex 2.*** He *cut off* a metre of cloth from the roll. ***Ex 3.*** The workman had a finger *cut off* by the machine he was operating.

(b) stop the supply of something to somebody. ***Ex 1.*** Our water supply has been *cut off* again. ***Ex 2.*** Her father *cut off* her allowance. ***Ex 3.*** The oil produing countries threatened to *cut off* all supplies of petrol to the customers unless their terms were met. ***Ex 4.*** Unless your outstanding account is paid within seven days of the date on this notice, we regret that we shall be obliged to *cut off* your supply of electricity.

(c) prevent somebody from leaving or communicating outside, a place, by surrounding him. ***Ex 1.*** The village was *cut off* from the outside world by the flood for more than month. ***Ex 2.*** The floods *cut* us *off* from our homes. ***Ex 3.*** The enemy soldiers were *cut off* from their regiment. ***Ex 4.*** The children were *cut off* by the tide and had to be carried up the cliff to safety.

(d) occupy a position to prevent or block. ***Ex 1.*** We *cut off* all their escape routes. ***Ex.2*** Although, their retreat had been *cut off*, they fought on to the bitter end.

(e) interrupt somebody speaking on the telephone by breaking the connection. ***Ex.1*** We were *cut off* in the middle of our conversation. ***Ex 2.*** Operator, I have just been *cut off*, while I was on the line to Calcutta. Please reconnect me. ***Ex 3.*** Just when she had reached the most interesting part of the story, we were *cut off*.

(f) disinherit somebody; leave somebody nothing in one's will. He *cut* his youngest son *off* with out a paisa.

Note : The word *cut off* is a noun used in the sense of limit; separation or division. ***Ex 1.*** There is no hard and fast *cut off* between semi-skilled and unskilled workers. ***Ex 2.*** The *cut off* point between great heat and excessive heat cannot easily be defined.

Cut open : open something by cutting. ***Ex 1.*** He fell and *cut* his head *open*.

Cut out : (a) stop functioning. ***Ex 1.*** One of the aircraft's engines *cut out*. ***Ex.2*** As we were circling the field preparatory to landing, the engine *cut out*.

(b) make something by cutting. ***Ex.*** The villagers *cut out* a path through the jungle.

(c) automatically stop providing heat or cool air. ***Ex.*** When the temperature of the room reaches 70 degrees, the convector heater *cuts out*.

(d) stop taking, eating, drinking or using; stop any harmful activity or bad habit; stop doing or saying something annoying. ***Ex 1.*** *Cut out* sweets in order to lose weight. ***Ex.2*** I am sick of you two squabbling-just *cut* it *out*. ***Ex 3.*** He has decided to *cut out* smoking and drinking. ***Ex 4.*** Why don't you *cut out* all this nonsense? ***Ex 5.*** In a vain attempt to regain her youthful figure, she *cut out* carbodydrates completely for about a fortnight.

(e) delete; leave something out; omit something. ***Ex 1.*** You can *cut out* the unimportant details. ***Ex 2.*** Before we can print this book, you will have to *cut out* all the four-letter words and slighting references to the political leaders.

(f) eliminate. ***Ex.*** He has managed to *cut out* his rival and many the girl he loves so passionately.

(g) take, by cutting from a piece of material, the shapes, required for making something. ***Ex.*** Before he could *cut* his dress *out*, he had to flatten the pieces of the pattern and pin them carefully to the material.

(h) cut out for: well matched; have the right abilities or qualities for. ***Ex 1.*** They are in deep love with each other. They seem to be *cut out* for each other. ***Ex 2.*** You are not *cut out* for legal profession. ***Ex 3.*** She is *cut out* for medical profession.

Cut out/out of : remove by cutting from. ***Ex 1.*** He *cut* the article on International Relations *out of* the newspaper. ***Ex 2.*** I am going to *cut* this advertisement *out* and send it to Priya Devi; she may be interested in the job. ***Ex 3.*** She showed me pictures of several towns that she had *cut out* of magazines.

Note : The word *cut out* is a noun. It is used to mean shape to be *cut out* of paper or cardboard. ***Ex.*** Where is the cardboard *cut out* of the Prime Minister?

Cut through : (a) make a path or passage through something by cutting. ***Ex 1.*** The prisoners managed to *cut* their way *through* the barbed wire round the camp and escaped.

(b) overcome or by-pass difficulties.***Ex.*** The government should devise ways and means to *cut through* the red tape of the bureaucracy as early as possible.

Cut up : (a) cause somebody to be emotionally upset. ***Ex 1.*** This news had *cut* him *up* beyond expression. ***Ex 2.*** He was very badly *cut up* by the sad and sudden demise of his youngest daughter in the prime of her youth.

(b) injure somebody with cuts and bruises. ***Ex 1.*** All the occupants of the two cars were badly *cut up* in the smash. ***Ex 2.*** He was badly *cut up* in the fight. ***Ex 3.*** Those fellows were not too gentle with him. They *cut* him *up* very badly.

(c) destroy somebody. ***Ex.*** Our army *cut up* the enemy's forces.

(d) cut or chop into pieces. ***Ex 1.*** The vegetables should be *cut up* into small pieces and dropped into the boiling water. ***Ex 2.*** You can *cut* this wood *up* very easily. ***Ex 3.*** This wood *cuts up* very easily with an ordinary saw.

Cut up for : be worth, or leave, a quantity of money at death. ***Ex.*** Ram Mehar is as mean as a miser but it would not surprise me if he *cuts up for* five million rupees.

4 Words Beginning With–D

Dab off : apply or remove something with light quick strokes. ***Ex 1.*** The maid *dabbed* the dirt *off* from the book. ***Ex 2.*** *Dab off* the thin film of water settled on the plates.

Dab on or onto : apply in small quantities. ***Ex 1.*** He *dabbed* paint *on* the picture. ***Ex 2.*** The furniture cream should be *dabbed on* with a soft cloth. ***Ex 3.*** She *dabbed on* the ointment with cotton wool.

Dabble in/at : take part in something without becoming seriously involved. ***Ex 1.*** Hejust *dabbles in* politics. ***Ex 2.*** She *dabbled in* what she called fine art.

Dally with : (a) treat somebody/something frivolously; consider or contemplate idly in one's mind. ***Ex 1.*** The government has been *dallying with* the idea of building a power station down here. ***Ex 2.*** We discussed a proposal with which he had been *dallying* for some time, but about which little had been done.

(b) appear to show an interest in somebody without intending a serious relationship. ***Ex 1.*** She merely *dallied with* his affections. ***Ex 2.*** He *dallied with* her for a bit, but quickly moved on when she showed signs of wanting a more permanent relationship.

Dam up : suppress, restrain, bottle up or hold back (emotions, etc.) ***Ex 1.*** He did his best to *dam up* his feelings. ***Ex 2.*** While speaking to his father, he *dammed up* his anger. ***Ex 3.*** I *dammed up* my resentment until I could no longer remain silent.

Damp down : restrain; control; make dull. ***Ex 1.*** The party spirit was considerably *damped down* by the news that all leave had been stopped. ***Ex 2.*** Don't do anything to *damp down* his spirits.

Dampen down : make something less strong; restrain. ***Ex.*** Nothing should be done to *dampen down* his ardent enthusiasm.

Dance across, along or down : move in a lively way. ***Ex.*** The bridal procession *danced across* the street.

Dangle before: offer prospects of wealth, etc. enticingly. ***Ex.*** The prospect of promotion was *dangled before* him in the recent past.

Dash off : write or draw something. quickly. ***Ex 1.*** He *dashed off* a letter to his father. ***Ex 2.*** She *dashed off* a sonnet before dinner.

Date back to : have existed since; originate in; go back in time to a particular date. ***Ex.*** Our friendship *dates back to* August, 1942, when he, along with me, was imprisoned for taking part in the freedom movement against the mighty British government.

Dawdle away : waste. ***Ex 1.*** He *dawdles* the hours *away* watching television. ***Ex 2.*** We *dawdled away* two hours playing badminton. ***Ex 3.*** Don't *dawdle away* your time.

Dawn on : become evident to somebody; gradually become clear to somebody's mind. ***Ex 1.*** In fine (finally), it *dawned on* me that she had been lying. ***Ex 2.*** The truth began to *dawn on* him. ***Ex 3.*** The sense of all that he had been saying suddenly *dawned on* her.

Deal in : (a) sell something; trade in something. ***Ex 1.*** Do you *deal in* cloth? ***Ex 2.*** They *deal in* rice, wheat, sugar and tea, etc.

(b) indulge in something; concern oneself with something. ***Ex.*** Don't make friends with him: he *deals in* gossip and slander.

Deal out : mete out; administer; distribute something. ***Ex 1.*** The judge *dealt out* harsh sentences to the rioters. ***Ex 2.*** The profits will be *dealt out* among the investors.

Deal with : (a) trade with; do business with; talk with in order to reach a settlement, etc. ***Ex 1.*** As we have *dealt with* the same firm for years, we can thoroughly recommend them to you. ***Ex 2.*** They are bad people to *deal with*; always late on delivery dates. ***Ex 3.*** Maharaj in jail was a myth, but Maharaj out of jail is a man, and one can *deal with* a man.

(b) handle; tackle; confront. ***Ex 1.*** Any complaint about the quality of our goods will be quickly *dealt with* by local branches. ***Ex 2.*** The galloping increase of traffic in recent years must be *dealt with*. ***Ex 3.*** The problem of unemployment is the most serious of those *with* which the government has to *deal*. ***Ex 4.*** How would you *deal with* an armed burglar? ***Ex 5.*** You must try to *deal* politely *with* angry customers.

(c) handle some offence. ***Ex.*** I shall *deal with* you when I get home from the office.

(d) be concerned with; cover; have something as a subject; discuss something. ***Ex 1.*** His first lecture *dealt with* corruption in government offices; this week he is talking about morality. ***Ex 2.*** The subject is not very well *dealt with* in her latest book. ***Ex 3.*** The next chapter *deals with* idioms.

(e) attend to; manage something. ***Ex 1.*** He *dealt with* an awkward situation very tactfully. ***Ex 2.*** Have not you *dealt with* that letter yet?

Deliver from : rescue somebody; save somebody; free somebody. ***Ex.*** May God, the Greatest, *deliver* us *from* evil.

Deluge with : send or give somebody/something in a very large quantity. ***Ex 1.*** I was *deluged with* phone calls this forenoon. ***Ex 2.*** We advertised the job and were *deluged with* applications.

Delve into : try to find information about something; study something. ***Ex 1.*** He *delved into* Sanskrit literature. ***Ex 2.*** He has been *delving into* accounts of daily life in the 16th century. ***Ex 3.*** I had to *delve* very hard *into* my memory to recall where I had seen her before.

Demand of : require; need. ***Ex 1.*** Have you any idea what a full-time political career with *demand of* you? ***Ex 2.*** As director of this institute, a great deal will be *demanded of* him.

Depart from : behave in a way not in accordance with what is usual or expected. ***Ex 1.*** While dealing with the case, you must not *depart from* the relevant departmental rules. ***Ex 2.*** The rules were rigid in principle, but sometimes they were *departed from* in practice.

Depend on/upon : (a) be sure, or confidently expect, that something will happen. ***Ex 1.*** You can never *depend on* his arriving on time. ***Ex 2.*** You can *depend on* her to be late. ***Ex 3.*** *Depend on* it, we shall not give up the plan. ***Ex 4.*** You can *depend on* his support for your proposal.

(b) believe that something will be reliable. ***Ex 1.*** You canno *depend on* this bus service-it is never punctual. ***Ex 2.*** You cannot *depend on* the train arriving on time. ***Ex 3.*** He is a man who can be *depend on* in a crisis.

(c) get income; material support or sustenance from. ***Ex 1.*** He *depends* for his livelihood *upon* a small income from investments. ***Ex 2.*** This town *depends* almost solely *on* the tourist trade. ***Ex 3.*** Children *depend upon* their parents for food and clothing.

(d) follow directly or logically from; be decided by something. ***Ex 1.*** A lot will *depend on* how she responds to the challenge. ***Ex 2.*** How much is produced *depends on* how hard we work. ***Ex 3.*** A great deal will *depend upon* the way the government responds.

(e) need somebody/something for a particular purpose. ***Ex 1.*** I have not got a car, so I have to *depend on* the buses. ***Ex 2.*** We *depend on* the radio for news.

Descend on/upon : (a) attack somebody/something suddenly. ***Ex 1.*** The police *descended on* their hide-out. ***Ex 2.*** Bands of bandits *descended upon* our isolated trading posts.

(b) visit somebody/something unexpectedly or inconveniently. ***Ex.*** His sister's family is *descending on* them this weekend.

Descend to : do or say something that is mean and unworthy of one; stoop to something. ***Ex 1.*** He *descended to* fraud with the sole purpose of amassing as much money as possible. ***Ex 2.*** I sincerely admire never to *descend to* foul language.

Describe as : call. ***Ex 1.*** She *describes* herself *as* a doctor. ***Ex 2.*** He *describes* himself *as* a business executive; in fact, he is a clerk. ***Ex 3.*** She *described* him *as* lacking in drive and initiative.

Detail off : choose or appoint for special duties. ***Ex 1.*** Half-a-dozen soldiers were *detailed off* for guard duty. ***Ex 2.*** The best technique is to *detail off* known stalwart supporters to enter into conversation with the other side before the meeting actually begins.

Dictate to : given orders to somebody; boss about. ***Ex 1.*** I refuse to be *dictated to* by you. ***Ex 2.*** You cannot *dictate to* people how they should live. ***Ex 3.*** Our factory workers will not allow themselves to be *dictated to* by the official union leadership. ***Ex 4.*** I shall not have him *dictating to* me.

Die away : become so faint or weak that it is no longer noticeable. ***Ex 1.*** The noise of the car *died away* in the distance. ***Ex 2.*** The breeze has *died away*. ***Ex 3.*** The thunder and lightning *died away* in heavy rain.

Die down : gradually become less strong, loud, noticeable, etc. ***Ex 1.*** Take it for granted that these rumours will soon *die down*. ***Ex 2.*** The storms are *dying down*. ***Ex 3.*** The tension between them had *died down* considerably. ***Ex 4.*** Her anger has *died down* a bit. ***Ex 5.*** The protests of the students are beginning to *die down*.

Die for : badly need or want. ***Ex 1.*** I am *dying for* a cup of hot coffee. ***Ex 2.*** He is *dying for* a bit of exercise. ***Ex 3.*** She was *dying for* a break away from her family and household commitments. ***Ex 4.*** What are you *dying for*?

Die from/of : have as the cause of death. ***Ex 1.*** The disease *from* which he *died* was at that time incurable. ***Ex 2.*** She *died of* cancer on her breast. ***Ex 3.*** Several beggars *died from* starvation. ***Ex 4.*** Five of the climbers marooned in the open *died of* exposure to biting cold.

Die of : be in an extreme state of. ***Ex 1.*** We are all *dying of* curiosity. ***Ex 2.*** As he has no work to do, he is *dying of* boredom. ***Ex 3.*** I am *dying of* thirst.

Die off : die one by one. ***Ex 1.*** The members of the family had all *died off*. ***Ex 2.*** A water shortage had struck the area and the wild life was *dying off* alarmingly in the intense heat. ***Ex 3.*** Afew persons *died off* through lack of food and proper medical attention.

Die out : become extinct; disappear, no longer be practised. ***Ex 1.*** With the development of transport and the building of new factories many of the traditional crafts have *died out*. ***Ex 2.*** Only those species sufficiently adaptable to cope with changing conditions survived. The others *died out*.

Dig in : position somebody or something below ground level by digging a trench or an emplacement. ***Ex 1.*** The tanks were *dug in* so that only the gun turrets remained visible above the ground. ***Ex 2.*** Our officers had *dug* their platoons *in* along the reverse slope of a ridge.

Dig oneself in : (a) protect oneself by digging a trench, etc. ***Ex.*** As soon as they had seized the enemy position, the infantry *dug themselves in*.

(b) establish oneself firmly in a place or job. ***Ex.*** He seems to have well and truly *dug himself in* on the ground floor.

Dig in/into : (a) sow, mix with soil, by digging. ***Ex 1.*** You will need to *dig* those young trees *in* a bit deeper, unless you want the wind to blow them over. ***Ex 2.*** Manure should be well *dug into* the soil.

(b) begin to eat hungrily or enthusiastically. ***Ex 1.*** Don't stand on ceremony-*dig in.* ***Ex 2.*** The boys *dug in* ravenously. ***Ex 3.*** Okay, *dig*

in. ***Ex 4.*** An enormous first course of pea and cheese did not prevent them from *digging into* the pudding.

Dig out/out of : (a) rescue by digging; get somebody/something out by digging. ***Ex 1.*** They *dug* the potatoes *out of* the ground. ***Ex 2.*** He was buried by an avalanche and had to be *dug out.* ***Ex 3.*** We mangaed to *dig out* the trapped miners. ***Ex 4.*** A whole family was *dug out* from underneath a tangle of fallen beams and masonry.

(b) catch or capture by digging. ***Ex.*** If you cannot smoke the rats out,you will have to *dig* them *out.*

(c) obtain by diligents earching or research. ***Ex 1.*** Where did he get hold of that information ? He managed to *dig* it *out of* some private library. ***Ex 2.*** Let us *dig* information *out of* books and reports. ***Ex 3.*** Devise proper ways and means to *dig out* the truth relating to this case.

(d) take out something not easy to get at. ***Ex.*** He *dug out* an old photo from the drawer.

Dig over : prepare ground thoroughly by digging. ***Ex.*** Who will *dig* the garden *over*?

Dig up : (a) break up by digging; prepare by digging. ***Ex 1.*** We shall *dig up* this land for a new garden. ***Ex 2.*** He has *dug up* the garden.

(b) reveal and remove something from the ground by digging. ***Ex 1.*** Police have *dug up* the body of his first wife. ***Ex 2.*** The archaeologists have *dug up* some interesting ancient remains.

(c) remove something from the ground by digging. ***Ex.*** We *dug up* the tree by its roots.

(d) discover; reveal something. ***Ex.*** Newspapers love to *dig up* scandals involving national leaders and other prominent persons in different fields of activities.

Digress from : turn or wander away from the main topic in speech or writing. ***Ex.*** Don't *digress from* the subject when lecturing.

Din in/into : tell somebody/something again and again in a forceful way. ***Ex 1.*** I *dinned* it *into* him that he had to manage things differently. ***Ex 2.*** We have been trying to *din* some sense *into* him. ***Ex 3.*** The importance of exports had been *dinned into* manufacturers by successive governments, but to little effect.

Dine out : dine either in a restaurant, or at a friend's house. ***Ex 1.*** Don't prepare anything for me tonight, I shall be *dinning out.* ***Ex 2.*** We sometimes *dine out* at one of our favourite places.

Dip into : (a) take money from. ***Ex 1.*** Mother had to *dip into* her holiday money to pay the milkman. ***Ex 2.*** The bank had to *dip into* its investments overseas to meet a financial crisis at home.

(b) make a brief study of. ***Ex 1.*** I *dip into* this book whenever I can. ***Ex 2.*** I cannot say that I know a great deal about modern weapons-I have just *dipped into* one or two books on the subject. ***Ex 3.*** I don't have time to *dip into* the report.

Direct to/towards : spend time and effort doing something; turn or aim something in a particular direction. ***Ex 1.*** Our efforts should be *directed towards* greater efficiency. ***Ex 2.*** We *directed* our steps *towards* home. ***Ex 3.*** He *directed* all his energies *to* finding a solution to the problem. ***Ex 4.*** Considerable thought had been *directed towards* improving the quality of the product.

Disagree with : (a) have a bad effect on one's health, etc. ***Ex 1.*** He is not feeling well; something he ate must have *disagreed with* him. ***Ex 2.*** Hot climates *disagree with* me. ***Ex 3.*** I feel sick; that curry *disagreed with* me.

(b) not match; be different. ***Ex 1.*** The total I have arrived at *disagrees with* the one on your bill. ***Ex 2.*** His estimate of the time *disagrees with* mine. ***Ex 3.*** The reports from Calcutta *disagrees with* those from Bombay.

Dish out : give away a lot of something; distribute. ***Ex 1.*** A few boys were *dishing out* leaflets to passers-by. ***Ex 2.*** He enjoys *dishing out* advice to everyone. ***Ex 3.*** I can *dish out* as much criticism as I get.

Dish up : offer or present something; provide. ***Ex 1.*** They are *dishing up* the usual arguments in a new form. ***Ex 2.*** In his latest article, he *dishes up* a mixture of reactionary opinions and thinly-disguised personal abuse.

Dismiss from : not think any further about something; put (thoughts, feelings, etc.) out of one's mind. ***Ex 1.*** He tried without success to *dismiss* her memory *from* his mind. ***Ex 2.*** Don't let the incident bother you, *dismiss* it *from* your thoughts. ***Ex 3.*** He could not *dismiss* those suspicions *from* his mind.

Dismiss as : consider somebody/something not worth thinking or talking about. ***Ex 1.*** He was *dismissed as* a dreamer. ***Ex 2.*** Her statement was *dismissed as* totally false.

Dispense with : get rid of somebody/something; manage without somebody/something; do without; set aside. ***Ex 1.*** He is not well enough to *dispense with* the pills. ***Ex 2.*** I can *dispense with* your asistance. ***Ex 3.*** Let us *dispense with* formality and proceed with our discussions on an informal basis.

Dispose of : (a) get rid of somebody/something that one does not want or cannot keep. ***Ex 1.*** He was forced to *dispose of* his old books. ***Ex 2.*** What is the better way of *disposing of* household waste? ***Ex 3.*** All the furniture has been *disposed of*.

(b) deal or finish with somebody/something that presents a problem; get rid of. *Ex 1.* Their objections were easily *disposed of* *Ex 2.* The president ruthlessly *disposed of* his rivals. *Ex 3.* Most of the opposition had been *disposed of*; only a few remained alive.

(c) have somebody/something available for use. *Ex.* 'People say that I *dispose of* considerable wealth, but it is not true. I have just enough to live a comfortable life, not a luxurious one.

Dive for : move quickly towards or in search of something. *Ex 1.* We *dive for* cover when the storm started. *Ex 2.* He *dived for* the gun to face the dacoits.

Dive in : begin eating hungrily. *Ex 1.* Don't wait for us to join you at the table: just *dive in*. *Ex 2.* Find a seat, then you can *dive in*.

Dive in/into : (a) move one's hand quickly into something. *Ex 1.* He *dived into* his pocket to make sure that his wallet was still there. *Ex 2.* Someone *dived* his hand *into* my handbag and made off with my purse.

(b) involve oneself completely in something. *Ex 1.* They say that he has *dived into* a new project.

Divorce from : separate somebody/something from something, in a false way. *Ex 1.* Most of our politicians are *divorced from* the real needs of the country. *Ex 2.* You cannot *divorce* science *from* ethical questions. *Ex 3.* What you say is totally *divorced from* truth.

Divvy up : distribute; share something out. *Ex.* They *divvied up* the winnings between them.

Do as/for : serve in place of; serve as a substitute for. *Ex 1.* Don't throw those bricks away. They will *do as* supports *for* my bookshelves. *Ex 2.* These pieces of scrap timber will *do* perfectly well *for* the frame of the bed. *Ex 3.* This bale of straw will *do as* a pillow.

Do away with : (a) get rid of something; abolish something. *Ex 1.* They want to *do away with* the monarchy. *Ex 2.* The death penalty has been *done away with* in many countries. *Ex 3.* We cannot *do away with* the Parliament.

(b) kill oneself or somebody. *Ex 1.* He tried to *do away with* himself. *Ex 2.* Don't *do away with* yourself.

Do down : speak of somebody/something in a critical or an unfavourable way; criticise or disparage somebody/something. *Ex 1.* Don't *do down* the present government. *Ex 2.* Don't *do* your friends *down*. *Ex 3.* It has become fashionable to *do down* traditional moral values. *Ex 4.* They are all incredibly catty and dishonest. They are trying to impress each other or *do* each other *down* the whole time.

Do for : (a) do housework for; clean and keep a houe tidy for. *Ex 1.* She has *done for* us for over ten years. *Ex 2.* As they cannot afford domestic help, they have to *do for* themselves.

(b) manage to obtain. ***Ex 1.*** What shall we *do for* fresh fruit while the fruit sellers are no strike? ***Ex 2.*** What did you *do for* coal during the miner's strike?

(c) ruin, destroy or kill somebody/something. ***Ex 1.*** Unless the government provides more cash, the steel industry is *done for*. ***Ex 2.*** I shall *do for* him one of these days. ***Ex 3.*** The bank will not come to the rescue for ever-we will be *done for* in six months.

(d) improve the appearance of somebody/something. ***Ex.*** That new hairstyle really *does* a lot *for* her.

Do in : (a) kill somebody or oneself. ***Ex 1.*** She was so depressed that she felt like *doing* herself *in*. ***Ex 2.*** I sincerely advise you not to *do* yourself *in*.

(b) exhaust somebody. ***Ex.*** Come in and sit down you look *done in*.

(c) injure (a part of the body). ***Ex.*** He *did* his back *in* lifting heavy furniture.

Do out : (a) clean out; make clean by scrubbing, sweeping, etc. ***Ex 1.*** The maid *did out* the parlour an hour ago. ***Ex 2.*** The courtyard needs to be *done out* thoroughly. ***Ex 3.*** Your desk needs *doing out*. ***Ex 4.*** Tell the servant to *do* the rooms *out* completely.

(b) make tidy or orderly (by removing scarp paper, unwanted clothes, etc.) ***Ex.*** You must *do out* your desk drawer: it is full of waste paper and unanswered letters.

Do out of : prevent somebody from having something in an unfair or dishonest way; deprive. ***Ex 1.*** I very much regret that Mohini has been *done out of* her promotion. ***Ex 2.*** He thinks that you *did* him *out of* that job. ***Ex 3.*** Tell me who *did* you *out of* a trip to Kashmir. ***Ex 4.*** Don't *do* him *out of* what he really deserves.

Do over : (a) clean or redecorate the surfaces of something. ***Ex 1.*** The paintwork is beginning to flake; it will need *doing over* soon. ***Ex 2.*** He has *done* the walls *over* in red. ***Ex 3.*** Go and *do over* the kitchen.

(b) beat up; attack and beat somebody severely. ***Ex 1.*** He was *done over* by a gang of thugs after a football match. ***Ex 2.*** Why did you *do* him *over*?

Do to : cause something to happen to something. ***Ex 1.*** What on earth have you *done to* your hair? Why have you had it cut in that way? ***Ex 2.*** What have you *done to* the television? It is not working properly.

Do up : (a) fasten. ***Ex 1.*** She asked me to *do up* her dress for her at the back. ***Ex 2.*** *Do* your files *up*. ***Ex 3.*** He was in his trousers and shirt, *doing up* his braces.

(b) be fastened. ***Ex 1.*** This skirt *does up* at the back. ***Ex 2.*** How does this jacket *do up*?

(c) renovate; modernize. ***Ex 1.*** Let me know who *did* the house *up* for you. ***Ex 2.*** We are getting a professional decorator to *do* the drawing-room *up*.

(d) make oneself more attractive by putting or make-up, different clothes, etc. ***Ex 1.*** I told her to *do up* and call at our house. ***Ex 2.*** She *did* herself *up* for the occasion.

(e) make into a bundle or parcel. ***Ex 1.*** You should *do up* some old clothes for the jumble sale. ***Ex 2.*** She *did* her hair *up* in a bun to keep it our of her eyes. ***Ex 3.*** *Do* that framed picture *up* in brown paper. ***Ex 4.*** He was carrying a parcel of books *done up* in brown paper.

(f) become exhausted. ***Ex.*** He felt really *done up* after the race.

Do with : (a) This phrasal verb is used with can and could to express a desire or need for something. ***Ex 1.*** You look as if you could *do with* (*i.e.* as if you need) a good night's sleep. ***Ex 2.*** I could *do with* a cup of hot coffee. ***Ex 3.*** She said she could *do with* a wash. ***Ex 4.*** My car could *do with* a good polish. ***Ex 5.*** You can both stop leaning against the wall: I can *do with* a helping hand.

(b) It is used in the negative with can and could in the sense of tolerate something. ***Ex 1.*** I cannot *do with* her insolence. ***Ex 2.*** If there is one thing I cannot *do with*, it is untidiness. ***Ex 3.*** He just cannot *do with* whinning children.

(c) It is used in questions with what. ***Ex 1.*** What have you *done with* (*i.e.* Where have you put) my umbrella? ***Ex 2.*** Tell me what you *did with* yourself (*i.e.* How passed the time) on Sunday. ***Ex 3.*** What are you going to *do with* (*i.e.* How are you going to use) the food left over from the party? ***Ex 4.*** She does not know what to *do with* herself.

Do without : (a) go without; exist, function, manage, without. ***Ex 1.*** If you don't like it, you will just have to *do without*. ***Ex 2.*** Most house-holders seemed to have decided to *do without* professional care for their window. ***Ex 3.*** You must buy sweets with your pocket-money or *do without*.

(b) not require. ***Ex 1.*** I can *do without* your advice. ***Ex 2.*** You could well have *done without* that happening. ***Ex 3.*** We can certainly *do without* Prem Kumar poking his nose in every five minutes. ***Ex 4.*** I cannot *do without* a secretary. ***Ex 5.*** If we cannot afford a car, we shall just have to *do without*. ***Ex 6.*** I could have *done without* being (*i.e.* I wish I had not been) woken up at 4 o'clock in the morning.

Dock from/off : take away a part of. ***Ex 1.*** The management keeps *docking* things *from* our wages. ***Ex 2.*** Something seems to get *docked off* your pay packet every month. ***Ex 3.*** The government *docks off* a lot in taxes.

Dole out : distribute as charity in small amounts. ***Ex 1.*** The food was *doled out* to the poor. ***Ex 2.*** They *dole out* just enough for each family. ***Ex 3.*** The government *doles out* something to help the victims of earthquake. ***Ex 4.*** Allowances are grudgingly *doled out* to the elderly.

Doll up : dress in a smart or showy way. ***Ex 1.*** I am going to get *dolled up* for the party. ***Ex 2.*** Sangeeta was *dolled up* without being over dressed. ***Ex 3.*** They are all *dolled up* and ready to go. ***Ex 4.*** Anju *dolled* herself *up* for the party. ***Ex 5.*** Manju *dolled* herself *up* smartly to go home and cut a dash. (be exciting and stylish in appearance or behaviour).

Done in : exhausted; be dog tired. ***Ex 1.*** What is the matter, Premlata? You look all *done in*. ***Ex 2.*** As I have been working for four hours, I am *done in*.

Doss down : lie down to sleep on a makeshift bed or on the ground. ***Ex 1.*** We *doessed down* on Kanta's floor after the party. ***Ex 2.*** These poor people *doss down* under a bridge.

Dote on/upon : show much. fondness for. ***Ex 1.*** He *dotes on* his grand children. ***Ex 2.*** Do you *dote upon* your wife?

Dotty about : very fond of or enthusiastic about somebody/something. ***Ex 1.*** She is *dotty about* this latest boyfriend. ***Ex 2.*** What are you *dotty about*?

Double back : turn back in the opposite direction, especially unexpectedly. ***Ex 1.*** The road ahead was flooded so we had to *double back*. ***Ex 2.*** Half-way through the wood we lost track of the fox; it must have *doubled back* on its track.

Double up : (a) bend, or cause somebody to bend, the body. ***Ex 1.*** He *doubled up* with severe pain. ***Ex 2.*** The humorous anecdote narrated by Rajni made Padmini *double up* with laughter. ***Ex 3.*** The impact of the blow *doubled* him *up*. ***Ex 4.*** The bystanders were *doubled up* with mirth.

(b) form pairs in order to share something; live two together in a room or flat. ***Ex 1.*** They don't mind *doubling up*. ***Ex 2.*** You two will have to *double up* tonight. ***Ex 3.*** We have only one room left: you will have to *double up* with him.

Dovetail with : bit together; combine neatly. ***Ex 1.*** My plans *dovetailed* nicely *with* hers. ***Ex 2.*** Your suggestions don't quite *dovetail with* the rest of the plan.

Doze off : fall into a light sleep. ***Ex 1.*** Try your best not to *doze off* during the film. ***Ex 2.*** After a substantial lunch, he *dozed off* in his armchair. ***Ex 3.*** He waited, hoping desperately that he would not *doze off*.

Draft into : conscript somebody. ***Ex.*** Ten thousand people were *drafted into* the army last year.

Drag down : (a) make somebody feel weak or depressed. ***Ex 1.*** Hot weather always *drags* me *down*. ***Ex 2.*** Hemlata cannot stand the intense heat-it really *drags* her *down*. ***Ex 3.*** His illness is *dragging* him *down*.

(b) bring somebody to a lower social level, standard of behaviour, etc. ***Ex 1.*** See to it that the children are not *dragged down* to this level. ***Ex 2.*** Nothing should be allowed to *bring* her *down* in the estimation of the general public in the society.

Drag in/into : (a) make somebody take part in an activity or be the subject of discussion, etc. against his will, or against the will of other interested persons. ***Ex.*** You are free to write what you like about me. But you must not *drag* my wife's name *in*.

(b) constantly and tiresomely introduce a particular topic into the conversation, and so on. ***Ex 1.*** Don't keep *dragging in* references to his medals won by him for his heroic deeds during the last war. ***Ex 2.*** Must you *drag* politics *into* everything? ***Ex 3.*** Why mut you always *drag* this subjet *in* when we are talking? ***Ex 4.*** I hate those people who are in the habit of *dragging* sex *into* every conversation.

Drag off : lead somebody against his will to. ***Ex.*** He will *drag* his wife *off* to parties, and she spends the whole evening trying to look inconspicuous in some corner.

Drag on : continue endlessly and tediously. ***Ex 1.*** The meeting *dragged on* for a little over a couple of hours. ***Ex 2.*** How much longer is the fil going to *drag on*? ***Ex 3.*** The partnership might have *dragged on* indefinitely if he had not decided on a clean break.

Drag out : (a) make something longer than necessary, thus causing tedium. ***Ex 1.*** Let us end the discussion here. I see no point in *dragging* it *out* any further. ***Ex 2.*** Let us not *drag out* this discussion, we have go to reach a decision.

(b) make somebody reveal or give information, etc. unwillingly. ***Ex.*** The police *dragged* a confession *out* of the suspect.

Drag up : (a) allow a child to grow up without proper discipline or training. ***Ex 1.*** Your children appear to have been *dragged up* rather than brought up. ***Ex 2.*** His children are allowed to roam the streets, and come and go as they please-they are simply being *dragged up*.

(b) deliberately recall or revive an event, usually unpleasant, from the past which is generally forgotten and should perhaps have remained forgotten; rake up. ***Ex 1.*** She *dragged up* that incident just to embarrass me. ***Ex 2.*** What made you *drag up* that particular episode in my murky past? ***Ex 3.*** Some newspapers have not anying better to do than to *drag up* the past scandals of well-known public figures.

Dragoon into : force somebody to do something; bully somebody into doing something. ***Ex 1.*** He was *dragoned into* joining the army by his father. ***Ex 2.*** Voices from loudspeakers *dragoon* housewives *into* buying unwanted soap powders. ***Ex 3.*** I was *dragooned into* going to the open by her.

Drain away : gradually decrease, disappear or fade. ***Ex 1.*** His life was slowly *draining away*. ***Ex 2.*** I feel as though all my strength has *drained away*. ***Ex 3.*** Her anger seems to have *drained away*.

Drain from : gradually reduce the volume or strength. ***Ex 1.*** You would be moving into a department *from* which the liveliest minds have been *drained*. ***Ex 2.*** The very will to survive had been *drained from* him.

Draw back : not take action, because one feels unsure or nervous. ***Ex.*** That country *drew back* from declaring war.

Draw in : (a) (of hours of daylight) : become shorter. ***Ex 1.*** The autumn days are *drawing in*. ***Ex 2.*** The days are beginning to *draw in* : I shall not get so much gardening done in the evenings.

(b) attract, bring in. ***Ex.*** This play is *drawing in* large crowds every night.

Draw in/into : make somebody take part in something, especially against his will. ***Ex 1.*** I found myself being *drawn into* another dreary argument. ***Ex 2.*** We organise various social activities, but not all the members want to be *drawn in*.

Draw off : (a) retreat. ***Ex.*** The enemy *drew off* as soon as we made a show of superior strength.

(b) remove. ***Ex.*** He *drew* his socks *off* and bathed his sore feet.

Draw on : (a) (of time or season) : approach. ***Ex 1.*** Night was *drawing on*. ***Ex 2.*** As winter *drew on* we felt the lack of an efficient way of heating the house.

(b) make somebody continue steadily forward on his course. ***Ex 1.*** The feeling that he was near his destination *drew* him *on*. ***Ex 2.*** He was *drawn on* by the hope of improving his own social position and that of his family.

(c) done clothing. ***Ex.*** He *drew on* his gloves, picked up his umbrella and went out.

(d) encourage to say something. ***Ex.*** She *drew* him *on* to tell her about what had happended.

(e) attract or entice. ***Ex.*** They *drew* investors *on* with visions of instant wealth.

Draw on/upon : use something. ***Ex 1.*** He *draws on* his childhood memories for the material of most of his stories. ***Ex 2.*** We *drew on* his experience throughout the project. ***Ex 3.*** Your expert knowledge will be *drawn upon* increasingly as negotiations proceed. ***Ex 4.*** Tell me something about the skills *drawn on* by your institute.

Draw out : (a) (of hours of daylight as summer approaches) : become longer. ***Ex.*** The summer days are *drawing out*.

(b) help to feel less shy or reserved; encourage somebody to talk, etc. ***Ex 1.*** From his mother, he had learnt the wonderful gift of *drawing* people *out*. ***Ex 2.*** He had chattered away to her in French; he had *drawn* her *out*, he had made her laugh. ***Ex 3.*** He is shy and needs to be *drawing out*. ***Ex 4.*** I managed to *draw* her *out*. ***Ex 5.*** I *drew* the old man *out* about his war experiences.

(c) prolong; make (an event, etc.) longer than usual. ***Ex 1.*** The meeting has been *drawn out* long enough. ***Ex 2.*** She *drew* the interview *out* to over an hour.

Draw out/out of : (a) produce from an inner space. ***Ex.*** He opened his safe and *drew out* a pistol.

(b) remove; extract from; pull out. ***Ex 1.*** He tore his hand trying to *draw* a nail *out of* a piece of wood. ***Ex 2.*** The stump was *drawn out* quite painlessly.

(c) elicit; persuade somebody to tell or offer. ***Ex 1.*** The police managed to *draw out of* him a full account of escape from captivity. ***Ex 2.*** The story was *drawn out* by slow degrees.

(d) depart from; leave. ***Ex.*** The last train to Hyderabad was *drawing out* as I ran into the station.

Draw to/towards : attract people to. ***Ex 1.*** Many people were *drawn to* him by his fondness for plain speaking. ***Ex 2.*** Thousands of educated people were *drawn towards* him by his erudite scholarship.

Draw up : (a) stop; come to a halt. ***Ex 1.*** A taxi *drew up* outside the house. ***Ex 2.*** A few policemen *drew up* in front of our office.

(b) arrange in a special order. ***Ex 1.*** Troops were *drawn up* in ranks. ***Ex 2.*** Ten thousand soldiers were *drawn up* in a hollow square, read for inspection by their unit commanders.

(c) bring near to; place close against. ***Ex 1.*** The table was *drawn up*, against the wall. ***Ex 2.*** Kamini made Rohini sit down in the easy chai and *drew up* the other.

(d) prepare, draft, compose; formulate; set out. ***Ex 1.*** A ne arrangement was *drawn up*. ***Ex 2.*** I instructed the lawyer to *draw up* the contract. ***Ex 3.*** He instructed a new will to be *drawn up*.

Dream away : spend time idly. ***Ex 1.*** She just sits by the window an *dreams away*. ***Ex 2.*** Don't *dream* the time *away*. ***Ex 3.*** He *dreamt* his life *away*, never really achieving anything.

Dream on : continue to hope for something that will not happen. ***Ex.*** You want a promotion? *Dream on*.

Dream up : devise up; think of (something foolish or imaginable)' concoct. ***Ex 1.*** Where on earth did you *dream* that *up*? ***Ex 2.*** Every. thing has worked wonderfully. This is much better than anything we ever *dreamt up*. ***Ex 3.*** *Dream up* a script in which the hero gets shot in the first act. ***Ex 4.*** For his first play, he has *dreamt up* a seedy bunch of riff-raff-drunks, Iay-abours and morons.

Dredge up : mention something that has been long forgotten, especially something that is unpleasant or embarrassing. ***Ex 1.*** Please *dredge up* the details of that episode in Cairo. ***Ex 2.*** He likes to *dredge up* unpleasant little facts about important people. ***Ex 3.*** His grandfather was a fine reconteur; *dredging up* quite effortlessly, and with a great wealth of detail, scenes and incidents from his early life.

Dress down : reprimand; scold; tell off, ***Ex 1.*** He *dressed* us *down* in no uncertain terms. ***Ex 2.*** Tell me why he *dressed* you *down* yesterday.

Dress up : **(a)** wear one's best clothes. ***Ex 1.*** Don't bother to *dress up*—come as you are. ***Ex 2.*** There is no need to *dress up*—it will all be very informal.

(b) put on fancy dress, etc. ***Ex 1.*** Children love *dressing up*. ***Ex 2.*** He was *dressed up* as a bandit.

(c) make something seem better or different by careful presentation. ***Ex 1.*** The facts are quite clear; it is no use trying to *dress* them *up*. ***Ex 2.*** The rumours have been *dressed up* as hard news. ***Ex 3.*** It is perfectly simple and understandable. You need not *dress* it *up*.

Drift along : go through life without aim or purpose. ***Ex 1.*** His upbringing seems to have left him incapable of sustained effort; he just *drifts along*. ***Ex 2.*** Those boys *drift along* doing nothing.

Drift apart : become gradually estranged; slowly lose interest in each other. ***Ex 1.*** He and his wife have never had a serious quarrel. Through mutual indifference, they have just *drifted apart*. ***Ex 2.*** They used to be close friends, but now they have *drifted apart*.

Drift away/off : move slowly, casually, away. ***Ex 1.*** The smoke pall *drifted away* to reveal the blackened shell of the building. ***Ex 2.*** He thought of a pleasure-garden where entertainment would vary with the weather and couples could *drift off* into the dark between a meal and a show.

Drill in/into : teach by persistent exercise, repetition. ***Ex 1.*** The language patterns were thoroughly *drilled in*. ***Ex 2.*** I simply don't believe that spoken skills can be *drilled into* learners in a language laboratory.

Drink away : relieve by taking alcoholic drink. ***Ex 1.*** He is trying to *drink* his trouble *away*. ***Ex 2.*** You cannot *drink* your sorrows *away*.

Drink down : drink until nothing remains. ***Ex 1.*** I know the medicine tastes nasty, but I *drank* it *down*. ***Ex 2.*** She got me to *drink* the medicine *down* in one gulp.

Drink in : **(a)** watch or listen to something with great pleasure or interest. ***Ex 1.*** They stood *drinking in* the beauty of the landscape. ***Ex 2.*** They *drank in* my stories. ***Ex 3.*** Shanti Devi stood and *drank in* the panorama. ***Ex 4.*** Please *drink in* what I am saying about Netaji Subhash Bose. ***Ex 5.*** You will be glad to know that a packed audience *drank in* every word I uttered in the course of my speech on Morality.

(b) absorb by eager attention. ***Ex.*** They sat outside on the terrace, *drinking in* the particular quality of the light at that time of day.

Drink off : drink in one long swallow. ***Ex.*** I *drank off* a mug of juice amid their cheers.

Drink up : drink until finished. ***Ex 1.*** Children, *drink up* your milk. ***Ex 2.*** She told me to *drink up*.

Drink to : express good wishes to somebody/something by drinking a toast. ***Ex 1.*** We *drank to* her health and happiness. ***Ex 2.*** Let us *drink to* the success of your plans.

Drive at : intend; mean; try to do or say. ***Ex 1.*** I don't know what you are *driving at*. ***Ex 2.*** What was she *driving at*?

Drive back : force to withdraw. ***Ex 1.*** The attacking force was *driven back* to its starting point. ***Ex 2.*** Our troops *drove back* the enemy with heavy losses. ***Ex 3.*** The police *drove* the spectators *back* behind the crash barriers.

Drive back on : force somebody as a last resort to use something he would prefer to avoid using. ***Ex 1.*** I had finished all my cigarettes, and could not any of Sanjay's lying about, so I was *driven back on* my pipe. ***Ex 2.*** The last retort of Arun's had *driven* Varun *back on* methods he seldom used. He turned to personal abuse.

Drive in : force to withdraw towards the main body of one's unit. ***Ex.*** Our piquets were *driven in* as a prelude to the main enemy attack.

Drive off : repel, repulse. ***Ex.*** The defenders *drove* the enemy *off* with heavy losses.

Drive on : incite. ***Ex.*** She *drove* her husband *on* to murder the man who teased her.

Drive out/out of : force to leave; make somebody forget or overlook. ***Ex 1.*** The intruders were *driven out of* the house at pistol point. ***Ex 2.*** Any misgivings they might have felt were *driven out* by the sight of her cheerful face.

Drivel on about : talk or write silly nonsense. ***Ex.*** He was *drivelling on about* the meaning of life.

Drone on : speak tediously and at length. ***Ex 1.*** Our managing director *droned on* for hours. ***Ex 2.*** Is there any easy way to stop him *droning on* about social customs.

Drool over : show in a ridiculous way how much one enjoys or admires somebody/something. ***Ex 1.*** He was *drooling over* a photo of Dilip Kumar, the tragic thespian. ***Ex 2.*** He is in the habit of *drooling over* his favourite meal.

Drop back/behind : move or fall into position behind somebody else. ***Ex.*** The two lovers *dropped behind* so as to be alone.

Drop in/in on : pay a casual visit to. ***Ex 1.*** She usually *drops in* at our place on her way home. ***Ex 2.*** They often *drop in* for coffee. ***Ex 3.*** He *dropped in* on us yesterday. ***Ex 4.*** They would just *drop in on* us for a chat at any odd moment.

Drop in/into : pay a casual visit to a place. ***Ex.*** Every evening, he *drops into* that roadside restaurant for a cup of coffee and sandwich.

Drop off : (a) decrease; fall off; become fewer or less. ***Ex 1.*** Interest in the book has *dropped off*. ***Ex 2.*** Sales have been *dropping off* badly. ***Ex 3.*** Traffic has *dropped off* since the by-pass opened. ***Ex 4.*** Takings at the pier have *dropped off* this season.

(b) fall into a light sleep; doze off. ***Ex 1.*** He *dropped off* and missed the end of the film. ***Ex 2.*** I felt myself *dropping off* in the middle of the second act. ***Ex 3.*** Just as I was *dropping off*, there was a loud bang from downstairs.

(c) alight; allow to alight. ***Ex 1.*** I *dropped off* at the corner of Netaji Subhash Bose Road. ***Ex 2.*** Get the driver to *drop* you *off* at the airport. ***Ex 3.*** I shall *drop* you *off* at your place on my way home.

Drop out : leave school, university, etc. without finishing one's course. ***Ex.*** She says she has *dropped out*, and will not attend college any more.

Drop out/out of : withdraw from; abandon. ***Ex 1.*** Since his defeat he has *dropped out of* politics. ***Ex 2.*** He *dropped out* before completing one circuit of the track. ***Ex 3.*** He was joining our party for the theater, but he has had to *drop out*. ***Ex 4.*** They have *dropped out of* our club. ***Ex 5.*** She has *dropped out of* the competition.

Drown out : make something impossible to hear by covering it with a louder noise; make inaudible. ***Ex 1.*** His screams were *drowned out* by the noise of the storm. ***Ex 2.*** The amplified music *drowned out* everything else. ***Ex 3.*** She turned up the radio to *drown out* the noise of the traffic.

Drowse away : spend time half asleep. ***Ex.*** He *drowsed away* a hot afternoon.

Drum in/into : (a) emphasise. ***Ex.*** I would like to *drum* this one point *in*.

(b) force into someone's head or attention; make somebody remember by frequent repetition. ***Ex 1.*** Our teacher used to *drum* our multiplication tables *into* us. ***Ex 2.*** He was determined to *drum* some elementary arithmetic *in*.

Drum on : makea drum-like sound on something; tap or beat against something. ***Ex 1.*** The rain *drumming on* the corrugated iron roof kept me awake last night. ***Ex 2.*** He was *drumming on* the table with his fingers. ***Ex 3.*** She was *drumming* her feet *on* the floor.

Drum out of : force somebody to leave a group, organisation, etc, often in disgrace. ***Ex 1.*** He was *drummed out of* the association. ***Ex 2.*** He has been *drummed out of* the army. ***Ex 3.*** His behaviour is so bad that he ought to be *drummed out of* decent society.

Drum up : try hard to get; obtain by canvassing or solicitation. ***Ex 1.*** He is going round firms *drumming up* interest in the project. ***Ex 2.*** The Prime Minister has managed to *drum up* ample support for the government's fiscal policy. ***Ex 3.*** They are trying to *drum up* public enthusiasm for their candidate. ***Ex 4.*** He could not *drum up* any support for his plans.

Dry down : dry completely. ***Ex.*** He *dried* himself completely *down* after a shower.

Dry off : (a) become dry. ***Ex 1.*** He has left the paint to *dry off*. ***Ex 2.*** Your clothes should have *dried off* by this time.

(b) make dry. ***Ex.*** Sita Devi *dried off* the towel.

Dry out : make or become completely dry. ***Ex 1.*** Her clothes will take hours to *dry out*. ***Ex 2.*** We waited for our wet clothes to *dry out*. ***Ex 3.*** The flood waters subsided and the hot sun *dried out* the wooden buildings.

Dry up : (a) no longer be available; be exhausted; come to an end. ***Ex.*** If foreign aid *dries up*, the situation will be desperate.

(b) stop talking. ***Ex 1.*** *Dry up* and listen to me. ***Ex 2.*** Now I am going to *dry up* and let someone else have his say.

(c) become unable to speak though shyness or nervousness, fail to produce words. ***Ex 1.*** The speaker suddenly *dried up* in the middle of his speech. ***Ex 2.*** The doctor *dried up* and looked blank. ***Ex 3.*** The priest did not *dry up* during the course of his harangue.

Duck out of : avoid or dodge. ***Ex.*** It is his turn to wash up but he will try and *duck out of* it.

Dust down : (a) remove dust from somebody by brushing or flicking. ***Ex.*** *Dust* yourself *down*—you are covered in chalk.

(b) reprimand. ***Ex 1.*** The Colonel *dusted* his men *down* for inefficiency. ***Ex 2.*** I shall not *dust* you *down*.

Dust off : begin to practise something, especially a skill or a language tha one knows but has not used for some time. ***Ex.*** You will have to *dust off* your French if you are going to Paris on an assignment.

Dwell on/upon : think, speak or write at length about something. ***Ex 1.*** One must not *dwell on* one's shortcomings. ***Ex 2.*** Let us not *dwell on* your past mistakes. ***Ex 3.*** I have no wish to *dwell upon* the unpleasant side of this business. ***Ex 4.*** He *dwelt upon* all the nasty aspects with considerable satisfaction.

Dwindle away : become gradually less or smaller. ***Ex 1.*** Her savings have *dwindled away* to nothing. ***Ex 2.*** The numbers attending these meetings have *dwindled away* terribly.

---

5 *Words Beginning With–E*

Earth up : cover with earth. ***Ex 1.*** The gardener conscientiously *earthed up* the young plants. ***Ex 2.*** We *earthed up* the celery this forenoon.

Ease across/along/away/into, etc. : move across, etc. slowly and carefully; move something across, etc. by the use of gentle pressure, careful judgement, etc. ***Ex 1.*** He *eased* himself *along* the hedge to reach the terrified boy. ***Ex 2.*** My foot was rather sore, but I managed to *ease* it *into* a large slipper. ***Ex 3.*** He *eased* his injured foot *into* his shoe.

Ease down : reduce speed. ***Ex 1.*** *Ease down*: there is a sharp bend ahead. ***Ex 2.*** There is a narrow bridge ahead, so you should *ease down*.

Ease of : (a) free somebody from suffering, etc. Walking helped to ease him of his pain. ***Ex.*** The doctor promised that the medicine he had prescribed would *ease* her *of* her suffering.

(b) take away from, by means of deception, cheating. ***Ex.*** In Delhi, as in all large cities, there are plenty of people ready to *ease* you *of* some money if they see that you are a stranger.

Ease off : (a) become less severe; slacken off; do something with less severity or intensity. ***Ex 1.*** The tension between the two countries has *eased off*. ***Ex 2.*** You are working too hard : you should *ease off*. ***Ex 3.*** He looked casually to left and right and, when the flow of traffic had *eased off*, crossed the road.

(b) remove slowly and gently. ***Ex 1.*** I *eased* the stamp *off* carefully. ***Ex 2.*** The nurse *eased* the bandage *off*.

Ease up : (a) move along, usually to make space for somebody. ***Ex.*** Please *ease up* a little, as there are several people without seats:

(b) become less pressing; do something with less intensity. ***Ex 1.*** I am very busy just now; wait until things have *eased up* a little. ***Ex 2.*** Don't take life so seriously, *ease up*.

(c) slow down. ***Ex.*** *Ease up*, we are going too fast.

(d) become less tense. ***Ex 1.*** I hope he will *ease up* now that he has got promotion. ***Ex 2.*** The situation should *ease up* now that the two sides are prepared to talk. ***Ex 3.*** The pain began to *ease up* after she was given a sedative.

Ease up/on : be more moderate with somebody/something. ***Ex.*** I should *ease up* on the cigarettes if I were you.

Eat away/away at : erode. ***Ex 1.*** The river is *eating away at* the bank. ***Ex 2.*** The sea water is *eating away* the base of the cliff. ***Ex 3.*** The sea has been *eating away* at the coast for years. ***Ex 4.*** You can see from here how the river bank is slowly being *eaten away*.

Eat in : eat at home. ***Ex.*** We are not going out: we are *eating in* tonight.

Eat into : (a) consume something; destroy. ***Ex 1.*** Acids *eat into* metal. ***Ex 2.*** The substances has begun to *eat into* the woodwork.

(b) consume a part of something; use unwillingly. ***Ex 1.*** The costs of the legal action against her *ate* deep *into* my savings. ***Ex 2.*** Paying for that new carpet has *eaten into* a small part of my savings. ***Ex 3.*** He has only been able to keep up appearances by *eating into* his capital.

Eat out : have a meal at restaurant, etc. rather than at home. ***Ex 1.*** I am too tired to cook tonight; shall we *eat out*? ***Ex 2.*** We need a baby-sitter tonight, because we are *eating out*. ***Ex 3.*** It is a long time since we last *ate out*. ***Ex 4.*** It is a good idea to *eat out* once in a while: a change of scene and cooking is good for you.

Eat up : consume; bother; worry; devour; obsess. ***Ex 1.*** I can tell you that there is something wrong by the way you have been behaving. What is *eating* you *up*? ***Ex 2.*** Curiosity was simply *eating* her *up*. ***Ex 3.*** She was simply *eaten up* with curiosity. ***Ex 4.*** He was *eaten up* with anger. ***Ex 5.*** Jealousy was *eating* him *up*.

Ebb away : grow less; become slowly weak or faint. ***Ex 1.*** Daylight was *ebbing away*. ***Ex 2.*** Their enthusiasm was soon began to *ebb away*. ***Ex 3.*** He felt his mental alertness and physical strength *ebbing away*. ***Ex 4.*** Life, he felt, was *ebbing away* from him.

Edge across/along/away/back/towards, etc. : move slowly and carefully. ***Ex 1.*** I *edged* my chair *towards* the door. ***Ex 2.*** The climber *edged*. carefully *along* the narrow rock ledge. ***Ex 3.*** The policeman slowly *edged* his way *toward*.

Edge out/out of : cause somebody/something gradually to lose a position or power. ***Ex 1.*** He was *edged out of* his job by his ambitious assistant. ***Ex 2.*** Their new product has *edged* all its competitors *out of* the market.

Egg on : encourage to do something. ***Ex 1.*** The older children were *egging* the younger ones *on* to steal money from their parents. ***Ex 2.*** He *egged* them *on* to fight those other boys. ***Ex 3.*** We don't want to do it, so stop *egging* us *on*.

End in : have as a result or culmination, conclusion. ***Ex 1.*** The arguments between the two drunks *ended in* a free-for-all in which about ten persons became involved. ***Ex 2.*** Their long struggle *ended in* failure. ***Ex 3.*** The argument *ended in* tears. ***Ex 4.*** The debate *ended in* shindig.

End off : finish something. ***Ex 1.*** We *ended off* the meal with coffee. ***Ex 2.*** He *ended off* his speech by telling a very funny joke. ***Ex 3.*** We *ended* the work *off* with a flourish.

End up : finish as; finally be or do something. ***Ex 1.*** If you take her too seriously; you all will *end up* in a mental home. ***Ex 2.*** Every time she tried to argue with her husband, she *ended up* crying her eyes out. ***Ex 3.*** Despite his strenuous efforts, he *ended up* unsuccessful after all. ***Ex 4.*** If you continue to steal, you will *end up* in prison. ***Ex 5.*** If he carries on driving like that, he will *end up* dead.

Engage in : take, or cause somebody to take, part in or be occupied in something. ***Ex 1.*** I have no time to *engage in* tittle-tattle. ***Ex 2.*** I *engaged* her *in* conversation. ***Ex 3.*** Are you *engaged in* business?

Engrave on : impress something deeply on. ***Ex 1.*** Memories of that terrible day are forever *engraved on* my mind. ***Ex 2.*** Her words were *engraved on* my memory: I could never forget them.

Enlarge on/upon : say or write more about something; add detail to something. ***Ex 1.*** Can you *enlarge on* what has already been said? ***Ex 2.*** Please *enlarge* a little *on* your recent suggestions for improving the club's premises. ***Ex 3.*** Don't *enlarge upon* the incident in which his two sons had come to blows.

Enter for : give name for competition, race, examination, etc. ***Ex 1.*** I have *entered for* the high jump. ***Ex 2.*** The teacher *entered* him *for* the examination.

Enter into : (a) begin something. ***Ex 1.*** They *entered into* negotiations with a business firm. ***Ex 2.*** I dared not *enter into* conversation with her. ***Ex 3.*** The two governments *enter into* preliminary discussions in the hope of reaching complete agreement at a full conference.

(b) give, provide, mention. ***Ex 1.*** There is no need to *enter into* a lot of unnecessary detail : just tell the court the main facts of the case. ***Ex 2.*** Let us not *enter into* details at this stage.

(c) be able to understand and appreciate something. ***Ex.*** Try to *enter into* the spirit of the occasion.

(d) form part of something. ***Ex 1.*** This possibility never *entered into* our calculations. ***Ex 2.*** The amount of money did not *enter into* their decision at all. ***Ex 3.*** He does not *enter into* out plans.

Enter on/upon : (a) begin something; make a start on something. ***Ex 1.*** He *entered upon* a new career. ***Ex 2.*** The President has just *entered upon* another term of office. ***Ex 3.*** When the Prime Minister *entered upon* for his second term of office, everyone hoped that he would show more wisdom than in his first.

(b) take possession of something; begin to enjoy something. ***Ex 1.*** He *entered on* his inheritance when he was 22. ***Ex 2.*** She expects to *enter upon* her inheritance sometime next year.

Entitle to : give somebody the right to enjoy something. ***Ex 1.*** I don't know that his rank *entitles* him *to* special treatment from the court. ***Ex 2.*** Your position as a friend of the family does not *entitle* you automatically *to* a share of the inheritance. ***Ex 3.*** You are not *entitled to* unemployment benefit. ***Ex 4.*** After a hard day's work, she felt *entitled to* a rest.

Entrap into : trick or deceive somebody; make somebody do or say something by a trick. ***Ex 1.*** Bhim Bahadur felt he had been *entrapped into* marrying her. ***Ex 2.*** Experienced guerilla fighters are not easily *entrapped into* revealing their positions.

Envelop in : surround. ***Ex 1.*** The whole business of the Managing Director's appointment has been *enveloped in* mystery from start to finish. ***Ex 2.*** The disappearance of his minor son is *enveloped in* mystery.

Exercise over : make use of something; employ. ***Ex 1.*** Teachers *exercise* authority *over* their pupils. ***Ex 2.*** People with strong personalities should be very careful how they *exercise* their influence *over* weaker people. ***Ex 3.*** He *exercised* some strange hypnotic power *over* that charming girl.

Expand on : develop or give more of. ***Ex.*** You mentioned the crying need for extra funding. Please *expand on* that.

Explain away : give excuses why one should not be blamed for, or why something is not important. ***Ex 1.*** He *explained away* his late arrival by blaming it on the crowded roads. ***Ex 2.*** You will find it difficult to *explain away* your use of such offensive language. ***Ex 3.*** He is trying to *explain away* the lipstick mark on his collar to his angry, tearful wife .. ***Ex 4.*** He advanced a theory to *explain away* some of the difficulties connected with this process.

Explode with/into : show sudden violent emotion; exclaim loudly as a result of. ***Ex 1.*** His wife *exploded with* rage for his arriving home at midnight. ***Ex 2.*** She *exploded into* loud laughter.

Eye up : look at somebody amorously in order to try to attract. ***Ex 1.*** He is a creep. He *eyed up* every woman at the party. ***Ex 2.*** Don't *eye up* ugly girls or women. ***Ex 3.*** Did you ever *eye up* anybody of the opposite sex?

---

6 Words Beginning With–F

Face away : look or point in the opposite direction. ***Ex 1.*** She *faced away* with embarrassment. ***Ex 2.*** She *faced away* in order to hide her blushes.

Face about : turn completely round. ***Ex.*** The officer told the soldiers to *face about.*

Face out : resist, oppose. ***Ex 1.*** You should *face out* your problems. ***Ex 2.*** I managed to *face out* their objections. ***Ex 3.*** He is a bully, but you should *face* him *out* straightway.

Face up to : accept and deal with something unpleasant or demanding honestly and bravely; confront. ***Ex 1.*** You must *face up to* the fact that you are no longer young. ***Ex 2.*** He is finding it difficult to *face up to* the possibility of an early death. ***Ex 3.*** He *faced up to* the problem. ***Ex 4.*** These are dangers which you must *face up to*. ***Ex 5.*** There is no running away from the facts; the truth just has to be *faced up to.*

Fade away : (of people) : (a) die. ***Ex 1.*** That old man is just *fading away*. ***Ex 2.*** She *faded away* and died. ***Ex 3.*** If you don't eat you will start *fading away.*

(b) disperse. ***Ex.*** The crowd just *faded away.*

(c) vanish quietly or discreetly. ***Ex 1.*** He *faded away* quietly and we never saw him again. ***Ex 2.*** He is an expert in *fading away* when he is not needed.

(d) become defunct in stages. ***Ex.*** These customs are *fading away* now.

Fade out : gradually become or make invisible ot inaudible. ***Ex 1.*** When you turn on a transistorised radio; the sound comes on immediately; when you turn off, it *fades out* gradually. ***Ex 2.*** *Fade out* the storm effect here, and turn up the music. ***Ex 3.*** The picture on the TV screen *faded out.*

Note : Fadeout is a noun used in the sense of *gradual weakening* (of sounds, pictures, etc.) ***Ex.*** I hope that during her television appearance, there will be no *fadeouts.*

Fag away : do very tiring work. ***Ex 1.*** He *fags away* for a pittance. ***Ex 2.*** She is *fagging away* in the office.

Fag out : make very tired; exhaust; tire out. ***Ex 1.*** This work will *fag* you *out*. ***Ex 2.*** Don't *fag* yourself *out* on their account. ***Ex 3.*** Running soon *fags* me *out*. ***Ex 4.*** He was completely *fagged out*. ***Ex 5.*** Standing on your feet all day really *fags* you *out*. ***Ex 6.*** After ten minutes of his conversation, I feel quite *fagged out.*

Fall about : laugh uncontrollably. ***Ex 1.*** Wall *fell about* when Bhagw Basu did his imitation of the tea-lady. ***Ex 2.*** Why are you *falling about*? ***Ex 3.*** Just the sight of that excessively corpulent and ugly woman is enough to make you *fall about*. ***Ex 4.*** People *fell about* whe she told them what she was doing.

Fall apart : break; fall to pieces; disintegrate. ***Ex 1.*** He tells me that you car is *falling apart*. ***Ex 2.*** The fact that your marriage has finally *fallen apart*, has saddened me beyond expression in language. ***Ex 3.*** She did what she could to keep the marriage from *falling apart*.

Fall away : (a) desert; leave. ***Ex.*** His supporters *fell away* as his populari declined.

(b) disappear; vanish. ***Ex.*** Bear in mind that in a crisis, old prejudic *fall away* and everyone works together.

(c) drop to a lower level; dwindle; diminish. ***Ex 1.*** Output from the power stations *fell away* steeply as restrictions on the movement coal took effect. ***Ex 2.*** The number of people coming to the club has *fallen away* a lot. ***Ex 3.*** Attendances are *falling away* steadily. ***Ex 4.*** The old customs have *fallen away* into disuse.

Fall back : (a) retreat; move or turn back. ***Ex 1.*** The enemy *fell back* as ou troops advanced. ***Ex 2.*** The army has begun *falling back* to prepared lines of defence.

(b) recoil. ***Ex 1.*** He *fell back* in surprise. ***Ex 2.*** She *fell back* in dismay when she saw him.

Fall back on : go to somebody for support or use something when in difficulty. ***Ex 1.*** At least we can *fall back on* candles if the electricity fails. ***Ex 2.*** We have some money to *fall back on*. ***Ex 3.*** It is good to-have a sincere friend to *fall back on*. ***Ex 4.*** She is completely homeless-at least I have my parents to *fall back on*.

Fall behind : be overtaken by somebody/something; fail to keep level with somebody/something; drop behind. ***Ex 1.*** This country has *fallen behind* several of its competitiors in the manufacture of cheap cotton goods. ***Ex 2.*** The major world powers are afraid of *falling behind* in the arms race. ***Ex 3.*** Many countries have *fallen behind* India in coal production.

Fall behind with : fall to pay for something or to do something for a period of time. ***Ex 1.*** They *fell behind with* the rent. ***Ex 2.*** He is *falling behind with* his payments for the cooker. ***Ex 3.*** Don't *fall behind with* the rent, or you will be evicted. ***Ex 4.*** I have *fallen behind with* my correspondence.

Fall down : collapse; be shown to be false or inadequate; fail; come to nought. ***Ex 1.*** The plan *fell down* because it proved to be too expensive. ***Ex 2.*** His plans have *fallen down*. ***Ex 3.*** Why did your scheme *fall down*?

Fall down on : fail to make a success of something; fail to do something properly or successfully. ***Ex 1.*** You should not *fall down on* your promises. ***Ex 2.*** Why did you *fall down on* the job?

Fall for : (a) be attracted to somebody; fall in love with somebody. ***Ex 1.*** They met, *fell for* each other and got married five weeks later. ***Ex 2.*** They say that you have *fallen for* her. ***Ex 3.*** She has *fallen for* him.

(b) allow oneself to be persuaded by something, especially unwisely. ***Ex 1.*** The salseman said that the car was in good condition, and I was foolish enough to *fall for* it. ***Ex 2.*** I never take my wife to the market. She *falls* for all that sales talk much too easily. ***Ex 3.*** Everyone seems to *fall for* her stunning beauty and charming manner.

Fall in : (a) collapse. ***Ex 1.*** The roof of their house *fell in* yesterday. ***Ex 2.*** The roof of the new tunnel has not been properly supported: it shows signs of *falling in.*

(b) form into ranks when on parade; form a military formation. ***Ex 1.*** The captain ordered the soldiers to *fall in.* ***Ex 2.*** Platoon sergeants *fell* their men *in* on the barrack square.

(c) (of legal matters) : expire. ***Ex 1.*** The lease of the building has *fallen in.* ***Ex 2.*** As the leases of these old properties *fall in*, they are being pulled down to make way for office blocks.

Fall in alongside/beside : join a person or group that is already walking or marching along. ***Ex 1.*** I *fell in* beside him and walked over the line. ***Ex 2.*** Onlookers left the pavement and *fell in alongside* the marching demonstrators.

Fall in/into : drop accidently into something. ***Ex 1.*** He thrust the hands farward and *fell* flat *in* the swimming pool. ***Ex 2.*** A very fat boy *fell* head foremost *into* a muddy puddle.

Fall in with : (a) join or rejoin after an absence; encounter; meet. ***Ex 1.*** We *fell in with* a party of nomads encamped by a water-hole. ***Ex 2.*** I crossed into West Bengal and *fell in with* our forces in Calcutta.

(b) slow support for somebody/something. ***Ex 1.*** She *fell in with* my idea at once. ***Ex 2.*** I have decided to *fall in with* your project. ***Ex 3.*** They have *fall in with* the general policy.

Fall into : (a) be divided into; have as components. ***Ex 1.*** The lecture series *falls* naturally *into* four parts. ***Ex 2.*** The four sections *into* which my argument may be said to *fall* are these.

(b) fall fast asleep; become comatose; move into a hypnotic state; pass into. ***Ex.*** The patient was given an injection and afterwards *fell into* a deep sleep.

(c) acquire, develop. ***Ex 1.*** He had *fallen into* the habit of calling at his brother's house on Friday evenings. ***Ex 2.*** He has *fallen into* undesirable habits.

Fall off : (a) become smaller or fewer; lessen; decrease; drop off. ***Ex 1.*** Attendances at our matinees have *fallen off* this season. ***Ex 2.*** Attendance at my lectures had *fallen off* considerabl ***Ex 3.*** dmissions to the advanced courses have *fallen off*.

(b) decrease in quality; worsen; deteriorate. ***Ex 1.*** His zeal has *fall off* considerably. ***Ex 2.*** It used to be my favourite restaurant but the standard of cooking has *fallen off* recently. ***Ex 3.*** I don't know who their enthusiasm has been *falling off*. ***Ex 4.*** Our-customers complai that the quality of our products has *fallen off*.

Fall on : take place on, occur on. ***Ex 1.*** What day does Diwali *fall on* ***Ex 2.*** Her birthday *falls on* Friday; the 14th August, 1994. ***Ex 3.*** Whe does your birthday *fall on*?

Fall on/upon : (a) be borne or incurred by somebody. ***Ex 1.*** The full cost of the wedding *fell on* me. ***Ex 2.*** When anything goes wrong, the blame usually *falls on* his younger brother.

(b) catch sight of; see. ***Ex 1.*** His gaze *fell upon* a small party of men moving up the hill-side. ***Ex 2.*** His eyes *fell on* the looking-glass. ***Ex 3.*** My eyes *fell upon* a group of young men running after a thief.

(c) attack fiercely. ***Ex 1.*** Bandits *fell on* the village and robbed many an inhabitant. ***Ex 2.*** The robbers *fell on* the unsuspecting travelled. ***Ex 3.*** A few desperadoes *fell upon* the cashier and robbed him of the cash.

(d) seize greedily. ***Ex.*** The children *fell upon* the food and ate it greedily.

Fall out : (a) happen; occur. ***Ex 1.*** I was highly pleased with the way things had *fallen out*. ***Ex 2.*** It is a matter of great satisfaction that everything *fell out* as we had planned.

(b) leave the parade. ***Ex 1.*** Hundred soldiers were told to *fall out* ***Ex 2.*** At the end of the drill parade, the battalion *fell out*. ***Ex 3.*** The troops *fell out* quickly after their march.

(c) quarrel with somebody. ***Ex 1.*** They *fell out* with each other just two days before their marriage. ***Ex 2.*** I don't want to *fall out* with her. ***Ex 3.*** Why did you *fall out* with my son?

Note : The word *fall-out* is a noun. It means *radioactive waste carried, in the air after a nuclear explosion*. ***Ex.*** It is the bounden duty of the government to protect people from radioactive *fall-out*.

Fall out of : fall from an enclosed space at a high level to a lower level. ***Ex.*** I am so glad you did not hurt yourself when you *fell out of* the bed.

Fall out with : get on bad terms with. ***Ex.*** He has a knack of *falling out with*, everyone.

Fall outside : not be something which one can handle, understand, etc. ***Ex.*** The future expansion of the maternity hospital *falls outside* the scope of the present inquiry.

Fall over : (a) fall forward and to the ground after slipping or tripping, when walking, etc. ***Ex 1.*** She slipped on a banana skin and *fell over*. ***Ex 2.*** He missed his footing and *fell over*. ***Ex 3.*** He *fell over* a chair an hurt his leg. ***Ex 4.*** That clumsy child is always *falling over* himself.

(b) (of a stationary object) : fall from an upright to a horizontal position. ***Ex.*** The monument *fell over* with a loud crash.

Fall through : come to nothing; fail to be completed. ***Ex 1.*** Our holiday plans *fell through* because of transport strikes. ***Ex 2.*** All his plans have *fallen through*.

Fall to : (a) begin to do something. ***Ex 1.*** She *fell to* eating with great gusto. ***Ex 2.*** He *fell to* brooding about what had happened to him. ***Ex 3.*** He *fell to* wondering again about who his enemy might be.

(b) become the duty and responsibility of somebody. ***Ex 1.*** It *fell to* me to inform him of his son's death. ***Ex 2.*** It *fell to* him to form an administration.

Fall under : be classified among something; be placed within a certain category. ***Ex 1.*** Please tell me what heading these items *fall under*. ***Ex 2.*** Which category does this item *fall under*? ***Ex 3.*** The entertainement of visitors *falls under* the heading of miscellaneous expenditure.

Fall within : be something which one is able to discuss or handle. ***Ex.*** The allocation of funds for research projects does not *fall within* the competence of this committee.

Fan out : spread out from a central point; move away from each other, while advancing. ***Ex 1.*** The army began to *fan out* north of Srinagar. ***Ex 2.*** The troops *fanned out* as they advanced. ***Ex 3.*** Police with tracker dogs were *fanning out* over the moor. ***Ex 4.*** The searchers *fanned out* across the mountainside to cover as much ground as possible. ***Ex 5.*** Did you *fan* your search party *out*?

Farm out : (a) arrange for somebody to be cared for by others. ***Ex 1.*** Two of my children were *farmed out* to their maternal-grandmother at an early age. ***Ex 2.*** Don't *farm* your baby *out* on that woman.

(b) send out or delegate work to be done by others. ***Ex 1.*** As we are very busy; we have to *farm out* a lot of work. ***Ex 2.*** The work of producing five thousand electrical components has been *farmed out* to small manufactures. ***Ex 3.*** The work has been *fanned out* to various people. ***Ex 4.*** Stop them *farming out* the information to all the other agencies.

Fart about/around : be silly; play the fool. ***Ex.*** Stop *farting about* and behave yourself.

Fasten on/upon : take and use somebody/something for a particular purpose; seize on somebody/something; choose, in a keen, alert way; for special comment or criticism. ***Ex 1.*** Defence counsel *fastened on* this flaw in his line of reasoning. ***Ex 2.*** He was looking for someone to blame and *fastened on* me. ***Ex 3.*** She *fastened upon* his suggestion as an excuse for her actions. ***Ex 4.*** Don't *fasten upon* his ideas so uncritically. ***Ex 5.*** I *fastened upon* the idea of going to New York.

Father on/upon : say that somebody is the father or originator of somebody/something. ***Ex 1.*** It is not my scheme; try *fathering* it *on* somebody else. ***Ex 2.*** Don't pin the blame on me : I had nothing to do with the plan. Try *fathering* it *on* somebody else.

Fathom out : find a reason or explanation for something; understand. ***Ex 1.*** Can you *fathom* it *out*? ***Ex 2.*** Dont tell me the answer; let me try to *fathom* it *out* for myself. ***Ex 3.*** I just cannot *fathom out* his intentions. ***Ex 4.*** She could not *fathom* him *out* at all.

Fatten on/upon : grow rich, fat, etc. at the expense of somebody else. ***Ex.*** There is gainsaying the fact that the owners of industry in India as a small and indolent class are *fattening on* the labours of others.

Favour with : do something for somebody; oblige somebody with something. ***Ex.*** I should be grateful if you would *favour* me *with* an early reply.

Fawn on : try to win somebody's favour by flattery or by obsequious behaviour. ***Ex 1.*** He *fawns on* anyone in an influential position. ***Ex 2.*** She likes to *fawn on* rich people.

Fear for : feel anxious about the health, etc. of somebody, or the future, development of events. ***Ex 1.*** I *fear for* her safety in this inclement weather. ***Ex 2.*** The miners' families *fear for* the lives of the men trapped underground. ***Ex 3.*** There is no need to *fear for* the future of the economy of India, the biggest democracy in the world. It is now on a sound course.

Feature in : have an important or prominent part in something. ***Ex.*** Does a new job *feature in* your future plans?

Feed on : be nourished or strengthened by something. ***Ex.*** Bear in mind that hatred *feeds on* envy.

Feed for : (a) have sympathy for somebody. ***Ex 1.*** It is easy to *feel for* people in need; it is harder to bring yourself to do something practical about it. ***Ex 2.*** I really *felt for* her when her husband died. ***Ex 3.*** Did you *feel for* her in her sorrow?

(b) search for something with the hands, the felt, a stick, etc. ***Ex 1.*** In the fog, he *felt for* the kerb with his walking-stick. ***Ex 2.*** He *felt* in his pocket *for* some money. ***Ex 3.*** She *felt* along the wall *for* the door.

Feel up to : consider oneself capable of doing something; feel equal to. ***Ex 1.*** If you *feel up to* it, we could walk into town after lunch. ***Ex 2.*** He does not *feel up to* the job. ***Ex 3.*** We could go on now if you *feel up to* it.

Fence in : (a) surround or enclose somebody/something with a fence. *Ex 1.* The grounds are *fenced in* to prevent tresspassing. *Ex 2.* He *fenced in* his garden. *Ex 3.* Thousands of acres of open range were *fenced in* to prevent cattlemen tresspassing on what had become private property. *Ex 4.* It is almost two acres in extent, neatly *fenced in* with tall palms.

(b) restrict the freedom of somebody. She felt *fenced in* by domestic routine. *Ex 1.* He felt *fenced in* by all these restrictions. *Ex 2.* I felt *fenced in* by domesticity, by my ten-to-five daily routine, by the social demands city life.

Fence off : (a) separate one area from another by means of a fence. *Ex 1.* One end of the garden was *fenced off* for chickens. *Ex 2.* The children cannot play in the front garden until it has been *fenced off* from the main road. *Ex 3.* He *fenced off* the whole plot of land.

(b) parry; resist. *Ex 1.* I *fenced off* his blow. *Ex 2.* The presiding officer neatly *fenced off* my question.

Fend for oneself : take care of or look after oneself; support oneself. *Ex 1.* You should learn to *fend for yourself*. *Ex 2.* I have no one to do the washing and heavy cleaning: I have to *fend for myself*.

Fend off : (a) defend oneself from something/somebody; fight something/ somebody off. *Ex 1.* He neatly *fended off* a job at his chest. *Ex 2.* He could not *fend off* my blow. *Ex 3.* They could not *fend off* our attack.

(b) parry. *Ex 1.* The Prime Minister had to *fend off* some awkward questions from reporters. *Ex 2.* He tried to kiss her but she *fended* him *off*.

Ferret about : (a) rummage. *Ex.* He *ferreted about* in the attic for old photographs.

(b) discover something by diligent searching or asking questions. *Ex 1.* He managed to *ferret out* quite a lot information. *Ex 2.* She will *ferret* it *out* for me if it humanly possible. *Ex 3.* He *ferreted out* my address from somewhere, and wrote to ask how I was doing. *Ex 4.* Try to *ferret out* the truth relating to this case.

Fetch up : arrive at a certain place or in a certain position : land up. *Ex 1.* Where on earth have we *fetched up* now? *Ex 2.* They *fetched up* in Baghdad eventually. *Ex 3.* We all *fetched up* simultaneously at the same spot. *Ex 4.* She left him a little time before she *fetched up* in Calcutta and came to you.

Fiddle away: waste. *Ex 1.* Don't fiddle away your time. *Ex 2.* He fiddled away a fortune in the recent past.

Fight back : fight with renewed force and strength; show resistance or retaliation; return by struggling hard to a position previously held. *Ex 1.* The enemy *fought back* ferociously. *Ex 2.* We shall *fight* them *back* if they attack. *Ex 3.* After a disastrous first half, the team *fought back* to level the match. *Ex 4.* Don't let them bully you.

Fight back. ***Ex 5.*** After several reverses, they *fought* their way *back* to their old seats on the Board of Directors.

Fight back/down : suppress (feelings, etc.); control hold in check. ***Ex 1.*** She *fought back* her tears. ***Ex 2.*** He *fought down* a sense of disgust. ***Ex 3.*** You should always *fight down* your anger.

Fight for : strive to obtain or accomplish something. ***Ex 1.*** They are *fighting for* freedom. ***Ex 2.*** We had to *fight for* independence from the British yoke for umpteen years.

Fight off : resist or repel somebody/something by fighting; not allow to approach. ***Ex 1.*** All the bombing attacks were *fought off* with heavy loss. ***Ex 2.*** We *fought off* repeated enemy attacks. ***Ex 3.*** He is *fight in off* a cold. ***Ex 4.*** *Fight off* your feeling of tiredness.

Fight out : settle by fighting; fight until a conclusion is reached. ***Ex 1.*** cannot help them to resolve their quarrel-they must *fight* it *out* between them. ***Ex 2.*** Don't interfere in a matrimonial squabble-let husband and wife *fight* it *out* among themselves.

Figure in : (a) include something in one's calculations. ***Ex.*** Have you *figured in* the cost of clothes for the children?

(b) appear as a character in; have a part in. ***Ex 1.*** Many characters in Tagore's Human Tragedy *figure in* more than one novel. ***Ex 2.*** He *figured* prominently in the discussions relating to the dispute between those two brothers.

Figure on : include something in one's plans; rely on something; count on. ***Ex 1.*** I ardently *figure on* your assistance. ***Ex 2.*** I *figure on* being in Tokyo in August.

Figure out : (a) come to understand somebody/something by thinking. ***Ex 1.*** I have never been able to *figure* her *out*. ***Ex 2.*** I cannot *figure out* why he quit his job. ***Ex 3.*** Have you *figured out* what is wrong with your car? ***Ex 4.*** *Figure out* why he has been behaving so oddly. ***Ex 5.*** She *figured out* how I had arranged the matter.

(b) discover something by using arithmetic; calculate something. ***Ex 1.*** The cost of the operation will need to be *figured out* precisely. ***Ex 2.*** Please *figure out* how much the project will cost.

Fill in : (a) take somebody's place for a short time; serve as a substitute. ***Ex 1.*** My partner is on leave this week, so I am *filling in* for him. ***Ex 2.*** We shall find someone to *fill in* for you. ***Ex 3.*** I shall *fill in* if absolutely necessary.

(b) complete; add what is necessary to make something complete. ***Ex 1.*** He *filled in* an application form. ***Ex 2.*** Please tell me how to *fill* the form *in*. ***Ex 3.*** *Fill in* your address at the bottom of the application form.

(c) fill something completely. ***Ex.*** The hole has been *filled in*.

(d) spend time while waiting for something. ***Ex.*** He *filled in* the rest of the day watching television.

Fill in on : give somebody full details about something. ***Ex 1.*** Can you *fill* me *in on* what has' been happening? ***Ex 2.*** Would you please *fill* me *in on* this point?

Fill out : (a) become fatter or larger; gain in weight. ***Ex 1.*** She has *filled out* a lot since I last saw her. ***Ex 2.*** Her cheeks have *filled out*. ***Ex 3.*** I have *filled out* a lot with all the nutritious good and regular exercise.

(b) make filler, more substantial by adding material. ***Ex 1.*** The manuscript might be usable, if the author could *fill* it *out* a little. ***Ex 2.*** As a series of episodes, I find this book entertaining; it would be even more successful if the story-line were *filled out*.

Fill up : become, or make completely full. ***Ex 1.*** The gutter has *filled up* with mud. ***Ex 2.*** *Fill up* the tank with Petrol. ***Ex 3.*** Following the heavy rains, the storage tanks were *filling up* again. ***Ex 4.*** Have you *filled up* all the buckets with water?

Filter in/into/through : Pass or flow slowly; become known gradually. ***Ex 1.*** New ideas are slowly *filtering into* people's minds. ***Ex 2.*** The news of the defeat started to *filter through*.

Find against : find somebody guilty in a court of law; decide against somebody; give a verdict against somebody. ***Ex 1.*** The court *found against* the defendant and ordered him to pay costs in the sum of ten thousand rupees. ***Ex 2.*** The judge *found against* the defendant.

Find for : decide in favour of somebody; give a verdict in favour of somebody. ***Ex.*** The magistrate *found for* the defendant.

Find out : discover a mistake, a loss, somebody's dishonesty, etc. ***Ex 1.*** He had been cheating the sales tax department but it was years before he was *found out*. ***Ex 2.*** One day someone will start asking questions and *find out* precisely why we have been losing so much money. ***Ex 3.*** You should send on another fifty thousand rupees to stop their *finding out*. ***Ex 4.*** I have *found out* the truth concerning the case. ***Ex 5.*** If you try to see her, be careful you are not *found out*. ***Ex 6.*** I finally *found out* what he was really like.

Finish off : end rapidly; destroy somebody/something. ***Ex 1.*** That fever nearly *finished* him *off*. ***Ex 2.*** The last bullet *finished off* the wounded animal.

Finish up with : have something at the end. ***Ex 1.*** We had a quick lunch and *finished up with* a cup of coffee. ***Ex 2.*** They had a quick lunch and a cup of coffee to *finish up with*.

Finish with : (a) end a relationship with somebody or a connection with something. ***Ex 1.*** She should *finish with* him-he treats her very badly. ***Ex 2.*** I have *finished with* gambling—it is a sheer waste of money. ***Ex 3.*** He has *finished with* gadding about—it is the quiet life for him now.

(b) no longer be busy with somebody; no longer be using something; have no further need of. ***Ex 1.*** Can you wait a minute? I have not *finished with* yet. ***Ex 2.*** Please put the saucepan away if you have *finished with* it. ***Ex 3.*** Have you *finished with* our lawn-mower yet?

Fire away : begin asking questions; begin to speak. ***Ex.*** I have got a couple of questions I would like to ask you. Right, *fire away*.

Firm up : (a) put something into a final fixed form. ***Ex.*** Have you *firmed up* a contract with them?

(b) make part of the body firmer and less fatty. ***Ex.*** Know it for certain that regular excercise will *firm up* your musles.

(c) make secure. ***Ex.*** We should try to *firm* this arrangement *up* a bit before putting money into the scheme.

Fish for : try to gain something by indirect methods. ***Ex 1.*** She is always *fishing for* praise. ***Ex 2.*** Don't be taken in by his charm: he is *fishing for* an invitation to the big party. ***Ex 3.*** She was a vain but constantly sought-aner attractive young woman : the *fished-for* compliments were never slow in coming.

Fish out/out of : take or pull something out of something after searching for it; extract; bring out. ***Ex 1.*** Several derelict cars are *fished out of* the canal every month. ***Ex 2.*** He *fished* a piece *of* paper *out of* his pocket.

Fish up : bring up like a fish. ***Ex 1.*** They have *fished up* something very peculiar in their nets. ***Ex 2.*** She put her hand into her bag and *fished up* several books.

Fit in/into : (a) succeed in finding time to see somebody or to do something. ***Ex 1.*** I shall try and *fit* you *in* after lunch. ***Ex 2.*** I had to *fit* ten appointments *into* one morning. ***Ex 3.*** Sorry, I cannot *fit in* any more callers this morning. ***Ex 4.*** She will have to be *fitted in* next wee. ***Ex 5.*** *Into* one hour on Friday afternoon I have to *fit* six appointments.

(b) find space or room for.***Ex 1.*** I don't see how we can *fit in* anymore chairs. ***Ex 2.*** Try to *fit* the record-player *into* the space beside the bookcase. ***Ex 3.*** There is no space to *fit* the children *in*.

Fit in : live in harmony; adjust to one's surroundings; be in harmony; be a smoothly fitting part of something. ***Ex 1.*** He has never done this type of work before, I am not sure he will *fit in* with the other employees. ***Ex 2.*** Do these plans *fit in* with your arrangements? ***Ex 3.*** How would they *fit in*, in this new country? ***Ex 4.*** The new boy *fitted in* well with his room-mates. ***Ex 5.*** The house *fits in* beautifully with its surroundings. ***Ex 6.*** This picture will *fit in* with your general decor. ***Ex 7.*** We must *fit* our plans *in* with yours.

(b) include. ***Ex.*** She has succeeded in *fitting* everything *in* her busy schedule.

Fit in with : match; suit; not clash with. ***Ex 1.*** Tell me whether the answer disappoints you or does not *fit in with* your temperament. ***Ex 2.*** Our holidays must be timed to *fit in with* yours. ***Ex 3.*** At least my ideas work. Because they *fit in with* the way life is lived.

Fit out : equip; supply to somebody or something, new equipment, stores, or clothes. ***Ex 1.*** The warship was *fitted out* with bigger guns. ***Ex 2.*** We must *fit* the expedition *out* with the best equipment. ***Ex 3.*** ram getting the children *fitted out* with clothes for their new school. ***Ex 4.*** I went to a large clothes shop where they could *fit* you *out* for anything.

Fit up : install; mount. ***Ex 1.*** The place has been *fitted up* with all modem conveniences. ***Ex 2.*** There is a room at the end of the garage to *fit up* a work-bench.

Fix on : (a) decide to have somebody/something; choose. ***Ex 1.*** They have *fixed on* Praveen Kumar as the new chairman of the board of directors. ***Ex 2.*** Have you *fixed on* a date for the wedding?

(b) direct one's attention, gaze, etc. at somebody/something. ***Ex 1.*** Throughout the meeting, his gaze was *fixed on* that charming young woman. ***Ex 2.*** Throughout the display, her attention was *fixed on* the horsemen in the foreground.

Fix up : (a) repair; redecorate,or adapt something. ***Ex 1.*** He *fixed up* the house before they moved in. ***Ex 2.*** I shall try to *fix* something *up* that suits everyone.

(b) arrange; organise. ***Ex 1.*** I have not done anything about my visit to Moscow. Please get a travel agent to *fix* it *up* for me. ***Ex 2.*** Try to *fix* me *up* an appointment for eleven tomorrow morning.

Fix up with : arrange for somebody to have something; provide somebody with something. ***Ex 1.*** I shall *fix* you *up with* a play to stay. ***Ex 2.*** She has got herself *fixed up with* a cosy flat.

Fix with : look intently at in an unfriendly or a hostile way. ***Ex 1.*** She *fixed* me *with* an angry stare. ***Ex 2.*** Why did you *fix* her *with* a hostile look?

Fizzle out : end or fail in a weak or disappointing way; come to nothing. ***Ex 1.*** After a promising start, their project soon *fizzled out*. ***Ex 2.*** Tell me why your protest *fizzled out*. ***Ex 3.*** The first and only attempt by the government to tax the Indian gambler *fizzled out*. ***Ex 4.*** The firework did not work properly, but just *fizzled out*. ***Ex 5.*** All his enthusiasm soon *fizzled out*.

Flag down : signal to stop. ***Ex 1.*** He *flagged down* a passing taxi. ***Ex 2.*** A student hitchhiking to Guwahati *flagged* me *down* on the Akbar Road, New Delhi, on Tuesday, the 4th August, at about 10.30 a.m.

Flake out : collapse or fall asleep from exhaustion. ***Ex 1.*** When I got home from the airport, I *flaked out* in the nearest armchair. ***Ex 2.*** They just *flaked out* when they got back. ***Ex 3.*** After the guests had gone and the dishes were cleared away, we simply *flaked out* in a couple of armchairs.

Flame up : flare up. ***Ex.*** Violence has *flamed up* again.

Flap across, away, by, etc. : fly with flapping wings. ***Ex 1.*** The big bird slowly *flapped away*. ***Ex 2.*** The heron *flapped slowly* off *across* the lake.

Flare up : (a) burn suddenly more intensely. ***Ex 1.*** The fire *flared up* as he put more logs on it. ***Ex 2.*** The bonfire *flared up* as I poured petrol on it.

(b) reach a more violent state; suddenly become angry; burst into a sudden rage. ***Ex 1.*** She *flares up* at the slightest provocation. ***Ex 2.*** Trouble may *flare up* any time in the city. ***Ex 3.*** The war will all *flare up* again and everyone says that it will be much worse than before.

(c) (of an illness); recur. ***Ex.*** Her back trouble has *flared up* again.

Note : *Flareup*, a noun, means sudden burst of fire, anger or trouble. ***Ex.*** The area commander in Kashmir reported a sudden *flareup* of fighting on his front.

Flash around : show or display something briefly. ***Ex 1.*** He is *flashing* his money *around*. ***Ex 2.*** I don't know why she *flashes* her diamonds *around* so much. ***Ex 3.*** The child is fond of *flashing* her new clothes *around*.

Flash across : cross like a sudden, bright light. ***Ex 1.*** A flight of aircraft *flashed* low *across* the field. ***Ex 2.*** A sudden smile of recognition *flashed across* her face.

Flash at : send a sudden bright look, etc. at somebody. ***Ex 1.*** Mother *flashed* a reassuring smile *at* the child. ***Ex 2.*** A good-looking young woman *flashed* a discreet glance *at* the handsome young man seated in the corner of the compartment.

Flash back : (of thoughts) : return to an earlier time. ***Ex 1.*** My mind *flashed back* to our previous meeting. ***Ex 2.*** The film suddenly *flashed back* to the hero's youth.

Note : Flash back is a noun used to mean part of a film, play and so on, that shows a scene earlier in time than the main story. ***Ex 1.*** The events that led up to the murder were shown in a series of *flash backs*.

Ex 2. The main action of the film portrayed the hero's adult life; scenes from his boyhood were shown in *flash back*.

Flash into : enter like a sudden bright light. ***Ex 1.*** An idea *flashed into* my mind. ***Ex 2.*** A small, brilliantly coloured bird *flashed into* view.

Flick from/off : remove something with a sharp tap or brushing movement of the fingers. ***Ex 1.*** The waitress *flicked* the bread crumbs *from* the table cloth and brought plates and glasses. ***Ex 2.*** He *flicked* the dust *off* with a cloth.

Flick through : turn over pages quickly, looking briefly at the contents. ***Ex 1.*** He *flicked through* a magazine while he waited. ***Ex 2.*** Patients in the waiting room idly *flicked through* magazines as they waited for their names to be called. ***Ex 3.*** Have you read the report yet? I have hardly had time to do more than *flick through*.

Flinch from : avoid thinking about or doing something unpleasant. ***Ex 1.*** Don't *flinch from* the facts. ***Ex 2.*** I shall never *flinch from* the task of telling the people the whole truth.

Fling at : express in a sudden, violent way. ***Ex 1.*** You should check your facts before *flinging* charges of corruption *at* half the board of directors. ***Ex 2.*** She thinks that all the criticism that had been *fling at* him might have dented his self-esteem-but nothing of the kind. ***Ex 3.*** You must be certain of your facts before you start *flinging* accusations *at* people.

Fling away : waste. ***Ex 1.*** Don't *fling* your money *away*. ***Ex 2.*** She told her daughter not to *fling* herself *away* on that dull job.

Fling off : **(a)** produce casually. ***Ex.*** He just *flung off* a remark about getting a new job.

(b) discard, get rid of. ***Ex.*** Shanti Devi has decided to *fling off* all restraints.

Fling off/out : move angrily or violently. ***Ex 1.*** He *flung off* the room in the presence of a few persons. ***Ex 2.*** Following an angry exchange with the Managing Director, Sachin gathered up his papers and *flung out* of the room.

Fling on : get dressed hurriedly and carelessly. ***Ex.*** She *flung on* her coat and ran to the bus-stop.

Fling up : give up, resign from. ***Ex 1.*** He says he will *fling up* the whole thing if they do not give him more money. ***Ex 2.*** I feel like *flinging* it all *up*.

Flip over : turn something over quickly. ***Ex.*** He *flipped over* the pages of the newspapers.

Flirt with : **(a)** pretend to be interested in something; think about something but not seriously. ***Ex.*** He is *flirting with* the idea of getting a job in the United States of America.

(b) behave so casually that one's life is put in danger. ***Ex.*** Don't *flirt with* danger.

Float about/around : **(a)** (of a rumour) be heard or talked about a lot. ***Ex.*** There is a rumour *floating about* of a new job in the organisation.

(b) (of an object) be in an unspecified space. ***Ex.*** Have you seen my keys *floating about* anywhere?

Flood in/into : come or arrive in great quantities or numbers. ***Ex 1.*** Donations have been *flooding in* since the appeal made for help over the radio. ***Ex 2.*** Thousands of applications *flooded into* the office.

Flood out : force somebody to leave home because of a flood. ***Ex.*** Thousands of people were *flooded out* when the canal burst its banks.

Flood with : arrive in great quantities for somebody/at something. ***Ex.*** The office was *flooded with* complaints.

Flop down : sit or lie down heavily or clumsily, because of tiredness. ***Ex.*** At the end of a working day, all he feels like doing is *flopping down* in an armchair to watch television.

Flow from : result from something; follow logically from. ***Ex 1.*** Many benefits will *flow from* this discovery. ***Ex 2.*** These consequences will surely *flow from* the court's decision. ***Ex 3.*** This is an important technical innovation *from* which will *flow* many a benefit to industry.

Flow in/into : arrive in a steady stream. ***Ex 1.*** The election results *flowed in* throughout the night. ***Ex 2.*** Requests for blankets, tents and medical supplies are *flowing into* the offices of the relief organisations.

Flow out of : leave in a steady stream. ***Ex.*** Profits are *flowing out of* the country.

Flow over : take place without affecting somebody. ***Ex 1.*** Office politics just seem to *flow over* him. ***Ex 2.*** He does not allow himself to be excited by the children's squabbles. The bickering and fisticuffs simply *flow over* him.

Flush out : bring out of concealment. ***Ex 1.*** The police intend to *flush* the bandits *out*. ***Ex 2.*** The security forces *flushed out* all the trouble makers.

Flutter about/around : (a) fly with quick light movements of the wings. ***Ex 1.*** A moth was *fluttering round* the lamp. ***Ex 2.*** Birds were *fluttering about* in the garden.

(b) move in a quick irregular way. ***Ex 1.*** She *fluttered* nervously *about*, going from room to room. ***Ex 2.*** Our hostess *fluttered about*, taking quick nervous puffs at her cigarette. ***Ex 3.*** Stop *fluttering about* the place. Sit down, and I shall buy you a cold drink.

Fly at : rush to attack somebody. ***Ex 1.*** They *flew at* him. ***Ex 2.*** Why are you *flying at* him? ***Ex 3.*** I shall *fly at* nobody.

Fly into : suddenly become very angry. ***Ex 1.*** The child *flew into* a rage and began scattering its toys about. ***Ex 2.*** I requested her not to *fly into* a temper with me.

Fob off : trick somebody into being satisfied with something inferior, an excuse, etc.; stop somebody achieving his aim or purpose by trickery or delaying tactics; cheat. ***Ex 1.*** He intends to *fob* him *off* again. ***Ex 2.*** Stop *fobbing* everyone *off* with false promises. ***Ex 3.*** I won't be *fobbed off* this time-I am determined to say what I think. ***Ex 4.*** You can not *fob* an expert *off* with cheap imitations. ***Ex 5.*** He might *fob* her *off* with six thousand rupees, if she happened to be in the mood.

Fob off on/onto : trick or deceive somebody into buying or accepting something inferior. ***Ex 1.*** Don't try *fobbing off* last year's goods on me. ***Ex 2.*** He tried to *fob* this rubbish *off* on them. ***Ex 3.*** Unscrupulous firms are *fobbing* these goods *off* onto the unsuspecting housewife. ***Ex 4.*** Last year's model was *fobbed off on* them.

Focus on : (a) concentrate on something. ***Ex.*** I am so tired that I cannot *focus on* anything today.

(b) concentrate one's attention, etc. on something. ***Ex 1.*** Please *focus* your minds *on* the following problem. ***Ex 2.*** He finds it hard to *focus* his thoughts *on* one thing for longer than five minutes. ***Ex 3.*** Public attention at the moment is *focussed on* the problem of unemployment.

Foist on : force somebody into accepting something not wanted; pass an unpleasant responsibility on. ***Ex 1.*** He is very religious but he does not try to *foist* his beliefs *on* everyone. ***Ex 2.*** I am sorry all this has been *foisted on* you. ***Ex 3.*** He *foisted* a bale of inferior cloth *on* a too eager customer.

Fold away : make or become more compact; fold to one side or for easy storage. ***Ex 1.*** The bed *folds away*. ***Ex 2.*** This kind of table *folds away* easily. ***Ex 3.*** She *folded* the clothes *away*.

Fold back : turn one part of a thing back over itself, fold to one side. ***Ex 1.*** The bed *folds back*. ***Ex 2.*** He *folded back* the bedclothes. ***Ex 3.*** *Fold back* the shutters, please. ***Ex 4.*** We drove in bright sunshine, with the hood of the car *folded back*.

Fold in/into : (in cooking) : mix one ingredient gently with another. ***Ex 1.*** *Fold in* the beaten whites of two eggs. ***Ex 2.*** She *folded in* sugar and flavouring.

Fold up : (a) collapse because of pain or great laughter. ***Ex 1.*** The boxer *folded up* in agony. ***Ex 2.*** The comedian had the audience *folding up*. ***Ex 3.*** From the moment he appeared on stage, the audience *folded up* in their seats. ***Ex 4.*** I jabbed him just once in the solar plexus and he *folded up*.

(b) end in failure; finish trading. ***Ex 1.*** Why did your business *fold up*? ***Ex 2.*** Please let me know why most of his ambitious schemes *folded up*. ***Ex 3.*** Several national newspapers have *folded up* in the past five years.

Follow on : (a) continue to follow : ***Ex.*** He *followed on* despite unspeakable hardships.

(b) continue. ***Ex 1.*** The story *follows on* from the death of the heroine. ***Ex 2.*** The later books *follow on* from the earlier ones. ***Ex 3.*** We shall *follow on* from where we left off.

Follow through : carry out or continue something to the end; complete something; continue doing something until a conclusion is reached. ***Ex 1.*** He takes several schemes in hand, but lacks the persistence to *follow* them *through*. ***Ex 2.*** You should *follow* the argument *through* to a conclusion. ***Ex 3.*** If you *follow* the policy *through* to its logical conclusion, you will find that it will succeed. ***Ex 4.*** He *followed* the path *through* to the end. ***Ex 5.*** Starting projects is one thing, *following* them *through* is another.

Follow up : (a) take further action on something; develop or exploit something. ***Ex 1.*** You should *follow up* your letter with a phone call. .***Ex 2.*** Don't rest on your laurels : *follow up* your success and start looking for new markets now. ***Ex 3.*** The general *followed up* the success, by attacking the enemy on all fronts.

(b) investigate something closely; follow where something leads. ***Ex 1.*** The night editor decides which of the stories that are phoned in should be *followed up*. ***Ex 2.*** The police *followed up* a clue relating to the murder of an industrial tycoon. ***Ex 3.*** I decided to *follow up* one or two hints that had been dropped at her coktail party.

(c) reinforce. ***Ex.*** She *followed up* the programme with another just as good.

Fool about/around : (a) behave foolishly or stupidly; play about/around with. ***Ex 1.*** Everyone knows that he has been *fooling around* with some girl at the office. ***Ex 2.*** Stop *fooling about* with that knife or someone will get hurt. ***Ex 3.*** Don't *fool around* on a rifle range. ***Ex 4.*** They love *fooling about*.

(b) waste time; be idle. ***Ex 1.*** Stop *fooling around*, do something useful. ***Ex 2.*** I was meant to be working on Sunday, but I just *fooled around* all day. ***Ex 3.*** Don't *fool about*, do your work.

Force back: try very hard not to show (an emotion). ***Ex.*** She *forced back* her tears.

Force down : (a) compel somebody/oneself to swallow something when he/one does not want to. ***Ex 1.*** After being ill I did not like eating but I managed to *force* something *down*. ***Ex 2.*** Yesterday she ate nothing. She has just now *forced* a glass of milk *down*.

(b) compel an aircraft to land. ***Ex.*** A bomb was found on board an aircraft. So, it was *forced down* to land.

Force on/upon : compel to accept; make somebody accept something against his will. ***Ex 1.*** She tried to *force* her ideas *on* me. ***Ex 2.*** Higher taxes were *forced upon* the people. ***Ex 3.*** She has *forced* a crisis *on* him.

Force up : cause to rise by applying strong pressure. ***Ex 1.*** Increasing the wages of the bus crews will *force up* fares. ***Ex 2.*** Imposing taxes on certain basic necessities of life will *force* the cost of living *up* very considerably.

Fork out : pay money reluctantly, unwillingly. ***Ex.*** Tell me why you are always *forking out* money for her school trips.

Form up : move into position in lines, as on parade. ***Ex 1.*** The troops had been *formed up* in review order. ***Ex 2.*** The battalion *formed up* by companies on the barrack square.

Foul up : mess something up; spoil something by behaving in a thoughtless or foolish way. ***Ex 1.*** The weather has really *fouled up* my holiday plans. ***Ex 2.*** Everything was just fine until she came along and *fouled* things *up*. ***Ex 3.*** His easy-going ways with other women have *fouled up* a good working partnership. ***Ex 4.*** When everything is running smoothly, why; must he step in and *foul* things *up*? ***Ex 5.*** They have really *fouled up* their chances of success. ***Ex 6.*** The whole business has been *fouled up* by his stupidity.

Note : The word *foulup* is a noun used in the sense of *spoiling or upsetting of arrangements, relationships,* and so on. ***Ex.*** We shall finish the project on time provided there are no *foul-ups* in supplying materials.

Frame up : produce false evidence against an innocent person to make him appear guilty. ***Ex 1.*** The accused man said that he had been *framed up*. ***Ex 2.*** In most cases in which a person is *framed up* by the police, the victim is too surprised, or ignorant, to help himself.

Note : The word *frame-up* is a noun. It means *situation in which false evidence is produced against an innocent person, so that he appears guilty.* ***Ex 1.*** I did not do it : it is a *frame-up*. ***Ex 2.*** Don't you see—it was all a *frame-up*? ***Ex 3.*** We have been expecting a *frame-up* for a long time. But this time we have got witnesses.

Freak out : (a) tempcrarily lose control of oneself; go crazy; act abnormally under the influence of drugs. ***Ex 1.*** This ordinary quiet guy just *freaked out* and shot ten persons. ***Ex 2.*** His party was really wild—everyone *freaked out* on drugs. ***Ex 3.*** He *freaked out* for many an hour.

(b) make somebody feel excessive pleasure or unease. ***Ex 1.*** Listening to a good stereo system always *freaks* me *out*. ***Ex 2.*** Listening to a tragic tale always *freaks* him *out*.

Note : *Freak-out* is a noun used to mean *wild and extreme experience, especially one produced by drugs.* ***Ex 1.*** His party last weekend was wild—a real *freak-out*. ***Ex 2.*** He was a victim of frequent *freak outs* in his youth.

Freeze off : show no enthusiasm for; keep at a distance by being too unfriendly. ***Ex 1.*** I offered my help, but she *froze* me *off*. ***Ex 2.*** They *froze off* his offers of help.

Freeze on to : attach oneself. ***Ex.*** He *froze on to* them and would not go away.

Freeze out : exclude somebody from business or from society by harsh competition or unfriendly behaviour. ***Ex 1.*** Small shops are being *frozen out* by the big supermarkets. ***Ex 2.*** They *froze* him *out* of everything they did. ***Ex 3.*** I don't know why they *freeze* me *out.* ***Ex 4.*** Some of the small traders are being *frozen out* by the big combines.

Freeze over : become covered with ice. ***Ex.*** The lake was *frozen over* until late spring.

Freeze up : freeze something so as to prevent normal use. ***Ex.*** The window has *frozen up* and I cannot open it.

Note : (a) The word *freeze-up* is used as a noun to denote period of weather during which temperatures are below *freezing-point.* ***Ex 1.*** After the last freeze-up, we put up insulation round the pipes. ***Ex 2.*** During last year's freeze-up, traffic was brought to a halt along the full length of the motorway.

(b) *Freeze-up* also means official fixing of wages, prices, etc. *for a period of time.* ***Ex.*** There was a price *freeze-up* last year.

Freshen up : wash and make oneself look clean and tidy after a journey, before a meeting, and so forth. ***Ex 1.*** I shall just go and *freshen* myself *up* before the interview. ***Ex 2.*** Go and *freshen* yourself *up* before the guests arrive.

Frighten away/off : frighten thus causing to stay away or go away. ***Ex 1.*** The alarm *frightened* the burglars *away.* ***Ex 2.*** Take it for granted that this job will not *frighten* her *off.* ***Ex 3.*** The children's shouts *frightened off* the birds.

Frighten into : cause somebody to do/not to do something by frightening him. ***Ex 1.*** The older boys *frightened* the younger ones into stealing money from their mothers' purses. ***Ex 2.*** The villagers were *frightened into* surrendering nearly all their grain by the drunken soldiers. ***Ex 3.*** News of the robberies *frightened* many people *into* fitting n locks to their doors.

Fritter away : waste time or money foolishly on small useless things ***Ex 1.*** Don't *fritter away* your money on gambling. ***Ex 2.*** Do you *fritter away* your time? ***Ex 3.*** Don't *fritter away* your money on things your, do not really need.

Frost over : become covered with frost. ***Ex 1.*** The car wind screen *frosted over* during the night. ***Ex 2.*** After the severe cold of last night, the windows *frosted over.*

Frown on/upon : disapprove of something. ***Ex 1.*** My parents always *frown on* late nights out. ***Ex 2.*** Gambling is *frowned upon* by many people. ***Ex 3.*** He *frowns upon* things like that. ***Ex 4.*** Does not she *frown upon* that kind of behaviour ? ***Ex 5.*** This is the kind of thing they *frown on* here.

---

7 Words Beginning With–G

Gad about/around : go from place to place for pleasure and excitement. ***Ex 1.*** While they *gad around* the world, their children are neglected at home. ***Ex 2.*** He *gads about* without a care in the world. ***Ex 3.*** They *gad about* a lot, going to expensive restaurants and shows. ***Ex 4.*** The way he *gads about*, I cannot see how he will pass his B.A. examination scheduled to commence on Monday, the 14th March, 1996, at 9.30 a.m.

Note : The word *gad about* is used as a noun in the sense of *person who habitually gads about*. ***Ex 1.*** As he is a *gad about*, I don't like to make friends with him. ***Ex 2.*** Unless one exercises some self-control, it is only too easy to become a *gad about*—going from one party to another, from one friend's house to another, and never doing anything useful.

Gain in : (a) acquire more of a moral or intellectual quality. ***Ex 1.*** The leader of the C.P.I.(M) in the Lok Sabha *gained* significantly *in* stature as a result of his speech on Jummu and Kashmir. ***Ex 2.*** You should always try to *gain in* wisdom.

(b) become heavier, taller, and so on. ***Ex 1.*** Parvati seems to have *gained* a lot *in* weight since I last saw her. ***Ex 2.*** Have you *gained in* height? ***Ex 3.*** Our army has *gained* greatly *in* striking power with the acquisition of one thousand of the most modern tanks in the world.

Gain on : (a) come closer to somebody/something pursued. ***Ex 1.*** You will have to drive faster-they are *gaining on* us. ***Ex 2.*** The Socialists are *gaining on* the Congress in the opinion polls. ***Ex 3.*** The police patrol car was *gaining on* the Maruti car when suddenly a shot was fired from it. ***Ex 4.*** Our troops were *gaining on* the enemy. ***Ex 5.*** The company is *gaining on* its rivals in volume of sales.

(b) move further ahead of somebody/something. ***Ex.*** The leading group of three continued to *gain on* the rest of the runners and were soon half a kilornetre clear of them.

Gain on/upon : erode. ***Ex.*** Year by year, the Sea *gained upon* the shore, and finally took toll of the houses that had once been the pride of the town.

Gallivant about : go from place to place for pleasure; gad about. ***Ex 1.*** He *gallivants about* as if he had all the time and money in the world. ***Ex 2.*** Stop *gallivanting about*, and settle down to something useful. ***Ex 3.*** You should spend less time *gallivanting about* and more with your children.

Gallop ahead : progress rapidly. ***Ex.*** India, the biggest democracy in the world, is *galloping ahead* in the race to develop new technologies.

Galumph down/into/up : walk, run, etc. noisily or clumsily. ***Ex.*** The children came *galumphing into* the house like a herd of elephants.

Galvanise into : shock somebody into action. ***Ex 1.*** The manager's arrival *galvanised* the workers *into* action. ***Ex 2.*** A shot rang out and *galvanised* the police patrol *into* action. They began to move in the direction from which the firing had come.

Gamble away : lose something by gambling. ***Ex 1.*** Don't *gamble away* all your money. ***Ex 2.*** Many a family fortune has been *gambled away* on the stock exchange. ***Ex 3.*** He has *gambled* his whole fortune *away*. ***Ex 4.*** Having *gambled away* half his salary at cards and spent the rest on drink, Bhim Bahadur had to borrow from his friends to pay the house rent and buy some food.

Gamble in : risk money by investing in. ***Ex.*** He *gambled* a large amount of money *in* oil shares.

Gamble on : act in the hope of something being successful, true, etc. despite the risk of loss. ***Ex 1.*** I shall not *gamble on* the weather being fine. ***Ex 2.*** Don't *gamble on* having his support. ***Ex 3.*** Only a dolt would *gamble* his life's savings *on* the stock exchange in the hope of making easy money. ***Ex 4.*** We must allow plenty of time to get to the airport we cannot *gamble on* the road being clear.

Gang up : organise or form groups, alliances, against; act together with somebody against somebody. ***Ex 1.*** It is not pleasant to see a lot of young men *ganging up* against their distinguished seniors. ***Ex 2.*** They are all *ganging up* against you. ***Ex 3.*** He has *ganged up* with some very disreputable persons.

Gang up on : join together to hurt or frighten somebody. ***Ex 1.*** Older boys are *ganging up on* younger ones. ***Ex 2.*** I hope they will not *gang up on* her and make her life miserable. ***Ex 3.*** Telling dirty jokes is a way that men *gang up on* women.

Gather around/round : (a) come together in a group and surround somebody/something. ***Ex 1.*** The boys *gathered around* the old man to his stories. ***Ex 2.*** *Gather round*, friends, and hear the news.

(b) come to somebody's side and give' him moral, physical or material support. ***Ex.*** When he was in trouble, his friends *gathered around* him.

Gather from : learn or understand. ***Ex 1.*** I *gathered from* the way she replied that she was not very enthusiastic. ***Ex 2.*** Did you' *gather from* what the man said that he intended to make a bid for the house or not. ***Ex 3.*** I *gather from* what he said that he will be giving up his job in the summer.

Gear to/towards : adapt something to a particular need or to an appropriate level or standard. ***Ex 1.*** Our effort is *geared to* a higher level of production. ***Ex 2.*** We are *gearing* our efforts *to* what the market really wants. ***Ex 3.*** Higher education is increasingly *geared towards* careers.

Gear up : become or make somebody/something ready for something. ***Ex 1.*** He *geared* himself *up* for the interview. ***Ex 2.*** The company is *gearing up* for the big export drive. ***Ex 3.*** I was all *geared up* to go on holiday, and now it has been cancelled. ***Ex 4.*** Science is not *geared up* to cope with the problems of human development. ***Ex 5.*** 'They are all *geared up* for the new sales compaign. ***Ex 6.*** Are you *gearing* yourself *up* for a full time job? ***Ex 7.*** The party organisation is ready to be *geared up* to the election, whenever it takes place.

Gen up : obtain information or provide somebody with information about something. ***Ex 1.*** I am fully *genned up* on the new project. ***Ex 2.*** He is all *genned up* about what to do and when to do it. ***Ex 3.*** I shall *gen up* on the legal position before I sign the contract. ***Ex 4.*** She *genned up* on the character before taking on the role.

Get about : (a) be able to move around after an illness, or in old age. ***Ex 1.*** He is *getting about* again after his illness. ***Ex 2.*** His material grandfather can *get about* with a stick. ***Ex 3.*** Her father is not able to *get about* since he had his stroke last year.

(b) move from place to place. ***Ex.*** Now that the traffic has been restricted in the centre of the city, it is easier to *get about*.

(c) (of news, rumour, etc.) circulate; spread from person to person; spread. ***Ex 1.*** It *got about* that the local government was recruiting teachers. ***Ex 2.*** The news of his resignation soon *got about*. ***Ex 3.*** I don't know how such a rumour *got about*. ***Ex 4.*** Bad news certainly *gets about*. ***Ex 5.*** The report has *got about* that you will not help us.

Get above oneself : have too high an opinion of oneself. ***Ex 1.*** She has been *getting* a bit *above herself* since winning her award. ***Ex 2.*** That young man is *getting above himself*. He has only been in this department two weeks and he is already telling his seniors how to do their work. ***Ex 3.*** He was restrained from *getting above himself* by a natural modesty

Get abreast of : draw or bring level with. ***Ex.*** It did not take India long to *get abreast of* American and Russian technology in guided missiles.

Get abroad : circulate; spread; get about. ***Ex.*** The news *got abroad* that the government had decided to impose a further tax on cigarettes and spirits.

Get across : (a) annoy, offend, irritate; form a bad relationship with; get on the wrong side of. ***Ex 1.*** Be careful how you talk to Champa Devi. She is an unpleasant person to *get across*. ***Ex 2.*** Those two men are so different in temperament that they were bound to *get across* each other. ***Ex 3.*** Don't *get across* me. ***Ex 4.*** She *got across* the headmaster who made life very difficult for her.

(b) make somebody understand something get something communicated. ***Ex 1.*** The speaker needs to know that his words are *getting across*. ***Ex 2.*** We managed to *get* our message *across*. ***Ex 3.*** It was difficult to *get across* the basic idea. ***Ex 4.*** Your meaning did not really *get across*. ***Ex 5.*** He is not very good at *getting* his ideas *across*. ***Ex 6.*** The comedian did not seem to be able to *get* his jokes *across* to his audience.

Get after : try to catch somebody accused of a crime or wickedness. ***Ex.*** It is for the police to *get after* the villains as fast as possible.

Get ahead/ahead of : progress well. ***Ex 1.*** By doing just a little extra homework each day, Sangeeta soon *got* well *ahead of* her classmates. ***Ex 2.*** We are *getting ahead* well with the project. ***Ex 3.*** You have to be sharp to *get ahead*. ***Ex 4.*** The bright young man can *get ahead* quickly in industry. ***Ex 5.*** As soon as he settled down to the routine his new job, Nitish *got ahead* splendidly.

Get along : (a) have a harmonious or friendly relationship with somebody; get on with somebody; succeed in doing something manage. ***Ex 1.*** He worked hard and was easy to *get along* with. ***Ex 2.*** They just can not *get along* together. ***Ex 3.*** Do you *get along* with your boss? ***Ex 4.*** We *get along* just fine. ***Ex 5.*** He *gets along* with her very well.

(b) leave a place. ***Ex 1.*** It is time we were *getting along*. ***Ex 2.*** Well, must be *getting along* now, or my husband will be wondering what has happened to me.

Get along/on : (a) make progress with a task, etc. ***Ex 1.*** How is Umesh *getting along* with the old car he bought last month ? ***Ex 2.*** *Get on*, you will be successful.

(b) have a harmonious relationship with; live or work together well. ***Ex 1.*** His wife and he do not *get on* very well. ***Ex 2.*** Your mother is immensely pious and good-natured-the easiest person in the world to *get along* with.

Get around/round : (a) gain the confidence, trust, favour of somebody, usually for a special purpose. ***Ex.*** The girl told her boyfriend that she would try and *get round* her father to lend the car for the day.

(b) tackle successfully; overcome. ***Ex.*** There seems to be no way of *getting around* the difficulty of keeping prices down when the cost of production goes on rising.

Get around/round to : find the necessary time for; reach the point of tackling something after setting other matters that must take priority. ***Ex.*** When I finally *got round to* buying the Diwali cards, it was too late. The shops were all sold out.

Get at : (a) gain access to somebody/something; reach somebody, something. ***Ex 1.*** The files are locked up and I cannot *get at* them. ***Ex 2.*** A sensible man keeps his savings in the bank-not in the house where some thief can *get at* them. ***Ex 3.*** I cannot *get at* her on the telephone. ***Ex 4.*** The village is very difficult to *get at*. ***Ex 5.*** They are having trouble *getting at* the information.

(b) start to work on. ***Ex 1.*** I wish the snow would thaw, in order that I could *get at* the garden.

(c) learn, ascertain, discover. ***Ex 1.*** What I am trying to *get at* is whether you want to marry the girl for her money, or because you love her very deeply. ***Ex 2.*** I have a determination to *get at* the facts. ***Ex 3.*** The members of the official board of inquiry had tremendous difficulty in *getting at* the truth of the matter: there seemed to be a conspiracy of silence. ***Ex 4.*** He wanted to *get at* the heart of this puzzling episode.

(d) suggest in an indirect way; imply; hint. ***Ex 1.*** I don't know what you are *getting at* exactly. ***Ex 2.*** The audience had no idea about what we were *getting at*.

(e) criticise; nag. ***Ex 1.*** Whenever his mother-in-law started talking about men who drink too much, he had a feeling that he was being *got at*. ***Ex 2.*** She is always *getting at* her husband. ***Ex 3.*** Whom are you *getting at* now?

(f) try to influence by improper means. ***Ex 1.*** The judge said that it was obvious from the man's behaviour in the witness-box that he had been *got at*. ***Ex 2.*** I should have won; I am sure the judges had been *got at*. ***Ex 3.*** The officer appears to have been *got at*.

Get away : (a) have a holiday. ***Ex 1.*** We have no chance of *getting away* this summer. ***Ex 2.*** I might crack up if I don't *get away* for a while. ***Ex 3.*** It is nice to *get away* in the autumn. ***Ex 4.*** I am hoping to *get away* for a few days at Diwali.

(b) escape from somebody or a place. ***Ex 1.*** The thief *got away* with a lot of money. ***Ex 2.*** Two of the dacoits *got away* from their captors. ***Ex 3.*** The convict *got away* from his guards.

(c) manage to leave the place one is in. ***Ex.*** It was nice of you to invite me to tea tomorrow, but I am afraid I cannot *get away* from the office.

(d) remove something. ***Ex 1.*** The nail had gone rusty in the wood and I could not *get* it *away*. ***Ex 2.*** *Get* all these dirty dishes *away*.

(e) assist somebody to leave a place for his own good. ***Ex 1.*** She must be *got away* from her children for a while and allowed to have a good rest.

Note : The word get away is a noun. It means escape. ***Ex 1.*** Their *get away* from the prison was very well planned. ***Ex 2.*** The thieves had made their *get away* down the stairs.

Get away from : (a) win, secrue, something/somebody in a struggle from. ***Ex.*** How are you going to *get* the ball *away* from the dog?

(b) escape from somebody or a place. ***Ex.*** Two of the prisoners *got away* from their captors.

(c) attract somebody back from. ***Ex.*** You will not be able to *get* her *away from* Paris now. She has fallen in love with the place.

(d) behave or do things in a different way. ***Ex 1.*** I shall not be able to *get away from* the office before 7 p.m. ***Ex 2.*** They wanted to *get away from* the rigid time-tables of the post.

Get away with : (a) steal and escape with. ***Ex 1.*** Bandits wearing, stocking masks over their faces raided the National Bank in New Delhi this morning and *got away with* ten lakh rupees. ***Ex 2.*** The cashier has *got away with* the takings.

(b) receive a relatively light punishment. ***Ex.*** For such a serious offence, she was lucky to *get away with* a fine.

(c) go unpunished; not suffer for. ***Ex 1.*** You cannot write to Head Office over your manager's head. You will never *get away with* breach of the rules such as that. ***Ex 2.*** Nobody *gets away with* insulting me like that. ***Ex 3.*** If you cheat in the examination you will never *get away with* it. ***Ex 4.*** He might have bribed the magistrate, and *got away with* it.

Get back : (a) return to one's home. ***Ex 1.*** What time did you *get back* last night? ***Ex 2.*** We only *got back* from our holidays yesterday.

(b) return to one's starting point. ***Ex 1.*** When Alok *gets back*, please, tell him that Alka phoned. ***Ex 2.*** When did you *get back* from Cairo? ***Ex 3.*** The nurse told the patient, who was wandering round the ward, to *get back* into bed at once.

(c) stand away; go to a reasonable, sensible distance. ***Ex 1.*** *Get back.* There is a bomb in this building. ***Ex 2.*** The police had great difficult in making the curious crowds *get back* and let the ambulance through.

(d) return something or somebody to its, his, place. ***Ex 1.*** He took the spring out of the clock, but now he cannot *get* it *back*. ***Ex 2.*** Did you *get* your books *back* to library in time? ***Ex 3.*** We are going to *get* you right *back* home where we can look after you properly.

(e) recover possession of. ***Ex 1.*** Don't lend him your dictionary. If you do, you will rever *get* it *back*. ***Ex 2.*** She has *got* her old job *back*. ***Ex 3.*** All he wants to do is *get* his girlfriend *back*.

(f) return to power after having lost it. ***Ex.*** The Communists hope to *get back* at the next election.

(g) punish or hurt somebody in return for something unpleasant done to one. ***Ex.*** I shall *get* him *back* for all the nasty things he said.

Get back at : retaliate against somebody; take revenge on somebody. ***Ex 1.*** I shall find a way of *getting back at* him. ***Ex 2.*** He *got back at* her for spoiling his evening.

Get back into : start being involved in an activity again. ***Ex 1.*** Japanese investors are *getting back into* the market. ***Ex 2.*** As his children are growing up, he would like to *get back into* research.

Get back to : (a) speak or write to somebody again later, in order to give a reply. ***Ex.*** I hope to *get back to* you on the question of costs by next week.

(b) return to something. ***Ex 1.*** Could you *get back to* the original question of funding? ***Ex 2.*** The student was glad to *get back to* his books after a vacation that had seemed too long. ***Ex 3.*** Let us just *get back to* the argument. ***Ex 4.*** He wanted to *get back to* sleep.

(c) contact somebody again after a short period of time. ***Ex 1.*** I shall *get back to* within an hour. ***Ex 2.*** I could not *get back to* you in time to tell you the new arrangements.

Get behind : not proceed at the necessary rate; not produce something at the right time; fall into arrears. ***Ex 1.*** I am *getting behind* with my work. ***Ex 2.*** He *got behind* with his payments for the car. ***Ex 3.*** Owing to her illness, Mohini could not keep up with the rest of the class and *got* badly *behind*.

Get by : (a) pass an obstacle. ***Ex 1.*** There was such a crowd outside the shop window that the young woman with the pram could not *get by*. ***Ex 2.*** I moved away from the doorway to let her *get by*. ***Ex 3.*** Let me *get by*, please. ***Ex 4.*** The traffic had come to a halt. Nothing could *get by* the accident.

(b) be accepted; pass scrutiny; be considered good, smart, etc.***Ex 1.*** He did not possess a dinner-jacket, but he was told that he would *get by* in a dark suit. ***Ex 2.*** He thought he could *get by* with the minimum of work.

(c) survive; get along; be successful in life or in a situation; manage; cope. ***Ex 1.*** She never seemed to have much money, but somehow she managed to *get by*. ***Ex 2.*** He *gets by* on very little money. ***Ex 3.*** How do you *get by* on such a small salary? ***Ex 4.*** He had managed to *get by* without much reading or writing. ***Ex 5.*** They slide through life, *getting by* as best as they can. ***Ex 6.*** His father had just enough land to *get by*.

(d) manage to cope with a difficult situation. ***Ex 1.*** You can *get by* in any Hindi conversation with a very limited vocabulary. ***Ex 2.*** It is possible to *get by* in a job interview by just talking about your interests.

Get down : (a) (of children) leave the table at mealtimes. ***Ex.*** The children sat through the meal in complete silence and spoke only to ask permission to *get down*.

(b) descend. ***Ex 1.*** A man escaped from the burning building by *getting down* a ladder. ***Ex 2.*** He *got down* from the bus. ***Ex 3.*** She has climbed up that tree, and now she cannot *get down*.

(c) make somebody depressed or demoralised. ***Ex 1.*** This wet weather is *getting* me *down*. ***Ex 2.*** Don't let the incident *get* you *down* too much. ***Ex 3.*** The bad news certainly *got* her *down*.

(d) assume a stooping kneeling position. ***Ex 1.*** She *got away* on her knees and prayed that her husband would survive the storm. ***Ex 2.*** He *got down* and began to pray. ***Ex 3.*** The woman *got down* on her knees and peered at the baby.

(e) swallow something with difficulty. ***Ex 1.*** The little boy *got* his medicine *down* with the help of a spoonful of jam. ***Ex 2.*** The medicine was so horrible that I could hardly *get* it *down*. ***Ex 3.*** He finds it hard to *get* food *down*.

(f) note or record something; write something down. ***Ex 1.*** Did you *get* her telephone number *down*? ***Ex 2.*** I *got down* every word of what he said. ***Ex 3.*** Make sure you *get* his confession *down*, and his signature at the bottom of it.

(g) cause to fall or descend; bring down. ***Ex 1.*** Nandini *got* the book *down* from the shelf. ***Ex 2.*** Will you give me a hand to *get* this trunk *down* the stairs?

Get down to : begin to do something; tackle something; give serious attention to something. ***Ex 1.*** Let us *get down to* some serious work. ***Ex 2.*** These are problems that we have never *got down to* tackling. ***Ex 3.*** He *got down to* business. ***Ex 4.*** You will never finish that job unless you forget everything else and *get down to* it.

Get home : (a) arrive at one's house; bring or take somebody at his house. ***Ex 1.*** What time did you *get home* last night? ***Ex 2.*** If you will come round for coffee, I shall *get* you *home* before ten o'clock.

(b) (of racing, athletics) : reach the winning port, target, etc. first. ***Ex 1.*** His horse *got home* by a nose. ***Ex 2.*** The hundred metres champion managed to *get home* by a second.

(c) make or become understood, hit the target. ***Ex 1.*** The T.Y. programme *got home* all right. ***Ex 2.*** Politicians are adept at *getting* their point *home*, even in the face of constant interruption from their opponents.

Get in : (a) arrive at destination. ***Ex 1.*** The train *got in* late. ***Ex 2.*** When do you normally *get in* from your work? ***Ex 3.*** What time does your flight *get in*?

(b) go inside. ***Ex 1.*** Never *get in* a stranger's car. ***Ex 2.*** I walked to the car, *got in* and drove away.

(c) enter a buiding, ***Ex.*** Nobody can *get in* the Parliament House without a pass.

(d) collect or gather something; bring back something. ***Ex.*** The farmers *got* the crops *in*.

(e) buy a supply of something. ***Ex 1.*** They *got* coal *in* for a month. ***Ex 2.*** Remember to *get in* some fruit.

(f) manage to do or say something. ***Ex 1.*** She talks so much that it is impossible to *get* a word *in*. ***Ex 2.*** I *got in* on hour's gardening between the showers.

(g) call somebody to perform a service. ***Ex 1.*** We have to *get* a plumber *in* to mend the burst pipe. ***Ex 2.*** I shall *get in* the police if they keep up this racket much longer.

(h) be elected to a political position. ***Ex 1.*** The party expects to *get in* at the next election. ***Ex 2.*** Our candidate stands a good chance of *getting in* Parliament. ***Ex 3.*** She *got in* by more than five thousand votes. ***Ex 4.*** The Congress *got in* with a small majority in the Punjab Legislative Assembly.

(i) succeed in saying something. ***Ex.*** He *got* a question *in* about the rates.

Get in/into : enter. ***Ex 1.*** The thieves *got in* through the floor by means of a tunnel. ***Ex 2.*** They *got into* the strongroom through the floor.

Get in on : take part in an activity. ***Ex.*** He is keen to *get in on* any discussions about the new project.

Get in with : try to become friendly with somebody in order to gain an advantage. ***Ex 1.*** He *got in with* a bad crowd at university. ***Ex 2.*** Have you noticed how she is trying to *get in with* the boss? ***Ex 3.*** She takes good care to *get in with* rich people. ***Ex 4.*** He managed to *get* well *in with* some of the local rich people by joining the golf club. ***Ex 5.*** I tried hard to *get in with* a charming girl sitting by herself, but she would not have anyting to do with me.

Get into : (a) enter reach a place. ***Ex 1.*** The thieves *got into* the house through a hole in the wall. ***Ex 2.*** I turned off the lights and *got into* bed. ***Ex 3.*** We *got into* the village at about one'o clock.

(b) (of a feeling) affect, influence or take control of somebody. ***Ex 1.*** *I* don't know what has *got into* her recently; she has become very bad tempered. ***Ex 2.*** He *gets into* a terrible rage if you just mention politics.

(c) put on a garment, etc. with difficulty. ***Ex 1.*** He cannot *get into* these shoes; they are too small. ***Ex 2.*** At the dress rehearsal the hero could not *get into* the armour he was supposed to wear.

(d) start a career in. ***Ex 1.*** He has *got into* accountancy. ***Ex 2.*** Do you intend to *get into* journalism?

(e) become involved in something; start something. ***Ex 1.*** He always *gets into* arguments with people. ***Ex 2.*** He was determined to *get into* politics.

(f) become involved in a difficult situation. ***Ex 1.*** Make sure you don't overspend and *get into* debt. ***Ex 2.*** He *got* himself *into* a frightful muddle recently.

(g) have a particular habit or behave in a particular way; acquire or develop something. ***Ex 1.*** She has *got into* the habit of sulking. ***Ex 2.*** I really need to *get into* a routine. ***Ex 3.*** He has *got into* bad habits.

(h) become interested in something. ***Ex 1.*** She is really *getting into* classical dance. ***Ex 2.*** How did you *get into* the habit of taking drugs? ***Ex 3.*** The children *got into* the habit of switching on the television as soon as they came in from school. ***Ex 4.*** Painting is a fascinating hobby once you *get into* it.

(i) be accepted as a member of an organisation. ***Ex 1.*** There was no chance of her *getting into* university. ***Ex 2.*** He failed to *get into* the government medical college in Calcutta.

(j) put on clothes with difficulty, or awkwardly. ***Ex 1.*** He became so fat that he could not *get into* any of his clothes. ***Ex 2.*** She was hopping on one foot to *get into* her shorts.

Get off : (a) dismount; alight from. ***Ex 1.*** The policeman told the child *get off* the pony. ***Ex 2.*** The absent-minded professor forgot to *get off* at New Delhi railway station and was taken on to Agra. ***Ex 3.*** When the train stopped, we *got off*. ***Ex 4.*** When did you *get off* the bus?

(b) not sit, stand, walk, drive, lying on, etc. ***Ex 1.*** We should *get off* the lake before the storm breaks, or we will get soaked. ***Ex 2.*** The children were told to *get off* the scaffolding round the building. ***Ex 3.*** She was *getting off* the bed.

(c) leave a place or start a journey. ***Ex.*** We *got off* immediately after breakfast.

(d) cause somebody to leave. ***Ex.*** She *got* the children *off* to school,

(e) fall asleep. ***Ex.*** When did you *get off* to sleep last night?

(f) cause somebody to fall asleep. ***Ex.*** She *got* the baby *out* to sleep by rocking it.

(g) leave work with permission. ***Ex.*** Normally I *get off* work at 5 : 30 p.m.

(h) stop discussing a particular subject. ***Ex 1.*** Let us *get off* the subject of dieting. ***Ex 2.*** Tell them to *get off* politics and get into the real issues here.

(i) send by post. ***Ex.*** Tell him to *get* these letters *off* by the first post tomorrow.

(j) remove something from something. ***Ex 1.*** Her finger was so swollen that she could not *get* her sing *off*. ***Ex 2.*** *Get* your shirt *off*.

(k) escape or nearly escape injury in an accident. ***Ex.*** She was lucky to *get off* with just a few bruises.

(l) escape or nearly escape punishment. ***Ex.*** I *got off* with a small fine.

(m) cause somebody to escape or nearly escape punishment. ***Ex 1.*** A good lawyer might be able to *get* you *off*. ***Ex 2.*** It was her youth that *got* her *off*, not her innocence.

(n) send a letter, parcel or message. ***Ex 1.*** He eventually *got* his letter *off*. ***Ex 2.*** *Get* this message *off* to the addressee.

(o) leave a place where one should not be. ***Ex 1.*** I told thein to *get off* our playground. ***Ex 2.*** The policeman told the noisy kids to *get off* the street.

(p) stop using. ***Ex 1.*** I told her to *get off* the phone. ***Ex 2.*** Will you kindly *get off* the phone-you have been on for hours.

(q) not to touch somebody/something. ***Ex 1.*** He kept trying to kiss her, so she told him to *get off*. ***Ex 2.*** *Get off* that cake, it is for tomorrow.

(r) persuade somebody to give something. ***Ex 1.*** They are more concerned with *getting* a meal *off* us. ***Ex 2.*** I shall *get* some money *off* my father.

Get off with : become friendly with, or deliberately attract a person of the opposite sex. ***Ex 1.*** We never thought that she would *get off with* anyone, let alone jailbird. ***Ex 2.*** He *got off with* my attractive lady secretary, a thing he no doubt imagined. I was secretly burning to do myself. ***Ex 3.*** Can't you get him off with that nice girl you keep talking about? ***Ex 4.*** Don't *get off with* his girlfriend. ***Ex 5.*** If a man is *getting off with* a girl, people notice it.

Get off on : become very excited. ***Ex.*** Rock-climbing is such a high (feeling of extreme pleasure)—I really *get off on* it.

Get on : (a) get dressed in; put into position; put on. ***Ex 1.*** I shall just *get* my things *on* and we shall go for a short walk. ***Ex 2.*** She *got* the kettle *on* for a cup a tea. ***Ex 3.*** He took the top off the jar but could not *get* it *on* again. ***Ex 4.*** *Get* your coat *on*.

(b) make progress; advance. ***Ex 1.*** The students *got on* so well that they had covered the course three weeks before the alloted time. ***Ex 2.*** How are you *getting on* these days? ***Ex 3.*** The work is *getting on* splendidly. ***Ex 4.*** He is *getting on* well at school.

(c) perform in a particular situation. ***Ex 1.*** How did you *get on* in your oral examination? ***Ex 2.*** He did not *get on* well in Indonesia.

(d) advance in age or grow old. ***Ex 1.*** He is *getting on* now, and is not as agile as he was. ***Ex 2.*** They are *getting on* in years now.

(e) (of time) pass; become late. ***Ex 1.*** Time is *getting on*, and we have not done all the work yet. ***Ex 2.*** The bus will be here for you in twenty minutes. Time is *getting on*. Please strat getting ready.

(f) be successful in life or career. ***Ex 1.*** You have to push yourself to *get on* in the academic world. ***Ex 2.*** He has certainly *got on* in the world. ***Ex 3.*** Some people *get on*, and others don't. ***Ex 4.*** I am always keen for my children to *get on*. ***Ex 5.*** She is ambitious and eager to *get on* in the world.

(g) cope with or manage. ***Ex 1.*** I simply cannot *get on* without an efficient lady secretary. ***Ex 2.*** We can *get on* perfectly well without him.

(h) detect or trace somebody; become aware of somebody's presence of activities. ***Ex.*** He had been stealing money from the company for years before the police *got on* to him.

(i) contact somebody by telephone or letter. ***Ex 1.*** He *got on* the phone to the President. ***Ex 2.*** *Get* her *on* the phone at once. ***Ex 3.*** If you wish to lodge a complaint, you should *get on* to the general manager.

(j) climb on; mount. ***Ex 1.*** He tried to *get on* the wall but it was too high. ***Ex 2.*** He *got on* the horse. ***Ex 3.*** She *got on* her bicycle and cycled off.

(k) get into something; enter. He *got on* the bus every morning.

(l) start doing or continue doing something. ***Ex 1.*** Let me *get on* with my dinner. ***Ex 2.*** We should *get on* with the meeting.

(m) have friendly relationship. ***Ex 1.*** Those two persons are not prepared to *get on* together. ***Ex 2.*** He has never really *got on* with his sister. ***Ex 3.*** They don't *get on* at all well together. ***Ex 4.*** I am *getting on* well with the managing director. ***Ex 5.*** We *get on* with them very well. ***Ex 6.*** I was surprised at how will you all *get on*.

(n) proceed; go on one's way. ***Ex 1.*** Well, we must be *getting on* now. ***Ex 2.*** Better *get on* while there is still light.

Get on at : criticise. ***Ex 1.*** Don't *get on at* her. ***Ex 2.*** I did not want him *getting on at* you.

Get on for : approach, draw near to, a stated age or time. ***Ex 1.*** This building must be *getting on for* hundred years. ***Ex 2.*** She is *getting on for* twenty years, and have become engaged. ***Ex 3.*** It was *getting on for* four o'clock. ***Ex 4.*** I have got to go. It is *getting on for* five, and I promised to meet my girlfriend at the golf club.

Get on/onto : mount, board. ***Ex 1.*** As the bus was full when it stopped at the school, the children could not *get on*. ***Ex 2.*** Before you can learn to ride a horse, you have to be able to *get onto* it. ***Ex 3.*** They helped him to *get* those sheep *onto* the cart.

Get on to : (a) contact, often by telephone. ***Ex 1.*** *Get on to* your lawyer and ask his advice. ***Ex 2.*** I shall *get on to* her right away. ***Ex 3.*** *Get* straight *on to* the department chief about it. ***Ex 4.*** I want you to *get on to* the Governor.

(b) trace, find, detect; become aware of somebody's presence or activity. ***Ex 1.*** The police will *get on to* the absconder soon. ***Ex 2.*** The police could not *get on to* the infiltrators. ***Ex 3.*** The murder squad followed every bit of information and eventually *got on to* the wanted man's trail in a remote area of Kashmir. ***Ex 4.*** The secret service *got on to* the enemy agent shortly after he arrived in the country and watched his every move.

(c) realise, become aware of. ***Ex.*** When she *got on to* the real reason for her husband being kept late at the office, the whole affair was out in the open.

(d) move from one activity, or phase, to another. ***Ex 1.*** That is something we shall *get on to* in the future. ***Ex 2.*** They *got on to* talking about old movies. ***Ex 3.*** When do you think we are going to *get on to* something useful? ***Ex 4.*** We don't *get on to* anatomy until next year.

Get on with : (a) make proress with a task. ***Ex 1.*** How is your son *getting on with* his Sanskrit? ***Ex 2.*** I am *getting on* very well *with* my French.

(b) continue doing sth, after an interruption. ***Ex 1.*** Put that novel away and *get on with* your work. ***Ex 2.*** As this letter has to be sent by post in twenty minutes, I must *get on with* it first. Then we shall have a cup of tea and a chat.

Get on without : manage, survive, keep going, without. ***Ex.*** How will he *get on without* a housekeeper? He has never had to look after himself before.

Get out : (a) become known, leak. ***Ex 1.*** Somehow the news *got out* that Dilip Kumar was in the Ashoka Hotel, and a big crowd gathered outside in the hope of seeing him. ***Ex 2.*** Don't let it *get out* that Premlata is coming to stay with us for a few days. ***Ex 3.*** Tell me how the secret *got out*.

(b) receive, draw, be given. ***Ex.*** In most walks of life, you only *get out* what you put in.

(c) say or utter something with difficulty. ***Ex 1.*** He was sobbing so hard that he could not *get* anything *out*. ***Ex 2.*** The young pretty woman was in such a state of shock after the accident that she could not *get* a word *out*. ***Ex 3.*** Although, the old man was deeply moved, he nevertheless managed to *get out* a short speech in which he profoundly thanked everyone for his retirement present. ***Ex 4.*** Do you sometimes find it difficult to *get* your words *out*?

(d) succeed in solving, or finding the correct answer to. ***Ex 1.*** Not a single boy in the class could *get* the problem *out*. ***Ex 2*** I managed to *get* that puzzle *out*. ***Ex 3.*** Can you *get* this sum *out*?

(e) leave. ***Ex.*** They decided to *get out* while there was still time.

Get out/out of : (a) go away; escape from danger. ***Ex.*** The police are coming. *Get out* at once.

(b) cause somebody to leave. ***Ex 1.*** We had to find some way of *getting* the nurse *out* for a few minutes, so that we could talk freely. ***Ex 2.*** Our car could not be *got out of* the garage because there were several other locked cars around it.

(c) leak; escape from. ***Ex 1.*** I don't know how the acid *got out*. ***Ex 2.*** The villagers were terrified when they heard that the lion had *got out* of its cage.

Get out of : (a) avoid; not do what one ought to do. ***Ex 1.*** His sons were experts at *getting out of* hard work. ***Ex 2.*** As I was out of sorts, I *got out of* going to the party last evening.

(b) lose, abandon. ***Ex 1.*** After living for two years in a hotel, I had completely *got out of* the way of doing things for myself. ***Ex 2.*** If you *get out of* the habit of smoking, you will soon feel better.

(c) cause to abandon. ***Ex.*** *Get* this child *out of* the habit of repeating everything I say.

(d) obtain, gain, from. ***Ex 1.*** Too many people spend their time wondering what they can *get out of* others, instead of what they can give to others. ***Ex 2.*** Don't imagine that I am going to *get* a huge profit *out of* this deal. I am probably going to lose money on it. ***Ex 3.*** There is nothing to be *got out of* this book: it is years out of date. ***Ex 4.*** She always *get* the best *out of* people .

(e) make somebody yield something; extract. ***Ex 1.*** The interrogators finally *got* a confession *out of* the prisoner. ***Ex 2.*** Nothing substantial could be *got out of* the minister.

Get over : (a) climb, cross. ***Ex.*** How did the cattle manage to *get over* the road?

(b) cause somebody to climb. ***Ex.*** We *got* ourselves safetly *over* the fence.

(c) surmount, overcome or master something. ***Ex 1.*** She cannot *get over* her shyness. ***Ex 2.*** I think the problem can be *got over* without difficulty. ***Ex 3.*** Let me know how to *get over* the linguistic problems in the country.

(d) become happy, healthy, calm, etc. again. ***Ex 1.*** He was disappointed at not *getting* the job, but he will *get over* it. ***Ex 2.*** She never *got over* the shock of losing her husband in the prime of his youth.

(e) fully believe, appreciate or understand. ***Ex 1.*** Anil could not *get over* it as Sunil solemnly handed over the money he had stolen. ***Ex 2.*** She could not *get over* the fact that someone so handsome could be so unlikeable.

(f) overcome, suppress, master. ***Ex 1.*** When I last saw Snehlata, she had almost completely *got over* her nervousness in the presence of strangers. ***Ex 2.*** He *got over* his difficulties. ***Ex 3.*** They don't appear to have *got over* their disappointment.

(g) travel over; cover a distance of. ***Ex 1.*** They only managed to *get over* ten kilometres. ***Ex 2.*** The athlete failed to *get over* the distance in the minimum time to qualify for the final.

(h) make clear; impress somebody with. ***Ex 1.*** He did not really *get* his meaning *over* to his audience. ***Ex 2.*** The lecturer, though he knew his subject inside out, was quite capable of *getting* anything useful *over* to the students. ***Ex 3.*** Dressed in deepest black, possessing more personal force than anyone else in the court, and more ability to *get* it *over*, Hemlata made a great impression.

Get over with : do something necessary but unpleasant. ***Ex 1.*** He will be glad to *get* the examination *over with*. ***Ex 2.*** Premlata wanted to *get* this miserable business *over with* as quickly as possible.

Get round : (a) avoid legally, if not honourably. ***Ex 1.*** The lawyer was well known for his skill at *getting round* the law, usually on technical points. ***Ex 2.*** They believed that there were no tax-laws that could not be *got round* somehow or others. ***Ex 3.*** I *got round* the problem in a novel way. ***Ex 4.*** To *get round* the law, their plays were staged in private houses.

(b) persuade somebody to agree to something or to do something which he first opposed. ***Ex 1.*** She knows how to *get round* her father. ***Ex 2.*** He could always *get round* her in the end. ***Ex 3.*** I *got* her *round* to my way of thinking.

(c) tackle something successfully; overcome something. ***Ex.*** What is the way of *getting round* the problem?

(d) evade or avoid without acting illegally. ***Ex.*** A clever lawyer found ways of *getting round* that clause of the law.

Get round to : finally do something after dealing with other matters; find the necessary time to do something. ***Ex 1.*** I did not *get round* to taking the examination. ***Ex 2.*** It took Kamini two years to *get round* to buying a Maruti car. ***Ex 3.*** I am very busy at the moment, but I hope to *get round to* answering your letter next week.

Get through : (a) use up or consume. ***Ex 1.*** People say that the old man *got through* a very large amount of money when he was young, and lived in poverty for the rest of his life. ***Ex 2.*** Sita *gets through* thirty

cigarettes a day. ***Ex 3.*** We *got through* a fortune while we were on holiday. ***Ex 4.*** Rohini has *got through* all the money her father left her.

(b) do or complete something. ***Ex 1.*** It is difficult to *get through* this amount of work in such a short time. ***Ex 2.*** Let us start; there is a lot of work to *get through*. ***Ex 3.*** I have *got through* a lot of correspondence today. ***Ex 4.*** My new secretary is very quick; she *gets through* a lot of work in a morning.

(c) manage to pass through. ***Ex 1.*** I don't know how such a large animal *got through* such a small hole. ***Ex 2.*** The water *gets through* every time it rains.

(d) reach, or bring to. ***Ex 1.*** If more supplies do not *get through*, thousands of refugees will die. ***Ex 2.*** The ammunition could not be *got through* to the troops, and they had to surrender.

(e) make contact with somebody, by telephone. ***Ex 1.*** I tried ringing you several times yesterday but I could not *get through* to you. ***Ex 2.*** I telephoned Ram in hospital and *got through* without difficulty. ***Ex 3.*** I have been trying for a whole hour to *get through* to you.

(f) be successful in; help to pass. ***Ex 1.*** Rajni *got through* the written papers but failed in the oral examination. ***Ex 2.*** He failed but his sister Nandini *got through*. ***Ex 3.*** It is hard work and nothing else that *gets* you *through*. ***Ex 4.*** The teacher *got* all his pupils *through* Sanskrit.

(g) be officially approved or accepted. ***Ex 1.*** The Bill *got through* Parliament and became a law. ***Ex 2.*** The opposition *got* the amendment *through* with a majority of 112. They think the Bill not *get through* Parliament.

(h) enable to survive. ***Ex.*** She needs her coffee to *get through* the day.

Get through to : (a) make somebody understand the meaning of what one is saying; communicate with somebody. ***Ex 1.*** I find her impossible to *get through to*. ***Ex 2.*** Try to *get through to* him that he is wasting his life in that job. ***Ex 3.*** The boy is just stupid: I cannot *get through to* him at all, even when I explain things in words of one syllable. ***Ex 4.*** As the injured man is in a dazed state, it is impossible to *get through to* him.

(b) succeed in reaching the intended place. ***Ex.*** The real emergencies were not *getting through to* the hospital.

(c) (of a player or team) : reach the next stage of a competition. ***Ex 1.*** Prem Kumari *got through to* the final. ***Ex 2.*** It was only luck that *got* us *through to* the next round.

Get through with : (a) finish or complete. ***Ex 1.*** As soon as I *get through with* my work, I shall join you. ***Ex 2.*** He finally *got through with* the subject. ***Ex 3.*** No sooner had the tedious job of decorating the house been *got through with* than a pipe burst in the attic and ruined everything. ***Ex 4.*** By the time we had *got through with* all the formalities, all we wanted to do was to go to the hotel and rest.

(b) finish dealing with somebody, implying physical attack or verbal correction. ***Ex 1.*** When I have *got through with* that scoundrel, even his own mother could not recognise him. ***Ex 2.*** When the nurse had *got through with* the grumbling patients, they felt thoroughly ashamed of themselves.

Get to : (a) reach; arrive at. ***Ex.*** We did not *get to* the hotel untill midnight. ***Ex 2.*** They *got to* the village at 4.30 p.m. ***Ex 3.*** unpleasant grin spread over the boy's face as he *got to* the juicy part of the novel.

(b) begin to do something; reach the point of doing something; annoy or anger. ***Ex 1.*** In his disturbed state, he *got to* screaming abuses at anyone who troubled him in any way. ***Ex 2.*** Lying in bed, unable to sleep, I *got to* thinking how nice it would be to go away and start a new life somewhere else. ***Ex 3.*** I *got to* thinking how lonel she must be. ***Ex 4.*** Her constant nagging is beginning to *get to* him

(c) affect strongly. ***Ex 1.*** Don't let that ugly incident *get to* you. ***Ex 2.*** The horror of war was beginning to *get to* him.

Get together : (a) meet socially; discuss something with a view to forming a common front. ***Ex 1.*** Let us *get together* next week and have a long chat about old times. ***Ex 2.*** Workers and supervisors *got together* to discuss their grievances. ***Ex 3.*** Do you think we could *get together* at Diwali?

(b) assemble or collect. ***Ex 1.*** Rebel leaders tried to *get* an army *together*. ***Ex 2.*** I want you to *get* your things *together*; so that we can leave at a moment's notice. ***Ex 3.*** Enough volunteers were *got together* to keep the place clean all through the summer.

(c) organise or, arrange. ***Ex 1.*** Our party *got together* a sizeable demonstration of support. ***Ex 2.*** I don't know whether he has *got* the time to get anything *together* yet.

(d) succeed in getting money needed. ***Ex 1.*** Almost all of the children had *got* the money *together* themselves. ***Ex 2.*** Somehow we have to *get* the fees *together*.

(e) control one's feelings. ***Ex.*** She *got* herself *together* enough to consult a lawyer.

Note : *Get-together* is a noun. It is used to denote an informal meeting or gathering. ***Ex.*** The firm had its annual *get-together* at the Ashoka Hotel.

Get up : (a) stand after sitting, kneeling, ere: rise. ***Ex 1.*** The class *got up* when the teacher came in. ***Ex 2.*** He *got up* slowly from the armchair. ***Ex 3.*** She *got up* and strode across the room.

(b) rise from bed. ***Ex 1.*** What time do you *get up* in the morning? ***Ex 2.*** I *get up* at 6.30 a.m., every morning.

(c) cause somebody to get out of bed; call or awake somebody out of bed. ***Ex 1.*** Could you *get* me *up* at 5.30 tomorrow? ***Ex 2.*** Don't *get* me *up* in the morning. ***Ex 3.*** She had to *get* the children *up* and dressed. ***Ex 4.*** If I had been *got up* earlier, I would not have missed the train.

(d) rise to one's feet from a chair, or the ground. ***Ex 1.*** When the Chairman asked if there were any questions, four persons *got up* at once. ***Ex 2.*** The man fell to the floor with a crash and could not *get up* again. ***Ex 3.*** He *got up* from the table and left the room as quickly as possible.

(e) arrange or organise something. ***Ex 1.*** They *got up* a play to amuse the children. ***Ex 2.*** I am *getting up* a grand party for your birthday. ***Ex 3.*** An impromptu dance was *got up* in her honour. ***Ex 4.*** The students *got up* a country-wide campaign in support of nuclear disarmament.

(f) dress in a special way; make beautiful or attractive. ***Ex 1.*** Mridula Devi was *got up* as an Indian princess. ***Ex 2.*** She knows how to *get* herself *up* effectively and attractively.

(g) acquire a knowledge; study or memorise something. ***Ex 1.*** I am busy *getting up* the Indian constitution for tomorrow's examination. ***Ex 2.*** He is *getting up* chemistry for his examination slated to begin on Friday, the 14th April, 1994, at 9.30 a.m. ***Ex 3.*** You must start *getting up* your lecture notes.

(h) mount. ***Ex.*** He *got up* on the horse by himself.

(i) climb; carry up. ***Ex 1.*** Your car will never *get up* that hill. ***Ex 2.*** How do you expect to *get* this table *up* all those stairs? ***Ex 3.*** He *got up* the tree without difficulty.

(j) prepare; arrange. ***Ex 1.*** She *got up* the dress for sale. ***Ex 2.*** The book has been *got up* very nicely by the designers and printers.

(k) dress. ***Ex.*** They *got* themselves *up* as pirates for the fancy dress ball.

Note : *Get-up* is a noun used in the sense of set of clothes, especially an unusual one; costume. ***Ex 1.*** She wears the most extraordinary *get-ups.* ***Ex 2.*** Do you like my *get-up*? ***Ex 3.*** He looked absurd in that *get-up*.

Get up against : (a) stand, sit, huddle very close to; place very near to. ***Ex 1.*** The child *got up against* the radiator in his efforts to keep warm. ***Ex 2.*** Can you help me to *get* this load of sand *up against* the tree, where it will stay dry?

(b) form a bad relationship with; find oneself in conflict with. ***Ex 1.*** Parvati is hopelessly headstrong; she always *gets up against* people in authority. ***Ex 2.*** I had only been working in the hotel for a week when I *got up against* the head waiter, and he began to make life unbearable for me.

Get up to : (a) raise to; cause to reach. ***Ex 1.*** It is inadvisable to pay too much attention to advertisements that promise to *get* you *up to* managerial status in one or two years.

(b) reach. ***Ex.*** The boy despaired of ever *getting up to* the high standard required for entry to the university.

(c) be occupied in, or be busy with something undesirable, foolish or surprising. ***Ex 1.*** What on earth will Shankar be *getting up to* next. First he bought antiques, then it was old houses, and now it is old ships. ***Ex 2.*** He has been *getting up to* his dirty tricks with young children again. ***Ex 3.*** He has *got up to* some new mischief. ***Ex 4.*** What did you *get up to* while I was away? ***Ex 5.*** When I found out what they used to *get up to* I was absolutely horrified. ***Ex 6.*** Don't *get up to* anything behind my back.

(d) reach (the specified point). ***Ex.*** I have *got up to* page 172 in the book.

Gibber away : chatter away like an ape; talk a lot without seeming to say anything important. ***Ex 1.*** What is he *gibbering away* about? ***Ex 2.***He *gibbered away* about his crazy ideas.

Ginger up : make somebody/something more vigorous or live ***Ex 1.*** Some dancing will *ginger up* the party. ***Ex 2.*** The Radical Party needs *gingering up*; it is dying on its feet. ***Ex 3.*** He is lazy. Please *ginger* him *up* a bit. ***Ex 4.*** The Prime Minister appointed some new ministers to *ginger up* his administration.

Gird on : fasten something on, especially with a best. ***Ex.*** The youngman *girded on* his father's sword and went forth to avenge him.

Give away : (a) (in a marriage ceremony) Lead the bride to bridegroom and give her to him. ***Ex 1.*** As her father was too ill to be present, the bride was *given away* by her paternal uncle.

(b) give something free of charge. ***Ex 1.*** I *gave away* most of my money to charity. ***Ex 2.*** These watches are only two hundred rupees each; we are almost *giving* them *away*.

(c) distribute or present something. ***Ex.*** The Chief Minister *gave away* the prizes at the college sports day.

(d) betray something/somebody; reveal something/somebody intentionally or unintentionally, ***Ex 1.*** He *gave away* state secrets to the enemy. ***Ex 2.*** The soldier *gave away* the secrets when the enemy tortured him.

(e) fail to take or use, through foolishness or neglect. ***Ex 1.*** Whether from laziness or ineptitude, he *gave away* his last chance to make his reputation as an actor. ***Ex 2.*** If you *give* your chances *away* like that, how can you expect to win the game?

(f) yield; give away. ***Ex.*** The floor of the dilapidated house *gave away* with the weight of hundred people who were sitting on it.

Give back : (a) return something to its owner. ***Ex 1.*** Please *give* me *back* my pen. ***Ex 2.*** He *gave back* everything he had taken.

(b) allow somebody to have or enjoy something again. ***Ex 1.*** The surgical operation *gave* him *back* the use of his legs. ***Ex 2.*** The dictator *gave* the people *back* their freedom.

Give for : (a) exchange for. ***Ex.*** She would have *given* her eyes *for* ballet dress.

(b) sacrifice for. ***Ex 1.*** He *gave* his life *for* his country. ***Ex 2.*** He has promised to *give* his life *for* you.

Give forth : emit; produce. ***Ex 1.*** The engine *gave forth* a horrible grinding noise, and stopped. ***Ex 2.*** On summer evenings, the flowers *gave forth* an almost intoxicating scent. ***Ex 3.*** The strange animal did not run away, but stood its ground *giving forth* a mooing sound.

Give in : (a) hand over something to somebody who is authorised to receive it. ***Ex 1.*** Please *give* your examination papers *in* to the teacher when you have finished. ***Ex 2.*** She *gave in* the documents as requested. ***Ex 3.*** Let me know who *gave* my name *in* for the cross-country run on Sunday.

(b) allow oneself to be defeated or overcome by somebody/something. ***Ex 1.*** The rebels were forced to *give in*. ***Ex 2.*** People say that Sudesh is a gusty player, she never *gives in*. ***Ex 3.*** Don't show any sign of *giving in* to the kidnapper's demands. ***Ex 4.*** Since she became the president of the Women' Freedom Association, she has totally stopped *giving in* to her husband on every point of difference between them; she sticks to her guns.

Give off : (a) display a particular quality. ***Ex 1.*** Politicians always *give off* an air of importance. ***Ex 2.*** Padma Devi *gave off* a tremendous intellectual aura.

(b) emit; release; produce. ***Ex 1.*** The acid *gives off* a characteristically pungent odour. ***Ex 2.*** The cooker is *giving off* a funny smell. ***Ex 3.*** The tremendous heat *given off* by the fire is wholly unbearable. .

(c) completely stop doing something. ***Ex 1.*** He never *gave off* doing bits of business for the amusement of friends or guests.

Give on to : have a view of something; lead directly to something ***Ex 1.*** The bedroom windows *give on to* the street. ***Ex 2.*** This door *gives on to* the courtyard. ***Ex 3.*** The door *gave on to* a path which skirted the house.

Give out : (a) come to an end; be exhausted. ***Ex 1.*** Her patience finally *gave out*. ***Ex 2.*** After a month their food supplies *gave out*. ***Ex 3.*** The haunted animal's strength finally *gave out*, and the hounds were upon it like lightning.

(b) hand out or distribute something. ***Ex 1.*** The teacher *gave out* the examination papers. ***Ex 2.*** You are not allowed to *gave out* leaflets without permission from the local authority.

(c) announce; make known. ***Ex 1.*** He *gave* the news *out* in a grave voice. ***Ex 2.*** The news of the King's death was *given out* in a radio broadcast. ***Ex 3.*** It was *given out* that the President of that country was shot. ***Ex 4.*** The accused man had *given* himself *out* to be a qualified doctor.

(d) send out or emit something. ***Ex 1.*** The radiator is *giving out* a lot of heat. ***Ex 2.*** Tail lights *give out* red reflections onto the wet road. ***Ex 3.*** She hugged her knees closer and *gave out* a loud girlish laugh.

(e) stop working. ***Ex 1.*** The engine *gave out*. ***Ex 2.*** The fuse in a plug will *give out* occasionally. ***Ex 3.*** Her voice was about to *give out*.

Give over : (a) stop doing something annoying. ***Ex 1.*** If you don't give over, I shall smack you. ***Ex 2.*** She asked me to *give over* humming ***Ex 3.*** *Give over* I cannot work with you chattering like that. ***Ex 4.*** *Give over* complaining.

(b) stop doing an activity. ***Ex.*** I *gave over* my restless re-arranging and sat by the windows.

Give over to : (a) use something specifically for something. ***Ex 1.*** The village hall is *given over to* civic functions and meetings. ***Ex 2.*** The period after supper was *given over* to games. ***Ex 3.*** He has *given* the building *over to* a charity. ***Ex 4.*** The response was so great that a whole page had to be *given over to* reader's letters.

(b) devote oneself completely to something. ***Ex 1.*** After his wife's death, he seemed to *give* himself *over to* despair. ***Ex 2.*** In her later years she *gave* herself *over to* writing full-time.

(c) let somebody have something. ***Ex 1.*** He *gave* the business *over to* his eldest son. ***Ex 2.*** We had it formally *given over to* us three weeks ago.

(d) abandon to. ***Ex 1.*** He *gave* himself *over to* drugs. ***Ex 2.*** Don't *give* yourself *over to* the gratification of your senses. ***Ex 3.*** The ruthless officers *gave* the city *over to* their men, who pillaged without mercy.

Give up : (a) abondon an attempt to do something. ***Ex 1.*** I *give up*; tell me what the answer is? ***Ex 2.*** She does not *give up* easily. ***Ex 3.*** They *gave up* without a fight.

(b) resign from. ***Ex 1.*** She *gave up* teaching to nurse her mother. ***Ex 2.*** For no apparent reason, Sanjay *gave up* his lucrative job in Delhi and emigrated to the USA. ***Ex 3.*** Don't *give up* your job when you get married.

(c) sell; dispose of; relinquish. ***Ex 1.*** I am afraid that business is so bad that we will have to *give* something *up*. ***Ex 2.*** Nothing could persuade her to *give up* her home: it was too big for her, but it was where she had always lived.

(d) surrender; no longer avoid or protect oneself/somebody from being captured. ***Ex 1.*** After a week on the run, he *gave* himself *up* to the police. ***Ex 2.*** When did he *give* himself *up* to the police?

(e) hand over custody of; abandon one's claim to. ***Ex.*** When she realised that she would have to *give up* her children, she dropped the idea of getting a divorce.

(f) no longer seek to avoid, or protect somebody from, capture. ***Ex.*** The pretty young woman became infatuated with the enemy agent and promised that she would conceal him in the attic of her home and never *gave* him *up* to the police.

(g) have no hope of a person's recovery. ***Ex 1.*** The doctors had *given* her *up* but she made a remarkable recovery. ***Ex 2.*** Everyone—the doctors, the nurses, his own family—had *given* him *up*, when he surprised them all by suddenly taking a turn for the better.

(h) no longer expect the arrival of somebody. ***Ex 1.*** There you are at last! We had *given* you *up*. Ex 2. Although, she had waited up until midnight, Champa Devi was actually surprised when she heard her husband calling her to open the door. She had almost *given* him *up*.

(i) stop having a relationship with somebody. ***Ex 1.*** I don't know why she does not *give* him *up*. ***Ex 2.*** Why don't you *give* her *up*?

(j) stop doing or having something. ***Ex.*** You should *give up* smoking; I *gave* it *up* last year.

(k) hand something over to somebody else. ***Ex 1.*** He had to *give* his passport *up* to the authorities. ***Ex 2.*** He *gave up* his seat to an old and weak woman.

(l) renounce, no longer hold. ***Ex 1.*** Just because the man she is going to marry is an atheist, there is no need for her to *give up* her own beliefs. ***Ex 2.*** Don't *give up* your own religion.

(m) no longer pursue one's efforts, etc. ***Ex 1.*** The income-tax officer was so beguiled by the young lady's charms that he *gave up* all thought of extracting further information from her—other than her telephone number. ***Ex 2.*** Old age and physical weakness forced her to *give up* her gay social life.

(n) admit defeat. ***Ex.*** Don't *give up* your fight against injustice meted out to you.

Give up on : abandon. ***Ex.*** So many women *give up on* men after pursuing them.

Glance off : be deflected off something. ***Ex 1.*** The ball *glanced off* goal post into the net. ***Ex 2.*** The tree was so hard that he blows of the axe simply *glanced off*. ***Ex 3.*** The bullet *glanced off* the soldier's badge and buried itself in a nearby tree. ***Ex 4.*** Every remark, however barbed, just seemed to *glance off* his incredibly tough hide.

Glare at : stare angrily or firercely. ***Ex 1.*** He did not shout, but just *glared* silently *at* me. ***Ex 2.*** The two men stood *glaring* drunkenly *at* each other, while the crowd looked on with amusement.

Glaze over : become dull and lifeless, often revealing lack of interest in something. ***Ex 1.*** After four glasses of alcoholic drink, his eyes *glazed over* and he remembered nothing more. ***Ex 2.*** It is obvious that their eyes *glazed over* at long lists of technical terms. ***Ex 3.*** She observed her guests' expressions *glazing over* with boredom at the insipidity of the conversation.

Glean from : obtain (news, information, facts), etc. from various sources, in small quantities and with effort. ***Ex 1.*** *From* what people said, I managed to *glean* that she was not coming. ***Ex 2.*** He always pretends that he gets his information straight from the highest authority, whereas he merely *gleans* what facts he can *from* clerks, and puts his own interpretation on them.

Glory in : take too much pleasure or pride in something. ***Ex 1.*** One should not *glory in* one's success. ***Ex 2.*** There are military leaders who seem to *glory in* slaughter. ***Ex 3.*** The actor *gloried in* his tremendous success with Delhi audience.

Gloss over : treat something briefly, or in a superficial or in an incomplete way; ignore; try to conceal or lessen. ***Ex 1.*** He *glossed* over the awkward facts relating to this case. ***Ex 2.*** I deplore the modern tending to *gloss over* the low standards in some of our schools. ***Ex 3.*** It is important that a politician's vices should be known and, if necessary, exposed. They should not be *glossed over.*

Glower at : look in an angry or threatening way. ***Ex 1.*** He sat *glowering at* his opponent. ***Ex 2.*** The child did not go away, but stood by the door *glowering at* his father.

Go about : (a) deal with; tackle; make a start at. ***Ex 1.*** I don't know how to *go about* this problem. ***Ex 2.*** They have *gone about* this matter the wrong way. ***Ex 3.*** She does not know how to *go about* the big black mole on her cheek. ***Ex 4.*** She will do anything for you if you *go about* it in the right way. ***Ex 5.*** He has not the faintest idea of how to *go about* finding a better job.

(b) move in society, among friends, etc; travel from place to place ***Ex 1.*** I sincerely advise you not to *go about* criticising your superiors. ***Ex 2.*** Is it dangerous to *go about* bareheaded when it is raining?

(c) circulate; be current; go around/round. ***Ex 1.*** The rumour is *going about* that she is going to marry a handsome, rich young man next month. ***Ex 2.*** Blood-curdling stories were *going about* concerning what they intended to do.

(d) keep, busy with something; continue to do something. ***Ex 1.*** Despite the threat of war, people *went about* their work as usual. ***Ex 2.*** Are you *going about* your daily routine? ***Ex 3.*** Just *go about* your work as if nothing had happened.

(e) change direction. ***Ex.*** The captain ordered the ship to *go about* and search for the missing man.

(f) move about a place. ***Ex 1.*** I could *go about* her house as freely as I liked. ***Ex 2.*** She learnt with difficulty to *go about* the streets amid cat-calls.

(g) keep company with; court with a view to marriage. ***Ex 1.*** His daughter is *going about* with a man who is old enough to be her father. ***Ex 2.*** How long have they been *going about* with each other? ***Ex 3.*** You used to *go about* with him very frequently. ***Ex 4.*** They seldom *went about* together.

Go after : (a) pursue; try to catch; chase. ***Ex 1.*** The police warned the public not to *go after* the escaped prisoner, as he was armed and dangerous. ***Ex 2.*** Some people *went after* the thief.

(b) try to get or obtain somebody/something. ***Ex 1.*** He *goes after* every young woman he meets. ***Ex 2.*** Don't *go after* ugly girls. ***Ex 3.*** We are both *going after* the same job. ***Ex 4.*** This is something you can *go after*. ***Ex 5.*** His son had *gone after* a job. **Ex 6.** You should *go after* your object with a single-mindedness.

Go against : (a) be unfavourable to. ***Ex 1.*** The court's verdict *went against* him. ***Ex 2.*** The war is *going against* us. ***Ex 3.*** They thought that the battle could *go against* them never for a moment entered into the general's calculations.

(b) be out of harmony with; be contrary to; conflict with. ***Ex 1.*** The idea of trying to cheat the income tax authorities *went against* his principles. ***Ex 2.*** Your thinking *goes against* all logic. ***Ex 3.*** Paying for hospital treatment *goes against* his socialist principles. ***Ex 4.*** This action *goes against* my conscience. ***Ex 5.*** Your conclusions *go against* all established opinions.

(c) resist or oppose somebody/something. ***Ex 1.*** Don't *go against* your parents' wishes. ***Ex 2.*** He *went against* the advice of his colleagues and resigned.

(d) have an adverse affect on. ***Ex.*** This misbehaviour will certainly *go against* his chances of promotion.

Go ahead : (a) proceed; do what one wants to do. ***Ex 1.*** As you have now fully recovered from your illness, you can *go ahead* and start up your new shop. ***Ex 2.*** The government has decided to *go ahead* with its plans to develop the backward areas of the country.

(b) make progress; go forward with. ***Ex 1.*** Once our policy is formulated, we intend to *go ahead* full steam. ***Ex 2.*** With the strike settled, work on the new bridge *went ahead* like wildfire.

(c) take place; be carried out. ***Ex 1.*** Despite the inclement weather, the fete will *go ahead*. ***Ex 2.*** The construction of the new airport will *go ahead* as planned.

(d) begin to do something without hesitation. ***Ex 1.*** May I start now? Yes, *go ahead*. ***Ex 2.*** The government intends to *go ahead* with its privatization plans.

Go ahead/ahead of : continue a journey in advance of others. ***Ex 1.*** A few carefully chosen men *went ahead* while the main body remained concealed in the valley. ***Ex 2.*** The scouts *went ahead* of the main force and reported back the strength of the enemy.

Go along : (a) continue; proceed with an activity. ***Ex 1.*** You may have some difficulty at first but you will find it easier as you *go along*. ***Ex 2.*** She made the story up as she *went along*. ***Ex 3.*** You will *get* more skilful at this job as you *go along*. ***Ex 4.*** They kept up their spirits by singing one song after another as they *went along*. ***Ex 5.*** They *went along* whistling to keep up their courage in the dark.

(b) progress; develop. ***Ex.*** Things are *going along* nicely.

(c) accompany somebody to a certain place. ***Ex 1.*** As everyone else was going to the fair, I decided to *go along* too. ***Ex 2.*** I have to go to the dentist this morning. Would you like me to *go along* with you?

Go along with : agree with somebody/something; accept something; share some body's opinion; act in agreement with. ***Ex 1.*** I cannot *go along with* you on that point. ***Ex 2.*** I don't *go along with* her views on co-education. ***Ex 3.*** I don't necessarily *go along with* all you say about politics.

Go around/round : (a) go from place to place; go from person to person; move in society. ***Ex 1.*** You cannot *go around* making up things about being assaulted by people who don't exist. ***Ex 2.*** Don't *go around* barefoot. ***Ex 3.*** It is the unprofessional to *go round* criticising your colleagues.

(b) (of a rumour, story, etc.) pass from person to person; circulate. ***Ex 1.*** Word *went round* that something important was in the offing; so the meeting was well attended. ***Ex 2.*** There is a rumour *going round* that you are having an affair with the attractive young lady secretary of your boss.

(c) keep company with; go about with; be often in the company of. ***Ex 1.*** He *goes round* with a bunch of thugs. ***Ex 2.*** I see that he has been *going around* with the same pretty girl for four months now. ***Ex 3.*** Though they have been *going round* for two years now, they still have not decided whether to marry or not.

Go at : (a) attack somebody physically ***Ex 1.*** She *went at* him with a big, thick stick. ***Ex 2.*** They *went at* each other furiously.

(b) argue or discuss something heatedly. ***Ex 1.*** The two sturdy women lost their tempers and *went at* each other tooth and nail. ***Ex 2.*** The committee has been in session for over a couple of hours on the question of proposed increase in membership fees, and they are still *going at* it hammer and tongs.

(c) make great efforts to do something; tackle. ***Ex 1.*** The villagers *went at* the building of a dam with a strong will. ***Ex 2.*** Once Manju decided to do something, she *went at* it for all she was worth.

Go away : (a) leave a place or somebody's presence; go off. ***Ex 1.*** We are *going away* for a period of twenty days for a holiday. ***Ex 2.*** I am tired of your constant complaints: *go away* and leave me in peace.

(b) fade; disappear. ***Ex.*** The smell still has not *gone away*.

(c) elope. ***Ex.*** He *went away* with his friend's wife.

Go back : (a) return. ***Ex 1.*** The children have to *go back* to school next week. ***Ex 2.*** This toaster is *going back* to the shop where I bought it—it does not work properly. ***Ex 3.*** You should never *go back* to the scene of your past romance.

(b) return to an earlier point in space, time, a discussion, etc. ***Ex 1.*** How far does your memory *go back*? ***Ex 2.*** Once you have taken this decision, there will be no *going back*. ***Ex 3.*** Can I *go back* to what you said at the beginning of the meeting? ***Ex 4.*** He *went back* to his childhood.

(c) retreat. ***Ex.*** The soldiers *went back* under heavy artillery fire.

(d) date back. ***Ex 1.*** Our family *goes back* to the time of Akbar, the Great. ***Ex 2.*** This festival *goes back* the Maurya period.

(e) revert. ***Ex.*** Species do not usually *go back* to earlier forms.

(f) extend back in space. ***Ex 1.*** The garden *goes back* to that wall. ***Ex 2.*** Our land *goes* all the way *back* to the field over there.

Go back on : retract; fail to fulfil; change one's mind about something. ***Ex 1.*** Poonam never *goes back on* her word. ***Ex 2.*** I promised you that I would help you. Well, I am not *going back on* that. ***Ex 3.*** Promises are made to be kept, and not lightly to be *gone back on.*

Go before : (a) exist or happen in an earlier time; precede in time. ***Ex 1.*** The meeting was different from any that had *gone before.* ***Ex 2.*** This topic had nothing to do with what had *gone before.* ***Ex 3.*** The present crisis is more than any that have *gone before.* ***Ex 4.*** Each stage depends on what has *gone before.* ***Ex 5.*** We have endeavoured to live up to the standards of those who have *gone before.*

(b) appear before, in order to explain one's actions, or to receive punishment; be presented for discussion, approval, etc. ***Ex 1.*** In my day, a boy who was caught smoking in school *went before* the headmaster and was probably beaten. ***Ex 2.*** My application to add a room to my house *goes before* the planning committee next week.

(c) be officially considered for judgement or decision. ***Ex.*** What is about the murder case? It has *gone before* the High Court.

Go between : (a) fit "well into a position between; pass between. ***Ex 1.*** This picture *goes* nicely *between* the portraits of your father and mother. ***Ex 2.*** Trying to avoid the jealousy of Anita while keeping on good terms with Sunita was like *going between* Scylla and Charybdis.

Note : (a) Scylla and Charybdis is an idiom. It means faced by a problem or danger that one can only avoid by facing another, equally unpleasant problem or danger.

(b) Go between is a noun used to denote an intermediary or messenger between two persons, especially between lovers. ***Ex 1.*** The little girl was absolutely unaware that she was being used as a *go-between* by her elder and the married man next door. ***Ex 2.*** He acted as a *go-between* and solved the problem faced by those two brothers.

Go beyond : exceed something; surpass something. ***Ex 1.*** His interests *went beyond* political economy. ***Ex 2.*** This' year's sales figures *go beyond* all our expectations. ***Ex 3.*** The matter has *gone beyond* ajoke. ***Ex 4.*** I expected Manju to be displeased with my decision, but her anger *went beyond* all reason.

Go by : (a) elapse; pass. ***Ex 1.*** As time *goes by,* his memory seems to get worse. ***Ex 2.*** A period of three weeks has *gone by* since I last saw her. ***Ex 3.*** In days *gone by,* it was hardly safe to travel anywhere by night.

(b) pass in front of somebody. ***Ex 1.*** As each contingent *went by*, there was a burst of applause from the watching crowd. ***Ex 2.*** The parade *went by* us, and soon silence descended once more on the square.

(c) be guided or directed by something. ***Ex 1.*** I shall *go* entirely *by* what my solicitor says. ***Ex 2.*** That is a good rule to *go by*. ***Ex 3.*** You should try to *go by* reason as far as possible.

(d) form an opinion or judgement from something. ***Ex 1.*** He has enough evidence to *go by*. ***Ex 2.*** You must bear in mind that it is not always wise to *go by* appearances. ***Ex 3.*** If past experience is anything to *go by*, the plane will be late. ***Ex 4.*** It is often a mistake to *go by* appearances: that poor-looking man is anything but poor. In fact, he is a millionaire. ***Ex 5.*** You can never *go by* what Chanchala Devi says.

(e) pass without being used or grasped. ***Ex.*** He hesitated just a little too long over the offer of a partnership in the firm; and when he finally made up his mind to accept, the opportunity had *gone by*.

(f) visit a place to do or get something. ***Ex.*** Let us *go by* the store for a minute.

(g) not let something affect one. ***Ex 1.*** He was able to let these *go by* without feeling any anxiety. ***Ex 2.*** I let his bitter comments on my meanness *go by* me.

Note : *Go-by* is a noun. It is used in the idiom give somebody the *go-by*. The idiom means *act of ignoring or disregarding somebody*. ***Ex 1.*** She gave me the *go-by* in the street yesterday. ***Ex 2.*** Anand accepted me in his rather pompous way, even when my own family had given me *go-by*.

Go down : (a) set, disappear below the horizon. ***Ex 1.*** We sat and watched the sun *go down*. ***Ex 2.*** The moon has *gone down*. ***Ex 3.*** As the sun *went down*, the whole sky became suffused with a red glow.

(b) sink, disappear below the surface of the sea; (of men) drown. ***Ex 1.*** Hundreds died when the ship *went down*. ***Ex 2.*** The captain stayed on board until all the passengers and crew had left; but he himself *went down* with his ship.

(c) be swallowed. ***Ex 1.*** A glass of milk would *go down* very nicely. ***Ex 2.*** This pill just won't *go down*. ***Ex 3.*** The food has *gone down*. ***Ex 4.*** A mouthful *went down* the wrong way and made him choke.

(d) collapse, fall. ***Ex 1.*** Sita tripped and *went down* with a bump. ***Ex 2.*** The wall *went down* with a crash. ***Ex 3.*** He *went down* on his knees and begged for mercy. ***Ex 4.*** The policeman hit the man once with his truncheon, and he *went down* like a felled ox.

(e) be reduced in amount; become lower. ***Ex 1.*** The price of rice is *going down*. ***Ex 2.*** Rice is *going down* in price. ***Ex 3.*** Her temperature has *gone down*.

(f) be lowered in level, size, etc. ***Ex 1.*** If our stocks of food *go down* much further, we shall have a hard winter: ***Ex 2.*** The flood waters are *going down*. ***Ex 3.*** The swelling on her rosy cheek has *gone down* a little.

(g) be reduced in force or degree; become less strong or violent. ***Ex 1.*** Let us wait for the wind to *go down*. ***Ex 2.*** If the wind does not *go down* before four o'clock, we shall not be able to take off today.

(h) leave university at the end of a term, or finally. ***Ex.*** Sudesh *went down* from the Allahabad University in 1989.

(i) be written down, recorded. ***Ex 1.*** Every word uttered in court *went down* for future reference. ***Ex 2.*** It all *goes down* in her notebook.

(j) be accepted or approved. ***Ex 1.*** His speech *went down* well with the conference. ***Ex 2.*** My idea *went down* well with her. ***Ex 3.*** That sort of behaviour will not *go down* at all well with your neighbour.

(k) go as far as. ***Ex 1.*** This history book *goes down* to the Mughal period. ***Ex 2.*** *Go down* to the bottom of the page and then stop.

(l) fail in an examination. ***Ex.*** I am afraid he has *gone down* again.

(m) be remembered or noted. ***Ex 1.*** You will *go down* in history as a great statesman. ***Ex 2.*** That remark will *go down* in history. ***Ex 3.*** This tradition should *go down* unchanged to posterity.

(n) become deflated. ***Ex.*** The tyre has *gone down*.

(o) break up at the end of an academic term. ***Ex.*** The students have all *gone down* for the summer holidays.

(p) diminish; lose value or tone. ***Ex 1.*** Our neighbourhood has *gone down* a lot. ***Ex 2.*** The pictures have *gone down* in value considerably.

(q) Specifically descend. ***Ex 1.*** She opened the cellar door and *went down*. ***Ex 2.*** *Go down* and see who is at the door.

Go down to : (a) be defeated by. ***Ex.*** The reigning champion *went down to* a hammer-blow in the sixth round.

(b) approach a river or the sea. ***Ex.*** They *went down to* the river to bathe.

(c) reach; get as far as. ***Ex 1.*** This volume only *goes down to* 1947. ***Ex 2.*** This book is no use to me; it only *goes down to* the General Election of 1957.

Go down with : become ill with. ***Ex 1.*** His youngest son has *gone down with* mumps. ***Ex 2.*** Sundari was unable to go into the office on Friday, the 14th March, 1995, because she had *gone down with* malarial fever.

Go for : (a) attack. ***Ex 1.*** She *went for* him with a long, thick stick. ***Ex 2.*** The newspapers really *went for* him over his defence of religious bigotry. ***Ex 3.*** When he arrived home drunk once again, his wife *went for* him with the rolling-pin.

(b) leave home or place of work to take exercise, etc. ***Ex.*** Her husband has just *gone for* a constitutional (a regular walk for one's health), but he will be back in half an hour.

(c) go somewhere to obtain or fetch somebody/something. ***Ex.*** As her baby had a high temperature, he *went for* the doctor.

(d) include; be true for. ***Ex.*** Your sister is a selfish girl—and that *goes for* you, too.

(e) be attracted by; like. ***Ex 1.*** I don't *go for* horror films. ***Ex 2.*** There is a very attractive girl sitting by herself over there. Why don't you go and chat her up? I don't *go for* such girls, thank you. ***Ex 3.*** She *goes for* young men who are tall, slim, healthy, handsome and rich. ***Ex 4.*** Do you *go for* mini skirts ?

(f) be sold for.***Ex 1.*** The old house, dilapidated as it was, *went for* five lakh rupees. ***Ex 2.*** How much do you think these paintings *go for*?

(g) apply to somebody/something. ***Ex 1.*** India has a high level of unemployment—but the same *goes for* many other countries in the world. ***Ex 2.*** What I said about Premchand *goes for* you, too.

(h) choose something. ***Ex.*** I think I shall *go for* the fruit salad.

(i) attempt to have or achieve something. ***Ex.*** Sangeeta is *going for* the world record in the high jump.

Go forth : (a) carry out some task or plan. *Ex.* That country is *going forth* in triumph from slavery into freedom.

(b) march or journey out. ***Ex 1.*** The army *went forth* amid tremendous applause and cheering. *Ex 2.* He *went forth* upon a journey to a far land.

(c) be sent out. ***Ex.*** The command *went forth* that all men of a certain age-group will be wholly looked after by the state.

(d) emerge. ***Ex.*** It is said that an inspired army can *go forth* only from an inspired nation.

Go home : (a) die. ***Ex 1.*** That poor old man is *going home* at last. ***Ex 2.*** Those old rose bushes are *going home*.

(b) hit the target; have the intended effect. ***Ex.*** He was a skilful debater, and his calculated sarcasm *went home*. His opponent flushed under the attack.

Go in : (a) (of the sun or moon). disappear behind a cloud. ***Ex.*** The sun *went in* and it grew colder.

(b) (of a batsman in cricket) go to the wicket at the start of one's innings. ***Ex.*** Who is *going in* next?

(c) be understood or assimilated. ***Ex.*** It is no use. I have read and reread the chapter on birth and rebirth of man, but nothing *went in*.

(d) fit. ***Ex 1.*** The key does not *go in*. ***Ex 2.*** It is too big to *go in* the car. ***Ex 3.*** All those things could easily *go in* the dining-room cupboard.

Go in for : (a) take an examination or take part in a competition. ***Ex 1.*** He is *going in for* his B.A. examination scheduled to take place on Tuesday, the 12th March, 1996 at 9.30 a.m. ***Ex 2.*** Which events is he *going in for* at the Olympics? ***Ex 3.*** Are you *going in for* the beauty competition? ***Ex 4.*** He *went in for* so many events, and so won none.

(b) choose something as a career. ***Ex 1.*** Are you thinking of *going in for* aching? ***Ex 2.*** His youngest son is *going in for* catering, and part of his course takes place in France.

(c) have as a hobby; pastime, etc.; have as a sport. ***Ex 1.*** You need something to take your mind off your work. So you should *go in for* collecting antiques or stamp-collecting, or golf. ***Ex 2.*** I *go in for* a lot of sport. ***Ex 3.*** She *goes in for* badminton and tennis.

(d) regularly practise; make a habit or practice of. ***Ex 1.*** I am not one of those people who *go in for* dieting-I am much too fond of eating. ***Ex 2.*** He *goes in for* a strange kind of phraseology in his letters.

Go into : (a) hit something. ***Ex 1.*** The car skided and *went into* a tree. ***Ex 2.*** The lorry must have *gone into* the side of the house at a tremendous speed.

(b) enter; insert a part of oneself, especially one's hand. ***Ex.*** Somebody keeps *going into* my desk and pinching my pens.

(c) be admitted temporarily; go to live in. ***Ex 1.*** Most university students have to *go into* digs (lodgings) for at least one or two years. ***Ex 2.*** I hear that your mother has had to *go into* hospital again, evidently she was not completely cured last time.

(d) begin to act or behave in a specified way. ***Ex 1.*** She *went into* a long explanation of the affair. ***Ex 2.*** Shanti *went into* peals of laughter. ***Ex 3.*** He *went into* fits. ***Ex 4.*** When she died, her husb and immediately *went into* a decline and followed her to the grave within a month.

(e) join an organisation in order to have a career. ***Ex 1.*** Two of his sons have *gone into* the army. ***Ex 2.*** His daughter has *gone into* teaching.

(f) wear a different kind of dress. ***Ex.*** People *go into* black clothes as a sign of grief.

(g) examine or investigate something carefully. ***Ex 1.*** He does not want to *go into* the minor details now. ***Ex 2.*** The matter is being *gone into*. ***Ex 3.*** The problem needs a lot of *going into*. ***Ex 4.*** Let us *go into* the question of costs.

(h) be spent or used to do something. ***Ex.*** Months of hard work have *gone into* the preparation of this highly valuable book.

(i) (of vehicle or driver) start the specified movement. *Ex 1.* The plane *went into* a nosedive. *Ex 2.* The lorry *went into* a spin on a patch of ice.

(j) be capable of dividing another given figure, so that the result is greater than one. *Ex.* Six *goes into* twelve, twice.

Go off : (a) go away; leave a place, room, etc. *Ex 1.* He had *gone off* to work. *Ex 2.* She *went off* to look at the flowers. *Ex 3.* He decided to *go off* on a visit of his own. *Ex 4.* They sold up their house and *went off* to live in Paris with their married daughter.

(b) explode; be fired. *Ex 1.* The gun *went off* by accident. *Ex 2.* The bomb *went off* in a crowded street.

(c) make a sudden loud noise; be sounded. *Ex.* The thieves ran away when the burglar alarm *went off*.

(d) fall asleep. *Ex 1.* Has not the baby *gone off* yet ? *Ex 2.* As soon as the baby has *gone off*; we will be able to relax and watch television.

(e) (of light, electric power, etc.) stop functioning. *Ex 1.* Suddenly the lights *went off*. *Ex 2.* The heating *goes off* at night.

(f) become unfit to eat or drink; go bad; turn sour. *Ex.* The milk has *gone off*.

(g) deteriorate; become worse in quality. *Ex.* His books have *gone off* in recent years.

(h) take place or happen in the way specified. *Ex 1.* The meeting *went off* well. *Ex 2.* How did the concert *go off*? *Ex 3.* He had the operation this morning and it all *went off* quite well.

(i) lose interest in somebody; lose one's taste for something. *Ex 1.* She seems to be *going off* her boyfriend. *Ex 2.* He has *gone off* drugs. *Ex 3.* You should *go off* smoking. *Ex 4.* He has *gone off* driving altogether after his accident. .

Go off into : suddenly enter a certain mental, state etc. *Ex.* Every time the baby started throwing his food about, his sisters *went off into* shrieks of laughter.

Go off with : (a) leave one's husband, wife, lover, etc. in order to have relationship with somebody else; elope. *Ex 1.* Her boyfriend *went off with* her best friend. *Ex 2.* He *went off with* his best friend's wife. *Ex 3.* His daughter *went off with* the milkman. *Ex 4.* She *went off with* another healthy and wealthy man after being married eight years.

(b) steal and carry away; run away with. *Ex 1.* Who has *gone off with* my pen? *Ex 2.* He had *gone off with* a large sum belonging to his maternal uncle. *Ex 3.* After twenty years of honest service, the cashier *went off with* five lakh rupees of the company's money.

Go on : (a) (of an actor or actress) walk onto the stage. *Ex.* She does not *go on* till Act 2. ,

(b) depart for the purpose of. ***Ex 1.*** None can deny the fact that only the rich can afford to *go on* safari these days. ***Ex 2.*** I should *go on* a refresher course—I am getting out of touch with modern techniques.

(c) continue one's journey. ***Ex 1.*** The explorers decided that they could not *go on* with darkness closing in. ***Ex 2.*** We all voted to *go on*, despite the signs of a thunderstorm on the horizon.

(d) continue a journey ahead of others; go ahead/ahead of. ***Ex 1.*** Alok said he would have to *go on*, as he was due at a meeting at eleven o'clock. The others could follow at their leisure.

(e) mount and travel on as a treat. ***Ex.*** The children *went on* everything at the fair, and then found they had not enough money to get the bus home.

(f) continue an activity or relationship; carry on. ***Ex 1.*** We cannot *go on* as though nothing has happened. It has happened. You have broken your promise. ***Ex 2.*** What I like about Anju Devi is that in spite of everything, she *goes on* trying. ***Ex 3.*** They cannot *go on* like this-they seem to be always arguing.

(g) (of a state of affairs) continue without change. ***Ex 1.*** After you left the firm, everything *went on* as usual. ***Ex 2.*** The cold war between the two countries seemed to *go on* and on. ***Ex 3.*** The present state of affairs cannot be allowed to *go on*. ***Ex 4.*** How much longer will this hot weather *go on*?

(h) elapse; pass by; go by. ***Ex 1.*** As the years *go on*, we grow both wiser and sadder. ***Ex 2.*** Things will improve as time *goes on*.

(i) continue speaking after a short pause. ***Ex 1.*** She hesitated for a moment, and then *went on*. ***Ex 2.*** He *went on* about his prolonged illness until I was tired listening. ***Ex 3.*** He *went on* to say that we were welcome any time we cared to come.

(j) add some new point to what has previously been said or written. ***Ex.*** After criticising our proposal in every detail, managing director *went on* to reassure us that there was nothing personal in his comments.

(k) happen, take place. ***Ex 1.*** Let me know what was *going on* there? ***Ex 2.*** What is *going on* between that couple over there? ***Ex 3.*** If you never read the newspapers, you will never know what is *going on* in the world.

(l) act according to; be guided by; base an opinion or a judgement on something. ***Ex 1.*** The police don't have much evidence to *go on* in this case. ***Ex 2.*** We cannot *go on* evidence like that. ***Ex 3.*** It is a mistake to *go on* the government's account of the talks with that country.

(m) be spent on. ***Ex.*** A lot of my money *goes on* books; but I think it is money well spent.

(n) begin to receive; get help from. ***Ex.*** A lot of people, who never expected to be unemployed, have had to *go on* the dole.

(o) be lit; start to function. ***Ex 1.*** Suddenly all the lights *went on*. ***Ex 2.*** What time do the illuminations *go on* tonight?

Go on about : talk about somebody/something for a long time in a boring or complaining way. ***Ex 1.*** People say that you *go on* sometimes. ***Ex 2.*** I know you don't like my smoking, but there is no need to *go on about* it. ***EX 3.*** I admit I was wrong in not keeping you informed of my plans. But please don't *go on about* it.

Go on at : complain to somebody about his behaviour, work etc.; criticise somebody; nag somebody. ***Ex 1.*** She *goes on at* her husband continually. ***Ex 2.*** Don't *go on at* that poor girl all the time. ***Ex 3.*** Why do you *go on at* the maid so often? She does her best.

Go on for : (a) be approaching a certain age. ***Ex 1.*** She is *going on for* twenty. ***Ex .2.*** He is six, *going on for* seven.

(b) (of time) approach; get near. ***Ex 1.*** It is *going on for* midnight. ***Ex 2.*** It is *going on for* one o'clock and I promised to see her at half past twelve.

Go on to : (a) pass from one item to the next, in an agenda, etc. ***Ex 1.*** The chairman said that as time was short, we should *go on to* the next item. ***Ex 2.*** I don't want any pudding, thank you. I would like to *go* straight *on to* the coffee.

(b) adopt as a new or temporary habit. ***Ex 1.*** The doctor told me that I would have to *go on to* a strict diet. ***Ex 2.*** Is it true that many women *go on to* the pill after they have had two children?

(c) change working arrangements to. ***Ex.*** The government says that if consumption of coal continues to fall, several big mines will have to *go on to* short time or stop production altogether.

Go on with : continue doing something after a pause or break. ***Ex 1.*** He paused to take a sip of water, and then *went on with* his story. ***Ex 2.*** If you don't finish painting the kitchen today, you can *go on with* it tomorrow.

Go out : (a) leave home to go to social events. ***Ex 1.*** She says that you *go out* a lot. ***Ex 2.*** Does he *go out* drinking most evenings? ***Ex 3.*** She has *gone out* riding and won't be back until six o'clock.

(b) be eliminated from a contest, competition etc. ***Ex.*** He *went out* in the first round of the tournament.

(c) end; depart. ***Ex 1.*** The year has *gone out*. ***Ex 2.*** The year, 1993, *went out* with the news of a major earthquake in Maharashtra. ***Ex 3.*** When March comes in like a lamb, it *goes out* like a lion.

(d) fade and die; cease. ***Ex 1.*** The light has *gone out* of her life. ***Ex 2.*** Her love for him has slowly *gone out*.

(e) stop burning, shining. ***Ex 1.*** I had just begun to go upstairs when the lights *went out*. ***Ex 2.*** When he arrived home, the fire had *gone out*.

(f) cease to be fashionable. ***Ex 1.*** Flared trousers *went out* years ago. ***Ex 2.*** The idea that women cannot do the same work as men is slowly but steadily *going out*.

(g) flow back or awayj ebb. ***Ex 1.*** The tide has *gone out*. ***Ex 2.*** The sea, at certain parts of the coast, *goes out* so far that it can no longer be seen.

Go out for : (a) make a great; concentrated effort to obtain. ***Ex 1.*** Don't trust that man. He just *goes out for* anything he can get. ***Ex 2.*** He *went out for* a job that would not disappear at the first signs of a depression.

(b) leave a building, go into the open air. ***Ex.*** She asked me to *go out for* some fresh air instead of watching television all day.

Go out of : (a) disappear from. ***Ex.*** As time went by and the old man became mellow, the fury *went out of* his parliamentary speeches.

(b) become reduced, less marked. ***Ex.*** When it was clear that nobody, was particularly interested in the matter, apart from the protagonists, the heat *went out of* the argument.

Go out to : (a) go overseas. ***Ex 1.*** My eldest son has *gone out to* New York for higher studiesin missile technology. ***Ex 2.*** She has decided to *go out to* Baghdad as an English teacher.

(b) be extended to, be offered to. ***Ex.*** Our hearts *go out to* all the victims of the earthquake in Maharashtra.

Go over : (a) check something; examine something. ***Ex 1.*** I have *gone over* the statement and it seems to be in order. ***Ex 2.*** You will have to *go over* the figures again; they don't balance out. ***Ex 3.*** *Go over* your work carefully before you hand it in.

(b) inspect something; look at something carefully. ***Ex 1.*** The surveyor *went over* the house thoroughly and advised us not to buy it. ***Ex 2.*** The prospective tenants *went over* the accommodation, but made no comment except to thank the old landlady for the trouble.

(c) clean something thoroughly. ***Ex.*** The maid *went over* the room quickly with a duster.

(d) inspect and repair. ***Ex.*** Would you please *go over* the engine of my car? It is producing a very strange noise.

(e) ponder, consider; examine or re-examine. ***Ex 1.*** I *went over* every detail of his story in an effort to discover whether it was true or not. ***Ex 2.*** The detective *went over* the facts in his mind for the tenth time, but still the vital clue eluded him.

(f) search. ***Ex 1.*** Awoman police-officer *went over* the girl from head to toe, but would not say what she was looking for. ***Ex 2.*** The police *went over* his house.

(g) rehearse; test one's knowledge of something learnt or studied; revise something. ***Ex 1.*** He *went over* the events of the day in his mind. ***Ex 2.*** Sushila *went over* her lines before the first night of the play. ***Ex 3.*** I cannot come out this evening. I am in the college play and must *go over* my lines again. ***Ex 4.*** The boys' mother used to *go over* their sums with them every evening.

(h) be received. ***Ex 1.*** How did her speech *go over*? ***Ex 2.*** His speech *went over* well. ***Ex 3.*** The news *went over* without much comment. ***Ex 4.*** Your talk to the Women's Institute *went over* very well.

Go over to : (a) cross a river, lake, etc.; go across to. ***Ex.*** A boat *goes over to* the island once a week with mail and provisions.

(b) transfer one's allegiance to; defect from ... to ... ; change from one side, system to another. ***Ex 1.*** Two Congress M.Ps *went over to* the Socialists. ***Ex 2.*** Mr. Ram Chandra, after years of dissatisfaction with the Janata Party, *went over to* the Congress.

(c) change from one habit to another. ***Ex 1.*** Sumitra has *gone over to* a milder brand of cigarettes. ***Ex 2.*** He has given up the piano and *gone over to* the flute.

(d) (of broadcasting) transfer to. ***Ex.*** We are interrupting the programme to *go over to* our news desk for an important announcement.

Go round/around : (a) go by a longer route than usual; make a detour along the outside perimeter of. ***Ex 1.*** As the front gate was shut, we had to *go round.* ***Ex 2.*** Don't blow your horn while you are *going round* the hospital. ***Ex 3.*** The main road was flooded, so we had to *go round* of narrow country lanes.

(b) be enough for everyone to have a share. ***Ex 1.*** Don't worry. There is enough chairs to *go round.* ***Ex 2.*** Do you have enough rice to *go around* ten people? ***Ex 3.*** There are not enough chairs to *go round.*

(c) move from place to place; move in society. ***Ex 1*** He *goes round* barefoot. ***Ex 2.*** Don't *go round* criticising your colleagues.

(d) (of rumour, story, etc.), pass from person to person; circulate. ***Ex 1.*** Many spooky stories began *going around.* ***Ex 2.*** There is a rumour *going round* that she is having an affair with the managing director of that company.

(e) (of illness) spread from person to person in a group or community. ***Ex.*** There is a lot of influenza *going round* at the moment.

(f) visit somebody or a place. ***Ex 1.*** I am *going around* to my parent's house later. ***Ex 2.*** Mamta sang up and asked me to *go round* to her. ***Ex 3.*** It was not until Friday evening that I was able to *go round* to their house.

(g) travel in a country or continent. ***Ex.*** I shall *go around* Europe myself.

(h) walk through every part of a room, house, etc. ***Ex.*** She *went round* the house making sure that all doors were locked.

(i) spin or turn continuously like a wheel. ***Ex 1.*** The wheels of the bicycle were *going around* very fast. ***Ex 2.*** The blue light is *going round* and around on top of the police car.

(j) do something repeatedly; be in the habit of doing something. ***Ex 1.*** They are always *going round* sticking posters. on walls. ***Ex 2.*** You must not *go round* telling people things that are not true.

(k) to regularly meet somebody and go to different places with him. ***Ex 1.*** He is an undesirable person. Don't *go round* with him. ***Ex 2.*** It is not wise for us to *go around* together like this.

Go through : (a) (of a bill, law, etc.) be officially approved or accepted. ***Ex 1.*** The bill *went through* Parliament. ***Ex 2.*** As soon as his divorcee has *gone through*, he will marry her.

(b) be successfully completed. ***Ex.*** The deal did not *go through*.

(c) be published in. ***Ex.*** The books 'Improve Your Vocabulary' and 'Interview Manual' authored by Abul Hashem were an immediate success, and have *gone through* six editions.

(d) study or examine something closely or systematically in order to find something. ***Ex 1.*** I always start the day by *going through* my mail. ***Ex 2.*** I have *gone through* all my pockets but I cannot find my keys. ***Ex 3.*** The lawyers *went through* the evidence. ***Ex 4.*** She *went through* the company's accounts, looking for evidence of fraud.

(e) discuss or study something in detail. ***Ex. 1.*** Let us *go through* the arguments again. ***Ex 2.*** They *went through* the details of the plan over and over again to make sure that there was no possibility of failure.

(f) rehearse something. ***Ex.*** Let us *go through* the last scene in Act Two again. We have not got it right yet.

(g) search. ***Ex 1.*** I *went through* the suspects clothes. ***Ex 1.*** The police *went through* the building with a fine tooth-comb, but they found no evidence that would help them to catch the thief.

Note : *With a fine tooth-comb* is an idiom. It means *closely* and *throughly*. ***Ex.*** Police experts are sifting all the evidence *with a fine tooth-comb*.

(h) perform something; take part in something. ***Ex 1.*** Certain formalities have to be *gone through* before one can emigrate. ***Ex 2.*** We have all *gone through* the required formalities. ***Ex 3.*** He *went through* his lessons. ***Ex 4.*** They *went through* the appropriate marriage procedure.

(i) experience, endure or suffer something. ***Ex 1.*** He would have *gone through* fire for the girl he loved so passionately. ***Ex 2.*** She has *gone through* a bad patch (*i.e.* a difficult or unhappy time) recently. ***Ex 3.*** He is amazingly cheerful considering all that he has *gone through*. ***Ex 4.*** The boy was *gone through* a lot since his father was killed. ***Ex 5.*** No one knows what I have had to *go through*.

(j) use up or consume something. ***Ex 1.*** I seem to be *going through* a lot of money at the moment. ***Ex 2.*** It did not take him very long to *go through* his inheritance. ***Ex 3.*** We have *gone through* five hundred envelopes bought last week.

Go through with : do what is necessary to complete or take a course of action. ***Ex 1.*** She decided not to *go through with* the abortion. ***Ex 2.*** He is determined to *go through with* the marriage despite his parents' opposition. ***Ex 3.*** He says that he cannot *go through with* the examination. ***Ex 4.*** A month before the wedding was due to take place, he received a letter from his fiancee saying that she could not *go through with* it (*i.e.* marriage), as she had fallen in deep love with someone else. ***Ex 5.*** The government was determined to *go through with* that legislation.

Go to : (a) be given to; be awarded to; be inherited by. ***Ex 1.*** Proceeds from this concert will *go to* charity. ***Ex 2.*** The first prize *went to* the youngest child in the class. ***Ex 3.*** After the sad and sudden demise of his father, the estate *went to* him. ***Ex 4.*** She was furious when her husband's entire possessions *went to* his housekeeper.

(b) incur; spend much money. ***Ex.*** Why don't you hire a caravan for a couple of weeks each year instead of *going to* the expense of buying one?

Go together : (a) match; be good, right, agreeable when worn, consumed, etc. at the same time; harmonise. ***Ex 1.*** Be frank and tell me whether this hat and coat *go* well *together*. ***Ex 2.*** People say that potatoes and rice do not *go together*. They make a stodgy meal.

(b) (of two or more things, qualities, states, etc.) be found in association with each other. ***Ex 1.*** Chastity and charity do not necessarily *go together*. ***Ex 2.*** Bullying and cowardice often *go together*. ***Ex 3.*** Fear and hatred seem to *go together*. ***Ex 4.*** This had been the basis of both wealth and military power; the two *went together*.

(c) court; keep company. ***Ex 1.*** That young man and that girl *go together*. ***Ex 2.*** They have been *going together* for over a year.

Go under : (a) sink below the surface of the river, sea, etc. ***Ex 1.*** The ship slowly *went under*. ***Ex 2.*** He thrashed about for some time before he *went under*. ***Ex 3.*** The lifeboat will sink and we shall *go under*. ***Ex 4.*** Just as the would-be rescuer reached the drowning man, he *went under* for the third time and was never seen again.

(b) become bankrupt; fail. ***Ex 1.*** His business has *gone under*. ***Ex 2.*** He has completely *gone under*. ***Ex 3.*** Their firm will *go under* unless business improves. ***Ex 4.*** He had no head for business, and it was not long before he *went under*.

(c) be known as; hide one's identity behind; pass by or under the name of. ***Ex 1.*** One of the robbers *went under* the guise of a respectable dealer in antiques. ***Ex 2.*** He is a cheat. He *goes under* the guise of a salesman.

Go up : (a) be built. ***Ex 1.*** New office blocks are *going up* everywhere. ***Ex 2.*** Everywhere you look, you can see skyscrapers, hospitals, schools, etc. *going up*.

(b) be blown up; be destroyed by fire or an explosion. ***Ex 1.*** The whole building *went up* in flames. ***Ex 2.*** Several buildings *went up* when the bomb exploded. ***Ex 3.*** With the outbreak of renewed hostilities on the border all our hopes for peace have *gone up* in flames.

(c) rise; become higher in price, level, etc. ***Ex 1.*** The price of sugar is *going up*. ***Ex 2.*** Sugar is *going up* in price. ***Ex 3.*** Unemployment has *gone up* again. ***Ex 4.*** Everything seems to be *going up* these days.

(d) (of the curtain on the stage of a theatre). be raised. ***Ex 1.*** In the first Act, the curtain *goes up* on a typical drawing-room of a businessman. ***Ex 2.*** There was a burst of applause as the curtain *went up*.

Go with : (a) have somebody as a boyfriend or girlfriend; keep company with. ***Ex 1.*** He *goes with* a different girl every week. ***Ex 2.*** Whom are you *going with*? ***Ex 3.*** How long have you been *going with* that young lady possessing stunning beauty? ***Ex 4.*** He never *went with* other women.

(b) be part of; be included with. ***Ex 1.*** We were immensely delighted

to find that a large rock garden *went with* the house. ***Ex 2.*** Crime does not necessarily *go with* poverty; some rich men are criminals. ***Ex 3.*** A new car *goes with* the job. ***Ex 4.*** Do the carpet and curtains *go with* the house?

(c) match; suit; combine well with; harmonise with. ***Ex 1.*** Her blouse does not *go with* her skirt. ***Ex 2.*** Her behaviour when under the influence of alcohol hardly *goes with* her high standards when sober.

(d) exist at the same time or in the same place as something; be commonly found together. ***Ex.*** Disease often *goes with* poverty.

Go without : manage without something; endure the lack of something. ***Ex 1.*** I had to *go without* breakfast this morning as I was in a hurry. ***Ex 2.*** How long can a human being *go without* food? ***Ex 3.*** He *went without* sleep for two days. ***Ex 4.*** Millions of the refugees were given food, but thousands had to *go without* and died of starvation.

Goad into : provoke something to do something or into a certain state. ***Ex 1.*** Her persistent questions finally *goaded* me *into* an angr reply. ***Ex 2.*** He weas trying to *goad* his lazy sons *into* action. ***Ex 3.*** She was being *goaded into* denouncing and mocking her best friend.

Goad on : continually urge and encourage somebody to do something. *Ex 1.* The older children *goaded* the youngsters *on* to break all the windows of the deserted house. *Ex 2.* The accused girls said that they were *goaded on* by their need to buy more and drugs. *Ex 3.* Stop *goading* them *on*.

Gobble up : use something up quickly; swallow. *Ex 1.* The house rent *gobbles up* half his earnings. *Ex 2.* Small family business are often *gobbled up* by larger firms. *Ex 3.* This project just *gobbled up* money. *Ex 4.* Imperial powers throughout history have always tended to *gobble up* their weaker neighbours.

Goof off : shirk responsibility; behave stupidly or irresponsibly; mess around. *Ex 1.* If you ask him to do anything, he will just *goof off*. *Ex 2.* He never *goofed off* into restaurants when he was on patrol.

Gouge out : remove something by digging into a surface with a sharp tool, one's fingers, etc. *Ex 1.* He *gouged out* a stone from a horseshoe. *Ex 2.* Some vandal had *gouged out* his initials on the newly finished altar. *Ex 3.* The heavy machine *gouged out* a deep trench across the field.

Grapple with : work hard to overcome a difficulty. *Ex 1.* He has been *grappling with* the problem for a long time. *Ex 2.* The government should *grapple with* the ever-growing unemployment in the country.

Grasp at : try to seize advantage of an opportunity. *Ex.* He tried to *grasp at* an opportunity to earn money.

Grass on : inform the police of somebody's criminal plans or activities. *Ex 1.* If anyone *grasses on* us, his life won't be worth living. *Ex 2.* Did you *grass on* your mates?

Grind away : work or study hard and long. *Ex 1.* He has been *grinding away* at his studies for about four hours. *Ex 2.* She has a biology examination on Tuesday, and she is *grinding away* at it to make up for lost time.

Grind down : treat somebody very harshly; oppress somebody. *Ex 1.* Most of the people of this country are *ground down* by penury. *Ex 2.* Don't *grind down* the poor. *Ex 3.* The small force of resistance fighters was *ground down* by the sheer weight of the occupying army. *Ex 4.* The dictator *ground* the people *down*.

Grind on : continue for a long time boringly and monotonously; move inexorably towards. *Ex 1.* The speaker *ground on*, oblivious of his listeners' boredom. *Ex 2.* Slowly the meeting *ground on*. *Ex 3.* The situation was out of our hands and the war machinery *ground* slowly, *on* towards disaster.

Grind out : produce (books, stories, etc.) with sustained but uninspired effort; churn out. *Ex 1.* He has been *grinding out* cheap romantic novels at the rate of six a year. *Ex 2.* The public relations people keep *grinding out* more information about how wonderful their companies are. ***Ex 3.*** Why don't you stop *grinding out*, the same old propaganda?

Grope after/for : feel or search about something as one does in the dark. ***Ex 1.*** That is a tricky question which left him *groping for* an answer. ***Ex 2.*** Scientists are *groping after* the secrets of the atom. ***Ex 3.*** The lecturer paused, *groping for* the most effective word to express his meaning. ***Ex 4.*** Throughout the ages men have *groped after* the meaning of the Universe and their own role in it.

Ground in : give somebody good teaching or basic training in a subject. ***Ex.*** Sushma *grounded* her pupils well *in* Arithmetic.

Ground on : base beliefs, etc. on something; give or provide something as basis. ***Ex 1.*** I always *ground* my arguments *on* facts. ***Ex 2.*** The government claimed that its policies were *grounded on* the realities of the situation and not on wishful thinking. ***Ex 3.*** There are innumerable people who *ground* their religion wholly *on* Nature.

Grovel to : behave with a show of humility or shame; humble or abase oneself before somebody. ***Ex 1.*** You will just have to *grovel to* the bank manager for a loan. ***Ex 2.*** Those who wished a favour of the king had to *grovel* on hands and knees *to* him.

Grovel about/around : move about on one's hands and knees. ***Ex.*** The boy was *grovelling about* under the table looking for a pin.

Grow away from : come to have a less close, less easy relationship with somebody; detach oneself; develop a separate life. ***Ex 1.*** Basanti has slowly *grown away from* us. ***Ex 2.*** Are you *growing away from* your mother? ***Ex 3.*** He has been *growing away from* these habits. ***Ex 4.*** It often happens that a girl, who in her early teens has been very close to her mother, suddenly *grows away from* her as she makes new friends and her horizon widens.

Grow in : become wiser, more worthy to lead, more important, etc. ***Ex 1.*** He has certainly *grown in* strength, but not, unfortunately, in wisdom. ***Ex 2.*** The Chief Minister was not an impressive figure when he took office, but has *grown* greatly *in* stature over the past two years.

Grow into : (a) become something with the passage of time. ***Ex 1.*** Shashikala is *growing into* a beautiful young woman. ***Ex 2.*** You have *grown into* an old miser. ***Ex 3.*** The small family business *grew into* a company of international importance. ***Ex 4.*** We did not meet again for six years. By then the rather punny boy had *grown into* a six-footer weighing hundred kilograms.

(b) become big enough to fit (clothes). ***Ex 1.*** The coat is too big for him now, but he will *grow into* it. ***Ex 2.*** It is a bit big, but the child will soon *grow into* it.

(c) become accustomed to. ***Ex 1.*** He has *grown into* the job. ***Ex 2.*** She is a good actress, but still needs time to *grow into* the part she is playing.

Grow on : (a) become more firmly established in somebody. ***Ex.*** Bear in mind that a habit *grows on* you, if you are not careful.

(b) come to have a greater attraction for somebody; win the liking of somebody. ***Ex 1.*** The books titled 'New Approach Learner's Grammar' (How to Write and Speak Effective English), 'Interview Techniques' and 'Model Interview's, and 'Common Errors in English' penned by Abul Hashem, have quickly and immensely *grown on* well educated people from different walks of life. ***Ex 2.*** She was someone whose charm *grew* slowly but steadily *on* him.

Grow out of : (a) become too big to wear. ***Ex 1.*** The boy is *growing out of* his shoes very fast; he needs a bigger size every four months. ***Ex 2.*** Pooja has *grown out of* her clothes. ***Ex 3.*** It cost a small fortune and he *grew out of* in four months.

(b) 'become too old for something and stop doing it. ***Ex 1.*** He has *grown out of* children's games. ***Ex 2.*** She has rather *grown out of* her taste for ice cream. ***Ex 3.*** Have you *grown out of* the beliefs acquired in childhood ?

(c) have something as a source. ***Ex 1.*** His present unfortunate position—six months in jail—*grew out of* his uncontrollable temper. ***Ex 2.*** My interest in the English language *grew out of* the time I spent in England during the Second World War. ***Ex 3.*** The plot to kill the king, *grew out of* the inordinate ambition of a few colonels. ***Ex 4.*** A broad socialist programme will surely *grow out of* our selfless social activities for the good of the poor and downtrodden.

(d) abandon with the passage of time or with maturity. ***Ex.*** Don't worry about Champa's tantrums. She will *grow out of* them.

Grow up : (a) (people or animals), reach the stage of full development; become adult or mature. ***Ex 1.*** What are you going to be when you *grow up*? ***Ex 2.*** Your children seem to have *grown up* quickly. ***Ex 3.*** She had *grown up* in Calcutta. ***Ex 4.*** Children should *grow up* with a fond attitude towards all humanity.

(b) develop. ***Ex 1.*** A close friendship gradually *grew up* between them. ***Ex 2.*** The idea has *grown up* that science cannot be wrong. ***Ex 3.*** Complaints and controversy *grew up* around the scene.

(c) behave or think as an adult ought to, face the realities of life as it is, not as a child might imagine it to be. ***Ex.*** When are you going to *grow up*?

Grow up into : become as one grows older. ***Ex.*** I punished him for not telling the truth. I am not going to let him *grow up* into a liar if I can help it.

Grub about/around : search for something intently but unmethodically. ***Ex 1.*** He found what he wanted by *grubbing about* in the library. ***Ex 2.*** Are you tired of *grubbing around* in the public library for material needed for your novel?

Grub up/out : dig something up; pull out of the ground, and get dirty in doing it. ***Ex 1.*** Birds were *grubbing up* worms. ***Ex 2.*** They *grubbed out* a dead tree. ***Ex 3.*** He was *grubbing up* hedgerows. ***Ex 4.*** They *grubbed up* roots and gathered berries.

Guard against : use care and caution to prevent something. ***Ex 1.*** Hasty reactions to provocation should be *guarded against*. ***Ex 2.*** You have been doing very well, but you should *guard against* over-confidence. ***Ex 3.*** Jealousy is something to be particularly *guarded against*. ***Ex 4.*** You need to *guard against* eating too much if you want to keep fit. ***Ex 5.*** Youmust *guard against* any tendency to take your privileges for granted.

Guess at : estimate; try to imagine. ***Ex 1.*** It is a mistake to *guess at* a woman's appearance from the sound of her voice. ***Ex 2.*** His origins can only be *guessed at*. ***Ex 3.*** We can only *guess at* the number of deaths it has caused. ***Ex 4.*** We shall have to *guess at* what went on there.

Gull out of : obtain by trickery from. ***Ex.*** The con-man *gulled* the unsuspecting villager *out off* every paisa he had with him.

Gulp back : restrain with an effort; prevent (expression of emotion) by swallowing. ***Ex 1.*** She *gulped back* her tears and tried to smile. ***Ex 2.*** I *gulped back* the furious reply I wanted to make.

Gun down : shoot somebody, especially so as to kill or seriously injure him. ***Ex 1.*** Nobody will ever know how many innocent people were *gunned down* in the war. ***Ex 2.*** Tell me where and when he was *gunned down*. ***Ex 3.*** Two dacoits were *gunned down* on the street by the police.

Gun for : seek an opportunity to expose somebody as inefficient, unconscientious, careless, or otherwise a vulnerable member of an organisation, class, etc; be looking for an opportunity to attack or criticise somebody. ***Ex 1.*** Who is *gunning for* you ? ***Ex 2.*** I do not wish to have half the university *gunning for* me. ***Ex 3.*** I sincerely advise you to be very careful over the next three weeks; your erstwhile employer is *gunning for* you. ***Ex 4.*** He had no idea that he was being *gunned for* until he was physically attacked by his enemies.

Gush over : be excessively demonstrative towards or about somebody. ***Ex.*** Pratibha *gushed over* her son's tremendous success at school.

---

8 Words Beginning With–H

Hack about : change and cut parts of a written matter. ***Ex.*** His book has been *hacked about* terribly by the editor.

Hammer away at : work hard at something. ***Ex 1.*** He *hammered away at* a very difficult problem till he got a solution. ***Ex 2.*** They were all *hammering away at* their work.

Hammer down : cause something to fall down, etc. by hammering. ***Ex 1.*** He *hammered* the door *down*. ***Ex 2.*** He *hammered down* the metal till it was the shape he wanted.

Hammer in/into : force somebody to learn something by repeating it many times. ***Ex 1.*** They have had English grammar *hammered into* them. ***Ex 2.*** I shall *hammer* some information *in* whether that child likes it or not. ***Ex 3.*** He intends to *hammer in* the point that his men will not accept the offer.

Hammer out : achieve something by great effort. ***Ex 1.*** After much discussion, the negotiators *hammered out* a compromise settlement. ***Ex 2.*** After prolonged discussion, the delegates *hammered out* a form of words that was acceptable to everyone. ***Ex 3.*** They *hammered out* a new policy which would satisfy both sides in the dispute.

Hand down (a) : pass on to a child below one in age or size. ***Ex 1.*** In poor families, clothes are generally *handed down* from one child to the next. ***Ex 2.*** He was dressed in a pair of trousers *handed down* to him by his elder brother.

Note : The word *hand-me-downs* is a noun. It means *used* or unwanted things, especially clothes that are given to another person; especially a younger brother or sister. ***Ex 1.*** I don't want your old *hand-me-downs*. ***Ex 2.*** The kids had to wear *hand-me-down* jackets.

(b) pass something on by tradition, inheritance, etc. ***Ex 1.*** These stories were *handed down* from generation to generation. ***Ex 2.*** Can you always observe the traditions *handed down* to us from the past? ***Ex 3.*** These ceremonies have been *handed down* through the centuries, and remain practically unchanged.

(c) pass sentence on somebody convicted of crime. ***Ex.*** The judge *handed down* very heavy sentences ranging from ten to fifteen years on all the accused.

(d) announce something formally or publicly. ***Ex 1.*** Let me know when the government will *hand down* the budget for the next fiscal year? ***Ex 2.*** The High Court will *hand down* its verdict on the sensational murder case on the 4th of the next month at 11.30 a.m. sharp.

Hand in : (a) submit, tender or surrender something. ***Ex 1.*** The Minister *handed in* his resignation in protest against the Cabinet's economic policy. ***Ex 2.*** Unserviceable articles should be *handed in* at the stores department of the factory. ***Ex 3.*** They *handed in* their examination papers to the invigilator on duty.

(b) give in by hand. ***Ex 1.*** Please *hand* this message *in* at the office as you go past. ***Ex 2.*** Someone *handed in* some money he had found in the street.

Hand on : (a) send or give something to another person. ***Ex.*** Please *hand on* the magazine to her.

(b) pass something to the generation following one's own. ***Ex 1.*** Property is something *handed on* from generation to generation. ***Ex 2.*** They *handed on* their knowledge to their children. ***Ex 3.*** They were choking with their experience of life and wanted to *hand* it *on*.

Hand out : (a) distribute something. ***Ex 1.*** Relief workers were *handling out* emergency rations to the survivors. ***Ex 2.*** Duplicated material illustrating the lecture was *handed out* to the students. ***Ex 3.*** The teacher *handed out* the books at the beginning of the lesson.

(b) offer. ***Ex.*** He likes *handing out* advice to everyone.

(c) give as charity. ***Ex.*** The Prime Minister *handed out* gifts of food and clothing to the survivors of the earthquake.

Hand over : (a) transfer a position of authority or power to somebody. ***Ex 1.*** I am resigning as chairman and *handing over* to my deputy. ***Ex 2.*** The king *handed over* power to an elected government. ***Ex 3.*** I shall be glad to *hand* this job *over* to her.

(b) surrender; deliver somebody/something, especially to authority. ***Ex 1.*** They *handed* the thief *over* to the police. ***Ex 2.*** India was under no obligation to *hand* him *over* to France.

(c) (at a meeting on Tv, etc. or on the telephone) : let somebody listen or speak to another person. ***Ex.*** I am *handing* you *over* now to our foreign affairs correspondent.

Hand (it) to : give somebody the praise or credit that he deserves. ***Ex 1.*** They are a clever lot, you have got to *hand* it *to* them. ***Ex 2.*** She has been wonderfully cheerful, and interested in everything you have really got to *hand* it *to* her.

Hang about/around : not move away; be standing about a place, doing nothing definite. ***Ex 1.*** Why are you *hanging about* here? ***Ex 2.*** Several unemployed persons were *hanging around* the streets.

Hang back : hesitate; show unwillingness to do something. ***Ex1.*** She *hung back* from asking the questions. ***Ex 2.*** Don't *hang back* when you get a chance to do something.

Hang behind : linger in a place after others. ***Ex.*** Two of the audience *hung behind* after the lecture to have a word with the speaker.

Hang on : (a) grip something firmly; hold tight. ***Ex 1.*** *Hang on* tight—we are off. ***Ex 2.*** The climber on the ledge *hung on* precariously, waiting for help.

(b) wait for a short time. ***Ex 1.*** *Hang on* a minute—I am nearly ready. ***Ex 2.*** *Hang on* and I shall come with you.

(c) (on the telephone) not replace the receiver; hold on. ***Ex.*** The line was engaged and the operator asked me to *hang on*.

(d) depend on something. ***Ex 1.*** Everything *hangs on* money at the moment. ***Ex 2.*** A great deal *hangs in* his decision. ***Ex 3.*** The survival of the government *hangs on* today's crucial vote.

Hang on to : (a) retain; not give or sell to somebody else. ***Ex 1.*** *Hang on to* those photographs-they may be valuable. ***Ex 2.*** I am *hanging on to* those shares-I think they will show a sizeable gain after the Budget is presented by the Government. ***Ex 3.*** Was he keeping his word to *hang on* to the picture?

(b) hold something tightly. ***Ex 1.*** *Hang on to* that rope and don't let go. ***Ex 2.*** We were both *hanging on to* the side of the boat.

Hang out : (a) spread damp clothes on a clothes-line, so that they can dry. ***Ex 1.*** I have just got two shirts to *hang out*—then we can go shopping. ***Ex 2.*** She *hung out* her blouses.

(b) have one's home; visit a place often; live, reside, spend a lot of time. ***Ex 1.*** Where do you *hang out* these days? ***Ex 2.*** He does not *hang out* at the factory. ***Ex 3.*** He spends a lot of time *hanging out* with friends.

(c) hold on : ***Ex 1.*** The striking workers *hung out* for more money before resuming work. ***Ex 2.*** I expect him to *hang out* until he gets what he wants.

Note : The word *hang-out* is a noun used to denote *place where one lives or which one visits often*. ***Ex 1.*** Where is your *hang-out*? ***Ex 2.*** This restaurant is a favourite *hang-out* for students. ***Ex 3.*** That coffee-house became one of his best liked *hang-outs*.

Hang over : (a) envelop something; possess somebody. ***Ex.*** He tried with a few good humoured remarks to break through the cloud of gloom *hanging over* his colleagues, but his words struck no response from them.

(b) be imminent; seem likely to occur soon; to worry much. ***Ex 1.*** The threat of deportation was *hanging over* him. ***Ex 2.*** I had the university examination *hanging over* me. ***Ex 3.*** Now that my Bar examinations are *hanging over* me, I don't want to take on any new outside commitments.

(c) continue. ***Ex.*** I expect this situation to *hang over* till Monday.

Hang together : (a) support or help one another; co-operate; stay united. ***Ex 1.*** We can come through any crisis if we *hang together*. ***Ex. 2.*** They all *hang together* in that village. ***Ex 3.*** We should all *hang together* in this emergency.

(b) (of statements) be consistent. ***Ex 1.*** Their accounts of what happened don't *hang together*. ***Ex. 2.*** All aspects of the struggle *hang together*. ***Ex 3.*** Her story *hangs together* well. ***Ex 4.*** The two parts of your statement do not *hang together*.

Hang up : (a) suffer inconvenience. ***Ex..*** We have been badly *hung up* through the inefficiency of the dispatch department.

(b) be emotionally upset or inhibited. ***Ex 1.*** She is really *hung up* on that young man. ***Ex 2.*** Are you *hung up* about your father?

(c) end a telephone conversation with somebody by replacing the receiver. ***Ex 1.***I was telling her all about the problem and then she just *hung up* on me. ***Ex 2.*** I did not have a chance to apologise-she *hung up* on me.

Hang upon : listen with devoted attention to. ***Ex 1.*** They *hung upon* their leader's words. ***Ex 2.*** He knew how to captivate her : she seemed to *hang upon* his lips.

Hanker after/for : have a strong desire for something; long for. ***Ex 1.*** Do you *hanker after* wealth? ***Ex 2.*** I *hanker after* fame and glory. ***Ex 3.*** They always *hankered after* a bungalow of their own.

Happen along : arrive or appear by chance and unexpectedly. ***Ex 1.*** She just *happened along* while we were waiting for the bus. ***Ex 2.*** He had to *happen along* just as we were about to settle the whole thing amicably.

Happen on/upon : find something by chance. ***Ex 1.*** I *happened on* just the thing I had been looking for. ***Ex 2.*** We *happened on* them in the street.

Hare off : run very fast. ***Ex.*** The boy was *haring off* down, the street, yelling.

Hark at : listen to somebody (implying that the previous speaker is being arrogant silly, etc.) : ***Ex 1.*** Just *hark at* him. What does he think of himself? ***Ex 2.*** Just *hark at* her—anyone would think that she owned the town.

Hark back : (a) refer back. ***Ex 1.*** She *harked back* to her youth. ***Ex 2.*** Let us *hark back* to what we were discussing earlier. ***Ex 3.*** To understand this entails *harking back* to a revelation I made earlier on.

(b) be similar to. ***Ex.*** The decorative use of bricks *harks back* to the old farmhouse style.

Harp on : talk repeatedly and tiresomely about something. ***Ex 1.*** She is always *harping on* about my faults. ***Ex 2.*** He *harps on* about how he has been cheated. ***Ex 3.*** This has been *harped on* many a time before.

Hash over : discuss something in great detail. ***Ex 1.*** Don't *hash over* the past events. ***Ex 2.*** They *hashed over* all their old problems.

Hash up : make a mess of something; do something badly; spoil something. ***Ex 1.*** He has *hashed up* our plans again. ***Ex 2.*** I am sorry I *hashed up* the arrangements.

Hatch out/up : think out and produce (a plot, plan etc.) ***Ex 1.*** Some disgruntled military officers *hatched up* a plot to overthrow the government. ***Ex 2.*** What mischief are those children *hatching up*?

Haul in : arrest somebody. ***Ex 1.*** Why did the police *haul* him *in*? ***Ex 2.*** Wait and get your evidence before you *haul* him *in*.

Haul off : take somebody to a place against his will. ***Ex 1.*** Several boys were dragged off buses and *hauled off* to ail. ***Ex 2.*** They tried to *haul* me *off* but I resisted.

Haul up : bring somebody to be tried in a court of law. ***Ex 1.*** This is the second time that he has been *hauled up* on a dangerous driving charge. ***Ex 2.*** He has been *hauled up* before the magistrate on a charge of assault. ***Ex 3.*** She was *hauled up* before the local judicial magistrate for disorderly conduct.

Have around/round : entertain at one's house. ***Ex.*** I shall be *having* a few persons *around* for tea, one of these evenings.

Have at : try to achieve or do something different and challenging. ***Ex.*** As things stand, I don't mind *having* a go *at* doing up the place.

Have back : allow a wife or lover from who one is separated to return. ***Ex 1.*** I shall never *have* her *back*. ***Ex 2.*** She says that she will not *have* him *back*.

Have down : have somebody to stay at one's house as a guest. ***Ex.*** They are planning to *have* their maternal grand children *down* for the weekend.

Have for : be interesting or attractive to somebody. ***Ex 1.*** The topic seemed to *have* a fascination *for* her. ***Ex 2.*** The novels of Rabindra Nath Tagore has always *had* an enormous appeal *for* me.

Have in : have somebody working in one's house. ***Ex.*** I am afraid we cannot *have* you to stay with us, we *have* the decorators *in* all this week.

Have on : (a) be wearing. ***Ex 1.*** She *had* nothing *on*. ***Ex 2.*** He *had* a fur coat *on*. ***Ex 3.*** Youshould not feel hot. You *have* nothing *on*.

(b) deceive. ***Ex 1.*** Don't *have* me *on*. ***Ex 2.*** She was *having* him *on*. ***Ex 3.*** I suspected we were being *had on* by the greengrocer, so we weighed the vegetables when we got back.

(c) have evidence to show that somebody is guilty. ***Ex 1.*** *Have* the police got anything *on* him? ***Ex 2.*** She *has* nothing *on* me legally and if she starts making complaints I can make plenty of counter-complaints against her.

Have out : discuss a matter frankly, often angrily with somebody until understanding is reached. ***Ex 1.*** After weeks of silent hostility, they *have* at last had it *out* with each other. ***Ex 2.*** I shall *have* the matter *out* with her this evening.

Have up : cause somebody to be accused of a crime, etc. in a law court. ***Ex 1.*** He was *had up* for exceeding the speed limit. ***Ex 2.*** If I see you hanging about these shops again, I shall *have* you *up* for loitering with intent.

Hawk about : spread news by talking. ***Ex.*** Please find out who has been *hawking* gossip *about* her.

Haze over : become dreamy; lose sharpness or focus. ***Ex 1.*** His eyes *hazed over* when he thought of her. ***Ex. 2.*** Whenever anyone mentions his name, her eyes *haze over*.

Head back : return. ***Ex.*** We changed our minds and *headed back* to Delhi.

Head for : move towards. ***Ex.*** I *headed for* the door. ***Ex 2.*** They were *heading for* Calcutta. ***Ex 3.*** If you go on with her, you ate *heading for* serious trouble. ***Ex 3.*** Is the world *heading for* disaster? ***Ex 4.*** He was *heading for* a personal triumph.

Head off : (a) get in front of somebody/something so as to turn him/it back or aside; divert from an intended direction. ***Ex 1.*** The boys fanned out, trying to *head off* the goats. ***Ex 2.*** We tried to *head* the men *off*, and get to the treasure first. ***Ex 3.*** The hunters decided to *head* the animals *off*. ***Ex 4.*** The first thing to be done was to *head off* the enemy from the tender spots and vital places.

(b) prevent somebody from moving to a topic that is boring, or embarrassing, by getting him to think about something else; prevent something unpleasant from happening. ***Ex 1.*** The speaker seemed intent on *heading off* awkward questions. ***Ex 2.*** The government allowed wages to rise faster than productivity in order to *head off* possible unrest. ***Ex 3.*** There is no gainsaying the fact that we do too little to *head off* disaster. ***Ex 4.*** Try your best to *head off* a quarrel between those two brothers.

Head towards : (of a situation) to get nearer. ***Ex.*** We are *heading towards* the general election.

Head up : to take charge of (a group or team). ***Ex.*** He *headed up* the football team at school.

Heap on/upon : award to, address to, in abundance; to praise or criticise somebody/something a lot. ***Ex 1.*** His popular following was fickle; honours were *heaped upon* him one moment, and curses the next. ***Ex 2.*** Why do you *heap* praise *on* that tomboy? ***Ex 3.*** He *heaps* praise *upon* a nymphet possessing stunning beauty.

Hear about : be given information about something. ***Ex 1.*** I have only just *heard about* your dismissal. ***Ex 2.*** You will *hear about* this later. ***Ex 3.*** The more I *hear about* her, the less I like her.

Hear from : (a) receive a letter, telephone call, etc. from somebody. ***Ex 1.*** How often do you *hear from* your sister-in-law? ***Ex 2.*** I have not *heard from* him for quite some time.

(b) listen to opinion of. ***Ex.*** The doctor says that he would like to *hear* more *from* the patient.

Hear of : (a) come to know of. ***Ex 1.*** I have never *heard of* you. ***Ex 2.*** When did you *hear of* his sad and sudden demise? ***Ex 3.*** I first *heard of* the firm, and had dealings with them, five years ago.

(b) have news of; have reports of the existence of. ***Ex 1.*** She disappeared two years ago, and was never *heard of* again. ***Ex 2.*** They started out to cross the Sahara Desert in a saloon car, and have not been *heard of* since.

(Note) hear of : refuse to consider or allow something. ***Ex 1.*** He would not *hear of* my walking home alone. ***Ex 2.*** I cannot let you pay my debts-I shall not *hear of* such a thing. ***Ex 3.*** He will not *hear of* you sharing in the expenses.

Hear out : listen until somebody has finished saying what he wants to say. ***Ex 1.*** The Prime- Minister was *heard out* in complete silence. ***Ex 2.*** Lakhs of people *heard* the globe-trotter *out* with tremendous interest. ***Ex 3.*** Please *hear* me *out*.

Heat up : (of a situation) start to change very quickly. ***Ex.*** Things are *heating up* so fast in the country that I don't want to make any rash predictions.

Hedge about/aruond : restrict or limit somebody/something; surround, as with a hedge. ***Ex 1.*** My life is *hedged about* with petty regulations. ***Ex 2.*** The king *hedged* himself *about* with armed guards. ***Ex 3.*** His freedom was *hedged around* with duties and restrictions.

Hedge in : restrict one's freedom of action; fence in. ***Ex 1.*** The whole matter is *hedged in* with umpteen difficulties. ***Ex 2.*** Custom *hedged* her *in* and made her helpless. ***Ex 3.*** He felt *hedged in* on financial matters. ***Ex 4.*** We are being increasingly *hedged in* by controls and restrictions.

Help along : assist the progress of. ***Ex.*** Respiratory diseases are often *helped along* by malnutrition.

Help off with : help somebody to remove. ***Ex.*** I *helped* her *off* with her coat.

Help on with : help somebody to put on. ***Ex 1.*** She followed her husband to the door and *helped* him *on with* his coat. ***Ex 2.*** He *helped* the ladies *on with* their wraps.

Help out : help somebody in a difficult situation or a crisis. ***Ex 1.*** He is always willing to *help* us *out* when we are short of staff. ***Ex 2.*** They *helped* us *out* a lot during those difficult months. ***Ex 3.*** Let me know whether a sum of five thousand rupees will *help* you *out* at the moment. ***Ex 4.*** Padmini finished her work and crossed to *help* Nandini *out* With hers.

Help to : serve somebody with. ***Ex 1.*** They were *helped to* some more vegetables. ***Ex 2.*** He *helped* himself *to* one of his own cigarettes. ***Ex 3.*** She was in the kitchen, *helping* herself *to* my biscuits.

Hem about/around : 'beset; surround. ***Ex 1.*** Our project was *hemmed about* by many an obstacle. ***Ex 2.*** I felt *hemmed around* by forces that I was absolutely powerless to overcome. ***Ex 3.*** His position was precisition the same as it had been before his attempt to face the problems that *hemmed* him *around*.

Hem in : (a) be enclosed by, ***Ex 1.*** The roads are *hemmed in* by tall buildings. ***Ex 2.*** The agricultural fields are *hemmed in* by hedges. **(b)** resirict the movement of; confine somebody. ***Ex 1.*** His marriage had *hemmed* him *in.* ***Ex 2.*** I felt *hemmed in* by convention. ***Ex 3.*** The enemy troops were *hemming* us *in.*

Het up about/over : be excited, irritated, annoyed, bothered. ***Ex 1.*** Father seemed terribly *het up over* something last Monday. ***Ex 2.*** What are you getting so *het up about*?

Hew across, through, etc. : make something by chopping. ***Ex.*** They *hewed* a path *through* the forest.

Hew away, off, etc. : remove something by chopping. ***Ex.*** We *hewed off* several dead branches of the tree with an axe.

Hew out : make something by hard work. ***Ex.*** He *hewed out* a brilliant career for himself.

Hinge on/upon: depend on. ***Ex 1.*** Everything *hinges on* the outcome of these talks. ***Ex 2.*** The success of the conference *hinges upon* the Cabinet decision which is expected at any moment.

Hit back : reply forcefully to verbal attacks; retaliate; counter-attack vigorously; resist actively. ***Ex 1.*** I *hit back* at my opponents in the debate. ***Ex 2.*** We must *hit back* against this tyranny. ***Ex 3.*** In a TV interview Mohini *hit back* at her critics. ***Ex 4.*** In a rousing speech to party loyalists, the Prime Minister *hit back* at those who sought to undermine the government's economic policy.

Hit it off : enjoy good relations with. ***Ex 1.*** How well do he and his boss *hit it off*. ***Ex 2.*** Do you *hit it off* with your boss. ***Ex 3.*** They had *hit it off* from the first evening.

Hit on/upon : find something by luck; suddenly devise or discover something. ***Ex 1.*** I *hit upon* a good title for my new novel. ***Ex 2.*** He *hit upon* the solution to the problem almost by accident. ***Ex 3.*** The committee eventually *hit upon* a formula that would be acceptable to all. ***Ex 4.*** Kamini *hit upon* an idea that seemed the answer to all of problems.

Hit out : make a vigorous attack with words or blows. ***Ex 1.*** In a rousing speech, the President *hit out* against the trade union. ***Ex 2.*** I *hit out* at government policy on unemployment. ***Ex 3.*** Do you *hit out* at hippie culture?

Hitch up : pull up with a quick movement. ***Ex 1.*** Rohini *hitched up* her skirt so as not to get it wet. ***Ex 2.*** He *hitched up* his trousers before sitting down.

Hive off : (a) become separate from a large group; form an independent body. ***Ex.*** Next year, the biochemistry section will *hive off* to form an independent, department.

(b) make part of an organisation independent; transfer work to another section or firm. ***Ex.*** The government has decided to *hive off* some parts of the nationalised industries to private enterprise.

Hold against : allow something to influence one's judgement or opinion of somebody. ***Ex 1.*** He is afraid that his criminal record will be *held against* when he applies for jobs. ***Ex 2.*** I don't *hold* it *against* him that he votes National Party. ***Ex 3.*** I don't *hold* it *against* her that she has spent two years in gaol. ***Ex 4.*** The fact that he has let you down once before should not be *held against* him.

Hold back : (a) hesitate to act or speak because of fear or reluctance. ***Ex 1.*** She *held back* from telling him what she though of him. ***Ex 2.*** He *held back*, not knowing how to break the terrible news. ***Ex 3.*** Police have *hold back* from going into a holy place to arrest him. ***Ex 4.*** I have noticed that he does not *hold back* in his discussions.

(b) prevent the progress or development of somebody. ***Ex 1.*** What are the prejudices which are *holding* you *back* in your career? ***Ex 2.*** Do you think that mixed-ability teaching *holds* the brighter children *back*? ***Ex 3.*** The rise in living standards has been *held back* in a long time.

(c) prevent somebody/something from advancing; control or restrain somebody/something. ***Ex 1.*** The thin police cordon was unable to *hold back* the crowd; they flooded on to the playground. ***Ex 2.*** The dam was not strong enough to *hold back* the flood waters.

(d) withold something; not release or grant something keep a secret. ***Ex 1.*** I think he is *holding* something *back*; he knows more than he admits. ***Ex 2.*** Don't *hold back* information relating to the road accident resulting in the death of ten persons. ***Ex 3.*** The scientists have been advised to *hold back* any announcement of their findings.

(e) control something; not express or reveal an emotion. ***Ex 1.*** She just managed to *hold back* her anger. ***Ex 2.*** He bravely *held back* his tears. ***Ex 3.*** Most of us were either crying or doing our best to *hold back* the tears.

(f) to keep in reserve to us.e later. ***Ex.*** They need money immediately and cannot *hold back* their goods to push the price up.

Hold down : (a) oppress somebody; control freedom of somebody; keep down. ***Ex 1.*** The people are *held down* by a vicious and repressive military regime. ***Ex 2.*** The dictator does not have enough forces to *hold down* the people.

(b) keep something down; keep something at low level. ***Ex 1.*** The rate of inflation must be *held down*. ***Ex 2.*** You must try your best to *hold down* expenditure.

(c) remain in a job for some time. ***Ex 1.*** Many government school boys have been unable to *hold down* a job. ***Ex 2.*** I fixed him up with work when he came out of prison, but he could not *hold* the job *down*. ***Ex 3.*** He could not *hold down* a job after his breakdown. ***Ex 4.*** What is the longest she has *held down* a job?

(d) hold for: apply in the case of; be valid for. ***Ex 1.*** What I have said *holds* as much *for* houses to rent as *for* houses to buy. ***Ex 2.***

The same requirement *holds* good *for* any applicant wishing to study natural sciences.

Hold forth : speak pompously and lengthily about something. ***Ex 1.*** He loves *holding forth* on any subject once hehas an audience. ***Ex 2.*** Ram introduced the carpenter, and *held forth* at great length on his prowess, personality, and intelligence. ***Ex 3.*** He was *holding forth* on the pleasures of travel.

Hold in : restrain, control or check something oneself. ***Ex 1.*** You must *hold in* your temper. ***Ex 2.*** He is incapable of *holding* himself *in*. ***Ex 3.*** Eventually, these feelings could be *held in* no longer: there were outbreaks of violence everywhere. ***Ex 4.*** Women are expected to *hold in* their anger. ***Ex 5.*** I am very good at *holding in* my emotions.

Hold off : (a) be delayed; not occur. ***Ex 1.*** The monsoon *held off* just for a month; then the rain fell in torrents. ***Ex 2.*** The rain *held off* just long enough for us to have our picnic.

(b) restrain oneself from diong something, esp. attacking somebody; keep at bay; prevent somebody from overwhelming oneself. ***Ex 1.*** Let us hope the gunmen will *hold off* for the duration of the cease-fire. ***Ex 2.*** He has been *holding* her *off* for many a month, but sooner or, later he will have to give in. ***Ex 3.*** It is a matter of great pleasure for me to say that she *holds off* from close friendships.

(c) resist sucessfully. ***Ex.*** Our troops *held off* superior enemy attacks for four days.

(d) delay something. ***Ex 1.*** Everyone *holds off* buying as long as they can, if they think the price still has a way to drop. ***Ex 2.*** Please *hold off* making your decision until next Monday.

Hold on : (a) wait or stop; hang on. ***Ex 1.*** Just *hold on* a minute while I get my breath back. ***Ex 2.*** *Hold on* a minute till I put my coat on. ***Ex 3.*** The telephone operator asked me to *hold on* until a connection was made.

(b) survive in a difficult or dangerous situation; hang on. ***Ex 1.*** They managed to *hold on* until help arrived. ***Ex 2.*** I don't think I can *hold on* much longer.

(c) keep something in position; fasten. ***Ex 1.*** The soles of his shoes were just *held on* by a few stitches. ***Ex 2.*** Use special adhesive for this job : ordinary glue won't *hold* the handle *on*. ***Ex 3.*** These nuts and bolts *hold* the wheels *on*.

Hold on to : (a) keep grasping or gripping somebody/something; not let go of somebody/something. ***Ex 1.*** Don't panic; just *hold on to* that rock and I shall come and fetch you down. ***Ex 2.*** I *held* firmly *on to* my briefcase.

(b) keep or retain something; not give or sell something to somebody else. ***Ex 1.*** It is not enough to take over the lead; we must *hold on to* it. ***Ex. 2.*** I should *hold on to* those bonds: they will appreciate (increase in value) considerably. ***Ex 3.*** I shall *hold on to* that house for the time being; house prices are rising sharply at the moment.

(c) keep arms around somebody. ***Ex.*** I stayed where I was on the sofa and *held on to* him.

(d) keep something. ***Ex 1.*** I permitted her to *hold on to* the money she earned. ***Ex 2.*** Politicians always want to *hold on to* power at all costs.

(e) look after something. ***Ex.*** Will you please *hold on to* my car for me for a week or so?

(f) continue to believe in a belief, idea or principle. ***Ex 1.*** You must *hold on to* your religion. ***Ex 2.*** I always *hold on to* my principle.

Hold out : (a) last; remain. ***Ex 1.*** We can stay here for as long as our supplies of food and water *hold out*. ***Ex 2.*** That so small a force was able to *hold out* against such heavy odds is certainly proof of bravery.

(b) resist an attack. ***Ex 1.*** Our battalion *held out* for a week in the face of heavy enemy assaults. ***Ex 2.*** They *held out* bravely against repeated enemy bombing.

(c) offer; afford. ***Ex 1.*** The forthcoming talks *hold out* the hope of real arms reductions. ***Ex 2.*** Doctors *hold aut* little of his recuperating. ***Ex 3.*** I am afraid that this case *holds out* very little hope. ***Ex 4.*** The prospect was *held out* of growing prosperity in the years to come.

(d) extend. ***Ex 1.*** I *held out* my arms to embrace the little child. ***Ex 2.*** She *held out* a hand and I shook it. ***Ex 3.*** He *held out* his hand for the briefcase.

(e) hold something, so that someone can take it or look at it. ***Ex.*** I took off my glasses and *held* them *out* to him.

Hold out for : deliberately delay reaching an agreement in the hope of gaining something. ***Ex 1.*** Having won the first round, the unions are likely to *hold out for* more than their original demand. ***Ex 2.*** The government employees' negotiators are *holding out for* a more generous pay settlement.

Hold out on : (a) refuse to give information, etc. to somebody; keep something secret from. ***Ex 1.*** He must know more than he will admit—I think he is *holding out on* us. ***Ex 2.*** I am not *holding out on* you. I honestly don't know where he is.

(b) refuse to yield or surrender. ***Ex.*** She is a little minx; she has been *holding out on* me.

Hold over : postpone or defer something. ***Ex 1.*** The final item on the agenda will be *hold over* until our next meeting stated to be held on Friday, the 8th instant, at 11.30 am. ***Ex 2.*** Let us *hold over* the matter until the next meeting.

Hold to : (a) stick to remain loyal to something. ***Ex 1.*** You should always *hold to* your religious beliefs very firmly. ***Ex 2.*** I shall *hold* firmly *to* what has already been agreed. ***Ex 3.*** I always *hold to* my convictions.

(b) make somebody keep a promise. ***Ex 1.*** We must *hold* the contractors *to* their estimates. ***Ex 2.*** You can have the car when I go out of station. I shall *hold* you *to* that.

Hold together : (a) remain united; unite. ***Ex 1.*** Our Party has *held together* wonderfully during the current crisis. ***Ex 2.*** A political party should always *hold together* in times of crisis.

(b) unite something; cause something to remain together. ***Ex 1.*** The country needs a leader who will *hold* the nation *together*. ***Ex 2.*** A group can *hold together* unless there is a general exodus.

Hold under : suppress; hold in submission; keep under. ***Ex.*** The country is *held under* by appeals to patriotism, some economic inducement, and, where necessary, force.

Hold up : (a) put somebody/something forward as an example; offer as a model to be imitated. ***Ex 1.*** She is always *holding up* her children as models of behaviour. ***Ex 2.*** Stop *holding up* your elder brother as an example to emulate it is bad for the young one's confidence. ***Ex 3.*** What do you *hold up* to the children as being desirable goals?

(b) obstruct or delay the progress of somebody/something. ***Ex 1.*** His application was *held up* by the postal strike. ***Ex 2.*** Our flight was **held up** by fog. ***Ex 3.*** Road-works on the motorway are *holding up* traffic. ***Ex 4.*** The traffic was *held up* by an accident.

(c) rob something using the threat of force or violence. ***Ex 1.*** Masked men *held up* a bank yesterday. ***Ex 2.*** Five dacoits *help up* a van carrying a factory payroll, and escaped with the money in a fast car. ***Ex 3.*** Robbers *held* him *up* at the point of a gun.

(d) remain in good condition after rough use. ***Ex.*** How did your boots *hold up*?

(e) remain convincing and effective. ***Ex 1.*** None of your stories will *hold up* in public. ***Ex 2.*** Did your arguments *hold up*?

Note : The word *hold up* is a noun. It means: **(a)** stoppage or delay. ***Ex 1.*** We should arrive in half an hour, barring *hold ups*. ***Ex 2.*** There was a *holdup* on the motorway. ***Ex 3.*** I missed my flight owing to a traffic *holdup*.

(b) robbery by armed robbers. ***Ex 1.*** After the *hold up*, the gang made their getaway in a stolen car. ***Ex 2.*** Several persons were killed in different *hold ups* in Delhi last month.

Hold with : agree with or approve of something. ***Ex 1.*** I don't *hold with* alcoholic drinks and wild parties. ***Ex 2.*** He does not *hold with* all this revolutionary talk. ***Ex 3.*** Do you *hold with* my views on education? ***Ex 4.*** I don't *hold with* lewd scenes on .the stage. ***Ex 5.*** Why did you enter for the contest if you don't *hold with* it ?

Hole up : hide; seek refuge; conceal oneself. ***Ex 1.*** The gang has *holed up* somehwere in the mountains. ***Ex 2.*** He had *holed up* at a local motel. ***Ex 3.*** The men were *holed up* on the top floor of the hotel. ***Ex 4.*** Where will you *hole up*?

Home in : (a) be directed or move towards. ***Ex 1.*** The torpedo *homed in* on its target. ***Ex 2.*** Football fans are *homing in* on the playground from miles around. ***Ex 3.*** The pilot *homed in* by means of radar, despite the poor visibility. ***Ex 4.*** The missile can *home in* on the target with pinpoint accuracy.

(b) pay more attention to, and deal in detail with, a subject. ***Ex 1.*** Kamlesh *homed in* on the things we were discussing. ***Ex 2.*** I *homed in* on the rampant corruption in the government offices throughout the country.

Hoot down/off : force to leave, stop speaking, with hoots of disapproval. ***Ex 1.*** The Minister tried to explain his policies in public, but he was *hooted off*. ***Ex 2.*** The proposal was *hooted down*. ***Ex 3.*** The audience *hooted* the speaker *off* the platform. ***Ex 4.*** The actor was *hooted off* the stage.

Hop in/into : get into a car. ***Ex.*** *Hop in*, I shall give you a lift to the airport.

Hop out : get out of a car. ***Ex 1.*** Where will you *hop out*? ***Ex 2.*** She *hopped out* of my car in front of the Hanuman Temple.

Hop off : go away. ***Ex.*** *Hop off*, I am very busy at the moment.

Horn in : muscle in; by cunning or force get oneself into a situation which seems profitable; intrude. ***Ex 1.*** They had come up for the day with no other motive than to *horn in* on her marriage. ***Ex 2.*** Don't *horn in* on our project. ***Ex 3.*** He always tries to *horn in* on an activity which seems very profitable. ***Ex 4.*** Don't allow anybody to *horn in* on our affairs.

Horse about/around : act in a noisy rough playful way. ***Ex 1.*** The boys were *horsing about* in the back garden. ***Ex 2.*** He loved to *horse around* with them. ***Ex 3.*** There was a certain amount of *horsing about* in the dressing-room after the game was over.

Hot up : (a) increase; intensify; become more exciting. ***Ex 1.*** With only a week to go before the election, things are really *hotting up*. ***Ex 2.*** The election campaign was *hotting up* all over the country. ***Ex 3.*** As the police closed in on the criminals, the pace of the investigation began to *hot up*. ***Ex 4.*** The documents finally arrived and the investigation was *hotted up*.

(b) become dangerous. ***Ex.*** Things were beginning to *hot up* in the Middle East again.

Hound down : find somebody/something after a persistent chase; hunt down. ***Ex 1.*** The police intend to *hound down* all dangerous criminals. ***Ex 2.*** He says that his political opponents are trying to *hound* him *down*, and make him look responsible for the crisis.

Hound out/out of : force somebody to leave somebody/a place. ***Ex 1.*** She was *hounded out* of her job by jealous rivals. ***Ex 2.*** We are determined to *hound out* law-breakers. ***Ex 3.*** By digging up a few unsavoury details about his past, they managed to have him *hounded out*. ***Ex 4.*** Do you want to get him *hounded out of* the Civil Service altogether?

Hover about/around : wait in a timid and uncertain manner; wait in an aimless way. ***Ex 1.*** I cannot work with you *hovering about* me like that. ***Ex 2.*** She is always *hovering around* the place annoying people. ***Ex 3.*** He *hovered about* outside, too afraid to go in. ***Ex 4.*** That fellow has been *hovering about* here for several days, and I would like to know what he wants.

Howl down : prevent a speaker from being heard by shouting scornfully, ***Ex 1.*** The students *howled down* the speaker, because they did not like his opinions. ***Ex 2.*** He was *howled down* by communists. ***Ex 3.*** The guest speaker was *howled down*, and it was some time before the chairman could restore order.

Huddle about/around : gather near something and stand or sit close to it. ***Ex 1.*** We all *huddled around* the radio to hear the news. ***Ex 2.*** They *huddled about* their crackling fires.

Huddle up : curl one's body up into a small space. ***Ex 1.*** The child was cold, so he *huddled up* against the radiator. ***Ex 2.*** He *huddled up* with his brother. ***Ex 3.*** There was a figure standing close to me, *huddled up* against the strong wind.

Hum with : be in a state of activity. ***Ex 1.*** The whole place was *humming with* life when we arrived. ***Ex 2.*** Our mill is very streamlined, scientific, and it fairly *hums with* wheels.

Hunger for/after : have a strong desire for somebody/something; long for somebody/something. ***Ex 1.*** He *hungered for* some contact outside his own circumscribed world. ***Ex 2.*** She *hungered for* my love. ***Ex 3.*** Whom did you hunger after ? ***Ex 4.*** The letters *for* which he *hungered* grew fewer, then stopped altogether. ***Ex 5.*** Why do our leaders *hunger after* power? ***Ex 6.*** Let me know what you *hunger for* so fiercely.

Hunt after/for : seek; look for. ***Ex.*** She was *hunting after* a particular kind of coat and finally found it.

Hunt down : pursue somebody/something until he/it is found. ***Ex 1.*** The police were intent upon *hunting down* the escaped convict. ***Ex 2.*** I hid, but they *hunted* me *down* in the end. ***Ex 3.*** Enemy soldiers left hiding out in the forest were *hunted down* by our troops.

Hunt out : search for, and find, something that was previously used and has been put away. ***Ex 1.*** I shall have to *hunt out* the children's old clothes to give to the rag and bone man when he calls. ***Ex 2.*** I have got the picture for you somewhere, but it will need some *hunting out*. ***Ex 3.*** Just let me *hunt* my bag *out*—it is here somewhere. ***Ex 4.*** He has been *hunting out* all the old family photographs.

Hunt up : search for something hidden and difficult to find. ***Ex 1.*** He has gone to *hunt up* references in the library. ***Ex 2.*** Where did you *hunt up* all the information? ***Ex 3.*** He has been busy *hunting up* the origins of his family. ***Ex 4.*** He is not likely to *hunt up* that particular page. ***Ex 5.*** Are you good at *hunting up* information?

Hurl at : yell; shout; utter something with force. ***Ex 1.*** She *hurled* insults *at* you. ***Ex 2.*** They egged on the boy to *hurl* abuses *at* her.

Hurry up : (a) make somebody/something do something more quickly or too quickly; speed something up. ***Ex 1.*** He is a good worker but he needs *hurrying up*. ***Ex 2.*** The nurse stood outside the washrooms to *hurry* us *up*.

(b) move more quickly or too quickly; do something more quickly. ***Ex 1.*** *Hurry up* and get ready—we are waiting. ***Ex 2.*** I wish the train would *hurry up* and come.

Hush up : prevent something from becoming generally known; suppress. ***Ex 1.*** They tried to *hush up* the scandal, but news soon leaked out. ***Ex 2.*** The government *hushed* the affair *up* to avoid a public outcry. ***Ex 3.*** They tried to *hush up* the small matter of ten thousand being missing from the till. ***Ex 4.*** The police had *hushed* the matter *up*. ***Ex 5.*** The incident did not remain altogether *hushed up*.

Hype up : publicise something in a wildly exaggerated way. ***Ex 1.*** The movie has been *hyped up* far beyond its worth. ***Ex 2.*** It has been *hyped up* out of all proportion.

---

9 Words Beginning With–I

Identify with : (a) give support to somebody; be associated with something. ***Ex 1.*** I refused to *identify* myself *with* the new political party. ***Ex 2.*** Of the 59 candidates, nearly a third were *identified with* revolutionary groups.

(b) be associated with somebody; give support to somebody. ***Ex.*** She finds it hard to *identify with* the boss.

Idle about/around : do nothing; be inactive; be idle. ***Ex 1.*** Stop *idling about* and help me clean up. ***Ex 2.*** I cannot have you *idling around* the house all afternoon.

Idle away : waste time. ***Ex 1.*** He *idles away* his time watching TV. ***Ex 2.*** Five old men are *idling away* the summer afternoon under the trees.

Impact on/upon : strong impression or effect on somebody/something. ***Ex 1.*** Her speech made a tremendous *impact on* everyone.

Impose on/upon : obtain a favour from somebody by using undue pressure. ***Ex 1.*** I hope it is not *imposing on* your hospitality, but could I stay to dinner? ***Ex 2.*** Relatives have *imposed* enormously *on* me lately.

Impress on/upon : (a) fix something in somebody's mind. ***Ex.*** Her words *impressed* themselves *on* my memory.

(b) make somebody keenly aware of something. ***Ex 1.*** *Impressed on* my office staff the importance of accurate records. ***Ex 2.*** You should *impress on* your children the virtue of always speaking the truth.

Improve up/upon : achieve or produce something of a better standard or quality than something else. ***Ex 1.*** The girl *improved on* her previous performance by swimming the distance in less than a minute. ***Ex 2.*** This achievement has never been *improved on*. ***Ex 3.*** He *improved on* his previous best performance in the 100 metres.

Inch forward, through, etc. : move slowly and carefully in the specified direction. ***Ex 1.*** He *inched* his way *through* the narrow passage. ***Ex 2.*** I *inched* the car *forward through* the dense fog.

Inform against/on : betray somebody to one's enemies, the police, etc. ***Ex 1.*** The Revolutionary Party deals ruthlessly with anyone who *informs against* one of its members. ***Ex 2.*** One of the criminals *informed on* the rest of the gang.

Inject into : change the tone of; introduce (new thoughts, feelings, etc.) into somebody/something. ***Ex 1.*** They *injected* a few new ideas *into* the project. ***Ex 2.*** Try to *inject* a bit of gusto *into* your performance.

Inquire after : ask about somebody's health or welfare. ***Ex 1.*** Several persons called to *inquire after* the baby. ***Ex 2.*** She *inquired after* my health. ***Ex 3.*** It is reassuring to be *inquired after* when you are ill.

Inquire into : try to learn the facts about something; investigate something. ***Ex 1.*** We must *inquire* further *into* the matter. ***Ex 2.*** The police are thoroughly *inquiring into* the case.

Interfere with : assault somebody sexually. ***Ex.*** The police reported that the murdered child had not been *interfered with.*

Introduce into : push something thin or fine into. ***Ex.*** A thin, hollow needle was carefully *introduced into* the patient's abdomen, and some fluid was drawn off.

Iron out : resolve something by discussion. ***Ex 1.*** He expects to *iron out* these difficulties at a special conference next week. ***Ex 2.*** They are experts at *ironing out* the problems that arise at international gatherings. ***Ex 3.*** There are no difficulties that cannot be *ironed out* if both parties are determined to reach an agreement.

Itch for : feel a strong restless desire for something. ***Ex 1.*** Pupils are *itching for* the lesson to end. ***Ex 2.*** Those two groups of boys are *itching for* a fight. ***Ex 3.*** He stood by the window, *itching for* the arrival of the postman and, he hoped, a reply to his proposal of marriage.

---

10 *Words Beginning With– J*

Jab into : force something into somebody/something. ***Ex.*** She *jabbed* her elbow *into* my side.

Jab out : force or push something out by jabbing. ***Ex 1.*** Be careful with that umbrella-you nearly *jabbed* my eye *out*. ***Ex 2.*** Don't wave that stick about. You will *jab out* somebody's eye. ***Ex 3.*** If you get a thorn stuck in your finger, don't try to *jab* it *out*. ***Ex 4.*** He *jabbed* the beetle *out* with a stick.

Jabber away : talk rapidly and indistinctly; talk repetitious nonsense. ***Ex 1.*** I am tired of these politicians *jabbering away* about matters of which they have no knowledge. ***Ex 2.*** What are those children *jabbering away*.

Jabber out : jabber aloud; say so rapidly as to reduce to nonsense. ***Ex.*** He *jabbered out* his prayers, to finish them as quickly as possible.

Jack in : leave something readily; abandon work, etc. ***Ex 1.*** I cannot take any more of this night-work. I shall have to *jack* it *in*. ***Ex 2.*** She cannot concentrate any more. She is going to *jack* it *in*.

Jack up : (a) raise; increase salary, payment, etc. ***Ex 1.*** Prices have *jacked up* a lot this year. ***Ex 2.*** My secretary requested me to *jack up* her salary with retrospective effect from the last month.

(b) arrange or organise something that is in disorder. ***Ex.*** Everything is falling apart; the whole system needs *jacking up*.

Jam on : apply (brakes) suddenly and forcibly. ***Ex.*** As soon as I saw the child in the road, I *jammed on* my brakes to prevent an accident.

Jangle on : irritate by making an unpleasant noise. ***Ex 1.*** Your voice *jangles on* my ears. ***Ex 2.*** The sound of that drill *jangles* horribly *on* the nerves.

Jar against/on : strike something with a harsh unpleasant sound. ***Ex.*** The ship *jarred against* the quayside.

Jar on/upon : be unpleasant to; seem discordant to. ***Ex 1.*** Turn the radio off. That music *jars on* my nerves. ***Ex 2.*** Her constant complaining *jars upon* my nerves.

Jar with : clash; be out of harmony; not match. ***Ex 1.*** Everything he said seemed to *jar with* our most firmly held convictions. ***Ex 2.*** His harsh criticism *jarred with* the friendly tone of the meeting. ***Ex 3.*** Your comments on future policy *jarred with* the proceedings of the meeting.

Jazz up : make something more lively; brighten; enliven. ***Ex 1.*** Take every step to *jazz up* the party. ***Ex 2.*** They have *jazzed up* the house.

Jerk out : utter something in an abrupt nervous manner. ***Ex 1.*** His words *jerked out* as he darted breathlessly about. ***Ex 2.*** He *jerked out* a request for monetary aid.

Jet from/ out of : come out in a jet or jets. *Ex.* Flames *jetted out of* nozzles.

Jockey for : manoeuvre to gain; move about pushing others aside in order to improve one's position. ***Ex 1.*** Rival trade unions continuously *jockey for* position. ***Ex 2.*** Don't you *jockey for* status in the society?

Jog along/on : continue in a steady manner, with little or no progress. ***Ex.*** For years the business just kept *jogging along*.

Jolly along : keep somebody in a good/friendly mood; encourage. ***Ex 1.*** You will have to *jolly* him *along* a bit but he will do a good job. ***Ex 2.*** The job will not be finished on time unless you *jolly* the workers *along* with an occasional bonus.

Jolt into/out of : make somebody act by giving him a sudden shock. ***Ex.*** He was *jolted out of* his lethargy and *into* action when he realised that he had only a short time to finish the article.

Jot down : make a quick short written note of something. ***Ex 1.*** I shall just *jot down* her telephone number before I forget it. ***Ex 2.*** Have you *jotted down* the licence number? ***Ex 3.*** *Jot down* the particulars in your notebook. ***Ex 4.*** I *jotted* some notes *down* on a pad.

Jump at : seize an opportunity eagerly; accept with enthusiasm. ***Ex 1.*** Private companies have not exactly *jumped at* the opportunity. ***Ex 2.*** Kavita *jumped at* the offer of a job. ***Ex 3.*** She said she would *jump at* the chance of going abroad.

Jump on : criticise or challenge somebody sharply. ***Ex 1.*** Our Mathematics teacher really used to *jump on* us when we got our answers wrong. ***Ex 2.*** I told her what I had thought of doing, and she just *jumped on* me and said it was ridiculous. ***Ex 3.*** Don't *jump on* a child for making up stories occasionally.

Jut out : (a) stick out so as to be more obvious; be out of line with; stand out from something. ***Ex 1.*** The balcony *juts out* over the garden. ***Ex 2.*** The road climbs to a high point that apparently *juts out* into the river. ***Ex 3.*** The pillar leaned into a steady overhang, *jutting out* at least twenty feet from the wave-washed base. ***Ex 4.*** Let us go to the headland that *juts out* into the sea. ***Ex 5.*** The stem of the ship *juts out* over the water.

(b) thrust forward to show determination; stick. ***Ex 1.*** His chin *juts out* rather a lot. ***Ex 2.*** Her teeth tend to *jut out* a little. ***Ex 3.*** His jaw was *jutting out* dangerously. ***Ex 4.*** Parvati *jutted out* her chin and went out into the street with a little flouncing movement of disdain.

---

11 Words Beginning With–K

Keel over : fall over; collapse, lose one's balance and fall. ***Ex 1.*** After a couple of drinks, he just *keeled over* on the floor. ***Ex 2.*** He suddenly *keeled over* with a heavily loaded tray. ***Ex 3.*** The old man walked into the room unsteadily, *keeled over* and fell unconscious.

Keep after : (a) not abandon the pursuit of. ***Ex.*** The police *kept after* the bandits till they finally trapped them in a cul-de-sac (street open at one end only).

(b) chivvy; continuously urge somebody to do something, often in an annoying way. ***Ex.*** Don't *keep after* the nurses all day long or they will all resign.

Keep ahead of : not lose one's position in front of others. ***Ex.*** If you want to *keep ahead of* your rivals, you will have to work very hard.

Keep at : (a) continue persistently in one's efforts; not abandon. ***Ex 1.*** The only way to get a good book written is to *keep at* it, day after day. ***Ex 2.*** He *kept at* the job till finished.

(b) make somebody work; force somebody to make a prolonged effort. ***Ex.*** Our English professor was a martinet. He *kept* us *at* our work all morning.

Keep away : (a) not go near. ***Ex 1.*** *Keep away* from the players. ***Ex 2.*** You should *keep away* from that woman: her husband is a very jealous and violent man. ***Ex 3.*** The more you *keep away* from the shops, the less money you will spend.

(b) prevent somebody from going near. ***Ex 1.*** *Keep* the children *away* from the river. ***Ex 2.*** It is the job of the police to *keep* the spectators *away* from the players. ***Ex 3.*** Why don't you *keep* your kids *away* from the street cattle? ***Ex 4.*** Her illness *kept* her *away* from work for three weeks.

(c) abstain. ***Ex.*** You should *keep away* from drugs and alcoholic drinks.

Keep back : (a) stay at a distance; prevent from going too close to. ***Ex 1.*** *Keep* well *back* from the road. ***Ex 2.*** The police could not *keep* the people *back* when they reached the barriers. ***Ex 3.*** The magician *kept* well *back* from the front of the stage.

(b) not let somebody know; hold something back; refuse to tell somebody something. ***Ex 1.*** I am sure she is *keeping* something *back* from us. ***Ex 2.*** The government decided to *keep back* the facts concerning the secret negotiations with the neighbouring country. ***Ex 3.*** The news of the army's defeat was *kept back* from the people for several days.

(c) not pay something to somebody. ***Ex.*** We agreed to let our employer *keep back* two per cent from our salary to go into a special fund for welfare purposes.

(d) prevent something from moving; restrain something. ***Ex 1.*** She was unable to *keep back* her tears. ***Ex 2.*** Millions of gallons of water are *kept back* by the dam.

Keep down : (a) not show where one is; not stand up; lie low. ***Ex 1.*** *Keep down*, you must not let anybody see you. ***Ex 2.*** There is somebody coming. *Keep down* and don't make a sound.

(b) repress or oppress somebody; control somebody. ***Ex 1.*** The people have been *kept down* for years by a brutal regime. ***Ex 2.*** The government intends to *keep down* the revolutionaries. ***Ex 3.*** You cannot *keep down* a whole population if they don't want to be *kept down*.

(c) not raise. ***Ex 1.*** *Keep* your head *down* and your eyeballs moving. ***Ex 2.*** Would you please *keep* your voice *down*? ***Ex 3.*** *Keep* your arms *down* and take a deep breath.

(d) prevent from increasing; not increase; hold down. ***Ex 1.*** The government should take prompt and proper steps to *keep* the cost of living *down*. ***Ex 2.*** You should manage to *keep down* your spending.

(e) restrain; control. ***Ex.*** You should try to *keep* your anger *down*.

(f) not allow something to multiply or grow. ***Ex 1.*** Use chemicals to *keep* pests *down*. ***Ex 2.*** There is no absolutely fool-proof way of *keeping* the flies *down* during the summer.

(g) retain something in the stomach. ***Ex 1.*** The medicine was so horrid that I could not *keep* it *down*. ***Ex 2.*** I cannot *keep* these powders *down* at all.

Keep from : (a) prevent from doing something. ***Ex 1.*** You should *keep from* doing anything rash. ***Ex 2.*** The temple bells *keep* him *from* sleeping. ***Ex 3.*** I hope I am not *keeping* you *from* work.

(b) avoid. ***Ex 1.*** *Keep* the children *from* swimming in the river. ***Ex 2.*** While you are recuperating from influenza, you should *keep from* getting wet or going back to work too soon.

(c) not let somebody know; *keep* back *from*; not tell, somebody. ***Ex 1.*** Manage to *keep* the news of his imprisonment *from* his parents. ***Ex 2.*** They don't *keep* anything *from* each other. ***Ex 3.*** I think we ought to *keep* the truth *from* him until he is better.

(d) prevent oneself from doing something; stop oneself doing something. ***Ex 1.*** She could hardly *keep* herself *from* laughing. ***Ex 2.*** I just-managed to *keep* myself *from* falling.

Keep in : (a) detain after normal school hours as a punishment. ***Ex.*** She was *kept in* at school for an hour for talking in class.

(b) restrain something; not express; not give vent to. ***Ex 1.*** He could scarcely *keep in* his indignation. ***Ex 2.*** Try to *keep* your emotions *in*. ***Ex 3.*** The policeman was provoked by the hostile crowd but he managed to *keep* his anger *in*, and dealt with the situation coolly and competently.

(c) maintain in a state of. ***Ex 1.*** The ballerina (female ballet dancer) took pride in the fact that she *kept* her mother and sister *in* luxury. ***Ex 2.*** Will you be able to *keep* your newly married tasty wife *in* the style to which she is accustomed ?

(d) give, allow, somebody a regular supply of. ***Ex 1.*** He won first prize in a lottery-enough to *keep* him *in* luxury for a year. ***Ex 2.*** Such jobs as he had from time to time barely *kept* him *in* existence. ***Ex 3.*** She earns enough to *keep* herself and all the family *in* good clothes.

(e) continue to be friendly with somebody, in order to gain some advantage. ***Ex.*** Have you noticed how she tried to *keep in* with the managing director?

Keep in with : remain in good terms with somebody, either to gain some advantage from him or to avoid being victimized by him. ***Ex 1.*** We shall have to *keep in with* him, in case we cannot ever pay the rent. ***Ex 2.*** In war time, people who before were always ready to accuse the butcher of giving short weight went to great lengths to *keep in with* him.

Keep off : (a) not begin. ***Ex 1.*** The fete will go ahead provided the rain *keeps off*. ***Ex 2.*** The thick clouds passed overhead, but fortunately the rain *kept off* the whole day. ***Ex 3.*** The thunderstorm, which had been brewing all evening, *kept off* until we were safely indoors.

(b) stay at a distance from; not walk on. ***Ex 1.*** *Keep off* the grass. ***Ex 2.*** Two large signs, with the words *Keep off* painted on them, had been attached to the sides of the boat.

(c) cause to stay at a distance. ***Ex 1.*** *Keep* those blasted squatters *off* my land. ***Ex 2.*** How can I *keep* the flies *off* this jam? ***Ex 3.*** One of the problems faced by the road-builders was how to *keep off* the fierce people whose land they were crossing. ***Ex 4.*** They lit a fire to *keep* wild animals *off*. ***Ex 5.*** *Keep* the dog *off* her.

(d) not eat or drink; prevent from eating, drinking or drug-taking. ***Ex 1.*** The only way to get your weight down is to *keep off* fattening foods, and cut out alcohol altogether. ***Ex 2.*** The doctor advised the woman to be *kept off* a solid food for at least two days. ***Ex 3.*** You can drink skimmed milk, but you have to *keep off* butter.

(e) avoid; not talk about. ***Ex 1.*** Please *keep off* the *subject* of politics while my father-in-law is here. ***Ex 2.*** He *kept off* the question of whose fault it was. ***Ex 3.*** By mutual consent, the negotiators *kept off* the religious issue, and concentrated on economic and political differences.

Keep on : (a) continue one's journey. ***Ex 1.*** *Keep on* past the Birla Temple; the stadium is about half a kilometre further on. ***Ex 2.*** The soldiers *kept on* towards their objective.

(b) continue doing something. ***Ex 1,*** The rain *kept on* all night. ***Ex 2.*** She *kept on* staring at me.

(c) continue to employ somebody. ***Ex 1.*** I intend to *keep* these men *on* at the factory. ***Ex 2.*** Only half the workforce will be *kept on* after this order has been completed. ***Ex 3.*** She is incompetent and not worth *keeping on*.

(d) continue to wear something. ***Ex 1.*** You do not need to *keep* your cap *on* indoors. ***Ex 2.*** Don't *keep* your socks *on* if they get wet.

(e) continue to rent or be the owner of. ***Ex.*** We are planning to *keep* the cottage *on* over the summer.

(f) continue talking in an irritating way. ***Ex.*** I shall mend the lamp just don't *keep on* at me about it.

Keep on at : (a) worry, pester, harrass with suggestions, requests, complaints. ***Ex 1.*** The children *kept on at* their mother to take them to the fair. ***Ex 2.*** Don't *keep on at* me about Sanjay getting a scooter for his birthday.

(b) not remove from; continue to employ. ***Ex.*** I am thinking of *keeping* my pupils *on at* school until they have taken their half-yearly examinations.

Keep out/out of : remain outside. ***Ex 1.*** There was a notice outside the gate bearing the words Ministry of Defence—Danger—*Keep Out*. ***Ex 2.*** We have tried everything to *keep* the moles *out of* the garden, but without success.

Keep out of : (a) avoid something; not expose oneself/somebody to. ***Ex 1.*** That child seems incapable of *keeping out of* mischief. ***Ex 2.*** *Keep out of* what does not concern you. ***Ex 3.*** *Keep* the children *out of* harm's way if you take them to the match.

(b) prevent somebody/something from entering a place. ***Ex 1.*** Mohini wore a hat to *keep* the sun *out of* her eyes. ***Ex 2.*** *Keep* that dog *out of* my study. ,

Keep to : (a) adhere to; follow: observe. ***Ex 1.*** The success of our enterprise depended on everyone *keeping* faithfully *to* the plan. ***Ex 2.*** Try to ensure that this time-table is strictly *kept to*.

(b) remain in; not leave. ***Ex 1.*** He was obliged to *keep to* his bed because of a fever. ***Ex 2.*** During the winter, a lot of people are forced to *keep to* the house, the weather being so cold and treacherous. ***Ex 3.*** He is old and infirm, and has to *keep to* the house.

(c) not wander from or leave (a path, road, etc.) ***Ex 1.*** *Keep to* the track—the moor is very boggy around here. ***Ex 2.*** If you would *keep to* the point, Miss Maya, we should all be very grateful to you.

(d) not express (a view, comment, etc.) *Keep* your opinions *to* yourself in future.

(e) avoid meeting people socially; not concern oneself with other people's affairs. ***Ex.*** Nobody knows much about him; he *keeps* himself very much *to* himself.

(f) not tell other people about something. ***Ex.*** I entreat you to *keep* this information *to* yourself.

Keep under : (a) maintain in a state of unconsciousness or strong sedation. ***Ex 1.*** Her pain was so intense that she was *kept under* by means of regular injections of morphine. ***Ex 2.*** He was *kept under* with a mixture of morphine and chloroform.

(b) suppress somebody; maintain control over somebody; hold under. ***Ex 1.*** The army managed to *keep* the population of the occupied country *under* for a few months, and then trouble began to break out. ***Ex 2.*** The local population is *kept under* by a brutal army of mercenaries.

(c) control or suppress something. ***Ex 1.*** Firemen managed to *keep* the fire *under*. ***Ex 2.*** The local volunteers managed to *keep* the outbreak of fire *under* and prevented it reaching a nearby petrol-station.

(d) keep observing; maintain a constant watch, etc. over. ***Ex.*** The plain-clothes officers were told to *keep* the suspected man *under* constant observation.

Keep up : (a) continue unabated; continue without stopping. ***Ex 1.*** Let us hope the sunny weather *keeps up* for Friday's tennis match. ***Ex 2.*** If this rain *keeps up*, all the crops will be ruined. ***Ex 3.*** The hurricane *kept up* for several days and left a swathe of destruction across the country.

(b) prevent from falling or sinking; not fall or sink; ***Ex 1.*** You should wear a belt to *keep* your trousers *up*. ***Ex 2.*** The children use waterwings to *keep* themselves *up* in the water whilst they are learning to swim.

(c) remain, maintain, at a high level. ***Ex 1.*** In spite of strikes, the national output managed to *keep up*. ***Ex 2.*** So long as the cost of raw materials *keep up*, prices of consumer goods will *keep up*, too.

(d) maintain; not allow to decline. ***Ex 1.*** They sang songs to *keep* their morale *up*. ***Ex 2.*** The troops, spirits were *kept up* by the occasional visit of well-known entertainers to their camps. ***Ex 3.*** I tried to *keep* my courage *up* by telling myself that the war would be over within a few weeks and then I could return to my family.

(e) maintain by expenditure of money and energy. ***Ex 1.*** He cannot afford to *keep up* a house in the city. ***Ex 2.*** The house is becoming too expensive for me to *keep up*.

(f) continue at a high level of intensity. ***Ex 1.*** The enemy *kept up* bombardment day and night. ***Ex 2.*** Ten persons crowded the narrow street and *kept up* an endless flow of sharp little fragments of repartee. ***Ex 3.*** The air force bomber command ordered that attacks on the industrial centres of the enemy country be *kept up* relentlessly. ***Ex 4.*** You are all doing a splendid job; *keep up* the good work.

(g) maintain, continue, produce with regularity. ***Ex.*** I can no longer *keep up* my annual subscription to the golf club, so I am tendering my resignation.

(h) continue to practise or observe something. ***Ex 1.*** Do you still *keep up* your French? ***Ex 2.*** We must *keep up* old traditions.

(i) prevent somebody from going to bed. ***Ex 1.*** I do hope we are not *keeping* you *up*. ***Ex 2.*** Don't *keep* her *up*. ***Ex 3.*** Don't *keep* your guests *up* talking until the wee hours.

Keep up with : (a) move or progress at the same rate as somebody/something. ***Ex 1.*** Show down—I cannot *keep up with* you. ***Ex 2.*** I cannot keep with all the changes in computer technology. ***Ex 3.*** Don't walk so fast. Your legs are longer than mine and I cannot *keep up with* you. ***Ex 4.*** He finds it difficult to *keep up with* the rest of the class in chemistry.

(b) rise or progress at the same rate as. ***Ex.*** The government has decided to ensure that old age pensions *keep up with* the ever-increasing cost of living.

(c) maintain the same social and material standards as. ***Ex 1.*** There is no gainsaying the fact that most people, in this competitive society, think that they must *keep up with* their neighbours. ***Ex 2.*** My salary is only about half of her husband's, and we just cannot *keep up with* them.

(d) learn about current events, etc. ***Ex 1.*** Sumitra is one of those intelligent and industrious young women who always *keep up with* the latest fashions. ***Ex 2.*** There is so much going on in the Bombay theatrical world that I just cannot find time to *keep up with* them.

(e) maintain contact with, through visits, correspondence, etc. ***Ex 1.*** For some years after his retirement, he *kept up with* a number of old colleagues, but as time went by he dropped them one by one. ***Ex 2.*** How many of your old school friends do you *keep up with*? ***Ex 3.*** We have *kept up with* each other ever since we left school.

Key to : (a) make something similar to something else. ***Ex.*** Mridula *keyed* her mood *to* that of the other guests.

(b) make something suitable for something else. ***Ex.*** The farm was asked to *key to* the needs of the local people.

Key up : make somebody excited, nervous or tense. ***Ex 1.*** The manager warned us not to get too *keyed up* before the big match. ***Ex 2.*** His anger surprised him, he was more *keyed up* than he had anticipated.

Keyed up : extremely tense. ***Ex.*** When his girlfriend left the house this morning, he was all *keyed up*. The examination had been on her mind for weeks.

Kick against : protest about, or resist, something; defy something; ***Ex 1.*** Don't *kick against* your transfer. ***Ex 2.*** It is no use *kicking against* the rules; you will be sufferer in the end. ***Ex 3.*** Don't *kick against* fate. What will be, will be.

Kick around : be present, alive or in existence. ***Ex 1.*** Some boys were *kicking around*, not doing anything much. ***Ex 2.*** I have been *kicking around* Asia since I saw you last. ***Ex 3.*** My Shirt is *kicking around* on the floor somewhere. ***Ex 4.*** This is our idea which has been *kicking around* for some considerable time.

Kick around/round : discuss informally. ***Ex.*** We shall *kick* some ideas *around* make a decision tomorrow.

Kick back at : kick somebody in retaliation; counter-attack. ***Ex.*** We ought to *kick back at* all these unfair allegations of corruption in our organisation.

Note : The word *kick back* is a noun. It denotes a bribe paid to a representative of a government or firm to encourage him to place an order; money paid to somebody who has helped one to make a profit, often illegally. ***Ex 1.*** People say that every job has its *kick backs*. ***Ex 2.*** He has systematically taken *kick backs* from the hiring agencies he works through.

Kick downstairs : (a) push somebody downstairs, with a kick. ***Ex.*** The irate husband seized his wife's lover and *kicked* him *downstairs*.

(b) demote. ***Ex.*** He was *kicked downstairs* to a job in the despatch section.

Kick in : break something inwards by kicking a damage. ***Ex 1.*** As the door was locked and I heard someone screaming for help, I *kicked* it *in* and rushed into the house. ***Ex 2.*** She *kicked* his teeth *in*.

Kick off : (a) start a football match by kicking the ball. ***Ex.*** Mohan Bagan *kicked off* and scored almost immediately.

(b) start. ***Ex 1.*** The party *kicked off* in great style. ***Ex 2.*** The match is due to *kick off* at 2.30.

(c) remove with a kick. ***Ex.*** He *kicked* his slippers *off* and dropped on to bed.

(d) begin (a meeting, etc.) ***Ex.*** I shall ask Madhu Rani to *kick off* the discussion.

Kick out/out of : expel somebody or send him away by force. ***Ex 1.*** We *kicked* him *out of* the club for fighting. ***Ex 2.*** A group of directors tried to *kick* the young tycoon *out of* his position as chairman, but he turned the tables on them.

Kick up : create; produce. ***Ex 1.*** The boys *kicked up* a terrible fuss. ***Ex 2.*** The prisoners, at a pre-arranged signal, began to *kick up* a hell of a row with the aim of attracting the attention of people passing the prison.

Kick upstairs : promote to a position carrying greater prestige or financial reward, but which, often carries less power. ***Ex.*** The only way for us to get rid of Mr. Bhagwan Bahadur is to *kick* him *upstairs*; then we shall be able to appoint Miss Madhuri, and get some life into the business.

Kid on : tease; tell somebody/something in just but with a serious expression on one's face. ***Ex 1.*** Don't *kid* us all *on*. ***Ex 2.*** Why did you *kid* her *on*?

Kill off : destroy or get rid of somebody/something. ***Ex 1.*** He *killed off* all his political opponents. ***Ex 2.*** A late frost *killed off* nearly all the apple-blossom, with the result that we had a very poor crop this year. ***Ex 3.*** The author *kills off* her hero in Chapter 8.

Kindle with : become bright; shine or glow. ***Ex.*** As the young lady; who is slim, tall and attractive, read her lover's lengthy letter, the colour came to her cheeks and her eyes *kindled with* excitement.

Kip down : lie down and go to sleep. ***Ex 1.*** We all piled out of the hot coach and *kipped down* for a couple of hours in the shade of some trees at the side of the road. ***Ex 2.*** He *kipped down* on the floor.

Kip out : sleep in the open air; ***Ex 1.*** Every night during the summer thousands of young people *kip out* on the beaches. ***Ex 2.*** These homeless people *kip out* on footpaths, open grounds, etc.

Kiss away : remove as a result of kissing; sympathise with somebody, ***Ex 1.*** She *kissed* my tears *away*. ***Ex 2.*** His wife helped him off with his coat and tried to *kiss* the anxiety *away*.

Knock about : (a) move; travel; lead an unsettled life. ***Ex 1.*** When he was a child, he used to *knock about* the market, trying to find a little work to earn a living. ***Ex 2.*** My elder son is *knocking about* the continent for several months. ***Ex 3.*** He spent a few years *knocking about* in Europe.

(b) beat; treat in a brutal manner. ***Ex 1.*** She gets *knocked about* by her husband. ***Ex 2.*** She tried to conceal her damaged eye behind dark glasses, but it was obvious to everyone in the office that her husband had been *knocking* her *about* again.

Knock about with : keep the company of. ***Ex 1.*** You ought to be more careful whom you are seen *knocking about with*. ***Ex 2.*** It is amazing that she is still *knocking about with* that good-for nothing follow. What on earth does she see in him ?

Knock back : (a) drink something quickly. ***Ex.*** He *knocked back* four glasses of water.

(b) cost. ***Ex.*** How much did your wife's new blouse *knock* you *back*?

Knock down : (a) strike somebody to the ground. He was *knocked down* by a bus.

(b) demolish something. ***Ex.*** These dilapidated houses are going to be *knocked down* soon.

(c) cause to fall. ***Ex.*** I *knocked down* my opponent three times in the first round.

(d) cause to reduce. ***Ex.*** I managed to *knock* his price *down* from ₹ 5680 to ₹ 5000.

(e) set something to a bidder. ***Ex.*** The painting was *knocked down* to an American dealer for ₹ 1256870.

Knock in/into : knock in/into by means of a hammer. ***Ex.*** The child tried hard, but could not *knock* the nail *in*.

Knock off : (a) stop doing something. ***Ex 1.*** What time do you *knock off* work in the office? ***Ex 2.*** Why don't you *knock off* that tedious job?

(b) reduce the price of. ***Ex 1.*** The greengrocer always *knocked* a little *off* the price of his fruit for the old age pensioners. ***Ex 2.*** The salesgirl *knocked* twenty ruppes *off* because the article was shop-soiled.

(c) write or compose rapidly or easily. ***Ex 1.*** He seemed to be able to *knock off* a limerick with the greatest of ease in a few minutes. ***Ex 2.*** This script shows every sign of having been *knocked off* in great haste. ***Ex 3.*** I *knocked off* two whole chapters in an hour.

(d) steal something. ***Ex 1.*** Thieves *knocked off* some watches from his shop. ***Ex 2.*** Dacoits *knocked off* a bank yesterday.

(e) remove something by striking it. ***Ex.*** I *knocked* her glass *off* the table.

(f) murder somebody. ***Ex.*** He had one of his elderly relatives *knocked off*, so that he could inherit the fortune.

Knock out : (a) make somebody unconscious by means of a blow, alcoholic drink, etc. ***Ex 1.*** Don't drink too much of this—it will *knock* you *out*. ***Ex 2.*** I *knocked* my inexperienced opponent *out* in the first round of the contest. ***Ex 3.*** The driver of the car was *knocked out* at the moment of impact.

(b) overwhelm or astonish somebody; render speechless. ***Ex 1.*** The film just *knocked* me *out*—it is the best thing I have ever seen. ***Ex 2.*** For a moment I was completely *knocked out* by the news of the sad and sudden demise of one of my fast friends. ***Ex 3.*** The letter informing the manager that his services would no longer be required *knocked* him right *out*.

Knock out/out of : remove by a blow/blows. ***Ex 1.*** Two of the child's teeth were *knocked out* in the accident. ***Ex 2.*** *Knock* the powder *out* of the tin gently.

Knock over : upset somebody/something by striking. ***Ex 1.*** He managed to *knock over* the box. ***Ex 2.*** He got *knocked over* by a car when he was six.

Knock together : make or complete something quickly and often not very well. ***Ex 1.*** He *knocked* bookshelves *together* from old planks. ***Ex 2.*** They *knocked* a few scenes *together* to make a play. ***Ex 3.*** The hut looked as if it had been *knocked together* by someone in a great hurry.

Knock up : (a) awaken somebody by knocking on his door, etc. ***Ex.*** Would you please *knock* me *up* at 7 o'clock tomorrow?

(b) prepare or make something quickly and without much planning. ***Ex 1.*** Even though they were not expecting us, they managed to *knock up* a marvellous meal. ***Ex 2.*** His mother was a marvel at *knocking up* a meal for an unexpected guest.

(c) drive or hit upwards with a blow. ***Ex.*** As the intruder rushed at me with a knife, I *knocked* his arm *up*, and hit him in the stomach with the poker.

(d) make tired, exhausted or ill. ***Ex.*** Please don't try to dig up the whole garden in one day: you will *knock* yourself *up*.

(e) score. ***Ex.*** The batsman *knocked up* over a hundred runs.

(f) make a woman pregnant. ***Ex.*** Why ever did she let him *knock* her *up*.

Know about : have knowledge of something; be aware of something. ***Ex 1.*** Not much is *known about* her background. ***Ex 2.*** Do you *know about* Rahim getting arrested? ***Ex 3.*** Did you *know about* your son's shocking behaviour at the meeting last afternoon?

Know from : be able to distinguish, separate or recognise the difference between. ***Ex.*** The nurse never seems to *know* one patient *from* another.

Know of : have information about or experience of somebody/something. ***Ex 1.*** Do you *know of* any way to stop a person snoring? ***Ex 2.*** I don't know her personally, though I *know of* her. ***Ex 3.*** There is only one way that I *know of* to pass examinations, and that is to work hard and be fully prepared. ***Ex 4.*** Do you by any chance *know of* a short cut to the Parliament House? ***Ex 5.*** I *know of* him, but I have never met him.

Knuckle down : begin to work seriously at something. ***Ex 1.*** *Knuckle down* and get the work done as required, ***Ex 2.*** If you want to pass that examination, you will have to *knuckle down* to some hard work.

Knuckle under : surrender; accept or admit defeat. ***Ex 1.*** As he refused to *knuckle under*, he was asked to leave. ***Ex 2.*** In spite of every argument, the recalcitrant students refused to *knuckle under*, and continued their occupation of the Vice-Chancellor's room.

Kowtow to : be submissive, humble or respectable to somebody/something. ***Ex 1.*** We refused to *kowtow to* the government's wishes on this issue. ***Ex 2.*** It is said that the poor *kowtow to* the rich. ***Ex 3.*** Don't *kowtow to* those people who are cruel, rude, dishonest, proud or untrustworthy.

---

12 Words Beginning With–L

Labour along : move along with effort. ***Ex 1.*** The damaged car was *labouring along*. ***Ex 2.*** He *laboured along*, groaning in pain.

Labour over : work hard and continuously at some difficult task; toil over. ***Ex 1.*** The editor *laboured over* the manuscript till early morning. ***Ex 2.*** Some kinds of writing are all the better for being *laboured over*.

Labour under : (a) have as a disadvantage or handicap. ***Ex 1.*** The new government removed many of the injustices *under* which the population had *laboured*. ***Ex 2.*** People are *labouring under* the handicaps of ignorance, penury and superstition.

(b) be misled or blinded by; be deceived by. ***Ex 1.*** Our political opponents *labour under* the delusion that support for our policies is dwindling. ***Ex 2.*** He *labours under* the illusion that he is a famous novelist.

Lace into : attack somebody physically or with words. ***Ex 1.*** She *laced into* him with a big stick. ***Ex 2.*** Don't *lace into* her with sarcastic remarks.

Ladle out : distribute something too lavishly. ***Ex 1.*** He likes to *ladle out* advice to one and all. ***Ex 2.*** He is not one to *ladle out* praise, so when he says 'Good,' he means it.

Lam into : thrash; hit somebody/something hard. ***Ex 1.*** What did the poor man say that made you *lam into* him like that? ***Ex 2.*** In the last round, the Indian boxer *lammed into* his opponent. ***Ex 3.*** Mother *lammed into* me for damaging her car. ***Ex 4.*** She *lammed into* me about the mistake I had made.

Land in : get somebody/oneself into difficulties, etc. ***Ex 1.*** Just look at the mess you have *landed* us *in*. ***Ex 2.*** Next year, I shall *land* you *in* gaol.

Land up : reach a final position or situation. ***Ex 1.*** His cap flew off in a strong wind and *landed up* in ther river. ***Ex 2.*** You will *land up* in prison, if you continue to act in this way. ***Ex 3.*** After knocking about the world for a couple of years, Lalita Devi *landed up* teaching Sanskrit in her home city.

Land with : oblige somebody to accept a burden or task. ***Ex 1.*** I have been *landed with* an extra set of B.A. English papers to mark. ***Ex 2.*** I have *landed* him *with* the job of fixing hotel rooms for the visitors. ***Ex 3.*** I found myself *landed with* four extra guests for dinner. ***Ex 4.*** Don't try and *land* me *with* your responsibilities.

Lap up : receive (praise, news, etc.) greedily or eagerly. ***Ex 1.*** He will take all the instruction you can give him-he just *laps* it *up*. ***Ex 2.*** She just *laps up* flattery. ***Ex 3.*** They *lapped up* the special treatment given them. ***Ex 4.*** I tell her all those lies and she just *laps* them *up*.

Lard with : add something pompous, flowery, etc. to one's words; embelish a speech or writing with something. ***Ex 1.*** He delivered a 168 Phrasal Verbs 169 lengthy lecture *larded with* obscure quotations. ***Ex 2.*** She *larded* her remarks *with* references to her importance in local affairs. ***Ex 3.*** His language was richly *larded with* oaths.

Lark about/around : behave playfully or irresponsively. ***Ex 1.*** Don't *lark about*: do some work. ***Ex 2.*** Why are you *larking around* here? ***Ex 3.*** Many a boy was *larking about* on the street corner.

Lash out : (a) make a sudden or violent attack, physically or verbally. ***Ex 1.*** The horse *lashed out* with its back legs at the passer-by. ***Ex 2.*** I was going to *lash out* at her, but I controlled myself. ***Ex 3.*** The opposition members *lashed out* at the government's economic policies. ***Ex 4.*** He is a politician in the making. He is fond of *lashing out* at his opponents.

(b) spend money freely or lavishly on something. ***Ex 1.*** Your father has really *lashed out* on your education. ***Ex 2.*** He *lashed out* on exquisite presents for his girlfriend. ***Ex 3.*** Why do you *lash out* on drinks and drugs which are so much injurious to health? Can't you put an end to it for ever?

Latch on : (a) understand an idea, etc. ***Ex 1.*** He is a bit slow but in the end he *latches on*. ***Ex 2.*** I have not really *latched on* to what you mean—could you explain it again? ***Ex 3.*** He has not *latched on* to what we are doing.

(b) become somebody's constant (and often unwelcome) companion; get into somebody's company. ***Ex 1.*** He always *latches on* to me when he sees me at a party. ***Ex 2.*** When a man is rejected, he may for a time *latch on* to some less attractive girl.

Latch on to : acquire. ***Ex.*** She has *latched on to* some very valuable pieces of property.

Laugh at : (a) show amusement at somebody/something. ***Ex 1.*** He *laughed at* the way the clowns kept falling over their big feet. ***Ex 2.*** The children *laughed at* the comedian. ***Ex 3.*** Did you *laugh at* her joke?

(b) mock or ridicule somebody/something; make fun of. ***Ex 1.*** Thoughtless children sometimes *laugh at* beggars and tramps. ***Ex 2.*** We all *laughed at* her when she said she believed in ghosts.

(c) disregard somebody/something; treat somebody/something; with indifference; scorn; dismiss as unimportant. ***Ex 1.*** He *laughs at* the difficulties-they just spur him on to further effort. ***Ex 2.*** Her mother's pleas to be careful were just *laughed at*. ***Ex 3.*** They *laughed at* your idea.

Laugh away : dispel, dismiss or drive away; by laughing, some unpleasant feeling or sensation in oneself or others. ***Ex 1.*** He *laughed away* the dangers. ***Ex 2.*** He tried without success to *laugh* her fears *away*. ***Ex 3.*** Can you *laugh* your toothache *away*?

Laugh down : reject or silence somebody/something by laughing scornfully. ***Ex 1.*** The audience *laughed* the speaker *down.* ***Ex 2.*** She *laughed down* my proposal.

Laugh off : try, by laughing, to pretend that something for which one is responsible has not happened or does not exist; show that one does not care about something. ***Ex 1.*** This is a mistake that cannot easily be *laughed off.* ***Ex 2.*** Your bungling has set the project back a month. It is a shame that now you are trying to *laugh* that *off.* ***Ex 3.*** An author has to learn to *laugh off* bad reviews.

Laugh out of : cause somebody to forget his problems, unhappiness, etc. by making him laugh. ***Ex.*** As she was in a bad mood, I tried to *laugh* her *out of* it.

Launch into : begin a long and involved speech, etc. often in a vigorous or violent way. ***Ex 1.*** He *launched into* a long series of excuses for his behaviour. ***Ex 2.*** She *launched into* another of her stories. ***Ex 3.*** Don't *launch into* a long and circumstantial narrative.

Launch out : (a) attack somebody physically or verbally. ***Ex.*** She suddenly *launched out* at me for no reason at all.

(b) start vigorously. ***Ex 1.*** Prem Lata wants to be more than just a singer and is *launching out* into films. ***Ex 2.*** He has *launched out* into a new line of business.

Lavish on/upon : give something to somebody/something abundantly and generously. ***Ex.*** He has only one child. He *lavishes* affection and care *on* her.

Lay about : (a) hit out in all directions. ***Ex.*** As we approached him, he *laid about* him with a big and thick stick.

(b) attack somebody/something with words or blows. ***Ex.*** She *laid about* him, calling him a liar and a cheat.

Note : The word *lay about* is a noun. It denotes somebody who habitually avoids work. ***Ex.*** He is a wretched, idle *lay about.* Don't make friends with him.

Lay aside : (a) put down or place something to one side. ***Ex 1.*** Hem Lata *laid aside* her knitting to rest her eyes for a moment. ***Ex 2.*** I *laid* my book *aside,* turned off the light and went to sleep.

(b) give up; abandon something. ***Ex 1.*** Now that your sons are growing up, certain of your responsibilities can be safely *laid aside.* ***Ex 2.*** Don't *lay aside* your studies.

(c) save something; keep something for future use. ***Ex 1.*** You should *lay* some money *aside* for your old age. ***Ex 2.*** You must *lay* something *aside* for your daughter's education. ***Ex 3.*** We have a little money *laid aside* for emergencies.

Lay before : present something to an official body for discussion, passing into law, etc. ***Ex 1.*** Here is a draft of the legislation the Law Minister intends to *lay before* Parliament. ***Ex 2.*** His proposals were *laid before* a select committee of members of Lok Sabha.

Lay down : (a) prescribe; indicate; give something as a rule, principle, etc. ***Ex 1.*** We had to *lay down* the general direction in which the answer lay. ***Ex 2.*** Follow the procedure *laid down* in our booklet. ***Ex 3.*** You cannot *lay down* hard and fast rules in this regard.

(b) build. ***Ex.*** Who will *lay down* the new-type tankers?

(c) resign; give up; cease to perform something. ***Ex 1.*** The old man has *laid down* his office, to make way for a younger man. ***Ex 2.*** Don't *lay down* your duties.

Lay in : stock up; provide oneself with a stock of something. ***Ex 1.*** You should *lay in* provisions against a shortage. ***Ex 2.*** We *laid in* a good supply of coal in the summer, when prices were low. ***Ex 3.*** She has *laid in* plenty of water and food.

Lay into : attack somebody violently or verbally. ***Ex 1.*** He really *laid into* her, saying she was arrogant and unfeeling. ***Ex 2.*** He *laid into* a man twice his size. ***Ex 3.*** At the committee meeting, the experts *laid into* each other fiercely.

Lay off : (a) stop doing or using something harmful, etc. ***Ex 1.*** He has smoked cigarettes for years, but now he is going to *lay off* them. ***Ex 2.*** I sincerely advise you to *lay off* drinks and drugs.

(b) stop doing something that annoys, irritates, etc. ***Ex 1.*** *Lay off* him. Can't you see that he is badly hurt. ***Ex 2.*** *Lay off.* You are messing up her hair. ***Ex 3.*** *Lay off* that girl.

(c) dismiss from work, usually for a short time. ***Ex 1.*** Many workers were *laid off* because of the lack of new orders. ***Ex 2.*** The factory has *laid off* fifty persons because of the drop in sales. ***Ex 3.*** The work force has been *laid off.* ***Ex 4.*** He is a skilled worker *laid off* from his job in a Bombay shipyard.

Lay on : (a) supply gas, water, etc. for a house, etc. ***Ex.*** I shall not move in until the electricity has been *laid on.*

(b) arrange something; provide something. ***Ex 1.*** Sightseeing tours are *laid on* for visitors. ***Ex 2.*** It is her birthday. That is why he *laid on* a party. ***Ex 3.*** They *lay on* all essential services.

Lay out : (a) spend money. ***Ex.*** I had to *layout* a big amount on that car.

(b) arrange something in a planned way. ***Ex 1.*** This is a well *laid out* garden. ***Ex 2.*** There is no gainsaying the fact that it is a well *laid out* magazine.

(c) make somebody unconscious; knock out. ***Ex 1.*** The boxer was *laid out* in the fourth round. ***Ex 2.*** If you slap my face-by God, I shall *lay* you *out.*

(d) spread out something ready for use or to be seen easily. ***Ex 1.*** Let us have a look at the beautiful jewellery *laid out* in the shop window. ***Ex 2.*** *Lay out* all the clothes you want to take on holiday. ***Ex 3.*** Tell the servant to *lay out* the clothes that I shall be wearing in the evening.

Lay over : stop at a place on a journey. ***Ex.*** We *laid over* in Hyderabad on the way to Madras.

Lay up : (a) stock; store something; save something. ***Ex 1.*** I have *laid up* large supplies of food. ***Ex 2.*** You will need to *lay up* a good supply of coal, if this winter is going to be like the last.

(b) accumulate. ***Ex.*** He is just *laying up* a lot of trouble for himself.

(c) take off the road, put out of use. ***Ex 1.*** My car is *laid up* at the moment. ***Ex 2.*** He *laid* a lorry *up* for repairs.

(d) cause somebody to stay in bed. ***Ex 1.*** About of malarial fever had *laid* him *up* for many a day. ***Ex 2.*** She is *laid up* with a broken leg.

Laze away : spend time idly. ***Ex 1.*** You cannot go on *lazing* your life *away*. ***Ex 2.*** He *lazed away* the whole afternoon.

Lead in : introduce; open one's remarks, speech, performance, etc. ***Ex.*** The chairman *led in* with some flattering references to the visiting speaker's record in the steel industry.

Note : The word *lead-in* is a noun used in the sense of *introduction to a subject, etc.* ***Ex.*** He told an amusing story as a *lead-in* to the serious part of his speech.

Lead off : start something. ***Ex 1.*** The chief editor of the Arnrit Bazar Patrika, Calcutta, *led off* with a general survey of the objectives to be aimed at. ***Ex 2.*** The singer *led off* with a popular ballad. ***Ex 3.*** The band *led off* by playing the National Anthem.

Lead on : persuade somebody to do, believe, etc. something by making false promises or claims. ***Ex 1.*** Travel brochures do *lead* you *on* with their promises of five-star treatment in luxury hotels. ***Ex 2.*** The salesman tried to *lead* me *on* with talk of amazing savings on heating , bills.

Lead up to : occur, one after the other, before something; prepare, have as a sequence; prepare, introduce or go before something. ***Ex 1.*** I lucidly narrated the events *leading up to* the outbreak of the war. ***Ex 2.*** The report describes the negotiations which *led up to* the settlement.

Leaf through : glance through something; turn over the pages of a book, etc. quickly; read in a brief, inattentive way. ***Ex 1.*** I cannot claim that I have read the article at all carefully : I have just *leafed through* it. ***Ex 2.*** Sneh Lata *leafed* idly *through* some old magazines as she waited for her taxi to arrive.

League together : form a league. ***Ex.*** We must *league together* against this threat.

Leak out : become known, despite efforts to keep it secret. ***Ex 1.*** The details relating to the military pact were supposed to be secret but somehow *leaked out*. ***Ex 2.*** The news about the details of her marriage *leaked out*.

Lean on : make somebody act as one wishes by threat or use of force, by blackmail, etc. ***Ex.*** If you don't pay soon, we shall have to *lean on* them a little.

Lean on/upon : depend on somebody/something. ***Ex 1.*** You can safely *lean on* her guidance. ***Ex 2.*** In a crisis, the chairman tends to *lean* overmuch *on* senior members of staff. ***Ex 3.*** You should *lean upon* your mother's advice.

Lean out/out of : bend out; put one's head out. ***Ex.*** Passengers are requested not to *lean out of* the windows.

Lean over : slant, incline, one's head and shoulders. ***Ex 1.*** He *leant over* and whispered something in her ear. ***Ex 2.*** Don't *lean over* me when I am trying to read the paper.

Leapt at : accept something eagerly, without hesitation. ***Ex 1.*** Shushmita *leapt at* the chance to go to America. ***Ex 2.*** The opportunity was laid before him and eagerly *leapt at*.

Learn off : learn by heart; memorise perfectly. ***Ex 1.*** He has *learnt* the poem *off*. ***Ex 2.*** The actor has *learnt off* his lines.

Learn up : learn as thoroughly as possible. ***Ex 1.*** I have *learnt up* as much French as I could for the trip. ***Ex 2.*** They have *learnt up* all they can about the subject.

Leave about/around : fail to put away carefully and tidily. ***Ex 1.*** Don't *leave* your toy soldiers *around* the house: I walk on them all the time. ***Ex 2.*** As he takes pride in his work, he does not *leave* things *about*.

Leave aside : disregard; not consider something. ***Ex 1.*** *Leaving* the expense *aside*, you actually need a second car? ***Ex 2.*** *Leaving* the matter of cost *aside*, we shall have to find time off from other work. ***Ex 3.*** I don't see how you can *leave aside* his neglect of his family.

Leave behind : (a) fail or forget to bring or take somebody/something. ***Ex 1:*** Wait-don't *leave* me *behind*. ***Ex 2.*** It will not rain: you can *leave* your umbrella *behind*.

(b) abandon as in a retreat. ***Ex.*** In their withdrawal, much of the heavy equipment had to be *left behind*.

(c) leave as a sign or record that somebody has acted or something has occurred. ***Ex 1.*** He was a ruler who *left behind* a legacy of bitterness. ***Ex 2.*** The storm *left behind* it a trail of destruction. ***Ex 3.*** Some rulers have *left behind* lasting memorial.

Leave for : abandon somebody/something in order to follow somebody/something else. ***Ex 1.*** He *left* advertising *for* a job in publishing. ***Ex 2.*** He *left* business *for* a new career as a social worker. ***Ex 3.*** At forty-five, she had been *left for* some new girlfriend.

Leave off : (a) stop; cease. ***Ex 1.*** He *left off* talking about his job. ***Ex 2.*** When did the rain *leave off*?

(b) refrain from putting on. ***Ex 1.*** Mohini *left* her coat *off* when she went out. ***Ex 2.*** Sweaters and other woollen clothes can be *left off* when warmer weather comes.

(c) avoid doing. ***Ex.*** I am afraid he has *left* it *off* again.

(d) stop something/doing something. ***Ex 1.*** It is time to *leave off* work. ***Ex 2.*** You should *leave off* whistling like that.

Leave on : (a) allow something to stay in place or position. ***Ex 1.*** He *left* his cap *on*. ***Ex 2.*** *Leave* the cloth *on*. I want to lay the table for supper.

(b) allow to stay alight or keep burning. ***Ex 1.*** Don't *leave* the light *on* when you go out. ***Ex 2.*** The electric fire had been *left on* overnight.

Leave out/out of : omit; not mention; not include; exclude. ***Ex 1.*** My name can be *left out of* this: I don't want to be involved. ***Ex 2.*** When you wrote the invitations, did you *leave* anyone *out*? ***Ex 3.*** Leave those people *out* from the invitations. ***Ex 4.*** *Leave* me *out of* this quarrel, please-I don't want to get involved. ***Ex 5.*** This word is wrongly spelt: you have *left out* a letter.

Leave out of : not take account of; not consider. ***Ex 1.*** Make sure that nothing is *left out of* account. ***Ex 2.*** He had *left out of* consideration the resentment of his former colleagues.

Leave over : (a) leave as a remainder (the best part having been consumed). ***Ex 1.*** No food has been *left over* after the meal. ***Ex 2.*** There are not any bits of cloth *left over*. ***Ex 3.*** The older children had the lion's share; the small ones had to make do with what was *left over*.

(b) reserve for attention at a later date. ***Ex.*** I regret that these matters will have to be *left over* until our next meeting slated to take place on Friday, the 14th instant.

(c) postpone. ***Ex.*** Let us *leave* the meeting *over* till next month.

Leave to : leave somebody in charge of something. ***Ex 1.*** The catering can be *left to* her. ***Ex 2.*** You have nothing to bother about. *Leave* it *to* me. ***Ex 3.*** It is *left to* the new Parliament to make amendments in the electoral laws.

Leave up : allow to remain in a raised position. ***Ex.*** The decorations can be *left up* for another day.

Leave up to : let some important decision, choice, etc. be made by somebody. ***Ex.*** I don't know how to raise the required amount of money. I *leave* it entirely *up to* you.

Lecture at : address in a formal, pompous manner, especially to scold or reproach. ***Ex 1.*** She is always being *lectured at* by her husband on her spending habits. ***Ex 2.*** My wife does not talk to me, she *lectures at* me.

Leech onto : attach oneself firmly and persistently to somebody. ***Ex 1.*** That neurotic is really *leeched onto* the doctor. ***Ex 2.*** The little boy is *leeched onto* me, and I cannot shake him off.

Lend : make more significant, believable, etc. ***Ex 1.*** This news *lends* some support to earlier reports of a ceasefire. ***Ex 2.*** It is these considerations that *lend* particular significance to the annual meeting of the party.

Lend itself to : (a) be suitable for, be well suited to something. ***Ex 1.*** The play *lent itself* admirably *to* presentation on an open stage. ***Ex 2.*** This is a novel which *lends itself* well *to* dramatization for television. ***Ex 3.*** The cellars *lend themselves to* conversion into a workroom and store.

(b) because of inherent weakness. etc. be liable or subject to ill use. ***Ex 1.*** None can deny the fact that any system of taxation *lends itself* to manipulation by clever or unscrupulous men. ***Ex 2.*** The various malpractices to which the election arrangements could *lend themselves* were pointed out by neutral observers.

Let down : (a) disappoint somebody; fail to help. ***Ex 1.*** She has been *let down* so much in the past that she trusts no one. ***Ex 2.*** Please come and support me. Don't *let* me *down*. ***Ex 3.*** We are counting on you not to *let* us *down*.

Note : *Let down* is a noun. It denotes disappointment. ***Ex.*** The dinner party held by him was a big *let down*.

(b) lower something. ***Ex 1.*** The hem of her dress needs to be *let down* several centimetres. ***Ex 2.*** Your skirt needs *letting down* a bit. ***Ex 3.*** Her parents had maintained their standards of value. She had *let* hers *down*.

(c) deflate something. ***Ex.*** Some joker has *let down* the back tyres of my car.

(d) make somebody's spirits sink. ***Ex.*** The bad news *let* him *down*.

Let in : make a garment, etc. narrower. ***Ex.*** Her skirt needs *letting in* at the waist

Let in for : make somebody assume responsibility for. ***Ex.*** He has been *let in for* a lot of extra duty.

Let in on : allow somebody to know about or take part in something that was previously hidden from him. ***Ex 1.*** He was *let in on* the plans without our consent. ***Ex 2.*** That would have involved *letting* a third person *in on* the scheme, my mother.

Let off : (a) allow somebody to disembark or alight from. ***Ex 1.*** I asked the captain of the ship to *let* me *off* at the next port of call. ***Ex 2.*** The guard did not *let* anyone *off* the train between stations.

(b) explode something; fire something off. ***Ex 1.*** Small boys *let* a few fireworks *off*. ***Ex 2.*** A brass cannon was *let off* dangerously with real gunpowder,

(c) not punish somebody severely. ***Ex 1.*** He was *let off* with a fine instead of being sent to prison. ***Ex 2.*** He got *let off* with probation becasue it was his first offence.

Let on : reveal; disclose. ***Ex 1.*** It does not do to *let on* too much. ***Ex 2.*** We did not *let on* about how rich we were. ***Ex 3.*** I am getting married next week, but please don't *let on* to anyone about it. ***Ex 4.*** Don't *let on* that I have given away his secret ingredient.

Let out : (a) utter (a cry; etc.). ***Ex 1.*** She *let out* a yelp of pain. ***Ex 2.*** The boy *let out* a scream of terror.

(b) reveal (a secret etc.). ***Ex 1.*** Who *let out* the details of the reshuffle in the Union Council of Ministers? ***Ex 2.*** Keep this information to yourself-don't *let* it *out* to the press.

(c) release somebody from an unpleasant obligation. ***Ex.*** He appeared just in time to propose the vote of thanks, which *let* me *out* nicely.

(d) make wider or looser. ***Ex.*** I have got so fat that I shall have to *let* the waistband *out* many centimetres.

Let through : allow to pass a test, etc. ***Ex 1.*** He is a hopeless driver, but the examiner *let* him *through*. ***Ex 2.*** A number of mistakes in the proofs were *let through*. ***Ex 3.*** Most of our party were *let through* customs without an examination.

Let up : slacken; ease; relax one's efforts. ***Ex 1.*** We must not *let up*, even though we are winning. ***Ex 2.*** Her mind never *let up* for an instant.

Note : *Let-up* is a noun. It means *reduction in strength, intensity, etc.*; *relaxation of efforts*. ***Ex 1.*** There is no sign of a *let-up* in the kidnappings for ransom. ***Ex 2.*** There will be no *let-up* till the escaped prisoner has been captured.

Level at : bring a change, etc. against somebody. ***Ex.*** What are the accusations *levelled at* the directors?

Level down : lower or reduce the high standards of a few to the level of the many, to achieve equality. ***Ex 1.*** Does the country as a whole benefit from *levelling down* the rewards and privileges of the rich? ***Ex 2.*** Some believe that the extension of higher education has *levelled down* university standards.

Lie behind : be the explanation for something; be the cause of. ***Ex 1.***What *lies behind* the recent Cabinet changes is the need to get rid of certain unpopular Ministers. ***Ex 2.*** I am not sure what *lay behind* his unpleasant remarks.

Lie down under : (accept an insult, etc.) without protest; submit to something meekly. ***Ex.*** We have no intention of *lying down under* these absurd allegations.

Lie over : await action/attention at a later date. ***Ex 1.*** There are several important matters *lying over* from last week. ***Ex 2.*** These items can *lie over* till our next meeting scheduled to be held on Monday, the 16th instant at 11.30 am.

Lie up : go into hiding, to escape pursuers or to attack enemies. ***Ex.*** The dacoits *lay up* by day, and by night sallied out to attack passers-by.

Lie with : be somebody's duty or responsibility. ***Ex 1.*** It *lies with* you to accept or reject the proposal. ***Ex 2.*** The decision on the matter *lies with* the Prime Minister.

Lift up : stimulate or inspire spiritually. ***Ex.*** Her very presence *lifted* us all *up*.

Light on/upon : discover by chance; happen to find. ***Ex.*** He had *lighted upon* a new method of refining the metal.

Light out/out of : leave hurriedly, to escape from somebody. ***Ex.*** On seeing the police coming, the gang *lit out of* the place.

Light up : become or make bright or animated. ***Ex 1.*** Her face was *lit up* with sudden excitement. ***Ex 2.*** His eyes *lit up* with joy. ***Ex 3.*** His eyes were still able to *light up* under the influence of curiosity or greed.

Note : *Lit or lighted* can be used in the past tense or as a past participle.

Limber up : warm up; loosen up; exercise in preparation for sport etc. ***Ex 1.*** I always do a few easy exercises to *limber up* before a match. ***Ex 2.*** The athletes were *limbering up* before the competition.

Line up : arrange or organise something. ***Ex 1.*** They have *lined up* some excellent entertainers for our show. ***Ex 2.*** He has *lined up* a live band for the party.

Note : The word *line-up* is a noun used to denote. **(a)** line of people formed for inspection, etc. ***Ex 1.*** There was a *line-up* of men in the indentification parade.

(b) any set of people, items, etc. arranged for a purpose. ***Ex 1.*** He will be missing from the team *line-up*. ***Ex 2.*** The film completes this evening's T.V. *line-up*.

Line up alongside/with : become the ally of; associate with. ***Ex 1.*** He is *lining up alongside* the most reactionary people in his party. ***Ex 2.*** Do not *line up with* dishonest persons.

Line up behind : follow somebody; take somebody as a leader. ***Ex 1.*** The majority of rank-and-file members are happy to *line up behind* the new leadership. ***Ex 2.*** Have you noticed the kind of support he has got *lined up behind* him?

Linger over : take more time than is normal or desirable, when completing a task or describing events. ***Ex.*** There is no gainsaying the fact that newspaper accounts of these disasters tend to *linger* rather nastily *over* the details.

Listen in : (a) listen to a radio programme or performer. ***Ex 1.*** He likes to *listen in* late at night. ***Ex 2.*** I just don't find such programmes worth *listening in* to. ***Ex 3.*** We *listened in* to some very interesting programmes last night.

(b) overhear (a conversation, etc.) ***Ex 1.*** She loves *listening in* to other people's gossip. ***Ex 2.*** Someone has been *listening in* to our telephone conversation.

Live down : live in such a way that (a past scandal, etc.) is forgotten. ***Ex 1.*** It will be very difficult to *live down* this humiliation. ***Ex 2.*** He will never *live* the scandal *down*. ***Ex 3.*** I can never hope to *live down* these shortcomings.

Life for : regard something as the aim of one's life. ***Ex 1.*** I *live for* my work. ***Ex 2.*** After she died, he had nothing to *live for*. ***Ex 3.*** He *lives for* the day when he can retire and grow roses. ***Ex 4.*** She *lives for* nothing but pleasure.

Live on : (a) continue to live or exist. ***Ex 1.*** He *lived on* for many a year after his wife died. ***Ex 2.*** These traditions will *live on* for centuries. ***Ex 3.*** The famous singer is dead but his music *lives on*. ***Ex 4.*** He will die, but his fame will *live on* after him.

(b) have something as one's food/diet. ***Ex 1.*** I *live on* fruit and vegetables. ***Ex 2.*** Can you *live on* air?

(c) depend on something for financial support. ***Ex 1.*** He *lives on* his salary. ***Ex 2.*** Do you *live on* charity? ***Ex 3.*** Do you know how little they manage to *live on*?

Live through : experience something and survive. ***Ex 1.*** He *lived through* both world wars. ***Ex 2.*** He had *lived through* the worst years of the depression.

Live together : (a) live in the same house, etc. ***Ex.*** They *live together* as husband and wife.

(b) live in the same house, as husband wife, but without being married. ***Ex.*** This man and that woman *live together*.

Live under : experience the rule of. ***Ex 1.*** The country is now *living under* a military dictatorship. ***Ex 2.*** He has *lived under* five Prime Ministers.

Live up to : behave in accordance with something. ***Ex 1.*** We cannot *live up to* our moral pretensions. ***Ex 2.*** He failed to *live up to* his principles.

Live with : accept or tolerate something. ***Ex 1.*** You have lost all your money; now you must learn to *live with* the situation. ***Ex 2.*** You must *live with* the fact that you are no longer as active as you were.

Load with : award honours to somebody in abundance. ***Ex.*** He was *loaded with* honours for the distinguished services he rendered to the country.

Lock away : store something securely and safely. ***Ex.*** Take good care to *lock away* your jewellery before going out of station.

Lock up : (a) put somebody in prison, a mental institution, etc. ***Ex.*** He has been *locked up* in jail.

(b) invest money so that it cannot easily be converted into cash. ***Ex.*** All his capital is *locked up* in the building's expansion programme.

Lodge in : enter and become fixed in something. ***Ex.*** The bullet *lodged in* his brain.

Look after : (a) make sure that one/somebody is safe and well; take care of oneself. ***Ex 1.*** You need to be properly *looked after*. ***Ex 2.*** He is good at *looking after* his own interests.

(b) be responsible for something. ***Ex 1.*** Who will *look after* the garden while you will be out of station? ***Ex 2.*** They *look after* the shop when he goes away. ***Ex 3.*** I am *looking after* his children this morning.

Look ahead : think about what is going to happen in future; project oneself into the future. ***Ex 1.*** Have you *looked ahead* to what you will be doing in five year's time? ***Ex 2.*** You can expect to find a multistorey building on this side. Of course, I am *looking ahead* four years when I tell you this.

Look around/round : (a) examine what is around one. ***Ex 1.*** I *looked around* the crowded hall, hoping to find an empty seat. ***Ex 2.*** He *looked round* him as he stood waiting for the bus to take him to school. ***Ex 3.*** He *looked round* when he heard the loud noise behind him.

(b) inspect or survey something; examine various options or possibilities. ***Ex 1.*** Was there anything you particularly wanted, sir? No, I am just *looking around*. ***Ex 2.*** We are going to *look round* a bit before deciding where to buy a house.

(c) visit a place as a tourist or sightseer. ***Ex.*** We shall *look around* the Birla Temple this afternoon.

Look at : (a) examine something closely. ***Ex 1.*** I can't tell you what it is worth, you must get an expert to *look at* it. ***Ex 2.*** Ask the accountant to *look at* the figure. ***Ex 3.*** The doctor ought to *look at* your badly swollen ankle. ***Ex 4.*** I am taking my car to the garage to be *looked at*. ***Ex 5.*** I have not had time to *look at* your article yet.

(b) think about, consider or study something. ***Ex 1.*** We shall *look at* the implications of the new law. ***Ex 2.*** The committee did not even *look at* his proposal. ***Ex 3.*** He would not *look at* a jab like that.

(c) view or regard something. ***Ex 1.*** The Indians *look at* life differently from the Americans. ***Ex 2.*** Her way of *looking at* things is not yours. ***Ex 3.*** *Looked at* from that point of view, the job becomes easy.

Look back : return in one's thoughts; cast one's mind back to something in the past; reminisce. ***Ex 1.*** People began to *look back* longing on the old regime. ***Ex 2.*** They like to *look back* on old times. ***Ex 3.*** Do you like to *look back* on your childhood?

Look beyond : place oneself imaginatively in the futrue. ***Ex.*** Try to *look beyond* your present hardships to future happiness.

Look down on/upon : despise somebody/something; regard somebody/something with contempt; consider somebody/something inferior to oneself. ***Ex 1.*** He *looks down on* the poor. ***Ex 2.*** Do you *look down on* people who have never been to university? ***Ex 3.*** She was *looked down on* because her humble background. ***Ex 4.*** The really unskilled people are *looked down upon* by everyone.

Look for : (a) hope for something; expect something. ***Ex 1.*** Don't *look for* any help from him. ***Ex 2.*** The chance which he had *looked for* was now freely offered to him.

(b) seek. ***Ex.*** We are *looking for* an ambitious young assistant.

Look forward to : anticipate something with pleasure. ***Ex 1.*** We are so much *looking forward to* seeing you again. ***Ex 2.*** He had been *looking forward to* leaving the hospital wards for a holiday in Kashmir. ***Ex 3.*** His retirement is very much *looked forward to* by the office staff.

Look in : make a short visit to somebody's house or place. ***Ex 1.*** The doctor *looked in* for a few minutes to see if everything was all tight. ***Ex 2.*** I shall *look in* at the party on my way home. ***Ex 3.*** Please *look in* on me next week.

Look into : (a) investigate or examine something. ***Ex 1.*** Her disappearance is being *looked into* by the police. ***Ex 2.*** A working group has been set up to *look into* the problem. ***Ex 3.*** I shall *look into* your complaints. '

(b) make a brief call or visit to. ***Ex.*** I must *look into* the garage on the way home to book a service for the car.

Look on : be a spectator at an event or incident. ***Ex 1.*** Passers-by just *looked on* as a young Woman was robbed. ***Ex 2.*** They stood *looking on* while the old man was viciously attacked by a gang.

Look on/upon : (a) regard or consider somebody/something to be somebody/ something. ***Ex 1.*** I *look upon* him as the betrayer of his country in its darkest hour. ***Ex 2.*** He was *looked on* as the leading authority on geography. ***Ex 3.*** She is *looked upon* as something of an authority on rare books.

(b) regard somebody/something in the specified way. ***Ex 1.*** He has always been *looked upon* with distrust by his wife. ***Ex 2.*** She was always *looked on* with suspicion by her mother-in-law. ***Ex 3.*** I *look on* his behaviour with contempt. ***Ex 4.*** Tell me, how do people *look upon* her in general?

Look out : (a) be careful; watch out. ***Ex 1.*** *Look out*, there is a car coming. ***Ex 2.*** *Look out*, Basanti, that step is not safe. ***Ex 3.*** Tell them to *look out*, the ceiling is threatening to fall in.

(b) search for something and find it. ***Ex 1.*** I must *look out* some old books for the jumble sale. ***Ex 2.*** I shall *look out* the photographs you want to see. ***Ex 3.*** Perhaps, he will *look out* one of his old girlfriends.

(c) be alert or watchful in order to see, find or be aware of somebody/something. ***Ex 1.*** You must *look out* for pickpockets. ***Ex 2.*** Please go to the station and *look out* for Anil. ***Ex 3.*** Police will be *looking out* for trouble makers at today's match. ***Ex 4.*** Do *look out* for spelling mistakes when you check your work.

Look over : (a) inspect or examine something. ***Ex 1.*** You must *look over* the car before you decide to buy it. ***Ex 2.*** The surveyor *looked over* our new plant near Hyderabad.

(b) examine something one by one, or part by part. ***Ex 1.*** Here is the mail. I have *looked* it *over*. ***Ex 2.*** I would like you to *look over* these documents. ***Ex 3.*** Would you *look* the applicants *over* and tell me what you think of them? ***Ex 4.*** He has *looked over* your work, and has some comments to make.

(c) revise. ***Ex.*** She is *looking over* her notes before the examination.

Look through : (a) read or examine something quickly. ***Ex.*** Pushpa *looked through* her notes before the examination.

(b) examine or read something carefully; examine or read (a number of things) one by one. ***Ex 1.*** Always *look* your work *through* before handing it in. ***Ex 2.*** I *looked* the proposals *through* before approving them.

(c) deliberately ignore somebody whom one can see clearly. ***Ex.*** She just *looked* straight *through* me.

Look to : (a) rely on or expect somebody to provide or do something. ***Ex 1.*** We are *looking to* you for assistance. ***Ex 2.*** Don't *look to* the government to reduce unemployment. ***Ex 3.*** She always *looks to* me for advice. ***Ex 4.*** Let this be a warning against *looking to* personal diplomacy to settle disputes between two countries. ***Ex 5.*** He is not the sort of man *to* whom one *looks* for reassurance.

(b) make sure that something is safe or in good condition; be careful about something. ***Ex 1.*** The country must *look to* its defences. ***Ex 2.*** You should *look to* your health.

Look up : (a) become/get better; improve. ***Ex 1.*** His prospects in life seem to be *looking up*. ***Ex 2.*** Business is *looking up*. ***Ex 3.*** The weather is *looking up*. ***Ex 4.*** Prospects for the small builder are *looking up*. ***Ex 5.*** Inflation is coming down; unemployment is coming down; things are definitely *looking up*.

(b) seek information about something; try to find something in a work of reference. ***Ex 1.*** I *looked* her *up* in Who's Who. ***Ex 2.*** *Look up* the time of the next train in the time-table. ***Ex 3.*** He *looked* the word *up* in the dictionary. ***Ex 4.*** I shall *look up* her number in the telephone directory.

(c) visit or contact somebody, especially after not having seen him for a long time. ***Ex.*** Do *look* me *up* the next time you are in Calcutta.

Look up to : admire or respect somebody. ***Ex 1.*** I always *look up to* her, for her academic brilliance, sharp intellectual ability; tenacity of purpose, amiability; suavity; and polite and polished manners. ***Ex 2.*** You must always *look up to* your parents.

Loosen up : relax. ***Ex 1.*** You should *loosen up* before playing any sport, ***Ex 2.*** Don't be so nervous *loosen up* a bit.

Lose in : become absorbed in something. ***Ex 1.*** I soon *lost* myself *in* the excitement of the film. ***Ex 2.*** He was *lost in* the intricacies of a new electric motor.

Lose out : suffer loss; be unsuccessful. ***Ex.*** If things go wrong, I am the one who will *lose out*, not you.

Lose out to : be overcome or replaced by. ***Ex 1.*** Has the cinema *lost out to* Try? ***Ex 2.*** The hard way, the grind, the moral lesson, duty; all were *losing out to* the easy way, money, charm, a well-known name.

Louse up : spoil or ruin something. ***Ex 1.*** You have really *loused* things *up* this time. ***Ex 2.*** We had just got her settled with a few reassuring words when you had to *louse* everything *up* by opening your big mouth.

Lumber with : pass to somebody else an awkward or inconvenient person, object or task. ***Ex 1.*** Don't *lumber* me *with* all this paperwork. ***Ex 2.*** Every summer, we get *lumbered with* our maternal grandfather for over a fortnight.

Lust after/for : feel a strong desire for somebody/something. ***Ex 1.*** Don't *lust after* women. ***Ex 2.*** He *lusted for* revenge.

---

13 Words Beginning With–M

Mad about/on : very interested in somebody/something; enthusiastic about. ***Ex 1.*** He is *mad about* her. ***Ex 2.*** Are you *mad on* football?

Mad with : very excited; frenzied. ***Ex.*** The crowd is *mad with* excitement.

Mad at/with : furious. ***Ex.*** Why were you *mad at* her?

Make after : chase or pursue somebody/something. ***Ex 1.*** The villagers *made after* the thief. ***Ex 2.*** They *made after* him on horseback.

Make at : move towards somebody to attack him. ***Ex 1.*** The dog *made at* the postman with his teeth bared. ***Ex 2.*** I *made at* her with a heavy ruler snatched from the table.

Make away/off : steal and hurry away. ***Ex.*** While they were having tea, two boys *made off* with their suitcases.

Make away with : commit suicide. ***Ex 1.*** I don't know why he *made away with* himself. ***Ex 2.*** Don't *make away with* yourself.

Make for : (a) move towards somebody/something; head for somebody/something. ***Ex 1.*** When the interval came, everyone *made for* the restaurant. ***Ex 2.*** I turned and ran when I saw the bull *making for* me. ***Ex 3.*** The ship *made for* the open sea.

(b) contribute to something; to ensure; help to make something possible. ***Ex 1.*** A big family is a wonderful interest. It *makes for* the stability of marriage. ***Ex 2.*** The large print *makes for* easier reading. ***Ex 3.*** Constant arguing does not *make for* a happy marriage. ***Ex 4.*** International football matches do not always *make for* better understanding between countries. ***Ex 5.*** This kind of thing *makes for* good human relations.

Make into : cause to become; transform into. ***Ex 1.*** He was not always a bully. You *made* him *into* one. ***Ex 2.*** Many of the cinemas have been *made into* restaurants.

Make of : understand the meaning or nature of somebody/something to be something. ***Ex 1.*** What did you *make of* the old lady? ***Ex 2.*** What do you *make of* it all? ***Ex 3.*** What are we to *make of* her behaviour? ***Ex 4.*** What do you *make of* the new manager? ***Ex 5.*** I can *make* nothing *of* the scribble in her notebooks.

Make off : escape. ***Ex 1.*** When the police arrived, the thieves *made off*. ***Ex 2.*** The dacoits *made off* in a stolen car.

Make off with : steal something and hurry away with it; decamp with. ***Ex 1.*** The cashier of our firm *made off with* a large amount of money. ***Ex 2.*** Three young women *made off with* our bags while we were not looking.

Make on : make a certain profit as the result of a business transaction. ***Ex.*** Parvati was prepared to sell me her car for what she paid for it : she would not *make* a rupee *on* the deal.

Make out : (a) manage; survive; fare. ***Ex 1.*** How are you *making out* with her? ***Ex 2.*** How did you *make out* while your wife was away? ***Ex 3.*** Let me know how he is *making out* in his new practice.

(b) understand the nature or character of somebody; work out. ***Ex 1.*** I really cannot *make* him *out*. Why does he offend the very people who try to help him? ***Ex 2.*** What a strange person he is? I can't *make* him *out* at all.

(c) manage to see somebody/something or read something. ***Ex 1.*** I could *make out* the expression on her face. ***Ex 2.*** Can you *make out* what that sign says? ***Ex 3.*** The outline of the house could just be *made out*.

(d) understand. ***Ex 1.*** I can't *make out* what she wants. ***Ex 2.*** I can't *make* it *out*, why does not he spend some of his money on a car that won't break down? ***Ex 2.*** I could never *make out* if they wanted our help or not.

(e) write out something; complete something. ***Ex 1.*** Applications have to be *made out* in triplicate. ***Ex 2.*** He *made out* a cheque for the required amount of money. ***Ex 3.*** The necessary documents will be *made out* in good time.

(f) claim; assert; maintain. ***Ex 1.*** He *made out* that he had been robbed. ***Ex 2.*** She is not as rich as people *make* her *out* to be. ***Ex 3.*** He *makes* himself *out* to be cleverer than he really is. ***Ex 4.*** It was not the cure everyone *made* it *out* to be.

Make over : (a) change or convert somebody/something; remake. ***Ex 1.*** She has *made* the coat *over* and it looks quite fashionable now. ***Ex 2.*** The basement has been *made over* into a workshop.

(b) transfer the ownership of something. ***Ex 1.*** He has *made over* the whole property to his eldest son. ***Ex 2.*** He has *made* the money *over* to charity.

Make up : (a) replace; make good. ***Ex 1.*** Our losses will have to be *made up* with more loans. ***Ex 2.*** He gave us ten thousand rupees to *make up* the deficit. ***Ex 3.*** You must *make up* the time you wasted this afternoon by working late tonight.

(b) provide a road with a hard surface to make it suitable for fast otor traffic. ***Ex.*** Half the roads in the town are still to be *made up*.

(c) invent something in order to deceive somebody. ***Ex 1.*** He *made up* an excuse for coming late. ***Ex 2.*** She *made* the story *up*. ***Ex 3.*** There is not any little girl called Mamta. He has just *made* her *up*. ***Ex 4.*** You can't go around *making up* things about being assaulted by people who don't exist. ***Ex 5.*** These entertainers *make* their stories *up* as they go along.

(d) arrange type, illustrations, etc. in colums or pages for printing. ***Ex.*** The way the front page is *made up* may need to be altered several times.

(e) form, compose or constitute something. ***Ex 1.*** Society is *made up* of people of widely differing abilities. ***Ex 2.*** What are the qualities that *make up* her character? ***Ex 3.*** These arguments *make up* the case for the defence.

(f) add more fuel to a fire, etc. ***Ex 1.*** If the stove is not *made up*, it will go out. ***Ex 2.*** The fire needs *making up*.

(g) apply cosmetics to the face to make it more attractive; prepare one's face or body for a performance in theatre or on film or television. ***Ex 1.*** She is always very heavily *made up*. ***Ex 2.*** She spent an hour *making up* before the party. ***Ex 3.*** It took her more than an hour to *make up* for the part of Sita.

(h) prepare by mixing together various ingredients. ***Ex 1.*** The doctor writes out a prescription and you get it *made up* at the chemist's. ***Ex 2.*** The pharmacist *made up* the prescription. ***Ex 3.*** The shop assistant *made up* the parcel expertly.

(i) prepare a bed for use; set up a temporary bed. ***Ex 1.*** We *made up* the bed in the spare room for our guest. ***Ex 2.*** I had a bed *made up* for me on the sofa.

(j) put something together from several different things. ***Ex 1.*** He *made up* a basket of food for the picnic. ***Ex 2.*** We *made up* a bundle of old clothes for a jumble sale.

(k) make complete. ***Ex 1.*** We recruited locally to *make up* our full compliment of labourers. ***Ex 2.*** We still need seven thousand rupees to *make up* the sum required. ***Ex 3.*** We have ten players, so we need one more to *make up* a team.

(l) fashion material into a garment. ***Ex.*** Can you *make up* this dress length for me?

Make up for : (a) compensate for something. ***Ex 1.*** Hard work can *make up for* a lack of intelligence. ***Ex 2.*** Nothing can *make up for* the death of a child. ***Ex 3.*** The beautiful autumn *made up for* the wet summer. ***Ex 4.*** Pay increases will not always *make up for* poor working conditions.

(b) make amends; redress; repay somebody for one's past failures, etc. ***Ex 1.*** How can I *make up for* the way I have treated you? ***Ex 2.*** You cannot *make up for* all that she had suffered because of you. ***Ex 3.*** His display of bad manners was scarcely *made up for* by his subsequent behaviour. ***Ex 4.*** He tried to *make up for* all the trouble he had caused.

Make up to : flatter; be pleasant to somebody in order to win favours. ***Ex 1.*** She is always *making up to* the boss. ***Ex 2.*** On his first day at the office, he started *making up to* the prettiest secretary. ***Ex 3.*** He is not the sort of man who likes being *made up to*.

Make with : (a) supply something quickly. ***Ex.*** Can't you see our tongues are hanging out? *Make with* the cold drinks.

(b) produce; create. ***Ex.*** We need some slogans for the promotion of the hairspray, so start *making with* the ideas.

Map out : plan or arrange something. ***Ex 1.*** Susanti has already *mapped out* her whole career. ***Ex 2.*** We have *mapped out* a plan of campaign. ***Ex 3.*** We must get the whole scheme clearly *mapped out* on paper before we start to order equipment. ***Ex 4.*** It was a well *mapped-out* itinerary, taking in all the places of historical importance in the area. ***Ex 5.*** Have you *mapped out* what you will do?

Mark down : (a) reduce the marks given to somebody in an examination, etc. ***Ex 1.*** He was *marked down* because his answers were too short. ***Ex 2.*** The boys at the top of the form were *marked down*, as the gap between them and the rest did not reflect their true merits.

(b) reduce the price of something. ***Ex.*** Many household articles have been *marked down* by 25% .

(c) single out; choose. ***Ex 1.*** I drove on to the Army House, which I had *marked down* for my brigade headquarters. ***Ex 2.*** He has been *marked down* for assassination.

Mark off : indicate the boundaries by marking. ***Ex 1.*** This area has been *marked off* for athletic practice. ***Ex 2.*** An area at the end of the side was *marked off* as a future playground.

Mark out : (a) choose somebody to receive something special. ***Ex 1.*** He has been *marked out* for early promotion. ***Ex 2.*** She was *marked out* for special training.

(b) indicate. ***Ex.*** They have marked out exactly what they intend to do.

Mark up : (a) increase the marks awarded to a student, etc. ***Ex.*** If we *mark up* Sonali Devi on two papers, she will just scrape a pass.

(b) increase the price of something. ***Ex.*** Cars have been *marked up* recently.

(c) put a price on. ***Ex.*** They have *marked up* all these items.

(d) prepare a manuscript for the printer by making corrections, inserting new material, etc. ***Ex.*** Let me know whether the editor has *marked up* the manuscript.

Marry above : marry somebody in a higher social class than one's own. ***Ex.*** People who *marry above* themselves in the social scale have the same kinds of problem as those who marry outside their religion or nationality.

Marry beneath : marry somebody in a lower social class than one's own. ***Ex.*** His father threatened to disinherit him if he *married beneath* himself.

Marry in/into : become a part of (a family; etc.) by marrying. ***Ex 1.*** He *married into* a rich family. ***Ex 2.*** She was not born into the nobility; she *married in.*

Marry off : arrange the marriage of one's daughter; get rid of (a daughter) by finding a husband for her. ***Ex 1.*** He has *married off* his daughter to a rich, handsome young lawyer. ***Ex 2.*** I don't know why they could not *marry* her *off*. ***Ex 3.*** When his last daughter is happily *married off*, he can afford to relax.

Marry up : (a) match. ***Ex.*** The two versions of the story don't quite *marry up.*

(b) join up or assemble correctly. ***Ex.*** The two halves of the structure did not *marry up*.

Match against/with : pit against; set somebody/something to complete with somebody/something else. ***Ex 1.*** I am ready to *match* my strength *against yours*. ***Ex 2.*** *Match* your skill *against* the experts in this quiz. ***Ex 3.*** You have been *matched with* one of the best amateur fighters.

Match up : (a) tally; be in agreement. ***Ex 1.*** Have you noticed how well the blouse goes with her long skirt ? The whole outfit *matches up* beautifully. ***Ex 2.*** The two statements don't *match up*.

(b) fit something to something else to form a complete whole. ***Ex.*** Please *match up* the torn pieces of the photograph.

Match up to : be as good as or equal to somebody/something. ***Ex.*** The film dit not *match up to* myexpectaions. .

Measure off : mark out a length or lengths of something. ***Ex 1.*** He *measured off* four metres of cloth. ***Ex 2.*** The assistant *measured off* a dresslength from the roll.

Measure out : give a measured quantity of something. ***Ex.*** Will you please *measure out* a dose of medicine?

Measure up : (a) reach the standard required or expected. ***Ex 1.*** The discussions did not *measure up* to her expectations. ***Ex 2.*** Differenciate between the genuine private detectives and others who do not *measure up* to our expectations.

(b) assess. ***Ex 1.*** We have been trying to *measure up* his chances. ***Ex 2.*** Did you try to *measure up* his intellectual ability.

Meet up : meet somebody; especially by chance. ***Ex 1.*** I *met up* with him at the supermarket, ***Ex 2.*** He *met up* with some old friends.

Meet with : (a) meet somebody; especially for discussion. ***Ex.*** The President *met with* senior Rashtrapati Bhawan aids at breakfast.

(b) encounter something; experience something. ***Ex 1.*** They *met with* stubborn resistance. ***Ex 2.*** They *met with* nothing but understanding from the doctors.

Melt away : disappear; ***Ex.*** The crowd *melted away* when the storm broke.

Melt into : (a) change by gradual degrees into something else. ***Ex.*** One colour *melted into* another. (e.g. in the sky at sunset).

(b) slowly disappear into something. ***Ex 1.*** The thief *melted into* the fog. ***Ex 2.*** The ship *melted into* the darkness.

Mess about/around : (a) behave in a foolish or boisterous way. ***Ex 1.*** Don't *mess about* in my presence. ***Ex 2.*** A few children were *messing about* in the next room.

(b) potter, work in casual, pleasant or disorganised way. ***Ex 1.*** He loves just *messing about* in the kitchen garden. ***Ex 2.*** He is *messing about* in a boat. ***Ex 3.*** Let me know whether he is *messing about* with his car.

(c) make a muddle of something; handle somebody/something roughly or inconsiderately; handle something clumsily or incompetently. ***Ex 1.*** Be nicer to her. You should not *mess around* with her like that. ***Ex 2.*** You cannot *mess around* with people like Bhim Bahadur. ***Ex 3.*** He has been *messed about* by the doctors for the past two years. ***Ex 4.*** Don't *mess* the files *around*.

Mess up : (a) make something untidy, dirty or disordered; mishandle; mismanage; disarrange. ***Ex 1.*** Don't *mess up* my hair, I have just combed it. ***Ex 2.*** He *messed up* your clean kitchen. ***Ex 3.*** I have sorted the list out; now don't *mess* it *up* again.

(b) bungle something; do something incompetently. ***Ex.*** He was asked to organise the trip, but he *messed* it *up*.

Mess with : interfere with somebody/something. ***Ex.*** Don't *mess with* him, he has got a violent temper.

Mete out : give or administer (punishment, rewards, etc.) ***Ex 1.*** Justice was *meted out* to the offenders. ***Ex 2.*** The judge *meted out* punishment impartially. ***Ex 3.*** The judgement *meted out* to the accused did not satisfy the public. ***Ex 4.*** The judge *meted out* severe penalties.

Mill about/around : crowd about in confusion; move about in a confused or disorderly way. ***Ex 1.*** Many girls were *milling about* in the corridor. ***Ex 2.*** Groups of fans were *milling around* in the streets after the match. ***Ex 3.*** The frightened animals were *milling about* in their pens. ***Ex 4.*** Conflicting fancies *milled around* in her mind.

Mind out : (a) take care to avoid danger, etc. ***Ex 1.*** *Mind out*, the dish is hot. ***Ex 2.*** You will trip over the cat if you don't *mind out*. ***Ex 3.*** *Mind out* for the traffic when you cross the road.

(b) allow somebody to pass. ***Ex 1.*** *Mind out*—you are blocking the passage.

Mislead into : make somebody do something by deceiving him. ***Ex 1.*** I *misled* her *into* thinking that I was very rich.

Miss out : (a) not include somebody/something. ***Ex 1.*** Today I shall *miss out* the sweet course. ***Ex 2.*** We shall *miss out* the last part of the play.

(b) forget or fail to include something. ***Ex 1.*** The printers have *missed out* a whole line here. ***Ex 2.*** Through an oversight, his name was *missed out* from the list of guests. ***Ex 3.*** No one is to be neglected or made to feel *missed out*.

(c) lose an opportunity to benefit from something or enjoy oneself. ***Ex.*** If I don't go to the party, I shall feel that I am *missing out*.

(d) fail to notice; not be present at; not experience. ***Ex.*** If he finds that his own paper has *missed out* on some important fact, his day is soured to begin with.

Mist over : (a) become covered with mist. ***Ex 1.*** The scene *misted over*. ***Ex 2.*** When I drink tea, my glasses *mist over*.

(b) become obscured. ***Ex.*** His brain *misted over* for a moment, cleared suddenly.

Mist up : cover or become covered by a film of water vapour. ***Ex 1.*** Our breath is *misting up* the car windows. ***Ex 2.*** He is as blind as a bat, his glasses have *misted up*.

Mistake for : wrongly suppose that somebody/something is somebody/something else. ***Ex 1.*** People are always *mistaking* him *for* his twin brother. ***Ex 2.*** He was *mistaken for* an enemy scout and badly beaten. ***Ex 3.*** She *mistook* a toad stool *for* a mushroom.

Mix up : (a) cause somebody to become confused. ***Ex 1.*** Now you have *mixed* me *up* completely. ***Ex 2.*** I think that she has been very *mixed up* and she feels as if she has had to fight the whole world.

(b) be unable to tell one thing or person from another. ***Ex 1.*** He is always *mixing* me *up* with my brother. ***Ex 2.*** One fault with his reading is that he still *mixes up* b and d.

(c) mix two or more things together, so that one does not know which is which; muddle up. ***Ex 1.*** The office *mixed up* our flight documents; Gita got mine and I got hers. ***Ex 2.*** The porter got our bags *mixed up*; I nearly walked off with someone else's.

Monkey about/around : behave in a foolish mischievous way. ***Ex 1.*** Don't *monkey about* in her presence. ***Ex 2.*** Stop *monkeying around*.

Monkey about/around with : play or interfere with something in a careless way. ***Ex 1.*** It is dangerous to *monkey about* in a workshop. ***Ex 2.*** Don't *monkey about with* a fire extinguisher.

Moon about/around : wander about aimlessly or listlessly. ***Ex 1.*** He spent the whole month *mooning around* at home. ***Ex 2.*** Don't *moon about*, and get on with some work. ***Ex 3.*** He is no longer *mooning around*, thank goodness. ***Ex 4.*** Tell him to stop *mooning about* the house.

Moon over : spend one's time dreamily thinking about somebody one loves. ***Ex.*** Whom are you *mooning over*? She has been *mooning over* her boyfriend.

Mop up : (a) absorb liquid using an absorbent cloth, mop etc. ***Ex 1.*** The maid *mopped up* the pools of water on the bathroom floor. ***Ex 2.*** He *mopped up* the pools that had formed under the leak in the ceiling.

(b) clear pockets of enemy troops left behind in the general advance. ***Ex 1.*** Our troops are *mopping up* the isolated pockets of resistance. ***Ex 2.*** There were still some *mopping up* operations to be undertaken.

(c) complete (the final parts of a task). ***Ex.*** They *mopped up* the last few bits of work.

Mope about/around/round : wander here and there in an unhappy or listless mood. ***Ex 1.*** He has been *moping about* the house all day. ***Ex 2.*** Can't you get her mind off that healthy and wealthy man? She has been *moping about* the place all weekend.

Mount up : become greater in amount. ***Ex 1.*** Our living expenses are *mounting up* day by day. ***Ex 2.*** His debts are beginning to *mount up*. ***Ex 3.*** Put aside hundred rupees a week and you will be surprised to find how quickly your savings *mount up*.

Move in : (a) take possession of a place. ***Ex 1.*** We are *moving in* on the 8th of the next month. ***Ex 2.*** The enemy *moved in* last night.

(b) move closer to somebody/something so as to handle, tackle or treat him or it. ***Ex 1.*** The tanks *moved in* to flush the snipers from their nests. ***Ex 2.*** Important changes are *moving in* on the industry. ***Ex 3.*** The army has begun to *move in* on the defenders.

Move on : progress; move to a better job, house, style of life. ***Ex 1.*** I have been in this job for four years now; it is time I was *moving on*. ***Ex 2.*** She has *moved on* to higher and better things.

Move over : move away so as to leave more room for another occupant of a bench, bed, etc. ***Ex.*** *Move over*, you are taking up more than half the bed.

Move towards : approach or move nearer to. ***Ex.*** We are *moving towards* a better understanding between our two countries.

Move up : (a) progress in one's work; rise socially, rise in rank. ***Ex 1.*** She is *moving up* in the world. ***Ex 2.*** He has *moved* very rapidly *up* the promotion, ladder. ***Ex 3.*** He will *move up* a rung or two when his qualifications are confirmed.

(b) rise financially; improve position. ***Ex 1.*** The exchange rate of the rupee *moved up* sharply in the recent past. ***Ex 2.*** Mining shares *moved up* to a new level.

(c) move into the battle area. ***Ex.*** Four battalions were *moved up* under cover of darkness to reinforce the front line.

Mow down : kill quickly in large numbers. ***Ex.*** The machine-guns *mowed down* the advancing lines of infantrymen.

Muck about/around : (a) mess about; behave in an aimless and silly way. ***Ex 1.*** Stop *mucking about*, and get down to some serious work. ***Ex 2.*** Many accidents 'are caused by children *mucking about* on railway lines.

(b) meddle. ***Ex.*** He keeps *mucking about* with things he does not understand.

(c) tinker for amusement. ***Ex.*** I am just *mucking around* with this old watch.

(d) irritate. ***Ex.*** She seems to enjoy *mucking* me *about*.

Muck in : share tasks or accommodation equally. ***Ex 1.*** Let us all *muck in* together, and we will soon finish the job. ***Ex 2.*** The officers had to *muck in* with their men. ***Ex 3.*** He is a lone wolf: never *mucks in* with the others.

Muck up : (a) spoil; ruin; mess up; make dirty. ***Ex 1.*** The children have *mucked up* the whole place. ***Ex 2.*** Don't *muck up* your clothes.***Ex 3.*** The weather really *mucked up* our outing.

(b) do something badly; bungle something. ***Ex 1.*** He really *mucked up* his chances by doing badly in the interview. ***Ex 2.*** They *mucked* my plans *up* completely.

Muddle along : live one's life in a foolish or helpless way, with no clear purpose or plan; manage somehow. ***Ex 1.*** We *muddle along* from day to day. ***Ex 2.*** We *muddle along*, you know, though we are not rich.

Muddle through : reach one's aims despite inefficiency, the lack of a plan or programme, etc. ***Ex 1***. We shall *muddle through*, don't worry. Ex 2. He expects that he will *muddle through* somehow. Ex 3. The Nationalist Party had a theory ten years ago, but it is no use for them now. They are just hoping to *muddle through* without it.

Muddle up : mix two or more things together, so that one does not know which is which; mix up; confuse. ***Ex 1.*** Their names have been *muddled up*. ***Ex 2.*** I am feeling rather *muddled up*. ***Ex 3.*** Don't *muddle* her *up*. ***Ex 4.*** The stamps were found *muddled up* in a drawer. ***Ex 5.*** My personal letters got *muddled up* with a batch of circulars.

Mug up : learn by intensive study, especially before an exam; swot up. ***Ex 1.*** He has been *mugging up* his Hindi. ***Ex 2.*** The candidate was able to offer a few facts hastily *mugged up* before the examination.

Mull over : think about or consider something long and carefully. ***Ex 1.*** I have not decided yet; I am *mulling* it *over* in my mind. ***Ex 2.*** Arguments for and against the proposal had been through *mulled over*.

Muscle in : use force or guile to get a share of, or participate in, something important or profitable. ***Ex 1.*** Don't try to *muscle in* on my property. ***Ex 2.*** They *muscled in* on the meeting. ***Ex 3.*** I wrote the book, and now she is trying to *muscle in* on its tremendous success by saying that she gave me the ideas.

Muse on/over/upon : think about, ponder, in an absorbed, dreamy way. ***Ex 1.*** He sat *musing on* the memories of his boyhood. ***Ex 2.*** Don't *muse upon* the events of the past. ***Ex 3.*** He *mused upon* the flattering comments made by that stunningly beautiful girl. ***Ex.* 4.** Her offer to lend me her seaside cottage was immensely pleasant to *muse on*.

Muss up : make untidy; disarrange; put something into disorder. ***Ex 1.*** Don't *muss up* my new dress. ***Ex.* 2.** Do you have the courage to *muss up* her hair? ***Ex.* 3.** Keep your hands to yourself. You are *mussing up* my hair.

Muster up : gain something by collecting it from other people or by drawing it from within oneself; summon something up. ***Ex 1.*** He *mustered up* all his courage for the ordeal. ***Ex.* 2.** Do your best to *muster up* public support for this cause. ***Ex 3.*** He could not *muster up* much enthusiasm for the project.

14 Words Beginning With–N

Nag at : (a) scold or criticise somebody continuously. ***Ex 1.*** He *nagged at* her all day long. ***Ex 2.*** She always *nags at* her husband.

(b) press somebody irritatingly to do something. ***Ex.*** She has been *nagging at* him to mow the lawn.

Nail down : (a) get somebody to say precisely what he believes or wants to do. ***Ex 1.*** Himadri Shankar is very difficult to *nail down*: you can never get him to speak his mind on anything. ***Ex 2.*** Try to *nail* him *down* on the subject of religious education. ***Ex 3.*** She says she will come, but I cannot *nail* her *down* to a specific time. ***Ex 4.*** I *nailed* him *down* to coming to our place at 6.30.

(b) define the character of somebody/something precisely. ***Ex 1.*** He had *nailed* Anil *down*, robbed of his mystery. His secret was out. ***Ex 2.*** Can we *nail* the concept *down* a little more precisely?

Narrow down : become restricted ***Ex 1.*** The field of inquiry has *narrowed down* to five persons. ***Ex 2.*** The police *narrowed* the search for the missing girl *down* to a few streets near the school.

Natter on : talk informally and aimlessly; chatter. ***Ex.*** He *nattered on* about his work for a couple of hours.

Nestle up : press close,to another person for warmth or comfort. ***Ex 1.*** The child *nestled up* to its mother and fell asleep. ***Ex 2.*** Nirmala *nestled up* against her mother and dozed fitfully.

Nibble at : show cautious interest in (an offer etc.). ***Ex*** She *nibbled at* my proposal, but would not make a definite decision.

Niggle about/over : criticise in a petty way; be fussy. ***Ex 1.*** Don't *niggle about* every rupee we spend. ***Ex 2.*** We had tremendous difficulty getting the agreement signed. Every little cause was *niggled over*.

Nip in : reduce the width of something; make narrow by nipping or pinching action. ***Ex*** She *nipped* the waist of the dress *in*.

Nod off : fall asleep. ***Ex*** I often *nod off* for a little while after lunch.

Noise abroad : make something known. ***Ex 1.*** It is being *noised abroad* that he has been arrested. ***Ex 2.*** Rumours of his dismissal were *noised abroad* in the office. ***Ex 3.*** It was *noised abroad* that he was taking up a new appointment.

Nose about/around : pry into or search something. ***Ex 1.*** The reporter was *nosing about* for news. ***Ex 2.*** Don't *nose about* in other peoples affairs.

Nose out : discover something by searching. ***Ex 1.*** He can *nose out* a news story anywhere. ***Ex 2.*** Trust him to *nose out* some choice piece of scandal.

Notch up : gain or achieve something; score something. ***Ex 1.*** He has *notched up* quite a few triumphs lately. ***Ex 2.*** Our teams have *notched up* a number of wins in matches against visiting sides. ***Ex 3.*** With this performance, Mohini has *notched up* her third championship title.

Note down : record something in writing; write something down. ***Ex 1.*** The policeman *noted down* every word he said. ***Ex 2.*** The date of the meeting was carefully *noted down*.

Number among : include somebody/something in a particular group. ***Ex 1.*** I *number* her *among* my closest friends. ***Ex 2.*** I *number* that crash *among* the most frightening experiences of my life.

Number off : Call out one's number in a sequence. ***Ex 1.*** The soldiers *numbered off*, starting from the right-hand man. ***Ex 2.*** The platoon *numbered off* from the right.

Nurse through : assist to survive or to get better. ***Ex 1.*** hope you will help to *nurse* this project *through*.

Nuzzle up to : press close to somebody/something, especially by pushing gently with the head. ***Ex 1.*** The child *nuzzled up* to me on the sofa. ***Ex 2.*** The children *nuzzled up* to their sleeping mother.

15 Words Beginning With–O

Ogle at : look or stare at, in a way that suggests sexual interest. ***Ex 1.*** Don't *ogle at* ugly women. ***Ex 2.*** Most women dislike being *ogled at* ***Ex 3.*** He *ogles at* all the attractive female secretaries in the office. ***Ex 4.*** She was embarrassed at being *ogled at* so persistently.

Open into : give access to something ; lead to something; allow one to reach something. ***Ex 1.*** The back door *opens into* the garden. ***Ex 2.*** The door of the cottage *opens into* an uninterrupted stretch of countryside.

Open out : (a) become wider; become visible. ***Ex 1.*** The road *opened out* into a dual carriage way. ***Ex 2.*** The view *opened out* in front of us as the fog cleared.

(b) develop (in personality, etc.) ***Ex.*** She *opened out* a lot while she was staying with us.

Open up : (a) talk freely and openly. ***Ex.*** She hoped that he would *open up* at once about his visit, but he did not.

(b) reveal. ***Ex*** His stories *open up* new world of the imagination.

(c) begin to fire. ***Ex*** A machine gun *opened up* from a concealed position.

Open with : start with something. ***Ex 1.*** The story *opens with* murder. ***Ex 2.*** I *opened* the conference *with* a concise speech.

Opt for : decide on something; choose something. ***Ex*** Fewer students are *opting for* science courses nowadays.

Opt out/out of : choose not to take part. ***Ex 1.*** He had simply *opted out of* every situation of trust he had been placed in. ***Ex 2.*** To *opt out* at this critical moment would be quite indefensible. ***Ex 3.*** I think I shall *opt out of* this game.

Order about/around : keep telling somebody to do this and that in a bossy way. ***Ex 1.*** Youhave got no right to *order* me *about* the place. ***Ex 2.*** Even as a boy he was always *ordering* his friends *about.*

Order out : order police or troops to parade to control civil disturbance, etc. ***Ex 1.*** As a dangerous situation was developing in some parts of Delhi, security forces were *ordered out* to control it. ***Ex 2.*** The government *ordered* the police *out* to restore order in the streets.

Own up : admit or confess that one is to blame for something. ***Ex 1.*** Nobody *owned up* to the theft. ***Ex 2.*** He *owned up* to the crime. ***Ex 3.*** They hoped that she would *own up* to having told a lie.

---

16 *Words Beginning With–P*

Pack away : eat. ***Ex.*** He can *pack away* more food than anyone else I know.

Pack in : (a) draw people in large numbers to a theatre, etc. ; crowd in; crowd or press together into a limited space. ***Ex 1.*** The people *packed in* as tightly as they could. ***Ex 2.*** That show has been *packing* them *in* for months. ***Ex 3.*** They *packed* all six of us *in* the tiny car.

(b) abandon; renounce; resign; stop working; give up. ***Ex 1.*** She has *packed in* her job. ***Ex 2.*** Smoking is bad for your health; you ought to *pack* it *in*.

(c) end a relationship with. ***Ex.*** She has *packed* her boyfriend *in*.

(d) stop functioning. ***Ex.*** The car engine *packed in* at the top of the big hill.

(e) lose interest in. ***Ex.*** He has *packed* his studies *in*.

Pack into : do a lot of things in a limited time. ***Ex.*** She managed to *pack* a lot of sightseeing *into* four days.

Pack it in : stop doing or saying something that angers or annoys somebody else. ***Ex.*** I am sick of your complaining—just *pack it in*.

Pack off : send somebody away, quickly and decisively. ***Ex 1.*** She *packed* the children *off* to bed. ***Ex 2.*** Wewere *packed off* to stay in the country.

Note : The expression the country in the said usage means *land away from towns and cities, typically with fields, woods, etc. and used for agriculture*. ***Ex.*** He lives in the *country*.

Pack out : fill to capacity; completely fill (a cinema, etc.) with people. ***Ex 1.*** A great throng *packed out* the lecture theatre and overflowed into the corridors. ***Ex 2.*** Opera houses were *packed out* whenever Madhu was singing.

Pack up : (a) stop doing; give up or abandon something. ***Ex 1.*** Business is terrible—I might as well *pack up*. ***Ex 2.*** If you don't know where you are going, you might just as well *pack up*. ***Ex 3.*** I shall tell her straight out that if she does not take this on, she may as well *pack up*.

(b) break down; stop operating or working. ***Ex.*** My car has *packed up*.

(c) put one's belongings into cases, etc. before leaving a place. ***Ex 1.*** He *packed up* the few possessions he had and moved out. ***Ex 2.*** She *packed up* her things and left.

Pack it up : stop an activity. ***Ex.*** The children were making an awful din and I told them to *pack it up*.

Pad about/along : walk with a soft sound of steps. ***Ex 1.*** The dog *padded along* next to its owner. ***Ex 2.*** He *padded about* the house in his slippers.

Pad out : make fuller by adding unnecessary material. ***Ex 1.*** The passage was tiresomely *padded out* with reference to the author's fashionable friends. ***Ex 2.*** The editor asked him to stop *padding out* his articles.

Pair off : from a pair, or pairs. ***Ex 1.*** Her parents tried to *pair* her *off* with a rich neighbour. ***Ex 2.*** The scouts *paired off* and began to patrol the area. ***Ex 3.*** Each girl in the party was *pared off* with a boy.

Pal up : become friendly with somebody. ***Ex 1.*** They have *palled up* again after the quarrel. ***Ex 2.*** In the first form, he *palled up* with a boy from the same village. ***Ex 3.*** Don't *pal up* with a disreputable person.

Pale at : show signs of fear at. ***Ex 1.*** The poor fellow, though no coward, *paled at* the mention of an injection. ***Ex 2.*** Meeting his mother-in-law for the first time was a prospect *at* which he *paled.*

Pale before/beside : become less important in comparison with something. ***Ex 1.*** Her beauty *pales beside* her mothers. ***Ex 2.*** Their other problems *pales* into insignificance *beside* this latest catastrophe.

Pall on/upon : become uninteresting or boring by being used, spoken, ere too long. ***Ex 1.*** His funny stories begin to *pall on* his listeners after the second time of telling. ***Ex 2.*** His glib manner *palls on* one within a short time of first meeting him.

Palm off : (a) dishonesly persuade somebody to accept something. ***Ex*** The salesman tried to *palm* us *off* with some shop-soiled sheets.

(b) persuade somebody to accept something/somebody by underhand means. ***Ex 1.*** He *palmed* his unwelcome guests *off* on the neighbours. ***Ex 2.*** Export rejects were *palmed off* in the street markets. ***Ex 3.*** We *palmed off* the unimportant equipment on somebody else. ***Ex 4.*** He is the kind of dealer on whom anything can be *palmed off.*

Pan out : turn out; develop; work out. ***Ex 1.*** It depends how things *pan out.* ***Ex 2.*** Nobody knows how the economy will *pan out* over the next few years. ***Ex 3.*** Don't spend too much time worrying how things are going to *pan out.* ***Ex 4.*** Things did not *pan out* well for her. ***Ex 5.*** Events may *pan out* better than expected.

Pander to : try to satisfy (a vulgar or immoral desire); gratify something/somebody. ***Ex 1.*** Many newspapers *pander to* the public love of scandal involving important persons. ***Ex 2.*** Many a monthly magazine *panders to* the public interest in the seamy and sensational. ***Ex 3.*** This is the kind of depraved appetite *to* which television often *panders.*

Paper over : (a) cover something with wall paper. ***Ex.*** We *papered over* the stains on the wall.

(b) attempt to conceal (a fault, difficulty or disagreement) quickly or imperfectly. ***Ex.*** We must try to *paper over* this disagreement.

Parcel out : divide something into parts or portions. ***Ex 1.*** He *parcelled out* the land into small plots. ***Ex 2.*** An extensive tract of land was *parcelled out* into small holdings.

Parcel up : make something into a parcel; wrap something up. ***Ex 1.*** He *parcelled up* the books. ***Ex 2.*** Tell him to *parcel up* two thousand copies of the book titled 'Improve Your Vocabulary' and post them to the distributors.

Pare down : reduce something considerably. ***Ex 1.*** We have *pared down* our expenses to a bare minimum. ***Ex 2.*** You will have to *pare down* your living expenses.

Pare off : remove (skin, peel, etc.) from something in thin strips. ***Ex.*** She *pared off* the thick peel with a sharp knife.

Part with : give away or relinquish something, ***Ex 1.*** I hate *parting with* my money. ***Ex 2.*** Despite his penury, he refused to *part with* the family jewels. ***Ex 3.*** She made them listen and even on occasion, *part with* money for her objects of charity. ***Ex 4.*** He is not the sort of man to *part with* hard-earned cash.

Partake of : resemble in part; contain something of the nature of. ***Ex 1.*** I cannot help thinking that his generosity *partakes* somewhat *of* patronage.

Partner off : become partners. ***Ex.*** We *partnered off* for the next dance. Pass away: die. ***Ex.*** His maternal grandfather *passed away* last year.

Pass by : (a) go past. ***Ex 1.*** The procession *passed right by my* front door. ***Ex 2.*** I saw the procession *pass by*.

(b) not touch or affect; leave alone; occur without affecting somebody/something. ***Ex 1.*** The whole business *passed* him *by*. ***Ex 2.*** She hoped that the great challenges of life would *pass* her *by*. ***Ex 3.*** Life's colourful pageant would best oblige him by continuing to *pass* him *by*. ***Ex 4.*** He feels that life is *passing* him *by*.

(c) not consider; avoid; ignore; pay no attention to. ***Ex 1.*** If you try to *pass* the problems *by*, they will remain to dog you. ***Ex 2.*** We cannot *pass by* this matter without protest.

(d) shun; avoid. ***Ex 1.*** He had a feeling that his friends were *passing* him *by*. ***Ex 2.*** He made quite a noise when one or other of his girlfriends *passed* him *by*.

Pass down : pass something from one generation to the next. ***Ex 1.*** The tradition has been *passed down* from father to son. ***Ex 2.*** The skill has been *passed down* over two generations. ***Ex 3.*** The accumulated knowledge which has been *passed down* on this subject is well presented in this volume.

Pass for : be accepted as somebody/something; be taken for. ***Ex 1.*** He speaks French well enough to *pass for* a Frenchman. ***Ex 2.*** She is 40, but I think she could *pass for* 25 without much trouble. ***Ex 3.*** Among the people of that small town, he *passed for* a man of considerable means. ***Ex 4.*** He looked at the collection of odds and ends that *passed for* China.

Pass into : become a part of something. ***Ex 1.*** Many foreign words have *passed into* the English language. ***Ex 2.*** His deeds have *passed into* legend.

Pass off : (a) take place and be completed. ***Ex.*** The demonstration *passed off* without incident.

(b) disappear; come to an end gradually. ***Ex.*** The numbness in your feet will soon *pass off*.

(c) turn attention away from, so as to avoid embarrassment. ***Ex.*** Even if someone else raised the subject of the lecture, he would *pass* it *off* as easily as he could.

Pass off as : represent somebody/something falsely as somebody/ something. ***Ex 1.*** She *passed* him *off* as her husband. ***Ex 2.*** He escaped by *passing* himself *off* as a guard. ***Ex 3.*** He *passed* his wife *off* as an official member of the party.

Pass on to : (a) hand something to the next person, or another person; get rid of something, by giving it to another person. ***Ex 1.*** *Pass* the letter *on to* whoever is next on the distribution card. ***Ex 2.*** If you cannot do the job yourself, *pass* it *on to* someone who can. ***Ex 3.*** *Pass* the book *on to* me when you have finished with it. ***Ex 4.*** She caught my cold and *passed* it *on to* her husband.

(b) move from one activity or stage to another. ***Ex 1.*** Let us *pass on to* the next item on the agenda. ***Ex 2.*** It seemed the most natural thing in the world for her to *pass on to* television from the theatre.

Pass out : faint; lose consciousness. ***Ex.*** He *passed out* when he heard the bad news,

Pass over : (a) not consider somebody for promotion. ***Ex.*** He was *passed over* in favour of a younger man.

(b) avoid something; ignore or disregard something. ***Ex 1.*** Sex is a subject I prefer to *pass over*. ***Ex 2.*** I chose to *pass over* her rude remarks.

(c) die. ***Ex.*** When did your grandfather *pass over*?

(d) scan; review; run through. ***Ex 1.*** I shall *pass* briefly *over* the events of last evening to refresh your memories. ***Ex 2.*** The Chairman *passed* quickly *over* the first four items to leave more time for the main business of the meeting.

Pass through : (a) go through a town, etc. stopping there for a short time but not staying. ***Ex 1.*** We came to say hello as we were *passing through*. ***Ex 2.*** Why don't you stay the night? No, thank you, we were just *passing through*.

(b) suffer; experience. ***Ex.*** She *passed through* a very difficult period after her marriage broke down.

Pass up : fail to grasp (a chance, opportunity, etc.). ***Ex.*** Don't *pass up* an opportunity to earn money.

Patch up : settle or resolve. They *patched up* their differences. ***Ex 1.*** The matter was *patched up* without resort to the police. ***Ex 2.*** We managed to *patch up* the dispute before any heads were broken.

Patter about/along/around : walk quickly with high footsteps. ***Ex.*** She *pattered along* the corridor in her bare feet.

Pay back : (a) repay money to. ***Ex 1.*** Have you *paid* me *back* the money you owe me yet? ***Ex 2.*** I shall *pay* her *back* next week.

(b) punish somebody or get one's revenge. ***Ex 1.*** I shall *pay* you *back* for the trick you played on me. ***Ex 2.*** She *paid* him *back* for his casual infidelities.

Pay for : suffer or be punished for something. ***Ex 1.*** I shall make him *pay for* his insolence. ***Ex 2.*** If we fail to act now, we shall find ourselves *paying for* inaction later on.

Pay off : (a) bring good results; be successful, prove profitable. ***Ex 1.*** My scheme has *paid off* handsomely. ***Ex 2.*** Occasionally the checking *pays off* and there is the excitement of a chase or an arrest. ***Ex.*** **3** The gamble *paid off*.

(b) pay in full as settlement of a debt, etc. ***Ex 1.*** He has *paid off* his debts. ***Ex 2.*** All her outstanding debts have been *paid off*. ***Ex 3.*** You will have to *pay off* your old loan before being allowed a new one. ***Ex 4.*** Have you *paid off* your creditors.

(c) average. ***Ex.*** He has managed to *pay off* old scores.

(d) discharge with a payment. ***Ex 1.*** I *paid* two of my servants *off*. ***Ex 2.*** The manager personally *paid off* the redundant employees. ***Ex 3.*** The ship's crew were *paid off* at the end of the voyage.

Pay out : (a) make a large payment for something. ***Ex 1.*** I had to *pay out* six thousand rupees to get the car repaired. ***Ex 2.*** He is *paying out* five thousand rupees a month on his mortage. ***Ex 3.*** He is tired of *paying out* on school fees and uniforms.

(b) release steadily, or in stages through the hands. ***Ex 1.*** He *paid out* the rope. ***Ex 2.*** Knoting the wire round a projecting stone cornice, he *paid* it *out* into the darkness.

(c) punish somebody in return for some injury one has suffered. ***Ex 1.*** Someone will try to *pay* you *out* if you trample too much on the feelings of others. ***Ex 2.*** He felt that he had been more than *paid out* for a few indiscretions.

Pay up : pay in full money that is owed for something. ***Ex 1.*** I shall take you to court unless you *pay up* immediately. ***Ex 2.*** Please *pay up* all you owe. ***Ex 3.*** My goods have vanished and the insurance company will have to *pay up*. ***Ex 4.*** You might as well smile and *pay up*.

Peak off : reach a maximum and fall off. ***Ex.*** The sales have begun to *peak off*.

Pell off : (a) leave a group and turn to one side. ***Ex.*** One squadron *peeled off* to attack enemy bombers.

(b) undress. ***Ex.*** She *peeled off* and went to bed.

(c) remove. *Ex.* She *peeled off* her clothes and went to bed.

Peg away : work hard and persistently. ***Ex 1.*** You are bound to find the answer in the end, just keep *pegging away*. ***Ex 2.*** He has been *pegging away* at his thesis for months.

Peg down : (a) pin somebody down; force or persuade somebody to be specific or make a definite promise. ***Ex 1.*** I *pegged* him *down* to a price for the work. ***Ex 2.*** The government agreed to *peg down* the retail price of certain basic foodstuffs.

(b) make somebody follow, or commit himself to, a particular course of action. ***Ex 1.*** It is proving very difficult to *peg* him *down* a definite date for completion. ***Ex 2.*** When it is a matter of getting a clear promise, he is hard to *peg down*.

Peg out : faint or collapse from exhaustion; die. ***Ex 1.*** His brother *pegged out* on the 28th of the last month. ***Ex 2.*** At this height, a climber can *peg out* from lack of oxygen. ***Ex 3.*** Several of the runners *pegged out* at the end of the course.

Pelt along, down, up, etc. : run very fast in the specified direction. ***Ex.*** They were *pelting along* the hill.

Pen in/up : shut somebody/something in, or as if in, a pen; restrict the movement or freedom. ***Ex 1.*** *Pen up* the chickens for the night. ***Ex 2.*** The flocks were penned in for the night as a protection against marauding wolves. ***Ex 3.*** She feels *penned in* by her life as a housewife. She can never get away from the kitchen stove or the children.

Pension off : (a) allow or force somebody to retire, and give him a pension. ***Ex 1.***He was *pensioned off* and replaced with a younger man. ***Ex 2.*** Has he been not *pensioned off* yet ? ***Ex 3.*** I think they will *pension* him *off* soon.

(b) no longer use something, because it is old and worn. ***Ex.*** The old printing press will have to be *pensioned off*.

People with : fill with people, imagination, etc. ***Ex 1.*** He believes the world is *peopled with* idiots. ***Ex 2.*** His dreams were *peopled with* strange, terrifying fantasies.

Pep up : make somebody/something move lively or energetic; stimulate somebody/something. ***Ex 1.*** Know it for certain that a walk in the fresh air will *pep* you *up*. ***Ex 2.*** It is a lively music to *pep up* the party.

Perk up : (a) become more cheerful, lively or vigorous, especially after illness or depression. ***Ex.*** He looked depressed but *perked up* when his girl-friend arrived.

(b) make somebody feel more cheerful or lively. ***Ex 1.*** A holiday will *perk* you *up*. ***Ex 2.*** This medicine will *perk* him *up*. ***Ex 3.*** What do you need to *perk* you *up*?

(c) make somebody look smarter. ***Ex.*** He had *perked* himself *up* for the party.

(d) make something look smarter, better, more vigorous, etc. ***Ex 1.*** *Perk up* the plants with a good watering. ***Ex 2.*** You need a bright red scarf to *perk up* that grey suit.

Permit of : tolerate; admit something as possible; allow or leave room for. ***Ex 1.*** The times we are living through do not *permit of* weakness of indecision. ***Ex 2.*** The situation does not *permit of* any delay. ***Ex 3.*** This problem does not *permit of* an easy solution.

Pick off : shoot after aiming carefully. ***Ex 1.*** A sniper hidden on a roof *picked off* four of the policemen on patrol. ***Ex 2.*** They *pick off* the officers first, so as to throw the attack into confusion.

Pick on : (a) choose somebody especially repeatedly, for criticism, blame or punishment. ***Ex 1.*** She felt that her parents were *picking on* her. ***Ex 2.*** He was constantly being *picked on* to do the dirty jobs. ***Ex 3.*** Why do you *pick on* me all the time?

(b) choose somebody for a task, especially an unpleasant one. ***Ex.*** He was *picked on* to announce the bad news.

Pick out : (a) choose from a number of people orthings ***Ex 1.*** I was *picked out* from thousands of applicants for the job. ***Ex 2.*** He *picked out* the ripest mangoes. ***Ex 3.*** We *picked out* the best items on the menu. ***Ex 4.*** Would you *pick out* the one you want?

(b) separate or distinguish from surrounding persons or objects. ***Ex 1.*** His house easily *picked out* from the rest: it has a large blue door. ***Ex 2*** I tried to *pick out* her face in the crowd pressing through the door. ***Ex 3.*** He was not able to *pick out* the figures clearly.

Pick over : look carefully at, in order to select the best or throwaway bad ones. ***Ex 1.*** You won't find any good tomatoes in that basket; they have been well *picked over.* ***Ex 2.*** The housewives *pick* the fruit *over* carefully before making their minds up which to buy. ***Ex 3.*** Customers were *picking over* the remnants left after the sale.

Pick up : (a) improve; become better; recover. ***Ex 1.***You will soon *pick up* after a day or two in bed. ***Ex 2.*** Her health and spirits *picked up* after a fortnight at the seaside. ***Ex 3.*** His health soon *picked up* after a few days' rest. ***Ex 4.*** We are waiting until the weather *picks up* a bit.

(b) continue; start again; manage to continue after an interruption. ***Ex 1.*** They will *pick up* where they finished yesterday. ***Ex 2.*** Let us *pick up* the story again at the point where Bhagwan has lost his job at the newspaper office. ***Ex 3.*** Because of the disturbance outside the window, I lost the thread of the discussion and had some difficulty in *picking* it *up* again. ***Ex 4.*** After the interruption, we *picked up* where we had left off.

(c) get to one's feet, especially after a fall. ***Ex 1.*** She *picked* herself *up* after the fall. ***Ex 2.*** *Pick* yourself *up* and brush yourself down.

(d) collect somebody; give somebody a lift in a car. ***Ex 1.*** The driver stopped to *pick up* a hitch-hiker. ***Ex 2.*** She *picked* me *up* at 7 o'clock.

(e) make casual acquaintance of. ***Ex 1.*** He just *picked* her *up* at a dance. ***Ex 2.*** He *picked up* the girl at a college disco. ***Ex 3.*** She is living with some man whom she *picked up* on holiday.

(f) rescue somebody (from the sea). ***Ex.*** Survivors of the air disaster were *picked up* by small boats.

(g) stop and seize somebody (for questioning); arrest somebody. ***Ex 1.*** He was *picked up* and taken for questioning. ***Ex 2.*** The police *picked* him *up* as he was trying to leave the country.

(h) reprimand somebody. ***Ex 1.*** The teacher *picked* him *up* for grammatical mistakes. ***Ex 2.*** I *picked* her *up* for using bad language.

(i) take hold of and lift somebody/something. ***Ex 1.*** I *picked up* your bag by mistake. ***Ex 2.*** He *picked up* the book from the floor. ***Ex 3.*** She *picked up* the phone and dialled her boyfriend's number.

(j) fall into company. ***Ex 1.*** She has *picked up* with some peculiar persons. ***Ex 2.*** He has *picked up* with a bad bunch of people.

(k) see or hear somebody/something, by means of apparatus. ***Ex 1.*** They *picked up* the yacht on their radar screen. ***Ex 2.*** The equipment *picked up* the signal from the satellite.

(l) learn or acquire without difficulty; learn by practising. ***Ex 1.*** I soon *picked up* French when I went to live in Paris. ***Ex 2.*** Rita is not very quick at *picking up* the local language.

(m) catch (an illness). ***Ex 1.*** When did you *pick up* the flu? ***Ex 2.*** She *picked up* a cold a few days ago.

(n) buy something, cheaply or luckily. ***Ex 1.*** We *picked up* most of the furniture at auctions in several cities. ***Ex 2.*** She is always on the prowl, *picking up* scraps of gossip.

(o) hear or learn (gossip, news, etc.) ***Ex 1.*** I *picked up* a very interesting piece of news. ***Ex 2.*** I entreated her to see if she can *pick up* anything about their future plans.

(p) collect something. ***Ex 1.*** Don't forget to *pick up* ice-cream on the way home. ***Ex 2.*** He is going to *pick up* his coat from the cleaners. ***Ex 3.*** I shall *pick up* something for dinner on my way home from the meeting. ***Ex 4.*** You can *pick up* the tickets an hour before the play begins.

(q) draw or derive something. ***Ex.*** The trolley-bus *picks up* current from an over-head wire.

(r) find something; locate something. ***Ex 1.*** They *picked up* the track on the other side of the river. ***Ex 2.*** Do you know how to *pick up* a scent?

(s) start to function again. ***Ex.*** The motor spluttered and seemed about to cut out; then it *picked up* again.

(t) recover; improve. ***Ex 1.*** The shares *picked up* after an early spate of panic selling. ***Ex 2.*** Sale of sweets *picked up* again before Diwali.

Pile in/into : enter something in a disorderly way. ***Ex 1.*** The taxi arrived and we all *piled in*. ***Ex 2.*** The children *piled* noisily *into* the bus. ***Ex 3.*** We *piled* all the luggage *in* and drove off.

Pile on/onto : burden somebody with an undue amount of something. ***Ex 1.*** Why is it that all the extra work gets *piled onto* me at Durga Pooja time?

Pile up : (a) accumulate; increase in quantity. ***Ex 1.*** Evidence was *piling up* against him. ***Ex 2.*** Her debts are *piling up* and she has no money to pay them.

(b) crash into each other, especially with each car hitting the one in front. ***Ex.*** Several cars *piled up* after ignoring the fog warning on the motorway.

Pile out : leave something in a disorderly way. ***Ex 1.*** We *piled out* of the back of the car and streched our cramped limbs. ***Ex 2.*** The police were waiting for the hooligans as they *piled out* of the train.

Pilot through : (a) cause to pass through various legislative, etc. stages; make sure that something, especially a bill is successful. ***Ex 1.*** He has successfully *piloted* his private member's Bill *through* its various stages in Parliament. ***Ex 2.*** The government *piloted* the Education Bill *through* both the Houses of Parliament.

(b) guide somebody/something. ***Ex 1.*** She *piloted* me *through* the crowd. ***Ex 2.*** Father *piloted* me *through* the academic career for a span of many a year.

Pin against/under : make it impossible for somebody to move/something to be moved; trap somebody between oneself and a tree, wall, etc. and prevent him from moving away. ***Ex 1.*** He was *pinned against* the fence by a boy twice his size; he could hardly breathe. ***Ex 2.*** A stout customer *pinned* the hapless assistant *against* the counter, and demanded to see the manager. ***Ex 3.*** I *pinned* him *against* the wall. ***Ex 4.*** The car was *pinned under* a fallen tree.

Pin down : (a) make somebody unable to move, especially by holding him firmly. ***Ex 1.*** He *pinned* her legs *down* under a heavy weight. ***Ex 2.*** He was *pinned down* by his attackers. ***Ex 3.*** Troops were *pinned down* in their trenches by accurate mortar fire.

(b) define exactly. ***Ex 1.*** What it was in her to *pin down* that pleased him so much. ***Ex 2.*** There is something wrong with this colour scheme but I can't quite *pin* it *down*.

(c) make somebody be specific or declare his intentions clearly. ***Ex 1.*** He is a very difficult man to *pin down*: he seems to enjoy being all things to all men. ***Ex 2.*** Have you tried *pinning* him *down* on the question of capital punishment.

(d) make somebody agree to something. ***Ex 1.*** I managed to *pin* him *down* to meeting us after work. ***Ex 2.*** You will find it difficult to *pin* him *down* to naming a price. ***Ex 3.*** They managed to *pin* her *down* to a particular time and place. ***Ex 4.*** I can't *pin* him *down* to a promise like that.

Pin on : make somebody seem responsible or take the blame for it. ***Ex.*** The bank manager was really to blame, he tried to *pin* it *on* a clerk.

Pine away : become ill or waste away becuase of grief. ***Ex 1.*** She has *pined away* dreadfully since her young passionate boyfriend broke things off. ***Ex 2.*** He lost interest in living and just *pined away*.

Pipe down : stop talking; be less noisy. ***Ex 1.*** He told the children to *pipe down* while he was talking on the phone. ***Ex 2.*** Tell them to *pipe down.*

Piss about/around : behave in a foolish, boisterous, time-wasting or unhelpful way; work in a casual disorganised way. ***Ex 1.*** Look just stop *pissing about*, for ten minutes. I have got work to do. ***Ex 2.*** Stop *pissing about*, get on with your work. ***Ex 3.*** We were *pissed around* for hours before they finally gave us the right form.

Piss off : (a) go away. ***Ex 1.*** Tell her to piss off. ***Ex 2.*** He told me to *piss off*, or he would clobber me.

(b) annoy or bore somebody. ***Ex 1.*** I am not interested in your haranque, don't *piss* me *off*. Leave me alone. ***Ex 2.*** Champa Rani is really *pissed off* with the job. She is looking for a way out-any way out.

Pit against : match against/with; set somebody or something in competition against. ***Ex 1.*** He will *pit* his wits *against* the bureaucracy of the tax office. ***Ex 2.*** He will *pit* himself *against* the reigning champion. ***Ex 3.*** Don't *pit* your puny wit *against* my massive intelligence.

Pitch in : (a) start working energetically. ***Ex.*** They all *pitched in* and soon finished the job.

(b) eat something with a good appetite. ***Ex.*** We had prepared supper for the team and they all *pitched in*

Pitch into : (a) start working energetically. ***Ex.*** They *pitched into* the work immediately.

(b) eat something With a good appetite. ***Ex.*** They *pitched into* the meal.

(c) attack somebody violently. ***Ex.*** The gang *pitched into* him and left him badly injured.

Pitch in with : offer help or support. ***Ex.*** They *pitched in with* liberal contributions of money.

Pivot on : depend on something central or essential; hinge on something. ***Ex.*** The whole discussion *pivots on* this one point.

Plan out : consider something in detail and arrange it in advance. ***Ex 1.*** Have you *planned out* your annual expenditure? ***Ex 2.*** The experts *planned out* a traffic system for the city.

Plane away/down/off : remove something using a plane. ***Ex 1.*** The cuts and scratches that the packers made on the desk can be *planned away*. ***Ex 2.*** He *planned away* the irregularities on the surface.

Plank down : (a) put something down heavily. ***Ex.*** He *planked down* his luggage on the floor.

(b) pay money at once. ***Ex.*** He *planked* the money *down* on the counter and asked for a cold drink.

Plant out : place (plants) in the ground, so that they have enough room to grow. ***Ex 1.*** We have *planted out* many tomato seedlings. ***Ex 2.*** These bulbs should now be *planted out*. ***Ex 3.*** When will you *plant* the flowers *out* in beds?

Play about/around : act or handle somebody/something in a casual irresponsible way. ***Ex 1.*** Don't *play around*, with another woman's husband. ***Ex 2.*** Why are you *playing about* with his expensive tools? ***Ex 3.*** He is *playing around* with a girl who is young enough to be his daughter. ***Ex 4.*** This is not a substance that can be *played about* by anybody.

Play along : (a) pretend to co-operate; act in accordance with; go along with. ***Ex 1.*** She was in charge, so I had to *play along* with her odd ideas. ***Ex 2.*** The minority parties will have to be persuaded to *play along*.

(b) keep waiting in suspense. ***Ex.*** They have *played* him *along* for some time now, without telling him what they really want.

Play at : (a) engage in casually or half-heartedly; do something only casually, without true interest. ***Ex 1.*** Office routine is just something he *plays at*; the one thing that really interests him is golf. ***Ex 2.*** Bear in mind that this is a job that needs to be tackled whole-heartedly-not *played at*. ***Ex 3.*** He is only *playing at* his job in the city, he is much more interested in being a racing driver.

(b) pretend for fun to be somebody or do something. ***Ex.*** Small boys usually like *playing at* soldiers, and small girls at nurses or mothers.

Play back : allow the material recorded on a tape, etc. to be heard. ***Ex 1.*** He rebound the cassette and *played* her voice *back* to her. ***Ex 2.*** I am going to *play back* part of the statement you made to the police.

Play down : try to make something appear less important than it is. ***Ex 1.*** The government is trying to *play down* its involvement in the affair. ***Ex 2.*** She tried to *play down* his part in the affair and play up her own. ***Ex 3.*** He has consistently tried to *play down* my part in the project. ***Ex 4.*** It must be borne in mind that in a crisis it is best to *play down* the emotional issues.

Play off against : oppose one person to another, for one's own adavantage; cause two persons or groups to oppose each other, for one's own advantage. ***Ex 1.*** She *played* her two rivals *off against* each other and got the job herself. ***Ex 2.*** He has *played* his enemies *off* against each other. ***Ex 3.*** I like to *play* one person *off against* another. ***Ex 4.*** It is a favourite occupation of some countries to *play* India, the biggest democracy in the world, and Pakistan *off against* each other.

Play on/upon : (a) rouse (somebody's feelings, etc.) for one's own purpose; exploit. ***Ex 1.*** He loves *playing upon* people's emotions. ***Ex 2.*** They *played on* his fears of losing his job to get him to do what they wanted. ***Ex 3.*** Her speech *played* heavily *on* the angry mood of her audience. ***Ex 4.*** Their memories of past injustices were cleverly *played on.*

(b) make use of words and expressions with a similar form but different meaning for humorous effect, etc. ***Ex 1.*** The writer *plays upon* the similarities between ordinary and technical language. ***Ex 2.*** The language of much advertising consists of *playing* elaborately *on* words.

Play out : (a) perform or enact something, especially in real life. ***Ex.*** Their love affair was *played out* against the background of a country at war.

(b) be exhausted; be finished. ***Ex 1.*** The argument is completely *played out.* ***Ex 2.*** I feel really *played out* after that game.

Play up : (a) cause somebody problems, pain or difficulties; annoy; torment; be a nuisance. ***Ex 1.*** His injured shoulder is *playing* him *up* today. ***Ex 2.*** Don't *play up* your teacher. ***Ex 3.*** She *played* him *up.* ***Ex 4.*** The children did their best to *play up.* ***Ex 5.*** The old wound has been *playing up* again lately. ***Ex 6.*** The engine began *playing up*.

(b) stress; emphasis. ***Ex.*** Depend on him to *play up* to the full his own part in reaching the settlement.

(c) try to make something appear more important than it-is. ***Ex.*** She *played up* her past achievements just to impress us.

Play up to : flatter somebody in order to win favour. ***Ex 1.*** He is always *playing up to* people who may be able to help him. ***Ex 2.*** He is the sort of man who dislikes being *played up to.* He prefers a more straightforward approach.

Play with : (a) consider lightly; toy with something; dally with. ***Ex 1.*** He is *playing with* the idea of starting his own business. ***Ex 2.*** She is not a woman to tolerate being *played with.* ***Ex 3.*** You can *play with* a woman's affections once too often.

(b) amuse oneself by handling; handle in a casual, absent-minded way; toy with. ***Ex 1.*** While we spoke, the general manager *played with* a carved paper knife.

Plod along : move slowly at some task. ***Ex.*** How is the work? Oh, I am *plodding along.*

Plod away : work steadily but slowly, and with difficulty. ***Ex 1.*** Chameli Devi is not content to *plod away* at a desk job for ever. ***Ex 2.*** He *plodded away* all night at the accounts but did not finish them in time. ***Ex 3.*** He is not the kind to make sharp leaps forward, he just keeps *plodding away*.

Plonk down : drop something or put something down roughly or heavily on a surface. ***Ex 1.*** He *planked down* the groceries on the kitchen floor. ***Ex 2.*** An apple *plank down* on her lap.

Plug away : work hard and steadily at something. ***Ex 1.*** He has been *plugging away* at his Sanskrit lessons for months. ***Ex 2.*** How is the French coming on? Oh, I keep *plugging away*.

Plump down : (a) fall or drop suddenly and heavily; place down quickly and decisively. ***Ex 1.*** He *plumped down* the heavy bags on the floor. ***Ex 2.*** The child was *plumped down* on the counter while she rummaged in her bag. ***Ex 3.*** He *plumped* his *money* down to secure one of the few remaining tickets.

(b) sink quickly and heavily. ***Ex.*** Mridula Devi glanced quickly around the crowded room and *plumped down* on the only available chair.

Plump for: choose or vote for somebody/something with confidence. ***Ex 1.*** The committee *plumped for* the most experienced candidate. ***Ex 2.*** The children *plumped for* a holiday in Kashmir. ***Ex 3.*** I wanted the red car, but wife *plumped for* the blue one with grey seats.

Ply with: (a) repeatedly give or offer somebody. (food, drink, etc.). ***Ex 1.*** He was *plied with* everything that would make his stay in hospital more comfortable. ***Ex 2.*** She *plied* me *with* luscious fruit .

(b) repeatedly ask somebody questions. ***Ex 1.*** I *plied* the little girl *with* cakes. ***Ex 2.*** People beseiged the shipping offices and *plied* the staff *with* inquiries.

Point up : give special emphasis to one particular aspect of something; show something very clearly. ***Ex 1.*** The recent disagreement *points up* the differences between the two sides. ***Ex 2.*** The recent wage increases *point up* still further the difference between this government and the last. ***Ex 3.*** This serves to *point up* an aspect of police work that the public fails to understand.

Poke about/around : search inquisitively; nose about/around; make unwanted inquiries. ***Ex 1.*** Why are you *poking about* among my private papers? ***Ex 2.*** Those detectives have been *poking about* here again.

Poke out of/through: be visible coming through; protrude. ***Ex.*** A pen was *poking out* of his pocket. .

Polish off : (a) finish something quickly; finish eating, writing, etc. ***Ex 1.*** He can *polish off* the rest of the typing in no time. ***Ex 2.*** *Polish off* the arrears of correspondence within five days. ***Ex 3.*** The rest of the Diwali pudding was *polished off* by the children. ***Ex 4.*** He *polished off* the food.

(b) finish off; defeat. ***Ex 1.*** His opponents in the eliminating rounds were quickly *polished off*. ***Ex 2.*** Having disposed of the main opposition, he could *polish off* the remainder at his leisure.

Polish up : work at something to improve its quality or effectiveness. ***Ex 1.*** I shall have to *polish up* my Hindi, it is getting a bit rusty.

Ex 2. Our sales techniques need *polishing up.*

Pore over: study something with close attention. ***Ex 1.*** He *pored over* geography. ***Ex 2.*** The child spends hours *poring over* her books. ***Ex 3.*** What are you *poring over*?

Potter about/around: (a) move from one place or thing to another in a leisurely way. ***Ex 1.*** He is *pottering about* the exhibition. ***Ex 2.*** Who is *pottering around* in the garden?

(b) work in an unhurried relaxed way, doing small or trivial tasks. ***Ex.*** They spent the weekend *pottering about* the house.

Pounce on/upon: choose in a keen, alert way for criticism, etc. ***Ex 1.*** This is the kind of careless mistake on which examiners love to *pounce.* ***Ex 2.*** The teacher would *pounce on* every slip the child made, however insignificant, and her up to ridicule before the whole class.

Pour in/into : arrive in a stream. ***Ex.*** Thousands of applications *poured into* the office in response to our advertisement for the post of a financial adviser.

Pour out: express or be expressed, freefy and fully. ***Ex 1.*** When she realised that we know the truth, the whole story came *pouring out.* ***Ex 2.*** Kanta Rani *poured out* her troubles to me over a cup of coffee.

Prevail on/upon: persuade somebody to do something. ***Ex 1.*** I *prevailed on* Mohini to make a speech after dinner. ***Ex 2.*** The judge was *prevailed upon* to show clemency.

Prey on/upon : (a) make somebody one's victim; exploit or attack. ***Ex 1.*** A confident trickster has been *preying on* rich widows for months. ***Ex 2.*** The villagers were *preyed on* by bandits from the hills.

(b) assail; deeply trouble. ***Ex 1.*** It appears that his impending trial has been *preying on* his mind. ***Ex 2.*** What is *preying on* your mind?

Prise off: use force to open (a box, etc.) or remove (a lid, etc.). ***Ex 1.*** She used a chisel to *prise off* the lid of the box. ***Ex 2.*** *Prise off* the cover with your thumbs.

Prise out/out of : force somebody to reveal something. ***Ex 1.*** Foreign espionage did its utmost to *prise out* these secrets. ***Ex 2.*** She *prised* the story *out* of him by threatening to inform his employers. ***Ex 3.*** She had promised not to talk, and nothing we could do to *prise* the information *out* of her.

Profit by : by studying one's mistakes, etc., ensure they are not repeated. ***Ex 1.*** He has been married twice, but does not seem to have *profited* much *by* the experience. ***Ex 2.*** We ought to *profit by* our mistakes. ***Ex 3.*** She is getting married again, after two divorces. This clearly shows that she has not *profited by* her experiences.

Profit from: benefit from, or be helped by something. ***Ex 1.*** I *profited* greatly *from* my years abroad. ***Ex 2.*** I have immensely *profited from* her sound and sincere advice.

Prop up : (a) use a prop, or props to raise something and prevent it from falling. ***Ex 1.*** The baby cannot sit unaided-she has to be *propped up* on pillows. ***Ex 2.*** The roof will have to be *propped up* while repairs are carried out.

(b) support something that would otherwise fail. ***Ex 1.*** The regime has been *propped up* by foreign aid. ***Ex 2.*** The government refuses to *prop up* inefficient industries.

Provide against: make preparations in case something happens. ***Ex.*** The government has to *provide against* a possible petrol shortage in the coming months.

Provide for : (a) supply somebody with what he needs, especially the basic necessities of life. ***Ex 1.*** They worked hard to *provide for* their large family. ***Ex 2.*** He did not *provide for* his wife and children in his will. ***Ex 3.*** He was always *provided* well *for* his family. ***Ex 4.*** If you decide to divorce, you must see to it that your wife is properly *provided for.*

(b) make such efficient arrangements that all possible difficulties can be overcome. ***Ex.*** Every possible failure of the electrical system has been provided for, generally by duplicating the circuits.

(c) (of a Bill, legal agreements, etc.) : establish the legal basis or authority for something to be done later. ***Ex 1.*** The Bill *provides for* the eventual self-government of the Territory. ***Ex 2.*** A clause in the agreement *provides for* the arbitration of all disputes by an independent body. ***Ex 3.*** Equal pay for women is *provided for* in the party manifesto. ***Ex 4.*** The right of individuals to appeal to a higher court is *provided for* in the Constitution ofIndia.

Pull ahead/ahead of: move in front of. ***Ex 1.*** The car *pulled ahead* as soon as the road was cleared. ***Ex 2.*** Our team has *pulled ahead* of the rest in the championship.

Pull apart : criticise severely. ***Ex.*** There is nothing more dispiriting than having your essays *pulled apart* in front of other students.

Pull at : draw smoke steadily from a pipe, etc. ***Ex.*** The old man *pulled* thoughtfully, *at* his pipe, before replying.

Pull back: retreat; withdraw somebody. ***Ex.*** The army *pulled back* after the battle.

Pull down: (a) destroy or demolish. ***Ex 1.*** The cinema he used to visit had been *pulled down.* ***Ex 2.*** A row of back- to-back houses is being *pulled down* to make way for new flats. ***Ex. 3.*** They *pulled* the old building *down.*

(b) leave somebody in a weak condition; weaken somebody. ***Ex.*** His protracted illness had *pulled* him *down* a lot.

(c) lower, draw down. ***Ex.*** His hat was *pulled* well *down* over his eyes, so that nobody should guess his true identity.

(d) cause to fall to a lower position. ***Ex 1.*** It was the written paper that *pulled* him *down*. ***Ex 2.*** He seemed all set to win a gold medal, but his performance in the third round *pulled* him *down*.

Pull in: (a) earn; draw. ***Ex 1.*** He is pulling in a regular salary. ***Ex 2.*** They are *pulling in* a lot of overtime on that job. ***Ex 3.*** I am *pulling in* ten thousand rupees a month.

(b) attract or draw to a place of entertainment, an opportunity of investment, etc. ***Ex 1.*** The play has *pulled in* large audiences. ***Ex. 2.*** They need to have a high rate of interest in order to *pull in* money from investors. ***Ex 3.*** The new show is certainly *pulling in* the crowds.

(c) fetch to the police for questioning. ***Ex 1.*** Two youths loitering near a bank were *pulled in* on suspicion. ***Ex 2.*** The police *pulled* him *in* last night.

Pull in/into: (a) enter; arrive at. ***Ex.*** Our train *pulled into* the station dead on time.

(b) move in towards something. ***Ex.*** The bus *pulled into* the side of the road.

Pull off: (a) remove something with some force. ***Ex 1.*** Please help me *pull* these boots *off*. ***Ex 2.*** See if you can *pull* the cloth *off* the table without disturbing the glasses.

(b) succeed in something; make a success of something; complete successfully. ***Ex 1.*** He *pulled* that deal *off* beautifully. ***Ex 2.*** They could not manage to *pull* it *off*.

Pull out: (a) detach; remove by pulling. ***Ex 1.*** The map is at the back of the book, and may be *pulled out* for easy reference. ***Ex 2.*** She *pulled out* a gun.

(b) move out or sideways. ***Ex 1.*** The boat *pulled out* into the middle of the river. ***Ex 2.*** A car suddenly *pulled out* in front of me.

(c) leave; depart from. ***Ex 1.*** The three-thirty train was *pulling out* of platform as I ran into the station. ***Ex 2.*** She arrived as the last train was *pulling out.*

(d) withdraw from something. ***Ex 1.*** We are *pulling* our troops *out* of the battle zone. ***Ex 2.*** The project become so expensive that we had to *pull out*.

(e) move out of a line of traffic, in order to overtake the vehicle in front. **Ex 1.** The car in front *pulled out* to overtake just as I was about to overtake it. ***Ex 2.*** Don't *pull out* of a line stationary vehicles unless the road behind you is clear.

(f) force oneself to emerge, recover from. ***Ex.*** He has been dogged by failures for years; now he is working strenuously to *pull out*.

Pull over: move or steer to one side. ***Ex 1.*** *Pull over* and let me pass. ***Ex 2.*** I shouted to the driver of the tractor to *pull over* and let me through.

Pull round: regain consciousness. ***Ex.*** How long will she take to *pull round* after her operation?

Pull through: recover (from illness); help to survive a period of danger/ crisis. ***Ex 1.*** The patient has an excellent chance of *pulling through*. **Ex *2.*** It was this spirit which *pulled* them *through* the darkest moments of the war.

Pull together: (a) act, work etc. with combined effort in a well organised way. ***Ex 1.*** After the shock of the electoral defeat, the party really began to *pull together*. ***Ex 2.*** If we all *pull together*, we should be able to get the country out of the mess it is in. ***Ex 3.*** The old habit of looking well after the wage earners is still alive; so is the stress on the need for all to *pull together*. ***Ex 4.*** I hope all members of staff will *pull together*.

(b) draw the parts of something closer to each other. ***Ex.*** It was Padmini Devi more than anybody who *pulled* the Party *together* after our defeat in the last election.

Pull oneself together: get control of oneself, one's feelings, etc. ***Ex 1.*** You must try to *put yourself together*-your family depend on you. ***Ex 2.*** She had her ups and downs, but she had always managed to *pull herself together* and have a good time. ***Ex 3.*** *Pull yourself together*.

Pull up: (a) come to a halt; stop; halt. ***Ex 1.*** He *pulled* his car *up* within a few metres of the wreckage. ***Ex 2.*** The driver *pulled up* at the traffic lights. ***Ex 3.*** The car *pulled up*.

(b) check, reprimand or correct. ***Ex 1.*** He was *pulled up* by the managing director. ***Ex 2.*** The police *pulled* him *up* for speeding. ***Ex 3.*** The soldier was *pulled up* for having an untidy uniform. ***Ex 4.*** Even his wife had to *pull* him *up* over his wrong-headed notions this afternoon.

(c) improve one's position in relation to somebody/something. ***Ex 1.*** At first the new boy was at the bottom of the class but he soon *pulled up* with the others. ***Ex 2.*** His mark in the Hindi paper *pulled* him *up* several places.

Pump in/into : (a) persuade or force somebody to learn something. ***Ex 1.*** She tried to *pump* some facts *into* his head before the examination. ***Ex 2.*** There is no gainsaying the fact that it is a hard job *pumping* facts and figures *into* unwilling pupils. ***Ex 3.*** *Pump* enough propaganda *in*, and people will believe anything.

(b) put money in, with a view to giving support, earning interest, etc. ***Ex 1.*** India's economy is booming and foreign companies are confidently *pumping in* capital. ***Ex 2.*** The firm *pumped* money *into* the development of the new product. ***Ex 3.*** There may be strong social reasons why the government should *pump* money *into* industries which, economically, seem no longer viable.

Pump out of : make somebody reveal something. ***Ex.*** I *pumped* the full story *out* of her little by little.

Push about/around: order somebody to do this and that in a bullying tone; order somebody about/around. ***Ex 1.*** Stop *pushing* people *about* as though they were children. ***Ex 2.*** I won't be *pushed around* by her any longer. ***Ex 3.*** You may be able to *push* your brother *around*, but you must not try it on with me. ***Ex 4.*** Stop *pushing* everybody *about*.

Push ahead/forward/on: (a) continue on one's way. ***Ex.*** Let us *push on* it is nearly nightfall.

(b) continue doing something in a determined way. ***Ex 1.*** I advised him to *push ahead* with his project. ***Ex 2.*** Now that problem is solved, there is nothing to stop us *pushing ahead*. ***Ex 3.*** Redevelopment must be *pushed on* with as far as money permits. *Ex 4. Push forward* with your plan to complete the inner ring road.

Push along: leave one's host. ***Ex.*** I am afraid I really ought to be *pushing along* now.

Push for : make repeated and urgent requests for; press for something. ***Ex 1.*** People are *pushing for* electoral reform. ***Ex 2.*** Don't push him too hardfor a settlement.

Push forward: force others to consider or notice something. ***Ex 1.*** He repeatedly *pushed forward* his own claim. ***Ex 2.*** He has never been one to *push* himself *forward*. ***Ex 3.*** She *pushed forward* her claim to be considered the rightful heir to the throne.

Push off : leave; go away. ***Ex 1.*** *Push off*, we don't want you here. ***Ex 2.*** He comes here periodically, looks up a few friends, and then *pushes off* again.

Push over: make somebody/something overturn or fall to the ground by pushing him/it. ***Ex 1.*** I was nearly *pushed over* by a crowd of boys suddenly pouring out of the school gates. ***Ex 2.*** two tables were *pushed over* in the scramble. ***Ex 3.*** Many a children was *pushed over* in the rush to leave.

Note: The word *push-over* is a noun. It denotes: (a) thing that is very easily done, especially a contest that is easily won. ***Ex.*** Winning that match was a *push-over*.

(b) client, opponent, etc. who is easily convinced or won over. ***Ex.*** Getting money from her is easy-she is a *push-over*.

Push through: get something accepted or completed quickly. ***Ex 1.*** Try to *push* the plan *through* the committee stage. ***Ex 2.*** We are trying to *push* legislation *through* before the Diwali recess. ***Ex 3.*** You cannot *push* proposals on this sort of scale *through* the Ministry of Finance.

Push up : increase at a steady rate. ***Ex 1.*** A shortage of building land will *push* property values *up*. ***Ex 2.*** Wage increases have *pushed up* the price of many household articles. ***Ex 3.*** The usual drinking parties at New Year will *push* the road death figures *up*.

Put about: (a) turn; change direction. ***Ex 1.*** The ship *put about* and headed for safety. ***Ex 2.*** The skipper *put* us *about* to avoid submarines that had been reported in that area.

(b) spread or circulate (false news, rumours, etc.). ***Ex 1.*** It is being *put about* that the Prime Minister may resign. ***Ex 2.*** Don't *put about* malicious rumours about ugly girls or women. ***Ex 3.*** It was *put about* that he was seeing a great deal of a certain charming young lady.

(c) inconvenience. ***Ex.*** Please don't *put* yourself *about* because of me.

Put above : regard or treat as more important than. ***Ex 1.*** The investigations reveal that few men were determined to *put* the integrity of the government *above* its survival. ***Ex 2.*** *Above* such considerations of cost we should *put* the welfare of the men who work the machines.

Put across : (a) communicate successfully; to somebody. ***Ex 1.*** He does not know how to *put* himself *across* at interviews. ***Ex 2.*** Hem Lata is very good at *putting* her ideas *across*. ***Ex 3.*** Padma Rani finds it hard to *put* herself *across* to a selection board. ***Ex 4.*** He was having difficulty *putting* his case *across*.

(b) trick somebody into accepting a claim, etc. that is worthless or untrue. ***Ex 1.*** Don't try to *put* anything *across* me. ***Ex 2.*** He *put* them *across* the police once, but they are not to be caught a second time.

Put aside: (a) set aside; place something to one side. ***Ex 1.*** She *put* the newspaper *aside*, and we had a long talk. ***Ex 2.*** He *put aside* his textbooks when he left school and never reopened them.

(b) abandon; forget; disregard; ignore. ***Ex 1.*** He *put aside* his grief; and went to work. ***Ex 2.*** They decided to *put aside* their differences. ***Ex 3.*** *Put aside* as that has happened and try to start again.

(c) save for spending later. ***Ex.*** I have a nice little sum of money *put aside* for a rainy day. ***Ex 2.*** He has managed to *put aside* a huge amount of money.

(d) reserve an item for a customer to collect later. ***Ex 1.*** If you would like to pay me a small deposit, I shall *put* the coat *aside* for you, sir.

Put at : calculate, estimate, to be. ***Ex 1.*** I would *put* your age *at* about twenty. ***Ex 2.*** What would you *put* the price of this car *at* ? ***Ex 3.*** He *put* her weight *at* seventy pounds.

Put away : (a) put something in a box, drawer, etc., because one has finished using it. ***Ex 1.*** The correspondence was all *put away* in numbered files. ***Ex 2.*** She *put* her clothes *away*. ***Ex 3.*** *Put* your toys *away* in the cupboard, when you have finished playing.

(b) garage. ***Ex.*** I am just going to *put* the car *away*.

(c) save money to use later. ***Ex 1.*** I have *put away* some money in the bank. ***Ex 2.*** You will have to *put* something *away* for your retirement.

(d) confine somebody in a prison or mental hospital. ***Ex 1.*** He was *put away* for seven years for armed robbery. ***Ex 2.*** She went a bit odd and had to be *put away*. ***Ex 3.*** He was *put away* for attacking young children.

(e) consume considerable quantities of food or drink. ***Ex 1.*** Sangeeta *put away* half a dozen cakes while my back was turned. ***Ex 2.*** I don't know how he manages to *put* it all *away*. ***Ex 3.*** They *put away* a lot.

Put back: (a) replace something. ***Ex.*** Please *put* the dictionary *back* on the shelf when you have finished with it.

(b) move the hands of a clock back to give the correct time. ***Ex.*** Your watch is fast; *put* it *back* ten mintues.

(c) move to a later time or date. ***Ex 1.*** This afternoon's meeting has been *put back* to next week. ***Ex 2.*** The date has been *put back* from March to April.

(d) slow; retard, delay. ***Ex 1.*** Drought has *put* our agricultural programme back to where we started from. ***Ex 2.*** The lorry drivers' strike has *put back* our deliveries by over a month. ***Ex 3.*** The strike has *put back* production considerably.

Put before: treat or regard something as more important than something else. ***Ex 1.*** He *puts* his children's welfare *before* all other considerations. ***Ex 2.*** Their determination is to *put* the development of the community *before* all other considerations.

Put by: save money to use in the future. ***Ex 1.*** Have a bit *put by* for a rainy day. ***Ex 2.*** She has a fair amount of money *put by*.

Put down. : (a) land; land (an aeroplane, etc.). ***Ex 1.*** The helicopter hovered over us looking for a place to *put down*. ***Ex 2.*** The plane *put down* at the airport. ***Ex 3.*** He *put* the glider *down* in a field.

(b) allow somebody to get off. ***Ex.*** The bus stopped to *put down* some passengers.

(c) suppress or abolish something by force or authority. ***Ex 1.*** Gambling should be *put down*. ***Ex 2.*** The dictator is determined to *put down* all political opposition. ***Ex 3.*** The government should introduce stringent measures aimed at *putting down* corruption in government offices.

(d) silence. ***Ex.*** If an editor and critic annoys the old-fashioned writers, they (editors and critics) must be cautioned, but not *put down* completely.

(e) destroy; kill. ***Ex.*** The horse broke a leg in the fall and had to be *put down*.

(f) record; write down; note down. ***Ex 1.*** *Put* the date *down* in your diary; so that you don't forget it. ***Ex 2.*** He *put down* everything in writing. .

(g) (in Parliament) table, include something on the agenda for a meting or debate. ***Ex 1.*** The Opposition parties plan to *put down* a censure motion on the government's handling of the Securities Scam affair. ***Ex 2.*** Some M.P.s are in favour of *putting down* a resolution which would come before the Congress Parliamentary Party.

(h) humiliate or snub somebody. ***Ex.*** He is always *putting* his wife *down* in public.

Put down as : (a) write, enter somebody/something in a record. ***Ex 1.*** When travelling abroad, Sadhu Ram often *puts down* the cost of entertainment *as* business expenses. ***Ex 2.*** She was *put down* in the hotel register *as* Sita. ***Ex 3.*** He *put* himself *down* on the application form *as* unemployed.

(b) consider to be; take to be. ***Ex.*** Noticing his military bearing, I *put* him *down as* a retired brigadier.

Put down for : (a) write down that somebody is willing to contribute to charity, buy something at sales, etc. ***Ex 1.*** *Put* me *down for* five tickets for Sunday's performance. ***Ex 2.*** How many Preference Shares shall I *put* you *down for*?

(b) enter a child's name for admission to a school. ***Ex 1.*** There is tremendous demand for places at English-medium public schools. Children's names are still *put down* at birth *for* those with the best academic records. ***Ex 2.*** Gita has *put* her daughter Rita *down for* Tagore International School.

Put down to: (a) enter an amount in a particular account. ***Ex 1.*** You can *put* the lunch *down to* my account. ***Ex 2.*** Expenditure on Diwali decorations was *put down to* petty cash. .

(b) regard as being due to; give as the explanation for; attribute something to something. ***Ex 1.*** The shortage can be *put down to* bad planning. ***Ex 2.*** I did notice that you were depressed, but I *put* it *down to* drink. ***Ex 3.*** What do you *put* her success *down to* ? ***Ex 4.*** I *put* it all *down to* her hard work and initiative.

Put forth: (a) sproud; display; send out. ***Ex.*** Spring has come and the hedges lire *putting forth* new leaves.

(b) exert; display. ***Ex.*** The day was superb, and here was the college *putting forth* its beauty.

Put forward: (a) advance, propose or suggest something for discussion. ***Ex 1.*** It is an explanation often *put forward* by Tripti Devi, she is convinced that economics is at the bottom of everything. ***Ex 2.*** I have *put forward* radical proposals for electoral reform. ***Ex 3.*** Anju Rani *put forward* several interesting ideas.

(b) propose, recommend. ***Ex 1.*** Can I *put* your name *forward* for golf club President? ***Ex 2.*** His name was *put forward* for inclusion in the Honours List. ***Ex 3.*** He was *put forward* as the man most likely to win the ear of the conference.

(c) move the hands of a clock forward to give the correct time. ***Ex 1.*** Clocks should be *put forward* one hour tonight at the beginning of official Summer Time. ***Ex 2.*** *Put* your watch *forward*, you are seven minutes slow.

Put in : (a) interrupt another speaker in order to say something; interject; interpose. ***Ex 1.*** But what about us ? He *put in*. ***Ex 2.*** She is carrying out an experiment, I *put in*.

(b) include or insert something in a story; narrative, etc. ***Ex 1.*** *Put in* the proper punctuation marks. ***Ex 2.*** If you are writing to your mother, don't forget to *put in* something about her coming to stay.

(c) manage to say something. ***Ex.*** Could I *put in* a word at this point.

(d) spend time working at something. ***Ex 1.*** Sudesh often *puts in* six hours' work a day. ***Ex 2.*** I must *put in* an hour's gardening this evening.

(e) instal or fit something. ***Ex 1.*** We *put* new central heating *in* when we moved here. ***Ex 2.*** We are having a new shower *put in*. ***Ex 3.*** We are *putting in* a completely new system of wiring and switches. ***Ex 4.*** We have pulled out the old pipes and *put in* copper ones.

(f) give duties to. ***Ex 1.*** We have *put in* a caretaker to keep an eye on people coming in and out of the building. ***Ex 2.*** A security man was *put in* to check on doors and windows.

(g) elect a political party to govern a country. ***Ex 1.*** The Congress Party headed by Mr. P.Y.N.Rao, the Prime Minister, was *put in* with an increased majority at the last general election. ***Ex 2.*** The electorate in West Bengal *put* the Communist Party of India (Marxist) *in* with a vastly increased majority at the last general election.

(h) submit, make, enter, something for. ***Ex1.*** I would like to *put in* for a posting in West Bengal. ***Ex 2.*** A claim has been *put in* for higher wages. ***Ex 3.*** Manju Devi is due for some leave and is thinking of *putting in* an application.

Put in for: (a) recommend somebody as deserving; propose somebody as being a suitable applicant for; ***Ex 1.*** He was *put in for* a medal for bravery. ***Ex 2.*** He is being *put in for* Padma Shri. ***Ex 3.*** She is being *put in for* something on the administrative side.

(b) apply formally for something. ***Ex.*** Are you going to *put in for* that job?

Put in/into: (a) call, dock, moor at. ***Ex 1.*** We shall *put in* at the next port for refuelling. ***Ex 2.*** The boats *put in* to shelter from the storm.

(b) devote, expend in doing something. ***Ex.*** A lot of careful planning was *put into* making the day a success.

Put inside: put in prison. ***Ex.*** He was *put inside* for breach of peace.

Put off : (a) postpone, delay or defer something. ***Ex.* 1.** It is no good trying to *put off* the evil day. ***Ex 2.*** I have been *putting* it *off* and not thinking about it, hoping that something would turn up. ***Ex 3.*** Anandi keeps *putting off* going to the dentist. ***Ex 4.*** We have had to *put* our wedding *off* until October. ***I'x 5.*** Today's meeting will have to be *put off*.

(b) discourage or prevent from : seeing one, making contact, collecting a debt, discussing an important matter, etc. ***Ex 1.*** He had *put* her *off* too often when she had wanted to talk. ***Ex 2.*** They went out nine or ten times and then she started *putting* him *off*, just a little, he was getting possessive. ***Ex 3.*** The grocer won't be *put off* with airy promises any longer; he wants his money.

(c) displease; repel. ***Ex 1.*** Don't be *put off* by her sharp tongue. ***Ex 2.*** Many people are *put off* by his surly behaviour. ***Ex 3.*** He could be a good salesman, but his manner *puts* customers *off*.

(d) distract from doing something; disturb while doing something ***Ex 1.*** Her delaying tactics are designed to annoy him and *put* him *off*. ***Ex 2.*** He was trying to pen, but the continuous noise outside his window *put* him *off*.

(e) cause somebody to lose interest in, or appetite for. ***Ex 1.*** My drill sergeant *put* me *off* the army for good. ***Ex 2.*** She was *put off* learning languages by incompetent teaching.

(f) allow somebody to alight or disembark; compel to alight. ***Ex 1.*** I asked the conductor to *put* me *off* at the cinema. ***Ex 2.*** If you make trouble, you will be *put off* the plane.

(g) discard; lay aside. ***Ex 1.*** He had *put off* all personal cares.

(h) send to sleep. ***Ex.*** Acup of tea will soon *put* you *off* to sleep again.

Put on : (a) done; get dressed in. ***Ex 1.*** What dress shall I *put on* for the party? ***Ex 2.*** *Put on* some good clothes. ***Ex 3.*** I don't know what dress to *put on*.

(b) light; switch on. ***Ex.*** Tell him to *put on* the light.

(c) grow heavier or fatter by a certain amount. ***Ex 1.*** In the month she had been with them, she had not *put on* any weight. ***Ex 2.*** How much did you *put on* over Dussehra ?

(d) impose on; place on. ***Ex 1.*** What will the government be *putting* a tax *on* next? ***Ex 2.*** The government is proposing to *put on* a new range of taxes to pay for social services.

(e) add to existing services. ***Ex.*** The Northern Railways are *putting on* ten extra trains to cope with the holiday traffic.

(f) produce or present a pray, an exhibition, etc. ***Ex 1.*** The local drama group are *putting on* a play at the Plaza. ***Ex 2.*** It was all agreed that this gallery was to *put on* an exhibition of paintings.

(g) assume a manner or a pose in order to impress or deceive; pretend to have something; assume or adopt something. ***Ex 1.*** He *put on* a silly face. ***Ex 2.*** She *put on* a wounded expression. ***Ex 3.*** Don't *put on* that innocent look; we know you ate all the biscuits. ***Ex 4.*** He seems very sincere, but it is all *put on*. ***Ex 5.*** She was obviously very good for him. So he did not have to *put on* an act for her. ***Ex 6.*** Her expensive voice and manner are all *put on*.

(h) apply something to one's skin. ***Ex.*** She is just *putting on* her make-up.

(i) make something begin to play. ***Ex 1.*** Do you mind if I *put* some music *on*? ***Ex 2.*** Tell him to *put on* a tape.

Put it on : pretend to be angry, sad, remorseful, and so on. ***Ex.*** She was not angry really, she was only *putting it on*.

Put on to : (a) help people to meet or speak; put in touch with. ***Ex 1.*** Afast friend of mine *put* me *on to* the Prime Minister. ***Ex 2.*** I shall *put* you *on to* a good accountant. ***Ex 3.*** He *put* me *on to* a famous lawyer. ***Ex 4.*** He insisted on being *put on to* the man in charge of the section.

(b) inform somebody of a person's whereabouts or activities, so that he can be caught. ***Ex 1.*** The police hunting the gang were *put on to* them by an anonymous telephone call. ***Ex 2.*** You cannot go to defrauding the sales tax department for good (for ever), somebody some day will *put* the tax man *on to* you. ***Ex 3.*** Sooner or later he will be spotted in the street, and the detectives will be *put on to* him.

(c) inform somebody of the existence of the advantageous or interesting; tell somebody about something. ***Ex 1.*** It was Anita who had *put* Sunita *on to* this club. ***Ex 2.*** I was *put on to* this cheap line in printed cotton by a friend in the trade. ***Ex 3.*** Who *put* you *on to* this restaurant?

Put out: (a) move towards the open sea, away from the shore. ***Ex 1.*** We *put out* to sea on the early morning tide. ***Ex 2.*** They will *put out* to sea from Bombay.

(b) eject, remove somebody by force. ***Ex.*** The next time he brings his noisy friends to the club, we shall have them *put out.*

(c) sprout; display. ***Ex 1.*** The plants *put out* early shoots. ***Ex 2.*** The trees are beginning to *put out* leaves.

(d) issue broadcast or publish, usually for a special purpose. ***Ex 1.*** Police have *put out* a description of the man they wish to question. ***Ex 2.*** The government has *put out* a pamphlet explaining the news rates of pension for retired people. ***Ex 3.*** Head Office has *put out* an official statement denying press reports of a possible take over.

(e) issue or circulate. ***Ex.*** A detailed description of the wanted man has been *put out* to all mobile patrols.

(f) broadcast, transmit, by radio or television. ***Ex.*** People clustered around the radio, listening to the news of the invasion *put out* by All India Radio.

(g) produce or generate something. ***Ex.*** The plant *puts out* six hundred new cars a week.

(h) exert; display. ***Ex 1.*** The Prime Minister's speech ended in an ardent appeal to party workers to *put out* all their energy and enthusiasm during the electoral campaign. ***Ex 2.*** Never had our supporters *put out* so much effort.

(i) make somebody unconscious. ***Ex 1.*** I *put* my opponent *out* in the fifth round. ***Ex 2.*** A whiff of ether will *put* you *out* in a few seconds. ***Ex 3.*** A few youths *put* the theif *out* with fists. ***Ex 4.*** The doctor *put* the patient *out* with an anaesthetic. Switch off. ***Ex 1.*** Tell the servant to *put out* the lamp. ***Ex 2.*** She drew the curtains and *put out* the lights.

(k) cause something to stop burning; extinguish. ***Ex 1.*** Ten firemen soon *put* the fire *out*. ***Ex 2.*** The fire brigade were still *putting out* small fires started by the plane crash.

(l) dislocate (a part of the body). ***Ex 1.*** She fell off her horse and *put* her shoulder *out*. ***Ex 2.*** He *put* his back *out* badly, falling down from the stairs.

(m) cause an inaccuracy in something; cause to be wrong. ***Ex 1.*** The devaluation of the rupee has *put* our estimates *out* by crores of rupees. ***Ex 2.*** The final totals can have been *put out* by as much as five per cent.

(n) inconvenience somebody; spoil or complicate somebody'; arrangements. ***Ex 1.*** I hope our arriving late did not *put* them *out*. ***Ex 2.*** I don't like to put out her. ***Ex 3.*** The hotel was seriously *put out* by the sudden cancellation of holiday bookings.

(o) upset or offend somebody. ***Ex 1.*** She was most *put out* by your rudeness. ***Ex 2.*** Why do you look so *put out*?

(p) give ajob, task, etc. to a worker or manufacturer who is not one's employee and will do the work in another place. ***Ex 1.*** A lot of proof-reading is *put out* to freelancers. ***Ex 2.*** All repairs are done on the premises and not *put out*. ***Ex 3.*** The manufacture of belts and buckles is *put out* to sub-contractors. ***Ex 4.*** Half of the work will be *put out* to other people.

(q) lend money to get interest on it. ***Ex 1.*** Banks are *putting out* more and more money to people buying their own homes. ***Ex 2.*** The building societies attract deposits from investors and then *put out* this money, at a higher rate of interest, to those wishing to buy houses.

Put oneself out: do something even though it is inconvenient for oneself. ***Ex 1.*** Please don't *put yourself out* on our account. ***Ex 2.*** She is always ready to *put herself out* to help others.

Put over on : persuade somebody to accept a claim, statement, story, etc. that is untrue or worthless. ***Ex.*** I am not the sort of man you can *put* something *over on*.

Put over to : convey, communicate something effectively to. ***Ex.*** This evening he was not *putting over* a story *to* an untried audience.

Put through: (a) conclude or complete successfully. ***Ex 1.*** We hope to *put through* the business deal. ***Ex 2.*** The government is *putting through* some radical social reforms. ***Ex 3.*** At the moment we are trying to *put through* a mass literacy programme. ***Ex 4.*** You will be glad to know that the airport redevelopment was *put through* in record time.

(b) cause to pass through various legislative or administrative stages. ***Ex.*** These proposals have to be *put through* several committees before they become part of the club constitution .

(c) provide for somebody, so that he or she can complete his or her education. ***Ex 1.*** He managed to *put* each of his six children *through* boarding school. ***Ex 2.*** She was *put through* university with money left by her maternal grandfather.

(d) allow somebody to speak to somebody by making a telephone connection. ***Ex 1.*** Could you *put* me *through* to the General Manager, please? ***Ex 2.*** I am trying to *put* a call *through* to Cairo. ***Ex 3.*** When Prem Lata comes on the line, you will *put* the call *through* to me.

Put to : (a) convey, express, communicate, to. ***Ex 1.*** Let me *put* the situation *to* you as I saw it in April and May. ***Ex 2.*** Your proposals will be *put to* the Board of Directors. ***Ex 3.*** The proposals were *put to* us very briefly and forcibly. ***Ex 4.*** The Prime Minister can *put* it *to* his supporters that there will almost certainly be a considerable swing back to the government. ***Ex 5.*** It might be *put to* the delegates that any reasonable demands would be headed.

(b) submit; pose. ***Ex 1.*** The audience is now invited to *put* its questions *to* our visiting speaker. ***Ex 2.*** To which of our experts do you wish *to put* that question?

(c) ask a meeting, etc. to vote on a particular proposal. ***Ex 1.*** Let us *put* the resolution *to* the meeting. ***Ex 2.*** The question of strike action must be *put to* union members. ***Ex 3.*** I propose that the matter be *put to* the vote, Mr. Chairman. ***Ex 4.*** The Secretary rose to *put* the motion *to* the assembly for its approval.

(d) make somebody suffer or undergo inconvenience, trouble, etc. ***Ex 1.*** I do hope we are not *putting* you *to* too much trouble. ***Ex 2.*** They have already been *put to* great inconvenience. ***Ex 3.*** She is ready to oblige anyone provided this does not *put* her *to* any trouble. ***Ex 4.*** You cannot imagine the trouble I have been *put to* by the Committee.

(e) suggest or submit to a witness, etc. ***Ex.*** The counsel for the defence harries her: I *put* it *to* you that you acted out of spice.

Put together: (a) assemble something; construct or repair something by fitting parts together. ***Ex 1.*** He *put together* a model aeroplane. ***Ex 2.*** He took the machine to pieces and then *put* it *together*. ***Ex 3.*** You took the things apart; now *put* it *together*.

(b) fit together pieces to make a whole. ***Ex.*** He had managed to *put together* a convincing case from the accounts of eye-witnesses. *Put towards* : give money as a contribution to a particular fund. ***Ex.*** You take care of the household expenses and I shall *put* half of my salary *towards* the cost of the holiday.

Put up : (a) raise or hoist something. ***Ex 1.*** Where will you *put up* the flags? ***Ex 2.*** *Put* your hand *up* if you want to ask a question. ***Ex 3.*** She has put her hair up.

(b) fasten in a place where it will be seen; display. ***Ex 1.*** The names of the successful candidates will be *put up* on the College Notice Board. ***Ex 2.*** We have already *put up* Diwali decorations all around the house. ***Ex 3.*** The team will be *put up* on the Notice Board.

(c) build; erect. ***Ex 1.*** These buildings were *put up* during the Moghal period. ***Ex 2.*** Let us *put up* a fence around the garden.

Ex 3. Many ugly blocks of flats were *put up* a few years ago. ***Ex 4.*** We are having a memorial to Rabindra Nath Tagore *put up* by public subscription.

(d) raise; increase. ***Ex 1.*** Every time a new tenant moves into that house, the landlord *puts up* the rent a bit more. ***Ex 2.*** The rate of interest was *put up* in the last Budget. ***Ex 3.*** His landlord is threatening to *put* the rent *up* by five hundred rupees a month.

(e) pretend to be, feel, or have done, something in order to hide one's true origins, activities, etc. ***Ex 1.*** Many people admire the tomboy for the facade she *puts up*. ***Ex 2.*** The fundamental secret of covering up inefficiency is the art of *putting up* a front.

(f) offer or present (a resistance, struggle, etc.) in a battle, game, etc. ***Ex 1.*** Very little resistance was *put up* by the surrounded men. ***Ex 2.*** The smuggler *put up* a fight but was finally overcome and arried off to jail. ***Ex 3.*** They surrendered without *putting up* much of a fight. ***Ex 4.*** Our team *put up* a splendid performance.

(g) state, advance, advocate; present (an idea, etc.) for discussion or consideration. ***Ex.*** I shall *put up* your proposal at the next meeting of the Board.

(h) advance or lend. ***Ex 1.*** When we had spent this huge amount, they *put up* another half-million. ***Ex 2.*** Awell-wisher had *put up* the money. ***Ex 3.*** How much can you *put up* at the moment ?

(i) prepare and provide (to be eaten). ***Ex 1.*** Get the hotel to *put up* some sandwiches for the journey. ***Ex 2.*** It is late, but I think we can *put* you *up* a cold meal.

(j) take food and lodging; provide food and lodging. ***Ex 1.*** They *put up* at the monastery rest-house. ***Ex 2.*** He *put up* at an inn for the night. ***Ex 3.*** I shall not *put* her *up* for the night.

(k) present somebody as a candidate in an election. ***Ex 1.*** The Nationalist Party hopes to *put up* a number of candidates in the general election. ***Ex 2.*** We shall *put* her *up* for treasurer at the next committee meeting slated to be held on Friday, the 8th of the next month, at 4.30 p.m. ***Ex 3.*** He was *put up* twice, but did not attract enough support.

(l) offer oneself as a candidate for election. ***Ex 1.*** I am not *putting up* for re-election to Parliament. ***Ex 2.*** Will you *put up* for election to the committee?

Put up to : (a) prepare somebody for ajob or task; instruct somebody in a job. ***Ex.*** Get an expert to *put* him *up to* the job in as short a time as possible.

(b) encourage to behave mischievously or unlawfully. ***Ex 1.*** He wants to get rid of income-tax. Somebody *put* him *up to* it. ***Ex 2.*** I cannot believe that he would do a thing like that on his own. He must have been *put up to* it by some of the older boys.

Put up with: tolerate or bear somebody/something. ***Ex 1.*** I don't know how she *puts up with* his cruelty to her. ***Ex 2.*** He just was not going to *put up with* all the caterwauling. ***Ex 3.*** There are some things that are not easily *put up with* and his damned impertinence is one.

Putty in : fix something in place with putty. ***Ex 1.*** They *puttied* a pane of glass *in* yesterday. ***Ex 2.*** Do you know how to *putty* a pane of glass *in* ?

Puzzle out: find the answer or solution to something by thinking hard. ***Ex 1.*** The teacher left the children to *puzzle out* the answer to the problem themselves. ***Ex 2.*** Follow that line of inquiry and I think you will *puzzle out* an answer. ***Ex 3.*** He spent the afternoon trying to *puzzle out* what had gone wrong with his car.

Puzzle over : think deeply about something in order to understand it. ***Ex 1.*** She has been *puzzling over* his strange letter for weeks. ***Ex 2.*** He had *puzzled over* the figures for hours without making head or tail of them. ***Ex 3.*** His scheme has been talked about in the press, and much *puzzled over* by the men who must provide the financial backing.

---

17 Words Beginning With–Q

Quarrel with : (a) disagree with somebody strongly and argue or sometimes fight with him. ***Ex 1.*** 'I don't want to *quarrel with* her', she said, 'She's my oldest friend.***Ex 2.*** She *quarrelled with* Rakesh over the lease.

(b) to be disagree with an idea, statement, or opinion; a slightly formal use. ***Ex 1.*** One may *quareel with* Pradeep's contention. ***Ex 2.*** I think Meera would *quarrel with* the use of the word madness. ***Ex 3.*** Royatly is intimacy. Nobody could *quarrel with* that.

Queen over : act in a way that shows somebody's thinking is better. ***Ex 1.*** A dozen cats *queened over* by the mother. ***Ex 2.*** All right, but don't you try to *queen* it *over* me.

Queue up : stand in a line of people and wait for something. ***Ex 1.*** Rekha had to *queue up* at the factory every morning to see if there was any work. ***Ex 2.*** People were *queueing up* for his autograph.

Quicken up : to quicken something up or if it quickens up, its speed increases. ***Ex.*** Start these movements slowly and then *quicken* them *up*.

Quieten down: become less noisy or active, or more calm. ***Ex 1.*** He had matured and *quietened down* considerably. ***Ex 2.*** A cunning stratagem to *quieten down* the rebellious peasants.

18 Words Beginning With–R

Rabbit on : talk lengthily or in a rambling and pointless way. *Ex.* Tell me what you are *rabbiting on* about.

Rail at/against: protest, complain or reproach somebody/something bitterly. *Ex 1.* She *railed at* her husband for his laziness. *Ex 2.* Don't *rail against* fate. *Ex 3.* The elderly people *railed against* further cuts in their standard of living. *Ex 4.* Many general practitioners *rail* vehemently *at* the volume of paperwork connected with the running of a surgery.

Rail in : enclose with railings or a fence; fence in. *Ex 1.* They *railed in* part of the pasture to prevent the cattle from wandering. *Ex 2.* The winners' enclosure was *railed in.*

Rail off : separate one place from another by means of rails. *Ex 1.* The bottom of the garden was *railed off* to stop the children straying into the road. *Ex 2.* They *railed* the meadows *off* from the new railway cutting. *Ex 3.* The villagers *railed off* a field from the road.

Railroad into : force somebody to do something. *Ex 1.* I won't be *railroaded into* buying a car I don't want. *Ex 2.* I am not going to be *railroaded into* joining a company with a shady past and a still more dubious future. *Ex 3.* In the course of the evening, he was *railroaded into* throwing down cream cakes and a packet of biscuits.

Railroad through : enact legislation by applying improper pressure. *Ex.* The Bill giving emergency powers to the military government was *railroaded through* with little respect for established parliamentary niceties.

Rain down: (a) flow or come down in large quantities. *Ex 1.* Tears *rained down* her rosy cheeks. *Ex 2.* Loose rocks began to *rain down* the hillside. *Ex 3.* Bits of plaster *rained down* on their heads from the ceiling, filling their hair and eyes. *Ex 4.* From these positions, accurate mortar fire was *rained down* upon reinforcement moving up through the valley.

(b) come down on somebody/something. *Ex.* Invitations *rained down* on the visiting writer.

Rain off : prevent (an event) from taking place because of rain. *Ex.* She told me that the match was *rained off* thrice.

Rain upon : be offered, or offer, abundantly or in great quantities to. *Ex 1.* We could not complain of our reception, food and cold drink *rained upon* us from the moment we entered the house. *Ex 2.* The distinguished guest was visibly embarrassed by the fulsome compliments that were *rained upon* him.

Raise with: introduce a subject in a discussion with somebody. *Ex.* He is likely to *raise* a number of important questions *with* the Chief Minister.

Rake about/around: search carefully here and there for something. *Ex 1.* She *raked around* in the files, but could not find the letter.

Ex 2. I *raked about* in the drawers for the pen.

Rake in : earn a lot of money. ***Ex 1.*** He *rakes in* a lot of cash. ***Ex 2.*** He is *rakin in* the profits. ***Ex 3.*** How much do you expect to *rake in* over the end of the month? ***Ex 4.*** The dealers can *rake in* another ten or fifteen per cent on the takings.

Rake through: examine documents, etc. carefully in search of evidence, etc. ***Ex 1.*** The police *raked through* every possible hiding-place to find the weapon. ***Ex 2.*** We shall *rake through* the place again before we give up the search.

Rake together/up: collect people or things with difficulty. ***Ex 1.*** We need to *rake up* two more players to form a team. ***Ex 2.*** I could not *rake together* enough money to buy new car.

Rake up: revive something which is now forgotten; drag up. ***Ex 1.*** Don't *rake up* the past. ***Ex 2.*** Why do you *rake up* old quarrels? ***Ex 3.*** He enjoys *raking up* old scandals about her. ***Ex 4.*** Old scores were *raked up*. ***Ex 5.*** Why did you have to *rake up* his political past ? He is a reformed character now.

Ram down: flatten by ramming; strike something firmly so that its parts pack tightly together. ***Ex 1.*** Ask them to *ram down* the soil. ***Ex 2.*** Broken bricks were *rammed down* in the trench to make a base for the concrete.

Ram home : make a point absolutely clear by example or illustration. ***Ex 1.*** The loss of all his belongings *rammed home* the need to insure against fire and theft. ***Ex 2.*** His point about sound navigation was *rammed home* by the disappearance of an aircraft over the sea.

Ramble on : continue to speak or write in a wandering, incoherent way. ***Ex 1.*** The old man *rambled on* about the past. ***Ex 2.*** Don't *ramble on* about your children. ***Ex 3.*** She *rambled on* about her unfulfilled ambitions. ***Ex 4.*** I had difficulty in reducing his draft chapter to coherent shape. The original had *rambled on* for ten pages.

Range over: include; cover; move about among. ***Ex 1.*** Her lecture *ranged over* a variety of highly useful topics. ***Ex 2.*** I find it very difficult to list all the fields *over* which his experience *ranges*.

Rap out: (a) say something abruptly and sharply. ***Ex 1.*** The officer *rapped out* the orders. ***Ex 2.*** Stand still, he *rapped out*, in a voice that froze the troops on parade. ***Ex 3.*** He always *raps* his instructions *out*, as though he were still in the army.

(b) express something by taps. ***Ex.*** The prisoner *rapped out* a message on the cell wall.

Rasp away/off: remove something with a rasp. *Ex.* The servant *rasped off* the rough edges.

Rat on: (a) break an agreement, a promise, etc.; fail to do something one has undertaken. ***Ex 1.*** We thought we could count on him backing us with cash but he *ratted on* the deal at the last moment.

(b) reveal a secret; betray somebody. ***Ex 1.*** She has *ratted on* us-here comes the headmaster. ***Ex 2.*** Nobody likes being *ratted on*, especially when so much depends on keeping things secret.

Ration out : distribute in fixed quantities; in a time of shortage. ***Ex 1.*** *Ration* the remaining water *out* among the survivors. ***Ex 2.*** The remaining stores of tinned milk were carefully *rationed out* among the children. ***Ex 3.*** They had to *ration* the petrol *out*; four gallons to each motorist while stocks lasted.

Rattle along/off: move with a rattling sound. ***Ex.*** The old bus *rattled along* the stony road.

Rattle away/on: talk idly and at length; chatter; talk in a sharp, fast and thoughtless way. ***Ex 1.*** I always found her company unendurable. She could *rattle on* for hours about absolutely nothing at all. ***Ex 2.*** He *rattled away* about his job, not noticing how bored she was.

Rattle off : say or repeat something quickly and meaninglessly. ***Ex 1.*** Ragini *rattled off* the poem she had learnt by heart. ***Ex 2.*** He *rattled off* a page of the telephone directory. ***Ex 3.*** Now read the poem again, and this time don't *rattle* it *off* like a machine-gun.
Ex 4. He *rattled off* the names of several dozen important people in the business.

Rattle through: say or do something rather quickly. ***Ex 1.*** He *rattled through* the list of names of the successful candidates. ***Ex 2.*** The old man *rattled through* his prayers. ***Ex 3.*** He always *rattles through* his work.

Rave about/over: talk with foolish enthusiasm of. ***Ex 1.*** She *raved about* her dressmaker, who could copy a Paris model for next to nothing. ***Ex 2.*** Your house in the country is nothing to *rave about*. ***Ex 3.*** The unspoiled fishing-village they had *raved about* so endlessly turned out to be a run-of-the-mill holiday resort.

Rave against/at : oppose somebody/something violently, wildly and incoherently. ***Ex 1.*** The patient began to *rave* incoherently *at* the nurses. ***Ex 2.*** The aging tyrant *raved against* his closest friends, accusing them of unimaginable crimes. ***Ex 3.*** There seemed no end to the hidden enemies at whom he *raved*.

Reach back: go back in the mind. ***Ex.*** I asked him to *reach back* and try to re-capture the atmosphere of the place in his boyhood.

Reach out: (a) make an effort to grasp. ***Ex 1.*** The farm means ease and security and wealth. That is what I have been *reaching out* for. ***Ex 2.*** All manner of opportunities will come your way, but you must *reach out* for them.

(b) try to communicate with, to make contact with. ***Ex.*** A party which does not *reach out* and take account of grass-roots feeling is like a head without a body.

(c) extend an offer of help. ***Ex.*** We have tried to *reach out* to these unfortunate people.

Read in : add in by inference. ***Ex 1.*** You should not try to *read in* to this matter, things which are not there. ***Ex 2.*** Don't *read* things *in* to what I say.

Read into: find something in the words of a speaker or writer which he did not intend; .assume that something means more than it does. ***Ex 1.*** Too much should not be *read into* the Prime Minister's statement, we cannot expect a sudden easing of the situation. ***Ex 2.*** Don't go *reading* things *into* my stories which I did not put there. ***Ex 3.*** You have *read into* his letter a sympathy that he cannot possibly feel.

Read out: Read something aloud, to others. ***Ex 1.*** She *read out* the letter to all of us. ***Ex 2.*** He *read* the proclamation *out*. ***Ex 3.*** The pupils took turns in *reading out* their work. ***Ex 4.*** After morning prayers, important notices are *read out* to the assembled school.

Read over/through: read completely, from beginning to end. ***Ex 1.*** Lalita Rani lifted out the topmost two letters, and he *read* them *through* again. ***Ex 2.*** *Read* the report *over* to yourself, and see if you find anything odd. ***Ex 3.*** He had to *read* the passage *through* many a time before he could understand it. ***Ex 4.*** The editor *read over* the manuscript. ***Ex 5.*** I would like you to *read* this passage *over* for me.

Read up : acquire a knowledge of a subject through reading. ***Ex 1.*** There is no need to attend classes in theory, you can *read* it *up* for yourself in the library. ***Ex 2.*** I knew nothing about the subject, but I could *read up* to pass a simple test.

Read upon : improve one's knowledge of something by reading; bring one's knowledge of something up to date by reading. ***Ex 1.*** We have so much to *read upon* in the subject; it is easy to get behindhand with one's knowledge. ***Ex 2.*** I must *read upon* developments in this field; I am getting badly out of touch. ***Ex 3.*** You must *read upon* Akbar, the Great, for the history examination.

Reason into: persuade somebody by reasoned argument to do something. ***Ex 1.*** Let me try to *reason* him *into* joining us. *Ex 2.* This is something he can be *reasoned into* given time. ***Ex 3.*** Renu Rani was *reasoned into* a sensible course of action.

Reason out : arrive at an answer through careful reasoning; find an answer to, by considering various possible solutions. ***Ex 1.*** The police tried to *reason out* how the thief had escaped. ***Ex 2.*** I keenly intend to *reason* this matter *out* if it is humanly possible. ***Ex 3.*** She is not good at *reasoning out* even simple problems. ***Ex 4.*** It is easy to *reason out* what the consequences of that action will be.

Reason out of : persuade somebody by reasoned argument not to do something, or to leave or abandon something. ***Ex 1.*** We tried to *reason* him *out of* this course of action, but without success. ***Ex 2.*** These were deeply held convictions and he could not be *reasoned out of* them easily.

Reason with: argue with somebody reasonably in the hope of convincing him. ***Ex 1.*** I *reasoned with* her for hours about the danger, but she would not change her mind. ***Ex 2.*** Have you tried *reasoning with* him? ***Ex 3.*** People tell me that she won't be *reasoned with*.

Recall to : make somebody aware or conscious again of something. ***Ex 1.*** The dangers that suddenly threatened *recalled* him *to* a sense of duty. ***Ex 2.*** He was *recalled to* a sense of propriety by the presense of distinguished visitors whom he dared not offend.

Reckon in : include something in a calculation; include as a part of a bill, estimate, etc. ***Ex 1.*** Don't bother to tip; the service charge has already been *reckoned in*. ***Ex 2.*** Why you submit your claim, don't forget to *reckon in* the money spent on petrol. ***Ex 3.*** Even ifwe *reckon in* profits from the new factory, we shall not be able to make an overall profit this year. ***Ex 4.*** When you did your expenses, did you *reckon in* your taxi fares?

Reckon on/upon: make one's plans in the sure knowledge that something will happen or be the case; depend on/upon. ***Ex 1.*** I shall always help in time of need; *on* this you can *reckon*. ***Ex 2.*** Her promises cannot always be *reckoned upon*. ***Ex 3.*** You need not *reckon on* my future. ***Ex 4.*** The next five years will show whether Ram Bahadur still has a political future *on* which he can *reckon*. ***Ex 5.*** Can I *reckon on* you to help us ? ***Ex 6.*** You cannot always reckon on having good weather.

Reckon up: find the sum, total, amount, of. ***Ex 1.*** A mechanic *reckoned up* the cost of repairing the damage to my car. ***Ex 2.*** When you *reckon up* the wastage of female staff through marriage, it is quite a total.

Reckon with: (a) take somebody/something into account; consider somebody/ something as important; expect to encounter. ***Ex 1.*** Himadri Shankar is a man to be *reckoned with*. ***Ex 2.*** I had not *reckoned with* the facts of my temperament, training and habits. ***Ex 3.*** I had not *reckoned with* the possibility of his turning up so soon. ***Ex 4.*** She had many difficulties to reckon with.

(b) tackle; overcome. ***Ex 1.*** All these problems had to be *reckoned with* as they arose, before they grew large enough to hinder progress. ***Ex 2.*** When you consider at the petty irritations and shortages they had to *reckon with*, it is a wonder that they kept their sense of humour.

(c) punish. ***Ex 1.*** Anyone not obeying the decrees of the new military government could expect to be reckoned with. ***Ex 2.*** The police *reckoned*, in a horrible fashion, *with* all those suspected of supporting the government in exile.

Reckon without: not include in one's plans or calculations; not take somebody/something into account; not consider somebody/ something as important. ***Ex 1.*** He is not the sort of man you can afford to *reckon without*. ***Ex 2.*** I had *reckoned without* their being prepared to lend me the money. ***Ex 3.*** The organizers of the garden party had clearly *reckoned without* the possibility of a freak thunderstorm. ***Ex 4.*** He *reckoned without* their interference. ***Ex 5.*** You must *reckon without* our help in this matter.

Recognize as : (a) be willing to accept that somebody or something has the rank or authority that are claimed for him or it. ***Ex 1.*** It is not certain that the Court will *recognize* him *as* his father's rightful successor. ***Ex 2.*** Everyone *recognized* her *as* the lawful heir to her father's large fortune.

(b) regard or consider somebody/something to be. ***Ex 1.*** This has long been *recognized as* the standard work on the Mughal period. ***Ex 2.*** In years to come, they will *recognize* him *as* one of the great founder-figures of our movement.

Recoil on/upon : strike back at the doer of an action, perhaps for the worse. ***Ex 1.*** An evil deed may *recoil on* the head of the doer. ***Ex 2.*** Neglect of his children *recoiled upon* him when he was of an age to need their support.

Recur to : come back into the mind; be recalled by somebody. ***Ex 1.*** The memory of the days we spent together often *recurs to* me. ***Ex 2.*** It *recurs to* me that he was the first person to help us in those difficult times. ***Ex 3.*** Our first meeting often *recurs to* my mind.

Reduce to : (a) make something appear to be of no value or importance, by revealing its faults, inconsistencies, etc. ***Ex.*** Our case was argued by an able barrister, who *reduced* the prosecutor's submissions almost *to* nothing.

(b) state in a more concise form; summarise as. ***Ex 1.*** I think we can *reduce* his rather lengthly statement *to* one or two essential points. ***Ex 2.*** Give us the basic facts to which you have *reduced* his argument.

(c) weaken the physical or nervous condition of somebody to a grave extent. ***Ex 1.*** Anxiety about the fate of his family *reduced* him *to* a nervous wreck. ***Ex 2.*** Weeks in an open boat had *reduced* the surviving crew members *to* skin and bones. ***Ex 3.*** Overwork has *reduced* him *to* a physical wreck. ***Ex 4.*** .The fire *reduced* the house *to* ashes.

Reck of: strongly suggest something unpleasant or suspicious. ***Ex 1.*** Their actions *reck of* corruption. ***Ex 2.*** His conversation *reck of* the literary world.

Reel off : say or repeat something rapidly without pause or apparent effort. ***Ex 1.*** He *reeled off* a set of instructions to be complied with by all office staff. ***Ex 2.*** Can you *reel off* a poem? ***Ex 3.*** Without apparent effort, he *reeled off* the names of those who had been associated with him in those early days.

Refer back: return a document, etc. to the sender for further clarification. ***Ex 1.*** The letter was *referred back* to us with a query. ***Ex 2.*** Accounts Department has *referred back* our travel claims.

Refer to : effect; concern; apply to ***Ex 1.*** What I have to say *refers to* all of you. ***Ex 2.*** There are few categories of workers *to* whom this order, does not *refer*.

Relieve of : (a) take something away from somebody, (to lighten his burden, etc.) ***Ex 1.*** Let him *relieve* you *of* that box; it looks terribly heavy. ***Ex 2.*** He was *relieved of* his post as General Manager. ***Ex 3.*** He was happy to be *relieved of* some of the detailed paperwork connected with the project.

(b) dismiss somebody from. ***Ex.*** The Commander-in-Chief was *relieved of* his command for concerning himself with questions, that were properly the responsibility of the politicians.

(c) steal something from somebody. ***Ex.*** Some light-fingered rogue had *relieved* him *of* his wallet.

(d) carry, take charge, etc. of somebody's personal effects. ***Ex.*** Let me *relieve* you *of* your coat.

Remember to : pass greetings from one person to another. ***Ex 1.*** She asked me to *remember* her *to* you. ***Ex 2.*** *Remember* me *to* everyone at home. ***Ex 3.*** He asked to be *remembered to* all his friends in tile department.

Remove from : dismiss somebody from a post, etc. ***Ex 1.*** He was *removed from* his position as Chairman. ***Ex 2.*** The new Managing Director *removed* her *from* her position as head of Sales Division.

Render into : express something in another language; translate something. ***Ex 1.*** It is really difficult to *render* poetry *into* other languages. ***Ex 2.*** *Into* how many languages have the plays of Tagore been *rendered*? ***Ex 3.*** It was a collection of short stories, badly *rendered into* Bengali.

Render up : hand over or surrender something; yield something; hand to the enemy in admission of defeat. ***Ex 1.*** After a prolonged siege, the town was *rendered up to* the insurgents. ***Ex 2.*** We shall never *render up* the fort to the enemy.

Report back: (a) return (from leave, etc.) ***Ex.*** The officer *reported back* from leave on Monday night.

(b) give a spoken or written account of somebody/something one has been asked to investigate. ***Ex.*** He was requested to *report back* to the committee on the complaint.

Rest on/upon: be based on something. ***Ex 1.*** All our hopes *rested on* this venture. ***Ex 2.*** *Upon* such slender evidence as this, did his case *rest*. ***Ex 3.***His fame *rests* more *on* his plays than on his novels.

Rest with: be somebody responsibility; be in somebody hands. ***Ex 1.*** The choice *rests* entirely *with* you. ***Ex 2.*** It *rests with* the committee to decide. ***Ex 3.*** Whether the talks are successful or not *rests with* a small number of men. ***Ex 4.*** It *rests with* you to settle your differences as best as you can.

Result in : have a specified effect or consequence; have as an outcome. ***Ex 1.*** Our efforts *resulted in* splendid success. ***Ex 2.*** The talks have *resulted in* a lessening of suspicion. ***Ex 3.*** The game *resulted in* a goalless draw.

Revolve around/about: have somebody/something as its chief concern; centre on somebody/something. ***Ex 1.*** She has no outside interests at all. Her whole life *revolves around* her husband and the children. ***Ex 2.*** The dispute at the moment *revolves about* whether other delegates should attend the conference. ***Ex 3.*** This is the point *about* which discussion now *revolves* and on which it has always been inconclusive. ***Ex 4.*** My life *revolves around* my job. ***Ex 5.*** He thinks that everything *revolves around* him.

Ride up: (of an article of clothing) : move gradually upwards; move out of position. ***Ex 1.*** Her skirt is *riding up*. ***Ex 2.*** 1 don't like this skirt because it keep *riding up*.

Riffle through : turn the pages of (a book, etc.) quickly and casually. ***Ex.*** As he was in a hurry, he *riffled through* the newspaper, and left for the airport.

Rig out: provide somebody with clothes or equipment; dress for a special occasion or in a strange manner. ***Ex 1.*** She was *rigged out* in an ancient green skirt of her mother's. ***Ex 2.*** Some of the crew were badly *rigged out*. ***Ex 3.*** He *rigged* the children *out* in special boots and trousers for their climbing holiday. ***Ex 4.*** She was *rigged out* in her best clothes.

Rig up: set up (a structure, etc.) quickly and/or with makeshift materials. ***Ex 1.*** The soldiers *rigged up* a shelter for the night. ***Ex 2.*** On one side of the room, they had *rigged up* a small bar.

Ring off: end a telephone conversation. ***Ex 1.*** She *rang off* before I could explain the case in detail. ***Ex 2.*** I shall have to *ring off* now, I have a train to catch.

Rip off: (a) cheat somebody. ***Ex.*** The shop tried to *rip* me *off*.

(b) steal something; rob. ***Ex 1.*** Somebody has *ripped off* his wallet. ***Ex 2.*** Is it surprising to find students *ripping off* books? ***Ex 3.*** He *ripped off* two young girls in the street yesterday.

(c) remove something by pulling sharply. ***Ex.*** He *ripped* the cover *off* a book.

Rise above : be superior to something; be capable of dealing with something; surmount or overcome something. ***Ex 1.*** He *rose above* her difficulties and became a tremendous success. ***Ex 2.*** Surely we can *rise above* petty personal jealousies. ***Ex 3.*** It must be hoped that the cricket club will *rise above* this anxiety.

Roam over : talk about various things, or various aspects of something. ***Ex.*** The speaker *roamed* freely *over* the events of the past week.

Roll by: pass in steady succession. ***Ex 1.*** Many years had *rolled by* since I last sat talking to her. ***Ex 2.*** She sits and watches the world *roll by*. ***Ex 3.*** Fifty years have *rolled by* since I left England.

Roll in : (a) arrive in a steady stream. ***Ex 1.*** Since the appeal was launched, cheques, postal orders and cash have kept *rolling in.* ***Ex 2.*** Offers of help are still *rolling in.*

(b) have a good deal of. ***Ex.*** They are *rolling in* money.

(c) arrive casually. ***Ex.*** She *rolled in* for work twenty minutes late.

Roll up : (a) (of a person or vehicle); arrive. ***Ex.*** He finally *rolled up* two hours late.

(b) arrive in an impressive or self-important way. ***Ex.*** The whole family *rolled up* to their daughter's first appearance on the stage.

Romp through: succeed easily (in a test, etc.) ***Ex.*** Kanta *romped through* her examination.

Root about/around: turn things over when searching in an untidy way. ***Ex.*** What are you doing *rooting around* in my desk?

Root for: cheer for somebody/something; support somebody/ something whole heartedly. ***Ex 1.*** We are *rooting for* the college football tealll. ***Ex 2.*** We are all *rooting for* you good luck with your job interview.

Root out : (a) destroy something completely. ***Ex 1.*** The government is determined to *root out* corruption. ***Ex 2.*** Agents were sent to *root out* elements hostile to the regime.

(b) find something after hard searching. ***Ex.*** He managed to *root out* a copy of the document.

Rope in/into : persuade somebody to. ***Ex 1.*** All her friends have been *roped in* to help organise the event. ***Ex 2.*** You should avoid being *roped into* organising the office party. ***Ex 3.*** He tried to *rope* me *in* on that swindle.

Rope off: enclose something with rope. ***Ex 1.*** The 'judges' enclosure was *roped off* from the spectators. ***Ex 2.*** The local police *roped off* the scene of the accident.

Rough out: shape, plan or sketch something roughly. ***Ex 1.*** I *roughed out* some ideas for the new buildings. ***Ex 2.*** He has *roughed out* some arrangements for the function tomorrow.

Rough up : (a) treat somebody roughly, with physical violence. ***Ex.*** Agang of youths set on him outside a cinema and *roughed* him *up.*

(b) make something untidy or uneven. ***Ex.*** Don't *rough up* her hair.

Round off : (a) end or complete something satisfactorily. ***Ex 1.*** He *rounded off* his career by becoming Cabinet Secretary, Government of India. ***Ex 2.*** The debate was *rounded off* by the chairman. ***Ex 3.*** I have *rounded off* my work. ***Ex 4.*** This somewhat abstract description is *rounded off* with a number of examples.

(b) take the sharp edges off something. ***Ex.*** She *rounded off* the corners of the table with sandpaper.

Round on/upon: attack somebody verbally in sudden anger. ***Ex.*** She was amazed when he *rounded on* her and called her a liar.

Round out: supply something with more explanation, detail, etc. ***Ex 1.*** He will tell you the plan in outline, and then I shall *round* it *out.* ***Ex 2.*** Your narrative is rather thin; it needs *rounding out,* filling with interesting detail. ***Ex 3.*** The original scheme has been *rounded out* with ideas from his colleagues.

Round up: cause somebody/something to gather in one place. ***Ex 1.*** The guide *rounded up* the tourists and led them back to the coach. ***Ex 2.*** I spent the morning trying to *round up* the documents I needed.

Rout out/out of : fetch somebody abruptly, forcibly, etc. ***Ex.*** We were *routed out* of our beds at 4 a.m.

Rub along: live together smoothly. ***Ex 1.*** They are *rubbing along* the same as ever. ***Ex 2.*** She and her boss have *rubbed along* together for years-for all the world like an old married couple

Rub in/into : constantly remind somebody that he is unfortunate, inferior or dependent in some way. ***Ex 1.*** She first arranged to meet me and then changed her mind, I called that *rubbing* it *in* a little too far. ***Ex 2.*** There is no need to *rub* it *in* that we lost by two goals. ***Ex 3.*** Father never failed to *rub* it *into* the family how much they depended on his money.

Rub off onto/on to : pass from one person or thing to another by contact or close association. ***Ex 1.*** Stay with him for a while and let some of the glory *rub off on to* you. ***Ex 2.*** If he remains in the group, some of his warmth and outgoingness may *rub off on to* the shyer people.

Rub out: kill, murder. ***Ex.*** A couple of mobsters were *rubbed out* in a fracas with the law.

Rule out : regard as impossible or undesirable; forbid. ***Ex 1.*** The possibility cannot be *ruled out* that improvement is largely due to absence of fatigue. ***Ex 2.*** He was *ruled out* as a possible candidate.

Run across : meet somebody or find something by chance. ***Ex 1.*** I *ran across* one of my former colleagues on a visit to Ankara. ***Ex 2.*** I ran across of her earliest recordings in a second-hand shop.

Run after : (a) chase somebody; run to try to catch somebody/something. ***Ex 1.*** Quick, *run after* him; he has left his wallet on the counter. ***Ex 2.*** Don't bother *running after* the bus-you will never catch it.

(b) follow persistently; pursue in the hope of attracting. ***Ex 1.*** He has been *running after* her for months, but she is not interested in him at all. ***Ex 2.*** I hate to feel that I am being *run after*, it only makes me run in the opposite direction. ***Ex 3.*** Don't *run after* an ugly girl. ***Ex 4.*** She had never before *run after* a man, and she was not very good at doing it seriously.

Run along: go away. ***Ex 1.*** Be a good girl and *run along*, I am busy. ***Ex 2.*** *Run along* now, children, I am busy.

Run around; move restlessly from one lover to another. ***Ex 1.*** When is he going to stop *running around* and settle for one girl ? ***Ex 2.*** She treated me right, she did not let me down. But I was not satisfied. That was why I had to *run around*.

Note : The word *run-around* is a noun. It is used in the idiom, give somebody or get the *run-around*. The idiom means treat somebody or be treated, in a deceitful or evasive manner. ***Ex 1.*** He has certainly been getting the *run-around* from her. ***Ex 2.*** He has been giving his wife the *run-around*.

Run at : run towards somebody as if to attack him, or towards something with the aim of jumping over it. ***Ex 1.*** A big fellow *ran at* me with a stick. ***Ex 2.*** He set his horse to *run at* the fence.

Run away: (a) escape from somebody/a place; suddenly leave somebody/ a place. ***Ex 1.*** He *ran away* from home when he was twenty. ***Ex 2.*** He *ran away* twice from his boarding school; he hated being cooped up in an institution.

(b) avoid somebody/something because one is shy, frightened, lacking confidence, etc. ***Ex 1.*** Don't *run away*. He will not eat you. ***Ex 2.*** Difficulties should not be *run away* from; they should be faced resolutely. ***Ex 3.*** Don't *run away* from a difficult situation. ***Ex 4.*** Don't *run away*-I want your advice.

(c) leave home, in the hope of marrying without parental consent; ***Ex 1.*** He has *run away* with the boss's daughter. ***Ex 2.*** He and the boss's daughter have *run away*.

Run away with: (a) steal and carry away; run off with. ***Ex 1.*** The cashier *ran away with* the day's takings. ***Ex 2.*** Someone in the office *ran with* the plans of the new engine.

(b) consume or use up a great deal of something. ***Ex 1.*** My new car really *runs away with* the petrol. ***Ex 2.*** Holidays abroad *run away with* a lot of money.

(c) win clearly or easily. ***Ex.*** Their team *ran away with* the first match in the series.

(d) gain complete control of; dominate. ***Ex 1.*** Don't let your temper *run away with* you. ***Ex 2.*** Her imagination tends to *run away with* het ***Ex 3.*** You tend to let your feelings *run away with you*. ***Ex 4.*** He is nota good man for this job, he lets a fondness for intrigue *run away with* the supervisor.

Run back over: review; reconsider; discuss or consider again. ***Ex 1.*** I shall *run back over* the procedure once again. ***Ex 2.*** I should like to *run back over* the past term, singling out events of particular importance.

Run down: (a) lose power or stop functioning. ***Ex 1.*** My car battery has *run down*; it needs recharging. ***Ex 2.*** If you leave the car lights on all night, the battery will *run down*.

(b) decline or reduce in size or number. ***Ex 1.*** They have been forced to *run* production *down*. ***Ex 2.*** Our manufacturing industry has been *running down* for many a year. ***Ex 3.*** The government will not *run down* military presence in Kashmir. ***Ex 4.*** The company is *running down* its sales force.

(c) knock' to the ground, collide with; hit somebody/something. ***Ex 1.*** The cyclist was *run down* by a lorry. ***Ex 2.*** The car *ran down* a pedestrian this forenoon.

(d) find eventually after a long search. ***Ex 1.*** I had a bit of trouble *running* Rohini *down*. ***Ex 2.*** The suspect was finally *run down* at the home of one of his associates. ***Ex 3.*** I finally *ran* the book *down* in the university library. ***Ex 4.*** The criminal was eventually *run down* in the woods near his home.

(e) disparage; be little; criticise unkindly. ***Ex 1.*** She is always *running* her husband *down* in public. I am surprised that he puts up with it. ***Ex 2.*** Don't *run down* your wife's cooking. ***Ex 3.*** He is always *running* his children *down* in public. ***Ex 4.*** She *runs* everyone *down*. ***Ex 5.*** He loves *running* people *down*.

Note: 1. The word *run-down* is a noun. It means: (a) reduction of tbe size of an industry, etc. ***Ex.*** Tell me something about the government's gradual *run-down* of the coal industry.

(b) detailed analysis or description of something; summary. ***Ex 1.*** Mamta gave me a *run down* on what had been happening while I was abroad. ***Ex 2.*** He can give us a *run down* on the lateSl developments. ***Ex 3.*** Go over to headquarters and try and get *run down* on the situation. ***Ex 4.*** I want a complete *run down* on how the accident happened.

Run down is also used as an adjective in the sense of : (a) tired and slightly ill, especially from working hard. ***Ex 1.*** You look pretty *run-down*; why don't you take a week's holiday? ***Ex 2.*** He emerged from his ordeal in a completely *run-down* condition.

(b) dilapidated; neglected; in bad condition. ***Ex 1.*** This is a *run-down* house, don't live in it. ***Ex 2.*** Don't work in a *run-down* industry. ***Ex 3.*** The whole district is in a terribly *run-down* state.

Run down to : extend to; stretch as far as. ***Ex.*** The grounds at Eastern Court *run down* to the water's edge.

Run for: offer oneself as a candidate for; stand as for. ***Ex 1.*** I have decided to *run for* President next year. ***Ex 2.*** Will you *run for* Mayor, Delhi Municipal Corporation?

Run in : (a) arrest somebody and take him to a police station. ***Ex 1.*** He was *run in* for dangerous driving on Saturday night. ***Ex 2.*** She was *run in* for drunk and disorderly behaviour. ***Ex 3.*** If you throw rotten mangoes at the speaker, you are liable to get *run in* for causing a breach of the peace.

(b) prepare (the engine of a new car) for normal use by driving it slowly and carefully for a certain distance. ***Ex 1.*** Don't expect me to get you home quickly-I am still *running* my car *in*. ***Ex 2.*** Don't drive your new car too fast until you have *run* it *in*. ***Ex 3.*** The point of *running* your engine *in* carefully is not to cause excessive friction between the new working parts.

Run into: (a) meet somebody by chance. ***Ex 1.*** I *ran into* an old friend whom I had not seen for years. ***Ex 2.*** I *ran into* myoid English master while on holiday in Paris. ***Ex 3.*** He *ran into* an old school friend at the supermarket this morning.

(b) collide with or crash into. ***Ex 1.*** He lost control of his car and *ran* it *into* a lamp-post. ***Ex 2.*** She *ran* her car *into* a tree while reversing. ***Ex 3.*** The bus went out of control and *ran into* a shop front.

(c) encounter (problems, etc.) ***Ex 1.*** The project is *running into* financial difficulties. ***Ex 2.*** He has *run into* trouble in his job. ***Ex 3.*** He has *run into* heavy debt. ***Ex 4.*** You should always try to avoid *running into* danger. ***Ex 5.*** His wild extravagance is *running* his family *into* the red (i.e. debt). ***Ex 6.*** We expect to *run into* a few snags before the machine is ready for production.

(d) extend to; be of the size; or order of. ***Ex 1.*** The book titled 'Office Procedure, Drafting and Noting' has *run into* four editions within the year. ***Ex 2.*** Her total income *runs into* six figures.

Run off: (a) drain or flow out of. ***Ex.*** Why don't you ever *run* the water *off* after you have had a bath.

(b) cause a race to be contested. ***Ex.*** The heats of the 200 metres will be *run off* tomorrow.

(c) reproduce, duplicate print or copy. ***Ex 1.*** Could you *run off* hundred copies of this document ? ***Ex 2.*** I have to *run off* fifty handouts on the duplicating machine. ***Ex.* 3.** They *ran off* ten thousand copies of the book titled 'Improve Your Vocabulary'. ***Ex.* 4.** We have already *run off* seven thousand copies of the book, titled 'Word Power'.

(d) leave in the company of somebody, having left ones husband, family, etc. ***Ex. 1.*** She has *run off* with her music teacher. ***Ex.* 2.** Why did she *run off* with one of her colleagues?

Run off with : steal something and carry it away. ***Ex 1.*** The treasurer has *run off with* the club's funds. ***Ex. 2.*** The cashier *ran off with* most of the firm's liquid assets. ***Ex. 3.*** If you leave your money lying about, someone is sure to *run off with* it.

Run on : (a) go on; continue without stopping. ***Ex. 1.*** The meeting will finish promptly-I don't want it to *run on*. ***Ex. 2.*** Do you know how her tongue *run on*? ***Ex.* 3.** He *ran on*, until most of his audience were restless with impatience.

(b) be concerned with; have something as a subject; ***Ex.* 1.** My thoughts kept *running on* recent events in the country. ***Ex.* 2.** Her talk *ran on* developments in the industry. ***Ex. 3.*** His thinking *runs on* familiar lines.

Run out: (a) become no longer valid; expire; come to an end. ***Ex. 1.*** The lease on their house *runs out* in a few months. ***Ex. 2.*** His contract *runs out* shortly. ***Ex. 3.*** The lease for that property will soon *run out*. ***Ex. 4.*** His passport has *run out*.

(b) be finished, used up or exhausted. ***Ex. 1.*** The petrol is *running out*. ***Ex. 2.*** We are *running out* of petrol. ***Ex. 3.*** Our time is *running out*. ***Ex. 4.*** We are *running out* of time. ***Ex. 5.*** Supplies are beginning to *run out*. ***Ex. 6.*** Your time has *run out*. ***Ex. 7.*** If his rice has *run out*, he goes to the paddy-stores. ***Ex. 8.*** If he has *run out* of rice, he goes to the paddy-stores.

(c) (of a rope, etc.) pass out; be passed out. ***Ex. 1.*** The rope *ran out* smoothly through a slot. ***Ex. 2.*** The sailor *ran* the line *out* neatly.

Run out at : work out at; reach a particular amount. ***Ex. 1.*** What does the cost of converting the present building *run out at* ? ***Ex. 2.*** The actual bill *runs out at* considerably more than the original estimate.

Run out/out of: finish; exhaust. ***Ex. 1.*** I have *run out of* money. ***Ex. 2.*** Stop at the next garage. We are *running out of* petrol.

Run out on : desert or abandon somebody who needs or expects one's support. ***Ex.*** The financial aid did not arrive on the promised date, giving us the unpleasant feeling of having been *run out on*.

Run over: (a) overflow. ***Ex. 1.*** Don't fill the kettle too full, it will *run over*. ***Ex. 2.*** Fetch the plumber; the cistern is *running over*.

(b) knock somebody down and pass over his body. ***Ex.*.** Four children were *run over* by a bus at that road junction last night.

(c) read or say something quickly, aloud, or to oneself, in order to learn it or refresh one's memory. ***Ex. 1.*** He *ran over* in his mind what he was going to say at the meeting. ***Ex. 2.*** Just *run over* my lines with me before the rehearsal begins. ***Ex. 3.*** I always *run over* my lines before going on stage. ***Ex. 4.*** She *ran over* her notes before giving the lecture.

(d) recapitulate. ***Ex.*.** Let us just *run over* the story again.

(e) visit briefly. ***Ex.*** I shall *run over* and see him tomorrow.

Run over with: overflow with; show an abundance of. ***Ex. 1.*** She is *running over with* health and vitality. ***Ex. 2.*** The children are *running over with* energy and mischief-I cannot keep them still for five minutes.

Run through: (a) pass quickly through something. ***Ex. 1.*** An angry murmur *ran through* the audience. ***Ex. 2.*** A snatch of their conversation kept *running through* his head. ***Ex. 3.*** Thoughts of revenge kept *running through* his mind.

(b) permeate something; be present in every part of something. ***Ex.* 1.** A deep melancholy *runs through* his poetry. ***Ex. 2.*** There is a deep-seated conservation *running through* our society.

(c) discuss, examine or read something quickly. ***Ex*..** He *ran through* the names on the list.

(d) review or summarise something. ***Ex. 1.*** Please *run through* the main points of the news. ***Ex. 2.*** Could we *run through* your proposals once again?

(e) spend or use up money carelessly or wastefully. ***Ex. 1.*** She *ran through* a lot of money in her first term at university. ***Ex. 2.*** He *ran through* no end of money while he was up at university. ***Ex. 3.*** The money inherited from his father was quickly *run through*.

Run to : (a) reach or extend to. ***Ex. 1.*** The book, 'Common Errors in

English', *runs to* more than 500 pages. ***Ex. 2.*** The book titled 'Interview Techniques' has already *run to* two impressions.

(b) be enough for something; have enough money for something. ***Ex.* 1.** Our funds won't *run to* a holiday abroad this year. ***Ex. 2.*** We cannot *run to* central heating in all rooms.

(c) amount to. ***Ex.*** His fortune *runs to* nearly ten crore rupees.

(d) tend to. ***Ex.*.** This author *runs to* sentiment in some of his novels.

Run up : (a) make a garment quickly. ***Ex. 1.*** She has *run up* a blouse. ***Ex.* 2.** She is willing to *run* me *up* a new dress. ***Ex. 3.*** She had not been able to get a bathing-costume to fit her. She had consequently *run up* two for herself.

(b) allow (a bill, etc.) to accumulate; cause to rise, sharply in amount. ***Ex. 1.*** He has been *running up* accounts at half a dozen big stores. ***Ex. 2.*** The extra grant will only just cover the deficit that we have *run up* already. ***Ex. 3.*** You will *run up* a huge gas bill, if you leave the heater on. ***Ex. 4.*** He has *run up* some astonishing debts.

Run up against: meet or encounter (a problem, difficulty, etc.) ***Ex. 1.*** The government is *running up against* considerable opposition to its privatisation plans. ***Ex. 2.*** She *ran up against* trouble in her new job. ***Ex.* 3.** The same opposition had been *run up against* when we last tried to introduce the measures.

Rush into: act, or cause somebody to act, hastily, without considering the consequences. ***Ex. 1.*** Don't let anybody *rush* you *into* joining; think it over. ***Ex. 2.*** We may eventually become members; but this is not something that should be *rushed into*. ***Ex 3.*** He did not want tl marry-she *rushed* him *into* it.

Rush out: produce something very quickly. ***Ex.*** Editors *rushed out* a piece on the plane crash for the late news.

Rush through: (a) cause something to become official policy, the law, etc. very quickly. ***Ex 1.*** Two Private Members' Bills were *rushed through* Parliament before the end of the session. ***Ex 2.*** The government has *rushed through* legislation making the carrying of firearms a serious offence.

(b) hasten; hurry through. ***Ex 1.*** They *rushed* the news *through*. ***Ex 2.*** You must *rush* this despatch *through* to headquarters.

(c) transport as quickly as possible. ***Ex.*** They are *rushing* men *through* to the danger zone as fast as they can get trucks.

Rustle up : prepare or provide somebody/something, at short notice. ***Ex 1.*** I shall *rustle up* a few sandwiches for you. ***Ex 2.*** I *rustled up* a few helpers to hand out leaflets.

19 Words Beginning With–S

Saddle with : place a particular burden on somebody; give to somebody the responsibility of looking after somebody/something. ***Ex 1.*** I am always being *saddled with* extra duties. ***Ex 2.*** He has been *saddled with* the job of organising the conference slated to be held on Friday, the 12th April, at 11.30 a.m. sharp. ***Ex 3.*** The boss *saddled* her *with* all the most difficult customers.

Sail across/into/past : move in a smooth or very confident way in the direction specified. ***Ex 1.*** Clouds are *sailing across* the sky. ***Ex 2.*** I *sailed past* her, ignoring her completely. ***Ex 3.*** The General Manager *sailed into* the conference hall. ***Ex 4.*** A back-bench critic of the official line *sailed in* the Minister at this point, his temper dearly roused.

Sail in : enter an argument or dispute energetically; attack somebody angrily or vigorously with words. ***Ex 1.*** Sunita *sailed in* with a furious attack on the Managing Director. ***Ex 2.*** Just as we thought the heat had gone out of the discussion, Anita *sailed in*.

Sally forth/out: (a) emerge suddenly, usually from a place where one is surrounded, and attack the enemy. ***Ex 1.*** The defenders *sallied forth* to attack the foe. ***Ex 2.*** The citizens *sallied out* in an attempt to break the siege. ***Ex 3.*** A large number of people *sallied out* against the besiegers. ***Ex 4.*** An army of housewives *sallied forth* to do battle in the annual sales at the big stores.

(b) set out somewhere or to do something. ***Ex.*** Party workers *sallied forth* in a drive to find new members.

Salt away: (a) save (money, etc.) secretly and dishonestly. ***Ex 1.*** He *salted away* most of the profit from our business. ***Ex 2.*** Allegations have been made that millions of rupees are being *salted away* illegally by speculators.

(b) save or invest for the future. ***Ex 1.*** She has *salted away* her money somewhere. ***Ex 2.*** He has got many thousand rupees *salted away* for his retirement. ***Ex 3.*** Now 'is the time to *salt* something *away* for your old age. ***Ex 4.*** The tycoon has *salted* his profits *away* in Switzerland.

Salvage from: rescue or preserve something worth while from a situation which has suffered damage. ***Ex 1.*** How can she *salvage* her reputation *from* the scandal ? ***Ex 2.*** There was very little, morally, that he had *salvaged from* the breakdown of his marriage. His self-confidence was so shaken that he was chary of forming any new relationship.

Sandwich between : put somebody/something between two other persons or things in a restricted space. ***Ex 1.*** The little girl *sandwiched* herself *between* two fat men on the bus. ***Ex 2.*** The car was *sandwiched between* two trucks.

Sass back: answer somebody rudely. ***Ex.*** I asked her to go and brush her teeth and she just *sassed* me *back*.

Saturate in/with: cause somebody/something to absorb a lot of something; fill somebody/something completely with something. ***Ex 1.*** The market is *saturated with* good used cars. ***Ex 2.*** We lay in the sun until our bodies felt *saturated with* the heat.

Savour of: suggest or indicate some bad feeling or attitude on the part of the speaker. ***Ex 1.*** The speaker's words *savoured* strongly *of* intolerance. ***Ex 2.*** Your remarks *savour of* impertinence. ***Ex 3.*** His remarks *savour of* hypocrisy.

Say about: make comments, observations, etc. about. ***Ex.*** What do you *say about* the prospects of a settlement in the rail dispute?

Scale down: reduce something. ***Ex 1.*** We are going to *scale down* the number of trees being felled down. ***Ex 2.*** Imports will have to be *scaled down* until exports begin to rise again. ***Ex 3.*** The effect of inflation is to *scale down* people's spending plans. ***Ex 4.*** Armies should be *scaled down*, but not if it meant giving one country an advantage over any other.

Scale up: increase something. ***Ex 1.*** We have *scaled up* production to meet demand. ***Ex 2.*** The salaries of teachers should be *scaled up* to correspond to those of people in comparable profession. ***Ex 3.*** It is now a matter of *scaling up* production of making forty thousand watches instead of one thousand.

Scare away/off: make somebody leave or stay at a distance by alarming or frightening him. ***Ex 1.*** They lighted a fire to *scare away* the wolves. ***Ex 2.*** He *scares* people *away* by being very brash. ***Ex. 3.*** Strangers never call at that house. I think the bulldog *scares* them *away*. ***Ex. 4.*** A lot of potential visitors are *scared off* by the look of the place-it seems too luxurious for them.

School in: train, discipline or control somebody/oneself. ***Ex. 1.*** You should *school* yourself *in* patience. ***Ex 2.*** He is a child who is well *schooled in* good manners. ***Ex 3.*** He is well *schooled in* many skills, such as movement at night, staying concealed, etc.

Scorch away/down/off: go in the direction, specified at a very high speed. ***Ex 1.*** Many motorcyclists were *scorching down* the road. ***Ex 2.*** The racing cars *scorched off* from the starting line. ***Ex 3.*** He *scorched away* on his motorbike.

Score off : make somebody appear foolish, by making a witty or unkind remark. ***Ex 1.*** She likes to *score off* people when she can. ***Ex 2.*** I know how to *score off* poeple who ask difficult questions. ***Ex 3.*** It is easy to *score off* those who are poor and old.

Score out: cancel something by drawing a line through it. ***Ex 1.*** Four of the names on the list have been *scored out*. ***Ex 2.*** Her name had been *scored out* on the blackboard.

Scrabble about : grope about with the fingers, trying to get hold of something. *Ex 1.* He *scrabbled about* under the table for the dropped pen. ***Ex 2.*** He *scrabbled about* on the desk for his pencil. ***Ex 3.*** Children *scrabbled about* on the floor for coins that had been thrown to them.

Scrape along/by: manage to live with difficulty. ***Ex 1.*** We *scrape along* somehow, although we have hardly any money. ***Ex 2.*** I can just *scrape along* on what my parents give me. ***Ex 3.*** He spent four years at college, *scraping along* on an allowance from her maternal uncle. ***Ex 4.*** They paid him a low salary; on which he was quite content to *scrape along* in the hope that something better would turn up. ***Ex 5.*** The first year in the new house was the hardest, but they just *scraped* by on a loan from the bank.

Scrape in/into : get in/into (ajob, a school, etc.) with difficulty. ***Ex 1.*** She just *scraped into* university with the minimum qualifications. ***Ex 2.*** How on earth did he get into the Indian Administrative Service? He must have *scraped in* by the barest margin, or perhaps he has influence among the selectors.

Scrape through: just manage to pass (a test, etc.); pass with the lowest acceptable mark. ***Ex 1.*** He got a comfortable pass in Chemistry; but barely *scraped through* in Botany. ***Ex 2.*** Sangeeta *scraped through* in the written papers, but may make up her marks in the oral. ***Ex 3.*** He ony just *scraped through* the test.

Scrape together/up: obtain something with difficulty, or by being careful; collect together with difficulty, money from various sources, to meet an emergency. ***Ex 1.*** Well, you will have *scrape* the money *up*. I am not going to dip into my funds to save you from a scandal. ***Ex 2.*** They *scraped together* an audience of seventy for the play. ***Ex 3.*** Can you *scrape up* enough money for a holiday?

Scratch out : erase something by scratching with something sharp. ***Ex 1.*** Her name had been *scratched out* of the list. ***Ex 2.*** I looked at the list; somebody had *scratched* my name *out*.

Scream past/through/sound : move quickly with a loud, piercing sound. ***Ex.* 1.** The wind *screamed through* the trees. ***Ex 2.*** Racing cars screamed *past*.

Screech along/past/through/over : move with a loud high-pitched sound. ***Ex.*** Ten jets were *screeching over* house-tops.

Screen from : protest somebody. (from blame, punishment, etc.) ***Ex 1.*** Everyone is angry with you, and I cannot *screen you* from their anger. ***Ex 2.*** You cannot *screen* your children *from* real life for ever. ***Ex 3.*** During her childhood, she had been carefully *screened from* contact with undesirable children.

Screw out of : (a) remove something from something by twisting. ***Ex.*** The maid *screwed* the water *out of* the sponge.

(b) force somebody to give something. ***Ex 1.*** Can't you manage to *screw* a bit extra *out of* your parents? ***Ex 2.*** They *screwed* the money *out of* her by threats.

Screw up: (a) tighten the muscles or the face or the eyes. ***Ex 1.*** The taste of the lemon made him *screw up* his face. ***Ex 2.*** She *screwed* her face *up* into an expression of the utmost seriousness.

(b) make somebody nervous or tense; tense up. ***Ex 1.*** Going to the dentist never seems to bother my wife, but I get terribly *screwed up* at the mere thought. ***Ex 2.*** The last few minutes before going on stage always *screw* him *up*, so he has a cigarette and a chat with someone in the dressing room to help him relax.

(c) mishandle; mismanage; mess up; ***Ex 1.*** Don't ask them to organise the trip, they will only *screw* everything *up*. ***Ex 2.*** We should never have left the arrangements to him. He *screwed* the whole thing *up* from start to finish. ***Ex 3.*** The opening stage of the attack was badly *screwed up* with the soldiers getting bunched into too narrow a front.

Scrub away/off: remove something by scrubbing. ***Ex 1.*** Please *scrub* the grease *away*. ***Ex 2.*** The servant *scrubbed* the dirt *off* the shelf.

Scrub out: cancel (a plan, etc.); regard as invalid something that has occurred. ***Ex 1.*** We wanted to go for a picnic, but we had to *scrub* it *out*, because of the rain. ***Ex 2.*** The whole programme has been *scrubbed out*; you will receive fresh orders shortly. ***Ex 3.*** We have *scrubbed out* event-L; move on to the next event. ***Ex 4.*** The researchers had to *scrub out* the first set of results and start again.

Seal in : keep something in by sealing. *Ex.* Our foil packets *seal* the flavour *in*.

Seal off : prevent anybody or anything entering or leaving an area, etc. ***Ex 1.*** Police *sealed off* all the exits from the building. ***Ex 2.*** It did not seem to occur to the security guards to *seal off* the entrances or order nobody to leave.

Search out : discover, reveal or bring to light something, by looking carefully for it. ***Ex 1.*** We went through drawer after drawer and eventually *searched out* a dusty portfolio. ***Ex 2.*** I have *searched out* some of her favourite recipes. ***Ex 3.*** He wants to *search out* an old school friend.

Search through : look carefully for something by moving steadily from one part of a book, room, etc. to another. ***Ex 1.*** You can *search through* his autobiography without finding a single reference to his first wife. ***Ex 2.*** There is no point in looking there, his personal papers have all been *searched through*.

Second to : transfer somebody from his normal point to another for special duties. ***Ex 1.*** Colonel Ramesh Gupta has been *seconded to* us to advise on the new signals procedure. ***Ex 2.*** She enjoyed the small, upcountry post *to* which she had been *seconded*.

See about: act to achieve, remedy, etc. something; deal with something; attend to something. ***Ex 1.*** That was how I got the idea of the market-garden, though I did not get round to *seeing about* it till now. ***Ex 2.*** I shall have to *see about* getting the roof mended. ***Ex 3.*** He said he would *see about* the electricity tomorrow.

See across: guide or escort somebody across. ***Ex 1.*** Ask a grown-up to *see* you *across* the road. ***Ex 2.*** I was there to make sure that the children were *seen* safely *across* the road.

See beyond : foresee and understand events, etc. which are at some distance in space or time. ***Ex 1.*** He is not the man to put in charge of the food supply; he cannot *see beyond* where the next meal is coming from. ***Ex 2.*** A man responsible for a large business must be able to *see beyond* short-term goals. He may need to plan for several years ahead.

See in : find somebody/something attractive or interesting. ***Ex.*** I cannot think what she *see in* that young man.

See into: investigate; inquire into. ***Ex 1.*** The police are *seeing into* the matter. ***Ex 2.*** We shall have to see into the case.

See off: (a) say or bid farewell to somebody. ***Ex 1.*** We all went to the airport to *see* her *off*. ***Ex 2.*** A number of friends and well-wishers came to *see* him *off* at railway station.

(b) drive or chase away. ***Ex.*** Some boys came round hoping to steal apples, but the farmer *saw* them *off* with a big heavy stick.

See out/out of: lead or guide somebody out of a building. ***Ex 1.*** Don't bother to come down. I can *see* myself *out*. ***Ex 2.*** She will *see* you *out* of the building.

See out: last until the end of something. ***Ex.*** We have enough coal to *see* the winter *out*.

See over/round: visit and examine or inspect a place carefully. ***Ex 1.*** I shall need to *see over* the house and grounds before I can make you any kind of offer. ***Ex 2.*** It took us two hours to *see* right *round* the Taj Mahal.

See through : (a) understand the true nature of somebody beneath a pleasant, deceptive appearance; not be deceived by somebody/something. ***Ex 1.*** Don't think you can fool me-I can *see* right *through* you. ***Ex 2.*** She learnt to *see through* the smooth exterior to the real person underneath. ***Ex 3.*** We all *saw through* him. ***Ex 4.*** I can *see through* your little game.

(b) ensure that somebody passes safely through a difficult time. ***Ex 1.*** Her courage and good humour *saw* her *through* the bad times. ***Ex 2.*** That overcoat will *see* me *through* the winter. ***Ex 3.*** I have only two thousand rupees to *see* me *through* until pay-day.

(c) not abandon a task, etc. until it is finished. *Ex*. He is determined to *see* the job *through*.

(d) handle a situation and bring events to a happy conclusion. ***Ex.*** Depend on him to *see* things *through*.

See to : take care that somebody is properly received, that something is made, tended, etc. ***Ex 1.*** Large sums of money would continue regularly to be moved, and their security must be *seen to*. ***Ex 2.*** This machine is not working; get a mechanic to *see to* it. ***Ex 3.*** I shall *see to* the arrangements for the next committee meeting.

See to it that : make sure that something, happens, in the case, etc. ***Ex 1.*** *See to it that* you are ready on time. ***Ex 2.*** The doctor has *seen to it that* the nurse did day duty only.

Seek out: look out for and find somebody/something. ***Ex 1.*** I *sought* her *out to* tell her of her tremendous success. ***Ex 2.*** He *sought out* and acquired all his early paintings. ***Ex 3.*** He *sought* her *out* again and he asked her what she really wanted. ***Ex 4.*** He *seeks out* all the new arrivals at the hotel and offers his services as a guide.

Seethe with : (a) be crowded. ***Ex.*** The streets were *seething with* excited crowds.

(b) be very angry, agitated, etc. ***Ex.*** She was *seething with* rage at his rude remarks.

Seize on/upon: recognize and exploit it, use it, etc. eagerly and at once. ***Ex 1.*** He will *seize on* any excuse not to go. ***Ex 2.*** Sushila Rani *seized on* my suggestion and began work immediately. ***Ex 3.*** He will seize upon any help he is given. ***Ex 4.*** The critics *seized upon* my mistakes and said I was ignorant. ***Ex 5.*** Sachin quickly *seized on* a basic flaw in the argument I was developing. ***Ex 6.*** Any weakness in your position will certainly be *seized upon* and exploited.

Seize up : become fixed or jammed because of overheating. ***Ex.*** Your engine will *seize up* if you do not put some more oil in it.

Sell off : get rid of by sales, goods which have not sold well, or plant which is inefficient, so as to free the money invested in them. ***Ex 1.*** We are going to *sell off* some of the stores which have been cluttering up our storeroom for so long. ***Ex 2.*** They have already undertaken to *sell off* one of their factories.

Sell out: (a) be all sold. ***Ex.*** The show has *sold out*. (i.e. there are no tickets left).

(b) sell one's entire stock of a particular article. ***Ex 1.***We have *sold out* of milk but we shall be getting some more in later. ***Ex 2.*** I am sorry, all the Sunday papers have gone, we have *sold out.*

(c) betray one's principles, one's side to somebody. ***Ex 1.*** She has *sold out* and left the party. ***Ex 2.*** He has *sold* us *out* to the enemy. ***Ex 3.*** The union leaders were accused of *selling out* to the employers. ***Ex 4.*** They have *sold* us *out* by agreeing to work during the strike.

Note : The word *sell-out* is a noun used in the sense of betrayal. ***Ex.*** The agreement is a compromise, not a *sell-out.*

Sell up : sell a business, house, etc. to pay one's debts, or because one is retiring or leaving the place/country. ***Ex 1.*** They have *sold up* and gone. ***Ex 2.*** I shall just have to *sell up* now, to get some ready cash. ***Ex 3.*** They are *selling up* next week, so go round if there is anything you want to collect before the sale.

Send after: ask somebody to follow a person, to tell him that he has left something behind, etc. ***Ex 1.*** Kamini had left without her umbrella, so I *sent* one of the boys *after* her: ***Ex 2.*** Nobody told him to leave. *Send after* him and bring him back.

Send away: make somebody leave or depart. ***Ex 1.*** If that boy comes around distributing trade leaflets again, *send* him *away* and tell him not to come back. ***Ex 2.*** I *sent* him *away* because I was totally tired of his idle chatter.

Send away/off: request by post; post money, a coupon, etc. to a dealer to obtain a special offer, free gift, etc. ***Ex 1.*** I have *sent away* for it. ***Ex 2,*** He wants to *send away* for some books. ***Ex 3.*** Have you *sent off* yet for your special guide to mountain expedition ? ***Ex 4.*** He *sent away* to one of the daily papers for a free scientist's almanac.

Send down : (a) expel (a student) from a university. ***Ex 1.*** He has been *sent down* for riotous behaviour. ***Ex 2.*** Many a student was *sent down* after incidents during the visit of a foreign Prime Minister.
(b) sentence somebody to imprisonment. ***Ex.*** He was *sent down* for ten years for armed robbery.

Send for: (a) send somebody to fetch help, etc., or a message asking for it. ***Ex 1.*** The plumber has been *sent for.* In the meantime, please help me mop up the water. ***Ex 2.*** She is ill, *send for* a doctor. ***Ex 3.*** We have sent for a mechanic to repair the T.Y. ***Ex 4.*** The boss has *sent for* me.
(b) make a request, or order for something. ***Ex 1.*** I am going to *send for* that book on wild birds. ***Ex 2.*** Don't delay. *Send* now *for* a free catalogue. ***Ex 3.*** We have *sent for* a fresh supply of paper.

Send in : (a) order so mebody to go to a place in order to deal with a situation. ***Ex.*** Soldiers were *sent in* to quell the riots.
(b) submit something to ajudge or assessor (in the hope of winning a prize, being accepted, etc.) ***Ex 1.*** Entries should be *sent in* to arrive by. 1stAugust. ***Ex 2.*** I shall not bother to *send in* the manuscript; it is sure to be rejected.
(c) submit something to an official, or one's superior, to inform him or obtain his approval. ***Ex. 1.*** If you want a visa, be sure to *send in* your application in good time. ***Ex 2.*** Situation reports were *sent in* three times a day, at 8 a.m.; 1 p.m. and 6 p.m.
(d) send something by post to a place where it will be dealt with. ***Ex.*** Have you *sent in* your application for the job?

Send off: (a) write to somebody to ask for something to be sent to one by post. ***Ex.*** I have *sent off* for those bulbs Isaw advertised in the paper.
(b) send something by post; dispatch something. ***Ex 1.*** Have you *sent* that letter *off* yet ? ***Ex 2.*** Why have not you got my letter? I *sent* it *off* last week.
(c) bid somebody farewell; see off. ***Ex.*** The whole family arrived on the quaside to *send* him *off.*
Note: The word *send-off* is a noun. It means act of saying goodbye to somebody. ***Ex 1.*** Rajni Devi was given a good *send-off* at the airport. ***Ex 2.*** The *send-off* was heart-warming.

Send on : (a) despatch, forward, letters, etc., after somebody has left, so that they reach him at his new address. ***Ex 1.*** Would be kind enough to *send on* any mail to my rrew address? ***Ex 2.*** Students are asked to leave their vacation addresses with office superintendent, in order that examination results can be *sent on*. ***Ex 3.*** I shall *send on* any letters that come for you.

(b) ask or get somebody to continue a journey ahead of others; cause to move on. ***Ex 1.*** The Managing Director had pressing business which kept him in Calcutta, so he *sent* his deputy *on* to represent him in Delhi. ***Ex 2.*** They *sent* the traveller *on* to the next village.

Send out: (a) emit; radiate; transmit. ***Ex 1.*** The sun *sends out* light and warmth. ***Ex 2.*** The oil-lamp *sent out* a gentle beam when you touched the knob. ***Ex 3.*** Some stars *send out* vast quantities of radiation. ***Ex 4.*** Long disused antennae *sent out* and receive all kinds of messages. ***Ex 5.*** This fire *sends out* a lot of heat. ***Ex 6.*** Does this lamp *send out* a powerful beam?

(b) produce something. ***Ex.*** The trees *send out* new leaves in spring.

(c) ask somebody to go from an office, shop, etc. to. ***Ex 1.*** The coffee they make over the road is so much better than the foul stuff we brew up here. Why don't we *send out* for some? ***Ex 2.*** I forgot to pick up the flowers on my way to the office. I suppose we could always *send* him *out* to collect them.

Send out/out of: tell or ask somebody to leave a place. ***Ex 1.*** What are you doing out in the corridor, Mr. Basu ? The Manager *sent* me *out* for throwing paper darts, sir. ***Ex 2.*** Let us begin with a game of Hide the Thimble, shall we ? Now, whom shall we *send out* of the room? ***Ex 3.*** The workmen in the building *sent out* for some biscuits.

Send to : arrange for somebody to attend a particular place, school, college, etc. ***Ex 1.*** He has *sent* his son *to* one of the best schools in the country. ***Ex 2.*** He was *sent to* prison for theft. ***Ex 3.*** Why do you *send* your children *to* a public school ?

Send up : (a) send somebody to prison. ***Ex.*** She says that you were once *sent up* for armed robbery.

(b) make fun of somebody/something, by copying in a comical way; satirize; ridicule by means of a mock-imitation. ***Ex 1.*** Comedians always *send up* members of the government. ***Ex 2.*** Do you *send up* political leaders ? ***Ex 3.*** He has constantly been *sent up* by his children: ***Ex 4.*** The students here love to *send up* the school staff. ***Ex 5.*** Do your son *send* you *up* ? ***Ex 6.*** There are many cartoonists who in their satirical sketches, *send up* fashionable young women who work for charitable causes. ***Ex 7.*** Do you *send up* the monarchy?

(c) blow up; destroy, by fire or explosion. ***Ex.*** A convoy of petrol lorries a mile to the rear was *sent up* in flames.

Note: The word *send-up* is a noun. It, denotes imitation intended to makefun of something or somebody. ***Ex.*** His book is a hilarious *send-up* of a conventional spy story.

Sentence to : declare that somebody is to have a certain punishment. ***Ex 1.*** The judge *sentenced* the murderer *to* fifteen years' hard labour. ***Ex 2.*** In some countries, those persons, who are convicted of murder, are-no longer *sentenced to* death. ***Ex 3.*** He has been *sentenced to* a fine of two thousand rupees.

Separate out: make or become distinct from each other. ***Ex 1.*** Oil and water always *separate out*. ***Ex 2.*** I have trouble in *separating out* the two parts of your argument. ***Ex 3.*** Let us *separate out* the various elements in the problem.

Serve as : be useful or suitable for a particular purpose. ***Ex 1.*** His unpunctuality *served as* an excuse to get rid of him. ***Ex 2.*** A hollowed stick *served* him *as* a spoon and a flat shell as a place.

Serve on : (a) act as a member of. ***Ex 1.*** I *serve on* the boards of several companies. ***Ex 2.*** She *serves on* the executive committee of the Delhi University.

(b) deliver a notice of the court to somebody. ***Ex 1.***.A summons was *served on* him to appear at the High Court. ***Ex 2.*** They have *served* a writ *on* him. ***Ex 3.*** Four summonses were *served on* him relating to four different criminal cases.

Serve out: (a) give a portion of food to many a person; distribute while serving. ***Ex 1.*** Shall I *serve out* the Soup, or would you like to help yourselves? ***Ex 2.*** She *served out* very ample helpings to her guests. ***Ex 3.*** The waiters *served out* the second course to the customers.

(b) serve, work, etc. until the end of a fixed period. ***Ex 1.*** You will have to *serve out* your notice before you leave a firm. ***Ex 2.*** The prisoners must *serve out* their time in jail.

Serve under : be a member of a force, organisation, etc. under the leadership of somebody. ***Ex 1.*** He is not the sort of man I would like to *serve under*. ***Ex 2.*** Do you want to *serve under* her?

Serve up : offer something to somebody for his consideration, entertainment, etc. ***Ex 1.*** She *served up* the usual excuses for being late. ***Ex 2.*** Why do the television networks keep *serving up* the same diet of old movies and second-rate variety programmes?

Note : *Serve* is also used as a noun to mean (in tennis.. etc.) act or manner of serving the ball. ***Ex 1.*** Whose *serve* is it? The said sentence is equivalent to : Whose turn is it to *serve*?

Set about: (a) attack verbally or physically. ***Ex 1.*** He *set about* the thief with a heavy stick. ***Ex 2.*** I shall *set about* him with a soup ladle if he teases me, said Mohini. ***Ex 3.*** A gang of boys *set about* a staunch supporter of the other team. ***Ex 4.*** They *set about* each other furiously.

(b) begin a task; start doing something purposefully and energetically. ***Ex 1.*** I don't know how to *set about* this job. ***Ex 2.*** Our government mind *set about* finding solutions to the country's economic problems. ***Ex 3.*** He *set about* the work methodically. ***Ex 1.*** She *set about* penning an essay.

Set against : (a) make somebody oppose or be hostile to (a friend, relative, etc.). ***Ex 1.*** Competing for the favours of a woman often *sets* friend *against* friend. ***Ex 2.*** A financial scandal of tremendous magnitude *set* father *against* son and brother against brother. ***Ex 3.*** She accused her husband of *setting* their children *against* her. ***Ex 4.*** The civil war *set* brother *against* brother.

(b) consider something good or positive as balancing or outweighing something bad or negative. ***Ex 1.*** You must *set* the initial cost of a new car *against* the saving, you will make on repairs. ***Ex 2.*** *Set against* her virtues, her faults don't seem nearly so bad. ***Ex 3.*** I know it is dearer to uy, than rent a house, but you must *set against* that the fact that I own what I pay for. .

Set apart: make somebody/something different from or superior to others. ***Ex 1.*** These qualities *set* her *apart* from the rest of the group. ***Ex 2.*** His lucid and elegant prose *sets* him *apart* from most other journalists. ***Ex 3.*** Exceptional gifts *set* him *apart* from other sculptors of his generation. ***Ex 4.*** For reasons he could not explain, he was made to feel different, *set apart*, from the other boys.

Set aside: (a) put aside, put something to one side. ***Ex 1.*** He *set aside* the papers he was marking and reached for his cigarettes and matches. ***Ex 2.*** I *set* the magazine *aside* for reading later. ***Ex 3.*** Work on the library extension had to be *set aside* while labour was diverted to more urgent projects. ***Ex 4.*** He *set aside* his book and began to eat an apple.

(b) save or keep money or time for a particular purpose. ***Ex 1.*** Don't eat all the tinned food. *Set* something *aside* for a possible emergency. ***Ex 2.*** I tried to *set aside* a few minutes each day to do some exercises. ***Ex 3.*** This was the day *set aside* for his execution in the local central jail. ***Ex 4.*** I sincerely advise you to *set aside* a bit of money every week.

(c) disregard or ignore something; abandon or reject something; dispense with; get rid of. ***Ex 1.*** I asked her to *set aside* her personal feelings on the matter. ***Ex 2.*** *Set aside* for a moment your instinctive dislike of the man. ***Ex 3.*** In these discussions, all formality was *set aside*. ***Ex 4.*** In dealing with her, I tried to *set aside* my instinctive mistrust of her. ***Ex 5.*** He *set* our objections *aside* and continued unaffected.

(d) cancel; annul or quash (a verdict, sentence, etc.) ***Ex 1.*** The magistrate's decision was *set aside* by the district and sessions judge. ***Ex 2.*** The Supreme Court has *set aside* the judgement of the High Court. ***Ex 3.*** The High Court's verdict was quashed and their prison sentences *set aside*.

Set back: (a) delay or hinder the progress of something. ***Ex 1.*** This interference is going to *set* us *back* considerably. ***Ex 2.*** This trouble will *set* his recuperation *back* if we are not careful. ***Ex 3.*** Financial problems have *set back* our building programme. ***Ex 4.*** Work on the new theatre has been *set back* three months. ***Ex 5.*** Shortage of right materials has *set* us *back*.

Note: The word *set back* is a noun used to denote thing that hinders the progress of something. ***Ex 1.*** Defeat in the by-election is a major *set back* to the ruling party. ***Ex 2.*** Hopes of an early end to the strike suffered a severe *set back* yesterday. ***Ex 3.*** They have suffered a *set back* because of the shortage of right materials. ***Ex 4.*** Two years

later, at the mid-term elections, his party suffered a very serious us *set back*.

(b) cost somebody (the specified amount of money). ***Ex 1.*** This new house will *set* him *back* nearly five lakh rupees. ***Ex 2.*** The new car has *set* me *back* a little over two lakh rupees. ***Ex 3.*** The meal is likely to *set* us *back* hundred rupees each. ***Ex 4.*** If you have dinner there, it will *set* you *back* two hundred rupees a head.

(c) place or situate something at a distance from something. ***Ex 1.*** Our house is *set* well *back* some distance from the main road. ***Ex 2.*** They have *set* the workshops well *back*, out of right of the house.

Set down: (a) allow to alight from; put down. ***Ex 1.*** The bus stopped to *set down* an old lady. ***Ex 2.*** The passengers will be *set down* at platform four. ***Ex 3.*** I *set* her *down* on the comer of her street. ***Ex 4.*** Woufd you mind *setting* me *down* at the next comer ? ***Ex 5.*** The bus stops regularly to *set down* and pick up passengers. .

(b) write something down; note or record something on paper. ***Ex 1.*** I shall *set down* three or four points while they are fresh in my mind. ***Ex 2.*** Why don't you *set* your ideas *down* on paper? ***Ex 3.*** If I can *set* it all *down* on paper, I shall.

(c) name or choose a day when a case is to be heard. ***Ex 1.*** The day *set down* for the trial has still to be announced. ***Ex 2.*** I did not know that the hearing of the case was *set down* for today.

Set forth : (a) start a journey; set out; leave home, base, etc. at the start of an expedition, campaign, etc, ***Ex 1.*** They *set forth* on the last stage of their mountain expedition. ***Ex 2.*** We shall *set forth* on the election campaign next week.

(b) make something known; declare, present or outline something. ***Ex 1.*** The Prime Minister lucidly and precisely *set forth* the aims of his government in a lengthy speech to party workers. ***Ex 2.*** These figures are more clearly *set forth* in tabular form.

Set in : begin and seem likely to continue; gain a hold and likely to spread. ***Ex 1.*** Winter has *set in*. ***Ex 2.*** A strong wind has *set in*. ***Ex 3.*** Those beams will need to be replaced; it looks as though woodworm has *set in*. ***Ex 4.*** Get those bulbs planted before the cold weather *sets in*. ***Ex 5.*** A new vague in trousers seems to have *set in*.

Set off: (a) begin (a journey; etc.) ***Ex 1.*** What time are you planning to *set off* tomorrow ? ***Ex 2.*** I shall set off on a journey round the world next-week. ***Ex 3.*** If you want to catch that train, we should *set off* for the station immediately.

(b) cause (a bomb, mine, etc.): to explode. ***Ex 1.*** He *set off* the bombs. ***Ex 2.*** Know it for certain that the slightest spark can *set off* the explosive stored here. ***Ex 3.*** Do be careful with those fireworks; the slightest spark could *set* them *off*. ***Ex 4.*** If the TNT is shaken or roughly handled, it will be *set off*.

(c) cause, prompt or stimulate something; ***Ex 1.*** The further decline of the money as reported in todays newspapers has *set off* a fresh

wave of setting. ***Ex 2.*** He *set off* her crying. ***Ex 3.*** The threatened action by miners may *set off* sympathy strikes by transport workers. ***Ex 4.*** Panic on the stock market *set off* a wave of selling.

(d) make something appear more attractive by contrast. ***Ex 1.*** The outfit *set off* her dark red hair. ***Ex 2.*** That jumper *sets off* the blue of her eyes. ***Ex 3.*** The formal beauty of the groves was *set off* by the perfection of the grey stonework. ***Ex 4.*** There is no gainsaying the fact that this dress *sets off* her complexion very well.

(e) balance, match (one thing against another). ***Ex 1.*** You can *set* these heavy expenses *off* against a probable increase in salary. ***Ex 2.*** The recent withdrawals from. his account can be *set off* by a refund of income tax.

(f) start to move. ***Ex 1.*** The cars *set off* in a cloud of dust. ***Ex 2.*** The police *set off* in hot pursuit of the escaped prisoner. ***Ex 3.*** Look education is like *setting off* on expedition into the jungle.

(g) cause somebody to start doing something; start somebody telling stories etc. ***Ex 1.*** Don't *set* him *off* talking politics or he will go on all evening. ***Ex 2.*** Her imitations always *set* me *off* laughing. ***Ex 3.*** She *set* him *off* on one of his interminable war stories. ***Ex 4.*** Yourjoke *set* all of them *off* laughing again. ***Ex 5.*** The look on his face is enough to *set* you *off*.

Set on : (a) attack somebody. ***Ex 1.*** He was *set on* by our dog as soon as he opened the gate. ***Ex 2.*** Why did you *set on* him?

(b) cause (a person or an animal) to attack. ***Ex 1.*** The farmer threatened to *set* his ferocious dogs *on* us. ***Ex 2.*** He was *set on* and beaten up in a dark alley.

Set out: (a) leave a place and begin a journey. ***Ex 1.*** We *set out* on the last stage of our journey. ***Ex 2.*** He *set out* at dawn. ***Ex 3.*** The reporters *set out* in high spirits. ***Ex 4.*** This morning the competitors *set out* on the last stage of the round-India cycle race.

(b) declare or state something. ***Ex 1.*** Recent changes in the tax law are clearly *set out* in the enclosed booklet. ***Ex 2.*** The staff side have already set out the safeguards which they think should be scrupulously observed. ***Ex 3.*** I *set out* my objections to the scheme presented by him. ***Ex 4.*** She *set out* the reasons for her resignation in a long letter.

(c) arrange or display items; present material in an orderly manner. ***Ex 1.*** Go and *set out* chairs for the meeting. ***Ex 2.*** Her work is always very well *set out*. ***Ex 3.*** You have not *set out* your ideas very lucidly in this article. ***Ex 4.*** He *set out* the pieces on the chessboard. ***Ex 5.*** The skirts were attractively *set out* to draw in the customers. ***Ex 6.*** I have seldom read such a well *set out* piece of work from a student. .

(d) begin work with the intention of achieving a particular aim. ***Ex 1.*** When I really *set out* to take care of somebody; I usually do the job properly. ***Ex 2*** ..The peasant *set out* to burn an acre of woodland in order to plant his maize. ***Ex 3.*** Ragini *set out* to break the world land speed record. ***Ex 4.*** I fully succeeded in what I *set out* to do.

Set to : (a) begin doing something energetically. ***Ex 1.*** She *set to* with il will and soon finished it. ***Ex 2.*** He is the fastest worker and *sets to* straight away; not stopping until the work is finished. ***Ex 3.*** She *set to* do all the housework. ***Ex 4.*** The engineers *set to* on repair work to the bridge. ***Ex 5.*** If we really *set to*, we can get the house cleaned in an afternoon.

(b) begin to fight or argue. ***Ex 1.*** The boys *set to* and had to be separated by a teacher. ***Ex 2.*** When those two women *set to*, the fur will really fly. ***Ex 3.*** Those two persons *set to* furiously

Set up : (a) make somebody healthier, stronger, more lively; etc. ***Ex 1.*** A cup of hot coffee will soon *set* you *up*. ***Ex 2.*** A week in the country will *set* her *up* nicely after her operation. ***Ex 3.*** He says that the sea air will *set* him *up*. ***Ex 4.*** This tonic will surely *set* you *up* again. ***Ex 5.*** A holiday will *set* him *up* after his illness.

(b) provide somebody with money to start a business, buy a house, etc. ***Ex 1.*** His father *set* him *up* as a bookseller. ***Ex 2.*** Her father will *set* her *up* in business. ***Ex 3.*** Winning all that money on the pools *set* her *up* for life. ***Ex 4.*** There was enough money left to *set* the youngest boy *up* as a photographer.

(c) erect something; place something in position. ***Ex 1.*** They *set up* their tents well before darkness fell. ***Ex 2.*** We shall *set up* camp here. ***Ex 3.*** He *set up* a little stall to sell tea. ***Ex 4.*** They *set up* a war memorial. ***Ex 5.*** Police *set up* road-blocks on routes leading out of the city.

(d) make ready for use. ***Ex.*** How long will it take to *set up* the projector ?

(e) establish or create something; institute something. ***Ex 1.*** The government has *set up* a working party to look into the problem of drug abuse. ***Ex 2.*** A fund will be *set up* for the dead men's families. ***Ex 3.*** The government has *set up* an emergency committee today to ensure the maintenance of milk supplies. ***Ex 4.*** He *set up* a school for poor children.

(f) begin to shout, protest, etc. loudly. ***Ex.*** As soon as he appeared on stage, the crowd *set up* such a commotion that the show had to be stopped.

(g) establish a record speed, time distance, etc. in a sporting event. ***Ex 1.*** She *set up* a new world record time in the 100 metres. ***Ex 2.*** The athletes *set up* several new records.

(h) cause or produce. ***Ex 1.*** Smoking *sets up* an irritation in the throat and bronchial passages. ***Ex 2.*** The doctor has no idea how the condition was first *set up*.

Note: The word *set-up* is a noun. It means structure of an organisation. ***Ex 1.*** What is the *set-up* in your company? ***Ex 2.*** The *set-up* in their business was far too hierarchical. ***Ex 3.*** By all accounts, this *set-up* has functioned with superbly improvised efficiency. ***Ex 4.*** It took him some time to find out what the *set-up* was at head office.

(i) consider somebody or oneself to be special in some way; have pretensions to being such a person. ***Ex 1.*** He likes to *set* himself *up* as an intellectual. ***Ex 2.*** I did not want to *set up* as better than anyone else. ***Ex 3.*** He has *set up* as something remarkable. *Ex 4.* He is not the wise, all knowing father he *sets* himself *up* as.

Settle down: (a) sit or lie in a comfortable position. ***Ex 1.*** She *settled down* in an armchair to read her book. ***Ex 2.*** Let us *settle down* to a quiet discussion of Hindi slang. ***Ex 3.*** He is a writer. He is not married. I don't know why, but writers often don't *settle down* like other people.

(b) adopt a more stable or quiet way of life; get used to a new way of life. ***Ex 1.*** When are you going to marry and *settle down*? ***Ex 2.*** He is settling down well in his new job. ***Ex 3.*** She says that you have no intention of *settling down* yet.

(c) make or become calm, peaceful, lesl restless, etc. ***Ex 1.*** The chairman tried to *settle* the audience *down*. ***Ex 2.*** After all the recent excitement, things have begun to *settle down* again. ***Ex 3.*** Wait until the children *settle down* before you start the lesson. ***Ex 4.*** Marriage has made him *settle down*.

(d) subside; lessen; ***Ex 1.*** Don't come back for a day or two until the noise and commotion have *settled down*. ***Ex 2.*** Go away for a minute while I try to *settle* her *down*.

(e) begin to give one's attention to something. ***Ex.*** The constant interruptions stopped me *settling down* to my work.

(f) establish oneself in ajob, trade, etc. ***Ex 1.*** He is a man whose one aim is to *settle down* in a safe job. ***Ex 2.*** Before you *settle down* to being an honest electrician, consider this offer.

Settle for : (a) accept something that is seen as not quite satisfactory. ***Ex 1.*** I had hoped to get one lakh rupees for myoid car but had to *settle for* a lot less. ***Ex 2.*** He wants to make a quick sale, so he will *settle for* a low price. .

(b) be ready to accept something simple, undemanding, etc. because one has modest tastes, or is lacking in ambition, etc. ***Ex.*** She was not prepared to *settle for* being an ordinary housewife.

Settle in/into: help somebody to move, or move into a new home, job, etc. ***Ex 1.*** We are a little disorganised after the move, but do come and see us when we have *settled in*. ***Ex 2.*** We had hardly *settled* the children *into* a new school when we were posted to another district and had to uproot them again. ***Ex 3.*** We only moved house last week and we have not *settled in* yet. ***Ex 4.*** The new family have *settled in*. ***Ex 5.*** I hope you are all *settling in* satisfactorily.

Settle on : (a) choose something; decide to take something. ***Ex 1.*** We must *settle on* a place to meet. ***Ex 2.*** Have you *settled on* the wallpaper you prefer ? ***Ex 3.*** I don't know what dress she finally *settled on*. ***Ex 4.*** After some discussion we *settled on* a date in early August. ***Ex 5.*** Now that the meeting-place has been *settled on*, can we talk about the agenda?

(b) transfer property, etc., to somebody's ownership. ***Ex 1.*** He *settled* part of his estate *on* his eldest son. ***Ex 2.*** The greater part of his fortune was *settled on* his four daughters. ***Ex 3.*** It ought to have beell enough to *settle* a lump sum *on* her, even if that might have meallt mortgaging the place.

Settle up : pay the money one owes before leaving a hotel, restaurant, etc. ***Ex 1.*** I am tired of this place: let us *settle up* and go. ***Ex 2.*** I am short of cash. Have you enough to *settle up* with the waiter? ***Ex 3.*** If you pay for both of us now, we can *settle up* later. ***Ex 4.*** Please *settle up* your bill before leaving the hotel. ***Ex 5.*** Will you *settle up* the outstanding bills? ***Ex 6.*** Let us *settle* the bill *up* together.

Settle with : punish somebody for an injury, insult, etc. that one has suffered; get even with. ***Ex 1.*** He may think that he has the better of us, but we shall *settle with* him before the week is out. ***Ex 2.*** He thinks he can laugh at me, but I shall *settle with* him soon. ***Ex 3.*** I hear Bhim Bahadur is back in town. It is just as well, I have got a score to *settle with* him.

Sew up : (a) arrange or settle a deal, etc. ***Ex 1.*** By the end of the meeting, everything should the nicely *sewn up*. ***Ex 2.*** When are you going to *sew up* the project? ***Ex 3.*** He has the whole matter *sewn up*. ***Ex 4.*** The deal was *sewn up* over a cup of hot coffee in the restaurant.

(b) organise an area, etc. especially for purposes of trade. ***Ex.*** Give me a good assistant and I shall have the area *sewn up* for you.

Shack up : live together although not married; live in an informal style with somebody to whom one is not married. ***Ex 1.*** Whom is he *shacking up* with these days? ***Ex 2.*** They have decided to *shack up* together in her flat. ***Ex 3.*** She has been *shacking up* with a long-haired poet for a couple of years.

Shackle with : impose some control or check on somebody, in order that he cannot speak or act freely. ***Ex 1.*** He is a bit young to *shackle* himself *with* the responsibilities of a family. ***Ex 2.*** Family doctors are anxious to provide a proper service for their patients, but they cannot give them the attention they need, if they are *shackled with* paperwork. ***Ex 3.*** Don't allow yourself to be *shackled with* superstition.

Shake down: (a) settle down and function properly; settle into harmony with one's companions, etc. ***Ex 1.*** The new office staff are *shacking down* well. ***Ex 2.*** The delegates were from many different backgrounds, but they quickly *shook down* in theirnew surroundings.

(b) settle properly into running order. ***Ex.*** Following extensive modifications after the accident to the turbine blades, the liner underwent further trials at sea to ensure that everything *shook down* properly.

(c) sleep somewhere where there is no proper bed. ***Ex 1.*** You can *shake down* on the floor. ***Ex 2.*** Let us *shake down* here.

(d) search somebody/something thoroughly. ***Ex.*** Police *shook* the club *down*, looking for narcotics.

Shake off : (a) rid oneself of somebody unwanted; escape from somebody; get rid of pursuers, etc. ***Ex 1.*** She tried to *shake* him *off* but he contiued to pester her. ***Ex 2.*** He *shook off* his pursuers. ***Ex 3.*** Our pilot dived into a bank of cloud in an attempt to *shake off* the enemy fighters. ***Ex 4.*** He *shook off* her unwelcome attentions and rushed into his room.

(b) get rid of something. ***Ex 1.*** I just cannot *shake off* his cold, ***Ex 2.*** You should *shake off* these expensive habits. ***Ex 3.*** I don't know how to *shake off* a fit of depression.

Shake up : (a) rouse somebody from a state of lethargy, apathy, etc.; discipline idle or unruly people by handling them vigorously. ***Ex 1.*** We have got to *shake up* all these people with old-fashioned ideas. ***Ex 2.*** What these recruits need is half an hour's drill on the square-that will *shake* them *up*.

(b) disturb; agitate. ***Ex 1.*** The death of her father *shook* her *up* more than she cares to admit. ***Ex 2.*** He feels rather *shaken up* after the accident. ***Ex 3.*** The bad news has *shaken* me *up* considerably.

(c) make somebody uncomfortable by *shaking*. ***Ex.*** When the aircraft finally landed, most of us felt badly *shaken up*.

Shame into: cause somebody to behave well by making him feel ashamed of his earlier wrong doing. ***Ex 1.*** She stared at him hard and eventually *shamed* him *into* giving up his seat to the old lady. ***Ex 2.*** They *shamed* him *into* apologising. ***Ex 3.*** Don't imagine that he can be *shamed into* admitting that it was all his fault.

Shape up: make progress; develop. ***Ex 1.*** How are the new boys in your team *shaping up*? ***Ex 2.*** He will *shape up* into an excellent footballer. ***Ex 3.*** Our plans are *shaping up* well.

Share with: tell somebody about something. ***Ex 1.*** I want to *share* my views *with* you. ***Ex 2.*** She will not *share* her secret *with* you.

Shorn of: be stripped or deprived of. ***Ex 1.*** The room looked bare, *shorn of* its rich furnishings. ***Ex 2.*** He is a deposed king *shorn of* his former power.

Sheer away/off : turn suddenly away from somebody/something dangerous or, unpleasant. ***Ex 1.*** She tends to *sheer away* from any discussion of her divorce. ***Ex 2.*** When he saw me coming, he *sheered off* in the opposite direction. ***Ex 3.*** This was a topic from which he always *sheered away*, as though unwilling to face the embarrassment it caused. ***Ex 4.*** He *sheers off* from hard work.

Sheet down: (of rain) fall heavily. ***Ex 1.*** The wind blew, the rain *sheeted down*, and we were all soaked. ***Ex 2.*** We sat gloomily by the hotel window, watching it *sheet down*.

Shell out: payout, often reluctantly. ***Ex 1.*** Don't expect me to shell out every time you want something. ***Ex 2.*** He *shelled out* a lot to get the car. ***Ex 3.*** I am tired of *shelling out* on repairs to this car. ***Ex 4.*** I know that when the collection box comes round, I shall be expected to *shell out* the most. ***Ex 5.*** He is expected to *shell out* for the dinner-party.

Shift for: manage to earn a living, run a home, etc. without help from others. ***Ex 1.*** If you are marooned on an island, I shall not be able to help you-you will have to *shift for* yourself. ***Ex 2.*** If he had not been able to *shift for* himself when his parents died, he would have starved. ***Ex 3.*** When their parents died, the children had to *shift for* themselves.

Shin up : climb up something using the hands and legs to grip. ***Ex 1.*** He *shinned up* a tree. ***Ex 2.*** Thieves got into the house by *shinning up* a drainpipe and forcing open the window. ***Ex 3.*** He *shinned up* onto the roof of the house.

Shin down: climb down. ***Ex 1.*** The boys *shinned down* from the roof of the house. ***Ex 2.*** He *shinned down* a rope.

Ship off : send somebody away. ***Ex 1.*** His children had been *shipped off* to boarding-school at an early age. ***Ex 2.*** As my youngest son had no prospects at home, he was *shipped off* abroad to make a career for himself.

Shoot down: (a) kill somebody by shooting. ***Ex 1.*** His victims were all *shot down* in cold blood. ***Ex 2.*** The local police *shot down* two dacoits in an encouter.

(b) cause to fall to the ground. ***Ex 1.*** We *shot down* two enemy fighter planes. ***Ex 2.*** You would be lucky to *shoot* a fighter plane *down* with a light machine-gun. .

Shoot off: (a) severe something by *shooting* with a gun. ***Ex.*** His arm was *shoot off* in the war.

(b) shoot into the air. ***Ex.*** People were *shooting off* pistols in the streets to celebrate the victory.

Shoot up : (a) terrorize a place by moving through it and firing into the air or at a house, etc. ***Ex 1.*** Nobody can scare them off, they will come back and *shoot* the place *up*, just for kicks. ***Ex 2.*** The gangsters ran into the restaurant and started *shooting* it *up*.

(b) rise or increase sharply. ***Ex 1.*** We shall do what we can to stop prices *shooting up* still further. ***Ex 2.*** My pulse rate would suddenly *shoot up* alarmingly.

(c) grow or increase in size quickly. ***Ex 1.*** The boy has *shot up* since we last saw him. ***Ex 2.*** The plants are just *shooting up*.

Shop around: (a) go from one *shop*, dealez etc., to another until one finds the best value for money; look *around* in shops, etc. seeking the best bargain. ***Ex 1.*** You should *shop around* a bit before making a decision. ***Ex 2.*** I *shopped around* till I got what I wanted at a price-I could afford. ***Ex 3.*** It will pay you to *shop around* a bit before deciding which car to buy. ***Ex 4.*** Don't buy the first car you see, *shop around* a bit.

(b) examine claims or programmes of various firms, schools, colleges, etc. before deciding which to join. ***Ex 1.*** Has your son decided which universities he is going to apply to ? Not yet. He is *shopping around* for a course with a good choice of options. ***Ex 2.*** You must *shop around* for the best school for your children.

Shore up : (a) support something: ***Ex.*** Padmini used this evidence to *shore up* her argument.

(b) prop up; protect by fiscal or other means. ***Ex 1.*** He expects us to *shore up* his inefficient firm. ***Ex 2.*** The government may need *shoring up* before the end of the year.

(c) support something with a wooden beam, etc. propped against it. ***Ex 1.*** You should *shore up* the side of the old house to stop it falling down. ***Ex 2.*** This canal bank has been *shored up*. ***Ex 3.*** It only needs a heavy storm to bring the whole house down. We will have to *shore* it *up*.

Shoulder in/into/through : move by pushing with one's shoulders. ***Ex 1.*** I *shouldered* my way *into* the room. ***Ex 2.*** They *shouldered* their way *through* the crowd.

Shout down: prevent a speaker from being heard by shouting while he is speaking; shout to prevent somebody from speaking. ***Ex 1.*** The crowd *shouted* the speaker *down*. ***Ex 2.*** Some angry persons *shouted down* one of the members of the committee as he tried to address them through a loud-hailer. ***Ex 3.*** Don't try to talk to them in their present mood, you will only get *shouted down*.

Shove off : leave; go away. ***Ex 1.*** *Shove off*, You are not wanted here. ***Ex 2.*** She *shoved off* about an hour ago. ***Ex 3.*** Well, you have said your piece. Now why don't you *shove off* and leave me alone ? ***Ex 4.*** I cannot stand his company any longer, let us *shove off* somewhere and have a cup of hot coffee.

Shove up : move along, in order to make more room. ***Ex.*** We can get one person more in if you don't *shove up*.

Show around/round: take visitors on a tour of a place; guide tourists round a place. ***Ex 1.*** If you are free at two o'clock on Friday, I shall be delighted to *show* you *around* the Taj Mahal. ***Ex 2.*** He is busy at the moment. He is *showing round* a party of visitors.

Show in/into: lead or conduct somebody into a place. ***Ex 1.*** When the guests arrive, please *show* them *into* the sitting-room. ***Ex 2.*** Don't keep Sushmita Sen waiting. *Show* her *in* at once.

Show off: (a) draw people's attention to somebody/something, especially out of pride or vanity). ***Ex 1.*** You will have to practise that trick a little more before you can *show* it *off*. ***Ex 2.*** Do you love *showing off* ? ***Ex 3.*** Her aunt liked to boast about her and *show* her *off* when she came home in uniform. ***Ex 4.*** He likes *showing off* how well he speaks Sanskrit. ***Ex 5.*** She was *showing off* her new husband at the party. ***Ex 6.*** This is a dress that *shows off* her figure well.

(b) try to impress others with one's wealth, abilities, intelligence, etc. ***Ex 1.*** Do stop *showing off-it* is embarrassing. ***Ex 2.*** The child danced around the room, *showing off* to everybody.

(c) display something, or make it appear, to advantage. ***Ex 1.*** The room, very plain, formal and grey, was intended primarily to *show off* the drawings that were hung there. ***Ex 2.*** The cut of her dress *shows off* her figure to perfection.

Note : The word *show off* is a noun. It means person who tries to impress others in speech or actions. ***Ex 1.*** Take no notice of him-you know what a *show off* he is. ***Ex 2.*** Are you a *show off* ?

Show out/out of: lead or conduct somebody from a place. ***Ex.*** We have concluded our discussion. Please *show* our visitor *out.*

Show over : take visitors on a tour of a place. ***Ex.*** I shall get you a guide to *show* you *over* the factory.

Show through: be visible underneath a covering. ***Ex.*** She has acquired very good French accent, but Her English speech habits still *show through.*

Show up : (a) be easily visible or apparent; make visible; reveal clearly. ***Ex 1.*** At times like these, the true character of the man *shows up*. ***Ex 2.*** Close study of the surface of the picture *shows up* a network of fine cracks. ***Ex.3.*** The dust on the shelf *shows up* in the sunlight. ***Ex 4.*** Close inspection *shows up* the cracks in the stonework.

(b) appear; arrive, often after a delay. ***Ex 1.*** It was ten o'clock when he finally showed up. ***Ex 2.*** We were hoping for a full team today but only five players *showed up*.

(c) make somebody feel embarrassed by behaving badly in his company. ***Ex 1.*** Don't show us up wearing something absurd. ***Ex 2.*** He *showed* me *up* by falling asleep at the concert. ***Ex 3.*** I can take our children anywhere. I am never afraid that they are going to *show* me *up* in some restaurant.

(d) show somebody to be (dishonest, disreputable, etc.) ***Ex 1.*** His diary *shows* him *up* to have been a greedy, arrogant man. ***Ex 2.*** Don't *show* yourself *up* for what you are. ***Ex 3.*** Should we expect him to tell the truth about himself if that truth would *show* him *up* as rather poor sort of fish.

Shower on/upon : be given, give to somebody freely, in abundance. ***Ex 1.*** We were quite embarrassed by people's kindness, offer of meals and shelter *showered upon* us. ***Ex 2.*** From the moment; Madhu Malti arrived, hospitality was *showered on* her. ***Ex 3.*** Gifts and praise were *showered on* the ballerina. ***Ex 4.*** Honours were *showered upon* me.

Shrink away/back: move back or withdraw from somebody/ something, through fear or disgust. ***Ex 1.*** He *shrank back*, he could not bear sharp voices. ***Ex 2.*** He always *shrank back* from actual commitment : he would rather be uninvolved. ***Ex 3.*** As he moved threateningly forward, she *shrank back* from him. .

Shrink from: be reluctant to do something. ***Ex 1.*** I *shrink from* hurting animals e ***Ex 2.*** Don't *shrink from* doing hard labour .

Shrink up: try to make oneself small and inconspicuous, (out of shyness). ***Ex.*** She had a tendency to *shrink up* whenever attention was focused on her.

Shrug off: dismiss something as being unimportant. ***Ex 1.*** He had a way of *shrugging off* criticism as though it were beneath his notice. ***Ex 2.*** I highly admire the way she is able to *shrug off* unfair criticism. ***Ex 3.*** He *shrugged off* their complaints. ***Ex 4.*** He just *shrugged* the whole affair *off*.

Shuffle off/out of : avoid doing (what one ought to do); get rid of; discard. ***Ex 1.*** He tries to *shuffle* his work *off* onto others. ***Ex 2.*** The maid *shuffled out of* the chores by saying she felt ill. ***Ex 3.*** He *shuffled off* his old friends When he became famous. ***Ex 4.*** He is running away because that is the only opportunity to *shuffle off* his responsibility. ***Ex 5.*** He tried to *shuffle off* his own responsibility onto the men who dig the nation's coal.

Shut away: put somebody/something away from others; isolate. ***Ex 1.*** I vehemently hate being *shut away* in the country. ***Ex 2.*** They feel very *shut away* in that remote little cottage. ***Ex 3.*** Do you want to be shut away in a mental hospital? ***Ex 4.*** What made him *shut* himself *away* in a remote mountain village?

Shut down : close; close down; cease production at; stop working.

Ex 1. The workshop has *shut down* and the workers are unemployed. ***Ex 2.*** They have *shut down* their factory. ***Ex 3.*** Our factory has been *shut down* from lack of orders. ***Ex 4.*** His shop has been *shut down* because of lack of trade. ***Ex 5.*** Some businesses will have to *shut down* if there is a recession.

Note: The word *shut-down* is a noun. It denotes process of closing a factory, etc. either temporarily or permanently. ***Ex 1.*** Frequent strikes are causing *shut-downs* in the steel industry. ***Ex 2.*** The government has ordered the *shut down* of two coal mines. ***Ex 3.*** The threat of a *shut down* in the newspaper industry has not been averted.

Shut in: (a) prevent somebody/oneself from getting out of a place; ***Ex 1.*** *Shut* myself *in* my study for hours almost daily. ***Ex 2.*** If you close that door, you can *shut* the noise *in*.

(b) surround. ***Ex.*** We are *shut in* by the hills here.

(c) trap or pinch something by closing something. ***Ex.*** I *shut* my finger *in* the car door.

Shut off: (a) stop the supply or flow of. ***Ex.*** You must *shut* the gas supply *off* if there is a leak.

(b) keep somebody/something away from something; separate; isolate. ***Ex 1.*** They feel *shut off* from all human contact on this island. ***Ex 2.*** Are you really *shut off* there? ***Ex 3.*** Their village is *shut off* from the world by.lakes and marshes. ***Ex 4.*** His deafness *shuts* him *off* from the lives of others.

Shut out/out of : exclude somebody/something; keep somebody/something out; block somebody/something; prevent somebody/something from entering. ***Ex 1.*** The Government wants to *shut* the refugees *out.* ***Ex 2.*** There trees *shut out* the view. ***Ex 3.*** I tried hard to *shut* all thoughts of her *out of* my mind. ***Ex 4.*** I cannot *shut out* the picture of the accident, ***Ex 5.*** You really cannot *shut* her *out of* your life so easily, ***Ex 6.*** It is impossible to *shut out* all news from the outside world. ***Ex 7.*** The window was open, but the rain *shut out* the air as effectively as a curtain. ***Ex 8.*** Ticket-holder? who arrive late may find themselves *shut out of* the stadium.

Shut up : (a) be quiet, stop talking. ***Ex 1,*** I asked them to *shut up* and let us hear the radio. ***Ex 2.*** Tell her to *shut up*. ***Ex 3.*** Can't you *shut* him *up* ? ***Ex 4.*** For heaven's sake, *shut* him *up* .' he has said quite enough already. ***Ex 5.*** Generals were in the greatest awe of the Prime Minister and *shut up* like an oyster in his presence.

(b) confine somebody; put something away under lock and key for sak keeping. ***Ex 1.*** We *shut* him *up* in his room. ***Ex 2.*** *Shut* the jewels *up* in the safe. ***Ex 3.*** The vital documents are kept *shut up* in a strong-box.

(c) close doors and windows of. ***Ex 1.*** He *shut* his room *up* securely and left the key with the guard. ***Ex 2.*** We *shut up* the house before going on holiday.

Shy away : avoid or move away from something because of fear; shyness, etc. ***Ex 1.*** Modern English writers tend to *shy away* from using the stage for direct auto-biographical expression. ***Ex 2.*** I have always *shied away* from close friendships. ***Ex 3.*** He *shies away* from problems. ***Ex 4.*** She *shies away* from the thought of contact as he makes to touch her shoulder.

Sick up: vomit something. ***Ex 1.*** He cannot keep anything down, he *sicked up* what little breakfast he had. ***Ex 2.*** The baby *sicked up* a little milk.

Sicken of: become weary of; become disgusted with something. ***Ex 1.*** I began to *sicken of* the endless violence shown on television. ***Ex 2.*** After a few weeks working for him, I *sickened of* his methods.

Side with: support somebody in an argument, dispute, etc.; put oneself on the same side as somebody. ***Ex 1.*** She *sided with* me against the others in the class. ***Ex 2.*** I *sided with* the minority against the official line. ***Ex 3.*** I am careful to *side with* the party most likely to win.

Sidle up/over/past: move or approach in a shy, nervous or furtive way. ***Ex 1.*** A young attractive lady *sidled over* to me, and asked if I recognised her. ***Ex ,2.*** She *sidled past*, trying to seem casual. ***Ex 3.*** The beggar *sidled up* and asked for money. ***Ex 4.*** A small man *sidled up* to me and pressed a piece of paper into my hand. ***Ex 5.*** If someone *sidles up* and offers to buy currency, pay no attention.

Sift through: examine something very carefully. ***Ex 1.*** He *sifted through* the piles of correspondence. ***Ex 2.*** The lawyer *sifted through* the evidence relating to the murder case.

Sigh for : feel a deep longing for something that is lost, far away, etc. ***Ex.*** He is an exile who constantly *sighs for* home.

Sign away: surrender or relinquish something by singing a document, etc. ***Ex 1.*** I shall never get married-it is like *signing* your life *away*. ***Ex 2.*** He has just *signed away* a fortune. ***Ex 3.*** He *signed away* all his nghts to the property. ***Ex 4.*** Read the document carefully, so that you know what you are *signing away*.

Sign for : sign a form, etc. to 'show that one has received something. ***Ex.*** The postman asked me to *sign for* the parcel.

Sign in : (a) write one's or somebody's name to show arrival. ***Ex 1.*** You must *sign* guests *in* when they enter the club. ***Ex 2.*** They *signed in* last night around eleven o'clock.

(b) help gain admittance by signing. ***Ex 1.*** She *signed* me *in* to her club. ***Ex 2.*** Can you find someone to *sign* me *in* ?

Sign out : write one's name or somebody's name to show departure. ***Ex 1.*** Soldiers *sign out* when they leave the barracks. ***Ex 2.*** He *signed out* at ten this morning.

Sign off : (a) stop work. ***Ex.*** He *signed* off early to go to the dentist. (b) end a letter. ***Ex.*** She *signed off* with Yours ever, Ragini.

Sign on : (a) register as an unemployed person. ***Ex.*** A lot of men *signed on* at the local Employment Exchange.

(b) sign or cause to sign an agreement or undertaking to work for somebody. ***Ex 1.*** Men who came forward as volunteers agreed to *sign on* for the duration of hostilities. ***Ex 2.*** We need to *sign on* sixty workers to boost production. ***Ex 3.*** He *signed on* yesterday and will start work on Monday. ***Ex 4.*** They *signed on* a large number of casual labourers last week. ***Ex 5.*** He *singed on* for five years in the infantry.

Sign over: formally transfer the ownership of something to somebody by signing a document, etc. ***Ex 1.*** She has *signed* her house *over* to me. ***Ex 2.*** Asenior executive *signed over* a delivery of five aircraft on behalf of his company. ***Ex 3.*** The top floor of the building was *signed over* for use as offices.

Sign up : join a club, enrol for a course, etc. ***Ex 1.*** He has *signed up* for a secretarial course. ***Ex 2.*** They have *signed up* a number of promising youngsters this season. ***Ex 3.*** Before you *sign up* for a course, make sure that the institute is attached to an established employment agency.

Simmer down: become calm after a period of anger, excitement, violence, etc. ***Ex 1.*** *Simmer down*, now, stop shouting. ***Ex 2.*** Things have *simmered down* since the riots last week. ***Ex 3.*** When things have *simmered down* a bit more, talks can be started. ***Ex 4.*** Give him a minute to *simmer down*-he is always like this when we discuss politics. ***Ex 5.*** His temper has *simmered down* and you may be able to . reason with him.

Sing out: (a) shout to get something. ***Ex.*** If you need anything, just *sing out* for it.

(b) shout an order. ***Ex.*** Just *sing out* what you want.

(c) shout out, perhaps melodiously. ***Ex.*** Sushmita *sang out* when she heard the good news.

Sing past/through : move with a humming, buzzing or whistling sound. ***Ex.*** A bullet *sang past* his ear.

Sing up : sing more vigorously or loudly. ***Ex 1.*** *Sing up*, let us hear you. ***Ex 2.*** *Sing up*, fellows, this is supposed to be a celebration, not a funeral. ***Ex 3.*** Tell the people at the back to *sing up*, I cannot hear them.

Single out: select somebody/something from others, for special comment, treatment, etc. ***Ex 1.*** Which would you *single out* as the best? ***Ex 2.*** Tell me why' he was *singled out* for punishment. ***Ex 3.*** He *singles out* in human nature the ugly elements-the elements that hurt him. ***Ex 4.*** I imagine, that to be *singled out* by the Chairman for a farewell luncheon is indeed an honour. ***Ex 5.*** We *singled* her *out* as one of the most talented students. ***Ex 6.*** He has been *singled out* for all the nasty jobs.

Sink down: (a) gradually disappear. ***Ex.*** The sun slowly *sank down* in the west.

(b) go down as fully as possible. ***Ex.*** He *sank down* out of sight when the enemy patrol came past.

Sink in : (a) be fully absorbed and understood. ***Ex 1.*** The scale of the tragedy gradually *sank in*. ***Ex 2.*** Mywarning obviously has not *sunk in* your thick skull. ***Ex 3.*** Her explanation took a long time to *sink in*. ***Ex 4.*** I don't know whether the facts have really *sunk in*. ***Ex 5.*** Has your flight *sunk in* yet?

(b) invest capital, etc. heavily in some project. ***Ex 1.*** They sank all their profits in property. ***Ex 2.*** A lot of their money had been *sunk in* mineral shares. ***Ex 3.*** In this particular tin-tack venture, he had *sunk in* half the sum left him by his father.

Sink into: (a) fall fast asleep. ***Ex.*** He has already *sunk into* sleep.

(b) fall to a lower physical or moral level. ***Ex 1.*** He *sank into* black depression. ***Ex 2.*** His maternal grandmother has *sunk into* a coma. ***Ex 3.*** Don't let yourself *sink into* despair.

Siphon off: (a) draw a liquid from one place to another. ***Ex 1.*** If you are short of petrol, you can *siphon off* a gallon from my tank.

(b) transfer somebody/something from one place to another, often unfairly or illegally; transfer funds from one person or account to another for dishonest purposes. ***Ex 1.*** She *siphoned off* profits from the business into her account. ***Ex 2.*** The big clubs *siphon off* all the best players. ***Ex 3.*** There is no doubt that a good deal of the money paid into the campaign fund has been *siphoned off* from it into private pockets. ***Ex 4.*** They have *siphoned* the money *off* for their own use. ***Ex 5.*** The department is good at *siphoning off* funds from one area to another.

Sit about/around: spend one's time sitting down, unwilling or unable to do anything; lounge idly; sit doing nothing. ***Ex 1.*** I have been *sitting around* waiting for the phone to ring all day. ***Ex 2.*** He just *sits about* all day. ***Ex 3.*** School discipline is very largely relaxed, and you have time to *sit about* and gossip. ***Ex 4.*** The foreign correspondents seemed to spend most of their time *sitting around* in restaurants.

Sit back: do nothing; relax after working; be inactive. ***Ex 1.*** I like to *sit back* and rest in the evenings. ***Ex 2.*** Are you going to *sit back* and let me do everything? ***Ex 3.*** After a long walk, it is pleasant to *sit back* with a cup of hot coffee and look out at the view. ***Ex 4.*** When we needed her help, all she did was *sit back* and twiddle her thumbs.

Sit down under: endure or suffer something without protest or resistance. ***Ex 1.*** You should not *sit down under* these accusations. ***Ex 2.*** He is a patient man, but not even he coulds *sit down under* that kind of provocation. ***Ex 3.*** Nobody can *sit down under* such insults.

Sit for: (a) be the Member of Parliament for (a constituency). ***Ex.*** I *sit for* New Delhi.

(b) take an examination. ***Ex.*** I shall *sit for* my B.A.examination next month.

Sit in : (a) occupy a building as a protest. ***Ex 1.*** The workers are *sitting in* against the factory closures. ***Ex 2.*** Some students are *sitting in* at the Principal's office.

(b) *sit in* a place, for a speacial purpose. ***Ex 1.*** She *sits in* for me sometimes, when I go shopping. ***Ex 2.*** He *sits in* with the patients' while the nurse has a rest.

(c) replace. ***Ex 1.*** She will *sit in* for me while I go to the shops. ***Ex 2.*** He is *sitting in* for his friend today ..

Sit in on : attend (a discussion, etc.) as an observer, not as a participant. ***Ex 1.*** The teachers allowed a pupil to *sit in on* their meeting. ***Ex 2.*** I *sat in on* the whole debate. ***Ex 3.*** I would like her to *sit in on* this meeting.

Sit on : (a) be a member of (a committee, board, jury; etc.); serve as a member of. ***Ex 1.*** A number of distinguished academics and teachers *sat on* the committee which recommended the expansion of higher education. ***Ex 2.*** This was only one of the many bodies on which Kanta Devi had *sat* during her life of public service. ***Ex 3.*** How many persons *sit on* the commission ?

(b) fail to deal with something; neglect or suppress a complaint, etc.; do nothing about something. ***Ex 1.*** They have been *sitting on* my application for over a couple of months. ***Ex 2.*** For many a week, they did nothing about my case, they just *sat on* it. ***Ex 3.*** Why did you *sit on* those student's applications for so long a period?

(c) stop somebody's bad or awkward behaviour; handle finnly somebody who behaves impertinently, etc. ***Ex 1.*** That young good-looking lady is becoming insufferable, she needs to be *sat on* firmly. ***Ex 2.*** I have to *sit on* the class when they get too rowdy. ***Ex 3.*** I don't like being *sat on* by the authorities. ***Ex 4.*** Tell me the details as to why the committee *sat on* you.

Sit out: (a) *sit out* doors. ***Ex.*** The garden is so lovely, I think I shall *sit out.*

(b) stay to the end of a performance, etc. (even though one may find it unpleasant). ***Ex 1.*** Why did you *sit out* a boring play? ***Ex 2.*** I found the show tedious-I don't know how I managed to *sit* it *out.* ***Ex 3.*** *Sit* the first bit *out* patiently-the game will liven up later. ***Ex 4.*** I somehow managed to *sit* the meeting *out*. ***Ex. 5.*** They *sat out* the play.

(c) not take part in a particular dance. ***Ex.*** I shall not *sit out* the rumba.

Sit through: remain in a theatre, etc. from the beginning to the end of a performance, etc. (even though one may dislike it). ***Ex 1.*** I did *sit through* the entire programme. I did not find it as bad as you seem to think. ***Ex 2.*** I cannot *sit through* four hours of the concert.

Sit up : (a) stay awake and out of bed till past one's usual bedtime (to wait for somebody or keep somebody company, erc.): ***Ex 1.*** They *sat up* till the small hours, exchanging tittle-tattle. ***Ex 2.*** I shall get back very late, so don't *sit up* for me. ***Ex 3.*** The nurse *sat up* with the patient all night. ***Ex 4.*** We *sat up* late watching a fild on T. ***Ex 5.*** They *sat up* all night talking. ***Ex 6.*** She *sat up* till three a.m., reading. ***Ex 7.*** I *sat up* with her, discussing her problems.

(b) move, or cause somebody to move, to an upright position after lying flat, slouching, etc. ***Ex 1.*** The patient is well enough to *sit up* in bed now. ***Ex 2.*** Don't slouch over your breakfast. *Sit up* straight. ***Ex 3.*** She *sat* the baby *up* to feed her.

(c) move to an upright position, in a tense, alert way, out of fear or surprise. ***Ex.*** She *sat up*, clapping her hands to her mouth, her eyes wide with fear.

Size up: form ajudgement or opinion of somebody/something. ***Ex 1.*** It is not easy to *size up* the situation. ***Ex 2.*** We *sized* each other *up* at our first meeting. ***Ex 3.*** She *sized* him *up* pretty quickly and decided to keep away from him. ***Ex 4.*** I was trying to *size* you *up*, but you did not fit into any type I knew.

Skate over/round : not deal with something directly; slide over; minimise; ignore; avoid. ***Ex 1.*** He always *skates over* difficulties. ***Ex 2.*** Will you be able to *skate round* this problem? ***Ex 3.*** She *skated round* the likely cost of the plan. ***Ex 4.*** He is so cautious and evasive, always *skating over* the surface, never coming to grips with the issues underneath. ***Ex 5.*** This is not something that can be *skated over*-let us get down to brass tacks.

Sketch out : outline something; give a general discription or account of something; draw roughly. ***Ex 1.*** The engineer *sketched out* proposals for a new road. ***Ex 2.*** I asked her to *sketch out* what she intends to do. ***Ex 3.*** Give me a pad and pencil and I shall *sketch out* what I have in mind. ***Ex 4.*** He *sketched out* the general picture first.

Skim from/off: (a) remove (cream, scum, etc.) from the surface of a liquid. ***Ex 1.*** She *skimmed* the cream *from* the milk. ***Ex 2.*** The gravy is too greasy, *skim off* some of the fat before you serve it.

(b) take the best part of a group. ***Ex 1.*** He always *skims off* the best students for his classes. ***Ex 2.*** In some areas, English-medium public schools are still able to *skim off* the best of the senior secondary school entry. ***Ex 3.*** The cream of manpower was *skimmed off* into the workers' battalions.

Skim over/through: read something quickly, noting only the main points. ***Ex 1.*** I don't have time to do more than *skim through* the book. ***Ex 2.*** She *skimmed over* the list, looking for one's name. ***Ex 3.*** I *skimmed through* the report in half an hour. ***Ex 4.*** Give me a moment to *skim through* these notes before the meeting. ***Ex 5.*** Don't read the book in detail, *skim through* it to get the general picture.

Skip off: leave a place furtively to avoid some unpleasant task. ***Ex 1.*** He skipped *off* with the stolen money. ***Ex 2.*** She *skipped off* without saying anything to anyone. ***Ex 3.*** They *skipped off* and left us to do the clearing away. ***Ex 4.*** I *skipped off* pretty smartly when the moment came to pay the bill.

Skirt around/round : avoid referring to or treating (a topic, an issue, etc.) directly. ***Ex 1.*** She *skirted around* the problem of the high cost. ***Ex 2.*** They usually prefer to *skirt round* problems rather than face them squarely. ***Ex 3.*** Let us not *skirt around* the awkward questions-let us try and answer them. ***Ex 4.*** The question of who is to pay has been *skirted around*. I suppose, that is because you assume that I shall foot the bill.

Skittle out: (in cricket) end the turn of opposing batsmen quickly. ***Ex.*** The whole side was *skittled out* for 10 runs.

Slack off/up : (a) reduce one's level of activity; slowly stop working . ***Ex 1.*** After intense work in the summer, we are *slacking off* now. ***Ex 2.*** Don't *slack off* now, just as we are getting to the end.

(b) reduce speed. ***Ex.*** *Slack off* as you approach the junction.

Slack up : stop working very hard. ***Ex.*** It is time to *slack up* a bit.

Slag off : say offensive and critical things about somebody unfairly. . ***Ex.*** She is always *slagging off* her old boss.

Slap down : stop somebody talking, making suggestions, etc. in a firm, unpleasant way. ***Ex 1.*** She tried to object, but the chairman slapped her down. ***Ex 2.*** Anyone who speaks out of turn in her presence is liable to be *slapped down*. ***Ex 3.*** Getting admitted to that club is likely to be tough for upstarts like you and me. You can try it if you don't mind being *slapped down*.

Slap on/onto: add something to the price of something. ***Ex.*** They have *slapped* 5 per cent *on* the price of sugar.

Slash back: economise severely. ***Ex.*** The government has *slashed back* on its spending.

Sleep around : have sex with many partners; move casually from one lover to another. ***Ex 1.*** Don't run after a girl who *sleeps around.* ***Ex 2.*** Men may not insist that their bride is a virgin any longer but they will still avoid a girl who is known to have *slept around.*

Sleep in: sleep on the premises where one works. ***Ex 1.*** Most of the hotel staff *sleep in*. ***Ex 2.*** Our maid *sleeps in.*

Sleep off: lose or get rid of something by sleeping. ***Ex 1.*** He is in an evil mood, but let us give him a night to *sleep* it *off*. ***Ex 2.*** He *slept* the party off. ***Ex 3.*** She *slept off* a bed headache. ***Ex 4.*** You will feel better when you have *slept* it *off*. ***Ex 5.*** It is usually possible to *sleep* these things *off*, and feel better afterwards.

Sleep on: not decide about something until the next day. ***Ex 1.*** Don't say now if you will take the job, *sleep on* it first. ***Ex 2.*** Let us *sleep on* it and try again tomorrow.

Sleep out: (a) sleep outdoors. ***Ex 1.*** Some vagrants have *sleep out* even in winter. ***Ex 2.*** It is very hot, let us *sleep out.*

(b) not steep at the place where one works. ***Ex 1.*** Our servant *sleeps out*. ***Ex 2.*** Do you like *sleeping out*?

Sleep through : not be woken up by. *Ex.* He *slept* right *through* the thunderstrorm.

Sleep together/with : have sex with somebody to whom one is not married. ***Ex 1.*** She is a very strictly brought-up girl; I doubt very much if she is *sleeping with* her boyfriend. ***Ex 2.*** Don't *sleep with* your girlfriend.

Slick down : flatten down one's hair close to the head with oil, etc. ***Ex.*** Hair was drawn up from the side of his head and *slicked down* over the bald patch on top.

Slide into: gradually pass into (a certain bad condition). ***Ex 1.*** Don't *slide into* bad habits. ***Ex 2.*** He *slide into* heavy debt. ***Ex 3.*** We must not *slide into* complacency.

Slide over: avoid dealing with (a topic, etc.) in detail; move quickly over something without tackling it. ***Ex 1.*** She discussed sales, but *slide over* the problem of how to increase production. ***Ex 2.*** He *slide over* the events of the previous day, wishing to spare his guests any embarrassment. ***Ex 3.*** This is not a matter that can be *slide over*; let us discuss it openly.

Slim down: reduce something in size or scale. ***Ex 1.*** We shall have to *slim down* the factory's work-force. ***Ex 2.*** The government has *slimmed* its budget *down* considerably.

Slip in/into : (a) enter quickly and quietly (without being noticed). ***Ex.*** Mother *slipped into* the children's room to make sure they were all asleep.

(b) mention something important in conversation, etc., so carefully that one does not appear to be drawing special attention to it. ***Ex 1.*** He liked, very casually, to *slip in* references to the important work he was doing. ***Ex 2.*** One or two appeals for funds were *slipped into* his opening address.

Slip into: put on, with a quick, easy movement. ***Ex 1.*** She got up, *slipped into* a dressing-gown, and peered out of the window. ***Ex 2.*** They are an old pair of shoes I can *slip into* to do the gardening.

Slip through: pass or enable to pass through, elude, something which is intended to control or check such movement. ***Ex 1.*** Some highly valuable information has *slipped through* the security network. ***Ex 2.*** We are unable to prevent a small number of defective parts *slipping through.*

Slip up : make a careless mistake. ***Ex 1.*** I *slipped up* and gave you the wrong phone number. ***Ex 2.*** He *slipped up* on the date of meeting. ***Ex 3.*** Somebody must have *slipped up* lady in your report.

Slobber over : show too much sentimental feeling for; show one's affection for somebody/something too openly, so that it embrasses other people. ***Ex 1.*** She is *slobbering* all *over* her boyfriend. ***Ex 2.*** I am always embarrassed by the way he *slobbers over* small children.

Slog away : work continuously, and in a hard, determined fashion at something. ***Ex 1.*** The accountant is *slogging away* at my accounts. ***Ex 2.*** She has been *slogging away* at her multiplication tables all morning. ***Ex 3.*** Keep *slogging away*, you have nearly broken the back of the problem.

Slop about/around : (a) move about in a lazy, casual way; slouch about/around: splash around. ***Ex 1.*** I have tried to get the boy interested in decorating the house, but all he does is *slop around.* ***Ex 2.*** I would like to know why some children like *slopping about* in puddles.

(b) move around in a small space. ***Ex.*** Water was *slopping about* in the bottom of the boat.

Slope off : go away, without being noticed, in order to avoid doing work, etc; go away furtively. ***Ex 1.*** She *sloped off* somewhere with her friends. ***Ex 2.*** Don't just *slope off* and leave us. ***Ex 3.*** Don't think that you can *slope off* just because my back is turned. ***Ex 4.*** Let us *slope off* somewhere quiet and have a cup of cold coffee.

Slosh about/around : move around noisily in something liquid. ***Ex 1.*** Children are *sloshing about* in puddles, ***Ex 2.*** Don't *slosh about* in the mud.

Slosh on : apply paint, etc., in a rough, vigorous way. ***Ex 1.*** Don't be afraid-*slosh on* plenty of bright colour. ***Ex 2.*** He was *sloshing* white wash *on* the wall. ***Ex 3.*** Be careful, you are *sloshing* paste *on* your jersey.

Slouch about/around: slop about/around; move about in a lazy, slovenly way. ***Ex 1.*** Why don't you stop *slouching about* with your hands in your pockets? ***Ex 2.*** He has been *slouching about* all day doing nothing.

Slough off : get rid of something; abandon something. ***Ex 1.*** Tell her to *slough off* her bad habits. ***Ex 2.*** Don't try to *slough off* your responsibilities. ***Ex 3.*** He had *sloughed off* all the petty cares of home and work.

Slow down: live or work less energetically ***Ex 1.*** You should *slow down* a bit and lead a less hectic life. ***Ex 2.*** He has *slowed down* a bit since his heart attack. ***Ex 3.*** You really ought to *slow down*-all these late nights are doing you no good. ***Ex 4.*** If I could find some way of *slowing* my father *down* I would; he is taking on far too much work.

Slow up : act, work, etc. less energetically because of age, poor health, etc. ***Ex 1.*** I think he is beginning to *slow up*-his latest book is much weaker than the previous one. ***Ex 2.*** He is over sixty, but he shows no signs of *slowing up*. ***Ex 3.*** *Slow up* a bit, or you will make yourself ill.

Slur over: avoid dealing with an unpleasant fact, a difficult problem, etc. ***Ex.*** She *slurred over* the high cost of her plan.

Smarten up : make oneself/somebody/something neater, tidier, etc. ***Ex 1.*** You will have to *smarten* yourself *up* a bit before going out. ***Ex 2.*** Try to *smarten* the house *up* before the visitors arrive. ***Ex 3.*** She has *smartened up* considerably since I last saw her. ***Ex 4.*** He has *smartened up* a lot in his general appearance.

Smash against/into/through: move, or cause to move, with great force into, against, etc., something. ***Ex 1.*** The car *smashed into* the wall. ***Ex 2.*** The elephant *smashed through* the trees.

Smash down: make something fall down by smashing it. ***Ex.*** The fireman *smashed* the door *down* to reach the children.

Smash in : make a hole, dent, etc. in something by hitting it with great force. ***Ex 1.*** Vandals *smashed* the door *in*. ***Ex 2.*** I shall *smash* her head *in*. ***Ex 3.*** The explosion had *smashed in* all the ground-floor windows.

Smell of : strongly suggest. ***Ex.*** It *smells* strongly *of* shady dealing.

Smell of : (a) detect somebody/something by smelling. ***Ex.*** Specially trained dogs can *smell out* drugs.

(b) discover something by finding and interpreting clues. ***Ex 1.*** The Intelligence Bureau *smelled out* a plot to kill those political leaders who are aged over fifty-eight. ***Ex 2.*** I can *smell out* trouble before it starts.

Smile on: approve of or encourage somebody/something. ***Ex.*** The board of directors did not *smile on* your plan.

Smoke out: drive somebody/something out by means of smoke. ***Ex 1.*** They *smoked out* a fox from a hole. ***Ex 2.*** He was determined to *smoke out* the leaders of the gang. ***Ex 3.*** The soldiers smoked the enemy out of their hiding places. ***Ex 4.*** The escaped convicts were *smoked out* of the house.

Smooth away: get rid of (problems, difficulties, etc.) smoothly and easily. ***Ex 1.*** Money helps to *smooth away* most problems. *Ex 2.* We shall *smooth away* any difficulties when we reach them.

Smooth down : restore feelings which have been upset or distrubed. ***Ex.*** Father is in a dreadful temper, Sudesh. Do what you can to *smooth* him *down*.

Smooth out: remove difficulties, etc., thus making a situation easier for somebody. ***Ex 1.*** The managing director has *smoothed out* some of the formalities, so you will get your certificate as arranged. ***Ex 2.*** There are some technical problems to be *smoothed out* before we can fly. ***Ex 3.*** She is good at *smoothing* these little problems *out*.

Smooth over: calm somebody, settle a quarrel, etc. by acting calmly and diplomatically. ***Ex 1.*** This was a genuine attempt to placate him and *smooth* this thing *over*. ***Ex 2.*** I was asked to *smooth* things *over* between them. ***Ex 3.*** They were now arguing furiously, with Umesh standing by and trying to *smooth* the quarrel *over*.

Snap at : (a) speak to somebody sharply and rudely. ***Ex 1.*** Why did you snap at him ? ***Ex 2.*** Don't *snap at* me like that. ***Ex 3.*** She *snapped at* him when he asked her what she was going to do.

(b) try to grasp something with the teeth by closing them quickly and sharply around it. ***Ex 1.*** The fish *snapped at* the bait. ***Ex 2.*** You must stop your dog *snapping at* visitors to the house.

(c) try to seize by accepting, agreeing, etc. quickly. ***Ex.*** He would *snap at* an opportunity to go abroad.

Snap out : explain something in a sharp or unpleasant way. ***Ex 1.*** He *snapped out* an angry reply. ***Ex 2.*** The colonel suddenly *snapped out* the information. ***Ex 3.*** The captain *snapped out* an order.

Snap up: buy or seize something quickly and eagerly. ***Ex 1.*** The cheapest articles at the sale were quickly *snapped up*. ***Ex 2.*** He *snapped up* the offer. ***Ex 3.*** If there are any bargains going on, he will *snap* them *up*. ***Ex 4.*** In this time of austerity, cotton stockings were *snapped up* as soon as they came into the shops.

Snarl up : make or become confused, tangled, jammed, etc. ***Ex 1.*** Traffic has *snarled up* the city centre. ***Ex 2.*** The machine *snarled* the material *up*. ***Ex 3.*** The traffic gets *snarled up* very often at that roundabout. ***Ex 4.*** Private traffic *snarled up* completely on the approach road to the docks. ***Ex 5.*** Extra demands at these hours *snarls up* the whole system.

Snatch at : (a) try to grasp something. ***Ex 1.*** He *snatched at* the ball but did not catch it. ***Ex 2.*** A man darted from a doorway and *snatched at* her bag. ***Ex 3.*** He *snatched at* the rope-ladder, but it eluded his grasp.

(b) grasp/seize or take advantage of something eagerly and quickly. ***Ex 1.*** You must *snatch at* every opportunity to earn money by fair means. ***Ex 2.*** It is my life-long principle to *snatch at* every opportunity to achieve fame and glory. **Ex 3.** They *snatched at* the opportunity of visiting the Rashtrapati Bhawan. ***Ex 4.*** There are a few vacancies on the production side every year, but they come and go quickly. You have to *snatch at* them. ***Ex 5.*** He was starving. He *snatched at* some food and ran.

Snatch from/out of : remove somebody/something from, quickly.
Ex 1. He was one of the few to be *snatched from* the holocaust.
Ex 2. The letter was *snatched out of* my hand before I could read it.

Sneak into/out of/past/away/off/in : go quietly and secretly. ***Ex 1.*** The servant stole the money and *sneaked out of* the house. ***Ex 2.*** The cat ate the food and *sneaked off*.

Sneak up : (a) approach quietly; staying out of sight until the last moment. ***Ex.*** Nandini loves *sneaking up* on her sister to frighten her. **(b)** move secretively. ***Ex.*** The thief *sneaked* quietly *up*.

Sneeze at : not consider lightly; take something seriously; worth considering or having; not to be despised. ***Ex 1.*** A prize of ten lakh rupees is not to be *sneezed at*. ***Ex 2.*** He says that the new job carries an increase of one thousand rupees a month. That is good money. Certainly not something to be *sneezed at*. ***Ex 3.*** Don't *sneeze at* his offer of help.

Sniff at : ignore or show contempt for something, reject or dismiss something as unworthy of. ***Ex 1.*** Her generous offer is not to be *sniffed at*. ***Ex 2.*** Don't *sniff at* his offer of monetary assistance. ***Ex 3.*** You should not *sniff at* this opportunity-you may not get another like it. ***Ex 4.*** The agreement the employers proposed was *sniffed at* by the workers.

Sniff out: discover somebody; find somebody out. ***Ex 1.*** The police were determined to *sniff out* the ringleaders. ***Ex 2.*** The culprit was *sniffed out* by the search-party. ***Ex 3.*** If is your job to *sniff out* abuses of power. ***Ex 4.*** He is off on his travels again, *sniffing out* adventure in Egypt.

Snipe at : make unpleasant critical remarks attacking somebody/something. ***Ex 1.*** They are always *snipping at* their political opponents. ***Ex 2.*** Film stars are often *sniped at* in the newspapers. ***Ex 3.*** He is not irritated when newspapermen *snipe at* him in their columns. It is a matter of patience born of long experience.

Snoop about/around: search or investigate (to find mistakes, signs that people are breaking rules, etc.) in a persistent, irritant, and secretive way. ***Ex 1.*** Some people were *snooping about* at night. ***Ex 2.*** The inspector of schools was *snooping around* the school entrance looking for late-comers. ***Ex 3.*** The house prefects *snoop around* the dormitories at night. ***Ex 4.*** A policeman is *snooping around* again. trying to find out if we have a licence for one gun.

Snow in/up : prevent somebody from going out by snowing heavily. ***Ex1.*** Wewere *snowed in* for four days in our cottage in the mountains. ***Ex 2.*** They were *snowed in* for several days.

Snow under : overwhelm somebody; have a heavy load of; overload. ***Ex 1.*** I was *snowed under* with work last week. ***Ex 2.*** She is *snowed under* with applications for the job. ***Ex 3.*** Don't give me any extra jobs: I am *snowed under* already. ***Ex 4.*** At that time we were being *snowed under* with requests for medical aid.

Snuff out : (a) put out; extinguish something. ***Ex 1.*** The candles on the long table were *snuffed out*. ***Ex 2.*** Go and *snuff out* the lamp.

(b) finish something; put an end to something; suppress something. ***Ex 1.*** His hopes were nearly *snuffed out*. ***Ex 2.*** The authorities *snuffed* out the rebellion almost as soon as it began.

Snuggle down: move under the bedclothes, to get warm and comfortable. ***Ex 1.*** *Snuggle down* here beside me. ***Ex 2.*** The children snuggled down in their beds. ***Ex 3.*** The little boy *snuggled down* with his toy and was quickly asleep.

Snuggle up : press up close to another person for warmth or comfort, out of affection or desire; cuddle up to. ***Ex 1.*** The little girls *snuggled up* to one another in the bed. ***Ex 2.*** She *snuggled up* to her boy friend in the darkened cinema. ***Ex 3.*** *Snuggle up* and I shall tell you a very interesting story.

Soak off/out: remove something by soaking in water. ***Ex 1.*** *Soak out* the stain from the shirt. ***Ex 2.*** He *soaked* the label *off* ajamjar. ***Ex 3.*** Rather than paint over the paper, you would do better to *soak* it *off*.

Soak through : make somebcdy including his clothes thoroughly wet. ***Ex.*** Don't stand out there, you will get *soaked through*.

Soak up: (a) take in liquid; absorb something. ***Ex 1.*** Use a paper towel to soak up the cooking oil. ***Ex 2.*** This sandy soil *soaks up* moisture very quickly. ***Ex 3.*** If you spill ink on the carpet, *soak* it *up* straight away.

(b) receive and absorb something; assimilate something. ***Ex 1.*** That girl is very intelligent. She *soaks up* new facts like a sponge. ***Ex 2.*** He was *soaking up* the sunshine.

Sob out: tell something while sobing; tell a story; etc. while crying bitterly. ***Ex 1.*** I listened sympathetically while she *sobbed out* the whole sorry tale. ***Ex 2.*** He *sobbed out* the story of his son's violent death. ***Ex 3.*** He *sobbed out* his account of the accident.

Sober down : make or become calm and serious, after a period of irresponsible or frivolous behaviour. ***Ex 1.*** Please *sober down* a bit; I have got some important news for you.

Sober up : make, or become, sober; cause somebody to recover from a drunken state. ***Ex 1.*** Give him some black coffeee that will help to *sober* him *up*. ***Ex 2.*** Put his head under the cold tap-that will *sober* him *up*.

Sad off : go away; clear off; leave. ***Ex.*** Don't stand for any trouble from him. Tell him to *sad off*.

Soldier on : continue bravely with one's work, despite difficulties. ***Ex 1.*** The walkers *soldiered on* although the weather was terrible. ***Ex 2.*** I shall *soldier on* whatever happens. ***Ex 3.*** Well, it is not easy, but we shall *soldier on*.

Sop up : take up with a cloth, etc. ***Ex 1.*** *Sop up* the water with a paper towel. ***Ex 2.*** Get a towel and *sop up* the water before it runs over the floor. ***Ex 3.*** I dislike her habit of *sopping up* the soup with a piece of bread.

Sort out: (a) separate something from a larger group. ***Ex.*** *Sort out* the smaller plants and throw them away.

(b) put something in good order. ***Ex.*** This room needs *sorting out*.
(c) find a solution to (a problem, etc.). ***Ex 1.*** I shall leave you to *sort* this problem *out*. ***Ex 2.*** Let us leave them to *sort* themselves *out*. ***Ex 3.*** I need to *sort* myself *out* a bit, before I start looking for a new job.
(d) deal with somebody by punishing or attacking him. ***Ex.*** I shall soon *sort* him *out*.
(c) arrange in classes or groups. ***Ex 1.*** Members of the armed forces have been *sorted out* by trades and occupations. ***Ex 2.*** He *sorted out* the different kinds of flowers.

Sound off : talk noisily and boastfully about something; speak loudly and pompously. ***Ex 1.*** Don't raise that topic, you will start Bhim Bahadur *sounding off* on his pet theory. ***Ex 2.*** I wonder when he will stop *sounding off* about this fabulous house he is building. ***Ex 3.*** He is always *sounding off* about how he would manage the firm.

Speak for : (a) act as a spokesman for somebody; speak on behalf of others. ***Ex 1.*** I cannot *speak for* Sudha Rani. ***Ex 2.*** I am *speaking for* all of us when I say how grateful we are to our hosts.
(b) give evidence on behalf of somebody. ***Ex.*** Are you prepared to *speak for* the accused?
(c) make a speech in support of something. ***Ex.*** I am prepared to *speak for* the reintroduction of the death penalty for violent crimes involving the use of explosives.

Speak of: indicate something; suggest something. ***Ex 1.*** He highly *speaks of* her honesty and intelligence. ***Ex 2.*** Her behaviour *speaks of* suffering bravely borne.

Speak on: give a talk, make a speech, on a particular subject. ***Ex 1.*** At our next meeting, he will be *speaking on* the early development of printing. ***Ex 2.*** The lecturer provided a list of topics *on* which he was prepared to *speak*.

Speak out: speak bravely and with conviction on a particular topic. ***Ex 1.*** I was the only one to *speak out* against the closure of the hospital. ***Ex 2.*** Have you got the courage to *speak out* against the corrupt politicians?

Speak to : (a) have a word with somebody in the hope of getting something done. ***Ex 1.*** There is something wrong with the plumbing. ***Ex 2.*** I shall have to *speak to* the landlord about it. ***Ex 3.*** Did you manage to *speak to* the managing director about my salary?
(b) scold, reproach somebody, with a view to changing his conduct for the better, reprimand somebody; tell off. ***Ex.*** Your children have damaged our kitchen garden. Can you *speak to* them?
(c) give information about (a subject) at a meeting. ***Ex.*** Will you *speak to* this item, Anita ?

Speak up : speak in a loud clear voice. ***Ex 1.*** Please *speak up*; we cannot hear you at the back. ***Ex 2.*** You should stop mumbling, and learn to *speak up*.

Speak up for: state clearly and freely what one thinks (on behalf of somebody). ***Ex.*** It is time to *speak up for* those who are suffering injustice.

Speed up: increase, or cause to increase, speed. ***Ex 1.*** We have *speeded up* production of the new car. ***Ex 2.*** The trian soon *speeded up.*

Spell out: (a) say alouid or write the letters of (a word) in their correct order. ***Ex.*** Please *spell* that word *out* for me again.

(b) make something clear and easy to understand; explain something in detail. ***Ex 1.*** My instructions seem simple enough-cdo I have to *spell* them *out* again? ***Ex 2.*** She is so stupid that you have to *spell* everything *out.* ***Ex 3.*** The magistrate *spelt out* the consequences of a crime of this kind. ***Ex 4.*** The possible economic benefits of the treaty were *spelt out* in detail in his recent book.

Spice with : add humour, etc. to a conversation, etc. to give it a more interesting flavour. ***Ex 1.*** I vividly remember some of the ancedotes *with* which her conversation was *spiced.* ***Ex 2.*** He was leading a boring life *spiced with* moments of intrigue. ***Ex 3.*** His stories are *spiced with* humour.

Spill over : (a) over flow from something that is full. ***Ex.*** The meeting *spilt over* from the hall into the corridor.

(b) be greater than, exceed, the number that a town or city can accommodate. ***Ex.*** New towns will have to be built to house the population of those suburbs of Delhi which have *spilled over.*

Spin along : move along rapidly on wheels. ***Ex.*** The car was *spinning merrily along* the road.

Spin out: make something last as long as pcssible. ***Ex 1.*** You should *spin* your money *out* until the next pay-day. ***Ex 2.*** They *spin out* the time by talking. ***Ex 3.*** She enjoys *spinning* a story *out* for as long as possible.

Spirit away/off: take or carry somebody/something away quickly, secretly or mysteriously. ***Ex 1.*** The ballerina was *spirited away* at the end of the concert before her fans could get near her. ***Ex 2.*** We were ushered smoothly to a table in the centre of the restaurant, and our coats and hats were *spirited away.* ***Ex 3.*** The speaker was *spirited off* by some officials before we had a chance to talk to him.

Splash about: sit or stand in water and make it fly about with one's hands or feet. ***Ex 1.*** Children were happlily *splashing about* in their bath. ***Ex 2.*** A party of boys was *splashing about* at the shallow end of the pool.

Splash across/through: move across, etc. with a splashing noise. ***Ex 1.*** We *splashed* our way *across* the stream. ***Ex 2.*** She *splashed through* the, puddles.

Splash down: land in water with a splash. ***Ex.*** The spacecraft *splashed down* in the Pacific.

Splash out: spend money on something in an impulsive or a carefree way. ***Ex 1.*** She *splashed out* on a new pair of shoes. ***Ex 2.*** Before you start *splashing out* on books and clothes, think of the bills you have to pay.

Split away/off: separate or divide something from a larger group or body. ***Ex 1.*** The group have *split away* from the official union. ***Ex 2.*** The storm has *split* the branch *off* from the main tree trunk.

Split on : give away information about a person that will get him into trouble. ***Ex 1.*** His friend *split on* him to the teacher. ***Ex 2.*** Don't *split on* me. ***Ex 3.*** Somebody must have *split on* him to a teacher.

Split up : end a marriage, friendship or relationship; separate. ***Ex 1.*** He and she have *split up*. ***Ex 2.*** He has just *split up* with his girlfriend. ***Ex 3.*** Who told you that she and I had *split up* ?

Spring back: return suddenly to its previous or usual position, having been pushed, bent, etc. ***Ex.*** The branch *sprang back* and hit him in the face.

Spring from: (a) orginate from something; have something as a source or origin. ***Ex 1.*** The authorities failed to remedy the grievances *from* which these disorders *sprang*. ***Ex 2.*** He *sprang from* peasant stock. ***Ex 3.*** Hatred often *springs from* fear. ***Ex 4.*** Her interfering ways *spring from* a desire to see her daughters comfortably married.

(b) appear suddenly or unexpectedly from. ***Ex.*** Where on earth did you *spring from*?

Spring on : present or introduce something to somebody suddenly; so that he is surprised, and may be unprepared. ***Ex 1.*** I hate to *spring* this *on* you at such short notice. ***Ex 2.*** Let us *spring* a surprise *on* her. ***Ex 3.*** He *sprang* a bad news *on* him. ***Ex 4.*** The headmaster *sprang* a revision of the time-table *on* us half-way through the term.

Spring out : appear suddenly from behind cover, with the intention or effect of frightening somebody. ***Ex 1.*** You did give me a fright, *springing out* at me like that. ***Ex 2.*** A masked man *sprang out* from a doorway.

Spring up: arise, develop, grow or appear quickly or suddenly. ***Ex 1.*** Weeds are *springing up* everywhere. ***Ex 2.*** New houses are *spring up* all over the city. ***Ex 3.*** A breeze *sprang up* as we were returning from the meeting. ***Ex 4.*** Doubts have begun to *spring up* in my mind. ***Ex 5.*** Milk bars have sprung up all over the city. ***Ex 6.*** Towards evening, a cold wind *sprang up*.

Spruce up : smarten up; make somebody; or oneself; clean and tidy. ***Ex 1.*** You should *spruce* yourself *up* for the interview. ***Ex 2.*** They were all *spruced up* for the party. ***Ex 3.*** Tell the children to get *spruced up* for the guests. ***Ex 4.*** The girls were all *spruced up* for the great occasion. ***Ex 5.*** I decided to go home and *spruce* myself *up*-to let everyone know that life had not got me down.

Spy out : explore and discover something illegal, etc., without being observed, and report it to the authorities. ***Ex 1.*** He was sent to *spy out* enemy positions. ***Ex 2.*** We *spied out* the exact location of the mortar.

Square up : pay somebody the money one owes, (esp. before leaving a restaurant, etc.) ***Ex.*** Can I leave you to *square up* with the waiter?

Squeeze out/out of: get something from somebody by applying pressure of various kinds such as violence, threats, etc. ***Ex 1.*** If you give in to the blackmailer, he will return to *squeeze out* another thousand rupees later. ***Ex 2.*** This government will *squeeze* every rupee it can, *out* of the unfortunate tax-payer. ***Ex 3.*** She *squeezed* a promise *out* of him.

Squeeze through: pass through a narrow passage, etc. by pressing in the sides of one's body. ***Ex 1.*** Turn your shoulders round the other way and you will manage to *squeeze through*. ***Ex 2.*** There was a small slit *through* which one could just *squeeze* by lying flat on one's stomach.

Squeeze up : move closer together; press, or cause somebody to press, tightly and uncomfortably against another person or thing. ***Ex 1.*** I had to sit *squeezed up* against the wall. ***Ex 2.*** *Squeeze up* a bit more and let the others sit down. ***Ex 3.*** There will be enough room if we all *squeeze up* a bit. ***Ex 4.*** Several hundreds were *squeezed up* against each other in one comer of the hall.

Stack up : measure up to something; compare with something. ***Ex.*** How well do you think this washing powder *stacks up* against your usual brand?

Stamp off : remove something by stamping with the foot. ***Ex.*** They *stamped* the mud *off* their shoes.

Stamp on : (a) crush something by bringing one's foot down heavily on it. ***Ex 1.*** He *stamped on* a spider. ***Ex 2.*** In her rage, she threw his papers on the floor and *stamped on* them.

(b) seek to control or suppress by vigorous action; quell something; control or suppress something by force. ***Ex 1.*** The rebellion was soon *stamped on* by the army. ***Ex 2.*** Anyone who steps out of line in this period of minority government can expect to be *stamped on* by the party whips.

Stamp out: (a) eliminate, get rid of, destroy or suppress something, by force or vigorous action. ***Ex 1.*** The police and the medical profession are trying to *stamp out* the increasing wave of drug addiction in young people. ***Ex 2.*** All resistance to the regime had been ruthlessly *stamped out*. ***Ex 3.*** Stern steps should be taken to *stamp out* corruption. ***Ex 4.*** The defenders were *stamped out* in the last attack.

(b) extiguish (a fire, etc.) by stamping. ***Ex.*** They *stamped out* the ambers of the camp fire.

Stand about/around: stand idly in a particular area; be still; doing nothing. ***Ex 1.*** The guests were *standing about* after dinner smoking and talking quietly. ***Ex 2.*** Don't just *stand around* doing nothing: give me a hand with the luggage. ***Ex 3.*** The unemployed men were just *standing about* with their hands in their pockets. ***Ex 4.*** I told her not to stand about doing nothing.

Stand apart : place oneself (through shyness, pride, etc.) at a distance from somebody. ***Ex 1.*** Tell her to *stand apart* from those young men. ***Ex 2.*** The general *stood apart* from his men, partly because he was naturally reserved, and partly because he found it profoundly distasteful to court popularity.

Stand as/for: be a candidate as representing a particular party or interest, for something. ***Ex 1.*** Are you prepared to *stand for* the vacant seat on the committee? ***Ex 2.*** He is *standing as* the official nominee *for* the post of general secretary. ***Ex 3.*** At this stage in my career, there are a few offices *for* which I am not prepared to *stand.*

Stand aside: (a) move to one side; move out of the way. ***Ex 1.*** *Stand aside* and let us pass. ***Ex 2.*** I *stood aside* to let her pass. ***Ex 3.*** People on the pavement were asked to *stand aside* and let the procession through.

(b) do nothing; take no part in events; remain at a distance from events. ***Ex 1.*** Don't *stand aside*, and let other do all the work. ***Ex 2.*** *Stand aside* and let others decide the important issues. ***Ex 3.*** I *stand aside* and let the current of events sweep past me. ***Ex 4.*** He *stood aside* meekly when the new policy was proposed. ***Ex 5.*** He just *stood aside* and allowed it to.happen,

(c) withdraw (as a candidate in an election). ***Ex.*** I *stood aside* in favour of another candidate.

Stand back: (a) move back; stand to the rear. ***Ex.*** The policeman asked us to *stand back.*

(b) be situated away from something. ***Ex 1.*** The house *stands back* a little from the road. ***Ex 2.*** The school *stands* well *back* from a busy thoroughfare. ***Ex 3.*** The big house *stands back* about half a mile from the main gates.

(c) distance oneself, mentally, from something in order to understand or judge it better. ***Ex.*** Sometimes an administrator must *stand back* from day-to-day business to grasp the wider pattern of events.

(d) withdraw or retreat from making decisions, influencing events, etc. ***Ex 1.*** These were vital discussions from which he could not afford to *stand back.* ***Ex 2.*** In my own case, two matters cannot have been right; both due to the fact that my mother ran the family and my father *stood back.*

Stand between: exist as an obstacle between somebody and something he wishes to achieve. ***Ex.*** Only two men *stood between* him and a coveted place on the board of directors.

Stand by : (a) observe events which require an active response without doing anything; be present but not do anything. ***Ex 1.*** A man may not *stand by* and watch another destroy himself. ***Ex 2.*** We cannot *stand* idly *by* while children go hungry. ***Ex 3.*** He *stood by* and watched. ***Ex 4.*** How can you *stand by* and let him treat his stepmother like that?

(b) be ready for action; be on the alert. ***Ex 1.*** The troops are *standing by.* ***Ex 2.*** The government ordered the military to *stand* *by*. ***Ex 3.*** Publishers of books *stand by*, ready to turn out a huge new edition. ***Ex 4.*** I told them to *stand by* for action.

(c) support or help somebody. ***Ex 1.*** He is the sort of friend who will *stand by* you through thick and thin. ***Ex 2.*** Our supporters continued to *stand by* us when the going was hardest. ***Ex 3.*** I shall *stand by* her whatever happens.

(d) true or faithful to: ***Ex 1.*** Imust *stand by* what I have said. ***Ex 2.*** She still *stands by* every word of what she said.

Stand down: (a) leave the witness box, after giving evidence. ***Ex 1.*** Unless you have further questions for him, I think this witness may *stand down*. ***Ex 2.*** He asked the witness to *stand down*.

(b) withdraw (as a candidate in an election); resign from one's position in favour of somebody. ***Ex 1.*** The President has *stood down* after five years in offie. ***Ex 2.*** The secretary is proposing to *stand down* in favour of a younger man. ***Ex 3.*** If she wants the job, I shall *stand down*.

(c) relax, or order somebody to relax, after an alert. ***Ex 1.*** The troops were *stood down*, it was a false alarm. ***Ex 2.*** The defenders *stood down* after the enemy disappeared. ***Ex 3.*** The soldiers *stood down*. ***Ex 4.*** The Colonel ordered the Soldiers to *stand down*. ***Ex 5.*** The troops were *stood down* only when it was clear that no attack was forthcoming.

(d) (of military) disband; end its life as an active unit. ***Ex.*** Certain regiments have chosen to *stand down* rather than be amalgamated with other units.

Stand for : (a) be an abbreviation of something. ***Ex 1.*** What does MK *stand for* in M.K. Gandhi? ***Ex 2.*** What does your second initial *stand for*?

(b) represent something. ***Ex 1.*** I vehemently condemn fascism and all it *stands for*. ***Ex 2.*** This symbol *stands for* strength and integrity. ***Ex 3.*** I dislike you and all you *stand for*. ***Ex 4.*** What on earth do these signs *stand for*.

(c) be in favour of. ***Ex 1.*** They had been wearing pyjamas until noon. I would not *stand for* it. ***Ex 2.*** If there is one thing I would not *stand for*, it is being treated like an office boy. ***Ex 3.*** Our party *stands for* communal tolerance.

(d) tolerate; PUl up with; bear. ***Ex 1.*** I shall not *stand for* this insolence. ***Ex 2.*** Nobody will *stand for* your intemperate language. ***Ex 3.*** Don't stand for her intemperate remarks. ***Ex 4.*** She *stands for* a lot of abuse from those children.

(e) offer oneself as a candidate. ***Ex 1.*** I am *standing for* Parliament. ***Ex 2.*** He is standing for re-election. ***Ex 3.*** Are you *standing for* Chairman?

Stand in: deputise; take somebody's place; act as a substitute for. ***Ex 1.*** I shall *stand in* for you any time. ***Ex 2.*** They are *standing* in while the others are unable to take part. ***Ex 3.*** My assistant will *stand in* for me while I am out of station. ***Ex 4.*** Another man *stands in* for the big star in the dangerous scenes. ***Ex 5.*** She is *standing in* for me tonight.

Note: The word *stand in* is a noun. It denotes person who acts as a deputy for on in place of somebody else, especially one who takes the part of an actor in dangerous scenes. ***Ex 1.*** In some minor scenes, her part is played by a *stand in*. ***Ex 2.*** She acted as a *stand in* during the period of my absce on leave.

Stand off: (a) dismiss workers (during an economic depression). ***Ex 1.*** If the slum continues, more workers will be *stood off*. ***Ex 2.*** We have already *stood off* forty men.

(b) keep or stay at a distance from the shore, etc. ***Ex 1.*** The ships *stood off* and waited for orders. ***Ex 2.*** The two fleets were *standing off* from each other.

Stand out : (a) be noticeable; be easily seen; be striking; be prominent. ***Ex 1.*** The first thing that *stands out* from the hold-up is that the routine precautions gave the bandits little trouble. ***Ex 2.*** The bold print *stands out* very well. ***Ex 3.*** Due to his height, he *stands out* in a crowd. ***Ex 4.*** Her talents *stand out* in comparison with the others. ***Ex 5.*** The primary colours *stand out* clearly from the others. ***Ex 6.*** Bright lettering *stands out* well against a dark background.

(b) be much better than somebody/something. ***Ex 1.*** Her work *stands out* from the rest as the best. ***Ex 2.*** Even as a schoolboy player, he *stood out* from the rest of the team.

(c) continue to resist. ***Ex 1.*** We managed to *stand out* against all attempts to close the company down. ***Ex 2.*** the workers are *standing out* for higher wages and better conditions. ***Ex 3.*** Let us *stand out* against this oppression.

Stand out for: delay reaching an agreement in order to get what one wants. ***Ex 1.*** They are *standing out for* a revision of the constitution. ***Ex 2.*** Our union leader is *standing out for* the original claim of two thousand rupees a month.

Stand outside : not be something which one wishes to consider, discuss, etc. ***Ex.*** The question of where these people are to be resettled has been allowed to *stand outside* the scope of the development plan.

Stand over: (a) postpone; defer; hold over; wait. ***Ex 1.*** There is no hrgency about this matter, it can *stand over* till next week. ***Ex 2.*** The project is to *stand over* till next year.

(b) supervise or watch somebody closely. ***Ex 1.*** You will have to *stand over* the new man until he learns the routine. ***Ex 2.*** He works better when someone is *standing over* him. ***Ex 3.*** I hate having someone *standing over* me all the time. ***Ex 4.*** Don't *stand over* me while I am cooking. ***Ex 5:*** She hates to have her boss *standing over* her.

Stand to: (order soldiers to) take up position against an attack; be on the alert, with weapons ready against enemy attack. ***Ex 1.*** The soldiers were *standing to* half the night. ***Ex 2.*** Units in the field are normally *stood to* just before dawn and dusk. ***Ex 3.*** The commandant told his men to *stand to.*

Stand up : fail to keep an appointment with somebody; fail to meet as agreed. ***Ex 1.*** First she agreed to come out with me, then she *stood* me *up.* ***Ex 2.*** She often *stands* boyfriends *up.* ***Ex 3.*** Don't *stand* me *up* again.

Stand up for: support somebody/something; speak, work, etc. in favour of somebody/something. ***Ex 1.*** You should always *stand up for* your girlfriends. ***Ex 2.*** You must *stand up for* your rights. ***Ex 3.*** I always *stand up for* my principles. ***Ex 4.*** Will you *stand up for* women's rights?

Stand up to : (a) resist; face; withstand a test, etc. ***Ex 1.*** That boy *stood up to* the big bully. ***Ex 2.*** *Stand up to* them. ***Ex 3.*** Your argument just will not *stand up to* close scrutiny. ***Ex 4.*** His position does not *stand up to* detailed examination.

(b) resist boldly. ***Ex 1.*** It was brave of her to *stand up to* those bullets. ***Ex 2.*** How will you *stand up to* your partner's antagonism? ***Ex 3.*** He thought of her as someone to be proud of, yet someone to be *stood up to* on occasion.

(c) remain in good condition in spite of; last well. ***Ex 1.*** Will this car *stand up to* winter conditions here? ***Ex 2.*** This cloth is designed to *stand up to* a lot of wear and tear.

Stare down : look intently at a curious or ill-mannered person who is doing the same, and continue looking until he is forced to lower his eyes. ***Ex.*** An inquisitive small boy looked at us from one corner of the railway compartment. Our eldest son looked back as intently at him, and did his best to *stare* him *down.*

Stare out: look intently at a curious or ill-mannered person who is doing the same, and continue looking until he is forced to stop; defeat by *staring.* ***Ex 1.*** Stop trying to *stare* me *out.* ***Ex 2.*** One boy *stared* fixedly at the new teacher as if he were some strange object. The teacher, for his part, sat calmly at his desk and *stared him out.* ***Ex 3.*** The two children were having a competition to see who could *stare* the other *out.*

Start in on : begin to criticise, scold or shout at somebody; harangue somebody. ***Ex 1.*** He *started in on* us again for poor work. ***Ex 2.*** The team were hardly settled in the dressing-room before the manager *started in on* them for slovenly; unaggressive play.

Start in to: begin to do something. ***Ex.*** We *started in to* a discussion of the idea.

Start off : begin, or cause somebody to begin, working on, doing, saying, etc. something. ***Ex 1.*** It is impossible to stop him talking once he *starts off.* ***Ex 2.*** What *started* him *off* on this crazy idea?
Ex 3. Don'tstart her off on one of her boring stories. ***Ex 4.*** The story-teller started off by describing a beautiful princess.

Starve into: force somebody to do something by not allowing him to get food. ***Ex 1.*** The dacoits were *starved into* surrender. ***Ex 2.*** They imagine that by blockading our ports, they can *starve* us *into* submission.

Starve of : keep somebody or something short of; deprive of. ***Ex 1.*** The railways are *starved of* first-class technical men. ***Ex 2.*** They had *starved* the workshop *of* vital components. ***Ex 3.*** His children felt *starved of* affection.

Starve out/out of : force somebody to leave a finding-place, etc. by stopping supplies of food. ***Ex 1.*** It took ten days to *starve* them *out of* the building. ***Ex 2.*** Having failed to bomb the occupants out, the enemy resolved to *starve* them *out*. ***Ex 3.*** They decided to *starve* the enemy *out*.

Stave in : break, smash, or make a hole in something. ***Ex 1.*** The side of the boat was *staved in* by the collision. ***Ex 2.*** The victim's skull had been *staved in* by a heavy instrument. ***Ex 3.*** He was admitted to hospital with two of his ribs *staved in*. ***Ex 4.*** Repeated batterings on the rocks had *staved in* one side of the craft.

Stave off : keep something off or away; delay something, especially temporarily. ***Ex 1.*** You should take suitable steps to *stave off* the pangs of hunger. ***Ex 2.*** Now it is too late to *stave off* trouble. ***Ex 3.*** This action will help to *stave off* later disasters of the same kind. ***Ex 4.*** Only the sure prospect of relief *staved off* utter despair. ***Ex 5.*** He stuffed down quantities of rice, trying to *stave off* increasing stabs of hunger.

Stay abreast: remain level with; remain informed about. ***Ex.*** It is difficult to *stay abreast* in one's reading when so much is being published in this country.

Stay away: keep a distance from somebody/something; not interfere with somebody/something. ***Ex 1.*** I have told him to *stay away* from your sister. ***Ex 2.*** Why don't you *stay away* from his sister?

Stay behind : remain at a place after others have left; remain behind. ***Ex 1.*** Many a student *stayed behind* after the lecture to ask questions. ***Ex 2.*** Will somebody *stay behind* to help with the washing-up ? ***Ex 3.*** They *stayed behind* after the party to help clear up. ***Ex 4.*** The teacher told him to *stay behind* after the class.

Stay down: (of food) remain in the stomach. ***Ex 1.*** She is so ill that nothing will *stay down*, not even water. ***Ex 2.*** The food seems to have *stayed down* this time.

Stay for/to: remain at somebody's house for a meal. ***Ex 1.*** Won't you *stay for* supper? ***Ex 2.*** Catch the last train, and you can *stay to* lunch. ***Ex 3.*** They had decided to *stay for* dinner, and Nitish had fussed because there was not enough food.

Stay in : (a) not go outdoors; remain in the house. ***Ex 1.*** The doctor advised me to *stay in* for a few days. ***Ex 2.*** *Stay in* for a few days until your cold is better. ***Ex 3.*** He does not usually *stay in* on Friday evenings. ***Ex 4.*** We *stayed in* all that week, while the rain poured down outside.

(b) remain at school after others have left, especially as a punishment. ***Ex 1.*** If this noise goes on for very much longer, you will all have to *stay in* after school. ***Ex 2.*** The teacher told two students to *stay in* after school.

(c) remain where it is, remain in position. ***Ex.*** Whatever he cut from his manuscript, those references would *stay in*.

Stay off: not eat, drink, smoke, etc. things which, if taken in excess, may be bad for one's health. ***Ex 1.*** You will have to *stay off* sweets and chocolates if you want to reduce weight. ***Ex 2.*** You must *stay off* drinks and drugs.

Stay on : (a) remain in position on top of something. ***Ex 1.*** His hat did not *stay on* properly. ***Ex 2.*** You cannot load any very large parcels onto the roof rack. They will not *stay on* in a strong wind, or if you are driving fast.

(b) remain alight; keep burning, running, etc. ***Ex 1.*** The T.Y. *stays on* all day at this place. ***Ex 2.*** The department's electricity bills are going to be high if half the lights are allowed to *stay on* after people gohome at night.

(c) remain at a place of study, with an employer, etc., after others have left. ***Ex 1.*** He *stayed on* at university to do research. ***Ex 2.*** A medical student becomes a senior figure in college as he *stays on* year after year.

Stay out: (a) remain outside the house, especially after dark. ***Ex 1.*** I don't like you *staying out* so late. ***Ex 2.*** You *stayed out* after midnight last night. What happened to you? ***Ex 3.*** Don't *stay out* half the night. ***Ex 4.*** My wife does not want me to *stay out* after 8 p.m. ***Ex 5.*** He usually *stays out* late on Tuesday nights. ***Ex 6.*** It is unusual for them to *stay out* so long.

(b) remain on strike; continue a stoppage of work. ***Ex 1.*** The miners *stayed out* for a span of a little over six months. ***Ex 2.*** The workers are prepared to *stay out* until their grievances are remedied.

Stay out of : remain at a point where somebody cannot reach one, or something cannot affect one. ***Ex 1.*** He told his son to *stay out of* trouble. ***Ex 2.*** I had been looking for her for years, but always she managed to *stay* just *out of* reach.

Stay up: (a) not go to bed; remain awake. ***Ex 1.*** Will you let us *stay up* till he comes ? **Ex .2.** She liked listening to records and *staying up* half the night. ***Ex 3.*** He *stays up* late most nights, reading business reports. ***Ex 4.*** It is not like you to *stay up* after midnight.

(b) remain in position where it has been mounted, hung, put, built etc. *Ex 1*. Your notice can *stay up* for a week, but then, it will have to come down to make room for others. ***Ex 2.*** Diwali decorations *stay up* just for a few days.

(c) not fall or sink. ***Ex 1.*** I am surprised that some of those cheap houses stay up as long as they do. ***Ex 2.*** My trousers only *stay up* if I wear a belt. ***Ex 3.*** If you do fall out of the boat, your life jacket will help you to *stay up* until we can fish you out.

Stay with: continue to listen attentively to somebody. ***Ex 1.***Please *stay with* me a moment longer-I am getting to the point of the story. ***Ex 2.*** Just *stay with* me a minute longer. I am sure I can convince you that We have a reasoable case. ***Ex 3.*** *Stay with* me just one moment, ladies and gentlemen, while I tell you about our new rub-on rub-off carpet cleaner.

Steel away/in/into/down/out/through : move in the specified direction, secretly and quietly, or without being noticed. ***Ex 1.*** He *stole into* the room. ***Ex 2.*** A tear *stole down* her rosy cheek. ***Ex 3.*** The morning light was *stealing through* the shutters. ***Ex 4.*** He *stole away* from his seat in the back row while the attention of the others was engaged. ***Ex 5.*** How did he *steal away* from the meeting? ***Ex 6.*** Don't *steal away* from your duties.

Steal over: gradually fill or take possession of somebody. ***Ex 1.***A sense of futility *stole over* him. ***Ex 2.*** The community spirit was beginning to *steal over* her.

Steal up on : (a) advance quietly and carefully to a place, thus taking the occupant by surprise. ***Ex.*** A small party *stole up on* the bridge under cover of darkness.

(b) (of a mood etc.) come to one gradually, without one knowing. ***Ex 1.*** I must not let madness *steal up on* me and take me by surprise.

Steam up : be excited, angry, enthusiastic or annoyed. ***Ex 1.*** He is all *steamed up* about losing the contract. ***Ex 2.*** Don't get *steamed up* about , it. ***Ex 3.*** I was very *steamed up* about this project. ***Ex 4.*** What was she getting so *steamed up* about? ***Ex 5.*** My wife came back all *steamed up* about modern decor, and painted the doors crimson.

Steel against/for : harden or toughen oneself in preparation for something. ***Ex 1.*** Citizens will probably *steel* themselves *for* a further levy. ***Ex 2.*** They had *steeled* themselves *against* possible failure in the examination. ***Ex 3.*** She had to *steel* her heart *against* pity.

Steep in : prevade or fill something thoroughly with something; give oneself/somebody a thorough knowledge of something. ***Ex 1.*** She says that you are *steeped in* ignorance. ***Ex 2.*** Delhi is a city *steeped in* history. ***Ex 3.*** Mridula Devi *steeped* herself *in* the literature of ancient India.

Steer away: avoid talking about a subject or topic. ***Ex 1.*** He managed to *steer* the discussion *away* from the subject of money. ***Ex 2.*** He likes to *steer away* from serious topics. ***Ex 3.*** She was *steering* all the conversation *away* from any talk of her divorce.

Stem from: arise from something; have something; as its origin or cause. ***Ex 1.*** It is a simple and pure veracity that discontent *stems from* low pay and poor working conditions. ***Ex 2.*** The present wave of strikes *stems from* discontent among the lower-paid workers.

Step aside: allow another person to take one's place, position, job, etc. ***Ex 1.*** She *stepped aside* to let me pass. ***Ex 2.*** It is time for me to *step* *aside* and let a younger person become chairman. ***Ex 3.*** They expect him to *step aside* and make way for a younger man. ***Ex 4.*** I am not ready to *step aside* yet.

Step back: move into an insignificant position. ***Ex.*** He does not want to *step back* from the centre of things.

Step down: resign (from a position of importance). ***Ex 1.*** He offered to *step down* if that would promote negotiations. ***Ex 2.*** The managing director of our company *stepped down* last month because of protracted illness.

Step forward : come forward; present oneself (to offer help or information). ***Ex 1.*** The organising committee has appealed for volunteers to *step forward*. ***Ex 2.*** I *stepped forward* and offered to pay the entire cost. ***Ex 3.*** When the appeal went out for volunteers to help with rescue work, many people *stepped forward*.

Step in: intervene (to help or hinder somebody/something). ***Ex 1.*** If the police had not *stepped in* when they did, there would have been serious violence. ***Ex 2.*** She really appreciates the way I *stepped in* and saw to things. ***Ex 3.*** It is known to one and all that the government has often had to *step in* to protect employees from employers. ***Ex 4.*** Seeing that I was lost for an answer, Sudesh *stepped in* to save the situation. ***Ex 5.*** The union leadership *stepped in* and made the strike official. ***Ex 6*** ? The government *stepped in* and settled the dispute. ***Ex 7.*** The policeare reluctant to *step in*.

Step off: (a) leave, get off or out of"a vehicle, etc. ***Ex 1.***As I *stepped off* the plane, I was surrounded by photographers. ***Ex 2.*** He *stepped off* the pavement, and was nearly knocked down by a taxi.

(b) (military) begin to march. ***Ex.*** When you *step off*, take a full pace of thirty inches.

Step out: walk faster; move more quickly. ***Ex.*** Tell the people at the front to *step out*-we will never be back in time for supper.

Step over: raise one's feet to cross an obstacle. ***Ex.*** We had to *step over* rows of outstretched legs to reach our seats in the stalls.

Step up : (a) increase; improve or enhance. ***Ex 1.*** Resources allotted to these operations should be *stepped up*. ***Ex 2.*** Their social position had been much *stepped up*. ***Ex 3.*** The factory has stepped up production. ***Ex 4.*** The tempo has been *stepped up*. ***Ex 5.*** We should *step up* the campaign for nuclear disarmament.

(b) be promoted. ***Ex.*** He has *stepped up* into the management of the firm.

Stick about/around: remain in a place waiting for something to happen, somebody to arrive, etc. ***Ex 1.*** *Stick around* for a while-the boss will soon be back. ***Ex 2.*** I did not want to *stick about* waiting for the bomb to explode. ***Ex 3.*** *Stick around*, we may need you.

Stick at: persevere; work steadily and persistently at something. ***Ex 1.*** If we *stick at* it, we should finish the job today. ***Ex 2.*** He will *stick at* it till he succeeds. ***Ex 3.*** I *stick at* my painting five or six hours a day, but nothing comes of it. ***Ex 4.*** You can get the report written inside a week, but you will need to *stick at* it. ***Ex 5.*** She never *stuck at* one job for more than a month.

Stick by : continue to support and be loyal to somebody. ***Ex 1.*** Her husband *stuck by* her in good times and bad. ***Ex 2.*** The older staff would *stick by* the firm through thick and thin. ***Ex 3.*** I shall *stick by* her whatever happens. ***Ex 4.*** She *stuck by* me to the end.

Stick down: (a) put or place something down. ***Ex 1.*** *Stick* it *down* anywhere you like. ***Ex 2.*** You can *stick* the table *down* in a corner for the time being. ***Ex 3.*** Where does the mail go? Oh *stick* it *down* over here. ***Ex 4.*** I just *stuck* this thing *down* here as I left. ***Ex 5.*** Tell me precisely why you *stuck* that doll *down* that hole.

(b) write something down. ***Ex 1.*** Tell them to *stick down* their names on this list. ***Ex 2.*** *Stick down* your name at the top of the form. ***Ex 3.*** He had *stuck* the formula *down* on the back of an old envelope.

Stick in/into: fasten something into a book, etc. with paste, etc. ***Ex.*** *Stick* these stamps *into* an album.

Stick on : fasten something to a surface with glue, paste, etc. ***Ex 1.*** *Stick* a label *on* your suitcase. ***Ex 2.*** Pictures of football stars were *stuck on* the wall by his bed.

Stick out: (a) jut out; project. ***Ex 1.*** I saw a pair of feet *sticking out* at the end of the blanket. ***E.. 2.*** We parcelled up the material securely, without leaving any ends *sticking out.*

(b) cause to project. ***Ex 1.*** Someone *stuck* a foot *out* and tripped me up. ***Ex 2.*** Don't *stick* your tongue *out* at me. ***Ex 3.*** Don't *stick* your head *out* of the car window.

Stick it/something out : continue with something to the end, despite difficulty or unpleasantness; endure something unpleasant. ***Ex 1.*** He hates the job-but he is determined to *stick it out* because he needs the money. ***Ex 2.*** He hated life in the city, but he would *stick it out* a bit longer for the sake of his family.

Stick out for: refuse to give up until one gets something one wants; hold out for; stand out for. ***Ex 1.*** The workers are in a fighting mood; they are *sticking out for* the full amount of their wage claim. ***Ex 2.*** We are going to *stick out for* fuller representation on the Council. ***Ex 3.*** They are *sticking out for* higher wages.

Stick to: (a) not move, stray or wander from. ***Ex 1.*** I find her lectures very confusing, she never *sticks to* the point. *Ex 2.* This is getting US nowhere. Let us *stick to* the facts.

(b) not abandon or change; hold to. ***Ex 1.*** Once we have sorted out a programme of events, we must try to *stick to* it. ***Ex 2.*** Flying is simple if you stick to the rules. ***Ex 3.*** I don't want to hear your opinions; *stick to* the facts. ***Ex 4.*** That is my story and I am *sticking to* it. ***Ex 5.*** You should *stick to* the point in the debate.

(c) continue doing something. ***Ex.*** *Stick to* the task until it is finished.

Stick together: be united; remain friendly and loyal to one another. ***Ex 1.*** If we keep calm and *stick together*, we shall be all right. ***Ex 2.*** New arrivals in a community are sometimes accused of *sticking together*.

Stick up : threaten people with a gun in order to rob them. ***Ex.*** Masked bandits *stuck up* a bank yesterday.

Note : The word *stick up* is a noun. It means robbery with a gun; hold-up. ***Ex.*** Don't move-this is a *stick-up*.

Stick up for: support or defend somebody/oneself/something; support a particular cause. ***Ex 1.*** If you don't occasionally *stick up for* yourself, nobody will *stick up for* you. ***Ex 2.*** He is always *stuck up for* the lower-paid workers in industry and that has won him a lot of grass-roots support. ***Ex 3.*** Don't allow those big boys to bully you; *stick up for* yourself. ***Ex 4.*** You should always *stick up for* your rights. ***Ex 5.*** Don't *stick up for* him. ***Ex 6.*** He always *sticks up for* her.

Stick with: stay close to somebody/something; continue to support or retain one's connection with somebody/something. ***Ex 1.*** I am *sticking with* my original idea. ***Ex 2.*** *Stick with* me and you will be all right. ***Ex 3.*** *Stick with* the Party you know you can trust.

Sting for: (a) swindle somebody; charge somebody too much money for something. ***Ex 1.*** He was *stung for* a sum of a little over six thousand rupees. ***Ex 2.*** How much did they *sting* you *for*?

(b) collect money from somebody which he is unwilling to give. ***Ex 1.*** On Diwali Day, the postman comes round and *stings* the public *for* ten rupees or so. ***Ex 2.*** At the airport he was *stung for* a few rupees for having excess luggage.

Stint of : give somebody a small supply of; keep somebody short of; restrict, limit somebody/oneself to a small amount of. ***Ex 1.*** She *stinted* herself *of* food in order to let the children have enough. ***Ex 2.*** Don't *stint* yourself *of* anything. ***Ex 3.*** They were *stinted of* all the things that made life easy and pleasant. ***Ex 4.*** He envied people who enjoyed the comforts of which he had to *stint* himself *for* so long.

Stir up : (a) rouse somebody to action. ***Ex 1.*** He needs stirring up. ***Ex 2.*** The men are being *stirred up* by outsiders. ***Ex 3.*** She loves to *stir* people *up*.

(b) cause trouble, discontent unrest, etc.; excite somebody; provoke somebody. ***Ex 1.*** The union leaders are *stirring up* discontent among the workers. ***Ex 2.*** Someone is *stirring up* trouble in the old part of the city. ***Ex 3.*** He hopes to *stir up* bloody revolution. ***Ex 4.*** He blamed for *stirring up* hatred between nations. ***Ex 5.*** Don't go round to that house *stirring up* between husband and wife.

Stoke up : (a) eat a lot; fill oneself with food. ***Ex 1.*** You should *stoke up* now-you may not get another meal today. ***Ex 2.*** He would *stoke up* with food for forty hours. ***Ex 3.*** She was *stoking up* as though this meal was going to be her last. ***Ex 4.*** Let us *stoke up* while there is time.

(b) stoke a fire; put fuel on a fire of an enclosed type (such as stove, furnace). ***Ex 1.*** He *stokes up* thrice a day. ***Ex 2.*** The furnaces have been *stoked up*. ***Ex 3.*** They *stoked up* the fires. ***Ex 4.*** It is his job to see that the boilers *stoked up* last thing at night.

Stoop to : lower one's moral standards to do something. ***Ex 1.*** He would *stoop to* anything to further his career. ***Ex 2.*** There is no folly to which he would not *stoop to* obtain what he wants. ***Ex 3.*** I would never *stoop to* cheating. ***Ex 4.*** He *stooped to* win her love.

Stop at : stay at; take board and lodging for a short time at. ***Ex 1.*** We *stopped* for a fortnight *at* a hotel in Hyderabad. ***Ex 2.*** They *stopped at* a camps ide for a week.

Stop away: not be present; be absent; stay away. ***Ex.*** Let me know what made you *stay away* from that particular task. It was one of the best he has given.

Stop behind : remain after a meeting, etc. has ended, to ask questions, etc.; remain behind; stay behind. ***Ex 1.*** The audience has invited to *stop behind* to discuss the play with its author. ***Ex 2.*** Will a few of you *stop behind* to help clear the chairs away.

Stop by : make a short visit to somebody's house, etc.; call in; call at somebody's house. ***Ex 1.*** Ask him to *stop by* and talk things over. ***Ex 2.*** Go and ask her to *stop by* for a chat.

Stop for: remain at somebody's house to have a meal; stay for. ***Ex 1.*** I would like you to *stop for* supper. ***Ex 2.*** She says she will *stop for* dinner.

Stop in : remain at school after others have left, as a punishment. ***Ex.*** If I have any more of this nonsense, the entire class will *stop in* after four o'clock.

Stop in/indoors: stay in indoors; remain inside a building. ***Ex 1.*** I shall stop in and look after the children. ***Ex 2.*** Babita usually *stops in* on Tuesday evenings. ***Ex 3.*** Don't *stop in* just for me. ***Ex 4.*** As it poured with rain all day, we had to *stop indoors*. ***Ex 5.*** I *stopped in* all weekend trying to shake off that damned cold.

Stop off : make a short break in a journey to do something. ***Ex 1.*** He *stopped off* at a restaurant to have a cup of tea on the way home. ***Ex 2.*** I shall *stop off* for a couple of days in Madras to visit our cousins. ***Ex 3.*** He *stopped off* on his journey to Calcutta to have a meal.

Stop on : remain at a place of study, etc. after others have left; stay on at. ***Ex 1.*** Kanta Devi *stopped on* for an extra year in the college to take a university scholarship. ***Ex 2.*** Some of the senior boys won't *stop on* at school for a month later than they have to.

Stop out: (a) remain out of doors. ***Ex 1.*** If you are going to *stop out* half the night, there is really not much point in your living at home. ***Ex 2.*** When she is angry with her husband, she *stops out* for hours. ***Ex 3.*** Don't *stop out* just because he is coming.

(b) remain on strike; continue a stoppage of work. ***Ex.*** The workers decided to stop out until their demands were met.

Stop out of : deduct a sum of money (from somebody's income). ***Ex 1.*** Students pay the college a deposit, and the cost of breakages is *stopped out of* that. ***Ex 2.*** He is paid four thousand rupees a month, and *out of* that about fifty rupees are *stopped* for tax and life insurance.

Stop over: break journey by air for sightseeing, etc. ***Ex 1.*** I expect she will *stop over* with us for a day or two on her way to Tokyo. ***Ex 2.*** I usually *stop over* with her in Paris. ***Ex 3.*** He *stopped over* in Lucknow for four days enroute for Patna. ***Ex 4.*** These are pictures of the Jumbo-jet passengers when they *stopped over* in Delhi.

Stop up : not go to bed until later than usual. ***Ex 1.*** I *stopped up* late to watch a film on T.Y.***Ex 2.*** We *stopped up* late to hear the midnight news. ***Ex 3.*** I shall be in late, but don't bother to *stop up* for me. ***Ex 4.*** She *stops up* till her husband gets home. ***Ex 5.*** Don't *stop up* for me, please.

Store up ; allow bad feelings to develop, fester, ere; harbour or nourish bad fee'ings. ***Ex 1.*** Don't *store up* hatred for the poor. ***Ex 2.*** Do you store up resentment towards me.

Storm about/around/off/out : move or walk in a very angry or violent manner in the direction specified. ***Ex 1.*** He was *storming about* the house. ***Ex 2.*** He *stormed out* of the room. ***Ex 3.*** After the argument, Sushma stormed off. ***Ex 4.*** Why are you *storming round* the school.

Storm across/in/through/into : attack violently and force a way across a place; enter a room, house, etc. noisily and aggressively. ***Ex 1.*** Six soldiers *stormed into* the house. ***Ex 2.*** They *stormed* their way *in*. ***Ex 3.*** She *stormed into* the meeting waving a piece of paper about. ***Ex 4.*** Tell them not to *storm into* my study like that. ***Ex 5.*** Just when we thought that we had the matter nicely settled, Anil *stormed in*, claiming that the vote was irregular.

Straighten out: (a) settle or resolve something; put something right; sort out; remove difficulties from something. ***Ex 1.*** We have inherited a very confused situation, which we are notrying to *straighten out*. ***Ex 2.*** The disagreement between them will not be *straightened out* overnight. ***Ex 3.*** Let us try to *straighten out* this confusion.

(b) make somebody understand how matters stand; remove doubt or ignorance in somebody's mind. ***Ex 1.*** She serously misunderstands certain aspects of our plan; I would like to *straighten* her *out* on these. ***Ex 2.*** You are clearly muddled about office procedures but I shall soon *straighten* you *out*. ***Ex 3.*** The police would have charged me with a traffic offence, if my local guide had not *straightened* them *out*. ***Ex 4.*** Can you come and *straighten* things *out* between them? ***Ex 5.*** I shall try to *straighten* the matter *out* once and for all.

Stretch out: (a) make something last or be enough to cover one's needs. ***Ex 1.*** He could not *stretch out* his money to the end of the month. ***Ex 2.*** I don't see how I can *stretch out* the houskeeping to the end of the month. ***Ex 3.*** Will the food *stretch out*? We have got two extra guests for dinner.

(b) relax by lying at full length. ***Ex 1.*** He *stretched out* on the floor, and fell asleep. ***Ex 2.*** A few holiday-makers *stretched* themselves *out* in the sun outside the window.

(c) extend; prolong. ***Ex 1.*** Shilpa Devi *stretched* the story *out*. ***Ex 2.*** I don't want to *stretch* the meeting *out*.

Strike as : appear or occur to somebody as having certain qualities. ***Ex 1.*** Long after the idea, whatever it was, had ceased to *strike* her *as* funny, she went on giving peal after peal, just for practice. ***Ex 2.*** He does not *strike* a stranger *as* a deeply religious man, but rather as a determined cleric preoccupied with social reform.

Strike down : make somebody unable to lead an active life; make somebody seriously ill or kill somebody. ***Ex 1.*** He was *struck down* by cancer at the age of forty. ***Ex 2.*** Many active professional men at the peak of their careers have been *struck down* by heart disease.

Strike into: make somebody afraid, especially by sudden, vigorous action. ***Ex.*** I cannot talk about my driving test. The mere thought *strikes* terror *into* me.

Strike off : remove somebody/somebody's name from something, especially from membership of a professional body. ***Ex 1.*** *Strike* her name *off* the list. ***Ex 2.*** The doctor was *struck off* for incompetence. ***Ex 3.*** Their names were *struck off* the roll of solicitors.

Strike on : get or find something unexpectedly. ***Ex.*** He *struck on* a brilliant new idea.

Strike out for/towards: move in a vigorous, determined way. ***Ex 1.*** Without hesitating, he *struck out* strongly for the beach. ***Ex 2.*** She stood looking up and down before she *struck out* for the bus-stop. ***Ex 3.*** They struck out on foot for the distant hills. ***Ex 4.*** He *struck out* strongly for the shore.

Strike out/through: remove something by drawing a line through it; cross something out. ***Ex 1.*** The editor *struck out* the whole paragraph. ***Ex 2.*** If you disagree with anything I have written, *strike* it *through*. ***Ex 3.*** Their names had been *struck through*, and were almost illegible.

Strike up : (Of band, orchestra; etc.) begin to play (a piece of music). ***Ex 1.*** The band *struck up* a waltz. ***Ex 2.*** Champa Rani *struck up* the first carol on the grand piano.

Strike up with : begin (a friendship, conversation, an acquaintance, etc., casually.) ***Ex 1.*** She is in the habit of *striking up* conversations *with* complete strangers. ***Ex 2.*** I had first *struck up* an acquaintance *with* her while waiting for a train. ***Ex 3.*** He would *strike up* conversations *with* people to hear them speak in the local accent. ***Ex 4.*** I hope you will *strike up* a lasting friendship *with* her.

String along : (a) deliberately mislead somebody, about one's own intentions, beliefs, etc.: deceive somebody into doing something which he might not otherwise do. ***Ex 1.*** Don't *string along* your boyfriends. ***Ex 2.*** I have a feeling that the young man is just *stringing* us *along*. Check his credentials. ***Ex 3.*** The ministers felt that they were being *strung along* by their advisors. ***Ex 4.*** She has no intention of marrying him-she is just *stringing* him *along*. ***Ex 5.*** They are *stringing* him *along* by offering him these occasional favours.

(b) tag along; stay with or accompany somebody casually or as long as it is convenient. ***Ex 1.*** Take my advice-*string along* with me. I know this business inside out. ***Ex 2.*** Can't you stop them *stringing along*-they are such deadful bores. ***Ex 3.*** She decided to *string along* with the others as he had nothing else to do.

String together : combine words, phrases, etc. to form meaningful statements. ***Ex 1.*** His sentences were so badly *strung together* that it was difficult to grasp their meaning. ***Ex 2.*** It was as much as he could do to *string together* a few words of French. ***Ex 3.*** I can just manage to *string* a few words of Sanskrit *together*. ***Ex 4.*** He had not prepared a speech but he managed to *string together* a few remarks at the end of the meeting.

String up: kill somebody by hanging, not legally. ***Ex l.*** If the crowd catch him, they will *string* him *up* on the nearest tree. ***Ex 2.*** Four of the rebel leaders were *strung up* as a warning to the others.

Strip away/off: remove something which is hiding the true nature of or intentions of somebody. ***Ex.*** You have to *strip away* the affected manners and speech to get at the real man underneath.

Strip down: remove all detachable parts of an engine in order to clean or repair it. ***Ex 1.*** The mechanic *stripped* the engine *down*. ***Ex 2.*** I shall have to *strip down* the mechanism to trace the fault. ***Ex 3.*** This motor needs to be *stripped down*.

Strip of: take something of value away from somebody. ***Ex 1.*** He was *stripped of* all his possessions. ***Ex 2.*** The General was *stripped of* his rank. ***Ex 3.*** Having been *stripped of* all his titles, he disappeared from pubic life.

Struggle along/on: manage to survive in spite of great difficulties. ***Ex 1.*** They *struggled along* for some years without much money. ***Ex 2.*** We are *struggling along* on a tiny income.

Strung up: made tense or nervous. ***Ex 1.*** He was *strung up* by having to attend so many official parties. ***Ex 2.*** On the evening of his big speech, he did not seem at all *strung up*.

Stub out: extinguish, put out, a cigarette by striking it against something hard. ***Ex 1.*** He *stubbed out* his cigarette in the ash-tray. ***Ex 2.*** Don't *stub* your cigarettes *out* on my mantlepiece. ***Ex 3.*** The place was littered with empty glasses and *stubbed-out* cigarettes.

Stump up : pay a sum of money required; pay up. ***Ex 1.*** I am tired of *stumping up* for school fees, books and uniform. ***Ex 2.*** I am always being asked to *stump up* extra cash for school outings. ***Ex 3.*** You get into trouble and I have to *stump up* the money for a fine to get you out of it. ***Ex 4.*** She expects me to *stump up* whenever she needs money.

Subject to : (a) bring (a country, etc. or a person) under one's control. ***Ex 1.*** Ancient Rome *subjected* most of Europe *to* its rule. ***Ex 2.***

Armed resistance showed that a minority at least was not prepared to be *subjected to* foreign rule.

(b) make somebody experience or undergo something. ***Ex 1.*** They *subjected* the beggar *to* ridicule. ***Ex 2.*** He was repeatedly *subjected to* torture. ***Ex 3.*** As a test, the metal was *subjected to* great heat. ***Ex 4.*** He vas *subjected to* severe criticism. ***Ex 5.*** The visiting speaker was *subjected to* very close questioning. ***Ex 6.*** It is remarkable how this one man in his small boat survived the hardships and privations *to* which he was *subjected.*

Submit to : yield to somebody/something; give way in the face of pressure. ***Ex 1.*** You should *submit to* office discipline. ***Ex 2.*** They *submitted to* the enemy. ***Ex 3.*** To such threats as .these I have no intention of *submitting.* ***Ex 4.*** They had to *submit to* superior force.

Subscribe to : agree with (an opinion, theory, etc.); support something. ***Ex 1.*** I don't *subscribe to* your views on this subject. ***Ex 2.*** Nobody will *subscribe to* such an inhuman code. ***Ex 3.*** He is a pessimistic view of man *to* which I have never *subscribed.* ***Ex 4.*** Do you *subscribe to* her optimistic view of the state of the economy of the country ?

Succumb to : die from physical strain, or overexposure to natural elements, etc. ***Ex 1.*** The climbers would have to face extremes of climate, *to* which many had *succumbed* before. ***Ex 2.*** Several children have measles, and the others are bound to *succumb to* it. ***Ex 3.*** The driver has succumbed to (i.e., died of) his injuries.

Suck in : ingratiate oneself. ***Ex.*** He is busy *sucking in* with his new boss.

Suck in/into : involve somebody in (a scandal an argument, etc.), unwillingly. ***Ex.*** I don't want to get *sucked into* the row about school uniform.

Suck up: try to please somebody by flattering, helping him, etc. ***Ex 1.*** She *sucks up* to him by agreeing with everything he says. ***Ex 2.*** I cannot stand the way he always *sucks up* to the teacher. ***Ex 3.*** Don't try to impress the new General Manager-he hates being *sucked up* to. ***Ex 4.*** He shamelessly *sucks up* to important people.

Suit to : make something suitable or appropriate for something! somebody; adapt something to something/somebody. ***Ex 1.*** Take care to *suit* the punishment *to* the offence. ***Ex 2.*** Tell them to *suit* the play *to* the audience. ***Ex 3.*** Do you really think that this work is *suited to* a class of beginners?

Sum up: (a) give a brief summary of. ***Ex 1.*** Now *sum up* your views in a few words. ***Ex 2.*** He *summed up* to everyone's satisfaction. ***Ex 3.*** I find it hard to *sum up* after such a wide-ranging debate. ***Ex 4.*** Can you *sum* it all *up* for us ? ***Ex 5.*** I *summed up* the way the members felt in a few words.

(b) (legal) review, and comment upon, the main points of a law case. ***Ex 1.*** In a packed and silent court-room, the judge began to *sum up.* ***Ex 2.*** The magistrate *summed* the matter *up* succinctly.

(c) form an opinion of somebody/something; assess somebody/something. ***Ex 1.*** She is good at *summing* people *up*. ***Ex 2.*** I cannot *sum* him *up* at all. ***Ex 3.*** I *summed* her *up* as a very competent manager. ***Ex 4.*** He *summed up* the situation at a glance.

(d) bring to a conclusion. ***Ex.*** He *summed up* the reminder with a few remarks of his own.

Summon up : evoke; prompt; gather strength; etc. by muster; cause something to come to the mind. ***Ex 1.*** She *summoned up* enough courage to tell them to go away. ***Ex 2.*** He could not *summon up* the strength to move. ***Ex 3.*** I cannot *summon up* much enthusiasm for this project. ***Ex 4.*** I had to *summon up* all my nerve to face my boss. ***Ex 5.*** This is a smell which *summons up* memories of my childhood. ***Ex 6.*** We find it hard to *summon up* thoughts of Panipat at the sight of the lake today.

Surrender to : (a) allow (a habit, an emotion, an influence, etc.) to control what one does. ***Ex.*** He *surrendered to* despair and eventually committed suicide.

(b) weaken, give way, in the face of some pressure. ***Ex 1.*** In an emergency, keep cool. Don't *surrender to* panic. ***Ex 2.*** Blackmail was one kind of pressure to which they were not prepared *to surrender*.

Sus out: investigate something carefully. ***Ex.*** I sent Champa Devi along to *sus out* the possibility of doing a deal with them.

Swan around/off: go around in a leisurely but irresponsible manner; wander off. ***Ex 1.*** He has just *swanned off* somewhere. ***Ex 2.*** Are you *swanning around* on holiday again? ***Ex 3.*** She was *swanning around* the city in her new sports car when she should have been at work.

Swarm with (of a place) : be unpleasantly crowded with or full of (people or things). ***Ex 1.*** The beach was *swarming with* bathers. ***Ex 2.*** The stables *swarmed with* flies.

Swear by: (a) name somebody/something as a guarantee of what one is promising. ***Ex 1.*** I *swear by* Almighty God, the Greatest, that I will tell the truth. ***Ex 2.*** He *swore by* all that is holy that he had been elsewhere at the time of accident.

(b) believe greatly in the usefulness or value of something; think highly of something. ***Ex 1.*** I always *swear by* their products. ***Ex 2.*** He *swears by* that shop. ***Ex 3.*** Many of my friends are using word processors but I still *swear by* my old typewriter.

(c) have great confidence in something as a remedy, etc. ***Ex.*** Take these tablets if you feel run down : I *swear by* them.

Swear in : introduce somebody officially or ceremonially to a new position, responsibility, etc. by getting him to swear an oath. ***Ex 1.*** The President was *sworn in* this morning. ***Ex 2.*** The Prime Minister has to be *sworn in* publicly. ***Ex 3.*** Let the witness be *sworn in*. ***Ex 4.*** The full committee has to attend when a new member is *sworn in*.

Swear off : declare that one will stop using something; promise to abandon, stop doing, something. ***Ex 1.*** He has decided to *swear off* smoking. ***Ex 2.*** I advise you to *swear off* drinks and drugs. ***Ex 3.*** I won't have a cigarette, thanks. I have *sworn off* them on doctor's advice.

Swear to : say definitely that something is true. ***Ex.*** I think I have met her before, but Iwouldn't *swear to* it.

Swear aside: dismiss comments, etc.; brush aside. ***Ex 1.*** He was so full of his own schemes, that he *swept aside* reasonable doubts. ***Ex 2.*** Interruptions were *swept aside* with a wave of the hand.

Sweep away: remove, abolish, by vigorous action. ***Ex 1.*** The government has *swept away* much of the old system. ***Ex 2.*** Successive governments have promised to *sweep away* the last vestiges of privilege in education. ***Ex 3.*** Newspaper editorials spoke of the need to *sweep away* corrupt practices in government offices.

Sweep in /into: (a) enter in a proud, lordly way. ***Ex.*** The procession *swept into* the hall, preceded by trumpeters.

(b) return, be returned, to office, easily, by a clear majority. ***Ex.*** The National Party *swept in* on a tide of discontent over rising prices, in the last election.

Sweep out/out of: leave a place in a proud, lordly way. ***Ex.*** Without a word, Kalpana turned and *swept out* of the room.

Switch around/round: alter the positions of people or things relative to each other. ***Ex 1.*** It is part of company policy to *switch* its young trainees *round* within departments and between departments. The idea is to give them early experience of all sides of the business. ***Ex 2.*** His father is always redecorating the rooms and *switching* the furniture *around*.

Switch off: make or become dull, bored, etc. ***Ex 1.*** I *switch off* when he starts talking about cars. ***Ex 2.*** Long lectures really *switch* me *off*. ***Ex 3.*** Parties *switch* him *off*.

Switch on : make somebody lively or excited. ***Ex 1.*** Her conversation does not *switch* me *on*-it leaves me cold. ***Ex 2.*** There are always plenty of *switched on* people at her parties.

Swoop away/up : seize or snatch the whole of something in one movement. ***Ex.*** The robber *swooped up* the banknotes.

Swot for: study hard (for a particular purpose). ***Ex.*** He is *swatting* every evening *for* his Bar examinations.

Swot up : by hard study, learn or revise something; mug up. ***Ex 1.*** I am *swatting up* my history. ***Ex 2.*** He is *swatting up* for his examinations. ***Ex 3.*** I shall have to start *swatting up* soon. ***Ex 4.*** I must *swot up* my Sanskrit. ***Ex 5.*** You will need to *swot up* your irregular verbs during the holiday. ***Ex 6.*** He seems to spend most of his time *swatting up*.

20 Words Beginning With–T

Tack onto: add something as an extra item. ***Ex.*** A cover charge was *tacked onto* the bill.

Tack on/onto: become, make somebody, a member or part of something larger; add something to the end of a document, etc. ***Ex 1.*** Sanjay *tacked* himself *onto* the end of a long queue at the bus-stop. ***Ex 2.*** The Bill was not allowed to go forward without further modification. Another clause was *tacked on* at the last minute.

Tackle about/on/over: speak to somebody frankly and boldly. ***Ex.*** He is always playing his radio at full blast: it is the proper time to *tackle* him *about* it.

Tag along: follow closely. ***Ex 1.*** Children are *tagging along* behind their mother. ***Ex 2.*** She always *tags along* with them. ***Ex 3.*** If you are going to the cinea, do you mind if I *tag along* with you ? ***Ex 4.*** I used to *tag along* on some of their evening outings. ***Ex 5.*** Wherever the four Party leaders went in their election campaigning, a gaggle of press and T.V. reporters was sure to *tag along* behind.

Tag around with : accompany. ***Ex.*** She *tags around with* him quite a lot.

Tag on : attach something; add something as an extra item. ***Ex.*** A postscript was *tagged on* to her letter at the end.

Tail off : (a) become smaller, weaker, fewer, etc; decrease gradually. ***Ex 1.*** We expect production to *tail off* at this time of the year. ***Ex 2;*** There is some *tailing off* in the demand for new cars at the end of the summer holidays. ***Ex 3.*** His enthusiasm has *tailed off*. ***Ex 4.*** The number of tourists starts to *tail off* in October. ***Ex 5.*** The actor's voice *tailed off* as he forgot his lines.

(b) fade into silence, usually because the speaker is shy or embarrassed. ***Ex 1.*** His feeble excuses soon *tailed off* into silence. ***Ex 2.*** Umesh was clearly overwhelmed by the occasion. After a few sentences, his voice *tailed off* into complete silence.

Tailor to : make or adapt for a special purpose. ***Ex 1.*** These are homes *tailored to* the needs of the elderly persons. ***Ex 2.*** Our Insurance policies are specially *tailored to* the earnings pattern of the insured person at different stages in his career. ***Ex 3.*** Experience has taught us to *tailor* our merchandie *to* the particular requirements of our individual overseas markets.

Take aback: shock or surprise somebody. ***Ex 1.*** She was *taken aback* by your rudeness. ***Ex 2.*** He was somewhat *taken aback* by the news that the police intended to prosecute him. ***Ex 3.*** Her reply *took* me so much *aback* that for a moment I was lost for words. ***Ex 4.*** I was quite *taken aback* by his attitude. ***Ex 6.*** Don't be *taken aback* by anything she says.

Take after: resemble in appearance or character. ***Ex 1.*** The baby really *takes after* his father. ***Ex 2.*** She *takes after* her mother.

Take against: begin to dislike somebody/something. ***Ex 1.*** Why have you suddenly *taken against* me. ***Ex 2.*** I don't know why she has suddenly *taken against* him.

Take apart : (a) (in sport) defeat somebody easily. ***Ex.*** We were simply *taken apart* by the opposition.

(b) criticise somebody/something severely. ***Ex 1.*** His second novel was *taken apart* by the critics. ***Ex 2.*** My first novel had rave notices; my second was *taken apart*.

(c) dismantle something. ***Ex.*** Let us *take* the radio *apart* and see what is wrong with it.

Take around/round: take as a companion, wherever one goes. *Ex 1.* He is beginning to teach his son the business. He *takes* him *around* with him in the car when he calls on customers. ***Ex 2.*** It is as though he cannot let the girl out of his sight. He *takes* her *around* all over the place.

Take away: (a) cause (a sensation, feeling, etc.) to disappear. ***Ex 1.*** The doctor has given him a few tablets to *take away* the pain. ***Ex 2.*** It is a universal veracity that nothing can *take away* the anguish of losing a child. ***Ex 3.*** He says that anxiety has *taken away* his appetite. ***Ex 4.*** What *takes* you *away* so early?

(b) remove somebody/something from somebody/something. ***Ex 1.*** Don't *take* these books *away* from the library. ***Ex 2.*** Tell me who has *taken away* his child.

(c) subtract. ***Ex.*** If you *take* six *away* from eight, that leaves two.

Take away from : *Ex.* The scandal *took away* greatly from his public image.

Take back: (a) agree to accept or receive back. ***Ex 1.*** We only *take* goods *back* if customers can produce the receipt. ***Ex 2.*** Under their guarantee, the dealers are obliged to *take* it *back*. ***Ex 3.*** After all his wife has gone through. I think he will be excessively lucky if she *takes* him *back*.

(b) retract or withdraw something. ***Ex 1.*** I wanted you to ask me to marry you, and you did. Now *take* it *back*, if you want to. ***Ex 2.*** 1 *takes back* what I said about you being very selfish.

(c) cause somebody's thoughts to return to a past time; recall earlier experiences to somebody; remind of earlief times. ***Ex 1.*** The smell of seaweed *took* him *back* to his childhood. ***Ex 2.*** Hearing those old songs makes *takes* me *back* a bit. ***Ex 3.*** Seeing Sunita again *took* me *back* to my first years as a teacher overseas. ***Ex 4.*** These photographs really *take* me *back* to my youth.

Take before : make somebody appear in a court, before somebody in authority, etc. to explain his actions or be punished. ***Ex 1.*** Prefects could deal with minor breaches of school rules; serious offenders were *taken before* the headmaster. ***Ex 2.*** She was hauled up for speeding and *taken before* the court.

Take by: in grasping somebody/something, take hold of a particular limb, or part. ***Ex 1.*** He *took* her gently *by* the wrist, and drew her aside. ***Ex 2.*** Don't take the knife by the blade; *take* it *by* the handle. ***Ex 3.*** I cshluabll. have you *taken by* the scruff of your neck and thrown out of the

Take down: (a) remove something from a higher level. ***Ex 1.*** She helped me *take* the curtains *down*. ***Ex 2.*** I *took down* my copy of the Ramayan and opened it at random.

(b) dismantle something; ***Ex 1.*** The workmen are now *taking down* the scaffolding round the building. ***Ex 2.*** The ornamental gates have been *taken down* and sold as scarp. ***Ex 3.*** They have *taken down* the iron railings on this side of partk.

(c) lower (a garment worn below the waist) without actually removing it. ***Ex 1.*** Why are you *taking down* your skirt? ***Ex 2.*** He was *taking down* his trousers.

(d) write something down in order to make a record of it. ***Ex 1.*** The reporters *took down* the President's speech. ***Ex 2.*** Anything you say may be *taken down* and used as evidence against you. ***Ex 3.*** My secretary *took down* all the points 1 made.

(e) humble somebody; humiliate somebody. ***Ex.*** They want to *take* him *down* a bit.

Take for : suppose, assume or consider somebody/something to be somebody/something. ***Ex 1.*** Do you *take* him *for* a fool? ***Ex 2.*** He speaks Hindi so well, that he is often *taken for* a native. ***Ex 3.*** I am sorry I spoke to you so familiarly: I *took* you *for* a close friend. ***Ex 4.*** Don't *take* him *for* an honest man.

Take from : (a) choose a text for reading or study from a larger work. ***Ex 1.*** I am going to *take* an extract *from* some recordings I have made of bird songs, and play it over to you.

(b) suffer, be the target of, attacks, etc. from. ***Ex.*** I have *taken* more than I can stand *from* those two persons.

(c) lessen, weaken, the effect or value of something; detract from something. ***Ex.*** His appearance in a shabby dressing-gown *took* somewhat *from* the impression of stem authority he wished to convey.

Take in : (a) allow somebody to stay in one's home, sometimes for payment ***Ex 1.*** She *takes in* lodgers. ***Ex 2.*** She was homeless, we *took* her *in*. ***Ex 3.*** Many households in the neighbourhood of the university add to their income by *taking in* students.

(b) deceive, delude, dupe or fool somebody. ***Ex 1.*** She *took in* completely with her story. ***Ex 2.*** Don't be *taken in* by his charming manner; he is completely ruthless. ***Ex 3.*** I am sorry you are all so easy to *take in*. ***Ex 4.*** The guid *took* the tourists *in*, and managed to get extra money out of them. ***Ex 5.*** You cannot *take* me *in* like that.

(c) absorb something into the body by breathing or swallowing it. ***Ex.*** Fish *take in* oxygen through their gills.

(d) make (a garment) narrower or tighter by altering, to fit a thinner person. ***Ex 1.*** The dress is not a bad fit, but it needs *taking in* a little at the waist. ***Ex 2.*** I shall have the waistband *taken in* for you a couple of inches. ***Ex 3.*** Her dress needs to be *taken in* at the waist.

(e) accept work for payment to be done in one's own home. ***Ex 1.*** She sometimes *take in* work to do at home. *Ex 2.* That woman, who is a widow with four children, *takes in* washing to supplement her income.

(f) include or cover something. ***Ex 1.*** The United Kingdom *takes in* England, Wales, Scotland and Northern Ireland. ***Ex 2.*** These points *take in* everything. ***Ex 3.*** Forensic science *takes in* criminology, which covers the causes of crime. ***Ex 4.*** These tours *took in* every part of India. ***Ex 5.*** My tour *took in* six Asian capitals. ***Ex 6.*** Her lecture *took in* all the recent developments in the subject.

(g) go to see or visit (a film, etc.) when one is in a place for a different purpose. ***Ex.*** I generally try to *take in* a show when I am in Paris on business.

(h) note something with the eyes; observe something. ***Ex 1.*** He *took in* every detail of her appearance. ***Ex 2.*** I *took in* the scene at a glance. ***Ex 3.*** The children *took in* the spectacle open-mouthed. ***Ex 4.*** Her eyes *taking in* nothing but the telephone.

(i) understand or absorb something that one hears or reads. ***Ex 1.*** I hope you are *taking in* what I am saying. ***Ex 2.*** Halfway through the chapter, I stopped. I was not *taking in* a single word. ***Ex 3.*** I could not *take in* this new situation or size up what her revelation meant to me. ***Ex 4.*** Did you *take in* what he said?

(j) escort in to dinner. ***Ex.*** He took her in on his arm.

Take off : (a) (of an aeroplane, etc.) leave the ground and begin to fly. ***Ex 1.*** The plane *took off* despite the fog. ***Ex 2.*** The helicopter took off smoothly.

(b) leave the 'ground by plane on a tour. ***Ex.*** The Prime Minister's party *takes off* for Moscow this morning for the next round of talks.

(c) remove or detach. ***Ex 1.*** The intense heat *took* most of the paint *off* the doors. ***Ex 2.*** He *took* the lid *off* the jar.

(d) remove (an item of clothing) from the body. ***Ex 1.*** *Take* your shoes *off* and dry your feet. ***Ex 2.*** He *took off* his coat.

(e) amputate. *Ex.* His leg had to be *taken off* above the knee.

(f) remove a bus, etc. from service. ***Ex 1.*** Several trains have been *taken off* this week. ***Ex 2.*** They had to *take* two of the buses *off* this route because of a shortage of crews. ***Ex 3.*** They have *taken* the local bus *off*. ***Ex 4.*** The 7 am. Express train to Bombay will be *taken off* next month.

(g) leave suddenly or hurriedly. ***Ex 1.*** They *took off* for the station at a run. ***Ex 2.*** I grabbed my hat and *took off* for the Town Hall. ***Ex 3.*** The moment he saw police car turn the corner, Jafar *took off* in the opposite direction.

(h) (commerce) begin to improve markedly; begin to show profit; rise very quickly. ***Ex 1.*** The book 'Word Power' has really *taken off* in recent years. ***Ex 2.*** Sales of home computers have *taken off* in recent years.

(i) leave a place. ***Ex.*** She has *taken* herself *off* to the country for a quiet weekend.

(j) mimic or imitate somebody in a satirical or amusing way. ***Ex 1.*** He likes to *take off* politicians. ***Ex 2.*** She *takes off* the Prime Minister to perfection. ***Ex 3.*** He *takes* that comedian *off* beautifully.

(k) no longer perform (a play, etc.); withdraw something. ***Ex 1.*** The show had to be *taken off* because of poor audiences. ***Ex 2.*** The play was *taken off* after libel charges had been laid against its author.

(l) have as a holiday or break from work. ***Ex 1.*** Everyone *takes* Dussehra *off*. ***Ex 2.*** He *took* the afternoon *off*. ***Ex 3.*** I am *taking* next week *off* work. ***Ex 4.*** You need rest. Why don't you *take* a fortnight *off* from work?

(m) remove somebody from (a job, etc.) ***Ex.*** The officer leading the inquiry has been *taken off* the case.

(n) remove an item from a menu in a restaurant. ***Ex* 1.** The mixed grill has been *taken off* the menu. ***Ex 2.*** We are running low on cabbage, you will have to *take* it *off* from the menu.

(o) deduct an amount of money from something. ***Ex 1.*** They *took* two rupees a gallon *off* the price of petrol. ***Ex 2.*** It is not so much a case of what taxes will be *taken off* in the next Budget as what new taxes will be put on. ***Ex 3.*** There is little prospect of the present levy being *taken off* betting.

(p) cause a product to be no longer on sale. ***Ex.*** Doctors recommended that the drug should be *taken off* the market.

(q) cause to lose weight. ***Ex 1.*** At the National Health Clinic, they guarantee to *take off* at least ten kg. in one course of treatment. ***Ex 2.*** We shall *take* a bit of surplus weight *off* you before you finish basic training.

(r) lead, accompany, away from one place to another. ***Ex 1.*** The guards *took* him *off* to prison. ***Ex 2.*** I *took* myself *off* because they did not want me there.

Take on : (a) become popular or fashionable. ***Ex 1.*** His idea never really *took on*. ***Ex 2.*** This song has really *taken on*.

(b) begin to have (a particular quality, appearance, etc.); assume something. ***Ex 1.*** She has *taken on* some irritating mannerisms. ***Ex 2.*** Her eyes *took on* a hurt expression. ***Ex 3.*** Now ShiJpa's hair has *taken on* a healthy shine. ***Ex 4.*** Our lives have *taken on* a certain regularity. ***Ex 5.*** In this context the words of Mahatma Gandhi *take on* a new significance.

(c) engage somebody; employ somebody; employ as a staff. ***Ex 1.*** We no longer have to *take on* a large number of temporary staff to do the checking. ***Ex 2.*** Are you going to *taken on* new staff? ***Ex 3.*** He was *taken on* as a graduate trainee. ***Ex 4.*** The candidates were to be *taken on* for four months' trial, after which five of the ten would be selected for permanent employment. ***Ex 5.*** They have *taken on* more men.

(d) (of a bus, ship, etc.) allow somebody/sOlflething to enter; take somebody/something on board. ***Ex 1.*** The bus stopped to *take on* more passengers. ***Ex 2.*** The ship *took on* more fuel at Bombay. ***Ex 3.*** The pilot refused to *take* any more passengers *on*.

(e) undertake something; decide to do something. ***Ex 1.*** I am not prepared to *take on* extra work. ***Ex 2.*** Vimla *took on* greater responsibilities when she was promoted. ***Ex 3.*** Don't *take on* more than you can cope with. ***Ex 4.*** I am beginning to regret that I *took* the job *on*; I am working overtime every evening. **Ex 5.** He blamed his own weakness for letting her *take on* to much work.

(f) express strong feelings of sorrow or displeasure. ***Ex.*** It is no good your *taking on*, because the matter is settled, signed and sealed.

Take out: (a) escort or company somebody to the theatre, a restaurant, etc. ***Ex 1.*** Have you *taken* her *out* yet? ***Ex 2.*** He *took* him *out* to dinner on his birthday.

(b) kill somebody or destroy something; put somebody/something out of action. ***Ex.*** Enemy missiles *took out* four of our fighters.

(c) obtain (an official document or service). ***Ex.*** He has *taken out* a life insurance policy for one lakh rupees.

(d) issue (a document that requires somebody to appear in court). ***Ex.*** The police have *taken out* summons against the drivers of both cars involved in the accident.

(e) remove something from something. ***Ex.*** She asked me to *take* my hands *out* of my pockets.

(f) withdraw money from a bank account. ***Ex.*** How much do you need to *take out* of the bank?

(g) deduct (an amount of money) from something. ***Ex.*** Monthly contributions to the pension scheme will be *taken out* of your salary.

(h) cause something to disappear from something. ***Ex.*** Cold water should *take* that stain *out* of your skirt.

Take out on : make somebody else the scapegoat for something one has done or suffered. ***Ex 1.*** I know how you must be feeling, but there is no need to *take* your resentment *out on* me. ***Ex 2.*** Don't *take* your bad temper *out on* me. ***Ex 3.*** She *took* her anger *out on* me.

Take over: (a) gain control of. ***Ex 1.*** Has the party been *taken over* Socialists? ***Ex 2.*** The army is threatening to *take over* if civil unrest continues. ***Ex 3.*** A foreign publisher is bidding to *take over* an important national newspaper. ***Ex 4.*** The firm has been *taken over* by an American conglomerate.

(b) take control of or responsibility for something; in place of somebody else. ***Ex 1.*** Sushma Devi will *take over* as Managing Director when Sushil Kumar retires. ***Ex 2.*** I have decided to *take over* her debts. ***Ex 3.*** When he fell ill, his son *took over* the business from him. ***Ex 4.*** Would you like me to *take over* the driving for a while? ***Ex 5.*** Some fellow has suddenly been taken ill, and I have got to *take over*.

(c) accept duty. ***Ex 1.*** I *took over* from him at six o'clock. ***Ex 2.*** The second shift has now *taken over*.

Take round: conduct somebody on a tour of. ***Ex 1.*** When you arrive inside the gate, an official guide is waiting to *take* you *round*. ***Ex 2.*** The Press Secretary is *taking* an American delegation *round* the University this afternoon.

Take to: (a) develop a liking for somebody/something; develop an ability for something. ***Ex 1.*** As he had reached the age of forty-four without getting married, it was obvious that he was not the sort of man who *takes to* matrimony like a duck to water. ***Ex 2.*** Sunita has really *taken to* that child. ***Ex 3.*** I did not *take to* her husband at all. ***Ex 4.*** I *took to* her the moment I met her. ***Ex 5.*** He has not *taken to* his new school.

(b) begin to do something as a habit. ***Ex 1.*** He has *taken to* smoking a pipe. ***Ex 2.*** He has *taken to* going on solitary walks. *Ex 3.* He has *taken to* drugs and drinks. ***Ex 4.*** She *took to* gardening in her retirement.

Take up: (a) absorb; soak up. ***Ex 1.*** The cloth is saturated; it cannot *take up* any more of the liquid. ***Ex 2.*** Blotting-paper *takes up* ink.

(b) continue; return to. ***Ex 1.*** She *took up* the story from where she had left off. ***Ex 2.*** This chapter *takes up* where the last one left off.

(c) fill or occupy (space or time). ***Ex 1.*** Some very important matter was *taking up* all his attention. ***Ex 2.*** My time is fully *taken up* with writing. ***Ex 3.*** This table *takes up* too much room. ***Ex 4.*** His bed *takes up* half the room. ***Ex 5.*** This work will *take up* a lot of my time.

(d) adopt somebody as a protege; help somebody; patronize somebody. ***Ex.*** A young actor will find it hard to make his way on the Calcutta stage unless he is exceptionally talented or has someone established to *take* him *up*.

(e) adopt something a hobby or pastime. ***Ex 1.*** He has *taken up* stamp collecting. ***Ex 2.*** I have *taken up* golf. ***Ex 3.*** Will you *take up* yoga? ***Ex 4.*** She has *taken up* the piano.

(f) interrupt somebody in order to contradict or criticise him. ***Ex 1.*** Mridula Devi *took* me *up* very sharply when I suggested that the job was only suitable for a man. ***Ex 2.*** I shall *take* you *up* on the point you just made.

(g) lift something up; raise something. ***Ex 1.*** She asked me to *take up* my pen. ***Ex 2.*** The carpets had to be *taken up* when the house was rewired.

(h) make (a garment, etc.) shorter; shorter. ***Ex 1.*** Your skirt will need *taking up*. ***Ex 2.*** She has *taken up* that dress.

(i) lift or displace for repairs. ***Ex 1.*** The pavement has been *taken up* again. ***Ex 2.*** The workmen have *taken up* that road.

(j) raise the question of something; raise or mention a topic in order to consider or discuss it. ***Ex 1.*** I shall *take up* this matter in Parliament next week. ***Ex 2.*** There are three points of detail that should be *taken up* before we move on. ***Ex 3.*** Much in the story has interesting parallels to the present time, but I shall not *take* these *up* at the moment.

(k) adopt or assume (a position, an attitude, etc.) ***Ex.*** Our troops *took up* defensive positions on high ground overlooking the river.

(l) accept something. ***Ex.*** She *took up* my offer of a cold drink.

Take up on : argue with somebody; question or challenge somebody. ***Ex 1.*** I must *take* you *up* on that point. ***Ex 2.*** I would like to *take* you *up* on what you said about unemployment. ***Ex 3.*** The insurance company guarantees to replace any parts of the car which are stolen, you should *take* them *up* on their guarantee.

Take up with : begin to be friendly with or spend a lot of time with somebody (unpleasant or disreputable). ***Ex 1.*** She has *taken up with* an unemployed actor. ***Ex 2.*** She has *taken up with* a man old enough to be her father. ***Ex 3.*** Don't *take up with* bad company.

Be taken up with : have much of one's time and energies occupied by somebody/something. ***Ex.*** He is very much *taken up with* voluntary work at the moment.

Be taken with : find somebody/something attractive or interesting. ***Ex 1.*** They were all very *taken with* her. ***Ex 2.*** I think he is rather *taken with* the idea.

Talk at : speak to somebody without listening to his replies. ***Ex.*** I don't like being *talked at*.

Talk away: (a) talk continuously. ***Ex.*** He *talks away* for hours without stopping.

(b) force to go away by talking. ***Ex 1.*** I am afraid you won't *talk* this problem *away*. ***Ex 2.*** You cannot *talk away* your enormous debts.

Talk back: reply insolently. ***Ex 1.*** Don't *talk back* like that. ***Ex 2.*** It is appalling the way that child *talks back* to his parents.

Talk down: (a) reduce to silence by talking; stop somebody speaking by talking loudly or persistently. ***Ex.*** He is an expert at *talking* the opposition *down*.

(b) bring (a pilot or an aircraft) to a landing by radio instructions from the ground. ***Ex 1.*** There is a particular need to *talk* aircraft *down* when visibility is poor or when several pilots are waiting to land. ***Ex 2.*** They *talked* the pilot *down* to a perfect landing, despite the fog.

(c) address somebody as though he were a social or intellectual inferior. ***Ex.*** Whatever their technical knowledge may be, adult students have a good deal of practical experience, they greatly resent being *talked down* to.

Talk into/out of : persuade somebody to do/not to do something. ***Ex 1.*** She *talked* her friend *into* lending her the car. ***Ex 2.*** I tried to *talk* her *out of* coming. ***Ex 3.*** I know you have got a smooth tongue, so don't even start to *talk* me *into* buying the car. ***Ex 4.*** He had better see the lawyer before anyone could say that he had been *talked into* anything. ***Ex 5.*** It is my own decision entirely. She has just been trying to *talk* me *out of* it. ***Ex 6.*** She is rather impulsive, but she can sometimes be *talked out of* making hasty moves.

Talk out: (a) resolve (a problem, etc.) by discussion. ***Ex.*** Let us *talk out* the problem sometimes soon.

(b) prevent from becoming legislation by spending all the parliamentary time. ***Ex.*** They have succeeded in *talking out* that piece of reform.

Talk over : discuss something fully with somebody. ***Ex 1.*** He *talked* this *over* with his wife. ***Ex 2.*** He and his wife *talked* things *over*. ***Ex 3.*** We must *talk* that matter *over* as early as possible. ***Ex 4.*** It goes without saying that it is best to *talk* these things *over* quietly.

Talk round: (a) persuade somebody to do something to which he was at first opposed; convince somebody. ***Ex 1.*** He is not the easiest man to win over; he will need some *talking round*. ***Ex 2.*** I may be able to *talk* her *round*, but I doubt it. ***Ex 3.*** They finally managed to *talk* him *round*. ***Ex 4.*** We finally managed to *talk* her *round* to our way of thinking.

(b) in conversation, avoid approaching a subject directly; discuss something without coming to the point. ***Ex 1.*** He is expert at *talking round* things without coming to any decision. ***Ex 2.*** They *talked round* the problem for hours. ***Ex 3.*** They wasted nearly a couple of hours *talking round* the real problem.

Talk to: reprimand, scold. ***Ex 1.*** That child needs to be *talked to* and you are the person to do it. ***Ex 2.*** I *talked to* her very sharply. ***Ex 3.*** Do you need to be *talked to* ?

Tart up : dress or decorate somebody/something in a gaudy way; smarten somebody/something up, cheaply or superficially. ***Ex 1.*** She has *tarted* herself *up* for her new boy-friend's benefit. ***Ex 2.*** She *tarted* herself *up* for disco. ***Ex 3.*** Don't *tart* yourself *up* : we are going to an official reception, not a students' dance. ***Ex 4.*** Let us *tart* the design *up* a bit and surprise everybody. ***Ex 5.*** They have *tarted up* the restaurant but the food has not improved.

Tax with : accuse somebody of something; bring somebody face to face with something he is believed to have done, and ask for an explanation. ***Ex 1.*** *Taxed with* the difference between her two statements, the girl broke down and confessed. ***Ex 2.*** I suspected that he had sold me defective goods, but when I *taxed* him *with* this, he strenuously denied it. ***Ex 3.*** He was *taxed with* negligence. ***Ex 4.*** She was *taxed with* having been negligent.

Tear apart: upset; disturb severely. ***Ex.*** The film was so harrowing that it *tore* him *apart*.

Tear away: force to move; leave somebody/something recultantly; leave or stop doing something with great unwillingness. ***Ex 1.*** I could not *tear* her *away* from that novel. ***Ex 2.*** Tell him to *tear* himself *away* from the television and come out for a walk. ***Ex 3.*** I found the programme absolutely fascinating. I could not *tear* myself *away*-even to finish an urgent letter.

Tear away/off: remove some superficial quality. ***Ex 1.*** *Tear off* the rhetorical top-dressing from his speech and you find there is very little solid content. ***Ex 2.*** If you *tore away* that elaborate manner he puts on for everybody, you would not find much underneath.

Tear down : bring something to the ground by pulling sharply; demolish something. ***Ex.*** They are *tearing down* these old houses to build a new office block.

Tear into: attack somebody/something physically or with words. ***Ex 1.*** The young man *tore into* his tormentors. ***Ex 2.*** The treatment meted out to his second play was savage. That he could survive being *torn into* to write another is a tribute to his resilence.

Tear off : write or draw rapidly; dash off. ***Ex 1.*** He *tore off* a letter to his maternal uncle while waiting in the airport lounge. ***Ex 2.*** Don't give me something you have *torn off* in an odd moment, Iwant a carefully considered plan.

Tear up : (a) destroy (a document, etc.) by tearing; ***Ex.*** She *tore up* all the letters Ihad sent her.

(b) vigorously renounce. ***Ex 1.*** The other side clearly does not regard such agreements as binding, they can be *torn up* at will. ***Ex 2.*** He accused the government of *tearing up* the negotiated agree- ment.

(e) reject; ***Ex 1.*** The workers have *torn up* the agreement with the management. ***Ex 2.*** He has decided to *tear* the contract *up*.

(d) break the surface of. ***Ex.*** The tanks have *torn up* the ground.

Tease out : **(a)** obtain by gentle persistence. ***Ex 1.*** I have *teased* the information *out* of her. ***Ex 2.*** Try to *tease out* all the significant factors in the problem.

(b) disentangle. ***Ex.*** She *teased out* the wool gently.

Tell against : be something which hinders or hampers somebody; weigh against. ***Ex 1.*** He is a very brave, aggressive player, but his weight is bound to *tell against* him in a game against a heavy pack of forwards.

Ex 2. Purnima tends to act impulsively, without consulting people higher up. That will *tell against* her in an old-fashioned firm, where they play everything by the book of rules.

Tell apart: be able to distinguish between two similar persons or things. ***Ex 1.*** Every day is identical with the one before. I literally cannot *tell* them *apart*. ***Ex 2.*** Even when magnified, the two organisms are difficult to *tell apart*.

Tell by/from: judge or deduce by observing something. ***Ex.*** You can *tell* just *from* looking at him that he is not a dolt.

Tell from: be able to distinguish one person or thing from another (which may be similar to, or different from, the first). ***Ex 1.*** I was less capable than Dinesh of *telling* truth *from* falsehood. **Ex 2.** Can you *tell* your priest *from* other priests at a meeting?

Tell off: (a) scold or reprimand; dress down. ***Ex 1.*** I *told* them *off* [or making so much noise. ***Ex 2.*** I was ten minutes late and Shanta Rani *told* me *off* in front of everyone. ***Ex 3.*** He did not like being *told off* for something he had not done. ***Ex 4.*** That child needs to be *told off*. ***Ex 5.*** I *told* her *off* severely. ***Ex 6.*** You will get *told off* if you are caught doing that.

(b) assign (a duty or task) to somebody. ***Ex 1.*** Ten men were *told off* to collect fuel. ***Ex 2.*** They were *told off* for guard duty.

Tell on : reveal somebody's activities to a person in authority. ***Ex 1.*** He caught his sister smoking and *told on* her. ***Ex 2.*** I assure you I shall not do it again. Please don't *tell on* me. ***Ex 3.*** Someone has *told on* him and the authorities are beginning to ask questions.

Tell on/upon: have a bad effect on. ***Ex 1.*** This work is *telling on* his health. ***Ex 2.*** Smoking will *tell upon* your health. ***Ex 3.*** She is looking distinctly run down. All these late nights are beginning to *tell on* her.

Temper with : mitigate something; moderate or soften the effects of something. ***Ex 1.*** Judges should *temper* justice *with* mercy. ***Ex 2.*** The academic rigour of her lectures is fortunately *tempered with* wit. ***Ex 3.*** *With* these few concessions to the tax-payer, the government hopes to *temper* the bleakness of its new measures.

Thin down: become slimmer. ***Ex.*** He has *thinned down* a lot since he went on a diet.

Thin out: become or make fewer or more widely scattered over an area. ***Ex 1.*** The crowds began to *thin out*. ***Ex 2.*** The gardener *thinned out* the lettuces. ***Ex 3.*** Periodic major floods had *thinned out* the population.

Think about : (a) recall somebody/something; reflect upon somebody/something. ***Ex 1.*** Do you ever *think about* your childhood? ***Ex 2.*** What are you *thinking about*? ***Ex 3.*** What is the use of *thinking about* the past?

(b) consider somebody/something; take somebody/something into account. ***Ex 1.*** Don't you ever *think about* other people? ***Ex 2.*** All he ever *thinks about* is money. ***Ex 3.*** What is the use of *thinking about* the past?

(c) consider or examine something to see if it is desirable, or practicable, etc. ***Ex 1.*** I shall *think about* it and let you know tomorrow. ***Ex 2.*** She is *thinking about* changing her job. ***Ex 3.*** This is something that needs to be *thought about* very carefully.

Think of: (a) consider something; take something into account. ***Ex 1.*** You cannot expect me to *think of* everything. ***Ex 2.*** There are so many things to *think of* before we decide.

(b) contemplate the possibility of something. ***Ex 1.*** They are *thinking of* moving to America. ***Ex 2.*** I did *think of* resigning, but I decided not to.

(c) imagine something. ***Ex 1.*** He is a wonderful organiser, he *thinks of* everything. ***Ex 2.*** Just *think of* the cost of the car. ***Ex 3.*** Let us now *think of* something nice to do. ***Ex 4.*** He never *thinks of* anyone but himself.

(d) have the idea of something. ***Ex 1.*** I could not *think of* letting you take the blame. ***Ex 2.*** She would never *think of* marrying someone so old.

(e) call something to mind; remember something. ***Ex.*** I cannot *think of* her name at the moment.

(f) suggest something; put something forward. ***Ex 1.*** Can anybody *think of* a way to raise money? ***Ex 2.*** We are still trying to *think of* a suitable title for the book. **Ex 3.** *Think of* a number, double it, and add your age. ***Ex 4.*** I know the prospect is a little bleak at the moment, but don't worry, we will *think of* something.

(g) have a certain opinion of. ***Ex 1.*** I know he does not *think* so highly *of* me. ***Ex 2.*** He is well *thought of* in government circles. ***Ex 3.*** I know, you do not *think* much *of* him, although you have hung around him for ages.

Think out : consider something carefully; plan something carefully, stage by stage. ***Ex 1.*** *Think out* your answer before you start writing. ***Ex 2.*** There is little opportunity to *think out* what the long-term solution may be. ***Ex 3.*** I shall have to *think* this matter *out* to the end.

Think over: reflect upon something; review past events in one's mind; consider carefully something that may affect the future. ***Ex 1.*** Please *think* it *over* and let me know. ***Ex 2.*** I hope you will *think* matters *over* before doing anything hasty. ***Ex 3.*** Let her *think over* what I have said. ***Ex 4.*** I would like more time to *think* things *over*. ***Ex 5.*** With the beginning of a new day, he had to *think* things *over* again, reconsider his position, and see where he was now.

Think up : invent or devise something; produce something by thought. ***Ex 1.*** There is no telling what he will *think up* next. ***Ex 2.*** Can't you *think up* a better excuse than that? ***Ex 3.*** He has *thought up* some astonishingly original schemes. ***Ex 4.*** There were two persons who *thought up* ideas of their own. ***Ex 5.*** He would have to *think up* some catchy names for these designs.

Thirst for: be eager for something; long for; desire ardently. ***Ex 1.*** Don't *thirst for* revenge. ***Ex 2.*** He was surrounded by savages *thirsting for* his blood. ***Ex 3.*** These advertisements are calculated to appeal to young men *thirsting for* adventure. ***Ex 4.*** She is *thirsting for* profound knowledge.

Thrash about/around : (a) make violent or convulsive movements. ***Ex 1.*** Swimmers are *thrashing about* in the water. ***Ex 2.*** Santoshi Devi was *thrashing about* in bed with a high temperature. ***Ex 3.*** We left the children *thrashing around* happily in the shallow end of the pool.

(b) act in a nervous, restless way. ***Ex 1.*** The drying fish *thrashed about* on the beach. ***Ex 2.*** Poonam was getting all worked up over her chemistry homework *thrashing about* for the answer to a quite simple problem.

Thrash out: (a) discuss something thoroughly and frankly. ***Ex 1.*** The two sides came together to *thrash* the matter *out* once and for all. ***Ex 2.*** Let us call a meeting to *thrash out* the problem.

(b) produce something (an answer, a solution, etc.) by frank and thorough discussion. ***Ex 1.*** After much argument we *thrashed out* a plan. ***Ex 2.*** Do your best to *thrash out* your conclusions.

Thread in : move with difficulty through something. ***Ex.*** The crowd was thick, and he had to *thread* his way *in* carefully.

Thread through : pass carefully through a crowd. ***Ex 1.*** The crowd was thick, and he had to *thread* his way *through* carefully. ***Ex 2.*** She *threaded* her way *through* the crowd with the dog at her heels.

Throw about/around: scatter something. ***Ex.*** Don't *throw* litter *about* like that. .

Throw around/round : surround or encircle something to control . movement in and out. ***Ex 1.*** The State government has *thrown* a cordon *around* the stricken area to contain the spread of the epidemic. ***Ex 2.*** A tight security ring was *thrown round* those parts of the city where violence was concentrated.

Throw oneself at: make over-eager advances to a man. ***Ex 1.*** Everyone can see that she is just *throwing herself at* him. ***Ex 2.*** She could not wait. She had to *throw herself* at the first man she met.

Throw away: (a) discard something as useless or unwanted. ***Ex 1.*** That is rubbish-you can *throw* it *away*. ***Ex 2.*** Don't *throw* your bus ticket *away* the inspector may want to see it.

(b) fail to make use of something. ***Ex 1.*** Don't *throw away* an opportunity to earn money by honest means. ***Ex 2.*** My advice was *thrown away* on her.

(c) (of actors, etc.) speak in a deliberately casual way. ***Ex 1.*** This speech is meant to be *thrown away*. ***Ex 2.*** He *threw away* a line with great effect.

Throw away on : waste something, or oneself, in foolish ventures, on undeserving people, etc. ***Ex 1.*** Any advice you might give is clearly *thrown away on* him. ***Ex 2.*** She thought that her daughter had *thrown* herself *away on* him. ***Ex 3.*** Think carefully. You may be *throwing* your savings *away on* shares that will be worthless in a few years.

Throw back: (a) raise, or remove, with a sharp movement. ***Ex 1.*** Padmini sat up in bed and *threw back* the bed-clothes. ***Ex 2.*** The curtains were *thrown back* to reveal a small boy cowering by the windows.

(b) repulse or repel vigorously. ***Ex.*** The attackers were *thrown back* in a series of fierce engagements.

Throw back on : force somebody to rely on something (because nothing else is available); force somebody to use, or resort to, something as a defence or support. ***Ex 1.*** The crisis *threw* them *back on* their own resources. ***Ex 2.*** The television broke down, so we were *thrown back on* our own resources. ***Ex 3.*** The failure of this policy *threw* the party leaders *back on* a scheme which had been put forward sometime previously. ***Ex 4.*** She has been *thrown back on* her savings. ***Ex 5.*** Triveni secretly enjoyed a situation in which she was *thrown back on* her own reserves of shrewdness and stamina.

Throw down: (Military) surrender. ***Ex 1.*** The men *threw down* their weapons. ***Ex 2.*** The general expected the enemy to *throw down* their arms soon.

Throw in : (a) include something with what one is selling or offering, without increasing the price, provide as a gratuitous extra. ***Ex 1.*** You can have the piano for four thousand rupees, and I shall *throw in* the stool as well. ***Ex 2.*** When we bought the bedroom suite, the manager of the shop *threw in* some sheets as well. ***Ex 3.*** If you are set on buying the house, we shall *throw in* the carpets and curtains at no extra cost.

(b) make (a remark, etc.) casually; interject. ***Ex.*** She *threw in* a remark about money. Throw in/into : insert into the course of; add as a contribution to. ***Ex 1.*** Could I just *throw in* the reminder that all these arrangements must be finally tied up by next week. ***Ex 2.*** He could never take these official meetings seriously-always *throwing* some outrageous comment *into* the proceedings.

Throw into : (a) begin to do something energetically. ***Ex.*** You should *throw* yourself *into* your work.

(b) confuse, disorganise, upset, etc. by sudden or violent action. ***Ex. 1.*** This unexpected change of plans *threw* everyone *into* confusion. ***Ex 2.*** Our arrangements were *thrown into* complete disarray by that interfering financial adviser from head office.

Throw oneself into: undertake, or become involved in, something with enthusiasm. ***Ex 1.*** Padma Devi tried again to *throw herself* with a will *into* life. ***Ex 2.*** The workers *threw themselves* whole heartedly *into* the task.

Throw off : (a) produce or compose something in a casual way; without apparent effort. ***Ex 1.*** I *threw off* a lines of verse. ***Ex. 2.*** The two men sat down over a cup of hot coffee and *threw off* a few songs and sketches for the evening's concert.

(b) manage to get rid of somebody/something. ***Ex 1.*** You should *throw off* your old habits. ***Ex 2.*** The downtrodden people have at last *thrown off* the yoke of imperialism. ***Ex 3.*** I always *throw off* a troublesome acquaintance. ***Ex 4.*** The visitor has to *throw off* the swarm of guides and hotel touts who cluster round the station entrance. ***Ex 5.*** I cannot manage the meeting tonight. I am still trying to *throw off* this wretched cold.

Throw oneself on/upon: rely entirely on somebody/something; entrust oneself to somebody/something; beg for kind or lenient treatment. ***Ex 1.*** He was clearly guilty and *threw himself* on the mercy of the court. ***Ex 2.*** The accused was guilty beyond any shadow of doubt; all he could now do was *throw himself* upon the mercy of the judge.

Throw on : put on hurriedly. ***Ex.*** She just *threw* her clothes on.

Throw out : (a) force (a trouble-maker, etc.) to leave. ***Ex 1.*** The drunk was *thrown out* of the room. ***Ex 2.*** We *threw* him *out* because of his bad behaviour.

(b) confuse or distract somebody; cause somebody to make a mistake; cause an error in something. ***Ex 1.*** Do keep quiet or you will *throw* me *out* in my calculations. ***Ex 2.*** Go and play your guitar somewhere else. I have nearly got this sum right, and I don't want you to *throw* me *out*. ***Ex 3.*** A tiny variation in temperature can *throw* us *out* in our results. ***Ex 4.*** It *throws* their calculations totally *out*.

(c) utter something in a casual or spontaneous way. ***Ex 1.*** I *threw out* some ideas at the meeting. ***Ex 2.*** When last I spoke to him, he was *throwing out* dire warnings of a financial crisis. ***Ex 3.*** I *threw out* a few suggestions as to how we might proceed in the case.

(d) reject (a proposal, an idea, etc.) ***Ex 1.*** Parliament has *thrown* that bill *out*. ***Ex 2.*** They just *threw* your ideas *out*. ***Ex 3.*** A proposal to extend the motorway into the Town Hall was *thrown out* in committee. ***Ex 4.*** The idea was put up to the finance committee, but they *threw* it *out*.

(e) build on. ***Ex 1.*** The workmen have *thrown out* an extension to the house. ***Ex 2.*** The fort commandant *threw out* some extra fortifications.

(f) disconcert. ***Ex.*** Your reply really *threw* her *out*.

Throw out/out of: remove forcibly; dismiss or expel. ***Ex 1.*** Now that you know why I am here, am I to be allowed to stay or are you going to *throw* me *out*? ***Ex 2.*** You know he got *thrown out* of college for failing his examinations.

Throw over: (a) end a relationship. ***Ex 1.*** This attractive young woman seduced him and taught him to drink, and then lightheartedly *threw* him *over*.***Ex 2.*** She has *thrown* him *over* for someone else. ***Ex 3.*** What happened to his long-standing love-affair with politics? Oh, he *threw* the party *over* years ago.

(b) desert or abandon. ***Ex.*** When he became rich, he *threw over* all his old friends.

Throw overboard : abandon; reject. ***Ex.*** Don't *throw overboard* the principle of concentration of effort.

Throw together : (a) bring people into contact with each other, often casually. ***Ex 1.*** The emergency situation has *thrown* them *together* again. ***Ex 2.*** It was funny to be *thrown together* in that way after such a long separation. ***Ex 3.*** Fate had *thrown* them *together*. ***Ex 4.*** As the only Indian speakers, we were rather *thrown together*.

(b) make or produce something hastily. ***Ex.*** She will just *throw together* a quick supper.

(c) assemble roughly or hurriedly; compose or compile in this way. ***Ex 1.*** They have simply *thrown* that machine *together*. ***Ex 2.*** Give me five minutes to *throw* a few clothes *together*, then we shall be off. ***Ex 3.*** You cannot *throw* a couple of good ideas *together* and expect a well-constructed essay somehow to emerge.

Throw up : (a) abandon; resign. ***Ex.* 1.** She had planned to do a management course but since then something had *thrown* it *up*. ***Ex 2.*** Why did you *throw up* your job at the income tax office? ***Ex 3.*** He has *thrown up* a perfectly good job and gone off somewhere. ***Ex 4.*** He has *thrown up* a very promising career.

(b) bring something to notice. ***Ex.*** His research has *thrown up* some interesting facts.

(c) produce or witness the appearance or development of. ***Ex 1.*** Bear in mind that not every generation *throws up* an author of his remarkable gifts. ***Ex 2.*** I was anxious that the Unions should grow naturally; this policy would ensure that the right leaders would be *thrown up* gradually.

Be through with : (indicating that a friendship, practice, etc. is ended) have finished. ***Ex 1.*** He is finally *through with* drugs. ***Ex 2.*** She is *through with* her new boy-friend. ***Ex 3.*** What are you *through with*?

Thrust on/upon: force somebody to accept somebody/something or to undertake something. ***Ex 1.*** He felt that she was tyring to *thrust* herself *upon* him-her attentions were too insistent to mean anything else. ***Ex 2.*** She is rather annoyed at having three extra guests suddenly *thrust on* her. ***Ex 3.*** Some men have greatness *thrust upon* them. ***Ex 4.*** I hope it has not put your housekeeper out having four extra guests suddenly *thrust upon* her.

Thumb through : scan a book, etc. turning, the pages with a quick movement of the thumb. ***Ex 1.*** I was *thumbing through* an old copy of a colour supplement when a secretary came in to say that the Managing Director was ready to see me. ***Ex 2.*** He was *thumbing through* the dictionary. ***Ex 3.*** He took down a standard textbook and quickly *thumbed through* to get a general idea of the lay-out.

Thunder against: speak in a loud and fierce voice to criticise or condemn. ***Ex 1.*** Reformers were *thundering against* rampant corruption in government offices. ***Ex 2.*** A back-bench M.P. *thundered against* what he called extravagant spending on the social services.

Tick away/by: (of time) pass; go by. ***Ex 1.*** Meanwhile the minutes kept *ticking away*. ***Ex 2.*** The minutes *ticked away* interminably.

Tick away: (of a clock, etc.) mark the passage of time. ***Ex 1.*** The station clock *ticked away* the minutes. ***Ex 2.*** The taxi driver had left his meter *ticking away* while I dashed into the house. When I emerged there was an extra fifty rupees to pay.

Tick off : rebuke or scold somebody. ***Ex 1.*** She got *ticked off* for careless work. ***Ex 2.*** The boss *ticked* them *off* about leaving work early.

Tick over: (a) (of engine) idle. ***Ex.*** I stopped the car but left the motor *ticking over.*

(b) live or function quietly, without achieving much success or making great progress; continue in a routine way. ***Ex 1.*** His business is just *ticking over*.***Ex 2.*** That machine *ticks over* very well. ***Ex 3.*** Everything in the office is *ticking over* very smoothly. ***Ex 4.*** How are you *ticking over* these days ?

Tide over: help somebody to live through, or manage, a difficult period, assist temporarily. ***Ex 1.*** Give me something, just to *tide* me *over* till I can get a decent, steady job. ***Ex 2.*** She could have found work other than nursing, to *tide* them *over* the years till her children could support themselves. ***Ex 3.*** This amount of money will *tide* you *over* until you receive your cheque. ***Ex 4.*** He needs some work to *tide* him *over* till his regular job starts. ***Ex 5.*** Will you please lend me seven hundred rupees in order to *tide* me *over* until I get my salary next week?

Tidy away : put something in a certain place, so that a room, etc. appears neat and orderly. ***Ex 1.*** Do *tidy* your papers *away*; your desk looks in a terrible mess. ***Ex 2.*** *Tidy* your toys *away* when you have finished playing. ***Ex 3.*** She *tidied away* the children's books. ***Ex 4.*** My husband always complains that I don't *tidy* everything *away*, so that he can never find what he wants.

Tidy out: remove unnecessary or unwanted items from something and arrange the rest neatly. ***Ex 1.*** Tell the maid to *tidy out* my drawers and letter trays. ***Ex 2.*** He decied to *tidy out* the upstairs rooms.

Tidy up: make somebody/something/oneself tidy. ***Ex 1.*** We need to *tidy* this room *up* before the guests start arriving. ***Ex 2.*** She got rather tired of constantly *tidying up* after the children. ***Ex .3.*** I shall just run upstairs and *tidy* myself *up*.

Tie down: (a) limit or restrict somebody/oneself to certain conditions, a fixed occupation or place, etc. ***Ex 1.*** I would like to take a job overseas, but there are too many things *tying* me *down* here. ***Ex 2.*** They were the rebellions few, the vagabonds, who were not *tied down* by a wife and family. ***Ex 3.*** I do not want to *tie* her *down* in any way. ***Ex 4.*** Children do *tie* you *down*, don't they? ***Ex 5.*** I refuse to be *tied down* by petty restrictions.

(b) (military) occupy or engage the attention of somebody, so that movement is difficult. ***Ex 1.*** Armour coming up in support was *tied down* by air strikes. ***Ex 2.*** Partisans operating from the mountains were able to *tie down* four enemy divisions.

Tie down to : oblige somebody to follow or conform to. ***Ex 1.*** I am *tied down to* what is stated in the departmental instructions, rules and orders. ***Ex 2.*** He is *tied down* to his duties. ***Ex 3.*** I hate being *tied* *down to a* regular work schedule. ***Ex 4.*** During the candidate's pre-election tour, his agent found it impossible to *tie* him *down to* the programme of visits he had prepared.

Tie in : make something correspond to/with; match or fit with; agree or be connected with. ***Ex 1.*** This evidence *ties in* with what we already know. ***Ex 2.*** This information completely *ties in*. ***Ex 3.*** Your story *ties in* with what they have been telling me. ***Ex 4.*** I want you to try and *tie* your story *in* with his. ***Ex 5.*** This evidence *ties in* very well with the picture which police have already built up. ***Ex 6.*** I managed to *tie in* my holiday arrangements with my work programme for the next month. ***Ex 7.*** You called him a drunk. That does not *tie in* with what I know of his habits.

Tie together: match. ***Ex 1.*** Their stories don't appear to *tie together*. ***Ex 2.*** He could not manage to *tie* the bits of the story *together*. ***Ex 3.*** You will have difficulty *tying* those loose ends *together*.

Tie up : (a) moor something or be moored. ***Ex.*** We *tied* the boat *up* alongside the quay.

(b) bind somebody with rope, etc., so that he cannot move or escape. ***Ex 1.*** The thieves left the night-watchman *tied up* and gagged. ***Ex 2.*** They *tied up* the prisoners.

(c) occupy somebody so that he has no time for other things. ***Ex 1.*** I am *tied up* in a meeting until 4 p.m. ***Ex 2.*** As far as I can tell, this editing will *tie* me *up* for the next fortnight. ***Ex 3.*** I am sorry; I shall not be able to get to your party after all. I am a bit *tied up* at the moment. ***Ex 4.*** The General Manager is *tied up* at the moment and cannot see you.

(d) complete (the arrangements or organisation of). ***Ex.*** I like to get all the arrangements for a holiday *tied up* a week in advance.

(e) agree. ***Ex.*** Your information and his certainly *tie up*.

(f) amalgamate. ***Ex.*** The two companies have finally *tied up*.

(g) tether. ***Ex.*** The cowboys *tied up* their horses.

(h) invest money, etc. in something, so that it is hard to draw upon for other purposes. ***Ex 1.*** All his capital is *tied up* in that firm. ***Ex 2.*** Most of his money is tied up in property. ***Ex 3.*** Bear in mind that it is unwise to *tie up* all your capital in one enterprise. ***Ex 4.*** I know nothing about where his money is *tied up*.

(i) bring (work, progress, etc.) to a halt; obstruct something. ***Ex.*** The strike by our factory workers *tied up* production for a span of a little over a month.

Tighten up : make or become more strict, effective, careful or vigilant. ***Ex 1.*** We shall have to *tighten up* on security in this department with immediate effect. ***Ex 2.*** The government has *tightened up* the regulations considerably since last year. ***Ex 3.*** The police are *tightening up* on drunken driving. ***Ex 4.*** He is responsible for reorganising and *tightening up* the local administration. ***Ex 5.*** Know it for certain that when a national currency is in difficulties, the rules governing the amount of money one can take abroad are invariably *tightened up*.

Tinge with : affect something slightly. ***Ex.*** Her admiration for my intellectual brilliance was *tinged with* envy.

Tingle with: be affected by an emotion. ***Ex.*** He was *tingling with* anger at your unpleasant remarks.

Tip off : give somebody an advance hint or warning. ***Ex 1.*** Someone *tipped off* the police about the robbery. ***Ex 2.*** We had been *tipped off* by Calcutta police that a man of this name was believed to have arrived in Delhi.

Note: The word *tip-off* is a noun used in the sense of hint of warning. ***Ex.*** Acting on a *tip-off*, the police arrested the heroin smugglers.

Tire of : no longer he interested in or attracted by; weary of; become uninterested in. ***Ex 1.*** I am *tired of* your title-tattle. ***Ex 2.*** After a week, he *tired of* eating cauliflower. ***Ex 3.*** She never *tires of* the sound of her own voice. ***Ex 4.*** The things *of* which he *tires* least are good company, music and gardening. .

Tire out: exhaust somebody physically or mentally. ***Ex 1.*** I am thinking about the future. I shall not be *tiring* myself *out* dodging trouble. ***Ex 2.*** The children have really *tired* me *out* today. ***Ex 3.*** He is quite *tired out*.

Tog out/up: dress up; put on smart clothes. ***Ex 1.*** His children *togged out* in their Sunday best. ***Ex 2.*** He *togged up* and went out. ***Ex 3.*** She *togged* herself *up* and went out. ***Ex 4.*** I don't want to go to party if it means that I should *tog up* in a dinner jacket.

Tone down: (a) make or become less intense. ***Ex 1.*** You should *tone down* the more offensive remarks in your article. ***Ex 2.*** Their enthusiasm has *toned down* since they discovered the cost of the outing. ***Ex 3.*** The editor had to *tone down* a few of my rather critical opinions.

(b) reduce or moderate. ***Ex.*** The rebels have *toned down* most of their demands.

Tone in: harmonise in colour. ***Ex 1.*** The new curtains *tone in* beautifully with the carpet. ***Ex 2.*** This colour *tones in* nicely with the general decor.

Tone up : make or become brighter, intenser, or more vigorous, lively, alert; improve in health. ***Ex 1.*** None can deny the fact that exercise *tones up* the muscles. ***Ex 2.*** More exercise and a change of diet-that is what you need to *tone* you *up*. ***Ex 3.*** After a quick dip and a brisk sub-down, his whole system felt *toned up*.

Tool along: drive in a casual and relaxed way. ***Ex.*** Make it a point never to *tool along* through crowded places.

Tool up : equip a factory with the necessary machine tools. ***Ex 1.*** The real cost in car-making is not design or raw materials, but the expense of *tooling up*. ***Ex 2.*** Every time there is a change in design, we have to *tool up* again.

Toss off : write quickly or casually; produce or compose something with little thought or effort. ***Ex 1.*** It is not enough in this job to be able to *toss off*, few bright remarks. It calls for real thought and understanding. ***Ex 2.*** She *tossed off* a sonnet. ***Ex 3.*** I *tossed* the article *off* for the local newspaper in half an hour. I

Tot up : add up; find the total of. ***Ex 1.*** Just *tot up* how much I owe her. ***Ex 2.*** He *totted up* the score. ***Ex 3.*** Let us *tot up* our expenses.

Tot up to : add up to something; equal something. ***Ex.*** The bill *totted up to* four hundred twenty rupees.

Touch at : (of a ship) stop for a period at a place; call at something. ***Ex 1.*** Our ship *touched at* Calcutta. ***Ex 2.*** Their ship will *touch at* Calcutta and Singapore.

Touch down: (of an aircraft) land (at an airfield, etc.) after a flight. ***Ex.*** The aeroplane *touched down* at Dum Dum airport today at 12.30 p.m.

Touch for: get somebody to give one money (as a loan, or by begging). ***Ex 1.*** He tried to *touch* me *for* a fiver. ***Ex 2.*** He is a bit tight with his money; definitely not the sort of man you can *touch for* a few rupees. ***Ex 3.*** She had been *touched for* a loan before; she was not going to be caught a second time.

Touch off : (a) cause something to explode or catch fire. ***Ex 1.*** They *touched off* the body-trap. ***Ex 2.*** His foot *touched off* the explosion. ***Ex 3.*** This explosive needs to be handled carefully, the slightest jolt will *touch* it *off*.

(b) cause some violent action to begin; spark off. ***Ex 1.*** His action has *touched off* a crisis. ***Ex 2.*** His arrest by the local police *touched off* a riot. ***Ex 3.*** Argument continued as to what exactly *touched off* the disturbances. ***Ex 4.*** Fresh violence was *touched off* when police moved in and dispersed the crowd.

Touch on/upon : mention or deal with a matter briefly; treat a matter briefly or superficially. ***Ex 1.*** Let me now deal more fully with the important question that was *touched upon* a few days ago. ***Ex 2.*** Your orrespondent had only *touched on* the fringe of the matter. ***Ex 3.*** I feel we should just *touch upon* some of these interesting points. ***Ex 4.*** He only *touched on* the matter for a few minutes.

Touch up : alter something by adding, or removing, small details; improve something by making small changes. ***Ex 1.*** I am going to *touch up* those scratches with a bit of paint. ***Ex 2.*** Protima Rani has two short articles almost ready for publication; they just need to be *touched up*. ***Ex 3.*** These photographs appeared on front pages of the dailies, in some cases after a generous degree of *touching up*.

Tough out: endure (a difficult situation) with determination. ***Ex.*** He had to *tough out* horrible hardships in his youth.

Toughen up : become worse or tougher. ***Ex 1.*** Her attitude has *toughened up* since you last saw her. ***Ex 2.*** The situation has *thoughened up* a bit. ***Ex 3.*** The law relating to kidnapping for ransom needs to be *toughened up*.

Tower above/over: (a) be of much greater height than others nearby; stand much taller or higher than somebody/something. ***Ex 1.*** Did you see the skyscrapers that tower over Calcutta ? ***Ex 2.*** At six feet, he *towers over* his father.

(b) greatly surpass others in ability, quality, fame, and so on. ***Ex 1.*** Dr JC Bose *towers above* all the scientists in the country of his time ***Ex 2.*** Netaji Subhash Bose *towered above* all other statesmen in India. ***Ex 3.*** As an original contributor to socialist thinking, and as a spell binding orator, Himardi Shankar Datta *towers above* all other members of the party. ***Ex 4.*** Shakespeare *towers over* all other Elizabethan dramatists.

Toy with : (a) consider something idly or without serious intent; dally with. ***Ex 1.*** He *toyed with* the idea of going back to his university town and getting a contract from his college. ***Ex 2.*** I have been *toying with* the idea of moving abroad.

(b) treat lightly or frivolously. ***Ex.*** He makes a great show of being fond of her in front of other people-just to show that he is not altogether heartless-but he is only *toying with* her really.

(c) handle or move something carelessly or absent-mindedly; play with. ***Ex 1.*** Tripti Devi was just *toying with* her food, as if she was not really hungry. ***Ex 2.*** He was *toying with* a pencil. ***Ex 3.*** He sat well back in his chair, his feet on the desk, *toying with* a glass paperweight.

Trace back: (a) find the source or cause of something by going back over a series of events, etc. ***Ex 1.*** Prem Lata *traced* her irrational fear of birds *back* to something which had happened to her as a child. ***Ex 2.*** The police have *traced* his disappearance *back* as far as day in April. ***Ex 3.*** His fear of water can be *traced back* to a childhood accident.

(b) be able, going back in time, to name one's ancestors in succession. ***Ex 1.*** He *traces* his descent *back* to an old Bengali family. ***Ex 2.*** How far *back* can he *trace* his family? ***Ex 3.*** On his father's side, he can *trace* his descent *back* to Mughal times.

Track down: find somebody/something by searching. ***Ex 1.*** I finally *tracked down* the reference in a dictionary of quotations. ***Ex 2.*** They *tracked down* the fox to its lair. ***Ex 3.*** It was almost forty-eight hours before the police *tracked down* the facts : there had been a series of brawls, involving ten constables. ***Ex 4.*** The police have *tracked down* the escaped convict. ***Ex 5.*** They hope to *track down* the source of the infection. ***Ex 6.*** We must try to *track* these people *down*.

Trade in: (a) be a dealer in. ***Ex 1.*** He *trades in* rice and wheat. ***Ex 2.*** Don't *trade in* drugs. ***Ex 3.*** In Calcutta, there are a number of business *trading* on a large scale *in* mustard oil and palm products.

(b) hand to a dealer a used article in part payment for a new one. ***Ex 1.*** He keeps a car for two years, then he *trades* it *in*. ***Ex 2.*** She *traded in* her old car for a new model.

Trade on/upon : use or exploit something unfairly to get something for oneself; use something for one's own advantage. ***Ex 1.*** His easy, forgiving nature was something *upon* which she was only too ready to *trade*. ***Ex. 2.*** When are you going to stop *trading on* your helplessness offering yourself all day to be petted and stroked? ***Ex 3.*** He trades on his father's reputation. ***Ex 4.*** You shou I not *trade on* her sympathy.

Traffic in : trade illegally or immorally. ***Ex 1.*** He *trafficked in* stolen goods. ***Ex 2.*** Do you traffic in heroin? *Ex 3.* Don't *traffic in* illicit alcohol. ***Ex 4.*** People *trafficking in* obsolete rifles and pistols still find a ready market for them.

Trail away off : fade into silence; gradually become quieter and then stop, especially because of shyness, confusion, etc. ***Ex 1.*** Let me know why your voice *trailed away*. ***Ex 2.*** Before the intimidating glare of the teacher his words *trailed off* into silence. .

Train on/upon: point something towards an object, so as to hit it, make it visible, etc.; aim at. ***Ex 1.*** I *trained* a gun *on* the fleeing dacoit. ***Ex 2.*** He *trained* a gun *on* a tiger. ***Ex 3.*** I *trained* my binoculars *on* the distant scene.

Translate into: express (ideas; feelings, etc.) in a different, more concrete form. ***Ex.*** We should *translate* our ideas *into* action.

Translate as : judge or guess that something has the specified meaning or intention; interpret something as something. ***Ex.*** I *translated* her silence *as* assent.

Travel over: look at, survey, consider, one by one. ***Ex 1.*** His eyes *travelled* slowly *over* the rows of faces in front of him. ***Ex 2.*** There are few problems *over* which his mind has *travelled* more searchingly than this one.

Trawl through: search through (records, etc.) ***Ex.*** The police are *trawling through* their files for similar cases.

Treasure up : keep something as precious or greatly loved. ***Ex 1.*** I shall *treasure up* these memories. ***Ex 2.*** I shall aways *treasure up* the memory of our meetings. ***Ex 3.*** I shall *treasure* her tremendous monetary assistance *up* in my heart till the last moment of my life.

Treat of: be about something; have as its subject; deal with. ***Ex 1.*** The second volume of the series *treats of* social changes after the 15 August, 1947. ***Ex 2.*** This is an essay *treating of* philosopical doubt. ***Ex 3.*** The book 'Interview Manual' *treats of* innumerable, highly valuable interview techniques.

Treat to : give or offer something to somebody that will afford him special pleasure. ***Ex 1.*** I *treated* each of the children *to* an apple. ***Ex 2.*** He decided to *treat* himself *to* a taxi. ***Ex 3.*** The whole school was *treated to* an extra half-holiday after the Covernor's annual visit. ***Ex 4.*** We wre treated *to* unusual sight of the Prime Minister singing on TV.

Treat with : negotiate with somebody. ***Ex 1.*** Don't *treat with* traitors. ***Ex 2.*** Though beaten almost to its knees, that small country had no thought of *treating with* the invader.

Trespass on/upon : take advantage of something in a selfish way; use something unreasonably; interfere in activities which are somebody else's concern. ***Ex 1.*** Don't *trespass on* my time. ***Ex 2.*** Why did you *trespass on* his area of responsibility in official matters ? ***Ex 3.*** I advised him not to *trespass upon* her privacy ***Ex 4.*** No ones privacy is so sacred that it cannot be *trespassed upon* occasionally.

Trick into: cause somebody to do something by means of a trick. ***Ex 1.*** She *tricked* him *into* marrying her. ***Ex 2.*** Don't let some backstreet traders *trick* you *into* signing a hire-purchase agreement. ***Ex 3.*** She was *tricked into* a disastrous marriage with a charming but absolutely unscrupulous young man.

Trick out : (a) cause somebody to lose something by means of a trick. ***Ex.*** My partner tried to *trick* me *out* of my share.

(b) decorate or ornament somebody/something. ***Ex 1.*** She *tricked* herself *out* in all her finery. ***Ex 2.*** She wore a floppy straw hat, *tricked out* with a yellow ribbon. ***Ex 3.*** We speedily produced a liberal edition of the pamphlet, *tricked out* prettily in red, white and blue, and ending with a resounding God Save the President.

Trigger off: be the cause of a sudden (often) violent reaction; set an action or a process in motion; spark off. ***Ex 1.*** The riots were *triggered off* by a series of police arrests. ***Ex 2.*** The smoke *triggered off* the alarm. ***Ex 3.*** His action has triggered off a crisis. ***Ex 4.*** The present dispute was *triggered off* by a rumour that some workers were to lose their jobs. ***Ex 4.*** Most of his stories are *triggered off* by word associations, or some odd juxtaposition of ideas.

Trim down: lessen or reduce. ***Ex 1.*** The government has *trimmed down* its expenditure. ***Ex 2.*** In a year of financial stringency, the department will have to *trim down* its spending on stationary and duplicating services. ***Ex 3.*** Do you know how much your figure needs *trimming down*. ***Ex 4.*** She needs to *trim down* her figure a bit.

Trim off: make smaller, make neat and trim, by cutting, clipping, etc. ***Ex 1.*** You will have to get some of that hair *trimmed off* before you go for your interview. ***Ex 2.*** The finance department has *trimmed* about fifty thousand rupees *off* our travel budget for the current year.

Trim up : tidy up by cutting neatly. ***Ex.*** You must *trim up* your beard before you go for your interview.

Trip up : be caused, or cause somebody, by a deliberate action to make a mistake, reveal a secret, etc. ***Ex 1.*** The lawyer was trying to *trip* the witnesses *up*. ***Ex 2.*** He *tripped up* in the interview and said something rather silly.***Ex 3.*** The witness *tripped up* rather badly under close cross examination. ***Ex 4.*** Be careful-there my be questions in the paper designed to *trip* you *up*.

Trot out: state or produce quickly and easily (often without careful thought) for somebody to hear or see. ***Ex 1.*** The accountant *trotted out* a few figures in support of his argument. ***Ex 2.*** I said that my theory seemed improbable when I first *trotted* it *out*. ***Ex 3.*** He always *trots out* the same old excuses for being late. ***Ex 4.*** She *trots* the same old stories *out* every time we see her. ***Ex 5.*** You must *trot out* some statistics to support your case. ,

Trump up : invent or construct something in order to make somebody appear guilty. ***Ex 1.*** They have *trumped up* a few ridiculous charges against her. ***Ex 2.*** The case against the prisoner was clearly *trumped up*; the authorities had evidently decided that an example should be made of a leading opposition figure. ***Ex 3.*** Ten persons, who were felt to be involved in the conspiracy case, were arrested on charges which were *trumped up*.

Trust in : have confidence in somebody/something. ***Ex 1.*** You must *trust in* divine providence. ***Ex 2.*** I always *trust in* God, the Greatest. ***Ex 3.*** Do you *trust in* your own judgement? ***Ex 4.*** Don't trust in her promises. ***Ex 5.*** I told you that it did not pay to *trust in* him-he has let us down again. ***Ex 6.*** We felt that we could *trust in* his wide experience of the property market.

Trust to : leave the result or progress of events to be decided by chance or by the unreasoning part of one's mind. ***Ex 1.*** It is not prudent on your part to always *trust to* luck. ***Ex 2.*** He does not *trust to* fate. ***Ex 3.*** You must have the whole project carefully planned in advance— don't just *trust to* luck. ***Ex 4.*** There is not much room for cold analysis in judging human character-you have to *trust to* intuition.

Trust with : confidently allow somebody to take care of. ***Ex 1.*** She is not the sort of woman whom you can *trust with* large sums of money. ***Ex 2.*** Is he reliable enough to be *trusted with* the details of the scheme?

Try on : act in a bold or impudent way to see if one's conduct, attentions, advances, etc. will be welcomed. ***Ex 1.*** She was just waiting for you to *try* it *on*, so that she could slap your face. ***Ex 2.*** You need not think that you can *try* anything *on* with the new financial adviser, he is a strict disciplinarian. ***Ex 3.*** The policeman warned the man not to *try* anything *on* with him. ***Ex 4.*** Don't *try* it *on* with me.

Try out: test somebody's abilities or character. ***Ex.*** She was *tried out* in the marketing section before a decision was made about his future.

Tuck away: **(a)** store or hide something. ***Ex 1.*** He had got a large amount of money *tucked away* in a Swiss Bank account. ***Ex 2.*** His farm is *tucked away* in the hills.

(b) eat; consume. ***Ex 1.*** He tucked away a huge breakfast. ***Ex 2.*** It is amazing that she can *tuck away* a lot of food.

Tuck up : cover somebody snugly with bed-clothes; make somebody comfortable in bed. ***Ex 1.*** The nurse had *tucked* the patient *up* and left him to sleep. ***Ex 2.*** The children are all safely *tucked up* in bed. ***Ex 3.*** *Tuck* the children *up* in bed.

Tumble to : realise the true character of somebody or grasp a hidden meaning etc.; understand what is being done, planned, etc. ***Ex 1.*** I have only just *tumbled to* what these people have been doing. ***Ex 2.*** It is time you *tumbled to* his tricks. ***Ex 3.*** I *tumbled to* what he was up to when I found some of his letters to her. ***Ex 4.*** He tries to keep his intentions well hidden, but it does not take too long to *tumble to* him.

Tune in : adjust the controls of a set, so that one receives a certain radio station; switch .on a radio. ***Ex 1.*** Don't forget-*tune in* again this time tomorrow. ***Ex 2.*** We always *tune in* to that programme. ***Ex 3.*** He *tuned in* to the B.B.C. World Service. ***Ex 4.*** *Tune in* next week at the same time.

Tune in to : make somebody sympathetically aware of somebody's feelings, thoughts, etc. ***Ex 1.*** It is a simple and pure truth that voters always elect the candidate who is most *turned in* to their needs. ***Ex 2.*** He has not the knack of *tuning in* to people. ***Ex 3.*** The lecturer could see from the expressions on the faces of his audience which students were really *tuned in* to what he was saying.

Turf out/out of : forcibly remove somebody/something; dispose of something; eject; expel. ***Ex 1.*** They have decided to *turf* these people *out*. ***Ex 2.*** He was *turfed out of* the club because he did not pay his debts. ***Ex 3.*** *Turf* that cat *out* if you want to sit in the chair. ***Ex 4.*** You would have more room in your wordrobe if you *turfed out* all your old clothes. ***Ex 5.*** The meeting was marred by a noisy disturbance and the ring-leaders had to be *turfed out* of the hall.

Turn about: face in the opposite direction. ***Ex 1.*** The Colonel ordered the troops to *turn about*. ***Ex 2.*** The company *turned about* and marched ten paces to the rear.

Turn against : make or become unfriendly or hostile towards somebody. ***Ex 1.*** She *turned against* her boyfriend. ***Ex 2.*** After the divorce, he tried his best to *turn* the children *against* their mother.

Turn aside : move away from or avoid somebody. ***Ex 1.*** He *turned* discreetly *aside* to wipe his nose. ***Ex 2.*** The government has *turned aside* from its collision course with the unions.

Turn away : (a) stop facing or looking at.somebody/something. ***Ex 1.*** She *turned away* in horror at the sight of so much blood. ***Ex 2.*** It was tempting to *turn away* from such a daunting task.

(b) refuse entry, hospitality, help, etc., to somebody. ***Ex 1.*** All seats were sold out in advance; many people hoping for last-minute cancellations had to be *turned away*. ***Ex 2.*** We hate to *turn away* from our Old Age Home anyone in need of food and shelter. ***Ex 3.*** Hundreds of people had to be *turned away* from the stadium. ***Ex 4.*** They have *turned* several *people* away because they have no more accommodation. ***Ex 5.*** It is unfortunate that we have to *turn* these beggars *away*. ***Ex 6.*** It is a universally accepted veracity that a doctor cannot *turn away* a dying man.

Turn back: return, go back, the way one has come. ***Ex 1.*** One of the party *turned back* to help a friend who had sprained an ankle.
Ex 2. The sight of the Red Fort was the end of her walk, and meant

she must *turn back*. ***Ex 3.*** The weather became so bad that we had to *turn back*. ***Ex 4.*** The project must go ahead; there can be no *turning back*. ***Ex 5.*** Our car was *turned back* at the frontier.

Turn down : (a) reject or refuse to consider somebody/something. ***Ex 1.*** He tried to join the army but was *turned down* because of poor health. ***Ex 2.*** I asked her to marry him but she *turned* me *down*. ***Ex 3.*** He was *turned down* by a large majority vote at the board meeting. ***Ex 4.*** I am always proposing to her and she always *turns* me *down*. ***Ex 5.*** The committee has *turned down* your application for a job. ***Ex 6.*** He was *turned down* by several publishers.

(b) adjust in order to reduce heat, noise, etc.; make less bright, intense or loud. ***Ex 1.*** I *turned down* the gas. ***Ex 2.*** He *turned* the wireless *down*. ***Ex 3.*** *Turn* that record-player *down*-I am trying to get some sleep.

Turn from: abandon; leave. ***Ex 1.*** Let us, at this point, *turn from* simple observation and enter the realm of speculation. ***Ex 2.*** He had no intention of going back to the life from which he had finally *turned from* so much indecision and struggle.

Turn in : (a) go to bed. ***Ex 1.*** It is late, I think I shall *turn in*. ***Ex 2.*** He usually *turns in* about midnight. ***Ex 3.*** When do you usually *turn in?*

(b) face or curve inwards. ***Ex 1.*** His feet *turn in* as he walks. ***Ex 2.*** His big toe *turns in*.

(c) hand somebody over to the police to be arrested. ***Ex 1.*** Please, don't *turn* me *in*. ***Ex 2.*** She threatened to *turn* him *in*. ***Ex 3.*** The farmer was in two minds whether to *turn* the poachers *in* or let them go.

(d) give back something that one no longer needs; return something. ***Ex 1.*** Don't forget to *turn in* all your camping gear before you leave. ***Ex 2.*** You must *turn in* your kit before you leave the army.

(e) abandon something; stop doing something. ***Ex 1.*** The job was damaging his health, so had to *turn* it *in*. ***Ex 2.*** He had to *turn in* his evening paper round, he found he had too much homework to do. ***Ex 3.*** All this travelling about the country is doing your health no good. Why don't you *turn it* in ?

Turn in on/upon oneself: move away from contact with others and become preoccupied with one's own problems. ***Ex 1.*** She has really *turned in on* herself since he left her. ***Ex 2.*** Avoid him. He is one of those bitter, disillusioned men who will *turn* you *in upon* yourself. ***Ex 3.*** Nothing was built, every activity was delayed, and the villagers *turned* bitterly *in upon* themselves, hoping for nothing better than food and peace.

Turn inside out: (a) make the inside face outwards. ***Ex 1.*** Are you quite sure you have not got the key on you ? *Turn* your pockets *inside out*. ***Ex 2.*** The wind *turned* his umbrella *inside out*. ***Ex 3.*** I *turned* all my pockets *inside out* looking for my keys. ***Ex 4.*** He *turned* his coat *inside out*.

(b) search thoroughly (with the result that things are in disorder). ***Ex 1.*** The police *turned* the place *inside out*. ***Ex 2.*** If you don't give us the evidence we want, we shall *turn* the place *inside out*.

Turn off: (a) leave one road in order to travel on another. ***Ex 1.*** Is this where we *turn off* for the airport? ***Ex 2.*** Is this where the road *turns off* for the airport? ***Ex 3.*** I told them to *turn off* about a mile further on.

(b) cause somebody to be bored or disgusted by something or not attractedro somebody; make somebody lose the appetite for, or interest in, something/somebody. ***Ex 1.*** This kind of treatment really *turns* me *off*. ***Ex 2.*** All that talk about abattoirs *turned* him *off*. ***Ex 3.*** It must be borne in mind that bad breath is guaranteed to *turn* a woman off. ***Ex 4.*** One sniff of his breath was enough to *turn* him *off* drink for ever. ***Ex 5.*** Pop music may *turn* you on, but it turns me *off*.

(c) stop the flow of, by turning a knob, tap, etc.; disconnect. ***Ex 1.*** Don't forget to *turn* all the lights *off* before you come up to bed. ***Ex 2.*** The electricity supply must be *turned off* at the mains before you alter the lighting circuit. ***Ex 3.*** Let her go to *turn off* the music. ***Ex 4.*** He *turned off* the water supply.

(d) stop (a radio, television, etc.) by pressing a button, moving a switch, etc. ***Ex.*** Let us *turn* the television *off*.

Turn on :Aa) attack somebody suddenly and unexpectedly (verbally or physically). ***Ex 1.*** He *turned on* her with a filthy oath. ***Ex 2.*** There is no need to *turn on* me just because rain spoiled the picnic. ***Ex 3.*** Why arc you all *turning on* him? ***Ex 4.*** His normally placid dog *turned on* the beggar and bit him in the leg.

(b) have something as its main topic. ***Ex 1.*** Our conversation *turned* mainly *on* what was to be done when the battle was over. ***Ex 2.*** The discussion *turned on* the need for better public health care.

(c) depend on. ***Ex 1.*** The question of a reprieve may *turn on* the age of the victim. ***Ex 2.*** The success of a picnic usually *turns on* the weather.

(d) excite or stimulate somebody. ***Ex 1.*** I think she is a marvellous girl-she really *turns* me *on*. ***Ex 2.*** I am not impressed by their choice of candidate. He is not likely to *turn* the voters *on*. ***Ex 3.*** Jazz music has never really *turned* me *on*. ***Ex 4.*** I find it hard to believe that she is often *turned on* by men with beards.

(e) connect; start the flow of; switch on. ***Ex 1.*** *Turn on* the television. ***Ex 2.*** He *turned on* the gas and lighted the oven. ***Ex 3.*** *Turn on* the water; please. ***Ex 4.*** Could you *turn on* the bath for me while you are upstairs? ***Ex 5.*** Who has *turned on* the central heating?

Turn out: (a) appear; be present at an event; assemble or attend. ***Ex 1.*** A large crowd *turned out* to welcome the Prime Minister. ***Ex 2.*** A vast crowd *turned out* to watch the match. ***Ex 3.*** Not many men *turned out* for duty. ***Ex 4.*** The people *turned out* to see him.

(b) prove to be; take place or happen; develop or progress iri a certain way. ***Ex 1.*** If the day *turns out* wet, we may have to change our plans. ***Ex 2.*** Things have *turned out* well. ***Ex 3.*** How did the party *turn out*? ***Ex 4.*** I hope all *turns out* well for you. ***Ex 5.*** He was not *turning out* very well. ***Ex 6.*** We need not have worried. Everything *turned out* all right in the end.

(c) produce somebody/something; train. ***Ex 1.*** Our factory *turns out* two hundred cars a month. ***Ex 2.*** This university has *turned out* some first-rate scholars. ***Ex 3.*** The press is ready to *turn out* a huge new edition. ***Ex 4.*** The most useful function of any nursing college is *turning out* a supply of fully trained doctors' wives.

(d) switch off; extinguish something. ***Ex.*** Remember to *turn out* the lights before you go to bed.

(e) empty something; remove the contents of something. ***Ex 1.*** Go and *turn out* your drawers. ***Ex 2.*** You must have the tickets on you somewhere. *Turn out* your pockets again.

(f) force somebody to leave a place. ***Ex 1.*** She got pregnant and was *turned out* of the house by her parents. ***Ex 2.*** His landlord is *turning* him *out* at the end of the month.

(g) dress smartly. ***Ex 1.*** She always *turns* her children *out* beautifully. ***Ex 2.*** The troops were smartly *turned out* for the drill parade.

(h) come to be known; transpire. ***Ex 1.*** It *turned out* that he was born in the Akbar Road, New Delhi. ***Ex 2.*** It *turns out* that this method does not work well. ***Ex 3.*** This method *turns out* not to work well.

Turn out to be: prove to be somebody/something. ***Ex 1.*** She *turned out to be* a friend of my younger sister. ***Ex 2.*** The job *turned out to be* harder than we thought. ***Ex 3.*** The symptom she had taken to the doctor had not *turned out to be* a false alarm. ***Ex 4.*** This *turned out to be* none other than the general manager's respectable relative.

Turn over : (a) do business worth; do business to a particular amount. ***Ex.*** Our company *turns over* ten million rupees a year.

(b) (of a shop) sell and replace its stock. *Ex.* A super market *turns over* its stock very rapidly.

(c) deliver somebody to; give into the custody of; hand over. ***Ex 1.*** Customs officers *turned* the man *over* to the police. ***Ex 2.*** The villagers *turned* the thief *over* to the police.

(d) pass the control or running of something to somebody. ***Ex 1.*** He *turned* the business *over* to his eldest son. ***Ex 2.*** They day-to-day management of the firm has been *turned over* to someone appointed from outside the company.

Turn to : (a) begin to work hard or vigorously. ***Ex 1.*** We *turned to* and got the whole house cleaned in an afternoon. ***Ex 2.*** The children *turned to* and cleared the dishes away.

(b) go to somebody/something for help, advice, etc. ***Ex 1.*** She has nobody she can *turn to*. ***Ex 2.*** The child *turned to* its mother for comfort. ***Ex 3.*** You can always *turn to* me. ***Ex 4.*** I have no one to *turn to.* ***Ex 5.*** The boy felt that there was no one he could *turn to* with his problems. ***Ex 6.*** It would have taken hours to work the sum out, so I *turned to* my pocket calculator. ***Ex 7.*** The more depressed he got, the more he *turned to* drugs.

Turn up: (commerce) (a) rise; increase; improve. ***Ex.*** There is no doubt about the fact that investment is *turning up* sharply.

(b) arrive; make one's appearance. ***Ex 1.*** We invited her to dinner but she did not even bother to *turn up*. ***Ex 2.*** We arranged to meet at the cinema at 5.30 p.m. but he failed to *turn up*. ***Ex 3.*** I don't know why he did not *turn up* on Tuesday. ***Ex 4.*** He will *turn up*. If he is not here by morning, we can start some inquiries.

(e) be found (esp. by chance) after being lost. ***Ex 1.*** I am sure your watch will *turn up* one of these days. ***Ex 2.*** Her purse eventually *turned up*. The boy, who took it, had got scared and dropped it behind some lockers.

(d) (opportunity) present itself; happen. ***Ex 1.*** He is still hoping that something will *turn up*. ***Ex 2.*** I have been putting off a decision, and trying not to think about it, hoping that something would *turn up*.

(c) cause something to face or point upwards. ***Ex 1.*** The collar of his overcoat was *turned up* against the bitter wind. ***Ex 2.*** Why don't you *turn up* your coat collar against the chill wind ? ***Ex 3.*** Her blonde plaits were *turned up* and tied with a neat black velvet bow. ***Ex 4.*** She *turned up* the palm of one hand in a gesture of resignation.

(f) shorten (a garment) by folding it at the bottom. ***Ex 1.*** These trousers are too long; they will need *turning up*. ***Ex 2.*** Does your skirt need to be *turned up* ? ***Ex 3.*** Who will *turn up* your jeans?

(g) expose something; discover something by digging. ***Ex.*** The soil had been *turned up* by the plough.

(h) increase the loudness of (a radio, television, etc.). ***Ex.*** I cannot hear the radio very well; could you *turn* it *up* a bit?

(i) make somebody feel physically sick; repel somebody morally or emotionally. ***Ex 1.*** The mere thought of flying *turns* her *up*. ***Ex 2.*** It *turned* me *up* to think of children being made to suffer.

Twist off : cause something to come or break off with a twisting movement; remove by turning. ***Ex 1.*** I cannot *twist off* the lid. ***Ex 2.*** He *twisted* the top *off*. ***Ex 3.*** The handles can be *twisted off*.

Twist up : distort; controt. ***Ex 1.*** Every time he tried to move, a sudden stab of pain *twisted* him *up*. ***Ex 2.*** His is a rather pitiful character, really-all *twisted up* with fear and jealousy.

21 Words Beginning With–U

Unbosom oneself to : reveal, disclose, one's secret thoughts, anxieties to. ***Ex 1.*** She *unbosomed herself* to me. ***Ex 2.*** Here was somebody to whom she could speak freely, to whom she could *unbosom herself*.

Unburden oneself to : reveal to somebody anxieties, sorrows, etc. which are a burden to one's thoughts or conscience. ***Ex 1.*** She longed for a sympathic person to whom she could *unburden herself*. ***Ex 2.*** To him, she *unburdened herself* fully of the anxieties which beset her. ***Ex 3.*** She *unburdened herself* of a secret to me.

Unfold to : make known; reveal. ***Ex 1.*** She *unfolded* her plans *to* her mother. ***Ex 2.*** The board of directors listened in silence as the details of the scheme were *unfolded to* them. ***Ex 3.*** The few men to whom I had *unfolded* the arrangements for the next day, were sworn *to* secrecy.

Unleash against/on/upon: set something free from control; release something in a powerful attack on. ***Ex 1.*** He *unleashed* a torrent of abuse *against* the unfortunate shop asistant. ***Ex 2.*** Let us appeal to all the countries of the world not to *unleash* the forces of nuclear power *against* each other. ***Ex 3.*** I am not going anywhere near his front gate, if it means having that ferocious bulldog *unleashed on* me.

Unload on/onto : pass a heavy or irksome burden on somebody else. ***Ex 1.*** The value of your holdings in falling. Better try to *unload* them *onto* somebody else. ***Ex 2.*** There is always somebody in the office *onto* whom the really unpleasant jobs are *unloaded*. ***Ex 3.*** Do you mind if I *unload* the children *on* you this afternoon ?

Uproot somebody/oneself from: force somebody/oneself to leave a place where he/one was born or has become settled. ***Ex 1.*** She *uprooted herself* from the farm and moved to Allahabad. ***Ex 2.*** Why did you *uproot yourself* from Delhi and move to Calcutta?

Urge on/upon: (a) recommend something strongly with reasoning or entreaty. ***Ex 1.*** I had another reason for *urging* caution *on* them both at this moment. ***Ex 2.*** The government *urged on* industry the importance of low pay settlements. ***Ex 2.*** That is a wise thought and I *urge* it *on* them.

(b) encourage or stimulate somebody to do something. ***Ex 1.*** I *urged* him *on* to try things out for himself. ***Ex 2.*** The President, reportedly *urged on* by his Prime Minister, has decided to attend the talks. ***Ex 3.*** *Urged on* by his colleagues and friends, he stood for election. ***Ex 4.*** The supreme need to find a solution to the problem *urged* him *on*. ***Ex 5.*** The General Manager *urged* his staff *on* to greater *efforts*.

Use out: (a) use until finished. ***Ex 1.*** I intend to *use* this jacket *out* before I buy another one.

(b) to exhaust. ***Ex.*** The resources of the area are *used out*.

Use up: (a) use until no more is left; ***Ex 1.*** I expect to *use up* quite a lot of paper during the next few months. ***Ex 2.*** He *used up* all the coins he had. ***Ex 3.*** The supply of coal has been *used up*, and we need more. ***Ex 4.*** He has *used up* all the glue.

(b) exhaust or tire 'something out. ***Ex.*** She *used up* a tremendous amount of energy.

Usher in: herald something; mark the start of something. ***Ex 1.*** The new government *ushered in* a period of prosperity. ***Ex 2.*** The Sepoy Mutiny of 1857 *ushered in* a new age. ***Ex 3.*** It would be unwise to assume that the April elections will *usher in* a new millenium.

---

22 Words Beginning With–V

Vamp up : (a) make something superficially attractive without making any genuine changes; make something new from old or existing material. ***Ex 1.*** He *vamped up* some lectures out of old notes. ***Ex 2.*** It is a musical comedy *vamped up* for the audience. ***Ex 3.*** They *vamped* it *up* a bit, and then sold it all right. ***Ex 4.*** The front office has been *vamped up* with strip lighting and a new coat of paint. ***Ex 5.*** There is no real change in the content of her lecture course-she has *vamped* it *up* a bit with one or two tricks of presentation.

(b) concoct; invent. ***Ex.*** They *vamped up* some ugly stories about her.

Varnish over: cover something unpleasant with a smooth surface; hide unpleasant aspects of something. ***Ex 1.*** Conflict is *varnished over* with polite words. ***Ex 2.*** The cracks and flaws in his old performance have been skilfully *varnished over*.

Veer away: (of conversation, somebody's behaviour or opinion) change suddenly or very noticeably. ***Ex.*** Their discussion *veered away* from religion and round to politics.

Vent on : express, get rid of, by attacking one person, the anger, etc. one feels against another; find or provide an outlet for an emotion. ***Ex 1.*** He *vented* his anger *on* his long-suffering wife. ***Ex 2.*** He longed to *vent on* Aruna all the spite he felt against his former associates.

Venture on/upon : dare to attempt something; attempt or undertake something involving risk or danger. ***Ex 1.*** He *ventured on* a trip up the Ganges. ***Ex 2.*** The hope of making further discoveries led them to *venture upon* a second voyage. ***Ex 3.*** The company secretary; who had never liked the project, but who also knew that stronger voice would be raised in support of it, *ventured* cautiously *on* a statement of the risks involved.

Verge on/upon: come close to; be approaching something; be similar to something; border on. ***Ex 1.*** As he is *verging on* 85 now, he needs constant attention. ***Ex 2.*** This is a situation *verging on* the ridiculous. ***Ex 3.*** He had taken over an old company *verging on* liquidation. ***Ex 4.*** She was not in that state *verging on* hysteria all the time. ***Ex 5.*** This action *verges upon* aggression. ***Ex 6.*** His behaviour *verges on* madness. ***Ex 7.*** I had a feeling of distrust *verging on* panic. ***Ex 8.*** It was the kind of smile that *verged on* laughter. ***Ex 9.*** These are games which *verge on* criminality

Vest in : legally confer rights, etc. on a person or body; confer something on somebody/something. ***Ex 1.*** Authority is *vested in* the people. ***Ex 2.*** By the powers *vested in* me, I declare you duly elected to the Lok Sabha. ***Ex 3.*** In India, the power to declare war is *vested in* the President.

Vie with: compete keenly with somebody for something; rival somebody for something. ***Ex 1.*** Businesses are *vying with* each other to attract customers. ***Ex 2.*** Two engineering companies were *vying with* each other to capture this valuable market. ***Ex 3.*** The members of the military board *vied with* one another in telling me agreeable things, and I kept looking around at them in astonishment. ***Ex 4.*** Several manufacturers are *vying with* one another for the coveted trophies.

Visit with: visit somebody for an informed talk or chat. ***Ex 1.*** Please stay and *visit with* me for a while. ***Ex 2.*** On Sundays, we usually *visit with* my father-in-law. ***Ex 3.*** We hope you will *visit with* us sometime. ***Ex 4.*** He went out to *visit with* some friends.

Vote down: reject or defeat somebody/something by voting. ***Ex 1.*** He proposed that the proceedings of the meeting should be recorded on tape, but the suggestion was *voted down*. ***Ex 2.*** Her proposal was *voted down*. ***Ex 3.*** Parliament *voted down* his proposals. ***Ex 4.*** The people have *voted* her *down*.

Vote in/into: elect somebody to a position of authority. ***Ex 1.*** The people have voted in a new government. ***Ex 2.*** They *voted* him *in* as president. ***Ex 3.*** All the Directors were *voted in* by proxies. ***Ex 4.*** The National Party was *voted in* for a second term of office, though with a greatly reduced number of seats. ***Ex 5.*** The Socialist Party was *voted into* power on a programme of wide-ranging social reform.

Vote out/out of : remove from a position of authority by voting at an election; reject through voting. ***Ex 1.*** The people have *voted out* the old government. ***Ex 2.*** They *voted* him *out* by a majority of 15. ***Ex 3.*** She was *voted out* of office. ***Ex 4.*** If you don't like the way the committee are going about things, you can always *vote* them *out* of office. ***Ex 5.*** If the present government is *voted out*, it will be on its general handling of the economic situation.

Vote through: approve or bring into force (a proposal, etc.) by voting. ***Ex 1.*** Parliament *voted* the bill *through* without a debate. ***Ex 2.*** The Legislative Assembly has *voted* the new reforms *through*. ***Ex 3.*** The committee *voted* the motion *through* by an overwhelming majority.

Vouch for: guarantee. ***Ex 1.*** I can *vouch for* her honesty. ***Ex 2.*** I cannot *vouch for* the truth of his story. ***Ex 3.*** I can *vouch for* the accuracy of my information.

23 *Words Beginning With–W*

Wade in : start doing something with determination and energy. ***Ex 1.*** The job has to be done, so let us *wade in* immediately. ***Ex 2.*** He did not stand about looking at all the jobs to be done: he *waded* straight *in*. ***Ex 3.*** Get to Champa Devi and watch her *wade in*.

Wade into: attack somebody/something vigorously. ***Ex 1.*** Mridula Devi *waded* straight *into* her critics with her opening remarks. ***Ex 2.*** He just *waded into* the bigger boy with both fists flying.

Wade through: read something that is long or difficult to read, without interest or enjoyment; proceed slowly and with difficulty with some task. ***Ex 1.*** I shall not be able to get away this weekend, I have got ten sets of examination scripts to *wade through*. ***Ex 2.*** She was *wading* through page after page of boring statistics. ***Ex 3.*** I *waded through*' a lot of work last night. ***Ex 4.*** This is a lot to *wade through*. ***Ex 5.*** A lawyer was *wading through* the two-hundred- page file.

Wage against/on: try to control by vigorous action; begin and carry on (a campaign, etc.). ***Ex 1.*** The government promised to *wage* a ceaseless war *against* price increases. ***Ex 2.*** For almost a year, they had *waged* a war of nerves *on* their neighbours.

Wait about/around: wait aimlessly, idly or impatiently. ***Ex 1.*** They *waited about* for another bus, but none came. ***Ex 2.*** The people seemed to be *waiting about* for something to happen. ***Ex 3.*** I am furious: you have kept me *waiting about* her for a whole hour. ***Ex 4.*** Show the visitor in as soon as she arrives. Don't make her *wait around* in the corridor.

Wait behind: stay after other people have gone. ***Ex 1.*** Kanta, you can *wait behind* when the class is dismissed, I want to have a word with you. ***Ex 2.*** The teacher asked me to *wait behind* after class today. ***Ex 3.*** She said that she would *wait behind* for me.

Wait in : stay at home. ***Ex.*** I *waited in* all day but she did not arrive.

Wait on : act as a servant for somebody; serve at a meal. ***Ex 1.*** He *waited on. us at dinner*. ***Ex 2.*** We were sitting around a dinner table, being *waited on* by uniformed waitresses.

Wait up: stay up; not to go to bed. ***Ex 1.*** I shall be home very late tonight, so don't *wait up* for me. ***Ex 2.*** I shall *wait up* till midnight. ***Ex 3.*** I shall not get in till after midnight, so don't bother to *wait up*.

Wake up : realise something; become aware of something. ***Ex 1.*** He has not yet *woken up* to the seriousness of the situation. ***Ex 2.*** He began to *wake up* to the danger he faced. ***Ex 3.*** It is time you *woke up* to the fact that you are not very popular. ***Ex 4.*** You should *wake up* and see the problems you have got on your hands. ***Ex 5.*** They should *wake up* to the problems they have got on their hand. ***Ex 6.*** He *woke up* too late to his predicament.

Walk abroad: spread far and wide. ***Ex.*** There death and destruction had already *walked abroad*.

Walk away/off with: (a) win easily. ***Ex 1.*** The official National Party candidate *walked away* with the election, his majority was a little over ten thousand. ***Ex 2.*** It is no good-they have lost. They should have *walked away* with the game.

(b) steal something. Ex. Somebody has walked off with my pen.

Walk into: (a) become caught in something that one is not expecting, because one is not careful. ***Ex 1.*** I set a trap for her and she *walked* right *into* it. ***Ex 2.*** He loves to set traps for the unwary, you would not be the first to *walk into* it.

(b) be appointed to (a job) without having to make an effort. ***Ex.*** Sushila simply *walked into* a decent job at the State Bank of India as soon as she graduated.

(c) strike against somebody/something while walking. ***Ex.*** He was not looking where-he was going and *walked* straight *into* an attractive young woman.

Walk off : reduce by energetic walking. ***Ex 1.*** We tried to *walk off* the effects of the heavy meal. ***Ex 2.*** I started back in a mood of deep depression, but had *walked* it *off* before I got home. ***Ex 3.*** I shall have to get out into the country more, and *walk off* some of this fat. ***Ex 4.*** He went out to *walk off* his disquiet in the night air. ***Ex 5.*** Tell me how to *walk off* my headache.

Walk off with : take or carry away somebody's property either intentionally or by mistake. ***Ex 1.*** Don't leave your suitcases unguarded. Somebody may *walk off with* them. ***Ex 2.*** He *walked off with* several watches. ***Ex 3.*** She wants to know what to do about the man who has *walked off with* her dictionary.

Walk on. : (theatre) have a small part Qrappear briefly in a play. ***Ex 1.*** Why don't you .comeand *walk on* in the Calcutta City Theature? ***Ex 2.*** When he first joined the company Prern Kumar was happy just to be able to *walk on*-to play the butler or the policeman.

Walk out : (a) (of workers) go on strike suddenly. ***Ex.*** Building workers *walked out* during the morning in protest at the sacking of a brick layer.

(b) (military) leave barracks with permission during off-duty hours. ***Ex 1.*** Soldiers are normally allowed to *walk out* in uniform or civilian dress. ***Ex 2.*** During the first weeks of basic training, recruits are not permitted to *walk out.*

(c) court; have a relationship with somebody. ***Ex 1.*** Is she engaged to him? That I don't know, but they ate *walking out.* ***Ex 2 .*** Do you *walk out* with him? ***Ex 3.*** They were *walking out* for years before they got married. ***Ex 4.*** Don't *walk out* with an ugly girl.

(d) leave (a meeting, etc.) suddenly and angrily. ***Ex 1.*** He *walked out* of the conference. ***Ex 2.*** Many of the audience *walked out* through sheer boredom. ***Ex 3.*** At various times, both teams of negotiators had *walked out* of the peace talks.

Walk out on: abandon or desert somebody. ***Ex 1.*** He had a row with his wife and just *walked out on* her. ***Ex 2.*** His girlfriend *walked out on* him. ***Ex 3.*** If I try to discipline him, he just *walks out on* me without listening. ***Ex 4.*** You cannot just *walk out on* us like this. ***Ex 5.*** Don't *walk out on* me.

Walk over: (a) thoroughly defeat somebody in a competition. ***Ex.*** The visiting team was too strong-they *walked* all *over* us.
(b) treat somebody badly or unkindly. ***Ex 1.*** You must not let him *walk over* you like that. ***Ex 2.*** Tell me why she *walks over* you.

Walk up : come and see (a circus, show, etc.) ***Ex.*** *Walk up* the greatest show on earth is about to begin.

Walk up to: approach somebody/something. ***Ex 1.*** A stranger *walked up to* me and shook my hand. ***Ex 2.*** He *walked up to* the desk and asked to see the Managing Director.

Wall in : enclose with a wall; surround somebody; so that he is not free to move. ***Ex 1.*** The garden has been *walled in.* ***Ex 2.*** The mass of faces pressed closer, *walling* him *in.*

Wall off : separate something with a wall. ***Ex 1.*** The garden has been *walled off* from its neighbours. ***Ex 2.*** Part of the yard has been *walled off.*

Wallow in : indulge oneself; take pleasure in something. ***Ex 1.*** They are absolutely *wallowing in* money. ***Ex 2.*** She is *wallowing in* luxury

Waltz off with : (a) steal something. ***Ex.*** He has just *waltzed off with* my pen.
(b) win something easily. ***Ex 1.*** She swept the board, *waltzing off with* four gold medals. ***Ex 2.*** He *waltzed off with* the history and geography prizes. .

Wander from/off/away: (a) leave the right place or way; stray from one's group. ***Ex 1.*** The shepherd set out to took for the sheep that had *wandered away.* ***Ex 2.*** Weseem to have wanderedfrom the path. ***Ex 3.*** The child *wandered off* and got lost.
(b) move or stray away in an absent-minded way from the subject one is concerned with. ***Ex 1.*** Don't *wander from* the subject, stick to the point. ***Ex 2.*** Don't let your mind *wander off* the main point at issue. ***Ex 3.*** Someone seated at the chairman's elbow would need to bring him back to the subject under discussion *from* which he all too easily *wandered.*

Wangle out of: avoid having to do something by scheming. **Ex.** It is bound to be a boring party-let us try to *wangle out of* it.

Want for : suffer because of a lack of something. ***Ex 1.*** Those children *want for* nothing. ***Ex 2.*** She did not *want for* help from her friends. ***Ex 3.*** He makes sure that his widowed mother *wants for* nothing. ***Ex 4.*** His children don't *want for* anything-they are well provided for.

Want out/out of: wish to be freed from something unpleasant; no longer what to be involved in. ***Ex 1.*** Don't imagine that you can depend on my support any longer; I *want out.* ***Ex 2.*** The ordinary people *want out* of their government's involvement in the war.

Ward off : keep away (somebody/something that is dangerous or unpleasant); find somebody/something off. ***Ex 1.*** He *warded off* the intruders. ***Ex 2.*** Take steps to *ward off* the danger ahead. ***Ex 3.*** The general *warded off* the enemy attack as best he could. ***Ex 4.*** This amulet is said to *ward off* evil spirits. ***Ex 5.*** He flung up an arm to *ward off* the blow.

Warm to : become more lively about something; become enthusiastic about something. ***Ex 1.*** Sensing the interest of the audience, the chairman *warmed to* his topic, giving the most entertaining, and convincing, speech of the evening. ***Ex 2.*** He grew ruder and louder as he *warmed to* his work.

Warm towards : feel a sympathetic interest in. ***Ex 1.*** I felt myself *warming towards* this big friendly man who had done so much to help us. ***Ex 2.*** She is not the sort of girl one *warms towards* easily—rather cold and aloof. ***Ex 3.*** He found himself *warming towards* her.

Warm up : become or make more lively and interested; enliven. ***Ex 1.*** The comedian told a few quick jokes to get his audience *warmed up.* ***Ex 2.*** The party has begun to *warm up.*

Warn off : give somebody notice that he must go or stay away; tell somebody to keep away. ***Ex 1.*** I had been *warned off* visiting her while she was still unwell. ***Ex 2.*** He *warns* everybody *off* who tries to be friendly with his girlfriend.

Wash away: remove or carry somebody/something away to another place. ***Ex. 1.*** His child was *washed away* in the flood. ***Ex 2.*** The footprints were *washed away* by the rain.

Wash over: occur all around somebody; or be expressed, without greatly affecting him. ***Ex 1.*** The recent criticism she has had seems to have *washed* right *over* her. ***Ex 2.*** The kids were making a tremendous din, and he sat there quietly typing his report. It all *washed over* him. ***Ex 3.*** He does not seem to mind what people say. All the recent criticism seems to have *washed* right *over* him.

Waste away: grow unhealthily thin or weak. ***Ex 1.*** He is just *wasting away*, and the doctors seem unable to help him. ***Ex 2.*** He was looking dreadful the last lime I saw him-he is *wasting away* to skin and bone.

Watch out: be careful to avoid danger, not to upset others, etc. ***Ex 1.*** You need to *watch out* here, because the ground is a bit boggy on either. side of the path. ***Ex 2.*** You will be in dire trouble if you don't *watch out.* ***Ex 3.*** *Watch out.* There is a car coming.

Watch out for: be alert so that one notices somebody/something; look out for somebody/something. ***Ex 1.*** I said I should be sick, and that I must *watch out for* symptoms. ***Ex 2.*** The staff were asked to *watch out for* forged banknotes.

Water down : (a) make (a liquid) weaker by adding water; dilute something. ***Ex 1.*** The milk had been *watered down*. ***Ex 2.*** You have to *water down* the medicine before drinking it.

(b) weaken the effect of something. ***Ex 1.*** The criticisms had been *watered down* so as not to offend anybody. ***Ex 2.*** They gave the press a *watered down* version of what really happened. ***Ex 3.*** I have considerably *watered down* his criticisms of the guilty men. ***Ex 4.*** Don't *water down* your argument.

Wave away/off: show, with a motion of the hand, that somebody must move or stay away. ***Ex 1.*** He *waved* them *away* impatiently. ***Ex 2.*** Nobody was allowed near the wreckage of the plane. Even those with press cards were *waved away*.

Wave aside : dismiss (an objection, etc.) as unimportant or irrelevant. ***Ex 1.*** Their criticisms were *waved aside*.

Wean away: cause somebody to stop doing something gradually. ***Ex 1.*** I *weaned* him *away* from drugs. ***Ex 2.*** Your son needs to be *weaned away* from the notion that everything will come easily to him.

Wear away: make or become thin, damaged, weak, etc. by constant use. ***Ex 1.*** The inscription on the coin had *worn away*. ***Ex 2.*** The steps had been *worn away* by the feet of thousands of visitors. ***Ex 3.*** Wind and rain have *worn away* the sharp ridges of these mountains. ***Ex 4.*** With the passing of the years, the finer detail of the carvings has almost *worn away*.

Wear down : become,or make, weaker by constant pressure, attack or nervous strain, etc. ***Ex 1.*** She was *worn down* by overwork, ***Ex 2.*** The strategy was designed to *wear down* the enemy's resistance. ***Ex 3.*** Under so much pressure from her parents, her will to independence, was slowly *wearing down*.

Wear off: disappear or be removed gradually. ***Ex 1.*** The novelty will soon *wear off*. ***Ex 2*** The pain is slowly *wearing off*.

Wear on : (time) pass tediously or slowly. ***Ex 1.*** The gloomy afternoon *wore on*. ***Ex 2.*** As the evening *wore on*, she became moreand more nervous. ***Ex 3.*** His life was *wearing on* towards its close.

Wear out: (a) become or make useless, threadbare or exhausted through use. ***Ex 1.*** I *worn out* two pairs 'of boots on the walking tour. ***Ex 2.*** Her patience had at last *worn out*.

(b) tire somebody out; cause somebody to become exhausted. ***Ex 1.*** They were *worn out* after a long day spent working in the fields. ***Ex 2.*** Just listening to his silly chatter *wears* me *out*. ***Ex 3.*** I have seen plenty of girls *wear* themselves *out* trying to run a home and a job. ***Ex 4.*** Anil *worn out* with anxiety and strain, followed from one house to the next.

Wed to : combine one thing or quality with another. ***Ex.*** In the design for the temple, he has *wedded* a traditional ground plan *to* modem structural methods.

Weed out : remove or get rid of, from amongst others that are valuable. ***Ex 1.*** I want you to *weed out* the trouble-makers. ***Ex 2.*** The examinations helps to *weed out* the unsatisfactory candidates. ***Ex 3.*** We shall have to *weed* the herd *out* carefully if we hope to improve the breed. ***Ex 4.*** Officers who could not stand the strain were to be *weeded out* and replaced. ***Ex 5.*** Natural selection has *weeded out* the weakest. ***Ex 6.*** Teachers should report on their own incompetent colleagues if they want to *weed* them *out* of the profession.

Weigh down : make somebody feel anxious or depressed. ***Ex 1.*** He was *weighed down* by worry and overwork. ***Ex 2.*** The responsibilities of the job are *weighing* her *down*. ***Ex 3.*** Don't let the cares of parenthood *weigh* you *down*. ***Ex 4.*** He seems altogether *weighed down* by all the extra work they are pushing on him.

Weigh in : bring forceful arguments to bear in a discussion; contribute confidently; support an enterprise; ***Ex 1.*** At that point, the chairman *weighed in* with a strong defence of the company policy. ***Ex 2.*** One man leapt to his feet and *weighed in* with a forceful appeal for'an allout strike. ***Ex 3.*** The whole family *weighed in* with offers of help. ***Ex 4.*** All of us will *weigh in* one hundred per cent to do what you want.

Weigh on: make (somebody/somebody's mind, etc.) anxious. ***Ex 1.*** The responsibilities *weigh* heavily *on* him. ***Ex 2.*** It has been *weighing on* my mind for days whether to tell her or not.

Weigh up : (a) assess, judge; consider carefully before forming a judgement. ***Ex 1.*** In splitsecond, Sudesh had everything *weighed up*. ***Ex 2.*** When you come to *weigh* things *up*, there is not any practicable alternative to this government.

(b) form an opinion, or make a judgement, or sornebody's character. ***Ex 1.*** He usually has someone *weighed up* within a few minutes of meeting him. ***Ex 2.*** The children had not *weighed up* their new teacher yet.

(c) consider alternatives carefully before choosing one of them. ***Ex.*** She was *weighing up* whether to stay with us or not.

Weigh with: be regarded as important by somebody; seriously considered by somebody. ***Ex 1.*** The social background of the applicants does not *weigh* at all *with* the interviewing panel. ***Ex 2.*** Trade considerations in particular bound to *weigh* heavily *with* us.

Weld together: unify, combine, strongly or solidly. ***Ex 1.*** The nation has been *welded together* by the shared experience of exile and persecution. ***Ex 2.*** The regime has succeeded in *welding together* many diverse elements-religious, racial and linguistic.

Wheel in/into: conduct or escort somebody into a place where he is to be interviewed or questioned. ***Ex.*** Who is next on the list, Miss Mohini? A Mr. Mohan. All right, *wheel* him *in*.

While away: pass (a period of time) in a leisurely way. ***Ex 1.*** I was glad of her company to *while away* an hour until the train carne. ***Ex 2.*** It is easy to *while away* few hours in a museum. ***Ex 3.*** *We whiled away* the time at the airport reading magazines. ‘

Whip in : compel to attend or to perform in some way. ***Ex.*** The party bosses *whipped* their followers *in* for the big vote.

Whip off : take off, or remove, with a sharp, snatching movement. ***Ex 1.*** As the boss entered, the men *whipped* their hats *off* and shuffled their feet uneasily. ***Ex 2.*** Gales uprooted trees and *whipped* the states *off* roofs.

Whip on : (a) drive somebody to work harder, go faster, etc. ***Ex.*** The fugitives wanted to rest, but the fear of capture *whipped* them *on*.

(b) make an animal go faster by striking it with a whip. ***Ex.*** The horses flashed past the post, *whipped on* furiously by their jockeys.

Whip out/out of: take out, produce, With a sharp, snatching movement. ***Ex 1.*** He *whipped* a piece of paper *out of* his pocket and waved it in our faces. ***Ex 2.*** How could you react if someone. entered your shop and *whipped out* a revolver?

Whip round: appeal to colleagues, etc. for money to help in a good cause. ***Ex.*** I shall *whip round* and raise a few thousand rupees for the office party.

Whip up: (a) arouse; creates (excitement, enthusiasm, etc.) in people or cause people to be enthusiastic, etc. ***Ex 1.*** A party orator *whipped* the crowd *up to* a state of frenzy. ***Ex 2.*** The speakers *whipped up* the emotions of the crowd. ***Ex 3.*** They are trying to *whip* up support for their candidate. ***Ex 4.*** The people were *whipped up* into a frenzy by the speaker. ***Ex 5.*** Competitive jouranlism had *whipped up* public in a rather strange stunt.

(b) prepare (a meal, etc.) very quickly. ***Ex.*** I can easily whip you up some refreshment.

Whistle for: wish for or expect something in vain. ***Ex 1.*** Neelam borrowed two of my books, and as far as she is concerned, I can *whistle for* them. ***Ex 2.*** If he wants his money now, he will have to *whistle for* it.

Whittle away: remove or take away little by little or one by one; gradually reduce or decrease something. ***Ex 1.*** He says that inflation has *whittled away* his savings. ***Ex 2.*** They are slowly *whittling away* our power. ***Ex 3.*** We had a pay rise in August but increases in the cost of food and fuel have *whittled away* the extra money.

Whittle down : reduce the size or importance of something by degrees. ***Ex 1.*** The number of employers is being *whittled down* in order to reduce costs. ***Ex 2.*** The research team has been *whittled down* considerably to staff other projects. ***Ex 3.*** The detective could not be expected to fool the smuggler unless his status was *whittled down*.

Ex 4. We have *whittled down* to a mass of evidence and produced two clear leads.

Win back: regain somebody/something after a struggle; get back or recover after a struggle. ***Ex 1.*** Valuable orders have been *won back* from our competitors. ***Ex 2.*** The party must try to *win back* the support it has lost. ***Ex 3.*** He hoped to *win* her love *back*.

Win out/through: come successfully through a difficult period; achieve success eventually. ***Ex 1.*** We are faced with a lot of problems but we shall *win through* in the end. ***Ex 2.*** He fought his trouble down and I thought he was going to *win out*. ***Ex 3.*** Do you look businesslike? If so; you may *win out* over some more experienced applicant. ***Ex 4.*** He settled to his task with a good will, and with his help we *won through*. ***Ex 5.*** The candidates all *won through*. ***Ex 6.*** Good will *win out*. ***Ex 7.*** They will *win out* in the long run.

Win over: persuade somebody to agree, to be on one's side, etc. ***Ex 1.*** She wanted to marry, but her mother could never be *won over*. ***Ex 2.*** After some argument, they were eventually *won over* to our side. ***Ex 3.*** This is a specious philosophy to which too many have been *won over*.

Wind down : (a) lower or bring down by turning a handle or wheel. ***Ex.*** He *wound down* the window of his car and leant out to ask the way.

(b) (of a clock or watch) become slack, causing the clock to go slow and stop. ***Ex 1.*** It is a one-day clock; the spring *winds down* in 24 hours. ***Ex 2.*** The watch *wound down* and stopped.

(c) move more slowly, or with less energy; lose momentum; come to an end slowly. ***Ex 1.*** The enthusiasm of the sales staff weakened and the whole campaign *wound down*. ***Ex 2.*** The proceedings began to *wind down*.

(d) (of a person) relax, after a period of stress or excitement. ***Ex 1.*** I felt tense, but now I am beginning to *wind down* a bit. ***Ex 2.*** This year has been frantically busy for us-I need a holiday just to *wind down*.

Wind up: (a) (of a person) arrive finally ina place; end up. ***Ex 1.*** You will *wind up* in hospital if you are not more careful. ***Ex 2.*** We eventually *wound up* in a super little hotel by the sea. ***Ex 3.*** I always said that he would *wind up* in jail. '

(b) finish (a speech, etc.) ***Ex 1.*** Before I *wind up*, there are two more things to be said. ***Ex 2.*** As we walked along, he *wound up* his story. ***Ex 3.*** If we all agree, let us *wind up* the discussion. ***Ex 4.*** I wound up . the debate for the Opposition. ***Ex 5.*** He wound up the meeting.

(c) cause somebody/something to reach a high level of excitement or agitation. ***Ex 1.*** She gets so *wound up* when she is arguing. ***Ex 2.*** Are you deliberately *winding* me *up* ? ***Ex 3.*** He is all *wound up*. ***Ex 4.*** By this time, he had *wound* the crowd *up* to fever pitch. ***Ex 5.*** In any political discussion, he always gets terribly *wound up*.

(d) stop or cause to stop functioning; cease activities. ***Ex.*** The smuggling organisation *wound up* its activities and prepared to disband.

(e) as a result of one's, manner of life, etc., get 'or experience something unusual. ***Ex 1.*** Don't carry on living at this pace, you will *wind up* with nervous exhaustion. ***Ex 2.*** Youwill keep your nose out of my affairs, unless you want to *wind up* in hospital. ***Ex 3.*** Mark my words, one day he will *wind up* running the company.

Wink at : pretend that one does not notice (had behaviour, etc.); deliberately, overlook or ignore. ***Ex 1.*** His wife has *winked at* his infidelity for years. ***Ex 2.*** Her extravagance is usually *winked at*, her husband thinks he is buying a quiet life. ***Ex 3.*** In this department, the General Manager *winks at* petty theft. ***Ex 4.*** I would like you to *wink at* their activities. ***Ex 5.*** Do you expect me just to *wink at* something like this? ***Ex 6.*** Don't *wink at* what they are doing.

Winkle out/out of : (a) get somebody/something out of a place slowly and with difficulty. ***Ex 1.*** Enemy troops hiding in the cellars had to be *winked out* one by one. ***Ex 2.*** I have dropped a coin between the floorboards; try to *winkle* it *out* of there. ***Ex 3.*** The children were finally all *winkled out* of their hiding places.

(b) obtain information, etc. from somebody with difficulty. ***Ex 1.*** She is very clever at *winkling* secrets *out of* people. ***Ex 2.*** See if you can *winkle* anything *out of* the wife; I shall question the husband.

Wipe out : (a) clean the inside of a vessel by rubbing with a cloth. ***Ex.*** Make sure that the inside of the tea pot is thoroughly *wiped out*.

(b) cancel out; remove; ***Ex 1.*** This year's losses have *wiped out* last year's profits. ***Ex 2.*** The museum's financial debt had been *wiped out*.

(c) destroy something completely. ***Ex 1.*** Some villages were *wiped out* in the bombing raids. ***Ex 2.*** The government is trying to *wipe out* drug trafficking. ***Ex 3.*** Asummer fire can *wipe out* all the pasture feed. ***Ex 4.*** Thousands of people were *wiped out* in that battle.

Wise up: make or become aware or informed of something. ***Ex 1.*** He was new here, but it did not take him long to *wise up* to what was going on. ***Ex 2.*** By this time, I had fully *wised up* to their little game. ***Ex 3.*** The new store detective was quickly *wised up* to the shoplifters' favourite methods.

Wish away: try to get rid of something by wishing it did not exist. ***Ex 1.*** The rising numbers seeking places in higher education cannot simply be ignored or *wished away*. ***Ex 2.*** These problems cannot be *wished away*, you know.

Wish on/onto: pass (an unpleasant or unwanted task, visitor, etc.) on to somebody. ***Ex 1.*** It is not ajob I would *wish on* anybody. ***Ex 2.*** I don't think we can *wish* the children *on* your parents while we are away. ***Ex 3.*** The school had had ten extra infants *wished on* it by the Education Department.

Witter on : speak in a lengthy and annoying way about something unimportant. ***Ex 1.*** What are you *wittering on* about? ***Ex 2.*** Don't *witter on* about unimportant matters.

Wolf down: eat something quickly and greedily. ***Ex 1.*** Don't *wolf down* your food. ***Ex 2.*** She *wolfed* her food *down.* ***Ex 3.*** He went into the kitchen in search of food and *wolfed down* an apple pie.

Work around/round: gradually approach (a subject, topic, etc.). ***Ex 1.*** It was a long time before he *worked around* to what he really wanted to say. ***Ex 2.*** Don't worry about the correspondence, I shall *work round* to it in time. ***Ex 3.*** By the time he *works round* to asking for a salary increase, it will be too late.

Work at : give thought, energy; etc. to getting rid of or solving something or problem ortask. ***Ex 1.*** You will crack this problem if you really *work at* it. ***Ex 2.*** There is no easy way round the difficulty, you will just have to *work at* it.

Work away: give continuous effort, thought, etc. to something. ***Ex 1.*** I found him *working away* in the library. ***Ex 2.*** Chemistry was a subject he did not mind *working away* at. ***Ex 3.*** He *works away* in his own room.

Work in/into : (a) insert something gradually, by moving it from side to side, etc. ***Ex.*** He *worked in* the key and opened up the classroom.

(b) include something by showing special care or cunning. ***Ex 1.*** When he wrote his essay, he *worked in* many a quotation. ***Ex 2.*** She always *works in* some reference to her father's money. ***Ex 3.*** He always contrives to *work* his war experience *into* the conversation. ***Ex 4.*** You won't get the story published unless you *work in* a bit of human interest.

Work off : get rid of something by work or activity. ***Ex 1.*** He *worked off* a large bank loan. ***Ex 2.*** Don't *work* off your anger on me. ***Ex 3.*** You can *work off* excess weight by regular exercise. ***Ex 4.*** I have *worked off* all my debts. ***Ex 5.*** He went into the garden and *worked off* his bad temper on the potato patch. ***Ex 6.*** One generally has to *work off* one's irritation on somebody. ***Ex 7.*** There is no need to *work* your disappointment *off* on me.

Work on : (a) give thought, effort, etc. to making or discovering something. ***Ex 1.*** For his doctorate, he is *working on* Mughal architecture. ***Ex 2.*** The manufacturers are *working on* a modification to the steering.

(b) be engaged in. ***Ex 1.*** I am *working on* a new book. ***Ex 2.*** The child was working on a jigsaw puzzle.

(c) seek to influence by constant attention. ***Ex 1.*** If I *work on* him, he may decide to help you. ***Ex 2.*** I shall have to *work on* her.

Work out: (a) turn out; develop in a specified way. ***Ex 1.*** Things *worked out* quite well. ***Ex 2.*** Nobody knows how things will *work out.*

(b) train the body by heavy physical exercise ***Ex.*** He *works out* regularly to keep it.

(c) be capable of being solved; solve. ***Ex 1.*** This is a problem that won't *work out*. ***Ex 2.*** I cannot *work* this puzzle *out*.

(d) calculate something. ***Ex 1.*** We have computers to *work out* our salaries these days. ***Ex 2.*** *Work out* how much one needs to spend in shops to earn these free gifts. ***Ex 3.*** Have you *worked out* the number of man hours lost through illness.

(e) find the answer to. ***Ex 1.*** He seems to have the problem nicely *worked out*. ***Ex 2.*** He *worked out* all the answers.

(f) understand somebody's nature. ***Ex 1.*** I have never been able to work her out. ***Ex 2.*** For as long as I have known him, I have never been able to *work* him *out*.

Work out at : be equal to something; have something as a total; amount to; come out at. ***Ex 1.*** The bill *works out* ₹ 95 each. ***Ex 2.*** What does that *work out at* ? ***Ex 3.*** His take-home pay *works out at* ₹ 8765 a month. ***Ex 4.*** What does his share of the bonus *work out at*?

Work over : beat somebody all over, to extract information, as a punishment, etc. ***Ex 1.*** He had been *worked over* by the gang for giving information to the police. ***Ex 2.*** A couple of the boys *worked* him *over* in a dark alley.

Work to : follow (a plan, etc.); be guided, governed, by a plan, etc. when doing something. ***Ex 1.*** Be careful with the money and *work to* a budget. ***Ex 2.*** Journalists have to *work to* tight deadlines. ***Ex 3.*** Magazines, photographers and dress houses *work to* tight schedules.

Work towards : strive to reach or achieve something. ***Ex 1.*** We are *working towards* common objectives. ***Ex 2.*** They have been *working towards* a new wages structure in the industry.

Work up : (a) develop or extend gradually. ***Ex 1.*** It took him some years to *work up* a market for his products. ***Ex 2.*** The retail side of the business was *worked up* by his father. ***Ex 3.*** He has *worked* the firm *up* from almost nothing.

(b) increase something in numbers or strength. ***Ex.*** Local organisations are trying to *work up* more support for the party before the eleetion.

(c) stimulate or make more keen. ***Ex 1.*** I went out for a brisk walk to *work up* an appetite for lunch. ***Ex 2.*** He does not seem to be able to *work up* any enthusiasm for his students.

(d) gradually change the shape or nature of something by thought, effort, etc. ***Ex 1.*** The mass of clay was *worked up* into a reclying figure. ***Ex 2.*** He is *working up* his notes on child language into a dissertation.

(e) raise somebody or oneself to a high point of excitement about something. ***Ex 1.*** She did not say when she was coming back. Arun got quite *worked up* about it. ***Ex 2.*** He can *work* the crowd *up* to the point where they would kill for his sake. ***Ex 3.*** Don't get all *worked up* over something which can easily be put right. ***Ex 4.*** He is *working* himself *up* into dreadful state over nothing.

Work up to : (a) develop what one is doing or saying to a high point. ***Ex 1.*** I felt, as he *worked up* to a climax, an impulse to stand up and shout. ***Ex 2.*** He took her out, all over the place. He was *working up* to a proposal of marriage. ***Ex 3.*** The story *worked up* to a splendid climax.

(b) prepare to say. ***Ex.*** What is he *working up* to?

Worm oneself/one's way along, through etc. : move slowly or with difficulty. ***Ex.*** They had to *worm* their *way through* the narrow tunnel.

Worm one's way/oneself into : establish in somebody's affection, confidence, and so on, esp. in order to deceive. ***Ex 1.*** They have *wormed themselves into* his affections. ***Ex 2.*** She used flattery to *worm herself into* his confidence. ***Ex 3.*** He *wormed his way into* a position of trust at the High Court. ***Ex 4.*** For the sake of his career, it was immensely important for Prem Kumar to *worm himself into* the Managing Director's confidence.

Worm out of : obtain information from somebody slowly and cunningly. ***Ex 1.*** Devise effective means to *worm* it *out of* her. ***Ex 2.*** Eventually I *wormed* the truth *out of* her. ***Ex 3.*** She was *worming out of* him shameful secrets about the Taran family. ***Ex 4.*** I have *wormed* all the information *out of* him. ***Ex 5.*** There are a few details of her private life that amply deserve to be *wormed out of* her soon.

Worry about/over: cause oneself anxiety over something, or trouble oneself about something. ***Ex 1.*** He *worries* himself sick *over* his eldest daughter. ***Ex 2.*** Look after yourself, my dear, and do not *worry about* me. ***Ex 3.*** He *worries about* the slightest thing. ***Ex 4.*** He *worried* himself sick *about* his missing son. ***Ex 5.*** Why do you *worry about* him?

Wrap up: (a) be quiet; shut up. ***Ex 1.*** Why don't you *wrap up* ? ***Ex 2.*** I wish he would *wrap up*. ***Ex 3.*** She *wrapped up* and went away.

(b) put on warm clothing so that it enfolds one completely. ***Ex 1.*** Now *wrap up* warm, it is freezing outside. ***Ex 2.*** The children were warmly *wrapped up* inscarves and anoraks. ***Ex 3.*** The nurse carried in a baby *wrapped up* in a thick shawl.

(c) complete (a task, a discussion, an agreement, etc.); finalise something; conclude something successfully. ***Ex 1.*** The salesman had already *wrapped up* a couple of deals by Lunch-time. ***Ex 2.*** They *wrapped up* the agreement on Friday. ***Ex 3.*** The whole thing has been *wrapped up*. ***Ex 4.*** He thinks he has got it all *wrapped up*. ***Ex 5.*** The sales team flew in at ten o'clock, *wrapped up* a few deals before lunch, and caught the afternoon plane back to Bombay.

(d) obscure (what one is saying) by using difficult or unnecessary words. ***Ex 1.*** Why does he have to *wrap* it all *up* in such complicated language? ***Ex 2.*** Make it a point never to *wrap up* your language by using ambiguous, difficult or unnecessary words.

Wrestle with : struggle to deal with or overcome something; fight inwardly morally with something. ***Ex 1.*** He was still *wrestling with* uncertainty over religious faith. ***Ex 2.*** These questions, long *wrestled with*; were not resolved. ***Ex 3.*** He has been *wrestling with* this problem for about week. ***Ex 4.*** The pilot was *wrestling with* the controls.

Wriggle out: escape. ***Ex.*** He is frightened so he wants to *wriggle out* before he gets caught.

Wriggle out of : escape something unpleasant by careful or cunning movements; avoid an unpleasant task by being cunning or by making excuses. ***Ex 1.*** Bimla managed to *wriggle out of* answering all the questions. ***Ex 2.*** It is your turn to take mother for a walk-don't try to *wriggle out of* it. ***Ex 3.*** They want to *wriggle out of* their responsibilities. ***Ex 4.*** You cannot *wriggle out of* this so easily.

Write back : write and send a letter in reply to somebody. ***Ex 1.*** I *wrote back* straight away to thank her for her kind invitation.

Ex 2. If the supplier sends you the wrong goods, *write back* to them at once.

Write down: (a) put something down in words on paper; record on paper (often as an aid to memory). ***Ex 1.*** *Write down* my phone number in your diary before you forget it. ***Ex 2.*** I *wrote* a few important notes *down* on the back of an envelope. ***Ex 3.*** I *wrote* my ideas *down* in order to clarify them. ***Ex 4.*** She *wrote* the information *down*.

(b) reduce the nominal value of (stock, goods, etc.) ***Ex.*** Have you *written down* the value of the unsold stock?

(c) classify. ***Ex.*** She has *written* you *down* as a fool.

Write in : write a letter to order something, state an opinion, etc. ***Ex 1.*** Thousands of people have *written in* to us for a free sample. ***Ex 2.*** To qualify for your free sample, all you do is *write in* to this address. ***Ex 3.*** Indignant viewers have been *writing in* to complain of the moral content of the plays.

Write in/into : (a) include something as a part of (a contract, an agreement, etc.); make a part of, or embody in, a legal document.

Ex 1. A penalty clause was *written into* the contract. ***Ex 2.*** A guarante to protect pension rights has been *written into* their contracts.

(b) include, or insert, something in a written text. ***Ex 1.*** Any alterations should be *written in* neatly to one side. ***Ex 2.*** The editor has *written* numerous suggestions *into* the margins.

Write off : (a) write to (an organisation, a company, etc.) to order something or to ask for information about something. ***Ex.*** I *wrote off* to the Radio Station for the special booklet. .

(b) cancel (a debt); recognise that something is a loss or failure. ***Ex 1.*** The firm has *written off* twenty lakh rupees, worth of bad debts. ***Ex 2.*** The debt has been *written off*. ***Ex 3.*** *They wrote* off ten lakh rupees. ***Ex 4.*** They *wrote off* five million rupees for depreciation of machinery.

(c) damage something so badly that it is not worth repairing. ***Ex.*** The driver escaped with minor injuries but the car was completely *written off*.

(d) regard somebody/something as a failure, beyond recovery, etc. ***Ex 1.*** He lost his match, but don't *write* him *off* as a future champion. ***Ex 2.*** Everyone they spoke to had *written off* the marriage before it began.

Write off as : regard somebody/something as unimportant, not worth listening to, etc. ***Ex 1.*** It is easy to *write* him *off* as just an eccentric old bore. ***Ex 2*** His political philosophy tends to be *written off* as an outdated fantasy. ***Ex 3.*** He cannot just be *written off* as a nincompoop.

Write out: (a) write something in full or in its final form. ***Ex 1.*** The lady doctor *wrote* me *out* a prescription for pain-killers. ***Ex 2.*** As I had no cash, I *wrote* her *out* a cheque. ***Ex 3.*** *Write* me *out* a full account of the accident. ***Ex 4.*** Did you *write out* a prescription to the medicine? ***Ex 5.*** She *wrote out* a testimonial for me.

(b) copy something. ***Ex.*** *Write out* this word twently times so that you learn how to spell it.

(c) remove (a character) from a continuing drama series on radio or television. ***Ex.*** After playing the part for over ten years, she was eventually *written out*.

Write up: (a) make a full written record of something. ***Ex 1.*** I *wrote up* my lecture notes. ***Ex 2.*** Tell him to *write up* the minutes of the meeting. ***Ex 3.*** Did you *write up* your diary? ***Ex 4.*** The basic experimental work has been done; what I have to do now is *write* it all *up*. ***Ex 5.*** For homework you can *write up* the rough notes you made in class. ***Ex 6.*** I *wrote up* the story of the young lovers. .

(b) write a review of (a play, etc.) or an account of an event. ***Ex 1.*** I am *writing up* the film for the local paper. ***Ex 2.*** He *wrote* the play *up* in the next edition of the paper. ***Ex 3.*** You can go home afterwards and *write* the film *up* in the paper.

Note: The word *write up* is a noun. It denotes written or published account of an event, review of a play, etc. ***Ex 1.*** My latest novel got an enthusiastic *write up* in the local press. ***Ex 2.*** Her latest play was given an ardent *write up* in the quality press.

24 Words Beginning With–X, Y and Z

Words Beginning With-Y

X out: stop thinking about somebody/something. ***Ex.*** When I thought of Padmini, I simply *Xed* her *out.*

Words Beginning With-Y

Yack away/on: talk cand often noisily. ***Ex.*** She kept *yacking on* about your wedding.

Yammer on: complain in a grumbling manner. ***Ex.*** Stop *yammering on* about the size of the bill.

Yank off: take off, or remove, with a sharp pull. ***Ex 1.*** The police *yanked* the offenders *off* to the police station. ***Ex 2.*** He seized my hand and in his great clasp and nearly *yanked* it *off*. ***Ex 3.*** She *yanked* the bed clothes *off* my bed.

Yank out/out of: extract with a sharp tug. ***Ex 1.*** I have to go to the dentist to have a few teeth *yanked out*. ***Ex 2*** Tap the nails up from the back, and *yank* them *out* with pincers.

Yap at : talk continuously in an annoying way. ***Ex.*** I vehemently hate people on trains or buses who keep *yapping at* me.

Yap away: talk noisily and foolishly. ***Ex.*** The child was *yapping away* about her new gaudy clothes.

Yarn away: tell stories continuously. ***Ex.*** They *yarned away* happily in the bar of the hotel.

Yearn for: be filled with longing; desire strongly; long for. ***Ex 1.*** He *yearned for* his home and family. ***Ex 2.*** Most people *yearn for* some truth in a relationship. ***Ex 3.*** He *yearned for* academic recognition. ***Ex 4.*** She *yearned for* a sight of her dear ones. ***Ex 5.*** He *yearned for* her whenever they were separated. ***Ex 6.*** Do you *yearn for* your wife and children?

Yell at : speak or say something in a yelling voice. ***Ex.*** She *yelled at* her husband about his constant drunkenness.

Yell out: cry or shout aloud. ***Ex 1.*** She *yelled out* in pain. ***Ex 2.*** The child *yelled out* in terror. ***Ex 3.*** When the captain *yelled out* my number, I had to rush forward. ***Ex 4.*** Don't squeeze his hand, it makes him *yell out* in pain.

Yield to : (a) allow oneself to be overcome by pressure; cease opposition to somebody/something. ***Ex 1.*** She *yielded to* temptation and had another biscuit. ***Ex 2.*** The government has not *yielded to* public opinion. ***Ex 3.*** The leader *yielded to* public pressure. ***Ex 4.*** If they won't *yield to* reason, we shall have to try other methods. ***Ex 5.*** Blackmail was a weapon to which they were not prepared *to yield*. ***Ex 6.*** To such persuasive arguments, she had *to yield* eventually. ***Ex 7.*** He was progressively *yielding to* her demands. ***Ex 8.*** Don't *yield to* the critics.

(b) be replaced or superseded by something. ***Ex 1.*** The cinema has largely *yielded to* the home video. ***Ex 2.*** Increasingly, farm land is *yielding to* property development. ***Ex 3.*** Radio has long been under pressure to *yield to* television. ***Ex 4.*** The swamp would *yield to* drier land.

(c) concede; admit that one is inferior to somebody/something. ***Ex.*** To speak the truth, *yield to* no one in my admiration for her work.

Yield up : (a) reluctantly give control of something to somebody; deliver somebody/something to somebody; surrerider to. ***Ex 1.*** The kidnappers have *yielded* two of their hostages *up* to the police. ***Ex 2.*** They *yielded up* the bulk of their supplies to enemy. ***Ex 3.*** The town would only be *yielded up* when ammunition and food supplies were exhausted. ***Ex 4.*** We will not *yield up* even an inch of our territory to the enemy.

(b) reveal something; disclose something. ***Ex 1.*** The universe is slowly *yielding up* its secrets to scientists. ***Ex 2.*** What are the methods ofmaking the brain *yield up* its secrets? ***Ex 3.*** I don't know what new mysteries will be *yielded up* to the scientist. ***Ex 4.*** In that year of plenty, the seas *yielded up* a rich harvest of fish. .

Yoke together: put together. ***Ex 1.*** The two lovers were *yoked together* in marriage. ***Ex 2.*** We did not expect to be *yoked together* in the same office.

Words Beginning With-Z

Zero in on : (a) aim guns, etc. at, or find the range of, (a particular target). ***Ex 1.*** The missile *zeroed in on* the tank. ***Ex 2.*** The bombers *zeroed in on* the enemy positions.

(b) fix attention on somebody/something; focus on somebody/something. ***Ex 1.*** Let us *zero in on* the key issues for discussion. ***Ex 2.*** The doctor concentrated on the heart, *zeroing in on* a single cell. ***Ex 3.*** I want to talk generally before I *zero in on* any speciality. ***Ex 4.*** By *zeroing in on* a particular lifestyle, we exclude a vast number of alternatives.

Zip along/into/through : move vigorously or quickly in the specified direction. ***Ex 1.*** She has just *zipped into* town to buy some food. ***Ex 2.*** After a slow beginning the play fairly *zips along* in the second Act. ***Ex 3.*** The car *zips along*, all right. ***Ex 4.*** The game got off to a sluggish start, but after half-time it fairly *zipped along*.

Zip up: fasten with zip. ***Ex 1.*** Will you *zip* me *up*, please? ***Ex 2.*** The dress *zips up* at the back. ***Ex 3.*** She *zipped up* the dress with difficulty. ***Ex 4.*** He packed his books into his briefcase and *zipped* it *up*. ***Ex 5.*** Does your jacket *zip up* at the front?

Zone off : make a separate zone. ***Ex.*** The business and commercial centre has now been *zoned off*, private cars are prohibited, and delivery vans may only enter and leave at specified times.

Zoom off: go somewhere in a hurry. ***Ex 1.*** In the summer we all *zoom off* to the Taj Mahal on our bikes. ***Ex 2.*** He *zoomed off* to Tokyo.